D0689104

GUIDE TO
MEDICAL & DENTAL SCHOOLS

BARRON'S
GUIDE TO
MEDICAL & DENTAL SCHOOLS

SECOND EDITION

Dr. Saul Wischnitzer
Director, Health Careers Consultants
Queens, New York

Barron's Educational Series, Inc.
Woodbury, New York • London • Toronto • Sydney

© Copyright 1985 by Barron's Educational Series, Inc.
Prior edition © 1982 by Barron's Educational Series, Inc.

Portions adapted from *Barron's Guide to Medical, Dental, and Allied Health Science Careers* by Saul Wischnitzer.

All rights reserved.
No part of this book may be reproduced
in any form, by photostat, microfilm, xerography,
or any other means, or incorporated into any
information retrieval system, electronic or
mechanical, without the written permission
of the copyright owner.

All inquiries should be addressed to:
Barron's Educational Series, Inc.
113 Crossways Park Drive
Woodbury, New York 11797

Library of Congress Catalog Card No. 85–11056
International Standard Book No. 0–8120–2788–4

Library of Congress Cataloging in Publication Data

Wischnitzer, Saul.
  Barron's guide to medical & dental schools.

  Bibliography: p. 319
  1. Medicine—Vocational guidance. 2. Dentistry—
Vocational guidance. 3. Osteopathy—Vocational
guidance. I. Title. II. Title: Guide to medical and
dental schools. III. Title: Barron's guide to
medical and dental schools. [DNLM: 1. Education,
Dental. 2. Education, Medical. 3. Schools, Dental.
4. Schools, Medical. W 19 W809b]
R690.W558   1985   610.69   85–11056
ISBN 0–8120–2788–4

PRINTED IN THE UNITED STATES OF AMERICA

5678   J00   987654321

CONTENTS

PREFACE AND ACKNOWLEDGMENTS   ix

LIST OF TABLES   xi

ABBREVIATIONS USED   xii

Part 1   **MEDICINE**   **1**

    1   **Medicine as a Career**   **3**

      Why study medicine?   3

      The need for physicians   4

      Desirable attributes for a medical career   5

      The major challenge to becoming a physician   5

      Physicians for the twenty-first century   6

    2   **Preparing for Medical School**   **7**

      High school   7

      College   8

      Nonacademic aspects
       of premedical education   14

    3   **Applying to Medical School**   **15**

      General considerations   15

      Selection factors   16

      The application   20

      Recommendations   25

      The interview   25

      The selection process   29

      Acceptance   30

      Ranking of medical schools   31

      Rejection   31

    4   **The Medical College Admission
       Test (MCAT)**   **34**

      Contents of the MCAT   35

      The value of the MCAT   36

      Preparing for the MCAT   36

      Model MCAT   37

    5   **Opportunities for Women and
       Minority Group Students**   **91**

      Doors are opening for women   91

      The women physician   94

      Current issues   94

      Current challenge   95

      Scholarships and support sources
       for women   95

Minority students in medicine 96
Financial aid for minority group
    members 96

6 Financing Your Medical Education **98**
The current financial aid crisis 99
Scholarships and loans 99

7 Medical Education **102**
The traditional program 103
The curriculum in transition 105
Other educational programs 106
The curriculum for the 21st century 107
Attrition in medical school 107
National medical board examinations 108
Postgraduate training: internship and
    residency 108

8 Medical Schools **112**
The medical scene in a nutshell 112
In-depth school profiles 134
Medical schools in development 201

9 Foreign Medical Study **202**
Admission 203
Transfer to U.S. schools 203
Internship and residency 204
Fifth pathway schools 204
Requirements for practice 205
Foreign medical schools 205

10 Osteopathy **210**
Basic philosophy 210
Educational data 211
Internship, residency and practice 212
Relationship between osteopathy and
    conventional medicine 212
Financial assistance 212
Basic data for osteopathic medical
    schools 213
Descriptions of the osteopathic medical
    schools 213

Part 2 **DENTISTRY** **217**
11 Dentistry as a Career **219**
Why study dentistry? 219

The need for dentists   220
Today's trends in dentistry   220
Dental specialization   221
Is dentistry for you?   222
Dentistry as an alternative to
    medicine   222

**12   Preparing for and Applying to
     Dental School**   **223**
Educational preparation   223
Application procedures   224
Admissions criteria   226

13   The Dental Admission Test (DAT)   **231**
Contents of DAT   232
The importance of the DAT   232
Preparing for the DAT   233
Sample DAT questions   233
Canadian DAT   234

**14   Opportunities for Women and
     Minority Group Students**   **235**
Doors are opening for women   235
Minority students in dentistry   236

15   Financing Your Dental Education   **239**
The current financial aid crisis   239
Scholarships and loans   240

16   Dental Education   **242**
Dental curriculum   242
Other educational programs   245
Postgraduate training   245

17   Dental Schools   **246**
The dental scene in a nutshell   246
In-depth school profiles   259

APPENDIX A   **277**

**Medical and Dental School Application
    Forms**
      AMCAS Application Form   278
      Sample Application from a non-AMCAS
        School   282
      AADSAS Application Form   288

APPENDIX B   **313**

Major Professional Organizations

APPENDIX C   **315**

   Regional Maps

BIBLIOGRAPHY   **319**

INDEXES   **320**

   Medical School Profiles 320
   Osteopathic School Profiles 321
   Dental School Profiles 321
   Subject 323

PREFACE AND ACKNOWLEDGMENTS

Of the many decisions facing you, the choice of a career is among the most important and it obviously requires the most careful consideration. The very competitive nature of our contemporary society has created marked pressures for an early choice, but the selection of a career is best determined after careful evaluation of your interests, abilities, and life goals. If you are considering medicine or dentistry, you will need the most current information about schools, admissions policies, and educational programs, as well as up-to-date data, to make the most realistic decision to overcome the barriers to success.

This book has been written to help you arrive at a decision and to provide you with both facts and advice on planning a career in medicine or dentistry, starting with high school and continuing through college. I have attempted to answer the most basic questions and to provide you with sources for more detailed information. Sound advice and current information are not only essential because of the strong competition that exists today but are also necessary because of the rapidly changing nature of medical education.

While your ultimate success naturally will depend on your abilities, the advice presented in this book can help you make the decisions that must be made during high school and college and which can be so crucial to achieving your goals.

In 1974 my book *Barron's Guide to Medical, Dental, and Allied Health Science Careers* was published. The favorable reception it was given resulted in the publication of new editions of the book in 1975 and 1977. With the very rapid increase in interest in health science careers, an expanded fourth edition of the book would have resulted in a volume that would be too cumbersome to be readily useful as a handbook for prospective students. Thus, it was decided to publish the book as two separate volumes: one dealing with medicine and dentistry, and the other with the allied health sciences. This volume is the second edition of the former.

Medicine and dentistry have been combined into a single volume because they are closely related. Among the considerations that they have in common are the facts that: (1) at the outset of one's study of the biological sciences in high school, a choice between the two careers need not be made; (2) a definitive career decision can be deferred until the junior year of college because of their common educational pathway; (3) in some cases applying to both medical and dental school may be desirable; (4) at some institutions medical and dental students take courses in the basic sciences together; (5) dental clinics are often located in hospitals that are centers for post-graduate medical as well as dental training; (6) medicine and dentistry overlap especially in surgical specialties relating to the mouth and neck. As a result of the interrelationship of these two sciences some dental schools award the Doctor of Dental Medicine (D.M.D.) degree rather than the traditional Doctor of Dental Surgery degree (D.D.S.).

In preparing this new edition, the facts and statistics concerning medical and dental careers have been updated so that the book is kept maximally useful. The following major changes or additions have also been introduced: (1) All medical and dental school profiles have been updated and new schools have been included, (2) the comprehensive data in Tables 6, 7, and 14 have been made current; (3) the sections dealing with the medical school selection process (Chapter 3) and with women and minorities in medicine (Chapter 5) have been substantially expanded; (4) a sample AMCAS application plus two sample essays have been incorporated into the text; and (5) the bibliography has been expanded.

The new material introduced into this edition stems in large measure from the author's experience over the past few years as a private, professional advisor in his capacity as Director of Health Careers Consultants. This has added a new and broader dimension to the book's perspective, as a result of exposure to a large pool of individuals with a variety of pre- and post-collegiate backgrounds at many different schools.

Special acknowledgment is made to the following organizations for allowing us to reprint copyrighted or previously published material in this book.

The Association of American Medical Colleges for permitting us to reprint its application form.

The American Association of Dental Schools Application Service for permitting us to reprint the AADSAS application form.

The American Dental Association for allowing us to use data in Tables 8, 9, and 10 from its *Handbook for Predental Advisors*.

Jonathan R. Cole, Professor of Sociology and Director of the Center for the Social Sciences, Columbia University, and James A. Lipton for permission to use their data in Table 3 from "The Reputations of American Medical Schools" in *Social Forces*, 55, 3 (March, 1977): 662–684. © Copyright 1977 by the University of North Carolina Press.

New York University School of Medicine for permitting us to reprint its application form, provided through the courtesy of New York University School of Medicine.

Hugo Seibel and Kenneth E. Guyer for permission to reprint Model MCAT from their book *Barron's How to Prepare for the New Medical College Admission Test*, © copyright 1983 by Barron's Educational Series, Inc.

The devoted efforts and expertise of Maxine K. Reed, Project Editor for this book at Barron's, is most gratefully appreciated.

Finally, I invite and welcome the comments of readers of this manual.

Saul Wischnitzer

LIST OF TABLES

1. Summary of required courses   10

2. Relationship of academic record to suggested number of applications   22

3. A ranking list of American medical schools   32

4. Percentage of women and minorities in 1984–85   92

5. Residency training for various specialties   110

6. Basic data on the medical schools   114

7. Basic data for osteopathic schools   214

8. The importance given to various sources of information concerning the dental school applicant   227

9. The importance given to dental admission test scores   229

10. 1983–84 dental school minority enrollment   237

11. Dental school courses and hours allotted   243

12. Major courses in the dental curriculum—by year   243

13. Dental schools providing opportunities to earn other degrees concurrently   245

14. Basic data on the dental schools   250

ABBREVIATIONS USED

AACOMAS	American Association of Colleges of Osteopathic Medicine Application Service
AADS	American Association of Dental Schools
AADSAS	American Association of Dental Schools Application Service
AAMC	Association of American Medical Colleges
AMA	American Medical Association
AMCAS	American Medical College Application Service
COTRANS	Coordinated Transfer Application System
DAT	Dental Admission Test
ECFMG	Educational Council for Foreign Medical Graduates
FLEX	Federation Licensing Examinations
GPA	Grade point average
LCME	Liaison Committee on Medical Education
MCAT	Medical College Admission Test
Med-MAR	Medical Minority Applicant Registry
MSKP	Medical Sciences Knowledge Profile
NBME	National Board of Medical Examiners
NIRMP	National Intern and Resident Matching Program
WAMI	Wyoming, Alaska, Montana, Idaho
WICHE	Western Interstate Commission for Higher Education

Part 1
MEDICINE

1

MEDICINE AS A CAREER

☐ Why study medicine?
☐ The need for physicians
☐ Desirable attributes for a medical career
☐ The major challenge to becoming a physician
☐ Physicians for the twenty-first century

Physicians are acknowledged practitioners of the art of medicine. They are expected to be people of high ethical standards since they are entrusted with the intimate details of life and death. They are expected to have the capacity and enthusiasm for difficult work extended over long hours, and they must be able to work efficiently under a chronic load of heavy responsibility.

Physicians are expected to be able to reason quickly and accurately and to have life-long desires to continually add to their accumulated body of medical knowledge by learning about new developments in their profession. They are expected to be able to communicate with their patients so as to teach them hygienic measures and to explain adequately the nature and significance of a disease. They are expected to be willing to serve the community in a capacity beyond that of their professional training. Physicians are people who have ordinary physical and emotional needs, yet who have a great purpose in life. Their practice can be the source of enrichment of their own life as well as the lives of others.

WHY STUDY MEDICINE?

The medical profession offers much to a young person. It provides an avenue for attaining satisfaction of many of the most fundamental human desires. Medicine can satisfy your intellectual curiosity; it permits you to successfully apply the enormous body of information that has been accumulated in recent decades to reduce pain and suffering and extend the average life span. At the same time, it presents the challenge of the many unsolved problems that await solution through laboratory or hospital work.

Medicine can satisfy your desire for human service by enabling you to bring help and comfort to others. Medicine can satisfy your desire to work in a profession that has prestige. While prestige is no longer granted automatically, it does come with the faithful discharge of responsibilities and obligations. Medicine can also satisfy your desire for a substantial income. This income, which is superior to that of most other professions, is earned by the long and difficult hours demanded of the physician. Medicine is a profession that can satisfy your desire for independent and individual achievement in a society that is becoming increasingly overstructured.

In seeking to become a physician, you are planning to join a fraternity of professional men and women who have a profound influence, both physically and emotionally, on the lives of many millions of people. The roots of medicine penetrate deeply into the history of humankind. Cave paintings reveal the existence of "healers" as far back as the Ice Age. The medical practitioners of ancient China developed acupuncture and a smallpox vaccination method. Western medicine is indebted to the "scientific" approach developed in ancient Greece and Rome by men such as Hippocrates and Galen. These advances were preserved through the Dark Ages by the Arab world. In medieval Europe medical science stagnated until the rebirth of learning and experimentation in the Renaissance.

In the United States during the Colonial Era, medicine was largely a hit-or-miss affair. The pushing of the frontiers westward developed a pioneer type of doctor. A step forward was achieved in the last half of the eighteenth century when medical schools in the United States began conferring the MD degree and it was no longer necessary to journey abroad to obtain one. In 1910 the Flexner Report brought about a revolution in medical education and placed it on a sound basis by establishing standardized requirements of medical education.

Well before the turn of this century, Americans made major contributions to medical science, especially in the battle against infectious diseases. In the last half of the twentieth century, American medicine has become a world leader. Thus, to become a physician means entering a fellowship with a healing tradition that extends back to the beginnings of civilization.

THE NEED FOR PHYSICIANS

Until about 1980, the increasing need for additional manpower in the health professions, and particularly medical manpower, has been shown in governmental studies of both urban and rural areas. Thus medical educators have strongly urged that efforts be made to increase the number of physicians and other health science personnel. As a result, increased financial support, especially from the federal government, has resulted in expanding first-year enrollment by both enlarging existing medical school class size and by establishing new colleges of medicine. Thus, for example, the number of first-year students increased from about 8000 in 1960–1961 to more than 11,000 in 1970–1971 and then to about 16,500 first-year places in the early 1980s. Almost all of the six two-year basic science schools have been converted to four-year MD-granting institutions. Also, in recent years, nine new schools became operational, thereby ultimately providing about 750–1000 additional places.

The increase in the number of medical schools and their class size has resulted in a significant narrowing of the gap between physician supply and demand. The number of active physicians has increased roughly 12% from 285,000 to 318,000 in the 1965 to 1970 period as against a population growth of only 5 percent. A similar rate of increase also occurred between 1970 and 1980 and is likely for the next ten-year period. Thus, on a numerical basis, the gap would apparently be closed by 1990 with an estimated 550,000 active physicians for an estimated population of 250 million people. A major federal study of future physician manpower needs, known as the GEMENAC report, projected an oversupply of physicians around 1990. This report has given rise (not surprisingly), to anxiety among some premedical and medical students, as well as to residents, regarding the need for their services in the twenty-first century.

There are a number of factors to consider when evaluating the conclusion of this report. First, as with all projections based on statistical analysis, they need not be self-fulfilling. Second, a major and unknown impact on the validity of the report's conclusions is the very significant (and long overdue) increase in the enrollment of women in medical schools; women now constitute more than 30% of the student population and their number may rise to 40% or more. An unknown, but perhaps significant, number of these women may initially opt for a specialty of their primary interest but later, to meet personal and/or family needs, gravitate to fields that demand less time. This may leave a void in the supply of physicians specializing in internal medicine, surgery and other time-intensive fields. Third, the number of American graduates of foreign medical schools will most likely diminish, in view of the drastic change in the "atmosphere" with regard to this option. Fourth, since the number of qualified applicants seems to be declining, there seems to be a tendency among some medical schools to reduce the size of their entering class, and a few schools may possibly close. Thus, the total number of medical school graduates, while currently stable, may diminish. All the while the population will undoubtedly continue to grow, increasing the demand for medical services (already being fueled by public health education programs). The increased number of physicians will, however, have its impact. It will require that prospective practitioners be more flexible in the choice of a specialty and in the location of their practice, and above all be very dedicated to their chosen profession.

DESIRABLE ATTRIBUTES FOR A MEDICAL CAREER

There are four basic qualities that are desirable and that are sought by medical school admissions officers.

1. *Intelligence.* Medical studies and practice require an ability to learn, retain, and integrate a vast amount of scientific data through study, experimentation, and experience.

2. *Scientific interest.* Medicine, while an applied science, rests upon an understanding of the fundamental biological and chemical activities which we define as *life*. An understanding of its dynamic processes requires a solid grounding in chemical, physical, and biological principles. What is especially desirable is a mastery of the scientific mode of inquiry and the attainment of good manipulative skills.

3. *Favorable personality.* A successful practice involves an ability to establish and maintain a good rapport with people at all levels. Thus, you must realize that you will have to treat people coming from different walks of life and associate with colleagues who have different backgrounds. It is very desirable to have warmth and empathy and, thus, be able to reflect a positive response to the needs, suffering, and fears of others in a manner that can provide both reassurance and respect.

4. *Physical growth and emotional strength.* Those who plan a career in medicine must possess the capability of enduring the rigorous physical and emotional demands of many years of study and training. You must be able to maintain the self-discipline required during such a prolonged preparatory period.

The four years of high school and first three years of college provide the opportunity to determine to what extent you possess these basic attributes. The grades you receive, especially in your science courses, will provide a basis for judging your intellectual ability. Your response to various science courses, as well as other contacts with experimentation and scientific inquiry in class or possibly in summer work, will enable you to evaluate your natural response to this area of studies. Your ability to get along with your fellow students and friends should provide a basis for judging your personality. Finally, how you stand up to the demands of your school work and personal problems will provide some basis for evaluating your inner tenacity and determination.

Objective self-analysis at the end of high school and at the end of each college year will help to insure that your choice of a medical career is realistic and will provide a stimulus for greater performance. Such analysis may, on the other hand, call for reconsideration and a possible change in your career goal. If this is the case after consultation with your guidance counselor and parents, the change should be made promptly in order to avoid loss of time and almost certain disappointment at a later date.

The aim of the self-evaluation should not be to determine if you are outstanding in all the basic attributes necessary for a successful medical career; rather you should ascertain if you are above average in the sum total, at least average in each, and do not have very serious deficiencies in any. What is to be sought is a determination of how close one actually comes to a hypothetical standard, realizing that there is a broad spectrum of acceptability determined by a balancing of all factors.

THE MAJOR CHALLENGE TO BECOMING A PHYSICIAN

The first step to becoming a physician is to decide that at all times you will be realistic and honest with yourself. Before you reach the stage of applying to a medical school, you should periodically reevaluate your abilities and the sincerity of your conviction to become a doctor. You should determine if you possess the intelligence, scientific aptitude, personality, and inner strength—that are essential for success as a physician.

All prospective medical school applicants must in time face the reality that each will be but one out of about 30,000–35,000 applicants competing for a place in freshman medical school classes. The competition is extremely intense and about 50% of the applicants fail to attain their goal (at least on the first try). You should also be aware that since each applicant applies to about ten medical schools, there are more than 300,000 applications to be processed. This means screening 500 to 7,500 applications to fill 50 to 250 places. The initial screening process rejects some individuals outright and ranks others for further action, determining if they merit a prompt interview or should be put on hold for an interview at a later date. It is, therefore, important to realize at the outset that in addition to your intellectual achievements and potential, the mechanics of the admission process itself is critical. Knowing which schools and how many schools to apply to, presenting your qualifications, writing your essay, and handling yourself well at interviews are all vital elements in achieving your goal. The admission process is the culmination of your efforts to become a physician. It involves marketing your personal assets to the maximum extent possible. It is therefore incumbent that you get to know your strengths and weaknesses to make sure that you accentuate the strengths and minimize or, if possible, even eliminate the weaknesses. The image that you indirectly project by means of the transcripts, recommendations, and MCAT scores submitted in your behalf, and that you directly project in your interview, will determine the success of your attempt to secure a place in a medical school. Once you have been accepted for admission, it is almost a certainty (because of the negligible failure rate) that in due course you will be awarded your medical degree.

PHYSICIANS FOR THE TWENTY-FIRST CENTURY

In the fall of 1984, after three years of study that involved hearings in different parts of the United States with leading medical educators, the Association of American Medical College's panel on General Professional Education of the Physician (GPEP) released a long-awaited report. It is one of the most comprehensive studies since the renowned Flexner Report (1910) that drastically reshaped medical education in the United States. It is believed that the GPEP report may have a very significant impact on medical education for the balance of this century. The GPEP recommendations are relevant to both premedical and medical students. For those planning a medical career, the following recommendations are of special interest:

1. College faculties should require that the education of all students encompass broad study in the natural and social sciences and in the humanities.

2. Medical schools should require only essential courses for admission; these should be part of the core curriculum that all college students must take.

3. Medical school admission committees' practice of recommending additional courses beyond those required for admission should cease.

4. Medical school faculties should modify their admission requirements so that college students who apply and have successfully pursued a wide range of study may be viewed as highly as the students who have concentrated in the sciences.

5. Medical school faculties should devote more attention to selecting students who have the values and attitudes that are essential for members of a caring profession, who have critical analytical abilities, and who have the ability to learn independently.

These recommendations should be borne in mind when you plan your program of college studies.

2
PREPARING FOR MEDICAL SCHOOL

☐ High school
☐ College
☐ Other aspects of pre-medical education

HIGH SCHOOL

High school is a period of social adjustment and a time when the student becomes increasingly aware of what adult responsibilities are. Thus, while high school is a transitional era, it is a critical one in that it is usually the time when your career goals become tentatively formulated. Career ambitions may change as you become exposed to new areas of knowledge and as old ones are explored more deeply, but it is advantageous to have some general educational goals rather than to drift aimlessly.

A final decision to choose medicine as a career need not be made in high school and probably should be deferred until the end of the sophomore year of college. Two questions, however, need to be answered in high school—Do you intend to go to college? Do you have a genuine interest in science? It is necessary to plan an educational program of high school studies that will make it feasible to gain admission to a suitable college as well as to test the validity of your preliminary career decision.

Program of Studies

Having decided to attend college and possibly become a premedical student, your high school program should include a selection of courses that meet at least the minimum requirements for admission to a liberal arts college.

The program should therefore include:

English: 4 years
Laboratory science: 2 years
Modern foreign or classical language: 2 years
Mathematics: 2½ years
Social studies: 2 years

You should enlarge upon these requirements as much as is feasible by taking electives to obtain a well-rounded academic background. Concentrate in a science with the aim of making your other college courses less demanding, and thereby enhance your chances of securing higher grades in all your courses. This approach can help strengthen your science course average, which is one of the factors in the medical school selection process.

Mastering good study habits is an essential that should be achieved in high school, since it will have a significant impact on your success in college. Set up regular hours for study, learn how to read quickly and effectively, and learn how to take lecture notes and develop test-taking skills. Good achievement in your academic studies, especially in science courses, should be a major challenge of your high school education.

During high school you should participate in a variety of extracurricular activities, including athletics and science clubs, especially premedical groups such as the Future Physician Club or Medical Explorer Post of the Boy Scouts of America. While in high school you should acquire a good ability to communicate—both orally and in writing. Seek help if there is a serious problem in these areas. Your summers should be spent profitably and should involve activities that bring you into active contact with people (e.g., camp counselor). Working in a hospital or laboratory may also provide some useful experience, but such activities are probably best deferred until the college years.

Take the appropriate college entrance examination required by the colleges you plan to apply to—either the Scholastic Achievement Test or the American College Test. If your scores are in the upper percentiles, you should feel encouraged about your potential success.

COLLEGE

The Selection of a College

There is a wide choice of colleges open to the high school graduate whose ultimate goal is medical school. Students should make their choice from one of the liberal arts colleges or universities accredited by one of the six regional accrediting agencies. This helps ensure that the school has met at least the minimum educational standards for institutions of higher learning. You should determine your personal preference either for a small school, with its opportunities for more personalized instruction and closer interaction with faculty and fellow students, or for a larger university, with its wider curricular and extra-curricular opportunities. Factors such as cost should also be carefully considered. Take into account also the size of the library, the student-faculty ratio, the local environment, and the academic pressures. In addition, evaluate each college keeping in mind the following items:

1. Does the college offer the premedical courses that are prerequisites for admission to medical school? Examine the school's catalog to determine this.

2. Does the college have dynamic and modern science departments and adequate laboratory facilities? Check the listing of faculty in the catalog (noting for example, the number of faculty with doctorate degrees). Visit the school and discuss with students the nature of the science and mathematics departments.

3. Does the college have a high academic reputation? Examination of the freshman class profile, which should be available from high school counselors, will shed light on this point.

4. Does the college consistently send a significant portion of its premedical graduates to medical school? This information is very helpful in assessing the school's reputation and the quality of its premedical students. Discuss this question with the college's seniors, its premedical advisor, and its science professors.

5. Does the college have a premedical advisory program? A knowledgeable and dedicated premedical advisor will help insure academic guidance, current information, and assistance at the time the student is planning to apply to medical and/or dental school.

A comparative evaluation of these and other issues involves reading the schools' catalogs and visiting each of the campuses under consideration. A visit offers the opportunity of meeting students, admissions and guidance personnel, and professors, and of discussing the aspects of the schools with those who are most familiar with them.

It is very important to give careful consideration to the college you select, for it will undoubtedly have a major impact upon your career. The undergraduate school at which you matriculate can affect your performance. In addition, it is one of the factors in the selection of medical students. Because of this, it is very desirable to secure a quality education at a well-established or prestigious college or university. A private school may give you an edge. To secure admission to a college that will improve your career potential requires competitive grades, attractive SAT scores, impressive recommendations, and personal achievement(s).

Program of Studies

You should realize at the outset of your college career that every medical school admissions committee will initially screen your application by viewing your grades as a whole. This is expressed by your grade-point average (GPA), which simply represents the total of your average for each academic year divided by the number of years you have attended college (usually three at the time you apply, plus any summer school work completed). Then your science course average, your achievement in your major and in the more challenging premedical requirements (e.g., organic chemistry and physics), and honors work or independent study, are all scrutinized. This means that it is imperative that you apply all your talents (and remedy any deficiencies) at the time you begin college studies. It is risky to wait until you are faced with serious academic problems to decide to buckle down to the demands of your courses. It is difficult, although certainly not impossible, to rectify the results of one unimpressive semester, let alone an entire year. Thus, for example, a B or 3.0 for your first freshman semester will give you a maximum B+ or 3.5 average for the year only if your second semester is straight A or 4.0. Similarly, a 3.0 for the entire freshman year would demand a perfect sophomore year to bring you up to a B+ level. In addition, a mediocre semester or a mediocre year can seriously undermine your self-confidence and raise doubts about the wisdom of your career decision. This type of situation is undoubtedly one of the underlying factors in the significantly high dropout rate among freshman premeds.

Your major. Historically, premedicine has changed to keep pace with advancements in medical education. In colonial America, premedical education as such was nonexistent. However, as medical education became more sophisticated, so by necessity did premedical education come into existence. During this century there have been varying trends in premedical programming. The older school of thought was that a specialized preprofessional program was mandatory. As a result, a formal "premedical major" with a prescribed program of study was established. A strong movement away from this approach began in the mid-nineteen fifties. Students were encouraged to select any major that was of interest, but if it was in one of the sciences (as was frequently the case) they were also urged to obtain broad exposure to the humanities and social sciences as well. Currently the pressure, due to diminished time allotted to the basic sciences in medical school, has given impetus to encouraging students to complete more science courses in college, so that the pendulum has swung in the direction of a science major. While completing a science major, students automatically take the required premedical courses.

The specific choice of which science to major in is yours alone. You should, before making a decision, evaluate your schools' science departments in terms of their requirements, quality of teaching, and grading attitudes. To do so, you should read the school catalog and talk to faculty members and senior-level students. The choice should be the one in which you will be academically most successful and in which you stand a good chance of developing a good relationship with members of the department staff. A correct decision as to your major will help ensure that your GPA, science cumulative average, and the quality of your recommendations—three important medical school selection factors—will be strong.

Most premedical students major in biology (zoology) or chemistry, but some major in biochemistry, physics, or even computer science, all of which have a relevance to medicine. However, choosing to major in a science unrelated to the art of healing, such as geology, mathematics, or astronomy, will certainly not disqualify an applicant any more than being a nonscience major does. This is true as long as you still demonstrate the necessary potential by superior work in the premedical science course requirements.

Premedical requirements. Regardless of your choice of a major, you should arrange to include the basic premedical science course plus lab requirements, namely, two years of chemistry and one each of biology and physics, in your first three years of college study. The purpose of premedical science course requirements is twofold: (1) to determine the compatibility between the student and science, since medicine academically is the science of the human body and (2) to provide the premedical student with a background on which to launch future studies in the basic medical sciences.

The required premedical science courses you take should not be those designed for the non-science major. If possible, stagger your laboratory courses so that you don't take too many at one time. These courses require additional time both in the laboratory and outside of the classroom. However, none of these courses should be deferred to the senior year. They are all needed in preparation for the MCAT. One or more of these courses may be in progress when taking the spring MCAT.

The course requirements are purposely limited in order to allow broad latitude for the planning of individualized programs. The following is a table of courses required by the medical schools. The symbol on the right indicates how many schools require those courses for admission.

Table 1. Summary of Required Courses

+ required by more than 100 schools
− required by less than 20 schools

COURSE	
Chemistry	
Inorganic (or General) Chemistry	+
Organic Chemistry	+
Qualitative Analysis	−
Quantitative Analysis	−
Physical Chemistry/Quantitative Analysis	−
Biochemistry	−
Other	−
Biology	
General Biology (or Zoology)	+
Embryology	−
Comparative Anatomy	−
Genetics	−
Cell Biology	−
Molecular Biology	−
Other	−
Physics	
General Physics	+
Other	−
Mathematics	
College Mathematics	−
College Algebra	−
Analytical Geometry	−
Trigonometry	−
Calculus	−
Other	−
Humanities	
English	+
Language	−
Other	−
Social and Behavioral Sciences	
Sociology	−
Psychology	−
Behavioral Science	−
Social Science	−
Other	−

It should be noted that some advanced science courses, as well as some nonscience courses, while not officially required for admission by some schools, may nevertheless be listed in their catalogs as "recommended" or "desirable."

In summary, while the premedical core studies in the sciences will usually absorb the greatest portion of one's time and energy, one must place these in the proper perspective of the entire program of undergraduate studies. For just as the patient should be viewed as a whole rather than as merely a collection of organ systems, so too should the person be educated as a whole in order to face both the academic as well as the nonacademic challenges that lie ahead. In essence this means that the student should attempt to secure a meaningful balance between the physical and biological sciences, and the humanities and social sciences. By this means the college experience will not only be more pleasurable but one's sense of purpose and ethical values will be developed, and a more humanistic physician can be developed even in a mechanistic society.

Special Educational Opportunities

Most liberal arts colleges offer special educational opportunities that can enhance the character of your program of study. These programs not only improve the quality of your college educational experience but also increase the strength of your medical school application and thereby improve your admission chances. You should not arbitrarily utilize any of these programs but should incorporate them into your program only if you are sure that they will definitely help you attain your career goal. The six special programs discussed below are advanced placement credit, honors courses, independent study, graduate-level courses, pass/fail courses, and summer school courses.

Advanced placement credit. When a student has acquired advanced placement credit for excelling in a science on the high school level, one or more required premedical science courses will be waived. As a result, there will be a gap in grade information in this area. It is frequently desirable in such cases to substitute a suitable number of elective courses for the waived courses. You should select substitute elective courses carefully, determining that your high school background is adequate, and discussing the course requirements with the instructor. You should also consider auditing the basic science course from which you have been excused in advance of taking the elective; this would not only provide a useful background but would also enable you to develop a set of lecture notes that could prove helpful for review when you are studying for the MCAT (see page 34). For example, if you should have your general biology requirement waived, you should review the principles of biology by yourself or audit a course if possible. This preparation is essential, even if you do not major in biology. In this case, your elective course grades will serve to indicate to the admissions committee your academic potential in this important area. If you do major in biology, a good grounding in its principles will serve you well for a variety of electives you choose in the course of your studies.

Honors courses. There is no question that completing an honors section of a course can strengthen your admission potential. This, however, is true only if you get an A in such a course. Receiving a B grade may serve to depress your GPA (and, where applicable, your science average) even though in reality a B in an honors section may be equivalent to an A in a standard section. In some cases, however, grades for honors courses may be weighted, in order to provide an equivalency factor. Thus, before enrolling in an honors section, you should determine, by talking to the instructor and students involved in the course, just how much additional work it requires, and how the grade is evaluated. If you have the time and are confident of your ability to master the requirements, then enrolling in an honors section is reasonable. In any case, the honors credit should be noted in your application documents. The course can be educationally rewarding and provide a good source for an impressive letter of recommendation.

Independent study. Another approach that can add significantly to the attractiveness of your credentials is satisfactory completion of an independent study program. Such an undertaking can demonstrate that you are willing and able to accept the responsibility of a special educational challenge. Your motives must, however, be sincere so that you will apply yourself maximally in order to ensure that your research is impressive and is completed on schedule. As a result of such an activity you will undoubtedly develop a special favorable relationship with your mentor, who will then be able to strongly support your candidacy for admission to medical school at the appropriate time.

Independent study should be undertaken only if you are sure that it will not have a negative impact on your educational responsibilities as a whole. You need to be especially careful in selecting a project that can be realistically completed by the date you set. It is best if you can complete any independent study project before you apply to medical school so that recommendations resulting from this work can be submitted when they can be most effective. A good time to carry out such a project may be the summer after you complete your junior-year studies. By then you should have completed all your premedical science course requirements and satisfactorily taken your MCAT. Your only remaining commitment will be preparing your application(s) to medical school. There is no objection, if time is available, to independent study during the regular academic year.

Graduate courses. Occasionally, the option of taking a graduate-level course is available to under-

graduates. You should not assume, unless specifically told, that you will be graded differently from the graduate students taking the course with you. Thus the note of caution regarding the impact of the grade from such a special course noted above in the discussion of honors work is also applicable here. Graduate courses can be demanding, and successful completion of such a challenge can demonstrate impressively your ability to respond effectively to the academic challenge of medical school. If you do successfully complete graduate courses, make sure to bring it to the attention of the medical school by noting it on your essay or in your interview.

Pass/fail courses. These are courses that your school permits you to take for credit without getting a grade. It is not advisable to take any courses in biology or chemistry on this basis since the implication would be that your level of performance was not satisfactory. Thus while the absence of a grade would preclude any negative impact on your GPA and science average, your image could suffer. On the other hand, taking a medically unrelated science (e.g., geology) or a nonscience course of special interest on a pass/fail basis is quite legitimate. It shows evidence of your desire to secure a broad education, if it is not done in excess.

Summer courses. There is no inherent objection to the completion of courses during the summer. Moreover, it may prove useful or even desirable to do so in order to get some required nonscience courses out of the way and thereby lighten your course load during the regular academic year. Thus some students take one or two nonscience courses at the end of their sophomore year so they can lighten their course load during their junior year when they have to take organic chemistry or physics and study for the MCAT.

It may even prove advantageous to take one or more science electives during the summer, if they are not offered at your school during the regular academic year, or if you cannot fit them into your schedule. In addition, summer electives can help improve your science average. Thus if your BCPM (biology, chemistry, physics, and math) average comes close to a critical level, taking summer courses can bring these figures up. It is worthwhile to consider attending summer school to do so. Again, it is important to realize that it will take an A or two As to do this, and that special care needs to be taken before utilizing this double-edged option.

Extracurricular and Summer Activities

Your nonacademic activities usually will not be decisive elements in your admission to medical school but they can be helpful. You would be well advised to participate in the premedical society, as well as other organizations that may be related to medicine less directly. Participation in community, political, or sports activities help in presenting a well-rounded and adjusted individual to admissions officers.

If possible, plan your summer activities so that they can be useful for your career goals. Such activities include hospital work, research, or other activities involving interpersonal contacts. For example, at the end of the freshman year, try to find activities that involve working with people, such as youth camp work or community projects. During the summer following the sophomore year, try to gain some hospital experience. Though summer positions in hospitals are not readily available, try for employment as an orderly, operating or emergency room assistant, or nurse's aide. Also consider a position as a clinical laboratory assistant or a position in a mental hospital or nursing home.

The summer between the junior and senior year could also be spent in hospital work. Students with an interest in research might try obtaining a position at a medical school or in a government laboratory. In addition, a summer spent participating in a research project can provide an understanding of scientific methods in action. It will afford experiences in designing experiments and in collecting and evaluating data.

When working on a summer project, make a definite effort to ensure that your supervisor becomes acquainted with both you and with your work. It may prove useful later when you begin securing letters of recommendation to be sent to the medical schools.

You, as a prospective professional, should take a job in a hospital not just to be able to list this activity on your application, but to be able to look at yourself and your reactions to the sick patient, to understand that medical practice is not all heroics and glory, but many hours of hard work. You should try to familiarize yourself with the roles of the various members of the health care team so that you recognize that each has a crucial function in the entire process. In this way you can see if it is the physician's role that is most compatible with your life goals.

Several excellent summer job opportunities exist in a few states at the following institutions:

California
Personnel Department, University of California, Lawrence Livermore Laboratory, P.O. Box 808–N, Livermore, California 94550.

Connecticut
Summer Student Research Fellowship, Department of Medical Education, Hartford Hospital, 80 Seymour Street, Hartford, Connecticut 06115.

Illinois
Summer Student Research Fellowship Program, Office of Research Administration, Michael Reese Medical Center, 29th Street and Ellis Avenue, Chicago, Illinois 60616.

Maine
Research Training Office, The Jackson Laboratory, Bar Harbor, Maine 04609.

New York
Research Participation Program, Roswell Park Memorial Institute, 666 Elm Street, Buffalo, New York 14263.

Institute of Society, Ethics, and Life Sciences, Hastings Center Internships, Hastings Center, 630 Broadway, Hastings-on-Hudson, New York 10706.

Health Policy Advisory Center, 17 Murray Street, New York, New York 10007.

Summer Scientific Work Program, Franklin General Hospital, 900 Franklin Avenue, Valley Stream, New York, 11582.

Office of Academic Relations, Brookhaven National Laboratory, Upton, New York 11973.

Pennsylvania
Mellon Research Summer Program in Psychiatry for Undergraduates, Western Psychiatric Institute and Clinic, 3811 O'Hara Street, Pittsburgh, Pennsylvania 15213.

Texas
Surgical Laboratory Program, Baylor College of Medicine, Texas Medical Center, Houston, Texas 77030.

The Premedical Advisor and/or Committee

The Premedical Advisor can help you in planning the sequence of courses needed to meet the requirements at most medical schools. He or she will also offer suggestions as to which schools to apply to, when to take the MCAT, and how to interpret the scores. The advisor is usually assisted by a committee of faculty members who evaluate your academic performance and potential as well as your overall fitness to study medicine. The Premedical Committee maintains a file of your records and evaluations by individual members.

It is the obligation of the advisor or committee to provide the medical schools with supporting information in your behalf. Some medical schools will utilize their own recommendation forms which they send out to be completed. Most rely on the college's forms and even accept them in lieu of their own. Undergraduate schools vary in the format they use to provide their evaluation. Many use a letter of recommendation drafted by the

_____ U N I V E R S I T Y
_____
_____

CONFIDENTIAL REPORT ON CANDIDATE FOR ADMISSION TO PROFESSIONAL SCHOOL

Date _____

The following evaluation is submitted for your guidance by the Health Sciences Advisory Office of _____ (the college of arts and sciences for men of _____ University). This evaluation is based on a careful study of written evaluations by, and consultation with, those members of the faculty who have had personal knowledge of the candidate and his work in both lecture and laboratory courses.

NAME OF CANDIDATE _____ I.D. No. _____

This student has completed _____ years of college. His cumulative average to date is _____ (A = 4).

Candidate for School of ( ) Medicine   ( ) Dentistry   ( ) Podiatry   ( ) Optometry   ( ) Other _____

	OUTSTANDING	VERY GOOD	GOOD	AVERAGE	POOR
PERSONAL ATTRIBUTES					
1. Appearance and Social Manner					
2. Maturity and Emotional Stability					
3. Communication Skills					
4. Interpersonal Relations					
5. Cooperation and Reliability					
6. Self-confidence					
ACADEMIC ATTRIBUTES					
7. Industry and Perseverence					
8. Originality and Resourcefulness					
9. Laboratory Skills					
10. Native Intelligence and Judgment					
11. Scientific Aptitude					

Summary evaluation of the applicant's
fitness for professional study and practice.*

*Determined by averaging the student's ratings of items 7 through 11 together with his cumulative academic average, according to a mathematical formula under which 4.0 is the highest possible rating. Students whose combined index falls between:

        3.7 and 4.0 are rated "outstanding"
        3.4 and 3.6 are rated "very good"
        2.9 and 3.3 are rated "good"
        2.3 and 2.8 are rated "average"
        2.0 and 2.2 are rated "poor"

_____
Health Sciences Advisor

REMARKS _____

_____

NOTE: The above student has waived his right to inspect and review this recommendation under the Family Education Rights and Privacy Act of 1974. Therefore please keep this document confidential.

advisor or a member of the committee who knows the student. It may include quotes about the applicant made by faculty members, and it will reveal the committee's consensus of the student's abilities and potential and may rate the applicant in comparison to others applying during the year from the same school. Some schools provide a letter of recommendation and a separate sheet of faculty comments. Others may provide a letter and a quantitative rating sheet (see page 13) and possibly also a comment sheet.

Attributes listed on rating sheets, and the ratings used, vary from school to school. However, in general they refer to the applicant's personal as well as academic attributes and attempt to portray them in a quantitative and objective manner.

In view of the generally high caliber of applicants to medical school, recommendations (and interviews) have assumed major importance in the application process. Thus, students should make themselves and their abilities well known to faculty members. Their knowledge of you should be as deep as possible so that they can rate you not only quantitatively but also qualitatively. Recommendations by science professors, whether they know you from course work or as an individual, are of special value. Of particular usefulness are evaluations from honors work or independent study supervisors who can evaluate such qualities as initiative, determination, and reliability.

Finally a word of caution about advisors. It is essential that you are courteous and respectful at all times in your dealings with members of your college faculty and especially with your preprofessional advisor. Your advisor will be responsible for transmitting the qualitative impression of the faculty to the medical schools. Thus your advisor's good will is most desirable and can be developed, not by ingratiating yourself, but by establishing a genuine relationship.

On the other hand, it is not necessary to accept your advisor's recommendations as the only truth if you have valid reasons to question it. As with physicians, there are both good and mediocre advisors. Moreover, there are no licensing or certification processes for accrediting advisors as there are for MDs or DDSs. The institution usually selects a member of its science faculty who may be interested in doing advisory work and assigns the responsibility to this individual, and in turn relieving that person of some teaching responsibilities. The quality of the advice you will receive will depend upon the advisor's innate ability, experience, conscientiousness, other academic responsibilities, and number of other advisees. Thus, the extent of personal attention students receive varies greatly. All too frequently, student counseling is provided on a "clinic"-type basis. Students frequently turn to upperclass-level premeds (especially seniors) for advice; their advice can be misleading since their experience is limited, even if they have been successful in getting into medical school. In the event that you have reservations about some important issue, you can seek to validate your advisor's recommendations by discreetly discussing it with another faculty member on a confidential basis, by asking a friend at another school to pose the same question or problem there, or by contacting a medical school admission office or a private counseling service.

OTHER ASPECTS OF PREMEDICAL EDUCATION

Aside from the intellectual and technical challenges that medical education presents, there are a variety of other considerations that must be faced by professional school students. Among these are the realizations that:

1. There is a great diversity in the patients that one sees. One is not surrounded by a homogeneous population, but by all types of people—rich and poor, young and old, educated and illiterate.

2. There are emotional as well as physical factors to be dealt with in patient care, including crises in the lives of patients.

3. The issues of pain and suffering, of dying and death are aspects of life that are distant from the young, healthy student who must learn to cope with them in a sympathetic, yet somewhat detached, manner.

4. There are ethical issues to consider that cannot be defined scientifically, such as who shall be born, who shall live, who shall die.

Medical school does not adequately prepare one for the aforementioned problems and thus it is the premedical experiences and training that tend to mold one's values on these subjective issues. Only by an indepth exposure to the human condition through literature, religion, and philosophy can the student develop the capacity to face the nonacademic aspects of the medical professions.

3

APPLYING TO MEDICAL SCHOOL

☐ General considerations
☐ Selection factors
☐ The application
☐ Recommendations
☐ The interview
☐ The selection process
☐ Acceptance
☐ Ranking of medical schools
☐ Rejection

GENERAL CONSIDERATIONS

There are two basic factors which determine admission to medical school independent of the personal qualifications of each candidate. These factors are the total number of first-year places available and the total number of applicants for admission. Presently about 48% of those that apply are accepted to American medical schools; about half of those that are rejected are considered qualified to attend medical school.

In the decade between the Great Depression and World War II, the number of medical schools remained substantially unchanged and the number of first-year students actually decreased slightly. In the next two decades (1940–1960), nine new schools were established and, as a result, first-year enrollment increased by about 50%. In the fifteen year period, 1960–1975, 27 new schools came into being, bringing with them nearly another 65% increase in enrollment. Over the past decade (1976–86), only seven new schools became operational. Currently, only three are being considered for development on the mainland. All of this suggests the end of the era of medical school expansion, at least for this century.

The total number of places in each year may change as a result of the opening up of new institutions or the enlarging of class size at existing schools. The data of the past twenty years indicates that two-thirds of the increase in enrollment has been due to the latter and one-third to the former.

This is understandable because new schools usually start with small enrollments and then expand.

Prospects for 1985–1990

The era of new medical school development and expansion has essentially ended. The goal set by medical educators to meet national health care needs of 15,000 first-year enrollments has not only been met but even surpassed. For the past several years approximately 17,000 freshman medical students enrolled each year. All indications are that the available number of freshman places has peaked, since few new schools are likely to open and significant expansion of first-year class size is very unlikely to take place. Moreover, in anticipation of the expected decline of 22-year-old prospective applicants, there may be an annual small reduction (about 100) in the number of places available. This would mean that by 1990 the number of first-year places will be about 16,500, and the total number of applicants will have declined to about 30,000. If the trends noted above are projected over a 15-year period (to the year 2000), first-year places will decline to about 15,500, while the applicant pool will number about 29,000.

First-Year Applicants

During the decade from 1950 to 1960, the number of applicants significantly decreased (from 22,000 to 14,000 per year) and there was a corresponding decrease in the applicant/acceptee ratio (from 3.1/1 to 1.7/1). From the early 1960s to its peak in 1974, there was a continual increase in the number of applicants (from 14,000 to 43,000 per year). Since then the number of applicants has markedly declined (to 35,000 in 1984). Therefore, the applicant/acceptee ratio has decreased from 2.8/1 to 2.1/1. The decreased applicant pool in part may be due to the fact that academically weak students decline to apply and thus in reality competition for a place in a freshman class is still very intense.

From what has been noted above, it is obvious that there was a significant increase in the odds of gaining admission by those who applied during the 1975–1984 period, when the applicant/acceptee ratio was about 2:1, over applicants of the preceding 10 years when the ratio was closer to 3:1. In the years 1985–1990, the competition may turn out to be slightly less than it has been since 1975. This would be due to a possible slow, but gradual, decline in the total number of applicants, which has been estimated to be about 1,000 per year. When one looks ahead into the next decade (1990–2000), the ratio is

expected to fluctuate just above and below the 2:1 mark.

While the 2:1 ratio does indeed present a formidable challenge, it need not be taken as reflecting any particular individual's chances for admission. It should rather be taken as a general reflection of the level of competition. The reason for this is that the applicant pool no longer consists almost entirely of white males as it did for well over half this century. The pool now contains a sizable female segment and a smaller minority segment, which together make up more than 40% of the freshman class each year. This situation makes it more difficult to define the exact odds for a particular individual to gain admission solely on the basis of the applicant/acceptee ratio. The problem of mathematically defining the intensity of competition is compounded by the fact that about one-fourth of the total applicant pool may be repeaters whose chances for admission usually are significantly less than are those of new applicants. Thus in trying to assess your own overall chances, a multiplicity of factors comes into play. These include sex, race, residency, age, and financial status, as well as intellectual achievement and potential.

Early Admission

Most of the applicants to medical school plan to have their baccalaureate degree before beginning medical study. Of the entering class for any recent year, less than 10% of the first-year students lacked their bachelor's degree.

There is considerable variation in policy regarding the admission of students after only three years of college study. The percentage of early admissions varies between none and 25%. In any case, only the exceptional student should consider applying for early admission, since only such an applicant will have a good chance of being accepted and the best chance of successfully completing his/her study. Applying early and not being accepted, however, does not prejudice your chances for admission the following year.

If you are interested in the early admission program, compare the colleges that offer such programs, using the information included in Table 6 (Chapter 8).

SELECTION FACTORS

The admission process is theoretically geared to recognize applicants who measure up to a hypothetical image of the person who, in the consensus of the medical school's admission committee, will prove to be a successful medical student and in time a qualified and dedicated practitioner. Those who are accepted may not have all the qualities that a committee seeks. There may even be some areas of weakness in a candidate's profile. The weaknesses however, can be offset by strengths in other areas so that on balance the applicant's overall picture is one that meets the standards that each school sets. In other words, one need not be the ideal candidate in order to achieve success.

It should also be realized, as was implied earlier, that some applicants may, at first glance, possess an impressive array of qualifications but nevertheless do not succeed in gaining admission. These candidates unfortunately proved unable to effectively project to the committee, either indirectly through their application or directly at their interviews, all the strengths they possess (as well as mask their deficiencies). Having solid credentials and being able to market yourself as a prospective good physician is the winning combination that will open the door to a place in a freshman medical school class.

Some selection factors, such as GPA or MCAT scores, can readily be put into quantitative terms, while others, such as personality or motivation, cannot. Nevertheless, both types of factors are important and have a strong bearing on the outcome of the admissions process. Specifically, they determine if you qualify to be placed at some point into the applicant interview pool and at a later time into the applicant acceptance pool.

Academic Achievement

Academic achievement is measured in terms of your grade point average, science course performance, and college(s) attended.

Grade Point Average (GPA). The application that each medical school receives on behalf of an individual applicant will contain a facsimile of the candidate's college transcript and where applicable any postgraduate record. It will show the courses taken and grades received during the regular academic year as well as during any summer. (Those high school courses and grades for which advanced placement credit were given are also listed). Courses that the applicant is taking or is planning to take are also frequently requested. This self-designed record is checked for accuracy against official transcripts sent by your school and will form the basis of your GPA.

Since 1975, the GPA of entering medical students has fluctuated, but the trend has been downward. In the most recent year for which data is available (1983), 45% had a 3.6–4.0 average, 53% had a 2.6–3.5 average, and 2% averaged below 2.6. These data suggest that applicants with a GPA below 3.0 will have serious difficulties securing any acceptances. It is thought by some, however, that for the 1985–1990 period, and

possibly even longer, there *may* be a decline in the number of A average students and an increase in the number of B or even C students admitted to freshman medical school classes. The assumptions beneath this projection are that the applicant pool is declining and that medical school admission committees may alter the priority of selection criteria. There is some reason to believe that increased emphasis will be placed on personal attributes and somewhat less on quantitative data such as GPA and MCAT scores. Nevertheless, even if this situation develops, applicants with higher undergraduate and science course averages and MCAT scores will be more competitive. They stand a better chance of being rated higher in the initial screening process, and they are more likely to have their entire application more thoroughly examined and to be granted an interview. Thus the quantitative factors will remain a very vital and for many, a critical element of the selection process. You should therefore strive to attain as high a level of achievement as is possible.

While the GPA is one of the major factors examined as part of the initial screening process, it is usually viewed in the context of the applicant's overall educational data. The reasons are that the GPA is subject to grade inflation, is relative to the college attended and the course of studies pursued, and only represents an overall level of performance rather than the direction of the performance.

Medical school admission officers know that grade inflation—namely, artificially high grades that do not accurately reflect the level of academic achievement—is a common phenomenon of undergraduate education. Thus while they do not minimize the value of a high GPA, they do not necessarily take it at face value. Admission officers seek to establish how authentic the GPA is by checking to see at which college the grades were earned. Thus an applicant with a good GPA attending a college with low admission selection standards will not be much better off than another applicant with somewhat lower grades who is enrolled at a more selective school. Also, the GPA is viewed in the context of the applicant's course of study. An applicant who met the premedical course requirements by completing bona fide courses designed for science majors will obviously be favored over one whose courses were intended for nonscience majors. Similarly, an applicant who is successfully completing a science major will tend to be more credible than one who is not doing so.

The breakdown of an applicant's GPA frequently provides a more significant insight into an applicant's achievement than does the numerical value of the GPA. Thus a consistent level of performance would tend to imply that this is the applicant's optimal achievement level. On the other hand, an erratic performance pattern, either upward or downward, may well reflect a person's response to the academic challenge being faced. An upward pattern suggests an ability to adjust to college, overcome an initial disappointing performance level, and then proceed to attain a high level of achievement even when the educational demands are increasing. A downward pattern would tend to indicate the reverse—namely, the inability to maintain a sustained high level of achievement in the face of increased educational pressures. In other words, when the values of GPAs are the same, a GPA with a consistently good achievement level and an upward pattern will have a greater impact on the screening and selection process than a similar GPA with a downward achievement trend.

Science Course Grades. The science course grades on your record is another factor considered in the admission process. This is reasonable since medicine is the application of scientific principles that are intensively studied during the first two years of professional school. While a straight A science average is certainly not mandatory for admission to medical school, a solid level of consistently good performance (3.5 or better) will serve to demonstrate the potential to cope with the intellectual demands of the basic medical sciences.

Your science grades and the effort it took to achieve them will also help you evaluate your own abilities and the wisdom of your career choice. Incidentally, it is not essential to enjoy all your premedical science courses, but a genuine interest in science is essential.

It should be emphasized that just as the GPA's impact is relative to the college attended, so too is the science course work judged. Similarly, the grade pattern for work completed over a three-year period can be of special value. Consistently good grades and an upward trend clearly present a positive image of your science potential.

College Attended. It has already been noted that the college attended affects the evaluation of an applicant's GPA and science course work by the admission committee. It also has an overall impact on admission chances in general, for three reasons. First, attendance at a university which has an affiliated medical school offers a degree of priority for acceptance into the university's own medical college. This is because medical schools traditionally accept a significant number of freshmen from their own college. Second, it appears, at least statistically speaking, that an applicant from a private undergraduate institution has a greater chance of acceptance at a private medical school. Third, coming from a college that has established a good medical school admission track record is a decided advantage. There is an initial favorable bias because of the positive image

that such an institution's name generates toward all its applicants.

Intellectual Potential

Your academic performance, usually after a three-year period of undergraduate studies, provides a reasonable measure of your intellectual potential. Its usefulness, however, is tempered by the status of the school you attend, by the possibility of grade inflation, and possibly by the impact of pass/fail grades. For these reasons there are two additional factors considered in obtaining a comprehensive and reliable determination of the future performance of a medical student. These factors are MCAT scores and recommendations.

MCAT Scores. The Medical College Admission Test (MCAT) is a day-long, standardized, multiple-choice examination (see page 34), which is given twice each year. It is designed to determine your basic, factual scientific knowledge and to assess your skills in data analysis, problem solving, and verbal comprehension. The MCAT determines your potential. The test is designed in such a manner that the value of memorization is deemphasized while analytic and synthetic intellectual capabilities are tested. This clearly implies that one of the major goals in college should be to develop "thinking" skills in exactly these areas. This can best be done over an extended period of time rather than by cramming for a few weeks or even months, and/or depending on commercial MCAT preparation programs.

The MCAT score is particularly important because it provides a quantitative measurement that easily lends itself, together with your GPA (and science average), to a screening formula. Because of the large volume of applications, such formulas are used by *some* medical schools as a rapid preliminary evaluation technique. The formula baseline figure, which can be adjusted during the admission season, can determine if your application deserves more careful examination. This may involve reviewing your recommendations, essay, and extracurricular activities to determine the possibility of an invitation for an interview. The MCAT score by itself will also be used to assess the validity of your academic record. This is especially true when the problem of grade inflation exists and when the academic caliber of a school is unknown or uncertain.

The MCAT is therefore an admission obstacle that must be overcome by all premedical students because almost all schools require this examination (for an exception, see the University of Rochester or Johns Hopkins profile, chapter 7). This examination should not be looked upon as a major admission barrier, but rather, from a positive perspective, as a potential asset that can enhance your admission potential. Thus, if you have a high GPA, good MCAT scores (above 60 total, ≈10 or better on each subtest) will confirm your status as an attractive applicant and thus speed processing your application toward the interview stage. On the other hand, if you are a borderline or weak applicant, impressive MCAT scores can significantly strengthen the chance of having your application reviewed more thoroughly. It is at this point that your letters of recommendation (see below) will have a special influence in determining your true intellectual potential.

Letters of Recommendation. Letters of recommendation supplement the quantitative data provided by transcripts and MCAT scores. They add a positive or negative tone to the overall impression that your college work and aptitude test have established. All medical schools expect recommendations, preferably from your Health Professions Advisory Committee or from several natural science faculty members at your school.

Personal Attributes

Aside from your academic achievements and intellectual potential, a number of personal attributes can have an impact of varying degree on your admission chances. These attributes can be placed into five categories, which will be discussed below.

Extracurricular and Summer Activities. See discussion in Chapter 2, pages 11 and 12.

Exposure to Medicine. This factor was, in part, discussed in Chapter 2, "Extracurricular and Summer Activities." It should be noted that in addition to unstructured observation and service opportunities as a hospital volunteer, some institutions offer formal premedical observation programs on a group basis. In the course of such a program, premedical students, like medical interns, rotate through various departments and may even be given lectures by attending physicians on the staff. Some students may receive a small stipend. Such programs can provide an invaluable opportunity for prospective medical students, by permitting them a direct personal view of the actual world of medicine and the realities of medical training. To learn about such exceptionally meaningful opportunities, make inquiries at the volunteer office of local hospitals; also ask your premedical advisor or senior premedical students who may have already participated in such a program.

Special Achievements. Medical schools usually look for applicants who, for one reason or another, stand out among the large pool of qualified individuals seeking admission. Therefore gaining acceptance into honor societies or receiving awards for scholastic achievement or service will strengthen your admission potential. Demonstrated leadership capacity will also enhance your appeal. Achievements such as serving as a student senator at your college, gaining election to an important student office, organizing a band, forming a volunteer group of students to visit the sick at your school infirmary or the elderly and handicapped in the neighborhood, or tutoring underprivileged youngsters would all be a strong plus on your credentials. These kinds of accomplishments demonstrate that you have initiative, concern for others, an ability to interact constructively as part of a team effort (a requirement for modern patient care), and the determination to succeed. All these qualities are desirable in applicants seeking to enter such professions as medicine.

Individual Status. Your individual status can have a significant bearing on your chances for admission. Five factors are involved: citizenship, state of residence, age, sex, and whether you are a minority group member. Each of these factors are discussed separately.

Citizenship. U.S. medical schools have more qualified applicants than places available to train them. Moreover the tuition paid by medical students covers only part of the actual training costs, with the balance made up by the school, state, and federal funding. Consequently, medical schools naturally have as their primary obligation the training of U.S. citizens and thus only rarely accept noncitizens into their freshman classes. Applicants not holding citizenship status, including Canadians, are clearly at a great disadvantage when applying for admission to U.S. schools. This handicap can be somewhat diminished if the applicant can secure a green card and establish permanent residency status, as well as initiate the first formal steps toward citizenship.

State Residence. The state where you reside is another major factor in determining your chances for success. Many state schools have significantly lower tuition levels for their residents and exclude nonresidents from admission as well. They have this policy because they are funded by state taxes and thus believe that their primary obligation is to train professionals who not only live in the state but who are likely to set up practice there. The state of your residence should be carefully considered when the time comes to make up the list of schools to which you plan to apply.

If your state has only a few medical schools, you need not consider this an insurmountable obstacle because there are quite a few private schools that do not discriminate against out-of-state residents, although they may demonstrate geographical preferences to applicants from a general section of the country.

To be classified as a legal or bona fide resident of a state, you usually must maintain domicile in that state for at least 12 months preceding the date of first enrollment in an institution of higher education in that state. Student status at an institution of higher education (for example, as an undergraduate) does not constitute eligibility for residence status with regard to graduate-level work in the same state. You must maintain residence in a non-student capacity for the prescribed time in order to gain residence status. The student's eligibility to establish residence is also determined by his/her status as an adult or a minor. A minor is any person who has not reached the age of 21 (18 in some states). For minors, the legal residence is that of his/her parents, surviving parent, or legal guardian. As a result of Supreme Court rulings, the right of state schools to charge higher fees for out-of-state students has been upheld, but it may now be easier for such nonresident students who are 18 or older to establish legal residence and thus take advantage of the lower rate.

Two groups of states generally offer prospective applicants a statistically better chance of admission: those with many freshman places and relatively few in-state applicants (e.g., Illinois, Texas) and those with no in-state medical school but with special admission arrangements with other state schools (e.g., Maine, Wyoming).

Age.   Medical schools prefer applicants who are in the 20–25 age group. Exceptions are made for select individuals, but the upper acceptance limit is usually about 35. The most favored applicants of the older group are those whose postcollege careers have been associated with medicine: research assistants, physician assistants, graduate students in one of the biomedical sciences, or holders of advanced degrees in one of these areas. Less attractive are applicants who would like to give up established careers as dentists, podiatrists, engineers, lawyers, accountants, or physicists, and who now seek to become physicians because of personal disillusionment with present activities. The latter group, seeking a career change instead of personal advancement, represent a higher risk than the former, because of concern that the pattern of giving up one's existing career might be repeated at a later time when this same individual is in medical school, training, or practice.

In the light of the aforementioned, an applicant whose age is above 25 (and preferably under 35) should present solid credentials in science course requirements, acceptable MCAT scores, good evidence of familiarity with the demands and responsibilities of a medical career, and above all, very convincing reasons for giving up a current career and seeking one as a physician.

That there exists a significant pool of postbaccalaureate students who become premeds is evident from the fact that there are schools (Columbia, Bennington, Goucher) that offer special programs designed so these students can meet the premedical science course requirements. In addition, the University of Miami offers an advanced placement program for those having a science Ph.D. Thus it is possible that highly motivated and well-qualified career changers can succeed in spite of inherent difficulties, if they can establish a strong case for themselves and present it effectively.

Sex.   The applicant's sex can influence the admission process. All medical schools accept both males and females as applicants and most encourage strongly motivated and well-qualified women to seek admission. Women currently make up about 33% of the national freshman class admitted. Some schools are more liberal in admitting women than others (see Table 4). A detailed discussion of women in medicine is found in Chapter 5.

Minority Status.   If you can claim minority status— namely, if you are black, American Indian/Alaskan native, Mexican American, Puerto Rican, Asian or Pacific Islander, or other Hispanic—you will be given special consideration, because most schools actively seek to enroll minority group members in their freshman classes. As a result, minority students currently make up about 15% of the national freshman class. A more detailed discussion of minority opportunities can be found in Chapter 5.

Personal Characteristics.   These include a wide variety of factors, such as personality, maturity, appearance, and ability to communicate, many of which become evident at the interview. They can have a decisive impact on your admission chances at that time.

In summary, there are more than ten factors that, to varying degrees, play a role in the admission process. An honest assessment of yourself in terms of each of these factors will give you an insight into your own chances for admission.

THE APPLICATION

How to Apply

There are currently two means of applying—directly to the school and indirectly through the American Medical College Application Service (AMCAS). The direct approach involves writing and submitting applications to any school that is *not* a member of the AMCAS. The application for each of these schools should be returned with a check covering the fee, which varies in amount from school to school. Table 6 in Chapter 8 gives the application fees for each of the non-AMCAS schools. In the Appendix to this guide, you will find a sample AMCAS application form as well as a sample form from a non-AMCAS school.

If the schools to which you wish to apply are members of the AMCAS, you must obtain an AMCAS Application Request Card from your Premedical Advisory Office or from AMCAS, Suite 301, 1776 Massachusetts Avenue, NW, Washington, D.C. 20036. The AMCAS Application Booklet will be sent to you and this booklet will serve as your application to all AMCAS schools to which you are applying. The cost is rather high—$30 for 1 school and $15 for each additional school. AMCAS reproduces your application (as well as your transcript and all your MCAT scores, but not your recommendations) for distribution to the schools, but the decision regarding admission continues to rest with the individual schools. Schools presently subscribing to AMCAS are indicated in Table 6, Chapter 8. It should be noted however, that after viewing your AMCAS application, some schools may require a final application and charge an additional fee of $10 to $60.

When applying, whether it be directly to the schools or through AMCAS, be sure to consider the following points:

1. All application forms should be filled out neatly; preferably use a typewriter.

2. All questions should be answered carefully, fully, and accurately.

3. Where free space is provided for any comments, such as on the AMCAS application, use the space judiciously. Thus, where some clarification of your academic record is desirable (such as a prolonged illness that was responsible for poor grades during a certain semester, or where a transfer to another school occurred), advantage should be taken of the opportunity to do so. An impressive essay on your motivation to become a physician is also appropriate (see discussion below).

4. The photograph submitted should be of good quality and should provide a favorable likeness.

5. Arrangements should be made for a transcript and the necessary recommendations to go to each non-AMCAS school. Only one copy of the transcript is needed for the AMCAS, but copies of your recommendations should be sent directly to all AMCAS schools.

When to Apply

The earliest date which medical schools begin accepting applications varies; the exact dates for each school are indicated in Table 6, Chapter 8. As a rule, your application should be submitted in July or August of the year preceding your planned enrollment. Naturally, the earlier your application is received, the earlier you will receive consideration. Thus, in the case of superior students, it may insure an early acceptance which would reduce anxiety and make it unnecessary to apply to additional schools. Moreover, prolonged delay in applying means that you will be competing for a smaller number of openings since part of the class may be filled by the time your application is received. Deadlines for receipt of applications at each college are also listed in Table 6, Chapter 8.

Early Decision Plan

From the students' point of view, applying to medical school is both an expensive and an emotionally trying experience. From the medical schools' point of view, selection is both a time-consuming and laborious process. To reduce the burden somewhat for both parties, the procedures of early decision have been introduced and adopted by some schools. Thus, if you are anxious to attend a particular school and you feel that you have a good chance of gaining admission, you should submit your application before the early decision deadline (usually August 1) to the selected school (but to none other at this time). Once your supporting data has been received, an interview will be scheduled if desirable and a prompt decision will be sent to you (usually about October 1). If this decision is in the affirmative you are obligated to accept the offer and refrain from seeking admission elsewhere. If you are rejected, you can then go ahead and apply to as many schools as you wish. Only if you have a sincere interest in attending a particular school and only if you have a good chance of being accepted should you use the early decision approach.

Medical schools participating in the early decision plan are indicated in Table 6, Chapter 8. It should be realized that schools offering this option will only fill a part of their freshman class by this means. The remainder of the places, which will probably be the bulk of the class, will be filled by students applying under the standard procedure.

Where to Apply

The decision as to which schools to apply to is in part determined by the total number of applications you plan to file. The estimated national average has been increasing and now is about nine per applicant. The actual number you should send out is best determined by your financial means and a realistic evaluation of your chances for gaining acceptance. A part of the financial considerations that should be taken into account is the cost for out-of-town interviews.

In general, one can suggest the following generalization regarding the number of applications that should be submitted in accordance with your academic record:

Table 2. Relationship of academic record to suggested number of applications

Academic Record	Number of Applications
A– to A+	5–15
B+ to A–	10–20
B to B+	15–25
C to B	25–40

The exact number of applications within each range should be determined by financial considerations, test scores, and possibilities for favorable interviews. A large volume of applications may be less important than selectivity as to which schools you should apply to, since in many cases, applications to some schools for some students are a waste of time, money, and effort.

Consider the following criteria when determining which schools you will apply to:

1. At which medical schools will you find students of your caliber; where have students from your undergraduate college gained acceptance in recent years?

2. Which schools can you afford to attend? Determine what your financial means are and exactly how much you can expect to pay for tuition and room and board without overextending yourself.

3. Which schools are located in areas that meet your personal needs? Do you prefer a large metropolitan area or a smaller town environment?

4. If you are planning to apply to an out-of-state school, does the school accept a significant number of nonresident students? Consider the possibility of schools located farther from home, even though these may not be the choices of your fellow students.

5. What schools offer curricula that are amenable to your style of intellectual endeavor? Carefully compare the curricula for differing schools to see which is the type in which you would be most comfortable.

The Essay

The AMCAS application is four pages long and the questions asked are straightforward. Detailed instructions are included.

Page two of the application is entitled "Personal Comments" and is completely blank. It enables you to communicate directly with the admission personnel who screen the applications and with those who evaluate the candidates. Your essay can thus be considered your brief or appeal for a place in the next freshman class. It affords you the opportunity to express yourself and to present your attributes in the most appealing manner possible, so the reader will want to get to know you personally by means of an interview.

One approach to drafting your essay can be to itemize all the information you wish to convey: biographical highlights, motivational factors behind your career choice, significant life experiences, and information about yourself or your past performance that needs elaboration or clarification. Having identified the key elements, you can next proceed to preparing a preliminary draft. The lead and concluding paragraphs probably deserve special attention since they will more likely be read during an initial scan of your essay. Once the draft is prepared, put it aside for a few days and then reread it and revise it as much as you feel is required. You may want to repeat this once again before your rough draft is completed.

You should next seek one or more outside reviewers to read and frankly criticize your essay. This may come from an able senior premed student, an English professor at your school, a young physician, or your premedical advisor. Since the essay is yours, you have the final decision of how much to revise your draft essay. It should be realized that the more people you ask, the more pressure for revision there will be. Thus, a reasonable cutoff point is desirable; that is when you are satisfied that your essay presents an honest image of you in the best possible light. When you reach that point, type your essay neatly and accurately and make sure that it stays within the allotted one page.

There is no "ideal" essay. Thus, the samples of conventional and unconventional essays shown on pages 23–24 are designed only to give you an insight into what other premeds have written. If your essay "sells" you as a potential attractive candidate, you have done your job.

Sample Conventional Essay

During my freshman and sophomore years at University A, I worked as a physical therapy assistant on a volumtary, parttime basis at Medical Center B in Hometown. In the course of this experience, the most important conversation I had relevant to my career goal was with a nurse. I had observed that she was exceptionally intelligent, inowledgeable and competent and I asked her why she had elected to become a nurse rather than a doctor. "A physician has to make a lifetime commitment to medicine; his profession must be his first priority. I am not prepared to have my profession dominate my life.? Her response did not surprise me, it only served to reinforce my commitment to a profession in which I had become actively involved.

For the summer of 1983, while I could have continued my work in physical therapy, I chose to seek a position which I felt would provide a new perspective from which to view medicine. Upon returning to Bigtown, I began working at the Department of Radiology of Medical Center C. My activities were concentrated in the Special Procedures Division where one of my duties involved assisting the nurses to prepare the patient and the room for the scheduled test. I observed the procedures which usually were angiograms, venograms, or percutaneous nephrostomies. I was usually provided with a detailed explanation in the course of the procedure which was informative and educational. At the conclusion of the procedure, I listened to the radiologist read the x-rays and learned about the patient's problems and the appropriate treatments mandated. The staff, after getting to know me, encouraged my spending time with many of the apprehensive patients to try to alleviate some of their anxieties and to be generally supportive. In addition, for one hour each day, I attended classes with the interns where I learned basic human anatomy, how to interpret some of the nuances of complicated x-rays and listened to a discussion of some of the interesting cases that occurred each week. My experiences at Medical Center C were so stimulating that I immediately applied for placement for the following summer and was accepted.

In June 1984, I began to work as a research assistant for Dr. Teicher, a surgeon at Medical Center C. The research concerns the reliability of the criteria for the diagnosis of appendicitis. The justification for the research is the problematic nature of diagnoses as evidenced by the significant negative laparotomy rate. The aim of this study is to assess the feasibility of increasing the diagnostic accuracy. A large part of my activities involves using the hospital computer to retrieve, study and evaluate appropriate patient charts in order to enlarge the statistical sample. My activities have not only made me more appreciative of the importance of medical research, but also it has shown me how some physicians combine their practice with clinical research.

After reading the recent article, "The Ordeal; Life As a Medical Resident" in The New York Times Magazine, my understanding of the strong commitment a physician must make was strengthened. Unlike the nurse in Hometown, I have been impressed by the many doctors who lead rich and rewarding home lives as well as being totally dedicated to their profession.

Besides a sense of dedication, I am aware that appropriate academic ability is needed to meet the demands of medical school and postgraduate training, I elected to attend University A because it is an excellent institution of high education and I wanted to be on my own so as to develop and self-confidence necessary to manage my life. My high academic performance and my science MCAT scores confirm my ability to handle the anticipated demands of the basic medical sciences. In the light of both my clinical exposure and educational preparation, I feel confident that I will be prepared for the demands of medical education, training, and practice. I look forward to beginning this exciting and challenging adventure.

Note: Names and places in this and the following essay have been disguised.

Sample Unconventional Essay

Raindrops pelted my body as I absently stared at the small concentric circles formed from the fusion of a raindrop and a puddle. I loosely gripped the 14-foot fiberglass pole with my perspiring hands, and thought: the pole vault--decathlon--third event--second day--the bar set at a logically impossible height, as Mr. Spock would say. Pressure. Whatever the outcome, I would not deny myself the challenge. So I strode down the slick runway, planted the pole, and launched myself up and over the bar--and subsequently into the giant sponge of a pit that sucked me into its depths. Of course, a requirement after a successful vault is back flip in the pit, which I immediately performed to the delight of the roaring crowd--all 23 of them. Thus ends another chapter in THE LIFE AND TIMES OF JOE WHITE.

Now let us turn to a later chapter, Joe White: The Road to Becoming a Physician.

My ambition to become a physician arose from my desire to help people. But not to help people like a waiter or a mechanic helps people. I want to help people who truly require my services. The first thing that anyone must do in order to help another is to care. I believe this to be the most important quality of a physician. And I believe that I possess this quality. I do, however, realize that it is not always easy to care about someone--especially if he does not seem to care about himself. My experiences with many different types of people will be valuable when caring for patients. However, my motives are not all so unselfish. I have always been fascinated with the structure and functions of the body. My high school and college educations have given me a broad background from which to build. By becoming a physician I will be able to further pursue my inquiry into the functioning of the body.

The road to becoming a physician may be full of potholes, detours, and do not enters. The way is not easy. But, I do not know the meaning of the word "quit" and do not intend to look it up.

Now that I have explained my motivation, let me explain my commitment. When I arrived at Chatham College, I obtained employment in the Health Center as an assistant laboratory technician/phlebotomist, where I have been working ever since. This job has provided me the important experience of interacting with patients. Then the director of the Health Center requested that I join his Student Health Advisory Committee, which functions to inform the student body of various health issues.

To obtain more knowledge about physicians and the practice of medicine, I served as a volunteer in a cardiology department. From this experience I learned much (relatively speaking) about cardiology and realized that the life of the physician was not all roses.

My academic life has not been limited to books. I worked with Dr. Jim Pike of Chatham College on epilepsy research. I enjoyed this very much and found it to be an interesting and informative experience.

There was much more to my life than scholastics. I spent many a night with the love of my life--hockey. My club team was able to successfully compete against division II and III teams. I also spent a good deal of time playing the gentleman's game of rugby.

Through my various activities I have encountered many different types of people. This fall I will be exposed to an entirely new environment. I will be taking a break from my regular science courses in order to study in Paris, where I hope to expand my cultural and intellectual horizons.

I hope that these excerpts from the book of my life have given you a little insight into me as a person. The next chapter is still in the planning stages, but after it is written I will be sure to send you a copy of Joe White: The Physician.

RECOMMENDATIONS

Letters of recommendation can have a significant impact if they describe you in realistic, qualitative terms (and when they rank you with respect to others applying from your class.) When the letter writers discuss not your quantitative achievements (midterm and final or course grades), but you as a person (in terms of your innate potential, motivation, personality, reliability), the communication will be effective. If your recommendation profile makes you stand out as a potentially quality medical student and physician, your admission chances will be significantly enhanced and the possibility of your being invited for an interview will be strengthened. If, on the other hand, your letters of recommendation are bland or noncommittal, your chances of getting an interview will be reduced.

It is your responsibility to see that recommendations in your behalf are sent to the medical schools. You can strengthen the quality of your recommendations by making sure that your Health Professions' Advisor gets to know you and has a favorable impression of you. In addition, you will usually be asked to select the instructors who will be called upon to submit their evaluations of you to the Health Professions' Committee or to send out separate letters of recommendation. It is clearly advantageous to ensure that these individuals really know you. This can best be achieved by asking appropriate questions during recitation periods, at personal conferences, or better still, in the course of doing a research or independent study project. All this requires appropriate initiative on your part, which can pay rewarding dividends at the time you apply to medical school.

Letters from prestigious professors, as reflected by their academic rank, are obviously more impressive and effective than those from teaching assistants or faculty instructors. It is not advisable to ask for a recommendation unless you are fairly confident that the individual knows you well enough and is known to follow through on such requests. Otherwise, you may end up with a perfunctory recommendation and even such a letter may be late in coming. Therefore, you should tactfully ask the people from whom you are requesting letters if they feel that they are in a position to write about you in a manner that will help your admission chances.

It is also appropriate to arrange to have letters of recommendation sent in your behalf (to your school committee or directly to the medical schools) by a hospital staff member where you have worked (in a volunteer or paid capacity), other employers or faculty members who have known you well as the result of working for them on a special project; these letters can supplement your committee's recommendation. Letters from clergy, family physicians, relatives, friends, or alumni (unless the latter know you exceedingly well) are not only ineffective but may be self-defeating. Such letters leave the clear impression that you have weak credentials that need such unsolicited outside support to merit attention.

In order to arrange that a committee recommendation be sent out in your behalf, your Advisory Office may require that you complete forms comparable to an AMCAS application (see page 13) and be interviewed by your Premedical Advisor and/or Advisory Committee. These proceedings can serve as a "trial run" in preparation for the actual application process. It is therefore advantageous for you to prepare, early in your upper junior semester, a short statement incorporating autobiographical highlights, an outline of your personal attributes, information about relevant medical exposure, and a brief discussion of your motives for selecting a medical career. This statement should be given to professors from whom you have requested recommendations at the time you request them, in order to facilitate their task; it can also be used in completing forms requested by your committee and later by AMCAS.

THE INTERVIEW

At the outset, it should be realized that the interview is not just a brief exchange between yourself and one or more representatives of the school that has requested your appearance. The interview should not be looked upon as a one-sided affair, but rather as an opportunity for a dialogue that has advantages for both the school and for you.

The medical school uses the interview to determine:

1. if your personal attributes are as appealing as your academic record (this goes, of course, for a student who is already academically acceptable), and if your personal attributes will enable you to overcome any deficiency that may appear;

2. if your personal attributes will place you in the overall acceptable range (if you are considered academically borderline);

3. the nature of, or permit clarification of, some apparent weakness and to determine if you have the personal attributes to overcome the deficiency (if you are considered to have some obvious academic or physical deficiency).

The interview will permit you to:

1. have an opportunity to sell yourself by projecting

as favorable an image as possible, and thus overcoming any shortcoming in your record;

2. familiarize yourself with the campus and with its facilities, as well as with members of its student body;

3. obtain firsthand answers to questions that may not yet have been answered.

Significance of the Interview

The receipt of the letter requesting that you come for an interview clearly indicates that the medical school is seriously interested. The large volume of applications has meant that admissions officers have become quite selective in granting interviews. Admissions officers have at their disposal only a limited number of interviewers who are usually faculty members and whose time is obviously very valuable. Thus, obtaining an invitation to come for an interview means either that they wish to confirm a tentative decision that you are acceptable or they think that you deserve a chance to prove that you merit admission in spite of some possible weakness. The interviewer will endeavor to appraise such personal qualifications as responsiveness, warmth of personality, poise, ability to communicate ideas clearly and concisely, and soundness of motivation.

In the interviewer's written report these criteria will usually be touched upon:

1. *Physical appearance:* Grooming, bearing and self-confident manner.

2. *Personality:* Friendliness, ability to establish rapport and charm, sense of humor.

3. *Communication skills:* Ability to express ideas clearly, with fluency and in an intelligent manner.

4. *Motivation:* Soundness of career choice, conviction of interests.

5. *Maturity:* Ability to undertake responsibility career entails.

6. *Interests:* What educational, social and cultural interests do you have?

7. *Level of concern:* Do you have a genuine interest in people, their problems and helping them solve them—empathy?

8. *Emotional stability:* Composure under pressure.

9. *Intellectual potential:* Have you truly demonstrated superior intellectual abilities?

10. Overall subjective reaction of the interviewer to the applicant.

Evaluate yourself in terms of items 1 to 9 as honestly as possible and work to improve your weaknesses. By subjecting yourself to mock interviews by your peers, you can determine where your weaknesses are, and how well you are doing to overcome them. Allow your mock interviewers to be honest and candid (even if it hurts your feelings).

Preparation for the Interview

There are a number of steps that you can take that will help to prepare you for your interview:

1. Read the catalog of the school and become familiar with any special facilities or programs it has to offer.

2. Discuss with fellow applicants from your college the nature of their experiences at interviews at various schools.

3. Dress neatly and be properly groomed.

4. Arrive for the interview early, so that you locate the interview site with time to spare for an adjustment to your surroundings.

5. If your interviewer is late, do not indicate annoyance for being kept waiting. (He/she probably was delayed by something important.)

6. Act naturally and avoid looking nervous.

7. Answer the questions raised without trying to anticipate what you think the interviewer may wish to hear.

8. Avoid controversial subjects and don't raise sensitive issues.

9. Be prepared to explain your specific interest in the school you are visiting.

10. If you inadvertently "flub" a question, don't let it upset you for the rest of your interview.

11. Be well rested, alert and honest. Do not exaggerate your scholastic achievements or extracurricular activities.

12. If you worked on a research (or other) project, be prepared to discuss it fluently, accurately and concisely.

13. If you have had exposure to medicine by working at a hospital, be prepared to discuss it if asked, or work it into the conversation in an appropriate manner.

14. If you can, find out the departmental affiliation of your interviewer in advance from an admissions office secretary, or by checking his name in the school catalog.

You may then be able to raise a topic of special mutual interest (e.g., if being interviewed by a surgeon, you may wish to mention that you saw an appendectomy).

15. Do not hesitate to ask questions about the school and its program—or about the interviewer's activities (e.g., how much time does he have for research).

16. Talk to a classmate who has had an interview at the school. Get his impressions of the school and interview. Remember that it is unlikely that you will get the same interviewer—but it is possible.

17. If the school is of special interest to you, you may wish to contact an alumnus in attendance or a recent graduate.

18. Bear in mind that the school is trying to get a sense of you as a person—to see what motivates you—to understand why you want to enter the health sciences, and to become convinced that you are a worthy, potential colleague.

19. Be prepared to answer some typical questions that frequently come up. Some of these are as follows:

Typical interview questions:

1. Why did you attend _____ College?

2. What are your extracurricular activities?

3. Why do you want to become a physician?

4. What books and newspapers do you read?

5. What do you do during the summer?

6. How will you finance your education?

7. What other schools have you applied to?

8. What do you plan to specialize in?

9. Why did you get a poor grade in _____ ?

10. Do you have any questions?

11. Which medical school is your first choice?

12. What kind of social life do you have?

13. Describe your schedule at _____ .

14. What were your favorite courses taken?

15. Did you participate in any special science projects in high school or college?

16. Will your religious convictions interfere with your studies or practice?

17. How did you arrive at your decision to become a physician?

18. What area of medicine do you wish to enter?

19. Describe a typical day in your life.

20. Do you feel you should have gone to a different college?

21. What do you do in your spare time?

22. Tell me about yourself and your family.

23. What do you think are the most pressing social problems?

24. Describe your study habits.

25. What are your hobbies?

26. What experiences led you to your career choice?

27. What are your plans for marriage and a family?

28. Why isn't (*name of school*) your first choice?

29. What are the characteristics of a good physician (or dentist)?

30. Why do you think you are better suited for admission than your classmates?

31. What is the status of the MD in modern society?

32. What has been your most significant accomplishment to date?

33. If you had great will power, how would you change yourself?

34. What are the characteristics of a mature person?

35. What can be determined about an applicant at an interview?

36. What books have you read recently?

37. Describe your research at _____ .

38. What is your opinion on _____ (major current event issues)?

39. What newspaper do you read and which columnist do you like the best?

40. How do you cope with frustrating situations?

41. What will you do if you are not accepted?

42. How do you rank among the preprofessional students at your school?

43. Have you ever worked with people, and if so in what capacity?

44. Who has had the greatest influence on your life?

45. What made you apply to our school?

46. What are your weaknesses?

47. Describe your exposure to medicine at _____ .

48. If you are accepted to more than one school, how will you decide which to attend?

49. How do you see yourself ten years from now?

50. Why did your grades go down in your _____ semester?

Atypical interview questions:

1. What is your favorite piece of music?

2. Do you know enough about hockey to compare the Bruins and the Rangers?

3. What would you do to improve the quality of life in large cities?

4. Describe the difference between lactose and glucose.

5. What movies did you see recently?

6. What do you think of Billy Martin?

7. If you were to have a year off, what would you do with it?

8. What is your favorite form of entertainment?

9. What is your opinion of socialized medicine?

10. What are physicians' obligations to their patients?

11. How would you respond to a patient who you learn is terminally ill?

12. How do your parents feel about your career goals?

13. What are characteristics of aromatic compounds?

14. Why do you think that life was based on the carbon atom?

15. What do you think about and how did you prepare for the MCAT?

16. Can you explain why your MCAT scores went up (down) when you took the test a second time?

17. Would you be willing to serve in an area where there is a physician shortage?

18. What specialty are you considering?

19. What message would you like me to convey to the admission committee in your behalf?

20. What were your most favorite and least favorite courses in college?

21. What demands do you think medicine will make upon you?

22. How will marriage and having a family fit in with your career plans?

23. Have you been interviewed or accepted elsewhere?

24. What are your thoughts about the expected physician surplus?

25. What are your views on: abortion, gay rights, capital punishment, etc.

The following steps will be of additional help in preparing for the interview:

1. Prepare rehearsed answers to the typical questions that may be asked at an interview. You can tape record your responses and hear how you sound.

2. See if you can appropriately fit or slip your rehearsed answers in during the interview in a manner which is casual and doesn't sound canned. The latter can be accomplished by pausing for a moment before answering a question that you are prepared for, acting as if you are preparing your answers.

3. Try to sell your favorable assets by fitting them into the interview (e.g., hospital work, research experience, community activities, research articles published etc.). Know your strengths thoroughly.

4. Try to establish a rapport with the interviewer from the very outset. Walk in with a greeting, a smile on your face and a firm handshake. On leaving, express your appreciation for the time the interviewer gave you.

5. Try to avoid, where possible, "Yes or No" answers. Rather, give the pros and cons of the issue and your views in a brief and concise manner. Show that you can be analytical while at the same time avoid being overly talkative.

6. If you don't understand the question, ask the interviewer to clarify it.

7. Look directly at your interviewer; act relaxed; avoid squirming in your seat; if you "flub" a question—forget it—go on, rather than become upset and ruin the remainder of your interview.

8. If you don't know an answer, admit it rather than guess wildly. If pressed for a reply, qualify it as being an "on the spur of the moment" judgment, that is open to change on further reflection.

9. Don't open up discussions on your own, such as on politics or religion. If asked, don't be defensive.

Interviewers seek a sense of confidence even on controversial issues.

10. Avoid disparaging your school or specific instructors or students. It will not make you look better.

You can improve your performance by preparing for it (as indicated in the preceding sections) and by learning from the mistakes you may have made at the interviews you have had. Thus, after each interview, evaluate your performance along the following lines:

1. Did I come across effectively?

2. Where did I flounder and become excessively talkative?

3. Did I keep my cool after a blunder?

4. Was there some basic information I should have known, but didn't?

5. Did my prepared responses come off effectively?

6. Did I sell myself, especially my assets, adequately and effectively?

7. Did I establish a good rapport and behave well-mannered?

8. Did I seem to show the appropriate interest in the school I was being interviewed at?

9. What would I have done differently?

With honest answers, you can then go on and prepare more effectively for the next interview. The results should be better. The first interview is usually the toughest. Try to schedule it with a school that is not your first choice, if this is at all possible.

THE SELECTION PROCESS

As an autonomous institution, each medical school has its own selection process and admission criteria (see profiles, page 137). There is considerable procedural variability among schools and one scheme cannot be applicable for all. Even the makeup of admission committees is not fixed, although 15 seems to be the average number of members, with representatives coming from the schools' basic and clinical science departments, each serving for terms of one to three years. Some schools have appointed students (usually seniors) to their admission committee as voting or nonvoting members.

The basic selection process takes three steps. At each step some of the variable approaches are noted.

Preliminary Screening

The first step is designed to narrow the large pool of applications that a school receives down to those who merit further serious consideration.

Screening personnel. After your application and supplementary supporting data (in whole or in part) have been received, your folder will be screened either by two admission officers independently or by a subcommittee of the admission committee.

Screening criteria. This is subject to variation and may include:

- Total GPA and MCAT percentile (with minimum GPA levels usually varying between 3.4 and 3.7 and MCAT levels between the 60th and the 80th percentiles).
- Total GPA, science GPA, nonscience GPA, and total MCAT scores.
- Quantitative data as well as letters of recommendation.
- Total application packet including letters of recommendation and application essay.

Supplementary application. Some schools have designed their own supplementary applications containing questions that they require you to answer (e.g., how do you see yourself ten years from now, what will medicine be like in the next century?) or that are optional (e.g., list the medical schools that you have applied to). Receipt of a supplementary application to be completed suggests that the school is interested in you. However, not all schools have supplementary applications and not getting one should not be interpreted as a lack of interest in you.

Interview

After you have been screened, your application will be rated to determine your eligibility for an interview. You may be invited for an interview promptly if your rating is high, relative to the established numerical standard; you may be placed on an interview-eligible list making it quite likely that you will be invited in due course; you may be placed on hold for future review; or you may be put on an ineligible list. The last classification may result in your receiving a rejection, which may or may not require full committee confirmation.

Determination

After your interview, a report drafted by the interviewer will be placed in your file. Your file subsequently will be presented to the entire committee.

It will then be discussed and rated, and depending on the rank it receives, an acceptance, hold, or rejection letter will follow.

ACCEPTANCE

The Executive Council of the AAMC has approved a set of guidelines regarding acceptance. Among the recommendations are:

1. That an applicant should not have less than two weeks in which to reply to an offer.

2. That medical schools should not notify applicants of acceptance before November 15 of each admission cycle.

3. That by April 1 any applicant holding more than one acceptance for more than two weeks (and having received all necessary financial aid information) should choose the school the applicant wishes to attend and withdraw from all others.

4. That after June 1 a medical school seeking to enroll an applicant already known to be accepted elsewhere should advise the school of its intentions.

5. That an offer of acceptance does not constitute a moral obligation to matriculate at that school.

When you receive notice of acceptance, you should promptly familiarize yourself with the regulations established by the particular school in its catalog or in instructions that have been sent to you.

Choosing Among the Acceptances

Naturally, if you have received only one acceptance, your course of action is restricted. If you receive multiple acceptances, then carefully consider each school so that you select the school that best meets your needs.

It is not in the best interest of the students or medical schools for an acceptee to hold on to more than one place at a time. The basic criteria in determining where to attend will be just as well known to the applicant at the time of notification of acceptance as a month or two later. If it is easy to make a choice, then it should be made promptly and a polite letter of withdrawal should be sent to the appropriate school(s). If, however, it is difficult to choose between schools, a choice should nevertheless be made rapidly (using the criteria noted below) rather than agonizing over the decision for a prolonged period. By making a decision with all deliberate speed you can then concentrate on other important matters. At the same time, this will enable the medical school(s) you have withdrawn from to offer the place(s) made vacant to others, perhaps even a student from your own school. (This is also the time to withdraw from schools you have not yet heard from if you would not attend if accepted.)

In making your selection, you should bear in mind that while all medical colleges in the country are acceptable, there are significant variations among them. Evaluate each school, keeping in mind the following criteria:

1. *Financial consideration*. You should evaluate tuition and living costs coupled with your financial means and offers of financial assistance.

2. *Location*. Consider the geographic location as well as the proximity of the school to where you wish to live.

3. *Faculty-student relationships*. What are the opportunities for informal and personal assistance and guidance in academic and general problems? What cooperation is there with the staff and administration? What is the role of the students in various policy-making organs of the school?

4. *Teaching program*. How recently has the curriculum been updated? How are the innovations working out in practice? Do the senior faculty members actively participate in teaching? Is the faculty as a whole interested in teaching or is their primary concern research and clinical services?

5. *Student performance*. Determine the current attrition rate and what percentage is due to academic failure. Of interest is also the number of students asked to repeat an academic year; compare the figure with the national average.

6. *Facilities*. Familiarize yourself with the character of the basic science teaching laboratories and what up-to-date equipment is available. How many hospital beds are available for teaching purposes, what kinds of hospitals are used (private, city, or state)?

7. *Student body*. What is the class size? What is their morale, attitude and enthusiasm for the school? Determine the nature of student competition—is it stimulating or cut-throat?

8. *Reputation*. Speak with recent graduates about the school's standing. Find out what percentage of the school's graduates are placed as interns in renown teaching hospitals.

RANKING OF MEDICAL SCHOOLS

There is a natural tendency to seek admission to the "best" medical school possible. The problem is identifying which medical schools are the best. It is quite possible that in reality the best school is the one that has accepted you and that is most suitable to *your own* special needs, rather than one which only has a distinguished reputation. Nevertheless, a list ranking medical schools can be useful; it may provide information that can help you decide which schools to apply to and which schools to select in case of multiple acceptances. Before referring to the ranking list provided here (Table 3), you should take the following considerations into account.

1. The ranking of a school should be only one of a number of factors affecting your final choice.

2. There is no official ranking list published by the medical establishment.

3. Formulating a ranking list that cannot be challenged is almost impossible, because there are so many variables to consider (size, curriculum, faculty, basic and clinical facilities, student services, supporting resources).

4. Since the educational philosophy of schools varies (for example, some are research oriented while others seek to train primary care physicians), one cannot objectively compare relative values. A judgment can be made only as to how well each meets its defined mission.

5. A list that ranks the schools in numerical order can be misleading, because it would suggest that a school ranked number 22 is superior to 21, when in reality the difference is based solely on minute statistical differences between the two, within the data collected.

6. The rankings presented here were determined some years ago; unfortunately, no recent studies of a comparable nature have been published. Many changes of various kinds have been implemented within medical schools in the intervening years, and these changes have undoubtedly modified the rankings as presented.

7. This study did not investigate the quality of the schools *per se*, but rather their *perceived* quality. "Perceived quality" refers to the mean rating given by the evaluators to the quality of the faculty, but to no other relevant factors.

8. The ranking list should not be used as a definitive measure of a school's status, but as a general estimate of its perceived reputation.

9. Only 94 schools were evaluated; if the school you seek is not on the list, it is one of the thirty that were not ranked.

10. The ranking list should not be used as a definitive measure of a school's status, but as a general estimate of its perceived reputation.

REJECTION

Each year about half of the applicants to medical school are rejected—about 15,000–20,000 men and women. If you unfortunately find yourself in this category, very careful evaluation of your future plans is needed.

Try to determine the reasons for your rejection. Weigh the advantages and disadvantages of the various alternatives that present themselves and then select a course of action that is realistic. Almost all rejected applicants fall into one of the six categories listed below:

1. Those that plan to reapply to U.S. medical schools the following year.

2. Those that plan to apply to foreign medical schools.

3. Those that will apply to enter a different health profession.

4. Those that will apply for admission to a graduate school to enter a career in teaching and research or in the basic medical sciences.

5. Those that plan a career in science education on the high school level or lower.

6. Those that will seek a non-science-oriented career.

Seriously consider the reasons why you might have been rejected. If your academic record has been consistently poor, your SAT and MCAT scores were low, and there were no genuine extenuating circumstances for your unimpressive performance, then you should consider either another health profession or a non-science career. If your academic record is good, but for obvious reasons—physical or mental health—you were considered unsuitable for a medical career, consider another health career, a career in science education, or a non-science program.

If you were a borderline candidate and you have had a consistently fair academic record at a recognized college, satisfactory test scores, a pleasant personality, good motivation, but were probably rejected because of a very competitive nature of admissions, then you should consider attending graduate school and studying

Table 3. Cole-Lipton Perceived Quality of 94 American Medical Schools

Harvard
Johns Hopkins University
Stanford University
University of California—San Francisco
Yale University
Columbia University
Duke University
University of Michigan
Cornell University
Washington University
University of Pennsylvania
University of Minnesota
University of California—Los Angeles
Albert Einstein
University of Chicago
University of Washington
Case Western Reserve University
University of Rochester
University of Colorado
University of California—San Diego
Mount Sinai
New York University
University of Texas—Southwestern
Vanderbilt University
University of North Carolina
Baylor
Tufts University
University of Wisconsin
Northwestern University
Emory University
Boston University
University of Iowa
University of Virginia
Ohio State University
University of Alabama
University of Florida
Dartmouth
University of Illinois
Tulane University
Georgetown University
University of Utah
University of Cincinnati
University of California—Davis
Pennsylvania State University
University of Pittsburgh
University of Vermont
Medical College of Virginia

Oregon Health Sciences University
SUNY Upstate Medical Center
Michigan State University
Indiana University
SUNY at Buffalo
University of Texas, Galveston
St. Louis University
Temple University
University of Miami
Medical College of Wisconsin
University of Maryland
University of Kansas
Albany Medical College
Bowman Gray
University of Arizona
University of Missouri
University of California—Irvine
George Washington University
SUNY, Downstate Medical Center
University of Texas, San Antonio
Wayne State University
Chicago Medical School
University of Oklahoma
University of Kentucky
University of Virginia
University of New Mexico
Medical College of Georgia
University of Tennessee
Louisiana State University—New Orleans
University of Arkansas
University of Connecticut
University of Louisville
Medical College of Pennsylvania
Hahnemann University
Loma Linda University
West Virginia University
University of Nebraska
New York Medical College
University of South Carolina
University of Mississippi
Medical College of Ohio
Howard University
Loyola University of Chicago
Creighton University
Rutgers
Meharry Medical College

for a career in teaching or research. If your test scores were low because of some unusual circumstances, you should consider retaking the examination and reapplying.

If you feel that your record, as a whole, is not exceptional but does reveal the possibility of considerable capability as reflected by occasional high performance in some key courses, high test scores, and so forth, you should seriously consider reapplying for schools the following year. You should also consider applying to foreign schools or beginning a non-science career. The schools you select to apply to the second time should be as close to those that would possibly accept you.

If you feel that you were rejected because of possible late application, delay in receiving or loss of supporting data, poor selection of schools to which you applied, too few applications submitted, poor performance at the interview, or some similar explainable factor, you should consider reapplying, as well as all other options open to you. A percentage of students who reapply do succeed, and therefore, you should feel encouraged to do so.

A study was made of the career choices of 98 unsuccessful applicants to an entering medical class. Of that group of 57 men and 41 women, it was discovered that 52% entered occupations outside the health care field. Forty-eight percent ultimately entered health-related occupations, of which 10 men and 2 women became physicians, 7 became dentists, 5 became pharmacists, 2 became podiatrists, and 1 became an optometrist. These data indicate that a medical career is still possible if one is rejected initially and that a career in one of the many health care professions is a realistic alternative.

A later study, consistent with the aforementioned findings, showed that unsuccessful applicants to medical school tended to reapply at least once and that 51% of those employed after being rejected initially were engaged in health-related occupations (with laboratory technology being the leading choice, especially for women). This study also noted that of the respondents who were still students, 29% of the men and 20% of the women were in health-related training. The largest group among men was in dental school and among women was in the study of microbiology or other medical sciences. Women were found to be less likely than men to enter doctoral-level health science study. Careers like the new mid-level health fields such as physician's assistant and nurse practitioner attracted a few rejected premedical students. This conclusion is strongly supported by an even more recent study of a larger sampling (1933) of unaccepted applicants to the medical school class. It was found that a majority had reapplied and that 27% had gained entrance to either a U.S. or a foreign medical school. Of those still unaccepted, about half were studying or working in health-related fields of study or occupations.

In any event, you should carefully consider the risks involved with medical study overseas before applying to such schools. See the chapter on Foreign Medical Study on the problems involved with transferring credits, obtaining American licenses, and other difficulties of foreign study. If you should decide to undertake an alternate health profession or graduate study, you must determine if you have sufficient motivation to do so. Without sufficient motivation, the chances for success are slim.

4

THE MEDICAL COLLEGE ADMISSION TEST (MCAT)

☐ Contents of the MCAT
☐ The value of the MCAT
☐ Preparing for the MCAT
■ Model MCAT

Essentially all applicants to the U.S. and Canadian medical schools, as well as some applicants to foreign schools, are expected to take the MCAT. It is given on a Saturday in April and in September at test centers located throughout the country and at some overseas locations. The test is administered and scored by The American College Testing Program, P.O. Box 414, Iowa City, Iowa 52243. Score reporting is the responsibility of the AAMC (MCAT Operations, Association of American Medical Colleges, One Dupont Circle, N.W., Washington, D.C. 20036). You can arrange to take the test by filing an application (frequently obtainable at your Premedical Advisory Office) along with the $55 examination fee and a recent snapshot.

Scores are sent automatically in mid-June or mid-November both to you and to your adviser. Your scores will also be sent automatically to AAMCAS schools. You can indicate on your test application six non-AAMCAS schools you wish to receive your scores; if you are applying to more than six non-AAMCAS schools, you must pay a small fee for each additional school. Special test centers are open on Sundays for students whose religious convictions prevent them from taking the exam on Saturday. An additional $5 is required for taking the exam on Sunday.

The MCAT can be retaken without special permission, but it is usually advisable to do so only if there is a significant discrepancy between your college grades and MCAT scores, if the test was taken before you completed your basic biology and chemistry courses, if you were quite ill or emotionally upset at the time the test was taken, or if you are encouraged by your premedical adviser or admissions committee member to do so. When the MCAT is taken twice, the AAMC recommends that the initial and retest scores on the Analytical Reading and Analysis of Quantitative Skills tests be averaged, and the retest scores for the Biology, Chemistry, and Physics tests be used, unless there is evidence that unusual circumstances might have affected scores on either exam.

As a general rule, you should take the MCAT at the session which you feel you could perform best. The overwhelming majority of students take the test in the spring and this is justified for a number of reasons:

1. Scores become available earlier and therefore prompter action on your application can be taken by admissions committee.

2. Additional knowledge accumulated between the two test periods does not significantly affect test scores.

3. Most schools interpret the scores in light of the actual course work completed at the time the exam was taken.

4. You still have the option of retaking the examination in the fall if you missed it in the spring or if you feel that the scores, for some reason, did not reflect your true capabilities.

5. A significant number of places may already be filled by the time the schools receive the scores from the fall exam (usually after Thanksgiving).

6. You can get a necessary hurdle out of the way and you can then concentrate better on your studies.

Students who have not had basic courses in chemistry and biology and who plan to take these courses during the summer and students whose academic record is B− or less and who will have additional time to study for the examination during the summer and therefore may perform better on the exam in the fall should give serious consideration to the later test administration. In any event, the exam should not be taken in the spring as if it were a trial run, with the intention of taking it definitively in the fall since medical schools are aware that the exam is taken twice and can secure both sets of scores.

Test scores are sent to the student usually 4 to 6 weeks after the test is taken. The student also receives a copy to be given to his or her advisor. The advisor receives a computer printout of the scores from those students electing to release them.

CONTENTS OF THE MCAT

The latest MCAT took several years to be fully developed. For some time the medical schools had asked for a pre-enrollment assessment of premedical students that would offer a better measure of professional aptitude, readiness, and promise than did the old MCAT. This new examination, introduced in 1977, requires a full day for its administration—both morning and afternoon sessions, with a break for lunch.

The MCAT consists of four separate subtests:

Skills Analysis: Reading (85 minutes)
Skills Analysis: Quantitative (85 minutes)
Science Knowledge: Biology, Chemistry, Physics (135 minutes)
Science Problems: Biology, Chemistry, Physics (85 minutes)

These subtests are described further as follows:

Skills Analysis: Reading. This test will assess various reading skills considered essential for both medical school and continuing medical education. Readings will be taken from medical textbooks, journals, and case histories and will aim to test the applicants' abilities to comprehend and analyze the selections.

Skills Analysis: Quantitative. The nonverbal test material will seek to evaluate the applicants' abilities to read graphs, charts, and tables and accurately translate and interpret this information. Another objective will be to assess reasoning and problem-solving skills, rather than basic computational skills. Basic and medical science as well as social science topics will be used as test material.

Science Subtests: Science Knowledge and Problems. The tests will assess knowledge of both scientific facts and principles and concepts, as well as test the ability to use these in a new setting. The skills measured will be the ability to apply scientific generalizations in given situations, the ability to identify essential elements of a scientific experiment and the ability to combine given information with known concepts. Scores will be given for each of the three basic sciences and in problem solving.

The tests are designed so that nearly everyone will have enough time to finish each section without undue pressure since the emphasis will be on one's preparation rather than on speed of response.

A full description of the test is included in *The MCAT Student Manual*, obtainable for $7.00 from AAMC, One Dupont Circle, N.W., Washington, D.C. 20036.

THE VALUE OF THE MCAT

The MCAT scores provide admissions committees with nationally standardized measures of both academic ability and achievement. This permits comparison of applicants even though they have widely different academic backgrounds. The scores attained on the MCAT do not by themselves determine admission and are supplemental in interpreting the academic record, since they help to shed light on the academic abilities of the applicant. The extent of their importance varies from school to school because committees place different degrees of stress on it. In general, the MCAT scores are significant in relation to the academic record of the individual. Where the scores are high or low for a student with a good or weak record respectively, they simply confirm the academic record. When they are significantly different from the student's record, they raise questions that can be critical in determining admissions. Thus a student with a poor record and high scores may have a greater potential than his record indicates. In such a case, more intensive evaluation of the applicant may be warranted, and he may be called for an interview which he otherwise may not have been granted. At the interview, the discrepancy between the academic record and the MCAT scores can be clarified, and the applicant will have an opportunity to "sell himself," perhaps significantly improving his chances for admission.

On the other hand, when the academic record is high and the MCAT scores are low, the applicant's interview will not be perfunctory but will be aimed at clarifying the discrepancy. He will have to convince the interviewer of his potential and overcome the uncertainty about his ability that has been created. One way of doing this is naturally to retake the test and perform significantly better.

PREPARING FOR THE MCAT

It can be said with a reasonable degree of assurance that you can improve your scores by studying for them. The use of vocabulary lists, available in various publications, can be helpful in improving verbal performance. The use of high school review books in geometry, intermediate algebra, and trigonometry can be helpful in preparing for the quantitative ability subtest. In addition, general and widespread reading of scientific journals and magazines will help boost your confidence in reading specialized articles. If you have been conscientious in your science courses, you should do well. A reading of high school or freshman college-level review books in biology, chemistry, and physics can be helpful.

There are a number of private coaching services that specialize in preparing students for aptitude tests including the MCAT. These are quite expensive and are not essential for the above average student who has done well on his college entrance examinations. It can be of help, however, for students who have difficulty with aptitude tests and for students with weak academic records and applicants needing an organized review program.

Timetable for the MCAT*

TOTAL TIME: 6 hours, 30 minutes, plus 1 hour for lunch, 2 10-minute breaks

135 minutes	Science Knowledge (125 questions)	38 questions on biology 49 questions on chemistry 38 questions on physics
Rest Period		
85 minutes	Science Problems (66 questions)	18 questions on biology 30 questions on chemistry 18 questions on physics
Lunch		
85 minutes	Skills Analysis: Reading (68 questions)	
Rest Period		
85 minutes	Skills Analysis: Quantitative (68 questions)	

*Format subject to change.

Model MCAT

The full-length Model MCAT that begins on page 45 will provide you with helpful practice. Be sure to take the model test under strict test conditions, timing each section as instructed. Remove the answer sheets on pages 39–40 and use them to record your answers. After completing the test, check your answers against the Answer Key on pages 89–90. Then, compute your MCAT scores using the Conversion Tables and the Self-Scoring Chart on pages 37–38. Doing this will help you to determine areas of strength and weakness. (If your computed MCAT is 7 or lower on any section, you should plan to work on that area.)

Conversion Table for Biology, Chemistry, and Physics Scores

To compute your MCAT scores for the Biology, Chemistry, and Physics sections, count the number of correct answers in each discipline from both the Science Knowledge section and the Science Problems section. This will give you your raw score for each of these subtests. Use your raw score to find your scaled score on the table below. (Note: The scaled scores on this conversion table are *approximated*.)

Biology

Raw Score	Scaled Score
0–3	1
4–6	2
7–10	3
11–13	4
14–17	5
18–21	6
22–25	7
26–29	8
30–33	9
34–37	10
38–41	11
42–45	12
46–49	13
50–53	14
54–56	15

Chemistry

Raw Score	Scaled Score
0–6	1
7–11	2
12–16	3
17–21	4
22–26	5
27–31	6
32–36	7
37–41	8
42–46	9
47–51	10
52–56	11
57–61	12
62–66	13
67–72	14
72–79	15

Physics

Raw Score	Scaled Score
0–3	1
4–6	2
7–10	3
11–13	4
14–17	5
18–21	6
22–25	7
26–29	8
30–33	9
34–37	10
38–41	11
42–45	12
46–49	13
50–53	14
54–56	15

Conversion Table for Science Problems, Skills Analysis: Reading, Skills Analysis: Quantitative Scores

To compute your MCAT scores for these sections, once again, count the number of correct answers in each area and then use the raw scores to locate your scaled scores on the table. (Note: The scaled scores on this table are *approximated*.)

Science Problems

Raw Score	Standard Score
0–5	1
6–10	2
11–14	3
15–18	4
19–22	5
23–26	6
27–30	7
31–34	8
35–38	9
39–42	10
43–46	11
47–50	12
51–54	13
55–59	14
60–66	15

Skills Analysis: Reading

Raw Score	Standard Score
0–5	1
6–10	2
11–15	3
16–20	4
21–24	5
25–28	6
29–32	7
33–37	8
38–41	9
42–45	10
46–49	11
50–54	12
55–59	13
60–64	14
65–68	15

Skills Analysis: Quantitative

Raw Score	Standard Score
0–5	1
6–10	2
11–15	3
16–20	4
21–24	5
25–28	6
29–32	7
33–37	8
38–41	9
42–45	10
46–49	11
50–54	12
55–59	13
60–64	14
65–68	15

Self-Scoring Chart

Now that you have computed your scaled scores for each of the six subtests, fill in the Self-Scoring Chart below so that you will have a clear picture of where your strengths and weaknesses lie.

	Total Possible	Raw Score	MCAT Score
Science Knowledge:			
Biology	_____	_____	_____
Chemistry	_____	_____	_____
Physics	_____	_____	_____
Science Problems	_____	_____	_____
Skills Analysis:			
Reading	_____	_____	_____
Quantitative	_____	_____	_____

Answer Sheet—Model MCAT

SCIENCE KNOWLEDGE

Biology

1. Ⓐ Ⓑ Ⓒ Ⓓ Ⓔ	11. Ⓐ Ⓑ Ⓒ Ⓓ Ⓔ	21. Ⓐ Ⓑ Ⓒ Ⓓ Ⓔ	31. Ⓐ Ⓑ Ⓒ Ⓓ Ⓔ
2. Ⓐ Ⓑ Ⓒ Ⓓ Ⓔ	12. Ⓐ Ⓑ Ⓒ Ⓓ Ⓔ	22. Ⓐ Ⓑ Ⓒ Ⓓ Ⓔ	32. Ⓐ Ⓑ Ⓒ Ⓓ Ⓔ
3. Ⓐ Ⓑ Ⓒ Ⓓ Ⓔ	13. Ⓐ Ⓑ Ⓒ Ⓓ Ⓔ	23. Ⓐ Ⓑ Ⓒ Ⓓ Ⓔ	33. Ⓐ Ⓑ Ⓒ Ⓓ Ⓔ
4. Ⓐ Ⓑ Ⓒ Ⓓ Ⓔ	14. Ⓐ Ⓑ Ⓒ Ⓓ Ⓔ	24. Ⓐ Ⓑ Ⓒ Ⓓ Ⓔ	34. Ⓐ Ⓑ Ⓒ Ⓓ Ⓔ
5. Ⓐ Ⓑ Ⓒ Ⓓ Ⓔ	15. Ⓐ Ⓑ Ⓒ Ⓓ Ⓔ	25. Ⓐ Ⓑ Ⓒ Ⓓ Ⓔ	35. Ⓐ Ⓑ Ⓒ Ⓓ Ⓔ
6. Ⓐ Ⓑ Ⓒ Ⓓ Ⓔ	16. Ⓐ Ⓑ Ⓒ Ⓓ Ⓔ	26. Ⓐ Ⓑ Ⓒ Ⓓ Ⓔ	36. Ⓐ Ⓑ Ⓒ Ⓓ Ⓔ
7. Ⓐ Ⓑ Ⓒ Ⓓ Ⓔ	17. Ⓐ Ⓑ Ⓒ Ⓓ Ⓔ	27. Ⓐ Ⓑ Ⓒ Ⓓ Ⓔ	37. Ⓐ Ⓑ Ⓒ Ⓓ Ⓔ
8. Ⓐ Ⓑ Ⓒ Ⓓ Ⓔ	18. Ⓐ Ⓑ Ⓒ Ⓓ Ⓔ	28. Ⓐ Ⓑ Ⓒ Ⓓ Ⓔ	38. Ⓐ Ⓑ Ⓒ Ⓓ Ⓔ
9. Ⓐ Ⓑ Ⓒ Ⓓ Ⓔ	19. Ⓐ Ⓑ Ⓒ Ⓓ Ⓔ	29. Ⓐ Ⓑ Ⓒ Ⓓ Ⓔ	
10. Ⓐ Ⓑ Ⓒ Ⓓ Ⓔ	20. Ⓐ Ⓑ Ⓒ Ⓓ Ⓔ	30. Ⓐ Ⓑ Ⓒ Ⓓ Ⓔ	

Chemistry

1. Ⓐ Ⓑ Ⓒ Ⓓ Ⓔ	14. Ⓐ Ⓑ Ⓒ Ⓓ Ⓔ	27. Ⓐ Ⓑ Ⓒ Ⓓ Ⓔ	40. Ⓐ Ⓑ Ⓒ Ⓓ Ⓔ
2. Ⓐ Ⓑ Ⓒ Ⓓ Ⓔ	15. Ⓐ Ⓑ Ⓒ Ⓓ Ⓔ	28. Ⓐ Ⓑ Ⓒ Ⓓ Ⓔ	41. Ⓐ Ⓑ Ⓒ Ⓓ Ⓔ
3. Ⓐ Ⓑ Ⓒ Ⓓ Ⓔ	16. Ⓐ Ⓑ Ⓒ Ⓓ Ⓔ	29. Ⓐ Ⓑ Ⓒ Ⓓ Ⓔ	42. Ⓐ Ⓑ Ⓒ Ⓓ Ⓔ
4. Ⓐ Ⓑ Ⓒ Ⓓ Ⓔ	17. Ⓐ Ⓑ Ⓒ Ⓓ Ⓔ	30. Ⓐ Ⓑ Ⓒ Ⓓ Ⓔ	43. Ⓐ Ⓑ Ⓒ Ⓓ Ⓔ
5. Ⓐ Ⓑ Ⓒ Ⓓ Ⓔ	18. Ⓐ Ⓑ Ⓒ Ⓓ Ⓔ	31. Ⓐ Ⓑ Ⓒ Ⓓ Ⓔ	44. Ⓐ Ⓑ Ⓒ Ⓓ Ⓔ
6. Ⓐ Ⓑ Ⓒ Ⓓ Ⓔ	19. Ⓐ Ⓑ Ⓒ Ⓓ Ⓔ	32. Ⓐ Ⓑ Ⓒ Ⓓ Ⓔ	45. Ⓐ Ⓑ Ⓒ Ⓓ Ⓔ
7. Ⓐ Ⓑ Ⓒ Ⓓ Ⓔ	20. Ⓐ Ⓑ Ⓒ Ⓓ Ⓔ	33. Ⓐ Ⓑ Ⓒ Ⓓ Ⓔ	46. Ⓐ Ⓑ Ⓒ Ⓓ Ⓔ
8. Ⓐ Ⓑ Ⓒ Ⓓ Ⓔ	21. Ⓐ Ⓑ Ⓒ Ⓓ Ⓔ	34. Ⓐ Ⓑ Ⓒ Ⓓ Ⓔ	47. Ⓐ Ⓑ Ⓒ Ⓓ Ⓔ
9. Ⓐ Ⓑ Ⓒ Ⓓ Ⓔ	22. Ⓐ Ⓑ Ⓒ Ⓓ Ⓔ	35. Ⓐ Ⓑ Ⓒ Ⓓ Ⓔ	48. Ⓐ Ⓑ Ⓒ Ⓓ Ⓔ
10. Ⓐ Ⓑ Ⓒ Ⓓ Ⓔ	23. Ⓐ Ⓑ Ⓒ Ⓓ Ⓔ	36. Ⓐ Ⓑ Ⓒ Ⓓ Ⓔ	49. Ⓐ Ⓑ Ⓒ Ⓓ Ⓔ
11. Ⓐ Ⓑ Ⓒ Ⓓ Ⓔ	24. Ⓐ Ⓑ Ⓒ Ⓓ Ⓔ	37. Ⓐ Ⓑ Ⓒ Ⓓ Ⓔ	
12. Ⓐ Ⓑ Ⓒ Ⓓ Ⓔ	25. Ⓐ Ⓑ Ⓒ Ⓓ Ⓔ	38. Ⓐ Ⓑ Ⓒ Ⓓ Ⓔ	
13. Ⓐ Ⓑ Ⓒ Ⓓ Ⓔ	26. Ⓐ Ⓑ Ⓒ Ⓓ Ⓔ	39. Ⓐ Ⓑ Ⓒ Ⓓ Ⓔ	

Physics

1. Ⓐ Ⓑ Ⓒ Ⓓ Ⓔ	11. Ⓐ Ⓑ Ⓒ Ⓓ Ⓔ	21. Ⓐ Ⓑ Ⓒ Ⓓ Ⓔ	31. Ⓐ Ⓑ Ⓒ Ⓓ Ⓔ
2. Ⓐ Ⓑ Ⓒ Ⓓ Ⓔ	12. Ⓐ Ⓑ Ⓒ Ⓓ Ⓔ	22. Ⓐ Ⓑ Ⓒ Ⓓ Ⓔ	32. Ⓐ Ⓑ Ⓒ Ⓓ Ⓔ
3. Ⓐ Ⓑ Ⓒ Ⓓ Ⓔ	13. Ⓐ Ⓑ Ⓒ Ⓓ Ⓔ	23. Ⓐ Ⓑ Ⓒ Ⓓ Ⓔ	33. Ⓐ Ⓑ Ⓒ Ⓓ Ⓔ
4. Ⓐ Ⓑ Ⓒ Ⓓ Ⓔ	14. Ⓐ Ⓑ Ⓒ Ⓓ Ⓔ	24. Ⓐ Ⓑ Ⓒ Ⓓ Ⓔ	34. Ⓐ Ⓑ Ⓒ Ⓓ Ⓔ
5. Ⓐ Ⓑ Ⓒ Ⓓ Ⓔ	15. Ⓐ Ⓑ Ⓒ Ⓓ Ⓔ	25. Ⓐ Ⓑ Ⓒ Ⓓ Ⓔ	35. Ⓐ Ⓑ Ⓒ Ⓓ Ⓔ
6. Ⓐ Ⓑ Ⓒ Ⓓ Ⓔ	16. Ⓐ Ⓑ Ⓒ Ⓓ Ⓔ	26. Ⓐ Ⓑ Ⓒ Ⓓ Ⓔ	36. Ⓐ Ⓑ Ⓒ Ⓓ Ⓔ
7. Ⓐ Ⓑ Ⓒ Ⓓ Ⓔ	17. Ⓐ Ⓑ Ⓒ Ⓓ Ⓔ	27. Ⓐ Ⓑ Ⓒ Ⓓ Ⓔ	37. Ⓐ Ⓑ Ⓒ Ⓓ Ⓔ
8. Ⓐ Ⓑ Ⓒ Ⓓ Ⓔ	18. Ⓐ Ⓑ Ⓒ Ⓓ Ⓔ	28. Ⓐ Ⓑ Ⓒ Ⓓ Ⓔ	38. Ⓐ Ⓑ Ⓒ Ⓓ Ⓔ
9. Ⓐ Ⓑ Ⓒ Ⓓ Ⓔ	19. Ⓐ Ⓑ Ⓒ Ⓓ Ⓔ	29. Ⓐ Ⓑ Ⓒ Ⓓ Ⓔ	
10. Ⓐ Ⓑ Ⓒ Ⓓ Ⓔ	20. Ⓐ Ⓑ Ⓒ Ⓓ Ⓔ	30. Ⓐ Ⓑ Ⓒ Ⓓ Ⓔ	

SCIENCE PROBLEMS

1. Ⓐ Ⓑ Ⓒ Ⓓ Ⓔ   18. Ⓐ Ⓑ Ⓒ Ⓓ Ⓔ   35. Ⓐ Ⓑ Ⓒ Ⓓ Ⓔ   52. Ⓐ Ⓑ Ⓒ Ⓓ Ⓔ
2. Ⓐ Ⓑ Ⓒ Ⓓ Ⓔ   19. Ⓐ Ⓑ Ⓒ Ⓓ Ⓔ   36. Ⓐ Ⓑ Ⓒ Ⓓ Ⓔ   53. Ⓐ Ⓑ Ⓒ Ⓓ Ⓔ
3. Ⓐ Ⓑ Ⓒ Ⓓ Ⓔ   20. Ⓐ Ⓑ Ⓒ Ⓓ Ⓔ   37. Ⓐ Ⓑ Ⓒ Ⓓ Ⓔ   54. Ⓐ Ⓑ Ⓒ Ⓓ Ⓔ
4. Ⓐ Ⓑ Ⓒ Ⓓ Ⓔ   21. Ⓐ Ⓑ Ⓒ Ⓓ Ⓔ   38. Ⓐ Ⓑ Ⓒ Ⓓ Ⓔ   55. Ⓐ Ⓑ Ⓒ Ⓓ Ⓔ
5. Ⓐ Ⓑ Ⓒ Ⓓ Ⓔ   22. Ⓐ Ⓑ Ⓒ Ⓓ Ⓔ   39. Ⓐ Ⓑ Ⓒ Ⓓ Ⓔ   56. Ⓐ Ⓑ Ⓒ Ⓓ Ⓔ
6. Ⓐ Ⓑ Ⓒ Ⓓ Ⓔ   23. Ⓐ Ⓑ Ⓒ Ⓓ Ⓔ   40. Ⓐ Ⓑ Ⓒ Ⓓ Ⓔ   57. Ⓐ Ⓑ Ⓒ Ⓓ Ⓔ
7. Ⓐ Ⓑ Ⓒ Ⓓ Ⓔ   24. Ⓐ Ⓑ Ⓒ Ⓓ Ⓔ   41. Ⓐ Ⓑ Ⓒ Ⓓ Ⓔ   58. Ⓐ Ⓑ Ⓒ Ⓓ Ⓔ
8. Ⓐ Ⓑ Ⓒ Ⓓ Ⓔ   25. Ⓐ Ⓑ Ⓒ Ⓓ Ⓔ   42. Ⓐ Ⓑ Ⓒ Ⓓ Ⓔ   59. Ⓐ Ⓑ Ⓒ Ⓓ Ⓔ
9. Ⓐ Ⓑ Ⓒ Ⓓ Ⓔ   26. Ⓐ Ⓑ Ⓒ Ⓓ Ⓔ   43. Ⓐ Ⓑ Ⓒ Ⓓ Ⓔ   60. Ⓐ Ⓑ Ⓒ Ⓓ Ⓔ
10. Ⓐ Ⓑ Ⓒ Ⓓ Ⓔ   27. Ⓐ Ⓑ Ⓒ Ⓓ Ⓔ   44. Ⓐ Ⓑ Ⓒ Ⓓ Ⓔ   61. Ⓐ Ⓑ Ⓒ Ⓓ Ⓔ
11. Ⓐ Ⓑ Ⓒ Ⓓ Ⓔ   28. Ⓐ Ⓑ Ⓒ Ⓓ Ⓔ   45. Ⓐ Ⓑ Ⓒ Ⓓ Ⓔ   62. Ⓐ Ⓑ Ⓒ Ⓓ Ⓔ
12. Ⓐ Ⓑ Ⓒ Ⓓ Ⓔ   29. Ⓐ Ⓑ Ⓒ Ⓓ Ⓔ   46. Ⓐ Ⓑ Ⓒ Ⓓ Ⓔ   63. Ⓐ Ⓑ Ⓒ Ⓓ Ⓔ
13. Ⓐ Ⓑ Ⓒ Ⓓ Ⓔ   30. Ⓐ Ⓑ Ⓒ Ⓓ Ⓔ   47. Ⓐ Ⓑ Ⓒ Ⓓ Ⓔ   64. Ⓐ Ⓑ Ⓒ Ⓓ Ⓔ
14. Ⓐ Ⓑ Ⓒ Ⓓ Ⓔ   31. Ⓐ Ⓑ Ⓒ Ⓓ Ⓔ   48. Ⓐ Ⓑ Ⓒ Ⓓ Ⓔ   65. Ⓐ Ⓑ Ⓒ Ⓓ Ⓔ
15. Ⓐ Ⓑ Ⓒ Ⓓ Ⓔ   32. Ⓐ Ⓑ Ⓒ Ⓓ Ⓔ   49. Ⓐ Ⓑ Ⓒ Ⓓ Ⓔ   66. Ⓐ Ⓑ Ⓒ Ⓓ Ⓔ
16. Ⓐ Ⓑ Ⓒ Ⓓ Ⓔ   33. Ⓐ Ⓑ Ⓒ Ⓓ Ⓔ   50. Ⓐ Ⓑ Ⓒ Ⓓ Ⓔ
17. Ⓐ Ⓑ Ⓒ Ⓓ Ⓔ   34. Ⓐ Ⓑ Ⓒ Ⓓ Ⓔ   51. Ⓐ Ⓑ Ⓒ Ⓓ Ⓔ

SKILLS ANALYSIS: READING

1. Ⓐ Ⓑ Ⓒ   15. Ⓐ Ⓑ Ⓒ   29. Ⓐ Ⓑ Ⓒ   43. Ⓐ Ⓑ Ⓒ   57. Ⓐ Ⓑ Ⓒ
2. Ⓐ Ⓑ Ⓒ   16. Ⓐ Ⓑ Ⓒ   30. Ⓐ Ⓑ Ⓒ   44. Ⓐ Ⓑ Ⓒ   58. Ⓐ Ⓑ Ⓒ
3. Ⓐ Ⓑ Ⓒ   17. Ⓐ Ⓑ Ⓒ   31. Ⓐ Ⓑ Ⓒ   45. Ⓐ Ⓑ Ⓒ   59. Ⓐ Ⓑ Ⓒ
4. Ⓐ Ⓑ Ⓒ   18. Ⓐ Ⓑ Ⓒ   32. Ⓐ Ⓑ Ⓒ   46. Ⓐ Ⓑ Ⓒ   60. Ⓐ Ⓑ Ⓒ
5. Ⓐ Ⓑ Ⓒ   19. Ⓐ Ⓑ Ⓒ   33. Ⓐ Ⓑ Ⓒ   47. Ⓐ Ⓑ Ⓒ   61. Ⓐ Ⓑ Ⓒ
6. Ⓐ Ⓑ Ⓒ   20. Ⓐ Ⓑ Ⓒ   34. Ⓐ Ⓑ Ⓒ   48. Ⓐ Ⓑ Ⓒ   62. Ⓐ Ⓑ Ⓒ
7. Ⓐ Ⓑ Ⓒ   21. Ⓐ Ⓑ Ⓒ   35. Ⓐ Ⓑ Ⓒ   49. Ⓐ Ⓑ Ⓒ   63. Ⓐ Ⓑ Ⓒ
8. Ⓐ Ⓑ Ⓒ   22. Ⓐ Ⓑ Ⓒ   36. Ⓐ Ⓑ Ⓒ   50. Ⓐ Ⓑ Ⓒ   64. Ⓐ Ⓑ Ⓒ
9. Ⓐ Ⓑ Ⓒ   23. Ⓐ Ⓑ Ⓒ   37. Ⓐ Ⓑ Ⓒ   51. Ⓐ Ⓑ Ⓒ   65. Ⓐ Ⓑ Ⓒ
10. Ⓐ Ⓑ Ⓒ   24. Ⓐ Ⓑ Ⓒ   38. Ⓐ Ⓑ Ⓒ   52. Ⓐ Ⓑ Ⓒ   66. Ⓐ Ⓑ Ⓒ
11. Ⓐ Ⓑ Ⓒ   25. Ⓐ Ⓑ Ⓒ   39. Ⓐ Ⓑ Ⓒ   53. Ⓐ Ⓑ Ⓒ   67. Ⓐ Ⓑ Ⓒ
12. Ⓐ Ⓑ Ⓒ   26. Ⓐ Ⓑ Ⓒ   40. Ⓐ Ⓑ Ⓒ   54. Ⓐ Ⓑ Ⓒ   68. Ⓐ Ⓑ Ⓒ
13. Ⓐ Ⓑ Ⓒ   27. Ⓐ Ⓑ Ⓒ   41. Ⓐ Ⓑ Ⓒ   55. Ⓐ Ⓑ Ⓒ
14. Ⓐ Ⓑ Ⓒ   28. Ⓐ Ⓑ Ⓒ   42. Ⓐ Ⓑ Ⓒ   56. Ⓐ Ⓑ Ⓒ

SKILLS ANALYSIS: QUANTITATIVE

1. Ⓐ Ⓑ Ⓒ Ⓓ   15. Ⓐ Ⓑ Ⓒ   29. Ⓐ Ⓑ Ⓒ   43. Ⓐ Ⓑ Ⓒ Ⓓ   57. Ⓐ Ⓑ Ⓒ
2. Ⓐ Ⓑ Ⓒ Ⓓ   16. Ⓐ Ⓑ Ⓒ   30. Ⓐ Ⓑ Ⓒ   44. Ⓐ Ⓑ Ⓒ Ⓓ   58. Ⓐ Ⓑ Ⓒ
3. Ⓐ Ⓑ Ⓒ Ⓓ   17. Ⓐ Ⓑ Ⓒ   31. Ⓐ Ⓑ Ⓒ   45. Ⓐ Ⓑ Ⓒ   59. Ⓐ Ⓑ Ⓒ
4. Ⓐ Ⓑ Ⓒ Ⓓ   18. Ⓐ Ⓑ Ⓒ   32. Ⓐ Ⓑ Ⓒ   46. Ⓐ Ⓑ Ⓒ   60. Ⓐ Ⓑ Ⓒ
5. Ⓐ Ⓑ Ⓒ Ⓓ   19. Ⓐ Ⓑ Ⓒ   33. Ⓐ Ⓑ Ⓒ   47. Ⓐ Ⓑ Ⓒ   61. Ⓐ Ⓑ Ⓒ
6. Ⓐ Ⓑ Ⓒ Ⓓ   20. Ⓐ Ⓑ Ⓒ   34. Ⓐ Ⓑ Ⓒ   48. Ⓐ Ⓑ Ⓒ   62. Ⓐ Ⓑ Ⓒ
7. Ⓐ Ⓑ Ⓒ Ⓓ   21. Ⓐ Ⓑ Ⓒ   35. Ⓐ Ⓑ Ⓒ   49. Ⓐ Ⓑ Ⓒ   63. Ⓐ Ⓑ Ⓒ
8. Ⓐ Ⓑ Ⓒ Ⓓ   22. Ⓐ Ⓑ Ⓒ   36. Ⓐ Ⓑ Ⓒ   50. Ⓐ Ⓑ Ⓒ   64. Ⓐ Ⓑ Ⓒ
9. Ⓐ Ⓑ Ⓒ Ⓓ   23. Ⓐ Ⓑ Ⓒ   37. Ⓐ Ⓑ Ⓒ Ⓓ   51. Ⓐ Ⓑ Ⓒ   65. Ⓐ Ⓑ Ⓒ
10. Ⓐ Ⓑ Ⓒ Ⓓ   24. Ⓐ Ⓑ Ⓒ   38. Ⓐ Ⓑ Ⓒ Ⓓ   52. Ⓐ Ⓑ Ⓒ Ⓓ   66. Ⓐ Ⓑ Ⓒ
11. Ⓐ Ⓑ Ⓒ Ⓓ   25. Ⓐ Ⓑ Ⓒ   39. Ⓐ Ⓑ Ⓒ Ⓓ   53. Ⓐ Ⓑ Ⓒ Ⓓ   67. Ⓐ Ⓑ Ⓒ
12. Ⓐ Ⓑ Ⓒ   26. Ⓐ Ⓑ Ⓒ   40. Ⓐ Ⓑ Ⓒ Ⓓ   54. Ⓐ Ⓑ Ⓒ Ⓓ   68. Ⓐ Ⓑ Ⓒ
13. Ⓐ Ⓑ Ⓒ   27. Ⓐ Ⓑ Ⓒ   41. Ⓐ Ⓑ Ⓒ   55. Ⓐ Ⓑ Ⓒ
14. Ⓐ Ⓑ Ⓒ   28. Ⓐ Ⓑ Ⓒ   42. Ⓐ Ⓑ Ⓒ Ⓓ   56. Ⓐ Ⓑ Ⓒ

Periodic Table of the Elements

Relative atomic masses are based on
$^{12}C = 12.00000$

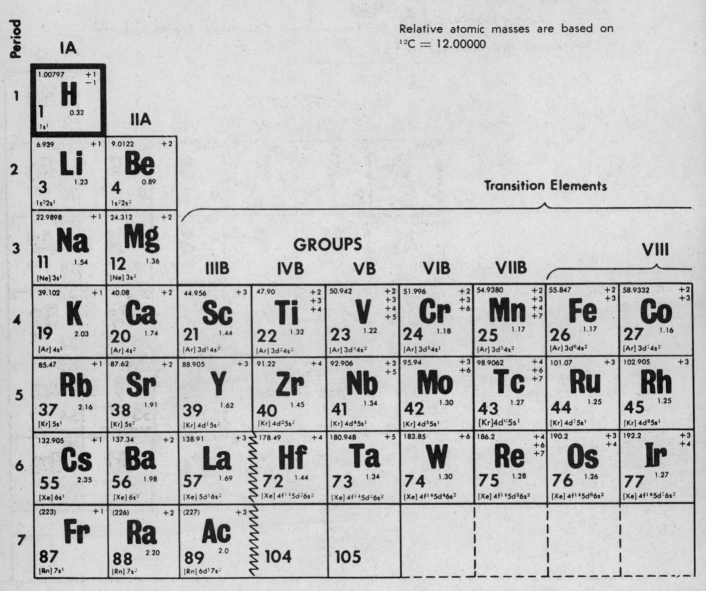

Numbers in parentheses are mass numbers of
most stable or most common isotope.

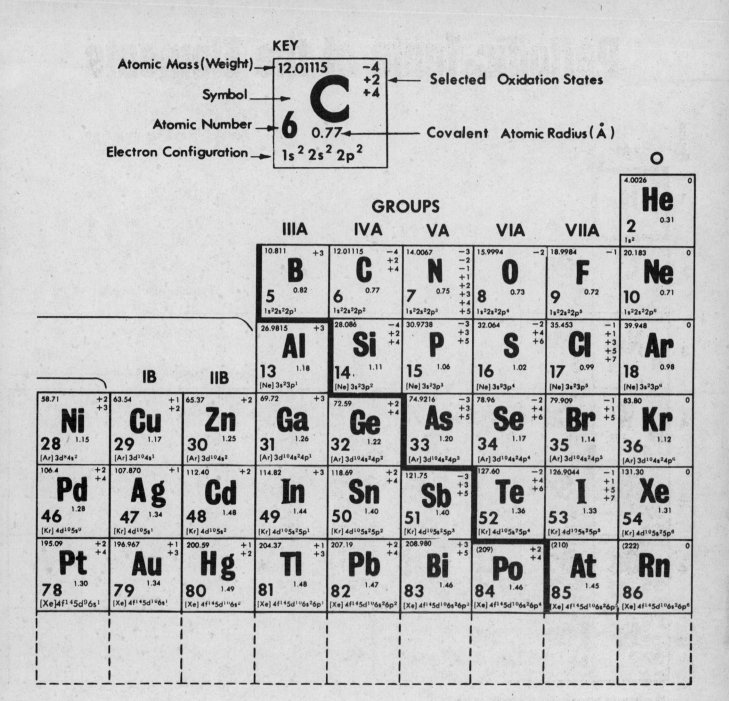

Model MCAT

SCIENCE KNOWLEDGE

135 MINUTES
125 QUESTIONS

The following questions are varied; therefore, you are advised to pay careful attention to the instructions for each portion. Use the periodic table of elements when necessary.

Biology

DIRECTIONS: Each of the statements or questions is followed by four or five suggested completions or answers. Choose the one that best completes the statement or answers the question, and mark the letter of your choice on the answer sheet. When you are unsure of an answer choose from among the possible correct ones after eliminating those that are definitely wrong.

1. Sperm utilize the substance _____ to penetrate the corona radiata of the egg in fertilization.
   (A) spermatase
   (B) chondroitin sulfatase
   (C) hyaluronidase
   (D) deoxyribonuclease
   (E) ribonuclease

2. During gamete production in the human female, the cell which undergoes the reduction divisions (meiosis) eventually produces _____ functional egg(s).
   (A) four
   (B) around three hundred
   (C) eight
   (D) one
   (E) around one hundred

3. A patient has suffered a cerebral hemorrhage that has caused injury and nonfunctioning of the primary motor area of his left cerebral cortex. As a result,
   (A) he cannot voluntarily move his right arm or hand nor his right leg or foot.
   (B) he feels no sensation on the left side of his body.
   (C) reflexes cannot be elicited on the left side of his body.
   (D) he cannot voluntarily move his right arm nor his left leg.
   (E) he feels no sensation on the right side of his body.

4. The pituitary (master) gland releases a gonadotrophic hormone which stimulates the production of testosterone by
   (A) spermatogonia.
   (B) interstitial cells of Leydig.
   (C) Sertoli cells.
   (D) epididymis.
   (E) ductus deferens.

5. The structure(s) responsible for the production of progesterone is (are)
   (A) ovarian follicle.
   (B) corpus albicans.
   (C) corpus luteum.
   (D) corpus spongiosum.
   (E) corpus cavernosum.

6. The sperm count of a normal 25-year-old male would be
   (A) one milion/ml.
   (B) one hundred million/ml.
   (C) one hundred thousand/ml.
   (D) four million/ml.
   (E) ten thousand/ml.

7. Each of the following is under control of the adenohypophysis EXCEPT the
   (A) thyroid.
   (B) adrenal medulla.
   (C) testis.
   (D) adrenal cortex.
   (E) ovary.

8. Mutations
   (A) are changes that take place and will always be passed on to the next generation.
   (B) are influenced by use and disuse of body parts.
   (C) occur spontaneously and cannot be produced experimentally.
   (D) are mainly due to diseases associated with development.
   (E) occur spontaneously and can also be produced by experimental means.

9. The functional unit of a striated muscle is known as the sarcomere. A sarcomere on an electron micrograph is the region between
   (A) two A bands.
   (B) two I bands.
   (C) two H bands.
   (D) two Z bands.

10. Bacteriophages are
    (A) quite dangerous to humans.
    (B) grown by innoculation of sterile broth.
    (C) reproduced only in living cells.
    (D) used as a source of vaccine against many bacterial diseases.
    (E) used in the production of vaccine against specific viral agents.

11. The czarinas of Russia and the queens of England popularized the disease hemophilia. These normal women produced sons suffering from hemophilia, a disease that is caused by a sex-linked recessive gene, h. The more common dominant gene, H, produces normal blood clotting. Genotypically these women must have carried
    (A) HH.
    (B) Hh.
    (C) hh.
    (D) none of the above.

12. Phenotype may be defined as
    (A) genetic make up of an individual.
    (B) hidden traits of an individual.
    (C) unrelated characteristics.
    (D) visible expression of genotype.
    (E) genetic material carried on the Y chromosome only.

13. Among the defense mechanisms available to humans to ward off their destruction by the environment is (are)
    (A) skin.
    (B) white blood corpuscles.
    (C) antibodies.
    (D) sebaceous secretions.
    (E) all of the above.

14. Alleles are genes which
    (A) arise during the cross-over process.
    (B) are linked to one chromosome only.
    (C) are always sex-linked and are transmitted from mothers to their sons.
    (D) occupy corresponding positions on homologous chromosomes.
    (E) are sex-linked and are transmitted from fathers to their daughters.

15. The neurotransmitter acetylcholine is released by
    (A) axon terminals.
    (B) dendrite terminals.
    (C) Golgi apparatus of neuron cell bodies.
    (D) Schwann cells.
    (E) node of Ranvier.

16. Two people are planning to have a family. The woman has blood type A/A and the man B/B. Their children might have the following
    (A) A and B.
    (B) B only.
    (C) A/B only.
    (D) A and B and A/B.

17. A man with blood cell genotype B/O marries a woman with type A/B. Their offspring could have any of the following
    (A) A/B, B/B, A/O, B/O.
    (B) A/B and B/O only.
    (C) A/O and B/B only.
    (D) none of the combinations above.

18. Of the pairs below which one is mismatched?
    (A) lymphatics: contain amino acids, salt, water, but no blood corpuscles
    (B) hepatic portal vein: drains the intestinal tract and carries nutrients
    (C) inferior vena cava: carries oxygenated blood and has a low blood pressure
    (D) hypothalamus: secretes releasing factors that influence pituitary-target organ relationships
    (E) pulmonary veins: carry oxygenated blood

19. A lack of iodine in the diet usually is associated with which disorder?
    (A) acromegaly
    (B) goiter
    (C) rickets
    (D) skin rash
    (E) tetanus

20. One enzyme that is important in protein digestion is
    (A) ptyalin.
    (B) trypsin.
    (C) maltose.
    (D) pancreatic lipase.
    (E) rennin.

21. If we examine the three types of muscles in respect to their characteristics, which of the series below is false?

	Characteristic	Cardiac	Skeletal	Smooth
(A)	No. of Nuclei	Several	Several	One
(B)	Position of Nuclei	Central	Central	Central
(C)	Striations	Present	Present	Absent
(D)	Control	Autonomic	Voluntary	Autonomic

22. Twinning is an interesting biological phenomenon. Identical twins usually result from fertilization of
    (A) two eggs by one sperm.
    (B) one egg by two sperms.
    (C) one egg by one sperm and separation of cells during the early cleavage division.
    (D) one egg and one polar body.
    (E) two eggs by two sperms.

23. The basic scientific finding that finally led to the development of the oral contraceptive (pill) used by many females in our society was that the preovulatory surge of LH can be prevented by the administration of
    (A) FSH.
    (B) estrogen.
    (C) progesterone.
    (D) ICSH.
    (E) androgen.

24. Dialysis (as is used for the treatment of chronic kidney ailments) differs from the process of osmosis in the respect that
    (A) both solvent and solute pass through the membrane.
    (B) solute selectively passes through the membrane only.
    (C) solvent selectively passes through the membrane only.
    (D) gases are the only substances that pass the membrane and blood is cleansed.

25. A foreign protein, when introduced into the body, is recognized and elicits an immunologic response; this substance is known as a (an)
    (A) antigen.
    (B) antibody.
    (C) complement.
    (D) vitamin.
    (E) enzyme.

26. Vasectomy is becoming a fashionable form of birth control in our society. In a vasectomy the _____ is (are) cut, a portion is removed, and the stumps are sutured.
    (A) epididymis
    (B) spermatic cords
    (C) oviducts
    (D) urethra
    (E) seminal vesicles

27. Sweating is a mechanism of temperature regulation by the body. This mechanism is usually far less effective in cooling the organism if the person is in an environment where the
    (A) wind is of hurricane proportion.
    (B) humidity is at least 0°.
    (C) humidity is almost 0°.
    (D) all of the above.
    (E) none of the above.

28. Hypersecretion of the hormone _____ will result in acromegaly (giantism).
    (A) TSH—thyroid stimulating hormone
    (B) STH—somatotropin (growth hormone)
    (C) ACTH—adrenocorticotrophic hormone
    (D) thyroxin
    (E) adrenalin

29. Conservation of body heat is aided by
    (A) constriction of the capillaries of the skin.
    (B) decreased respiratory activity.
    (C) decreased heart rate.
    (D) decreased sweating.
    (E) all of the above.

30. Testosterone is produced by
    (A) spermatogonia of the testes.
    (B) interstitial cells of the testes (Leydig cells).
    (C) the glans penis.
    (D) the prostate gland.
    (E) Sertoli cells.

31. Glucagon, which is produced by the pancreas, and epinephrine, which is produced by the adrenal glands, are hormones which
    (A) raise blood sugar level.
    (B) lower blood sugar level.
    (C) do not affect blood sugar markedly.
    (D) markedly increase liver glycogen.

32. Abnormal blood clots (thrombi) occur more frequently in people with
    (A) prothrombin deficiency.
    (B) impeded venous blood flow.
    (C) vitamin K deficiency.
    (D) platelet deficiency.
    (E) none of the above.

33. Growth hormone releasing factor is
    (A) a precursor of growth hormone.
    (B) the same as growth hormone (somatotropin).
    (C) a hypothalamic releasing factor.
    (D) a dietary stimulant regulating positive nitrogen balance.
    (E) an enzyme.

34. The large intestine functions mainly in
    (A) absorption of water.
    (B) excretion of water.
    (C) absorption of sodium and potassium.
    (D) finishing the digestive process.
    (E) excretion of digestive enzymes.

35. Blood pH is influenced by respiration; experimental hyperventilation in a physiology laboratory will result in the student's blood pH being
    (A) lowered.
    (B) raised.
    (C) unaffected.
    (D) raised to pH6.

36. Heart beat is initiated by the
    (A) vagus nerve.
    (B) sympathetic nervous system.
    (C) A-V (atrio-ventricular) node.
    (D) Purkinje system.
    (E) S-A (sino-atrial) node.

37. The graph below depicts the results of an experiment in which cells were grown on a complete culture medium that was never replaced.

    The probable cause of cell death from the five options listed below is
    (A) depletion of nutrients.
    (B) overcrowding.
    (C) buildup of toxic wastes.
    (D) answers A and B
    (E) answers A and C

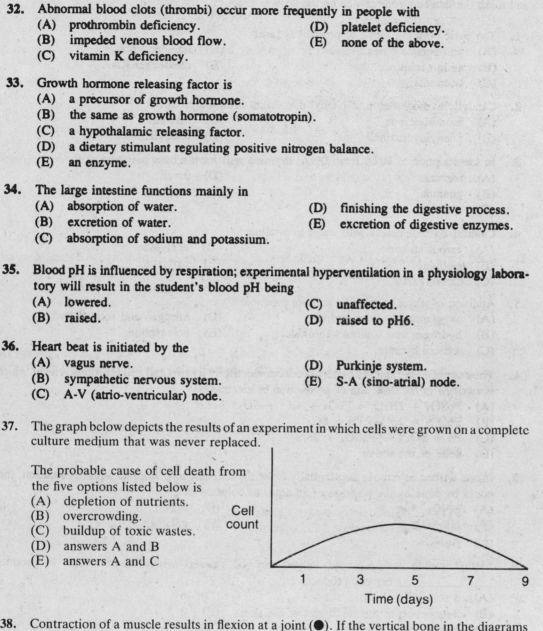

38. Contraction of a muscle results in flexion at a joint (●). If the vertical bone in the diagrams below is fixed, the natural sites for the muscle's origin and insertion would best be reflected in diagram
    (A) A
    (B) B
    (C) C
    (D) D
    (E) E

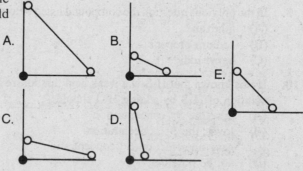

Chemistry

DIRECTIONS: Each of the statements or questions is followed by four or five suggested completions or answers. Choose the one that best completes the statement or answers the question, and mark the letter of your choice on the answer sheet.

1. The basic building block of proteins is (are)
   - (A) nitrogenous bases.
   - (B) amino acids.
   - (C) ammonia.
   - (D) transfer RNA.
   - (E) messenger RNA.

2. Catalytic hydrogenation of phenyl diazonium bromide produces
   - (A) bromobenzene.
   - (B) phenylhydrazine.
   - (C) benzene.
   - (D) phenylamine.

3. In transcription of RNA from DNA, thymine will form a base pair only with
   - (A) adenine.
   - (B) guanine.
   - (C) cytosine.
   - (D) uracil.
   - (E) thymine.

4. Calcium carbide reacts with water to produce
   - (A) carbon dioxide.
   - (B) methane.
   - (C) carbohydrate.
   - (D) acetylene.
   - (E) ethylene.

5. Addition of water to metallic sodium produces
   - (A) oxygen and sodium hydride.
   - (B) hydrogen and sodium hydroxide.
   - (C) sodium hydrate.
   - (D) nitrogen and sodium hydride.
   - (E) no reaction.

6. The common lead storage battery produces electricity by two hall cell reactions, one of which is (written in the direction of production of electricity)
   - (A) $PbSO_2 + 2H_2O \rightarrow PbO_2 + 4H^+ + SO_4^= + 2e^-$
   - (B) $PbSO_4 + 2e^- \rightarrow Pb + SO_4^=$
   - (C) $Pb + SO_4^= \rightarrow PbSO_4 + 2e^-$
   - (D) none of the above

7. If one wished to remove substantially all of the chloride ions from an aqueous solution, this could be done by the addition of an aqueous solution of
   - (A) KNO_3.
   - (B) Na_2SO_4.
   - (C) $AgNO_3$.
   - (D) starch.
   - (E) gelatin.

8. Methyl iodide and n-propyl iodide may be reacted with sodium metal to produce _____ organic products.
   - (A) 2
   - (B) 3
   - (C) 4
   - (D) 6
   - (E) 8

9. In the previous question the compound listed below that would be produced in greatest yield is
   - (A) n-hexane.
   - (B) sodium propane.
   - (C) hexyl iodide.
   - (D) n-butane.
   - (E) none of the above.

10. If it is known that H_2S is a weak acid that ionizes to form $2H^+$ and $S^=$. lowering the pH of a solution of H_2S by adding HCl should
    - (A) raise the $S^=$ concentration.
    - (B) lower the $S^=$ concentration.
    - (C) have no effect on $S^=$ concentration.
    - (D) not be possible.

11. Which of the following aqueous solutions will have the lowest freezing point?
    (A) 1 M NaCl   (D) 0.5 M BaSO$_4$
    (B) 0.3 M Na$_2$SO$_4$ (E) H$_2$O
    (C) 1.5 M glucose

12. Consider this reaction Fe^{++} $\rightleftharpoons$ Fe^{+++} + e$^-$
    (A) The reaction toward the right is an oxidation.
    (B) The reaction toward the right is a reduction.
    (C) The reaction toward the left is a reduction.
    (D) A and C are correct.
    (E) None of the above is correct.

13. A negative iodoform test (i.e., no yellow precipitate) will be the result when NaOH + I$_2$ is reacted with
    (A) CH$_3$ —CH —CH$_3$
                  |
                  OH

    (B) CH$_3$ —C —CH$_2$ —CH$_3$
                ‖
                O

    (C) Ø —C —CH$_3$
             ‖
             O

    (D) CH$_3$ —CH$_2$ —CH$_2$ —C = O
                                |
                                H

14. The hydronium ion is
    (A) a protonated water molecule.
    (B) formed by removal of H$^-$ from a water molecule.
    (C) really a free radial rather than an ion.
    (D) an ion with the formula of H$_2$O$^+$.
    (E) an uranium byproduct.

15. The alpha helix in a protein is classified as the
    (A) primary structure.   (D) quaternary structure.
    (B) secondary structure.   (E) permanent structure.
    (C) tertiary structure.

16. The neutralization of 50 ml of 0.25 N H$_2$SO$_4$ will require _____ ml of 0.50 N NaOH.
    (A) 25   (D) 2.5
    (B) 50   (E) none of the above
    (C) 0.25

17. The smallest organic ring compound that may be synthesized contains _____ carbon atoms.
    (A) 3   (D) 6
    (B) 4   (E) 7
    (C) 5

18. Factor(s) that influence(s) enzymatic activity is (are)
    (A) temperature.
    (B) pH.
    (C) concentration, substrate, cofactors
    (D) enzyme poisons.
    (E) all of the above.

19. A zwitterion is a molecule containing
    (A) both cationic and anionic functions.
    (B) more than one cationic or anionic function.
    (C) polar and nonpolar groups.
    (D) a Z^+ charge.
    (E) none of the above.

20. Prolonged boiling of animal fat with lye is called
    (A) ecology.
    (B) stain removal.
    (C) saponification.
    (D) alchemy of glyceridization.
    (E) conjugation.

21. Without considering stereoisomers the number of possible dibromoisomers of n-butane is
    (A) 3.
    (B) 4.
    (C) 5.
    (D) 6.
    (E) 8.

22. The reaction of HBr with 1-propene in the presence of peroxides will produce primarily
    (A) 1-bromopropane.
    (B) 2-bromopropane.
    (C) 1,2-dibromopropane.
    (D) 2-bromopropene.
    (E) 1,3-dibromopropane.

23. Theoretically, the ring monobromination of 4-bromo-1,2-diisopropylbenzene could produce _____ isomers.
    (A) 1
    (B) 2
    (C) 3
    (D) 4
    (E) 5

24. In a titration of iodine with sodium thiosulfate, the formation of a blue color on the addition of colorless starch solution indicates that
    (A) all of the iodine has not been oxidized.
    (B) the glassware has not been washed sufficiently.
    (C) all of the iodine has not been reduced.
    (D) a blue complex of starch, iodine, and sodium thiosulfate has been produced.
    (E) the temperature is above 50°C.

25. Of the compounds listed below which has the greatest affinity for combining with hemoglobin?
    (A) nitrogen, N_2
    (B) carbon dioxide, CO_2
    (C) oxygen, O_2
    (D) helium
    (E) carbon monoxide, CO

26. Use of helium is preferred over use of hydrogen in airships (e.g., blimps) because
    (A) helium has a lower density.
    (B) helium is chemically less reactive.
    (C) both of the above.
    (D) none of the above.

27. Nucleotides are composed of two types of sugars:
    (A) glucose and maltose.
    (B) glucose and ribose.
    (C) maltose and deoxyribose.
    (D) ribose and deoxyribose.
    (E) none of the above.

28. The process of fermentation can be considered to be
    (A) oxidation.
    (B) dehydration.
    (C) aerobic respiration.
    (D) anaerobic respiration.
    (E) hydrolytic.

29. Low molecular weight mercaptans are often added to natural gas to
    (A) increase the flammability.
    (B) slightly retard the burning.
    (C) produce a pleasant deodorant during burning.
    (D) provide a stench which is helpful in the detection of gas leaks.
    (E) prevent corrosion of the pipelines.

30. In the reaction sequence used in breakdown of glycogen in the liver or muscle—glycogen →
    glucose-1-phosphate → glucose-6-phosphate → glucose—the first step is
    (A) catalyzed by phosphorylase.
    (B) catalyzed by pepsin.
    (C) catalyzed by pancreatic amylase.
    (D) nonenzymatic.
    (E) catalyzed by trypsin.

31. An inorganic cation has been precipitated from water by the addition of NaOH. When we find
    that the precipitate may be redissolved upon the addition of NaOH or dilute HNO_3, we may
    conclude that the precipitate was
    (A) colloidal.   (D) amorphous.
    (B) amphoteric.   (E) crystalline.
    (C) anthromorphic.

32. The inorganic cation in the question above could be
    (A) silver.   (D) nickel.
    (B) ferric.   (E) barium.
    (C) aluminum.

33. Transuranium elements are
    (A) found on earth as a result of bombardment by particles from the planet Uranus.
    (B) found naturally in abundance greater than that of uranium isotopes.
    (C) man-made elements with more than 92 protons in the nucleus.
    (D) elements that have been postulated but not found naturally or produced artificially.

34. The particles which spin around the nucleus of an atom and are negatively charged are the
    (A) neutrons.   (D) electrons.
    (B) positrons.   (E) ions.
    (C) protons.

35. Below are listed the major differences between compounds and mixtures. Which one is an
    incorrect pairing?

	Mixture	Compound
(A)	Physical union	Chemical union
(B)	No new substances are formed	New substances are formed
(C)	Can be separated by physical means	Can be separated by physical means
(D)	Elements form no definite proportions	Elements form definite proportions

36. 2,4-D (2,4-dichlorophenoxyacetic acid) is a potent stimulator of plant metabolism. Most
    sensitive to it is (are)
    (A) monocotyledons.   (D) Kentucky blue grass.
    (B) dicotyledons.   (E) Kentucky fescue grass.
    (C) phytoplankton.

37. Solids
    (A) are rigid and have a definite form.
    (B) possess molecules which vibrate very slowly in a fixed position.
    (C) possess molecules which are close together.
    (D) have all of the above characteristics.
    (E) have none of the above characteristics.

38. Which of the following reactions is a decomposition reaction?

(A) $CO_2 + H_2O \rightarrow H_2CO_3$

(B) $2HgO \xrightarrow{\Delta} 2Hg + O_2$

(C) $Zn + CuSO_4 \rightarrow ZnSO_4 + Cu$

(D) $HCl + NaOH \rightarrow NaCl + H_2O$

(E) $2H_2 + O_2 \rightarrow 2H_2O$

39. Which of the following is an incorrect statement?

(A) Ions have a charge equal to the number of electrons gained or lost.

(B) The fewer ions formed, the greater the electric current carried by an electrolyte.

(C) Atoms and ions of the same element have different properties.

(D) Certain substances break up into ions when dissolved in water.

(E) All of the above.

40. Which of the following structural formulas is not properly identified?

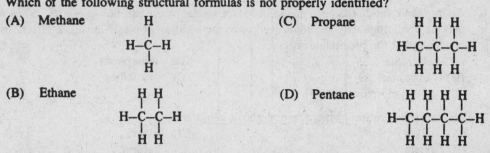

(A) Methane

(B) Ethane

(C) Propane

(D) Pentane

41. The pH of a weak solution of ammonium hydroxide has been measured. If ammonium chloride is now added

(A) the pH will increase.

(B) the pOH will decrease.

(C) the acidity will decrease.

(D) the pH will decrease.

(E) no pH change is observed.

42. Black and white photographic film is based on the light-catalyzed chemical reaction

(A) $gelatin_c \rightarrow gelatin_B + H_2O$.

(B) $Cd^{++}He \rightarrow Cd^+$.

(C) $quinone_1 \rightarrow quinone_2 \rightarrow hydroquinone$.

(D) $Ag^+He \rightarrow Ag^o$.

(E) none of the above.

43. According to the principle of LeChatelier, a higher pressure applied to the reversible reaction $N_2 + 3H_2 \rightleftarrows 2NH_3$ would be expected to result in

(A) shifting the equilibrium to the left.

(B) shifting the equilibrium to the right.

(C) no change in the equilibrium.

(D) increased percentages of NH_3 and H_2.

(E) increased N_2 and decreased H_2.

44. The neutron was discovered by

(A) Marie and Pierre Curie.

(B) Ernest Rutherford.

(C) James Chadwick.

(D) Enrico Fermi.

(E) Albert Einstein.

45. Reaction of acetic anhydride with toluene (methylbenzene) in the presence of $AlCl_3$ produces

(A) an aromatic ester.

(B) an aromatic acid.

(C) an aromatic ketone.

(D) an aromatic anhydride.

(E) an aromatic lipid.

46. In order to produce polyvinyl alcohol we would expect to
  (A) polymerize the monomer, vinyl alcohol.
  (B) polymerize another vinyl monomer and convert the polymer to polyvinyl alcohol.
  (C) hydroxylate polyethylene.
  (D) ask for another task. This one has not been done successfully.

47. Acetaldehyde, in the presence of NaOH, will
  (A) not react.
  (B) be converted to acetic acid.
  (C) produce 3-hydroxybutanal.
  (D) produce ethyl acetate.
  (E) do none of the above.

48. The graph below reflects the frequency distribution of velocities of gas molecules. The mean velocity is shown by number

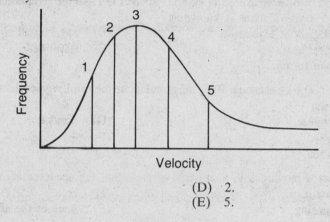

  (A) 1.
  (B) 4.
  (C) 3.
  (D) 2.
  (E) 5.

49. The acyclic *A* shown below hydrolyzes less readily than the cyclic ester *B*. This reactivity difference is due to

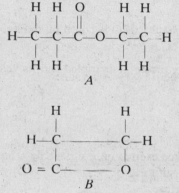

  (A) puckering of the ring.
  (B) electronic delocalization.
  (C) bond angle strain.
  (D) steric strain.
  (E) different hybridization of carbons.

Physics

DIRECTIONS:. Each of the statements or questions is followed by five suggested completions or answers. Choose the one that best completes the statement or answers the question, and mark the letter of your choice on the answer sheet.

1. If the uniform acceleration near the surface of the earth is about 9.8 m/sec.^{2} for a free-fall, what is the velocity at the end of 2 seconds of fall (neglect friction)?
   - (A) 19.6 m/sec.
   - (B) 17.0 m/sec.
   - (C) 14.6 m/sec.
   - (D) 12.2 m/sec.
   - (E) 9.8 m/sec.

2. The amount of heat measured in calories needed to raise the temperature of 1 gram of substance by 1 degree Celsius is known as
   - (A) coefficient of expansion.
   - (B) specific heat.
   - (C) heat of fusion.
   - (D) mechanical equivalent of heat.
   - (E) latent heat.

3. If a force of 30.6 kg acts on a 60 kg mass, calculate the resulting acceleration. (1 kg of force = 9.8 newtons)
   - (A) 0.5 m/sec.^{2}
   - (B) 2 m/sec.^{2}
   - (C) 5 m/sec.^{2}
   - (D) 6 m/sec.^{2}
   - (E) 9.8 m/sec.^{2}

4. If an object is moving with a constant acceleration, the net force acting on that body is
   - (A) constant.
   - (B) increasing.
   - (C) decreasing.
   - (D) zero.
   - (E) none of the above.

5. What is the potential energy of a 10 kg steel ball which has been raised vertically 9 m above the floor?
   - (A) 90 joules
   - (B) 98 joules
   - (C) 441 joules
   - (D) 882 joules
   - (E) 1938 joules

6. If the mass of a moving projectile is tripled and its velocity is doubled, the kinetic energy will be multiplied by
   - (A) 2.
   - (B) 6.
   - (C) 8.
   - (D) 12.
   - (E) 16.

7. The direction of the force exerted on a surface by a liquid at rest is
   - (A) tangential to the surface.
   - (B) parallel to the surface.
   - (C) normal to the surface.
   - (D) 45° to the surface.
   - (E) 30° to the surface.

8. The volume of a confined gas varies inversely with the absolute pressure provided that the temperature remains unchanged. This statement is known as
   - (A) Avogadro's law.
   - (B) Bernoulli's law.
   - (C) the gas law.
   - (D) Dalton's law.
   - (E) Boyle's law.

9. Which ratio below best defines the efficiency of simple machines?
   - (A) $\dfrac{\text{useful work output}}{\text{work input}} \times 100\%$
   - (B) $\dfrac{\text{work input}}{\text{work output}} \times 100\%$
   - (C) $\dfrac{\text{theoretical mechanical advantage}}{\text{actual mechanical advantage}} \times 100\%$
   - (D) $\dfrac{\text{centrifugal force}}{\text{centripetal force}} \times 100\%$
   - (E) $\dfrac{\text{useful work input}}{\text{useful work output}} \times 100\%$

10. You are standing 1000 m from the point where a steel block strikes the sidewalk. How long will it take the sound to reach your ears if the speed of sound in air at 0°C is about 333 m/sec.?
    (A) 1 second
    (B) 2 seconds
    (C) 3 seconds
    (D) 4 seconds
    (E) 5 seconds

11. In simplest terms, the energy of a wave is directly proportional to the square of its
    (A) period.
    (B) length.
    (C) reflection.
    (D) refraction.
    (E) height.

12. Shadows consist of two portions, the umbra and the penumbra. Which statement below applies ONLY to the umbra?
    (A) It is circular in shape.
    (B) It is always the longest portion.
    (C) It is a partial shadow.
    (D) It receives no light from any part of the source.
    (E) It receives light from part of the source.

13. What is the work done in joules if a 100-kg ball is raised to 3 m above the floor in 1 second?
    (A) 300 joules
    (B) 980 joules
    (C) 1960 joules
    (D) 2940 joules
    (E) 3240 joules

DIRECTIONS: Below are listed five basic unit names and five phrases of definition for these units. Match the correct definition with the correct unit name.

Questions 14-18:
    (A) The work done when a force of 1 newton is extended through a distance of 1 meter.
    (B) The quantity of heat needed to raise the temperature of 1 gm of water 1°C.
    (C) The amount of force that will give 1 kg of mass an acceleration of 1 m/sec.².
    (D) The resistance of a device in which heat is generated at 1 watt by a current of 1 ampere.
    (E) The magnetic flux through a surface.

14. newton

15. joule

16. ohm

17. calorie

18. weber

19. Which of the statements below is correct?
    (A) If a road is properly banked for the speed of the vehicle, the resultant force on the vehicle is a horizontal centripetal force.
    (B) The resultant force action on a vehicle will be that which maintains it in a circular path.
    (C) There is no tendency for the vehicle to skid if a road is banked for the speed at which the vehicle is moving.
    (D) The angle of bank for a road is obtained from a consideration of the centripetal force required.
    (E) All of the above statements are correct.

20. How far will a body free-fall in 1 second if released from rest?
    (A) 0.0 m
    (B) 4.9 m
    (C) 9.8 m
    (D) 14.7 m
    (E) 19.6 m

21. A resultant force of 45 kg is acting on a body whose acceleration is 10 m/sec.^{2}. Calculate the mass of the body.
    (A) 4.5 kg
    (B) 44.1 kg
    (C) 450 kg
    (D) 980 kg
    (E) 1960 kg

22. $F = Gm_1m_2/d_2$ is the equation representing Newton's law of universal gravitation. Which of the statements below is true?
    (A) G is called the gravitation constant.
    (B) The law can be used to calculate the mass of an object on another planet if the mass and radius of that planet are known.
    (C) Knowing the value of G, one can easily calculate the mass of the earth.
    (D) The force of attraction of the earth for a body is equal to the force of attraction of the body for the earth.
    (E) All of the above are true.

23. Two forces of 45 kg-f and 40 kg-f act on a body in opposite directions. What is the resultant force?
    (A) 5 kg-f
    (B) 40 kg-f
    (C) 45 kg-f
    (D) 85 kg-f
    (E) 90 kg-f

24. A good floor lamp has a wide heavy base to increase its stability through
    (A) raising the center of gravity.
    (B) lowering the center of gravity.
    (C) banking.
    (D) neutral equilibrium.
    (E) none of the above.

25. When analyzed, most complicated machines are found to consist of a combination of various simple machines. Which machine below is NOT a simple machine?
    (A) wheel-and-axle
    (B) pulley
    (C) lever
    (D) electric motor
    (E) inclined plane

26. Calculate the velocity of a test sled that is propelled by a device that has 2500 joules of available energy to propel a sled of 50 kg mass.
    (A) 50 m/sec.
    (B) 25 m/sec.
    (C) 10 m/sec.
    (D) 5 m/sec.
    (E) 1 m/sec.

27. Using the figure below as a reference, identify the true statement. The large tank is full of water and is exposed to the atmosphere.

    d_1 = diameter of opening
    v_1 = velocity at d_1
    v_2 = velocity at d_2

    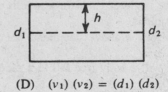

    (A) $v_1 > v_2$
    (B) $v_2 > v_1$
    (C) $v_1/v_2 = 1$
    (D) $(v_1)(v_2) = (d_1)(d_2)$
    (E) none of the above

28. If the density of a given body is 10 gm/cm³, what is its specific gravity?

(A) 0.01 gm/cm³
(B) 1.0 gm
(C) 0.01
(D) 10.0
(E) 1.0

29. The amount of a liquid's cohesive force per unit of length is called

(A) apparent weight.
(B) adhesion.
(C) depression.
(D) surface tension.
(E) capillary rise.

30. When light is reflected from a surface it can be either regular reflection or diffuse reflection. The essential difference between regularly and diffusely reflecting surfaces is that

(A) the regularly reflecting surface is coarser than the diffusely reflecting surface.
(B) only mirrors reflect in a regular manner, every other surface reflects diffusely.
(C) regularly reflecting surfaces are smoother than diffusely reglecting surfaces.
(D) light can not be reflected from a diffusely reflecting surface.
(E) all of the above are essential differences between regularly and diffusely reflecting surfaces.

31. If a color disc composed of red, orange, yellow, green, blue, indigo, and violet pie-shaped sections is rapidly rotated, which color will your eye see?

(A) black
(B) brown
(C) red
(D) white
(E) blue

DIRECTIONS: Given below are some fundamentals of electricity, followed by phrases defining these fundamentals or equations symbolically representing these characteristics. Match the fundamental with the correct identifying item.

Questions 32-36:

(A) Ratio of charge to potential difference
(B) Ratio of work done to unit charge in moving the charge from point 1 to point 2 (voltage)
(C) $V = I$ or $V = IR$
(D) $F = \dfrac{KQ_1Q_2}{d^2}$
(E) $P = I^2$ or $P = IR$

32. Ohm's law
33. Joule's law
34. capacitance
35. potential difference
36. Coulomb's law

37. With reference to the circuit diagram shown below, the correct heat loss shown in resistor R_1 is

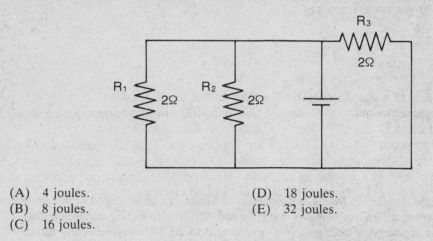

(A) 4 joules.
(B) 8 joules.
(C) 16 joules.

(D) 18 joules.
(E) 32 joules.

38. If the block in the diagram below has a mass m and lies at rest on a rough surface having a coefficient of friction of static force S_f, the frictional force is

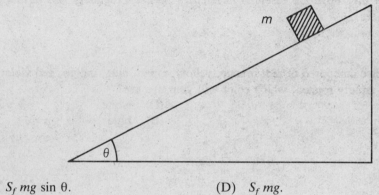

(A) $S_f\, mg\, \sin\theta$.
(B) $mg\, \sin\theta$.
(C) $mg\, \cos\theta$.

(D) $S_f\, mg$.
(E) $S_f\, \tan\theta$.

STOP. If you finish before the time limit is up, go over your work for this section. DO NOT look at any other sections of the model examination. When your time limit is up, go on to the next section.

SCIENCE PROBLEMS

85 MINUTES
66 QUESTIONS

The following questions require you to use your knowledge of science to solve problems.

DIRECTIONS: The following questions are in groups. Preceding each series of questions is a paragraph or short explanatory statement, a formula or set of formulas, or a definition. Read the written material and then answer the questions. Eliminate those choices that you think to be incorrect and mark the letter of your choice on the answer sheet.

In uniformly accelerated motion the following equations hold:
$$V = V_0 + at$$
$$X = V_0 t + \tfrac{1}{2} a t^2$$
when X = displacement, V = velocity at time t, V_0 = initial velocity, t = time, and a = acceleration. A ball is projected directly upward at a velocity of 15 m/sec.

1. What is the distance above the ground after 3 seconds?
   (A) 0 m
   (B) 0.9 m
   (C) 1.8 m
   (D) 2.7 m
   (E) 3.6 m

2. What is its velocity at that point?
   (A) 14.4 m/sec. upward
   (B) 14.4 m/sec. downward
   (C) 29.4 m/sec. upward
   (D) 29.4 m/sec. downward

3. What is the highest point this ball will reach?
   (A) 9.80 m
   (B) 11.48 m
   (C) 38.66 m
   (D) 22.95 m
   (E) 1.53 m

In the dark, bromine adds to double bonds to produce dibromo additional compounds. The addition of bromine to conjugated dienes can produce 1,2-dibromo-3-alkenes or 1,4-dibromo-2-alkenes.

4. The reaction of 1 mole of 1,3-butadiene with 1 mole of bromine would be expected to result in production of
   (A) 1,4-dibromo-3-butene.
   (B) 1,4-dibromobutane.
   (C) 1,2-dibromo-2-butene.
   (D) 1,3-dibromo-2-butene.
   (E) none of the above.

5. Another example of the reaction of bromine with conjugated dienes is that in which bromine reacts with
   (A) acetylene.
   (B) allene (propadiene).
   (C) 1,4-pentadiene.
   (D) B and C.
   (E) none of the above.

6. The formation of 1,4-addition products with conjugated dienes is evidence of
   (A) ionic mechanism.
   (B) free radical mechanism.
   (C) radiant energy.
   (D) A and B.
   (E) none of the above.

The solubility of compound R in water is 5 gm/100 ml. The distribution coefficient between water and ether, $K_{H_2O/ether}$, is 2 at room temperature.

7. Extraction of 50 ml of water containing 1.0 g of compound R with 50 ml of ether will result in _____ of compound R being in the ether phase.
   (A) 1.0 g
   (B) 0.5 g
   (C) 0.33 g
   (D) 0.1 g
   (E) 0.05 g

8. A second extraction of the remaining aqueous solution by another 50 ml of ether would result in the extraction of an additional
   (A) 0.1 g.
   (B) 0.2 g.
   (C) 0.3 g.
   (D) 0.5 g.
   (E) 0.55 g.

9. In order to remove 0.8 g in the first extraction it would be necessary to use _____ of ether.
   (A) less than 150 ml
   (B) 200 ml
   (C) 300 ml
   (D) 400 ml
   (E) more than 475 ml

Assume that the membrane of a neuron is unimolecular, and that an impulse travelling along the nerve involves the same type of ions regardless of location along the fiber. While examining with the oscilloscope the nature of an impulse traveling along the sciatic nerve of a test animal, an unusually large spike is visualized and seems out of phase.

10. One can assume that the unusually large spike height visualized is
    (A) typical of a repeated nerve impulse.
    (B) an artifact.
    (C) not typical of a nerve impulse but definitely a result of the nerve's physiology.
    (D) all of the above.
    (E) none of the above.

11. The usual wave function seen while studying neural impulses is an example of
    (A) an all or none response.
    (B) a gradient response.
    (C) subthreshold transmission.
    (D) all of the above.
    (E) none of the above.

12. The spike height of the wave can be altered by
    (A) external application of a saline solution to the nerve.
    (B) injecting a saline solution into the nerve fiber.
    (C) increasing the voltage of the applied stimulus.
    (D) all of the above.
    (E) none of the above.

A block weighing 1 kg = 1000 grams is totally submerged in a liquid whose specific gravity is 1.25. The apparent weight of this body in the liquid is 800 grams.

13. What is the buoyant force?
    (A) 125 gm
    (B) 200 gm
    (C) 800 gm
    (D) 1000 gm
    (E) 1800 gm

14. What is the volume of the body or that of the displaced liquid?
    (A) 50 cm³
    (B) 160 cm³
    (C) 270 cm³
    (D) 350 cm³
    (E) 450 cm³

15. Calculate the density of the body.
    (A) 1 gm/cm³
    (B) 2 gm/cm³
    (C) 3 gm/cm³
    (D) 6.25 gm/cm³
    (E) 5 gm/cm³

Use the following graph to answer questions 16-18:

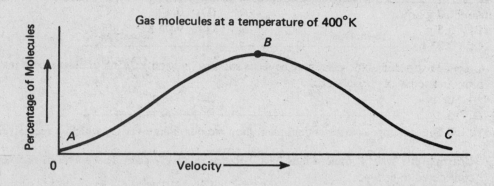

Gas molecules at a temperature of 400°K

16. In the graph above, point B is
  (A) the escape velocity.
  (B) the average velocity.
  (C) the most probable velocity.
  (D) the maximum velocity.
  (E) B and C

17. Point C indicates
  (A) cessation of motion.
  (B) escape velocity.
  (C) maximum velocity.
  (D) an improbable velocity under these conditions.
  (E) an impossible velocity under these conditions.

18. If the above velocity plot were changed to 500°K, the peak of the curve would
  (A) be displaced to the right.
  (B) remain unchanged.
  (C) be displaced to the left.
  (D) have three maxima.
  (E) be flattened to such an extent that no maximum could be observed.

The equilibrium constant for the reaction $C + D \rightleftharpoons E + 2F$ may be represented by the equation:

$$K_{eq} = \frac{[E]\,[F]^2}{[C]\,[D]}$$

19. Doubling the concentration of C will
  (A) double the equilibrium constant.
  (B) halve the equilibrium constant.
  (C) increase the equilibrium constant by a factor of 3.
  (D) increase the equilibrium constant by a factor of 4.
  (E) do none of the above.

20. Doubling the concentration of D would result in
  (A) an increase in the concentration of E.
  (B) an increase in the concentration of F.
  (C) a decrease in the concentration of C.
  (D) all of the above.
  (E) none of the above.

21. The greatest change in the equilibrium constant would be noted upon
  (A) doubling the concentration of A.
  (B) doubling the concentration of B.
  (C) doubling the concentration of C.
  (D) doubling the concentration of D.
  (E) none of the above.

The A B O blood grouping system is explained on the basis of a single triallelic system with genes A, B, and O operating at a single genetic locus. Phenotypic and genotypic characteristics may be expressed as follows:

Phenotype	Genotype
A	A/A; A/O
B	B/B; B/O
O	O/O
AB	A/B

The A and B genes appear to be codominant; they are dominant over O, which is recessive.

22. Utilizing this system, transfusions have become relatively safe. The universal recipient is considered to be type
(A) A.
(B) B.
(C) O.
(D) AB.
(E) Rh.

23. These individuals carry on their red blood cells the following agglutinogens
(A) A.
(B) B.
(C) O.
(D) A,B.
(E) None.

24. A person of blood type A can receive blood of type(s)
(A) A.
(B) B; A.
(C) O.
(D) A; O.
(E) A; AB.

The equation of Snell's law is $\dfrac{\sin \theta_i}{\sin \theta_r} = \dfrac{N_r}{N_i}$ where θ_i = angle of incidence, θ_r = angle of refraction, N_r = index of refraction of pass through medium, and N_i = index of refraction of incident medium.

A beam of light is traveling through air and strikes a medium whose index of refraction is 1.414 at 45° with a normal to the glass.

25. The ray of light as it enters will
(A) bend toward the normal.
(B) bend away from the normal.
(C) be totally reflected.
(D) travel along the normal.
(E) do none of the above.

26. The index of refraction can be defined as the velocity of light in a vacuum divided by the velocity in the medium ($N = \dfrac{C}{S}$). If this is the case, another valid expression for Snell's law is

(A) $\dfrac{S_i}{S_r} = \dfrac{N_r}{N_i}$

(B) $\dfrac{\sin \theta_i}{\sin \theta_r} = \dfrac{C_i}{S_i}$

(C) $\dfrac{\sin \theta_i}{\sin \theta_r} = \dfrac{C_r}{S_r}$

(D) $\dfrac{\sin \theta_i}{\sin \theta_r} = \dfrac{S_i}{S_r}$

(E) $\dfrac{\sin \theta_i}{\sin \theta_r} = \dfrac{S_r}{S_i}$

27. What is the velocity of the light in the medium if $\sin \theta_i = 0.707$, $\sin \theta_r = 0.500$, and the velocity of light in a vacuum is 3.0×10^8 m/sec.?
(A) 1.4×10^8 m/sec.
(B) 2.1×10^8 m/sec.
(C) 2.8×10^8 m/sec.
(D) 3.5×10^8 m/sec.
(E) 4.2×10^8 m/sec.

Two containers of equal volume are filled with helium gas at different temperatures and pressures.

28. If container X is at 760 torr and 0°C while container Y is at 137°C and 1140 torr, then container X (compared to container Y) has
    (A) fewer atoms of gas and a higher average velocity.
    (B) more atoms of gas and a lower average velocity.
    (C) an equal number of atoms of gas and an equal average velocity.
    (D) fewer atoms of gas and a lower average velocity.
    (E) none of the above.

29. Increasing the number of atoms in container X while retaining the volume constant would result in
    (A) increased pressure.   (D) decreased temperature.
    (B) decreased pressure.   (E) Choices A and C.
    (C) increased temperature.

30. If containers X and Y (above) had been at the temperatures and pressures given but container Y had contained argon rather than helium, then container X (compared to container Y) would be observed to have
    (A) fewer atoms of gas and a higher average velocity.
    (B) more atoms of gas and lower average velocity.
    (C) an equal number of atoms of gas with an equal average velocity.
    (D) an equal number of atoms of gas with an unknown average velocity.
    (E) none of the above.

A muscle fiber is a single muscle cell. Each fiber is composed of numerous cylindrical fibrils running the entire length of the fiber. The fibril exhibits light and dark bands—the I and A bands respectively. The I band is bisected by the M line. There is a somewhat lighter band within the A band that is called the H band. These striations are produced by the arrangement within the fibril of myofilaments; myosin is the thick myofilament while actin is considered the thin myofilament.

31. A sarcomere is the area between
    (A) two A bands.   (D) two Z bands.
    (B) two H bands.   (E) two M bands.
    (C) two I bands.

32. During contraction the lengths of the thick and thin myofilaments
    (A) increase.   (C) remain the same.
    (B) decrease.

33. If we could imagine observing a contraction under a light microscope we would see the narrowing of the
    (A) H and I bands.   (D) H bands only.
    (B) A bands.   (E) I bands only.
    (C) Z bands.

Given the circuit diagram below:

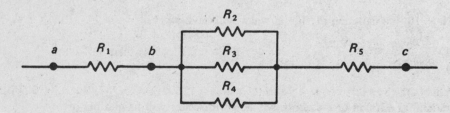

with the resistors R_1 = 5 ohms, $R2$ = 2 ohms, R_3 = 4 ohms, R_4 = 12 ohms and R_5 = 5 ohms. The current through the circuit is 10 amps.

34. Calculate the potential differences across R_1.

(A) 10 volts
(B) 20 volts
(C) 30 volts
(D) 40 volts
(E) 50 volts

35. Calculate the resistance in the parallel resistors.

(A) 1.2 ohms
(B) 5.6 ohms
(C) 6.0 ohms
(D) 18 ohms
(E) 28 ohms

36. Calculate the potential difference across the parallel resistors.

(A) 12 volts
(B) 60 volts
(C) 120 volts
(D) 180 volts
(E) none of the above

An unknown organic compound is observed to react with phenylhydrazine to form a crystalline derivative. Mild oxidation produces one or more acidic compounds.

37. The compound could be

(A) acetone.
(B) 1,3-butadiene.
(C) ethylene glycol.
(D) butanol.
(E) all of the above.

38. Another compound fulfilling the requirements would be

(A) glycerol.
(B) ethanol.
(C) acetic acid.
(D) aniline.
(E) none of the above.

39. If oxidation with permanganate and then oxidation with periodic acid is performed prior to the reactions with phenylhydrazine and the mild oxidation (treatment and results mentioned above), the compound could be

(A) 2-butene.
(B) acetone.
(C) 2-butanone.
(D) butane.
(E) 2-butanol.

Strong acids such as HCl are considered to be completely ionized unless they are at very high concentrations.

40. A 1×10^{-4} M solution of HCl in water will have a pH of

(A) 11.
(B) 7.
(C) 9.
(D) 4.
(E) less than 3.

41. A 1:10,000 dilution of the above solution with water will have a pH of

(A) greater than 8.5.
(B) 8.
(C) 7.
(D) 6.
(E) less than 5.6.

42. A mixture of 10 ml of 1×10^{-4} M HCl with 90 ml of the diluted solution of the previous question will have a pH of

(A) 0.4.   (D) 5.
(B) 3.1.   (E) greater than 6.2.
(C) 4.

The diagram illustrates a typical single neuron; the basic unit of the nervous system. Neurons connect with each other and in that manner an impulse is conducted and transmitted throughout the body. Two types of cell processes are indicated.

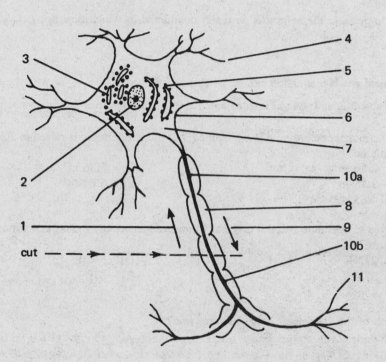

43. An impulse on the skin will be picked up by

(A) 4.   (D) 10.
(B) 6.   (E) 11.
(C) 7.

44. The genetic material of the cell is located in

(A) 2.   (D) 7.
(B) 3.   (E) 9.
(C) 5.

45. Protein synthesis is carried out under the direction of

(A) 3 in 5.   (D) 2 in 7.
(B) 2 in 3.   (E) 5 in 2.
(C) 2 in 5.

A person has been in an accident and the physician is conducting a neurological examination. Sensation is lost over several fingers and the examiner fears that a nerve has been cut. Note the cut indication on the diagram.

46. Which process would completely degenerate?
(A) 4
(B) 8
(C) 10a
(D) 10b
(E) 11

47. Retrograde degeneration would be visible in
(A) 2.
(B) 3.
(C) 6.
(D) 10b.
(E) 11.

48. The impulse in the neuron is normally conducted in which direction?
(A) 9
(B) 1

The general gas law equation can be written as follows: $\frac{PV}{T} = \frac{P_0V_0}{T_0}$ with the temperature and pressure in absolute units. A gas is maintained at 0°C in a volume of 5 m³ at atmospheric pressure.

49. If the atmospheric pressure is maintained, but the temperature is raised to 20°C, what will be its volume?
(A) 2.50 m³
(B) 3.75 m³
(C) 4.65 m³
(D) 5.36 m³
(E) 6.65 m³

50. At what temperature will this original volume of gas occupy 2.5 m³ at 4 atmospheres absolute pressure?
(A) 273°K
(B) 373°K
(C) 456°K
(D) 546°K
(E) 679°K

51. Which of the statements below is (are) true?
(A) $\frac{P}{P_0} = \frac{T}{T_0}$
(B) $\frac{V}{V_0} = \frac{T}{T_0}$
(C) $PV = P_0V_0$
(D) $\frac{PV}{T} = \frac{P_0V_0}{T_0}$
(E) all of the above

On the Celsius scale (°C) the freezing point of water is 0° and the boiling point is 100°. On the Fahrenheit scale (°F) they are respectively 32° and 212°. The absolute Kelvin scale lists as absolute zero a temperature of −273°, and therefore the Kelvin and Celsius scales differ only in the choice of point zero. Kelvin temperature is, therefore, 273 plus the Celsius temperature. For calculations the following formula may be utilized:

$$\text{Celsius equals } \frac{5}{9} \times \text{(Fahrenheit} - 32)$$

52. 104°F is _____ degrees on the Kelvin scale.
(A) 40
(B) 377
(C) 169
(D) 113
(E) 313

53. 45°C will equal _____ degrees F.
    (A) 145
    (B) 318
    (C) 313
    (D) 113
    (E) 90

54. The normal body temperature for human beings on the Celsius scale is
    (A) 98.6°
    (B) 40°
    (C) 30°
    (D) 37°
    (E) 32°

A newly synthesized, weakly ionized acid is being studied. It is found to have an ionization constant of 1×10^{-7}.

55. A 0.1 N solution of the acid will have a pH of
    (A) 4.
    (B) 5.5.
    (C) 6.1.
    (D) 6.9.
    (E) none of the above.

56. A tenfold dilution of the above solution with water will have a pH between
    (A) 3.5 and 4.5.
    (B) 4.6 and 5.5.
    (C) 5.6 and 6.7.
    (D) 6.75 and 7.1.
    (E) none of the above.

57. Assuming the acid is highly soluble in water, prediction of pH at very high concentrations might be in error because of
    (A) higher temperatures in the solution.
    (B) errors in that area of logarithm tables.
    (C) decreased ionization at higher concentrations.
    (D) all of the above.
    (E) none of the above.

Compound V is known to contain only carbon, hydrogen, and oxygen. Elemental analysis reveals 40.0% carbon and 6.67% hydrogen.

58. The empirical formula of compound V is
    (A) CH_2O.
    (B) CH_3O.
    (C) CH_4O.
    (D) none of the above.
    (E) not possible to determine with the data given.

59. If the molecular weight of the compound is twice the molecular weight of the empirical formula, then the molecular formula is
    (A) $C_2H_4O_2$.
    (B) $C_2H_6O_2$.
    (C) $C_2H_8O_2$.
    (D) none of the above.
    (E) not possible to determine with the information from this question and the previous one.

60. With the information from the two previous questions, compound V could be
- (A) methanol.
- (B) methyl ether.
- (C) formaldehyde.
- (D) glucose.
- (E) none of the above.

For the base pyridinium hydroxide the K_b is 1×10^{-9}

$$PyrOH \rightleftharpoons Pyr^+ + OH^-$$

$$K_b = \frac{[Pyr^+][OH^-]}{[Pry\,OH]}$$

61. The pH of a 0.1 M solution of PyrOH would be
- (A) 4.
- (B) 5.
- (C) 6.
- (D) 7.5.
- (E) greater than 8.5.

62. A hundredfold dilution with water would produce a solution with a pH
- (A) greater than 10.
- (B) between 8.5 and 9.5.
- (C) between 7.5 and 8.5.
- (D) between 6.5 and 7.5.
- (E) less than 6.3.

63. The terms pH and pOH are always related in the following manner:
- (A) pH/pOH = 1.
- (B) pH/pOH = k.
- (C) pH + pOH = 100.
- (D) pH + 1/pOH = 14.
- (E) none of the above.

Using the illustration below when both surfaces 1 and 2 are exposed to the atmosphere, P_1 and P_2 are gauge pressure, and h_1 and h_2 are heights. The Bernoulli equation for this situation is

$$h_1 + \frac{P_1}{W} + \frac{V_1^2}{2a} = h_2 + \frac{P_2}{W} + \frac{V_2^2}{2a}$$

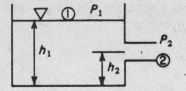

64. The values of P_1 and P_2 are such that
- (A) $P_1 = P_2 = 0$.
- (B) $P_1 > P_2$.
- (C) $P_2 < P_1$.
- (D) $P_1/P_2 = 0$.
- (E) $P_2/P_1 = 0$.

65. The velocity of the fluid leaving point 2 is constant and can be expressed as
- (A) $V_2 = [(h_1 - h_2)(2a)]^{\frac{1}{2}}$
- (B) $V_2 = (P_1/P_2)ah$.
- (C) $V_2 = (P_1/P_2)V_1$.
- (D) $V_2 = V_1$.
- (E) none of the above.

66. If an identical outlet were placed at exactly the same point on the left side of the container, the velocity would be

(A) computable.

(B) zero.

(C) $\frac{1}{2}V_2$.

(D) $2V_2$.

(E) none of the above.

STOP. If you finish before the time limit is up, go over your work for this section. DO NOT look at any other sections of the model examination. When your time limit is up, go on to the next section.

SKILLS ANALYSIS: READING

85 MINUTES
68 QUESTIONS

The following questions are to be answered based on your careful reading of selections from scientific writings.

DIRECTIONS: Read each passage carefully, then answer the questions following it. Consider only the material within the passage in answering the questions. Eliminate those choices that you think to be incorrect and mark the letter of your choice on the answer sheet.

The origin of the ovarian follicle has long been a subject of confusion. It is generally recognized that germ cells arise extragonadally during fetal development and migrate to the prospective gonadal region. There is still confusion, however, concerning the manner by which these germ cells enter the gonad and become enveloped by the follicular epithelium.

In their study of ovarian development in mice, Doctors Odor and Blandau suggested that stromal cells within the ovary surround the germ cells which have migrated into this region. The stromal cells thus become the follicular epithelium. Observations of previous investigators, however, suggest that the situation in the primate may be different. Witschi in 1948 described the migration of germ cells in humans. He stated that these cells were present in the endoderm (the epithelium of the presumptive gut), the mesothelium (an epithelium lining the body cavity) adjacent to the gut, and the mesenchymal tissue (which lies between these two epithelia). According to Dr. Witschi, the cells within the endoderm leave this epithelium and migrate through the mesenchymal tissue to the presumptive gonadal region which is a thickening of the mesenchyme of the body wall covered by a continuation of the same mesothelium found in proximity to the gut. In another investigation, Dr. Gillman described the presence of cords of cells within the fetal ovary. These cords were continuous with the mesothelium of the ovary. Initially these cords were devoid of germ cells; however, in the later stage of development the germ cells which had been seen in the stroma were incorporated into the cords. These cords subsequently split up into follicles. More recently, Dr. Merchant has reexamined ovarian development in the rat. By injecting a mitotic poison into a pregnant female at the time of germ cell migration, he has produced offspring which are lacking germ cells. In these animals follicles are absent but epithelial cell cords which are continuous with the ovarian mesothelium are present. Other investigators have also noted the presence of cords in the ovaries of normal laboratory animals.

Studies of human ovaries during the early stages of development are difficult because of technical as well as legal and medical problems. Nevertheless, observations by this investigator of ovaries from human and monkey fetuses after germ cell migration, confirm Gillman's observation that germ cells are present in the epithelial cords and that from these cords follicles are produced. However, this investigator is not in agreement with the proposed method by which the germ cells become incorporated into the cords. We have observed germ cells in the ovarian mesothelium which is in continuity with the epithelial cords. At the points of continuity, dividing cells within the mesothelium are oriented so that their mitotic spindles are perpendicular to the plane of the mesothelium. One daughter cell from such a division would be retained in the mesothelium, while the other would become part of the underlying cord. These observations suggest that the germ cell-containing cords arise from inward growth of a germ cell containing mesothelium. An extension of this conclusion would be that it is the germ cells which are found in the mesothelium in the region of the gut rather than those in the gut itself which are the cells that populate the gonad; and that this region of the mesothelium because of differential growth is, at a later time, positioned over the stroma of the presumptive gonad where the inward growth takes place.

The following statements are related to the passage above. Based on the information given, select:
- (A) if the statement is *supported by* the information in the passage.
- (B) if the statement is *contradicted by* the information in the passage.
- (C) if the statement is *neither supported nor contradicted by* information in the passage.

1. The manner by which the germ cells are enveloped by follicle cells is generally agreed on.

2. Germ cells arise within the ovary by differentiation of ovarian stromal cells.

3. In primates follicles arise by splitting off of ovarian cords.

4. Ovarian cords grow from the ovarian mesothelium.

5. Germ cells are moved by ciliary action.

6. The author believes that germ cells move independently of surrounding cells.

7. Due to less rigid abortion laws, studies on humans will increase and allow for the solution of the problem.

Does the order of a child's birth in a family have a bearing on his or her personality and on the type of adult he or she will grow up to be, or is the entire theory of ordinal position simply a bag of tricks that makes for interesting cocktail party conversation but little else?

While it has been the highlight of numerous debates and most certainly the subject of various studies, ordinal position remains a little-understood personality variable.

Consider the oldest child in a family of three children. Parents often claim that their first-born has a solid head on his or her shoulders, behaves in a mature manner, and is capable of getting along with adults. This important family member often exhibits a quiet front, yet is able to take the lead, care for his or her siblings and act like a miniature adult. Parents view the first-born as an intelligent individual who will grow up to be a pillar of the community.

What on earth happened to the second-born (again in a family of three children) to make him or her so different from the eldest? This child is much more lively, less willing to take orders, does not show the same interest in adults, and often has difficulty communicating with them. He or she may even become a "problem" child in school. Teachers have been heard to complain that "B— is not in the least like A— was. . . ." Could it be that the second-born is striking out in an attempt to find his or her own place? The problems of the second child in a family seem to intensify even more when the "baby" comes along and moves him or her into the "middle-child" position. Now he or she has to contend not only with a successful older brother or sister, but also with the youngest who seems to be the favorite. The youngest, on the other hand appears not to feel the need to measure up to anyone and goes along his or her own way to develop into an often exuberant, well-rounded individual. Because he or she is the baby, the mother doesn't expect this third sibling to function like a miniature adult, and she considers "cute" a great number of the actions that were viewed as unsatisfactory in the case of the other children.

Surely the questions related to ordinal position will provide research material for years to come. The problem is much like that of the chicken and the egg in that it is difficult to tell whether the numerical place a child occupies in a family *or* the attitudes which parents have developed in connection to child-rearing through years of trial and error, have the greatest effect on his or her personality.

The following statements are related to the information presented above. Based on the information given, select:

    (A) if the statement is *supported by* the information in the passage.
    (B) if the statement is *contradicted by* the information in the passage.
    (C) if the statement is *neither supported nor contradicted by* information in the passage.

8. It is a proven fact that the first-born always grows up to be a responsible citizen.

9. Ordinal position has been the topic of research for many years.

10. Parents often claim that first-born children behave in a more mature manner than later-born.

11. To date, ordinal position is a little-understood personality variable.

12. Second-born children who later move into the "middle-child" position achieve on a higher plane in school than do second-born who remain in the same position.

13. Comparison to older siblings, by teachers and other adults is the best method for stimulating the middle child to work harder.

14. By the time the third child comes along, mothers no longer seem to put the same emphasis on certain aspects of behavior that they did when raising their first-born.

15. The best place to discuss ordinal position is at a cocktail party, because it is such an interesting topic of conversation.

16. The youngest child is most adversely affected by his or her family position because he or she has more than one sibling to live up to.

17. The "baby" of the family is often a child with an outgoing personality.

Two systems modulate, integrate, and control the activities of the body; they are the nervous and endocrine systems. The response in nervous control is rapid while control via the endocrine system is fairly slow and longer lasting. The endocrine glands are ductless glands and secrete their products called hormones into the capillaries (bloodstream). Hormones are substances that are secreted into the bloodstream and travel to their target organs to elicit their effects. The product of the target organ may also feed back upon the organ that stimulated its activity and production; and manipulate in this respect its cycle of function. It may shut off the supply of stimulating hormone; this activity is called a negative feedback. The controlling mechanism can be though of as a neuro-endocrine-somatic tissue relationship, or the brain affecting the pituitary gland, which in turn affects the target organs, which then elicit their effect upon the body tissues and cells. Hormones cannot be classified into one chemical class; they are, however, all organic substances and may be proteins, peptides, amino acids (or amino acid derivatives), and steroids, or prostaglandins (derivatives of essential fatty acids). Generally the glands which produce protein hormones embryologically originate from the alimentary tract; they are the anterior pituitary, thyroid, parathyroids, and pancreas. Glands which produce steroid products are derived from the celomic mesothelium and are the testes, ovaries, and adrenal cortex. Glands whose products are small molecular weight amines arise from cells of nervous tissue derivation and are the neurohypophysis and the adrenal medulla.

The following statements are related to the information presented above. Based on the information given, select:
  (A) if the statement is *supported by* the information in the passage.
  (B) if the statement is *contradicted by* the information in the passage.
  (C) if the statement is *neither supported nor contradicted by* information in the passage.

18. Nervous impulses are conducted quickly and produce long-acting effects.

19. The endocrine system achieves its functions via the bloodstream.

20. Releasing factors produced by the hypothalamus affect the pituitary gland.

21. Hormones are similar in nature.

22. The pancreas produces hormones that are proteins.

23. Steroids are produced by the reproductive organs.

24. The cells of the adrenal medulla may be thought of as postganglionic sympathetic cells.

Contraction in a skeletal muscle is triggered by the generation of an action protential in the muscle membrane. Each motor neuron upon entering a skeletal muscle loses its myelin sheath and divides into branches with each branch innervating a single muscle fiber, forming a neuromuscular junction. Each fiber normally has one neuromuscular junction which is located near the center of the fiber. A motor unit consists of a single motor neuron and all the muscle fibers innervated by it. The motor end plate is the specialized part of the muscle fiber's membrane lying under the nerve.

The impulse arriving at the end of the motor neuron causes liberation of acetylcholine from vesicles in the nerve terminal. The acetylcholine acts at specific sites normally found only on the motor end plate section of the fiber membrane and increases the permeability of the motor end plate. The resulting $Na+$ influx produces a depolarizing potential called the end plate potential. This in turn depolarizes adjacent areas of the fiber membrane, triggering an action potential which is propagated in both directions from the central neuromuscular junction toward the fiber ends. Normally the magnitude of the endplate potential is sufficient to discharge the muscle membrane, so that each impulse in the nerve ending produces a response in the muscle. The acetylcholine is rapidly destroyed by the enzyme acetylcholinesterase which is found in high concentrations at the neuromuscular junction.

The following statements are related to the information presented. Based on the information given, select:

(A) if the statement is *supported by* in the passage.
(B) if the statement is *contradicted by* the information in the passage.
(C) if the statement is *neither supported nor contradicted by* information in the passage.

25. The contraction of skeletal muscle is quicker and of shorter duration than the activation of smooth muscle.

26. Acetylcholinesterase is released at the motor end plate.

27. Motor neurons are myelinated.

28. Acetylcholine is produced by muscle.

29. While there is a sodium ion influx, potassium ions leave the cell.

30. Sodium ion influx plays a role in the conduction of a nerve impulse.

31. Magnitude of the end plate potential is of critical importance.

Primogeniture was the custom of allowing the oldest member of a family, in most situations this meant the oldest male member, to inherit all lands and possessions of his parents, to the exclusion of his siblings.

The ordinal position of being the first-born male therefore carried much power, as the first-born was considered to be intelligent, level-headed, and capable of taking over as family protector and landlord once the father died. Theoretically the oldest would be unselfish and see to the care of the younger family members, but in actuality this was often not the case.

The custom of primogeniture was particularly popular during the federal period and was practiced in many countries of Europe, especially in France and England where, for example, a fief descended intact to the oldest son. One European country where this custom was not in force during the Middle Ages was Germany.

Outlawed in the United States and no longer the mode of inheritance in Europe for today's population as a whole, primogeniture was in evidence as late as the 1920s and can still be seen in degree with some of Europe's royal families.

The following statements are related to the information presented above. Based on the information given, select:

(A) if the statement is *supported by* the information in the passage.
(B) if the statement is *contradicted by* the information in the passage.
(C) if the statement is *neither supported nor contradicted by* information in the passage.

32. Countries in Europe that have royal families still practice the custom of primogeniture

33. Ordinal position was of utmost importance in medieval Europe

34. In Germany during the federal period the oldest son could be certain of inheriting his father's fief intact.

35. In the United States each sibling recieves the same amount of inheritance.

36. Modern society often calls upon the first-born male to be the executor of his parents' will.

37. The first-born male was thought to be the most intelligent level-headed sibling and therefore considered the proper landlord of his parents' holdings.

38. Under the primogeniture custom, younger brothers and sisters were granted their fair share.

39. France and England were two of the countries where primogeniture was practiced during the federal period.

40. Today the royal family of England carries on this custom.

41. The oldest child—whether male or female—*always* inherited everything.

A term that has been very much in vogue over the past five years or so is that of behavior modification or the changing of a subject's behavior from an unacceptable to an acceptable pattern.

While it may be argued that behavior is continually being altered and modified, the term as used here refers to a very structured approach by which the undesirable behavior is identified and specific monitored steps are undertaken to modify and move it into the path of becoming acceptable. A token system is included so that progress in the correct direction can be rewarded immediately.

This type of management system has been widely used by educators, especially at the elementary level, so that when children come home on any given afternoon with scores of M&M's in their pockets, mothers realize that teachers are busily modifying some aspect of behavior and that the candy is the reward system. Education does not, however, have a monopoly on behavior modification techniques. They have proven to be successful in certain scientific areas as well as many other fields.

Consider the person who has a weight problem yet claims to consume very little at meal time. Often this frustrated soul will eat next to nothing morning, noon, and evening, thus convinced that he or she is starving, but will forget to account for the 20 sidetrips to the refrigerator.

Such a person would be wise to use behavior modification techniques. Two charts are called for in this case. The first to cover every waking hour for one week with a check to indicate the times when something was eaten. The second could be identical except that the subject would now make a conscious effort to reduce the checks and give a token each time this happens. Thus, for instance, for each check missing a dime could be thrown in a kitty and saved for a nonfood splurge later on. Hopefully the subject would eventually alter his or her previous habit without the need for charting.

The following statements are related to the information presented above. Based on the information given, select:
- (A) if the statement is *supported by* the information in the passage.
- (B) if the statement is *contradicted by* the information in the passage.
- (C) if the statement is *neither supported nor contradicted by* information in the passage.

42. The only way behavior can be altered is through use of a token system.

43. Doctors should suggest behavior modification to their overweight patients.

44. One area where this technique is used frequently is in elementary education.

45. Overweight people often eat too many carbohydrates and too little proteins.

46. Behavior modification can be classified as a type of management system.

47. In order to be successful, a person using behavior modification must first identify the undesirable behavior and then plan specific structured steps to change it.

48. Problem identification is an important facet of the behavior modification process.

49. Just because they are in vogue does not mean that behavior modification techniques are reliable.

50. Charting a specific behavior is often one way of pinpointing the undesirable action.

51. Once the problem has been spotted behavior modification will always eliminate it.

The major structural and functional cellular unit of nervous tissue is the neuron. The neuronal cell body or soma, like all cells, contains a distinct nucleus and nucleolus and a cytoplasm rich in organelles.

Prominent among these organelles are mitochondria, the Golgi apparatus, and profiles of rough-surfaced endoplasmic reticulum. Extending from the neuronal cell bodies are numerous appendages which are characterized as either axons or dendrites. The dendrites are generally multiple in number and from their primary shafts secondary, tertiary, and higher order branches arise.

Frequently, extending from the dendritic surfaces are numerous spines or gemmules which are reminiscent of thorns extending along the branches of a rose bush. The dendrites and their associated spines provide a greatly increased neuronal surface area which ultimately allows for increased interaction with other neuronal elements. Unlike their dendritic counterparts, the axons are usually singular and generally are quite long and thin. Many axons are encompassed by a lipoprotein sheath known as myelin and this myelin sheath displays periodic discontinuities referred to as the Nodes of Ranvier. At terminal points these axons transmit impulses to the dendrites of other neurons and such sites of contacts between individual neurons are called synapses. In the human nervous system there are approximately 8 billion neurons, all of which display great variability in both size and form. Also, in addition to these 8 billion neurons, there exist 80 billion supportive elements known as glial cells. In view of both the number and complexity of the neurons and their supportive elements, it is readily apparent as to why our present understanding of nervous tissue interaction and function is quite limited.

The following statements are related to the passage. Based on the information given, select:
(A) if the statement is *supported by* the information in the passage.
(B) if the statement is *contradicted by* information in the passage.
(C) if the statement is *neither supported nor contradicted by* information in the passage.

52. Axons and dendrites are appendages of neuronal cell bodies and as such are structurally and functionally the same.

53. It is apparent from the passage that dendrites greatly increase the neuronal surface area.

54. It can be deduced from this article that the neurons and glial cells are structurally and functionally comparable.

55. The site of functional contact between two individual neurons constitutes a synapse.

56. It is clear from the preceding passage that the precise nature of nervous tissue interaction has been completely elucidated.

Local anesthetics are frequently used and because of this widespread clinical use, knowledge concerning the effects of these drugs at the cellular level is desirable. Most local anesthetics produce a cytotoxic effect; tissues that are affected usually degenerate, and the fragments are phagocytised. This process is followed by a phase of regeneration. There is evidence that the severity of the effect—recognized by the size of the lesion produced—varied with the potency of the anesthetic, the concentration of the anesthetic, the route of administration, and the sequence of injections. The significance of potency—that is, the variability of effect produced by different local anesthetics at the same concentration—was clearly demonstrated when tetracaine produced more severe lesions than lidocaine which in turn produced more severe lesions than procaine. The severity of the lesion increased as the concentration increased. Differences in route of injection were apparent as more severe lesions were produced following intramuscular injection of the anesthetic when compared with subcutaneous injection. Muscle degeneration and subsequent regeneration is found irrespective of the sequence of injection (as for example, one large dose or two smaller doses). No muscular damage has been found following an injection when the same volume of physiologic saline, instead of the anesthetic, is administered. Limited information is available concerning the effect of local anesthetics on enzyme activity in the highly ordered metabolic machinery of the cell.

The following statements are related to the passage above. Based on the information given, select:
(A) if the statement is *supported by* the information in the passage.
(B) if the statement is *contradicted by* the information in the passage.
(C) if the statement is *neither supported nor contradicted by* information in the passage.

57. All local anesthetics are alike.

58. Local anesthetics are used more often by dentists than physicians.

59. Potency and concentration may be considered one and the same.

60. Severity of lesion and concentration show a direct relationship.

61. Physiologic saline can be substituted for an anesthetic.

62. General anesthesia does not result in any damage.

63. Tissues are sensitive to local anesthetics.

The blood vessels of the mammalian brain normally provide a barrier that blocks the passage of certain molecules which readily permeate other body tissues. This unique property of the brain vasculature is referred to as the blood-brain barrier and in normal functional states this property prevents the entrance of numerous intravascular probes such as horseradish peroxidase into the substance of the brain. However, in experimental studies of brain dysfunction, such as seen in mechanical brain injury, a disruption of the blood-brain barrier occurs, and experimental probes such as horseradish peroxidase now enter the brain's substance. The mechanism of this blood-brain barrier dysfunction in brain injury is poorly understood. Some contend that the mechanical stress of the injury physically disrupts the vessels and allows for peroxidase leakage through defects in the vascular walls. However, others argue that brain injury activates cellular mechanisms which allow the blood vessels to rapidly uptake substances such as horseradish peroxidase and then to both deposit them within and ultimately flood the substance of the brain tissue.

To date few substantive experimental data have been advanced to support any of the above-stated theories of blood-brain barrier dysfunction in instances of mechanical brain injury. However, research continues, for medical scientists realize that any rational therapeutic treatment of brain-injured patients, is totally dependent upon the elucidation of those mechanisms involved in blood-brain barrier dysfunction.

The following statements are related to the passage. Based on the information given, select:
(A)   if the statement is *supported by* the information in the passage.
(B)   if the statement is *contradicted by* the information in the passage.
(C)   if the statement is *neither supported nor contradicted by* information in the passage.

64.   The blood-brain barrier is a structural rather than a physiological barrier.

65.   The mechanisms responsible for blood-brain barrier dysfunction in brain injury have been identified and it is apparent that blood-brain barrier dysfunction is related to vasogenic shock.

66.   This passage implies that the appropriate therapeutic management of the head-injured patient awaits the elucidation of the those mechanisms responsible for blood-brain barrier dysfunction in brain trauma.

67.   The blood vessels of the human brain normally provide a barrier which blocks the passage of certain substances which readily permeate the body tissues.

68.   Mechanical brain injury may physically disrupt the integrity of the brain's vasculature.

> STOP.   If you finish before the time limit is up, go over your work for this section. DO NOT look at any other sections of the model examination. When your time limit is up, go on to the next section.

SKILLS ANALYSIS: QUANTITATIVE

85 MINUTES
68 QUESTIONS

The following questions are to be answered based on your knowledge of basic mathematical principles and relationships.

DIRECTIONS: Read each passage carefully, study each table or chart, then answer the questions following it. Consider only the material presented in answering the questions. Eliminate those choices that you think to be incorrect and mark the letter of your choice on the answer sheet.

Diet	Losing Weight	Mortality
Balanced Diet	4%	2%
Diet A	90%	74%
Diet A + Vitamin C	84%	72%
Diet A + Vitamin B	4%	2%
Diet A + Vitamin A	88%	76%

Groups of 50 mice were fed the diets listed in the table, and the percentage losing more than 10% of their initial body weight and the percentage mortality after 30 days were recorded.

1. The study was designed to determine
   (A) what vitamins are missing from a balanced diet.
   (B) what vitamins aid in losing weight.
   (C) what vitamins were missing from diet A.
   (D) what mice need that humans do not.

2. The best conclusion to be drawn from this study is that
   (A) diet A is a good reducing diet.
   (B) diet A lacks B vitamins.
   (C) vitamin C is not necessary for life.
   (D) vitamin A is necessary for life.

3. The difference between percentage losing weight and percentage mortality within each group is best explained by
   (A) individual variation among mice within each group.
   (B) variations in importance of the different vitamins.
   (C) the fact that the effectiveness of vitamins is reduced by purification and later addition to food.
   (D) the fact that some mice were overweight and therefore were not resistant.

The epiphyseal cartilage plate is very sensitive to somatotrophin (growth hormone) and, therefore, can be used as an assay for this compound. Species variations exist and other hormones such as estrogen, thyroxine, and several antibiotics also have an effect upon cartilage growth. The assay must be carried out on hypophysectomized animals.

The following experiments were conducted as can be seen from the table:

Test Groups	No. of Animals	Cartilage Growth in μ	
		1 Injection Daily	2 Injections/Day (½ amount each time)
Control (normal) (saline)	20 (10/injecting group)	100	100
Hypophysectomized (saline)	20	60	60
Hypox + 100 mg STH	20	150	160
Hypox + 300 mg STH	20	180	195
Stressed normal animals (saline)	20	175	190
Hypox & stressed (saline)	20	50	50
Stressed normal + 100 mg STH	20	200	210
Hypox, stressed + 100 mg STH	20	110	120

4. The reason the assay must be carried out on hypophysectomized rats is
   (A) just to add another sophisticated method to the experiment.
   (B) because the pituitary produces its own growth hormone and it might interfere with the assay.
   (C) to study the pituitary composition of growth hormone.
   (D) to obtain the animals' own growth hormone.

5. These experiments show
   (A) the route of administration was critical.
   (B) the route of administration made no difference.
   (C) the route should be adjusted from procedure to procedure.
   (D) none of the above.

6. Twice daily administration proved to be
   (A) less effective in eliciting a response.
   (B) more effective in eliciting a response.
   (C) of no great consequence in the experiment.
   (D) none of the above.

7. Stressed animals
   (A) do not need growth hormone.
   (B) produce substances that act like growth hormone.
   (C) produce growth hormone that has an additive affect upon stress factors.
   (D) both B and C.

The following experimental protocol was carried out. Bean seeds were picked for their uniformity and 20 were planted/pot. One hundred percent germination was observed; and when the seedlings were 9 days old, the seedlings of uniform growth were selected for treatment with X-rays. Four hundred r units/minute were applied at a distance of 30 cm from the object. Seedlings were exposed up to 60 minutes with up to 24,000 r. After exposure, seedlings were placed in a greenhouse and kept at uniform light, temperature, and moisture conditions. Seedlings were measured as indicated in the table.

CODE

I		II	
1	From ground to cotyledon (a mark was made on the seedling near the ground with india ink)	A	0 minutes — control
		B	7.5 minutes — 3,000 r
2	Cotyledon to 1st node	C	15 minutes — 6,000 r
3	Petiole length of 1st leaf	D	30 minutes — 12,000 r
4	Midrib of 1st leaf	E	60 minutes — 24,000 r
5	From 1st node to tip of the plant (when included)		

EXPERIMENTAL RESULTS

		10 Days					17 Days					33 Days			
	A	B	C	D	E	A	B	C	D	E	A	B	C	D	E
1	6.20	6.58	7.30	5.45	4.43	7.08	6.73	8.00	6.99	5.82	7.21	6.73	8.00	7.00	6.05
2	2.17	2.16	2.30	1.15	.76	8.06	7.11	5.36	2.50	1.63	8.07	7.11	5.48	2.65	1.65
3	.87	1.11	1.10	0.65	.53	4.12	4.50	4.15	2.13	1.70	4.33	4.61	4.86	2.30	1.90
4	3.00	3.23	3.02	2.03	1.86	5.44	5.27	5.68	5.33	4.97	5.50	5.50	6.13	5.91	5.25
5											12.56	11.38	5.27		

8. The purpose of this experiment was
   (A) to observe the germination rate.
   (B) to check for uniform growth rate.
   (C) test output and scatter of the X-ray machine.
   (D) observe X-ray effect on growth.

9. The control plants reached a height at the termination of the experiment of _____ cm and little stunting could be observed in the plants that received 3000 r units. They were only 2.66 cm shorter than the controls.
   (A) 25.11   (C) 37.67
   (B) 27.84   (D) 18.06

10. When 12,000 r units were employed, plant growth did not go beyond the first node and these plants were 18.19 cm shorter than the controls. Growth from the mark on the stem to the cotyledon is comparable to control plants but growth beyond the cotyledon is greatly diminished.
   (A) This cannot be determined from the data given.
   (B) These statements are absolutely correct.
   (C) Too many assumptions are made.
   (D) All of the above are confusing statements.

11. As seen from the table, the plants exposed to 24,000 r units show a marked effect. Growth from the cotyledon to the first node is greatly decreased. This was the part most affected; the midrib lengths were not affected.
   (A) The statements are unfounded.
   (B) The statements are partly true.
   (C) The statements are correct.
   (D) Too many assumptions are made.

Both sexes carry a complete complement of sex-linked genes. A female, however, with the XX arrangement will only exhibit a recessive gene if she has received it from both parents (a rare event if we are dealing with an uncommon gene of the population); while in the male with the XY arrangement the recessive gene cannot be masked since there is no partner X chromosome and, therefore, a larger number of recessive genes are expressed (examples are hemophilia and color blindness). A man receives his X chromosome from his mother and passes it on to his daughters not his sons. His daughters in this respect are the carriers of his sex-linked traits and their sons will be the affected ones. Let us illustrate with an example. The normal czarinas of Russia produced sons suffering from hemophilia, a disease that is caused by a sex-linked recessive gene, h. The more dominant gene, H, produces normal blood clotting. Genotypically, these women must have carried Hh (X_H and X_h). A daughter, depending on the father ($X_H Y$ or $X_h Y$), could have carried $X_H X_h$ or $X_H X_H$ while a son could have been born either with an $X_H Y$ or a $X_h Y$ (hemophilic) chromosomal complement.

The following statements are related to the information presented above. Based on the information given, select:
   (A) if the statement is *supported by* the information given.
   (B) if the statement is *contradicted by* the information given.
   (C) if the statement is *neither supported nor contradicted by* information given.

12. A cattle breeder has in a herd a Y-linked trait. A male calf sired by a bull carrying this trait is born. The chances of the inheritance of the trait are 50%.

13. A female calf was born; the chances of exhibiting the trait are zero.

14. If the sex in the above cross is known, there is no doubt about whether a calf has the trait.

15. All males would exhibit the trait.

16. Females in this case would not be the carriers of this trait.

Melanoma tumors were implanted into three strains of mice. Experiments were then performed to determine the types and amounts of host serum antibodies produced against the lipid components of the virus contained in the melanoma cells. The results are summarized in the table below.

Host	Ag A Phenotype	Mg Equivalent Day 40 Post Implant	Antilipid Antibody Day 60 Post Implant
Strain 1	3/3	4.5 ± 0.3	6.3 ± 1.7
Strain 2	1/3	3.4 ± 0.4	5.5 ± 1.3
Strain 3	1/1	1.3 ± 0.1	1.3 ± 0.3

The following statements are related to the information presented above. Based on the information given, select:

(A) if the statement is *supported by* the information given.

(B) if the statement is *contradicted by* the information given.

(C) if the statement is *neither supported nor contradicted by* information given.

17. Strain 1 produced less antilipid antibody at both time periods measured than the other two hosts.

18. On the basis of this information, Strain 1 animals are less resistant to melanoma-type cancers than either Strain 2 or 3 animals.

19. All three hosts produced more antibody at 60 days than they did at 40 days.

20. An Ag A phenotype containing three seems to be related to higher antibody production.

21. If it has a 1/3 Ag A phenotype, a mouse resulting from a cross of Strain 2 with one of Strain 3 would probably be a better antibody producer than a sibling having a 1/1 Ag A phenotype.

During wound healing, proliferation of cells in epithelial tissues, connective tissues, and vascular tissues occurs in order to fill in and resurface the defect caused by necrotic (dead) tissue. In experimental studies of the cellular kinetics of wound healing, it is often necessary to assess the amount of proliferation in various cell populations. Because cells replicate DNA within 8 to 12 hours before dividing, determination of the frequency of DNA synthesis at a particular time among cells in a population is a good index of the rate of cell division. DNA synthesis can be determined by tagging replicating DNA with radioactive thymidine. By the procedure of autoradiography, the nuclei of cells which have incorporated radioactive thymidine can be identified on histological sections. The percentage of cells labeled with radioactive thymidine is called the labeling index.

The following table includes data on the labeling index of endothelial cells which form the lining of blood vessels.

^{3}H-THYMIDINE INDEX IN WOUND HEALING

Wound Age	Amount of Epidermal Resurfacing	Endothelial Labeling Index
1 day	0%	3.5%
2 days	0%	13.3%
3 days	0-5%	10.5%
6 days	60-70%	5.6%
10 days	90-100%	2.5%

The following statements are related to the information presented. Based on the information given, select:

(A) if the statement is *supported by* the information given.
(B) if the statement is *contradicted by* the information given.
(C) if the statement is *neither supported nor contradicted by* information given.

22. The ^{3}H-thymidine labeling index, and hence the amount of endothelial proliferation, increased before epidermal resurfacing had become evident.

23. The endothelial labeling index, after day two, decreased both with advancing wound age and with advancing surface coverage.

24. The increased endothelial proliferation at two and three days led to the formation of new blood vessels, which then induced epidermal resurfacing.

25. Endothelial proliferation ceases when the wounds are 90-100% resurfaced with epidermis.

26. Synthesis of DNA may not lead to cell division, but rather may lead to an increase in the ploidy of the cell.

Androgen compounds are responsible for maintaining the secondary sex organs and characteristics of organisms. An endocrinology class was divided into 4 groups to conduct a blind experiment and at the end was asked to compare results. Each group received a compound and injected a similar amount. The experimental protocol in male animals was: 1) Unoperated control animals; 2) Unoperated control animals receiving vehicle only; 3) Bilaterally castrated (testes) animals; and 4) Bilaterally castrated animals receiving unknown. The results were summarized in table form.

Experimental Groups	Prostate Weight-mg Student Groups				Seminal Vesicle Weight-mg Student Groups			
	1	2	3	4	1	2	3	4
Unoperated Control	33	31	29	34	68	65	63	67
Unoperated Control and Vehicle	31	32	30	31	69	70	65	64
Bilaterally Castrated	10	9	7	8	12	14	10	15
Bilaterally Castrated and Unknown	37	33	28	31	70	64	61	59

The following statements are related to the information presented above. Based on the information given, select:

(A) if the statement is *supported by* the information given.
(B) if the statement is *contradicted by* the information given.
(C) if the statement is *neither supported nor contradicted by* information given.

27. Different compounds were used by the different groups.

28. The compounds used were in the androgen group.

29. The parameters used were not the proper ones.

30. The prostate gland is most sensitive to a lack of androgens.

31. These experiments were not properly controlled.

32. The results obtained are probably not statistically significant.

33. When these data are plotted on graph paper, it is found that the percentage of increase in organ weight corresponds to a dose relationship.

34. Bilateral castration removes a major source of sex hormones.

35. In the absence of the testes, the hypophysis exhibits an increased production of gonad stimulating hormones.

36. The absence of androgens affects the behavior of the animal.

In the laboratory experiment, red blood cells were placed into 0.5M solutions and the appearance of the solutions was observed two hours later with the naked eye.

Solution	Cells
0.5M glucose	no change
0.5M sucrose	no change
0.5M urea	hemolysis of RBCs
0:5M glycerol	hemolysis of RBCs

37. The solutions of urea and glycerol are _____ to the red blood cells.
(A) isotonic
(B) hypotonic
(C) hypertonic
(D) none of the above

38. The reason for these results is that:
1. the number of particles in the urea and glycerol solutions is greater than that in the glucose and sucrose solutions.
2. glucose and sucrose form coatings around the red blood cells which prevent their breaking.
3. glucose and sucrose enter the cells but are immediately metabolized, therefore water does not enter the cells.
4. urea and glycerol can enter the cell, water follows them into the cell because it is then in greater concentration outside.

(A) 1 and 2
(B) 1 and 3
(C) 3 and 4
(D) 4

39. The property of the cell membrane that allows for this phenomenon to be demonstrated is called
(A) diffusion.
(B) osmosis.
(C) impermeability.
(D) semipermeability.

A 75-kg person and a 1-kg steel ball fall simultaneously from an airplane 5000 feet above ground level. The following graph and table summarize the kinetic data for the first few seconds of the fall.

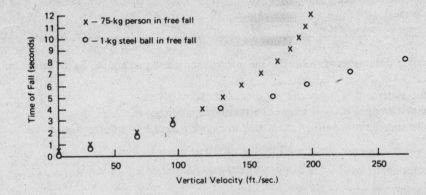

Time of Fall (sec.)	Vertical Velocity (ft./sec.)		Distance of Fall (feet)	
	Person	Steel Ball	Person	Steel Ball
1	32	32	32	
2	64	64	96	
3	96	96	192	
4	115	128	307	
5	126	160	433	
6	141	192	574	
7	152	224	726	
8	159	256	895	
9	163		1058	
10	166		1224	
11	169		1393	
12	170		1563	

40. The greatest increase in downward velocity for the person occurs
  (A) during the first 5 seconds of the fall.
  (B) between 3 and 6 seconds of the fall.
  (C) between 6 and 9 seconds of the fall.
  (D) between 8 and 12 seconds of the fall.

41. Comparing the first 5 seconds with seconds 8-12 of the person's fall, the later velocity changes can be explained by
  (A) the force of gravity being greater than atmospheric resistance.
  (B) the force of gravity being less than atmospheric resistance.
  (C) atmospheric resistance approaching the acceleratory force of gravity.
  (D) none of the above.

42. After 7 seconds of the fall, how far is the steel ball from the person (vertical distance)?
  (A) 96 feet   (C) 144 feet
  (B) 108 feet   (D) 170 feet

43. Assuming the person's velocity does not change after 12 seconds (170 ft./sec.), the person will hit the ground
  (A) 20 seconds after start of the fall.
  (B) 24 seconds after start of the fall.
  (C) 32 seconds after start of the fall.
  (D) Cannot be calculated from data provided.

44. The person will hit the ground how many seconds after the steel ball? (Assume ball's velocity remains constant after 8 seconds of fall).
  (A) 6 seconds   (C) 9 seconds
  (B) 8 seconds   (D) 11 seconds

Gerbils were used for this experiment. One group served as a control; one group was thyroidectomized and maintained on 1% calcium gluconate since the parathyroids were probably removed also; one group received daily injections of thyroxin; and one group that was thyroidectomized and maintained as described above also received daily injections of thyroxin. Oxygen was measured in a standard manner. The following were the results.

Groups	Initial Body Weight gm	Final Body Weight gm	Thyroid Gland Weight mg	Liter of O_2 Consumed hour/ meter^2
Normal	143	150	5.0	1.54
Hypothyroid	160	174	0.0	0.16
Hyperthyroid	123	120	8.0	7.33
Hypothyroid + thyroxin	164	158	4.9	1.23

The following statements are stated on the information presented above. Based on the information given, select:
  (A) if the statement is *supported by* the information given.
  (B) if the statement is *contradicted by* the information given.
  (C) if the statement is *neither supported nor contradicted by* information given.

45. The quantity of heat liberated by an organism as calculated on the basis of respiratory exchange is decreased by deficiencies and elevated by excesses of the active thyroid principle.

46. After total thyroidectomy the basal metabolic rate falls to 10% of its normal value.

47. Hypothyroid animals probably exhibited sluggishness.

48. Hypothyroidism is accompanied by a depression of the oxidative processes in the tissues and slight obesity probably due to the relatively slow burning of the consumed food.

49. Thyroxin probably is the active thyroid principle.

50. Animals can be made hyperthyroid if given thyroxin.

51. In thyroidectomized animals, glucose absorption is slower in the intestinal tract.

A manufacturer is testing a newly designed line of autoclaves that will be marketed. Calibration of timers and temperature controls are critical to insure destruction of bacteria.

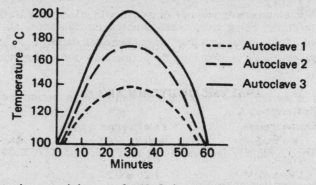

52. Bacteria X requires a minimum of 140°C for at least 20 minutes to be destroyed. Only _____ could possible be used.

(A) autoclave 1
(B) autoclave 1 and 2

(C) autoclave 2 and 3
(D) autoclave 3

53. Virus Y requires 180°C or more. The technician would not place material in

(A) autoclave 1.
(B) autoclave 1 and 2.

(C) autoclave 2 and 3.
(D) autoclave 3.

54. Bacteria Z will only grow when the temperature is below 160°C. Therefore to be destroyed it can not be put into

(A) autoclave 1.
(B) autoclave 1 and 2.

(C) autoclave 2 and 3.
(D) autoclave 3.

The pineal complex is implicated in the modulation of reproductive functions of the golden hamster. Surgical removal of the eyes produced atrophy of the testes and seminal vesicles within four to six weeks, and simultaneous pinealectomy prevented the atrophy. In the following experiment the drug MTPH was injected subcutaneously daily for 30 days to learn if there was an enhancement of atrophy. The results are summarized below.

Treatment	Number of Hamsters Treated	Organ Weight (mg/100 g body weight)	
		Testes	Seminal Vesicles
Untreated Control	6	2884	722
Blinding	6	1695[a]	396[a]
Pinealectomy	6	2600	544
Blinding, Pinealectomy	6	2580	577
MTPH, No Surgery	6	3069	699
MTPH, Blinding	6	1419[a]	398[a]
MTPH, Pinealectomy	6	2875	591
MTPH, Blinding, Pinealecomy	6	2635	577
[a]($p < 0.05$)			

The following statements are related to the information presented above. Based on the information given, select:

(A) if the statement is *supported by* the information given.
(B) if the statement is *contradicted by* the information given.
(C) if the statement is *neither supported nor contradicted by* information given.

55. Drug MTPH increased the testicular atrophy in blinded hamsters when compared with blinded hamsters not receiving MTPH.

56. Drug MTPH increased the seminal vesicle atrophy in blinded hamsters when compared with blinded hamsters not receiving MTPH.

57. Drug MTPH had no effect on atrophy, either testicular or seminal vesicles.

58. Drug MTPH had no effect on the weights of testes or seminal vesicles.

59. Drug MTPH when administered without surgery would affect reproductive organ weight.

The table represents the results obtained in a certain experiment analyzing hydrocarbon A with a new fluorometric procedure.

ANALYSIS OF HYDROCARBON A

Sample	Hydrocarbon A Concentration, mole/ml	Fluorescence in delta units	Determinations
Blank	0.00	0.00	40
1	2.95×6^{-14}	1.26 ± 0.24	40
2	4.12×6^{-14}	2.21 ± 0.35	40
3	7.36×6^{-14}	3.48 ± 0.48	40
4	10.63×6^{-14}	4.84 ± 0.60	40
5	14.79×6^{-14}	6.67 ± 0.67	40
6	22.21×6^{-14}	10.14 ± 0.54	40
7	29.50×6^{-14}	13.42 ± 0.61	40

The following statements are related to the information presented above. Based on the information given, select:

(A) if the statement is *supported by* the information given.

(B) if the statement is *contradicted by* the information given.

(C) if the statement is *neither supported nor contradicted by* information given.

60. The table represents data for multiple analysis of hydrocarbon A exhibiting a range of 3×6^{-14} to 30×6^{-14} moles/ml.

61. Average deviations varied from 20% for the lowest concentration to 5% for the highest.

62. The variations in the blank obviously affected the reliability of the analysis more at the higher concentrations.

63. A fluorescence of 53.68 units corresponds to a hydrocarbon A concentration of 118 moles/ml.

Serum Vitamin K levels in the Tra-la bird of Upper Zulu were investigated. The following were the results.

SERUM VITAMIN K (μg/100 ml), PROTEIN (g/100 ml), AND BODY WEIGHT (g) FOR BIRDS

Birds	Daytime		Nighttime		
	Vitamin K	Protein	Vitamin K	Protein	Body Weight
Mature: Males	21.42	6.12	31.00	6.21	3370
Females	20.91	6.02	29.99	6.12	3200
Newborn: Males	14.97	5.71	17.79	5.69	1616
Females	14.19	5.49	17.46	5.71	1700

The following statements are related to the information presented above. Based on the information given, select:

(A) if the statement is *supported by* the information given.

(B) if the statement is *contradicted by* the information given.

(C) if the statement is *neither supported nor contradicted by* information given.

64. Mature males are about 5% heavier than females, while in the newborn the converse is true.

65. There is a definite correlation between body weight and the levels of Vitamin K and protein under investigation.

66. A diurnal rhythm is exhibited by Vitamin K levels.

67. Light influences protein synthesis.

68. After analysis of the table the reader comes to the conclusion that these experiments were well controlled.

STOP.   If you finish before the time limit is up, go over your work for this section. DO NOT look at any other sections of the model examination. When your time limit is up, go on to the next section.

Answers—Model MCAT

SCIENCE KNOWLEDGE

Biology

1. C	9. D	17. A	25. A	33. C
2. D	10. C	18. C	26. B	34. A
3. A	11. B	19. B	27. B	35. B
4. B	12. D	20. B	28. B	36. E
5. C	13. E	21. B	29. E	37. E
6. B	14. D	22. C	30. B	38. D
7. B	15. A	23. C	31. A	
8. E	16. C	24. A	32. B	

Chemistry

1. B	11. A	21. D	31. B	41. D
2. B	12. D	22. A	32. C	42. D
3. A	13. D	23. C	33. C	43. B
4. D	14. A	24. C	34. D	44. C
5. B	15. B	25. E	35. C	45. C
6. C	16. A	26. B	36. B	46. B
7. C	17. A	27. D	37. D	47. C
8. B	18. E	28. D	38. B	48. B
9. D	19. A	29. D	39. B	49. C
10. B	20. C	30. A	40. D	

Physics

1. A	9. A	17. B	25. D	33. E
2. B	10. C	18. E	26. A	34. A
3. C	11. E	19. E	27. C	35. B
4. A	12. D	20. B	28. D	36. D
5. D	13. D	21. B	29. D	37. D
6. D	14. C	22. E	30. C	38. A
7. C	15. A	23. A	31. D	
8. E	16. D	24. B	32. C	

SCIENCE PROBLEMS

1. B	15. E	29. E	43. A	57. C
2. B	16. E	30. D	44. A	58. A
3. B	17. D	31. D	45. C	59. A
4. E	18. A	32. C	46. D	60. E
5. E	19. E	33. A	47. A	61. E
6. A	20. D	34. E	48. A	62. D
7. C	21. E	35. A	49. D	63. E
8. B	22. D	36. A	50. D	64. A
9. D	23. D	37. D	51. E	65. A
10. B	24. D	38. E	52. E	66. A
11. A	25. A	39. A	53. D	
12. C	26. D	40. D	54. D	
13. B	27. B	41. C	55. A	
14. B	28. E	42. D	56. B	

SKILLS ANALYSIS: READING

1. B	15. C	29. C	43. C	57. B
2. B	16. B	30. A	44. A	58. C
3. A	17. A	31. B	45. C	59. B
4. A	18. B	32. B	46. A	60. A
5. C	19. A	33. A	47. A	61. C
6. B	20. A	34. B	48. A	62. C
7. C	21. B	35. C	49. C	63. A
8. B	22. A	36. C	50. A	64. C
9. A	23. A	37. A	51. B	65. B
10. A	24. C	38. B	52. B	66. A
11. A	25. C	39. A	53. A	67. A
12. C	26. A	40. C	54. C	68. A
13. B	27. A	41. B	55. A	
14. A	28. B	42. B	56. B	

SKILLS ANALYSIS: QUANTITATIVE

1. C	15. A	29. B	43. C	57. A
2. B	16. A	30. B	44. C	58. A
3. A	17. B	31. B	45. A	59. B
4. B	18. C	32. B	46. A	60. A
5. D	19. B	33. B	47. A	61. A
6. B	20. A	34. A	48. A	62. C
7. D	21. A	35. C	49. A	63. C
8. D	22. A	36. C	50. A	64. A
9. B	23. A	37. B	51. C	65. B
10. C	24. C	38. D	52. C	66. A
11. C	25. B	39. D	53. B	67. B
12. A	26. C	40. A	54. A	68. B
13. A	27. B	41. C	55. B	
14. A	28. A	42. D	56. B	

5

OPPORTUNITIES FOR WOMEN AND MINORITY GROUP STUDENTS

☐ Doors have opened for women
☐ The woman physician
☐ Current issues
☐ Current challenges
☐ Financial aid and support sources for women
☐ Minority students in medicine
☐ Financial aid for minority group members

DOORS HAVE OPENED FOR WOMEN

It is generally agreed that there has been a long standing prejudice against women in medicine in the United States. This prejudice is reflected in national enrollment averages such as 4.5% in 1929 and 5.5% in 1955. Since 1970, however, there has been a dramatic increase in the enrollment of women. The 1971 survey showed that 10.8% of the total medical student population were women. By 1975, enrollment doubled to 20% of the total 55,818 medical students. For the 1983-84 academic year, freshman women made up more than 32% of the freshmen class. Male and female acceptances were approximately the same (49% and 47%, respectively). About 75 U.S. medical schools currently have a total female enrollment of greater than 30% (see Table 4). The impact of increased enrollment of women is shown by the fact that in the 40-year span between 1930 and 1970 only 14,000 women graduated from medical school, while over the 10-year period between 1970 to 1980 more than 20,000 women graduated.

The increase in total enrollment that has taken place is not due to an improved aptitude on the part of women students applying or an increase in the number of women obtaining their baccalaureate degree. Rather the increase is probably due to the following reasons: (1) a perceptible change in society's attitude toward women in medicine, particularly in the educational climate; (2) the realization that women make up a vast and untapped source of medical talent; (3) the obvious difference between the proportion of female doctors in this country as against other countries; and (4) the increase in the trend of women toward becoming wage earners, reflecting a changing cultural pattern.

Table 4. Percent of Women and Minorities, 1984–85. First-year class

School	% of women	% of minorities
Albany Medical College, Union University	32	05
Albert Einstein College of Medicine, Yeshiva University	41	10
Baylor College of Medicine	35	18
Boston University School of Medicine	36	11
Bowman Gray School of Medicine, Wake Forest University	31	3
Brown University Program in Medicine	51	34
Case Western Reserve University School of Medicine	44	9
Chicago Medical School, University of Health Sciences	27	1
Columbia University College of Physicians and Surgeons	30	13
Cornell University Medical School	40	21
Creighton University School of Medicine	32	7
Dartmouth Medical School	46	11
Duke University School of Medicine	31	4
East Carolina University School of Medicine	na	na
East Tennessee State University College of Medicine	38	11
Eastern Virginia Medical School	32	19
George Washington University School of Medicine	34	3
Georgetown University School of Medicine	na	na
Hahnemann University School of Medicine	30	11
Harvard Medical School	45	15
Howard University College of Medicine	46	93
Indiana University School of Medicine	na	na
Jefferson Medical College, Thomas Jefferson University	26	38
Johns Hopkins University School of Medicine	na	na
Loma Linda University School of Medicine	24	10

na = data not available

Table 4. Cont.

School	% of women	% of minorities
Louisiana State University School of Medicine in New Orleans	33	10
Louisiana State University School of Medicine in Shreveport	22	7
Loyola University of Chicago Stritch School of Medicine	36	3
Marshall University School of Medicine	40	9
Mayo Medical School	16	6
Medical College of Georgia	27	6
Medical College of Ohio	37	9
Medical College of Pennsylvania	60	10
Medical College of Virginia, Virginia Commonwealth University	37	7
Medical College of Wisconsin	27	8
Medical University of South Carolina College of Medicine	na	na
Meharry Medical College School of Medicine	35	80
Mercer University School of Medicine	33	7
Michigan State University College of Human Medicine	48	22
Morehouse School of Medicine	47	78
Mount Sinai School of Medicine, City University of New York	39	11
New Jersey Medical School, University of Medicine and Dentistry	35	17
New York Medical College	31	9
New York University School of Medicine	24	5
Northeastern Ohio Universities College of Medicine	31	4
Northwestern University Medical School	38	12
Ohio State University School of Medicine	33	7
Oral Roberts University School of Medicine	25	na
Oregon Health Sciences University School of Medicine	26	5
Pennsylvania State University College of Medicine	34	11
Rush Medical College	34	6
Rutgers Medical School, University of Medicine and Dentistry	31	9
Saint Louis University School of Medicine	23	2
Southern Illinois University School of Medicine	32	17
Stanford University School of Medicine	34	13
SUNY at Buffalo School of Medicine	39	16

Table 4. Cont.

School	% of women	% of minorities
SUNY at Stony Brook School of Medicine	na	na
SUNY Downstate Medical Center College of Medicine	29	9
SUNY Upstate Medical Center College of Medicine	39	12
Temple University School of Medicine	25	8
Texas A & M University College of Medicine	19	14
Texas Tech University School of Medicine	27	19
Tufts University School of Medicine	na	na
Tulane University School of Medicine	32	22
Uniformed Services University School of Medicine	18	14
University of Alabama School of Medicine	21	10
University of Arizona College of Medicine	51	11
University of Arkansas College of Medicine	26	11
University of California—Davis School of Medicine	39	13
University of California—Irvine, College of Medicine	37	17
University of California—Los Angeles, School of Medicine	na	na
University of California—San Diego, School of Medicine	34	na
University of California—San Francisco, School of Medicine ..	40	43
University of Chicago Pritzker School of Medicine	na	na
University of Cincinnati College of Medicine	33	4
University of Colorado School of Medicine	na	na
University of Connecticut School of Medicine	50	6
University of Florida College of Medicine	28	20
University of Hawaii Burns School of Medicine	34	50
University of Illinois College of Medicine	31	25
University of Iowa College of Medicine	na	na
University of Kansas School of Medicine	33	6
University of Kentucky College of Medicine	32	3

na = data not available

Table 4. Cont.

School	% of women	% of minorities
University of Louisville School of Medicine	31	6
University of Maryland School of Medicine	38	37
University of Massachusetts Medical School	44	7
University of Miami School of Medicine	36	22
University of Michigan Medical School	31	21
University of Minnesota, Duluth School of Medicine	48	4
University of Minnesota Medical School, Minneapolis	na	na
University of Mississippi School of Medicine	25	5
University of Missouri Columbia School of Medicine	30	4
University of Missouri Kansas City School of Medicine	56	10
University of Nebraska College of Medicine	30	3
University of Nevada School of Medicine	29	10
University of New Mexico School of Medicine	45	19
University of North Carolina School of Medicine	na	na
University of North Dakota School of Medicine	25	9
University of Oklahoma College of Medicine	na	na
University of Pennsylvania School of Medicine	na	na
University of Pittsburgh School of Medicine	35	13
University of Rochester School of Medicine	29	17
University of South Alabama College of Medicine	35	6
University of South Carolina School of Medicine	31	14
University of South Dakota School of Medicine	26	4
University of South Florida College of Medicine	31	17
University of Southern California School of Medicine	30	8
University of Tennessee College of Medicine	21	3
University of Texas Medical Branch at Galveston	25	10

Table 4. Cont.

School	% of women	% of minorities
University of Texas Medical School at Houston	37	10
University of Texas Medical School at San Antonio	30	29
University of Texas, Southwestern Medical School at Dallas	32	14
University of Utah School of Medicine	25	5
University of Vermont College of Medicine	52	0
University of Virginia School of Medicine	23	4
University of Washington School of Medicine	37	5
University of Wisconsin Medical School	na	na
Vanderbilt University School of Medicine	28	1
Washington University School of Medicine	29	11
Wayne State University School of Medicine	30	6
West Virginia University School of Medicine	32	2
Wright State University School of Medicine	28	12
Yale University School of Medicine	na	na

na = data not available

THE WOMAN PHYSICIAN

A profile of the typical woman physician emerged from a comprehensive study that was conducted in 1957 covering graduates from a 15-year period. In terms of their personal life, it showed that 57% of all female doctors are married and that these women have, on the average, 1.8 children (as against the national average of 2.3 children in all medical families). Other findings were that half of the married physicians are part of a husband-wife doctor team and the women doctors are slightly more likely to be divorced than the female in the general population. More recent studies have updated this profile and have shown that female doctors marry in the same proportion as nonphysicians and that nearly 70% of them have children. Moreover, female physicians were much more likely to have had working mothers than male doctors, indicating the importance of role models in developing career decisions.

In terms of their professional lives, it was found that women tend to practice in larger cities and that a large number (over one-third) worked either on a fixed salary or in what could be characterized as "fixed-hours" positions. Also, women have a slightly higher tendency to specialize than men, with the most popular fields being pediatrics, psychiatry, anesthesiology, and pathology. Other fields having significant appeal to women are obstetrics-gynecology, internal medicine, family practice, and public health. As to the critical issue of the time women spend in practice, the aforementioned study indicated that, while they clearly practiced less than men, the difference is not so significant as to support the long-standing argument that "a woman is a waste of a medical education." Thus, about half were found to have been in full-time practice all of their professional life and 87% in full- and part-time practice. The greatest loss occurred when women dropped out for a number of years to raise a family.

Since the 1957 study was conducted, extensive change has occurred. Opportunities for women to function in a full-time profession while raising a family have increased. In addition, feelings of the importance of a career for a woman have continued to grow, while attitudes concerning the traditional family patterns have changed.

The prospects for women in medicine are more encouraging now than at any other time in the past century. While undoubtedly prejudice still exists in some quarters, it is balanced by favorable discrimination on the whole. This is clearly evident from a review of the percentages of women accepted in recent years; it not only established that an equal percentage of women to men were accepted from their respective applicant pools, but also that women achieved this equal percentage with a lower average of multiple applications. Thus it can be anticipated that more women will be accepted to medical school in the coming years, and that changes will be made that will facilitate both the pre- and postgraduate training of women physicians so that they can live relatively normal family lives while simultaneously obtaining further training.

Group practice, part- or full-salaried positions with hospitals, health departments, medical schools, or pharmaceutical companies are but some of the ways in which women can enjoy a medical career with regular and reasonable hours. With the increase in number and size of such health care providers as the Kaiser Permanente Plan, H.I.P., and the virtual certainty of some form of national health insurance plan, the number of these positions most assuredly will increase.

CURRENT ISSUES

A few years ago, a two-day conference titled "Woman MD" was held at Johns Hopkins University School of

Medicine. In attendance were 200 female doctors from across the country who met to study the impact of the increase in the number of women entering medicine. Among the major issues raised were that:

1. Women physicians were looked down upon for showing feelings of tenderness and sadness towards patients and their families, thereby violating what is considered implicit medical standards of behavior. It was pointed out, however, that demonstrating sensitivity and compassion is not incompatible with the need for the doctor to also demonstrate strength.

2. Women physicians often wind up in specialties they did not originally want because of family obligations.

3. Women physicians, especially young ones, were concerned that they would not be able to have both a career and a family unless they found a mate who would help with the housework and child rearing—or unless they were untiring "superwomen."

In a summary of the symposium, the women doctors were warned of two "pitfalls": an intolerance of the emotional responses of the other sex in times of stress and possible reverse discrimination if they tried to change the medical system too much.

In general, the attitude of young women physicians toward their professional futures is optimistic. The forces responsible for changes have been the trailblazing efforts of older women, together with changes in societal values and laws. Having become firmly convinced that medicine is a suitable career choice, more and more women are applying to medical schools and discriminatory barriers afe falling.

CURRENT CHALLENGES

There are two major challenges facing prospective physicians: choosing a specialty and establishing a balance between professional and personal life.

Because of increased enrollment of women in medical schools, both the number and percentage of women residents have increased. Women are being trained in specialties that were once the exclusive domain of men. Until 1977, more than one-third of the medical specialties had no women residents. Within the next five years, women were enrolled in accredited postgraduate training programs of *all* specialties.

While such traditional choices as pediatrics, psychiatry, pathology and anesthesiology continue to attract many women, a very significant trend toward other areas of specialization has also taken place. Family medicine,

internal medicine, and radiology have become increasingly popular. Specialties such as obstetrics/gynecology and surgery are also attracting increased numbers of women. The number of women obstetrics/gynecology residents doubled between 1980 and 1985, and women now make up about 40% of those entering this area. There is reason to believe that the proportion of women training in this field will continue to increase. In surgery and the surgical subspecialties, the number of women has tripled in a little more than a decade. Thus on an overall basis, the percentage of women who have chosen the traditional specialties has decreased while the percentage of those electing to enter the nontraditional fields has increased.

Attempts are being made to improve conditions for women during their residencies. Some hospitals are considering allowances for maternity leaves. This is feasible in larger programs where a woman's on-call time can be absorbed by others. Another possibility for the future is the introduction of shared residencies where two individuals extend their residency training period by sharing a common vacancy. This may be the ideal solution for dual-physician couples who have a common specialty interest (but need not necessarily be a couple in order to succeed). This solution may be especially useful since intermarriage between physicians is increasing and some studies have shown that 50 percent of women physicians marry another doctor.

FINANCIAL AID AND SUPPORT SOURCES FOR WOMEN

The following are financial aid sources specifically for women students. Additional details are available from the organizations listed below:

1. American Association of University Women Educational Foundation. Contact: Director, Fellowships Office, American Association of University Women, 2401 Virginia Avenue, NW, Washington, D.C. 20037.

2. American Medical Women's Association Loan Fund. Contact: American Medical Women's Association, Inc., 465 Grand Street, New York, N.Y. 10002.

3. Educational Financial Aid Sources for Women. Contact: Clairol Loving Care Scholarship Program, 345 Park Avenue, New York, N.Y. 10022.

In the past several years a number of support groups that aim to facilitate women's adaptation to the demands of residency have been established. They include:

Dual Doctor Families, 6900 Grove Road, Thorofare, New Jersey 08086.

Shared Residencies (Drs. Frazer and Somjen), 1125C Grant Boulevard, Woodlawn Gardens, Syracuse, New York 13203.

American Medical Student Association, Women in Medicine Task Force, c/o Susan Trovan, 6626 Southwest 63rd Terrace, South Miami, Florida 33143, or Becky Williams, 4351 South Sacramento, Chicago, Illinois 60632.

American Medical Women's Association, 2302 East Speedway #206A, Tucson, Arizona 85719.

Association of American Medical Colleges, Special Assistant to the President on Women's Issues, One Dupont Circle, NW, Washington, D.C. 20036.

MINORITY STUDENTS IN MEDICINE

The academic medical community has responded, in the last few years, in a positive manner to provide greater opportunities for members of minority groups to secure admission. There are intensive efforts to enroll minority group members: blacks, American Indians/Alaskan natives, Mexican Americans, Puerto Ricans, Asians or Pacific Islanders, or other Hispanics. This policy has been especially effective as reflected by the fact that for 1983–84, minority group members made up both 15 percent of the first-year class and of the total medical student enrollment. This represents a significant increase over the less than 5 percent representation about two decades ago. Facilitating this process is the fact that many schools have a specific person to deal with minority affairs. Thus, if you are a member of a minority group, you should direct all your inquiries to "Director of Minority Affairs."

A special service that has been initiated to assist such students is the Medical Minority Applicant Registry (Med-MAR). This service enables any minority student applying to medical school to have his basic biography (except GPA and MCAT scores) circulated to all U.S. medical schools without charge. A list of such students is published two times a year. To get put on this list, you should identify yourself on the questionnaire as a member of a minority group at the time you take the MCAT, or contact the

Minority Student Information Clearing House
Association of American Medical Colleges
One Dupont Circle, NW, Suite 200
Washington, D.C. 20036.

You should also consider that some medical schools may waive their application fee for minority group students with economic need. The AMCAS fee can also be waived because of financial need, but the MCAT fee is never waived.

The increase in the number of blacks being admitted to medical school has had an impact on their total enrollment and on the number of blacks graduating. As expected, the number of blacks undertaking graduate education, that is, securing special teaching by means of residencies, has increased significantly over the past decade. The majority of blacks initiating residency training do so at hospitals located in California, Maryland, New Jersey, New York, and Pennsylvania. The majority of blacks in residency programs are being trained in five specialties: family practice, internal medicine, obstetrics-gynecology, pediatrics, and surgery.

The percentage of minority applicants most recently admitted is shown in Table 4.

To help disadvantaged or minority group students, some schools arrange special summer programs prior to the formal beginning of medical school for candidates already admitted. In addition, a variety of flexible curricular alternatives are available in some schools for such students as they progress through medical school. For specific information on these programs, contact the office of Minority Students Affairs at the individual schools.

Summaries of special minority admissions programs are outlined for individual schools in the special features section of the schools' profiles (see page 137).

FINANCIAL AID FOR MINORITY GROUP MEMBERS

The following listing gives a brief idea of the scholarships and loans available for minority group students. Additional information is available from each of the sources cited.

1. National Medical Fellowships, Inc. For minority group students. Contact: Executive Secretary, 250 West 57th Street, New York, New York 10019.

2. Doorstep, Inc.—Racial Minority Student Financial Assistance Fund. For minority group members. Contact: Executive Director, 1196 South Washburn, Topeka, Kansas 66604.

3. American Medical Association and Research Foundation. Contact: Foundation, 535 North Dearborn, Chicago, Illinois 60610.

4. National Scholarship Service and Fund for Negro Students. Contact: Executive Director, NSSFNS Application Department, 1501 Broadway, New York, New York 10019.

5. United Student Aid Funds, Inc. For low-income families. Contact: Executive Director, 8085 New Road, Indianapolis, Indiana 46220.

6. Emergency Scholarships. For American Indian students. Contact: Association on American Indian Affairs, 432 Park Avenue South, New York, New York 10016.

7. Bureau of Indian Affairs. For American Indians and Eskimos. Contact: Director, Higher Education Program, 500 Gold, S.W., Albuquerque, New Mexico 87103.

8. National Hispanic Scholarship Fund, P.O. Box 748, San Francisco, California 94101.

Additional information is available from the AAMC by writing to the Minority Student Opportunities in U.S. Medical Schools, AAMC, 1 Dupont Circle, NW, Washington, D.C. 20036.

6

FINANCING YOUR MEDICAL EDUCATION

☐ The current financial aid crisis
☐ Scholarships and loans

The high cost of medical education raises problems for many students. Various sources of financial assistance are presently available so that once accepted, however, a student can feel relatively assured that there will be adequate financial support forthcoming, if not in scholarships, then in loans. Recent proposed cuts in the federal aid to medical schools have included mostly attempts to cut back on research and building grants. These cuts in funding would affect the research being done primarily by staff professors and would threaten the future of research and the training of research scientists. In addition, other proposals include the substitution of a loan program instead of scholarships for students. Needless to say, educators have been decrying these cuts and have been urging a reassessment of financial allocations.

How do medical students meet their expenses? Usually from multiple sources including gifts and loans from families, their own earnings, and, if married, their spouses' earnings. Scholarships and loans form another major source of financial assistance, with about 50% of all students currently being helped by either of these means. Employment during medical school is strongly not advised, but work during the summers is possible. In light of this situation, it is important that prospective medical students anticipating the need for financial assistance undertake long-term planning early in their careers. Once the student has been accepted and has decided to attend a school, the financial aid office should be contacted for information and assistance. In most cases, financial aid is provided solely on the basis of need.

In determining how to finance your medical education, keep the following points in mind:

1. The most important sources of current financial information are the individual schools.

2. Those students who have been accepted and are considering enrolling at a school should request relevant information from the school's financial aid officer.

3. Some federally funded programs exist (see below) that provide financial aid for medical school students in return for a specified number of years of service.

4. Students who are accepted and are planning to enroll at a school should obtain current information as to tuition and fees (and any projected increases), room and board, and other expenses.

5. Students who have decided to enroll at a school should arrange to obtain specific information about a personal aid package by requesting an interview with the school's financial aid officer.

6. Students should realize that the financial aid picture is a changing one and that the general pattern of aid has been toward a declining level of support.

7. Financial aid awards are usually made on the basis of demonstrated need established by a financial analysis system. There are three national organizations that analyze the information provided by the students and their families. The results are sent to the individual medical schools. The schools then determine the award to be made.

8. Public medical schools are less expensive for both residents and, generally, for nonresidents also than private schools. This applies to both tuition and fees as well as all other expenses.

9. In 1984–85, the average cost of tuition for a freshman medical student at a public school was about $4000 for residents and $8000 for nonresidents, and $13,000 at private schools. All other expenses totaled about $7500 on the average.

10. The total average expenses (tuition, fees, living) for 1984–85 for a freshman thus can be estimated as $11,500 for a resident attending a state school and $15,500 for a nonresident. For a student attending a private school, the average total expenses were about $20,500.

THE CURRENT FINANCIAL AID CRISIS

During the past several years, there has been a marked escalation in tuition and other costs related to medical education. This inflationary spiral will continue for the foreseeable future. It is taking place unfortunately at a time when financial aid programs are being cut. This situation has caused a rising deficit between what monies are needed by medical students and what financial aid is available to them. To aggravate the situation, in 1979, legislation reducing federal grants to medical and osteopathy schools by 20% was approved. These schools will receive approximately $1,100 per student. Congress is being asked to end the grants entirely, citing fears that there will be a surplus of health personnel by 1990. In addition, it has become increasingly difficult to receive bank loans through the Federally Insured Student Loan Program, and private sources of support to medical students are also on the decline. All this strongly suggests that very careful consideration be given to financing one's medical education well before one considers applying for admission. In 1976, a Health Manpower bill was passed that will require almost every recipient of a federally supported medical scholarship to serve at least two years with the National Health Service Corps in areas of need.

SCHOLARSHIPS AND LOANS

Scholarships largely come from two sources: medical schools and the federal government. All medical schools have some scholarships or tuition-remission grants available that are awarded on the basis of financial need and scholastic performance. The school catalogs usually give the necessary details. The federal government provides most of the funds which the medical schools as well as banks and other lending institutions make available to students.

Scholarships

Scholarships for First-Year Students of Exceptional Financial Need. U.S. citizens or permanent residents who have been accepted and are planning to enroll as freshmen in medical school, and have exceptional financial need, can apply for such a scholarship. While funds under this program are very limited, they do provide for tuition as well as a stipend (currently about $6000) for all other educational expenses. No service payback is required. School financial aid officers are the best sources of information concerning these scholarships.

Armed Forces Health Professions Scholarship Program. All three armed forces offer scholarships to U.S. citizens who have been accepted or are already enrolled at a medical school in the U.S. or Puerto Rico. These scholarships provide full tuition and payment of educational expenses, plus a substantial stipend (currently in excess of $6000). Recipients must serve one year of active military duty for each year they receive support, with the usual minimum being 3 years. Premedical advisors generally have, or can secure, information concerning the individual programs sponsored by the Army, Navy, and Air Force.

National Health Service Corps Scholarship Program. These scholarships are provided by the U.S. Public Health Service, on a competitive basis, to students enrolled at U.S. medical schools. They provide for tuition, educational expenses, and a substantial stipend (currently about $6000). Support may be provided for up to 4 years, and the stipend is subject to annual cost-of-living adjustments. Recipients of such a scholarship, usually upon completion of postgraduate training, must provide one year of service in health manpower shortage areas for each year of financial support provided (with the minimum being 2 years). The service may be fulfilled as salaried federal employees of the National Health Service Corps, or as self-employed private practitioners.

Loans

Health Education Assistance Loan Program. This program provides insured loans of up to $15,000 a year (with a maximum of $60,000 for 4 years). Interest is not to exceed 12% during the life of the loan, and the principal is repayable over a 10- to 15-year period starting 9 months after completion of postgraduate training. It is also possible (if funds are available) to repay the loan in part or in whole by arranging a service contract through the Department of Health and Human Services.

Health Professions Student Loan Program. This program is administered by the medical schools and gives a student who has exceptional need the opportunity to borrow the cost of tuition and up to $2500 for other expenses per year. The interest rate is 7% and is applied after completion of residency training. The loan is repayable over a 10-year period.

National Direct Student Loan Program. Administered by the U.S. Office of Education this program enables a student to borrow up to $12,500 (including loans received as an undergraduate). The interest rate is 5% and repayment can extend over a 10-year period. Repayment begins 6 months after completing school.

Guaranteed Student Loan Program. This program is also administered by the U.S. Office of Education. It permits a student to borrow up to $5000 per year, the maximum not to exceed $25,000 (including undergraduate loans). The sources of these guaranteed funds are banks, savings and loan associations, or other participating lending institutions. Interest is at 9% and repayment begins 6 to 12 months after completing one's studies.

Other Loan Sources. Medical schools have loan funds provided by philanthropic foundations, industry, or alumni. Interest rates and repayment policies are determined by the individual schools.

Funds in the form of scholarships and loans in varying amounts are available from many other sources. There are, however, restrictions as to eligibility based on residence, ethnic group, or other requirements. Sources of some of these programs are:

1. Joseph Collins Foundation, One Chase Manhattan Plaza, New York, New York 10005

2. National Medical Fellowships, Inc., 250 West 57th Street, New York, New York 10019

3. New England Board of Higher Education, 40 Grove Street, Wellesley, Massachusetts 02128

4. Armed Forces Health Professions Scholarship Program. Commander, USA MEDDPERSA, HQDA (SGPE-PDM), 19 Half Street, SW, Washington, D.C. 20314; Commander, Navy Recruiting Command, 4015 Wilson Boulevard, Arlington, Virginia 22203; United States Air Force, Recruiting Service, Medical Recruiting Division, Randolph Air Force Base, Texas 78148

5. American Medical Association, Education and Research Foundation, 535 North Dearborn Street, Chicago, Illinois 60610

6. Educational and Scientific Trust of the Pennsylvania Medical Society, 20 Erford Road, Lemoyne, Pennsylvania 17043

7. USA Funds Endorsement Center, 6610 North Shadeland Avenue, P.O. Box 50827, Indianapolis, Indiana 46250

8. National Health Corps Scholarship Program, Bureau of Health Manpower, Center Building, Room G-15, 3700 East-West Highway, Hyattsville, Maryland 20782

9. Robert Wood Johnson Student Loan Guarantee Program. Write to address given under item 7.

There are many sources of information regarding specialized financial aid programs which are offered to state residents or to those entering particular specialty fields. For additional information on such programs, consult the following books:

1. *Medical Scholarship and Loan Fund Program*, published by the AMA, 535 North Dearborn Street, Chicago, Illinois 60610.

2. "Financial Information for Medical Students" which is Chapter 6 in the *Medical School Admission Requirements*, published by the AAMC, One Dupont Circle, NW, Washington, D.C. 20036.

3. *FIND: Financial Information National Directory-Health Careers*, published by the AMA, 535 North Dearborn Street, Chicago, Illinois 60610.

4. "The Health Education Assistance Loan Program: A New Way to Help Finance Your Health Professions Education." Heal, P.O. Box 23033, L'Enfant Plaza, Washington, D.C. 20024.

5. "Where to Get Health Career Information," published by the National Health Council, Inc., 1740 Broadway, New York, New York 10019.

6. "The Health Field Needs You! Sources of Financial Aid Information," published by the Bureau of Health Professions, Health Resources and Service Administration, DHHS, Parklawn Building, 5600 Fishers Lane, Rockville, MD 20857.

In addition, there are several programs for minority group students. Information on these programs is included in Chapter 5.

7

MEDICAL EDUCATION

☐ The traditional program

☐ The curriculum in transition

☐ Other educational programs

☐ The curriculum for the 21st century

☐ Attrition in medical school

☐ National medical board examinations

☐ Postgraduate training: internship and residency

Until the early 1900s, medical education in the United States was unstructured and unregulated. A person wishing to become a doctor would usually seek some didactic training at a medical school and/or spend time as an apprentice with one or more physicians. Since a license to practice was not needed, many unqualified individuals were engaged in the healing arts. The caliber of many medical schools was also open to serious question.

In 1910, after an investigation into the state of affairs existing in medical education, Abraham Flexner proposed a program of reorganizing medical education in a way that would insure that only qualified individuals would enter the profession. With the adoption of the Flexner Report, many medical schools of borderline quality became defunct while others significantly improved their standards. Another result was that medical education became a structured four-year program consisting of two years of basic sciences or preclinical training followed by two years of clinical experience. This educational program was essentially the same in all medical schools.

To ensure the maintenance of high standards, today all medical schools must obtain and maintain legal accreditation. The status of their educational programs are periodically evaluated by the Liaison Committee on Medical Education (LCME) of the Association of American Medical Colleges. This has not restricted medical schools, however, from introducing modifications in their traditional program. The traditional program, nonetheless, still forms the basis of the medical education process.

THE TRADITIONAL PROGRAM
The First Year

This introductory phase is devoted to the study of normal human biology, which includes anatomy, biochemistry, and physiology. The scope and emphasis within each of these areas is gradually being altered as new experimental approaches result in fresh data. Thus, for example, while the time allotted in gross anatomy is being diminished, the time spent on histology (microscopic anatomy) is being increased, with more emphasis being placed on ultrastructural and histochemical findings. Most schools incorporate clinical demonstrations within basic science lectures so as to relate subject matter to actual medical problems. Many schools offer some introductory lectures in the behavioral sciences and genetics during the first year.

The first year is about 35 weeks long, with about 35 hours of required class work per week. Half or more of the class time is spent in lectures, the rest is spent in the laboratory.

The Second Year

The second year is the bridge between the preclinical sciences and the clinical subjects that occupy the bulk of the final two years of study. This year establishes the scientific basis for understanding abnormal states of human biology. The standard courses taken during the sophomore year are pathology, microbiology, pharmacology, physical diagnosis, clinical laboratory procedures, and introductions to certain specialty fields such as public health and psychiatry.

Pathology is probably the keystone course of the sophomore year. It provides an introduction to the essential nature of disease and, in particular, the structural and functional changes which cause or are caused by disease. During the second semester, the more common diseases of each organ system and each organ are studied. The teaching process in pathology involves formal lectures, clinical pathological conferences, and laboratory exercises in pathological histology.

Microbiology provides an introduction to disease processes. It involves a study of the microorganisms which invade the body. The basis of mechanism of infection and immunity is analyzed. One of the most effective means of combating disease is by means of drugs. Pharmacology concerns itself with the chemistry of the natural and synthetic drugs and their action in the healthy and diseased human body. The full impact of this subject comes to the forefront during the lengthy laboratory exercises in which experimental animals are frequently used to measure the effects of drugs.

The groundwork provided by the aforementioned courses, together with those completed during the first year, provide a great deal of fundamental information about the human body in illness and in health. The next step is to become familiar with the practical techniques required to determine the nature of a patient's illness. An introduction to this procedure is provided by the course in physical diagnosis. This phase of preclinical study gives a strong psychological lift. You learn the art of taking a medical history and examining a sick patient. The sophomore year ends with a framework for the clinical years well established.

The Third Year

While the junior year is highlighted by considerable exposure to clinical experience, the formal educational process continues during this period with lectures, conferences, and seminars in medicine, surgery, pediatrics, obstetrics, and gynecology, as well as other specialties and subspecialties. The educational process is usually closely integrated with presentation of relevant patient cases. The emphasis in this early clinical training period is on the diagnosis of disease. The principles of treatment noted will be emphasized later.

Juniors are assigned various patients for a "workup," obtaining a history and physical examination. To carry out the former, the junior medical student learns to interrogate the patient so as to elicit and organize the chronological story of his or her present illness, obtain information as to the general state of his or her past and present health, secure vital data concerning the patient's family history, occupation, and social life. Supplementing this is a physical examination using manual manipulative and instrumental aids (stethoscope and ophthalmoscope). All the information is then integrated to provide preliminary diagnosis. The student then decides whether laboratory tests, X-rays, or special studies are needed. A faculty member reviews the entire "workup" and makes adjustments or confirms the order for diagnostic tests. This preliminary stage of clinical training, like all initial educational experiences, is of special importance. It helps develop a critical approach that tends to avoid the hazards that result from insufficient gathering of information, careless observation, or improper evaluation of the obtained data.

The initial diagnostic training is provided as part of service in the outpatient clinics and in the hospital wards. Later in the year, having attained proficiency in working up new patients, the student serves as a full-time clinical clerk in various clinical departments and in their outpatient clinics. As an apprenticing diagnostician, he or she is introduced into a variety of specialties. The aim of these experiences is not only to introduce the student to possible areas of specialization, but to teach techniques of detecting all kinds of illness, regardless of specialization. Generally, the student will spend one quarter on medicine, another on surgery, a third on obstetrics-gynecology and pediatrics, and a fourth on electives.

As a clerk in medicine the student will rotate among various outpatient clinics and become familiar with groups of diseases that are classified as cardiovascular, allergic, infectious, rheumatic, neurological, gastrointestinal, and dermatological. Teaching clinics in these subspecialties are conducted by members of the medical school's faculty.

Short periods of time (several weeks each) are usually allotted to otolaryngology (diseases of the ear and throat) and ophthalmology. The student learns the basic diagnostic techniques in these specialties and has an opportunity to study the medical and surgical treatments used in these areas.

The clerkship in surgery enables the student to apply the newly acquired diagnostical training. The student gains insight into the process of determining when an operation is required as well as the need for pre- and post-surgical care. If assigned to the emergency room, he or she may have an opportunity to perform, under supervision, minor surgery such as treatment for infections of fingers, draining of abscesses, or suturing of lacerations. Many institutions offer as an elective a course in operative surgery where animals are treated as patients. Participation by the third-year student in such a program provides him or her with an opportunity for training as a surgeon, first assistant, scrub nurse, and anesthetist.

The student develops a foundation in the physiology of the human female in the first year and in pathology of diseases of the female urogenital system in the second year; he or she is now prepared for the clinical exposure to gynecological diseases, and during the third year, the student participates in conferences, ward rounds, lectures, surgery, and outpatient clinics. It is quite common for the student to deliver about a half dozen babies. These are naturally performed under the close supervision of a resident in obstetrics. Aside from the training in child birth, the student learns about the medical and emotional problems of prenatal care. In the outpatient obstetric clinic the student has the opportunity to examine and counsel women in pregnancy. This provides an especially favorable opportunity to develop the doctor-patient relationship.

The clerkship in pediatrics is devoted to the study of children and their diseases. The life span covered is from shortly after childbirth to adolescence. The student is taught to recognize the need not only for diagnosis of pediatric diseases but to anticipate them and thus better help to insure that the child will develop into a healthy adult. The preparation for the pediatric clerkship is frequently initiated in the latter part of the second year with lectures and some clinical experience in the fundamentals, such as heart sounds, X-rays, and e.e.g.'s of infants and children. Work in the clinics and wards becomes more intensive in the third year when the student is exposed to varied medical and surgical problems of children's diseases. The fourth year then provides additional opportunity for pediatric training along with greater responsibility.

During the third year, the student-instructor relationship becomes more personalized and an exchange of views begins to take place; the student assumes the status of a junior colleague. The junior medical student's responsibilities are carefully demarcated and essentially restricted to taking medical history and carrying out a physical examination. The acute illnesses the student sees in the wards and the explicit problems he or she handles in the clinics are often "classical," and therefore the student is free from the necessity of coping with diagnostic and therapeutic uncertainties that fall outside a limited area.

The Fourth Year

In the fourth year, the student's activities are frequently divided into four quarters. One is devoted to surgery (including general, orthopedic and urological), another to medicine, a third to pediatrics, psychiatry, neurology and radiology, and a fourth to elective study. There is usually considerable latitude in the arrangement of the order in which the program may be carried out.

In the surgical clerkship, the senior may frequently be assigned his or her own cases. He or she will, under careful supervision, be responsible for the patient workup, help arrange for laboratory tests, and contribute to discussions involving the diagnosis. The student will participate in preparing the patient for surgery, and, in the operating room, can expect to serve as third or fourth surgical assistant. He or she may be assigned to keep watch over the patient in the recovery room and be responsible for routine post-operative check-ups until the patient is discharged. The aim of the limited surgical experience of the senior student is not to secure specialized training, but to gain diagnostic experience so as to have a balanced insight into the usefulness of surgical intervention in the process of healing the sick. The exposure in surgery will be a very wide one, ranging from tonsillectomy to cardiac surgery.

In the block of surgical time devoted to orthopedics, the senior is exposed to the diagnosis and treatment of diseases of the joints and vertebral column, as well as fractures and deformities of the bones of the body. In urology some surgical and medical experience is gained by coming into contact with patients suffering from diseases of the kidney, bladder, prostate gland, and reproductive organs.

The quarter devoted to clinical clerkship in medicine is rather similar to that in surgery; naturally the nature of the patient's illness and the method of treatment differs. Nevertheless for the fourth-year student, there are workups to be made, tests to be ordered, and diagnoses to be reached. Several times a week the student and his or her supervisors will go on rounds and the student will participate in the discussions about the patients' conditions, treatments, and prognoses. During the clerkship period, the senior will be on call twenty-four hours a day and must be ready to assist in emergencies and to comfort patients through periods of stress. Naturally, throughout this period, the house staff—the interns and residents—will bear the direct responsibilities for prescribing treatment and directing emergency care. But the senior medical student nevertheless gains firsthand insight into the responsibilities that must be assumed in postgraduate training.

THE CURRICULUM IN TRANSITION

Since the mid-1960s, there has been increased pressure from medical students to introduce greater flexibility into the course of study. In response to such pressure, most schools have established committees (sometimes including students) to reevaluate and update their curricula. In many schools, new curricula have been introduced which have modified the traditional program using one or more of several different approaches.

1. Determining a "core curriculum" that places the emphasis on principles rather than only on facts.

2. Greater correlation between basic and clinical sciences. In the first year, the student is exposed to some clinical experience as patients having illness related to the subject being studied and presented.

3. Greater emphasis placed on function than structure. This approach is reflected in two ways; by a decrease in the amount of time allotted to morphological studies (anatomy, for example) and by an integration of material presented by different departments.

4. Introduction of multiple-tract systems. This offers students who have completed the core curriculum, which is the reduced required common experience of all students, to choose one of several pathways having different emphasis depending upon their ultimate career goals. Thus, there is a differentiation of exposure depending upon interest, need, and ability.

5. Use of interdisciplinary and interdepartmental courses. These frequently replace departmental offerings, especially in the basic sciences. The combined viewpoints of several basic medical sciences are presented in an integrated fashion as each organ system is discussed, rather than being taught in the classical manner at varied times through separate courses. The organ systems are muscular, skeletal, nervous, cardiovascular, respiratory, gastrointestinal, hematopoietic, renourinary, integumentary, endocrine and reproductive. This type of teaching is known as "back to back"; that is, the normal aspects of the anatomy, chemistry, physiology, and pharmacology are considered in relation to abnormal or pathological principles.

6. Use of visual aids. These and other modern methods of instruction are much more widely used, although their effectiveness cannot yet be evaluated.

7. Taking qualifying examinations. In many schools students are encouraged to take such examinations before beginning certain basic science courses. If successful, they may proceed to other areas or disciplines without further course work in the subject they demonstrated competence in.

8. Introduction of more elective time. This permits the student to spend additional time in areas of special interest thus facilitating the choice of and preparation for a specialty or becoming more proficient in a selected area.

9. Accelerating the program of studies. A small number of schools have offered their most promising students opportunities to complete their studies in less than four years. The seventeen schools listed below have standard four-year programs with an acceleration option for a three-year program.

Baylor College of Medicine
Howard University
Johns Hopkins University
Medical College of Georgia
Medical College of Ohio
Medical College of Virginia
Northwestern University
Ohio State University
SUNY at Buffalo
University of Alabama

University of Connecticut
University of Illinois at Chicago
University of North Carolina
University of Tennessee
University of Texas Medical School at Galveston
University of Virginia
University of Washington

The number of schools shortening their curriculum increased during the early 1970s. However, the enthusiasm for the three-year program has markedly diminished, and all schools have reverted back to a four-year program.

10. Lengthening the program of studies. If it proves necessary, some medical schools permit students to extend their educational program for a year. Among such schools are:

Boston University
Creighton University
Howard University
Medical College of Wisconsin
Stanford University
University of California, San Diego
University of California, San Francisco
University of Hawaii

Since there now exists a diversity of curricula because of the many possible variations, it is advisable for the prospective applicant to become familiar with the programs offered by the school in which the applicant is interested.

OTHER EDUCATIONAL PROGRAMS

In addition to the changes in curriculum being introduced at many schools, special programs of varying nature are now also available at some schools to specially qualified students.

Integrated Programs (BA or BS-MD Programs)

This program permits the selected students to participate in combined undergraduate and medical school curricula thus enabling them to obtain the MD degree in six or seven years from the time they graduate from high school. In such cases, individual students can obtain their baccalaureate degree while enrolled in medical school. The following list includes schools presently offering such a program:

Albany Medical College
Boston University School of Medicine
Brown University Program in Medicine
Case Western Reserve University
Hahnemann University
Howard University
Jefferson Medical College
Johns Hopkins University
Louisiana State University—Shreveport
Medical College of Pennsylvania
Medical College of Wisconsin
Northeastern Ohio Universities
Northwestern University
Texas A & M University
University of Florida
University of Miami
University of Michigan
University of Missouri—Kansas City
University of Wisconsin
Washington University—St. Louis

Independent Study

A few schools offer certain students the possibility of completing the required courses at their own pace. Such students must meet with faculty advisers regularly to demonstrate their progress and they must pass the standard comprehensive examinations for promotion and graduation.

Combined Programs

This arrangement permits a combination medical degree program with those of other fields such as engineering, statistics, law, physics, chemistry, administration, dentistry, agriculture, and others. Schools offering such programs will be identified in the special features section of their profiles.

MD-MS, MD-PhD Programs

These programs permit combined study for an MS or PhD degree in a basic medical science, along with study for the MD degree. Average time for these programs ranges from six to seven years. A special Medical Scientist Training Program sponsored by the National Institutes of Health offers annual stipends and full tuition coverage for six to eight students accepted into the program at the schools offering it. The Medical Scientist Training Program is available at:

Albert Einstein Columbia University
Duke University
Mount Sinai

New York University
Stanford University
University of California at Los Angeles
University of California at San Diego
University of Chicago
University of Florida
University of Iowa
University of Pennsylvania
University of Washington
University of Wisconsin
Washington University
Yale University

Elective Programs

Almost all schools now offer opportunities for students to pursue such activities as independent study, honors programs, and special research projects, either at home or elsewhere during the academic year or in the summer.

THE CURRICULUM FOR THE TWENTY-FIRST CENTURY

The AAMC's report on the General Professional Education of the Physician (GPEP) made a series of important recommendations that undoubtedly will affect medical education significantly in the next century. They will affect not only admission policies of medical schools but also undergraduate medical instruction. Some of the recommendations of the panel of experts in the field of medical education were:

1. Medical facilities should develop procedures and adopt explicit criteria for the systematic evaluation of student performance.

2. Medical schools should emphasize the development of independent learning and problem-solving skills.

3. The level of skills and knowledge that a student should reach in order to enter graduate medical education (residency training) should be defined more clearly.

4. Medical schools should encourage their students to concentrate their elective programs on the advancement of their general professional education rather than on the pursuit of a residency position.

5. Medical students' general professional education should include an emphasis on the physician's responsibility to work with individual patients and communities to promote health and prevent disease.

Obviously each medical school will interpret these guidelines for curriculum changes according to its own philosophy of education. This will serve to add greater variability to the learning experiences one can have at different institutions. It will obviously be another significant factor to consider when selecting a medical school.

ATTRITION IN MEDICAL SCHOOL

If you have been accepted to a U.S. medical school you are one of a select number of students who have survived the successive academic prunings of elementary school, high school, college, and medical school selection procedures. In addition you rank in the upper 50% of all students entering graduate and professional schools. Medical schools seek to graduate as many of their entrants as possible; thus you stand a better chance of successfully completing your medical education than students in other professional schools in the U.S. or medical students in practically every other country. While the attrition rate in American professional schools is relatively high, that for medicine has consistently been relatively low. Nevertheless, any loss of medical students is a loss to society and is especially painful when one considers the many rejected yet qualified applicants who were denied an opportunity to study medicine.

It is therefore encouraging to report that the overall dropout rate has remained very low over the past few years. The withdrawals from the total student enrollment in a recent year were 751, or 1.85% of the enrollment. Moreover, even this figure may in reality be artificially high because one-fifth of the students (143, or 0.35%) withdrew to pursue advanced study and are expected to return to medical school. In addition, less than one-third of the withdrawals or dismissals (223) were for academic reasons, the remainder (385, or 1%), for other reasons. Thus in actuality the true attrition rate is closer to 0.5%. This means that admissions committees have been able to select from the large pool of qualified applicants those most likely to succeed. If accepted, you should feel confident that with consistent hard work you will most likely complete your course of studies.

An analysis of student records over an extended period has provided significant information regarding the relationship of various student characteristics to attrition that can help you assess your own chances for success and indicate when extra care and effort may be called for. Successful students are more likely to have attended an undergraduate college with a sizable premedical program which they found to be both difficult and competitive. The premedical grades of academic dropouts are substantially lower than are the grades of both successful students and nonacademic dropouts. The average test scores for dropouts are much lower than those of successful students. Unsuccessful students report almost twice as many personal problems as do successful students. Older students have a much higher dropout rate than do younger students. Women have a somewhat higher attrition rate than do men. It should be noted, however, that studies have shown that the academic dropout rate was the same for both sexes but the dropout rate for nonacademic reasons (e.g., marriage or pregnancy) was almost three times higher in females. The dropout rate did not differ significantly for married students or for those reporting similar time allocations to study, part-time employment, or extracurricular activities. Successful students tend to be influenced by a desire for independence and for prestige, whereas, unsuccessful students are most likely to be influenced by such additional factors as reading and by religious and service motivation.

The following are some specific suggestions that can reduce your chances of dropping out of medical school. Prior to entering medical school you should obtain a strong background of fundamental knowledge in the sciences and develop good study habits; seek opportunities to test your motivation for a career in medicine by exposure to health science related work (e.g., lab assistant, hospital aid, volunteer work with handicapped, visiting hospitals and medical schools); and seek admission to medical schools where you can most likely gain admission and which are most suited to your abilities and interests.

If you fail at the end of a year and are offered a chance to repeat, accept the opportunity to do so if you still want to study medicine. The chances are high that you, like many previous repeaters, will finally successfully complete your studies. Should you decide to withdraw voluntarily, do so only after consultation with appropriate faculty and administrative members of your school.

NATIONAL MEDICAL BOARD EXAMINATIONS (NMBE)

There is no national medical licensing body in the United States. It is the function of the individual states to determine who shall practice within their borders and to maintain high standards of medical practice in accordance with their own rules and regulations. In recognition of the thoroughness and widely accepted standards of the National Board examinations, its certificate is accepted by the medical licensing authorities of the

District of Columbia, Puerto Rico, and all states except Louisiana and Texas.

The National Board of Medical Examiners have established three qualifying examinations which are referred to as Part I, Part II, and Part III. Part I is given in June and September and is a two-day, multiple-choice examination in the basic medical sciences including various aspects of behavior. It tests not only the candidate's knowledge, but also the subtler qualities of discrimination, judgment, and reasoning. Part II is given in April and September and is similar to Part I but covers the clinical sciences; it is usually taken during the senior year. In addition to covering a broad spectrum of knowledge in each of the clinical areas, sets of questions are presented that are designed to explore the extent of knowledge of clinical situations and test the ability to bring information from many different clinical and basic science areas to bear upon these situations. Part III is given in March and May and is a test of clinical competence. By use of special testing techniques it determines how the candidate uses his knowledge in the interpretation of clinical data and in the evaluation, diagnosis, and management of clinical problems. To qualify for Part III, the student must have passed the first two parts, have obtained his MD degree from a U.S. or Canadian school, and have served at least six months in an approved hospital internship or residency. Certification, however, is not awarded until satisfactory completion of one full year of internship or residency.

POSTGRADUATE TRAINING: INTERNSHIP AND RESIDENCY

Internship

When the internship first became an established part of medical education, its purpose was straightforward and uniform: a *rotating* internship, with nearly equal portions devoted to medicine, surgery, pediatrics, and obstetrics-gynecology, which provided the first extended clinical experience and the first supervised responsibility for the welfare of living patients. These experiences were deemed necessary, and usually sufficient, to complete the preparation of a young physician for independent practice.

The purpose of an internship is no longer obvious, nor is it uniform. The internship does not provide the student's first practical experience with problems of diagnosis and treatment; that function is now served by undergraduate clinical clerkships. Nor is it sufficient to provide the final education experience preceding independent practice; the additional training of a residency is generally considered necessary to fulfill that purpose.

The nature of the internship has also changed over the years. Aside from the original rotating format, more recently two other types have come into use: *mixed* internships—providing training in two or three fields with prolonged concentration in one of them; and *straight* internships—devoting time entirely to single areas, such as medicine, surgery, or pediatrics.

While medical school curricula are the corporate responsibilities of faculties, internship programs are not the corporate responsibilities of hospitals. The responsibility of insuring a truly educational internship is usually that of an individual head of a service or heads of several independent services. An inevitable result of such highly individualized and fragmented responsibility is that internship programs vary widely in the extent to which they duplicate the experience already gained in the clinical-clerkship, in the amount of routine and sometimes menial service required, and in their educational quality.

As a result of the questionable value of the internship in the educational process and the very high percentage of physicians taking residencies, its usefulness as a distinct program came into serious question. At its annual convention in December, 1968, the AMA adopted a resolution that "an ultimate goal is unification of the internship and residency years into a coordinated whole." Further steps toward implementation of this resolution were subsequently adopted and the goal was set that by July 1, 1978, all internship programs would be integrated with residency training to form a unified program of graduate medical education. This means that the internship year becomes the first year of residency and that one person is assigned as program director in a specialty at a given institution and is responsible for the entire program. That person has the option of requiring or recommending a specific type of "internship year" (e.g., rotating, mixed, or straight) acceptable as part of the residency program, or even assign the trainee to an outside hospital for his or her internship year. A significant amount of flexibility has been introduced so as to permit the graduating MD to secure postgraduate training that is specifically designed for individual interests and career goals. It will also facilitate long term plans and insure a more stable personal life.

Intern and Resident Matching Program

Almost all graduates of U.S. and Canadian medical schools secure internship appointments in U.S. hospitals through the National Intern and Resident Matching Program (NIRMP). Foreign medical graduates are eligible to participate if they have passed the ECFMG examination in September or earlier. The matching is carried out in March for internships that usually start July 1.

In the fall of the senior year, every medical student applies to the hospitals to which he or she would like an appointment. Sometime during the winter, after the student's marks have been submitted to the hospital's chief of staff, the student will be asked to visit the hospital. He or she may be interviewed by one or several attending physicians as well as the director of the training program. After the interviews are completed in the early spring, the future intern makes up a list of hospitals to which he or she has applied, with the number one choice at the top, the last choice at the bottom. All the participating hospitals submit similar lists of the students they have interviewed. The lists are gathered in a central office, fed into a computer, and pairings are made. The senior medical student then gets an appointment at the hospital highest on his list that wants him. This program, which was instituted in 1952, avoids a great deal of chaos and anguish, since previously neither students nor hospitals knew where they were at until the last moment.

As of March, 1974, candidates have been matched by NIRMP to first-year positions in six specialties. Because all specialty boards have made significant modifications in their requirements to adjust to the plan for integrated postgraduate training, senior medical students may now apply for a first year of graduate medical education either in one of the existing types of internships or in a first-year of residency in most specialties. For additional information contact: NIRMP, State National Bank Building, Suite 1150, Evanston, Illinois 60201.

The current average salaries for interns (first post-MD year) and residents are in the $20,000 to $30,000 range. However, as a result of the deterioration of their financial status because their salaries have not kept up with inflation and their education indebtedness has increased, many residents hold second jobs. Married people, especially those with children, are the most likely to be forced to supplement their incomes.

Residency

After internship comes residency. The function of this extended period of training has changed greatly since its start a century ago. At that time a residency was a special period of additional clinical education for a few promising and scholarly young physicians who wished to become the teachers or leaders in medicine. Residency training in the past few decades has become standard for the average physician and more than 1500 American hospitals offer such programs. Completing an approved residency and passing a written and/or oral examination given by a specialty board are the basic requirements for certification as a specialist.

In the early 1900s, nearly half of all medical school graduates entered general practice. By the 1960s, this figure had shrunk to about 20%. A recent study concerning medical specialization showed that the distribution of entrants into specialty training has been relatively constant over the last decade. Economic factors are comparatively minor in determining medical specialization, while up to 87% of the sampling indicated intellectual interests to be a major determining factor. Most recruits are entering internal medicine, surgery, psychiatry, obstetrics-gynecology, and pediatrics. Female physicians have generally favored fixed-schedule specialties (anesthesiology, radiology, psychiatry, pediatrics, public health) and work settings (state hospitals and industry).

The length of residency training varies among the different specialties and is indicated in Table 4.

It should be noted that many of the specialties listed have subspecialties that may require additional training beyond that listed in Table 4. Thus, among the many subspecialties of internal medicine are cardiology and hematology; of pathology are forensic and neuropathology; and of surgery are plastic and thoracic surgery.

Table 5. Residency Training for Various Specialties

Specialty	Nature of Work	Prerequisite Training Year(s)	Prerequisite Training Area	Training Period Minimum	Training Period Maximum
Allergy	Treatment of illness due to hypersensitivity to a specific substance or condition	Two	Medicine	One	Two
Anesthesiology	Producing a partial or total loss of pain by use of drugs, gases or other means	One	Clinical Base	Two	Three
Child Psychiatry	Treatment of emotional disorders of children	Two	General Psychiatry	Two	Two
Colon and Rectal Surgery	Treatment of diseases of the lower bowel	Three	General Surgery	Two	Two
Dermatology	Treatment of skin diseases	One	Medicine	Two	Three
Diagnostic Radiology	Use of specialized X-ray techniques for diagnosis	One	Clinical Base	Three	Three
Family Practice	Evaluating total health needs and providing routine treatment	—	—	Three	Three
Forensic Pathology	Use of pathological methods in criminal investigations	Three	Pathology	One	Two
Internal Medicine	Treatment of diseases and organs with medications	One	General Surgery	Four	Four
Neurosurgery	Surgery of the nervous system	One	General Surgery	Four	Four
Neurology	Treatment of nervous system with medications	One	Clinical Base	Three	Five
Neuropathology	Diagnosis of pathological condition of the nervous system	Four	Pathology	One	Two
Nuclear Medicine	Treatment of disease by radiation therapy	Two	Medicine, Path or Radiology	Two	Two
Obstetrics	Care during pregnancy and labor and treatment of diseases of genital and reproductive system	One	Clinical Base	Three	Four
Ophthalmology	Care and treatment of eye diseases	One	Optional	Three	Four
Orthopedic	Treatment of skeletal deformities and injuries of the bones and joints	One	General Surgery	Three	Four
Otolaryngology	Treatment of ear, nose and throat diseases	One	General Surgery	Three	Four

Table 5. **Residency Training for Various Specialties—Cont'd**

Specialty	Nature of Work	Prerequisite Training		Training Period	
		Year(s)	Area	Minimum	Maximum
Pathology	Diagnosis of structural and functional changes in the body tissues due to diseases	—	—	Three	Four
Pediatrics	Care of infants and children and treatment of their diseases	—	—	Three	Four
Pediatric Cardiology	Treatment of heart diseases in children	Three	Pediatrics	Two	Two
Physical Medicine and Rehabilitation	Treatment by physician and mechanical means to permit maximum restoration of function	Half	Medicine and Surgery	Two	Three
Plastic Surgery	Surgery to repair or restore injured, deformed or destroyed parts of the body, especially by transferring tissue	Three	General Surgery	Two	Three
Preventive Medicine and Public Health	Prevention of disease for individuals and for public in general	One	Public Health	Three	Four
Psychiatry	Treatment of mental disease	One	Clinical base	Three	Three
Radiology	Diagnosis of disease by radioactive means	One	Clinical base	Three	Three
Surgery	Treatment of diseases by surgical intervention	—	—	Four	Seven
Therapeutic Radiology	Treatment of diseases by radioactive methods	One	Clinical base	Three	Three
Thoracic Surgery	Surgical treatment of chest diseases	Four	General Surgery	Two	Two
Urology	Treatment of kidney and bladder diseases	Two	General Surgery	Three	Three

Family Practice

Public demand for a single, competent physician for the entire family has grown as the availability of such physicians continues to diminish. To meet this need, the specialty of family practice evolved. This specialty differs from the others in that it is defined in terms of functions performed rather than limited by treatment of certain diseases or parts of the body or on the basis of the patients' chronological age.

The specialist in family practice must acquire a basic core of knowledge in all areas of medicine. Being the physician of first contact, he is responsible for evaluating the patient's total health needs over an extended period of time. Family practice is thus a specialty in breadth rather than a specialty in depth.

Career Placement

National trends in career placement are not available and specialty imbalances change from year to year as well. The activities of the AMA Physician's Placement Service for the past few years do provide insight into what is happening, however. The AMA's statistics show that there is a general pattern of undersupply of physicians for general and family practice and an oversupply of anesthesiologists, dermatologists, pediatricians, psychiatrists, radiologists, surgeons, and urologists. The only area other than general practice in which there currently seems to be a shortage is otolaryngology, with less specialists in this field in proportion to the opportunities available. Note, however, that the oversupply of particular specialists reflects the desires for prime locations, rather than a national oversupply.

8

MEDICAL SCHOOLS

■ The medical scene in a nutshell

■ In-depth school profiles

☐ Medical schools in development

This chapter consists of two components: a table and school profiles. The table in "The Medical Scene in a Nutshell" provides numerical data dealing with many school characteristics and serves as a quick source of information and a means for easily comparing features of schools you may be interested in. The "In-Depth School Profiles" offer detailed information that distinguishes the individual schools.

THE MEDICAL SCENE IN A NUTSHELL

Table 6, Basic Data on the Medical Schools, contains the kind of information that will be useful in helping you decide which schools to apply to. At a glance you can see and compare application data, admission statistics, academic statistics, and expenses.

Please note that while the information in this table is as up-to-date and accurate as possible, it is recommended that you check the individual medical school catalogs prior to applying.

How to Use This Table

The following list explains the column headings in Table 6.

Application Fee In most cases, this fee is required

only at the time you submit your supplementary application. The preliminary application is usually the AMCAS application fee that is paid when submitting the form.

Earliest and Latest Filing Dates These are usually firm dates.

Number of Applicants This column gives an idea of how many applications were received for the 1984–85 class.

Applicants Accepted The columns indicate the men, women, and out-of-state students accepted for the 1984–85 class. The ratio of the total number of men and women accepted to the total number of applicants gives an indication of the competitive nature of admission at each school.

Class Size The figures in this column refer to the 1984–85 class.

Percentage with Four Years of College This shows the relative chances of a third-year student gaining admission.

Percent Interviewed This indicates the relative importance of being granted an interview at a specific school.

Percent Residents This indicates the desirability of a student to apply to a specific out-of-state school.

Percent Women The actual number of women accepted is shown in Column 6.

Mean MCAT Scores The mean test scores for entering first-year students. These scores can serve as a guide to the standards and competitive nature of each school.

Mean GPA The mean grade point average for accepted nonresidents. It is usually somewhat lower for residents (less 0.2; where A=4.0).

Deposit The amount of money that must be sent in to hold a place in the class. It may be applied toward eventual tuition cost and in some cases is refundable.

Tuition 1984–85 tuition costs (annual) for first-year students.

Other Expenses This estimate covers the minimum room and board, fees and other expenses excluding microscope cost, for first year.

The following abbreviations are used in Table 6:

B	Biology score on the MCAT
C	Chemistry score on the MCAT
P	Physics score on the MCAT
SA R	Skills Analysis: Reading score on the MCAT
SA Q	Skills Analysis: Quantitative score on the MCAT
SP	Science Problems score on the MCAT
na	Information not available

Table 6. Basic Data on the Medical Schools

School	Fee	Filing Dates Earliest	Filing Dates Latest	Number of Applicants	Men	Women	Out-of-State	Class Size	% with 4 years College
ALABAMA									
*University of Alabama School of Medicine	$25	6/15**	11/1	790	161	48	22	151	100
*University of South Alabama College of Medicine	$25	6/15**	11/1	634	97	31	6	64	97
ARIZONA									
*University of Arizona College of Medicine	$ 0	6/1	11/1	649	61	49	2	88	100
ARKANSAS									
*University of Arkansas College of Medicine	$10	6/15	11/15	356	101#	35#	0	136	90
CALIFORNIA									
*Loma Linda University School of Medicine	$35	6/15	11/1	2260	108#	35#	70	143	99
*Stanford University School of Medicine	$55	6/15**	10/15	5891	132	58	0	86	100
*University of California – Davis School of Medicine	$35	6/15	11/1	3376	57#	36#	3	93	100
*University of California – Irvine College of Medicine	$35	6/15	11/15	92	58#	34#	0	92	100
*University of California – Los Angeles School of Medicine	$30	6/15	11/1	4443	na	na	na	140	100
*University of California – San Diego School of Medicine	$35	6/15	11/1	4098	na	na	na	122	100
*University of California – San Francisco School of Medicine	$35	6/15	11/1	4497	85#	56#	22	141	100
*University of Southern California School of Medicine	$45	6/15**	11/1	3790	96#	40#	19	136	100
COLORADO									
*University of Colorado School of Medicine	$20	6/15**	11/1	882	na	na	na	132	98

* AMCAS school
** early decision available
na data not available
figures given are for men and women *enrolled*

Admission Statistics			Academic Statistics	Expenses		
Class Profile						
% Interviewed	% Residents	% Women	Mean MCAT	Deposit	Tuition Res/Nonres	Other
99	97	21	B-9.5 C-9.11 P-9.39 SP-9.14 R-8.95 Q-9.52	$ 50	$ 2,904 $11,616	$7,060
100	98	35	B-9.67 C-9.11 P-9.05 SP-9.14 R-9.14 Q-8.67	$ 50	$ 3,600 $ 7,200	$5,336
52	98	51	B-10 C-9.3 P-9.6 SP-9.3 R-9.4 Q-9.0	$ 0	$ 3,470 n/app	$7,230
100	100	26	B-9.7 C-9.5 P-9.1 SP-9.3 R-9.4 Q-9.1	$ 0	$ 3,500 $ 7,000	$4,334
100	51	24	Required—scores not available	$6,000	$12,500 $12,500	$5,500
100	na	34	B-11.49 C-11.95 P-12.12 SP-12.24 R-10.26 Q-10.72	$ 0	$11,424 $11,424	$6,895
100	97	39	B-11.2 C-11 P-11 SP-11.1 R-9.9 Q-9.6	$ 0	$ 1,684 $ 5,044	$8,000
100	100	37	B-10.8 C-10.8 P-10.9 SP-10.6 R-9.0 Q-9.5	$ 0	$ 1,384 $ 4,948	$5,800
100	na	na	Required—scores not available	$100	$ 1,344 $ 4,908	$7,500
100	88	36	B-11.7 C-11.9 P-12.3 SP-12.1 R-10 Q-10.6	$ 0	$ 1,365 $ 4,929	$5,660
100	84	40	B-11 C-11 P-12 SP-11 R-10 Q-10	$ 0	$ 1,438 $ 5,002	$8,070
100	86	30	B-11 C-11.1 P-11.1 SP-11.1 R-9.4 Q-9.8	$100	$13,320 $13,320	$8,995
100	na	na	Required—scores not available	$200	$ 6,348 $26,337	$5,840

Table 6. Basic Data on the Medical Schools continued

School	Fee	Filing Dates Earliest	Latest	Number of Applicants	Men	Women	Out-of-State	Class Size	% with 4 years College
CONNECTICUT									
*University of Connecticut School of Medicine	$35	6/15**	12/1	1504	94	69	16	88	100
Yale University School of Medicine	$45	6/1**	11/1	2917	na	na	na	102	100
DISTRICT OF COLUMBIA									
*George Washington University School of Medicine	$40	6/15**	12/31	6772	97#	50#	143	147	97
*Georgetown University School of Medicine	$40	6/15**	11/15	7091	na	na	na	205	100
*Howard University College of Medicine	$25	6/15	12/15	4412	140	139	266	117	91
FLORIDA									
*University of Florida College of Medicine	$15	6/15	11/15	1574	61#	24#	2	85	100
University of Miami School of Medicine	$50	7/1**	12/15	907	89#	49#	5	138	83
University of South Florida College of Medicine	$15	7/1**	10/5	863	66#	30#	2	96	97
GEORGIA									
*Emory University School of Medicine	$40	6/15	10/15	3873	126	59	116	110	100
*Medical College of Georgia	$ 0	6/15	12/1	1211	175	57	3	180	100
*Mercer University School of Medicine	$25	6/15**	12/1	1129	16#	8#	0	24	96
*Morehouse School of Medicine	$30	6/15**	12/15	2079	17#	15#	12	32	100
HAWAII									
*University of Hawaii Burns School of Medicine	$ 0	6/1**	12/1	424	37#	19#	3	56	100

* AMCAS school
** early decision available
na data not available
\# figures given are for men and women *enrolled*

Admission Statistics			Academic Statistics	Expenses		
Class Profile						
% Interviewed	% Residents	% Women	Mean MCAT	Deposit	Tuition Res/Nonres	Other
100	99	50	B-10.3 C-10.1 P-10.1 SP-10.1 R-9.5 Q-9.5	$100	$ 3,425 $ 7,980	$9,575
100	7	na	Required—scores not available	$100	$10,500 $10,500	$7,620
100	3	34	B-10.4 C-10 P-10.3 SP-10.1 R-9.0 Q-8.8	$ 0[1]	$18,500 $18,500	$7,250
100	na	na	Required—scores not available	$100	$19,600 $19,600	$8,950
100	10	46	B-8 C-7.4 P-7.7 SP-7.5 R-7.0 Q-6.5	$175	$ 4,500 $ 4,500	$9,253
100	98	28	B-10.04 C-10.02 P-10.08 SP-10 R-8.86 Q-9.38	$ 0	$ 2,674 $ 6,081	$3,980
100	95	36	B-10.1 C-10.1 P-10.1 SP-9.9 R-9.0 Q-9.1	$ 50	$10,491 $10,491	$7,450
100	98	31	B-10.2 C-9.9 P-10 SP-9.9 R-9.1 Q-9.2	$ 0	$ 2,591 $ 5,999	$7,529
100	52	31	B-10.1 C-10.3 P-10.4 SP-10.2 R-9.6 Q-9.3	$ 50	$10,450 $10,450	$7,373
100	99	27	B-9.57 C-9.16 P-9.12 SP-9.16 R-8.72 Q-8.29	$ 50	$ 2,715 $ 8,142	$6,171
100	100	33	Required—scores not available	$100	$10,500 $10,500	$8,607
100	38	47	B-7.43 C-6.53 P-6.46 SP-6.68 R-7.0 Q-6.0	$100	$ 9,000 $ 9,000	$8,834
100	95	34	B-10 C-9.6 P-9.8 SP-9.6 R-8.7 Q-9.1	$ 90	$ 3,020 $11,570	$5,930

[1] $3,000 prepayment due in July

Table 6. Basic Data on the Medical Schools continued

School	Fee	Filing Dates Earliest	Filing Dates Latest	Number of Applicants	Men	Women	Out-of-State	Class Size	% with 4 years College
ILLINOIS									
*Chicago Medical School, University of Health Sciences	$55	7/1**	11/15	5191	110#	40#	100	150	100
*Loyola University of Chicago Stritch School of Medicine	$35	6/15**	11/15	5387	83#	47#	59	130	100
*Northwestern University Medical School	$45	6/15**	11/15	5927	237	122	217	171	100
*Rush Medical College	$40	6/15**	11/15	2757	111#	57#	40	168	100
*Southern Illinois University School of Medicine	$ 0	6/15**	11/15	1022	49#	23#	0	72	100
*University of Chicago Pritzker School of Medicine	$25	6/15**	11/1	2957	na	na	na	104	99
*University of Illinois College of Medicine	$20	7/1**	12/1	3018	402	181	80	331	100
INDIANA									
*Indiana University School of Medicine	$20	6/1	12/15	1380	na	na	6	290	100
IOWA									
*University of Iowa College of Medicine	$10	6/15**	12/1	1000	na	na	na	175	95
KANSAS									
*University of Kansas School of Medicine	$15	6/15**	11/1	843	135	63	30	192	100
KENTUCKY									
*University of Kentucky College of Medicine	$ 0	7/1**	11/15	982	64#	31#	9	95	99
*University of Louisville School of Medicine	$15	6/15**	11/15	862	86#	38#	9	124	98
LOUISIANA									
*Louisiana State University School of Medicine in New Orleans	$20	7/1	11/15	806	117#	58#	0	175	na

* AMCAS school
** early decision available
na data not available
\# figures given are for men and women *enrolled*

Admission Statistics			Academic Statistics	Expenses		
Class Profile						
% Interviewed	% Residents	% Women	Mean MCAT	Deposit	Tuition Res/Nonres	Other
100	33	27	B-9.74 C-9.46 P-9.70 SP-9.49 R-8.48 Q-8.58	$100	$17,900 $17,900	$9,145
100	55	36	B-10.3 C-9.7 P-10.2 SP-9.9 R-8.8 Q-8.9	$ 0	$11,100 $13,600	$7,622
100	53	38	B-11 C-11 P-11.1 SP-11 R-9.8 Q-10	$ 0	$13,815 $13,815	$7,000
100	76	34	B-10.6 C-10.3 P-10.3 SP-10.4 R-9.3 Q-9.3	$100	$ 4,900 $ 9,100	$4,017
100	100	32	B-9.11 C-8.51 P-8.75 SP-8.6 R-8.01 Q-7.68	$100	$ 3,963 $11,889	$6,017
100	na	na	Required—scores not available	$ 50	$ 9,995 $ 9,995	$7,800
100	91	31	B-10.08 C-9.98 P-10.03 SP-9.94 R-9.02 Q-8.99	$100	$ 3,774 $11,332	$4,544
na	na	na	Required—scores not available	$ 0	$ 3,500 $ 7,500	na
100	na	na	Required—scores not available	$ 50	$ 3,920 $ 8,520	$5,588
100	87	33	B-9.9 C-9.6 P-9.8 SP-9.9 R-9.4 Q-9.2	$ 50	$ 4,830 $ 9,630	$5,625
100	90	32	B-9.0 C-9.0 P-9.0 SP-9.0 R-8.0 Q-9.0	$100	$ 3,180 $ 7,169	$7,600
100	93	31	Required—scores not available	$100	$ 3,191 $ 7,180	$7,781
na	100	33	B-9.2 C-8.7 P-8.8 SP-8.8 R-8.6 Q-8.1	$ 0	$ 2,200 $ 7,400	$9,896

Table 6. **Basic Data on the Medical Schools** *continued*

School	Fee	Filing Dates Earliest	Filing Dates Latest	Number of Applicants	Men	Women	Out-of-State	Class Size	% with 4 years College
*Louisiana State University School of Medicine in Shreveport	$20	6/15	11/15	732	75#	22#	100	100	92
*Tulane University School of Medicine	$50	7/15	12/31	4781	101#	47#	110	148	100
MARYLAND									
*Johns Hopkins University School of Medicine	$50	6/15**	11/1	2657	na	na	na	120	100
*Uniformed Services University School of Medicine	$ 0	6/15	11/1	3965	128#	29#	na	157	100
*University of Maryland School of Medicine	$20	6/15**	12/1	1692	172	87	62	152	100
MASSACHUSETTS									
*Boston University School of Medicine	$50	7/1**	11/1	6894	na	na	na	135	54
Harvard Medical School	$45	5/1	10/15	3214	91	75	141	165	na
*Tufts University School of Medicine	$50	6/15**	11/1	6518	na	na	na	145	100
*University of Massachusetts Medical School	$18	6/15**	11/1	900	na	na	0	100	100
MICHIGAN									
*Michigan State University College of Human Medicine	$20	6/15**	11/15	2145	55#	51#	19	106	98
*University of Michigan Medical School	$20	6/15**	11/15	3090	115#	52#	34	167	na
*Wayne State University School of Medicine	$25	6/15**	12/15	1916	251	123	41	256	99
MINNESOTA									
*Mayo Medical School	$40	6/15	11/15	1271	24#	16#	20	40	100
*University of Minnesota – Duluth School of Medicine	$ 0	6/15**	11/15	596	25#	31#	1	48	100

* AMCAS school
** early decision available
na data not available
\# figures given are for men and women *enrolled*

Admission Statistics			Academic Statistics		Expenses		
Class Profile							
% Interviewed	% Residents	% Women	Mean MCAT	Deposit	Tuition Res/Nonres	Other
na	100	22	B-9 C-9 P-9 SP-9 R-9 Q-9	$ 50	$ 2,200 na	na
100	25	32	B-10 C-10 P-10 SP-10 R-10 Q-10	$100	$ 9,720 $14,520	$7,520
100	na	na	Not required after 1985	$ 0	$10,300 $10,300	$8,220
100	na	18	B-10.6 C-10.4 P-10.7 SP-10.8 R-9.6 Q-9.5	$ 0	n/app n/app	$6,000
100	85	38	B-10 C-10 P-10 SP-10 R-10 Q-10	$100	$ 4,816 $ 9,630	$2,147
100	27	36	B-9.3 C-9.2 P-9.2 SP-9.0 R-8.3 Q-7.9	$500	$15,800 $15,800	$8,000
100	15	45	B-11.62 C-11.92 P-12.14 SP-12.01 R-10.31 Q-10.68	$ 0	$12,100 $12,100	$8,000
100	na	na	na	$100	$15,425 $15,425	$9,000
100	100	44	B-10.7 C-10.3 P-10.7 SP-10.5 R-9.5 Q-9.7	$ 0	$ 5,532	na
100	87	48	B-9.5 C-8.7 P-8.8 SP-8.8 R-8.8 Q-8.3	$ 50	$ 6,000 $11,000	$5,800
100	80	31	B-10.6 C-10.8 P-11 SP-10.8 R-9.4 Q-9.8	na	$ 5,928 $11,312	$4,090
100	95	30	B-10 C-9.7 P-9.8 SP-9.7 R-8.8 Q-8.7	$ 50	$ 5,330 $10,660	$8,325
100	20	16	B-10 C-10 P-10 SP-10 R-10 Q-10	$100	$ 7,000 $14,000	$7,200
100	98	48	B-9.6 C-9.3 P-9.5 SP-9.4 R-9.1 Q-8.8	$ 0	$ 6,065 $12,131	$6,475

Table 6. **Basic Data on the Medical Schools** *continued*

School	Fee	Filing Dates Earliest	Latest	Number of Applicants	Men	Women	Out-of-State	Class Size	% with 4 years College
*University of Minnesota Medical School, Minneapolis	na	na	na	na	na	na	na	na	na
MISSISSIPPI									
*University of Mississippi School of Medicine	$ 0	7/1**	12/1	554	82#	28#	0	110	100
MISSOURI									
*St. Louis University School of Medicine	$45	6/15**	12/15	4284	121#	37#	113	158	99
*University of Missouri – Columbia School of Medicine	$ 0	6/15**	11/15	1016	77#	33#	1	110	100
University of Missouri – Kansas City School of Medicine	$ 0	9/1**	11/15	404	52	58	6	90	100
*Washington University School of Medicine	$35	6/15**	11/1	5467	85#	34#	88	119	100
NEBRASKA									
*Creighton University School of Medicine	$40	6/15**	12/15	5772	78#	32#	81	110	99
*University of Nebraska College of Medicine	$ 0	6/1	11/15	348	94	36	3	120	100
NEVADA									
*University of Nevada School of Medicine	$35	6/15**	11/1	435	34#	14#	3	48	100
NEW HAMPSHIRE									
*Dartmouth Medical School	$50	6/15**	11/1	4000	111	83	167	86	100
NEW JERSEY									
*New Jersey Medical School, University of Medicine and Dentistry.	$25	6/15**	12/15	2300	111#	59#	8	170	100
*Rutgers Medical School, University of Medicine and Dentistry	$25	6/15**	12/15	2630	90#	40#	11	130	100

*   AMCAS school
** early decision available
na data not available
\# figures given are for men and women *enrolled*

Admission Statistics			Academic Statistics	Expenses		
Class Profile						
% Interviewed	% Residents	% Women	Mean MCAT	Deposit	Tuition Res/Nonres	Other
na	na	na	na	na	na	na
100	100	25	B-9 C-8.5 P-8.8 SP-8.6 R-9 Q-8.3	$100	$ 5,000 $11,000	$7,500
100	29	23	B-10.8 C-10.7 P-10.8 SP-10.7 R-9.3 Q-9.7	$100	$13,550 $13,550	$4,043
100	99	30	B-9.9 C-9.9 P-9.4 SP-9.7 R-9.3 Q-9.4	$100	$ 4,631 $ 7,459	$10,620
100	94	56	Not required	$100	$ 5,362 $ 8,582	$4,783
100	26	29	B-11.3 C-11.2 P-11.6 ℒℬ SP-11.4 R-10.2 Q-10.6	$100	$12,800 $12,800	$7,265
74	28	32	B-9.9 C-9.6 P-9.8 SP-9.5 R-8.4 Q-8.7	$100	$ 9,990 $ 9,990	$6,510
100	97	30	B-8.9 C-9.1 P-9.2 SP-9.0 R-9.1 Q-8.9	$100	$ 2,822 $ 5,020	$7,000
100	94	29	B-10.3 C-9.8 P-9.9 SP-9.9 R-8.9 Q-8.3	$ 0	$ 4,180 $ 9,900	$7,200
100	16	46	B-10 C-10 P-10 SP-10 R-10 Q-10	$ 0	$13,780 $13,780	$5,380
100	95	35	B-10.2 C-9.8 P-9.8 SP-9.7 R-8.6 Q-8.5	$100	$ 7,175 $ 8,965	$7,500
100	92	31	B-10.01 C-10 P-10.03 SP-10.2 R-9.0 Q-9.0	$ 50	$ 7,175 $ 8,965	$8,440

Table 6. **Basic Data on the Medical Schools** *continued*

School	Fee	Application Data Filing Dates Earliest	Latest	Number of Applicants	Admission Statistics Applicants Accepted Men	Women	Out-of-State	Class Profile Class Size	% with 4 years College
NEW MEXICO									
*University of New Mexico School of Medicine	$10	6/1**	12/1	401	40#	33#	7	73	100
NEW YORK									
Albany Medical College, Union University	$60	7/1	11/1	2682	161	97	64	127	100
*Albert Einstein College of Medicine, Yeshiva University	$50	6/15	11/15	5525	178	294	177	176	100
Columbia University College of Physicians and Surgeons	$40	7/1	10/15	3268	103#	45#	69	148	100
*Cornell University Medical School	$45	6/15	11/15	5861	123	78	122	101	100
Mount Sinai School of Medicine, City University of New York	$50	8/1	10/31	2797	64#	41#	27	105	98
*New York Medical College	$50	6/15**	12/1	3933	124	56	134	182	97
New York University School of Medicine	$40	8/15	12/15	4059	295	101	47	155	99
*SUNY at Buffalo School of Medicine	$40	6/15	12/1	3090	82#	53#	3	135	100
SUNY at Stony Brook School of Medicine	$50	7/1	12/15	2361	na	na	na	100	100
*SUNY Downstate Medical Center College of Medicine	$50	6/1	12/15	3215	142#	58#	9	200	91
*SUNY Upstate Medical Center College of Medicine	$50	7/15	12/15	3355	na	na	na	145	na
University of Rochester School of Medicine	$50	7/1	11/1	2871	158	97	96	106	100
NORTH CAROLINA									
*Bowman Gray School of Medicine, Wake Forest University	$40	7/1	11/1	3847	163	85	103	108	100

*   AMCAS school
** early decision available
na data not available
\# figures given are for men and women *enrolled*

Admission Statistics			Academic Statistics	Expenses		
Class Profile						
% Interviewed	% Residents	% Women	Mean MCAT	Deposit	Tuition Res/Nonres	Other
100	90	45	B-9.49 C-9.25 P-9.19 SP-9.23 R-9.11 Q-8.52	$ 0	$ 1,320 $ 3,586	$6,469
100	76	32	B-10 C-9.9 P-10 SP-9.9 R-9.2 Q-9	$100	$14,200 $14,200	$5,365
100	72	41	B-11.1 C-11.2 P-11.4 SP-11.1 R-9.7 Q-10.0	$100	$13,100 $13,100	$6,950
100	53	30	Required—scores not available	$ 0	$12,250 $12,250	$8,215
100	54	40	B-11.2 C-11.3 P-11.1 SP-11.1 R-9.9 Q-10	$100	$13,660 $13,660	$6,740
100	74	39	B-10.4 C-10.3 P-10.5 SP-10.1 R-8.9 Q-8.5	$100	$13,000 $13,000	$7,525
100	74	31	B-9.52 C-9.27 P-9.44 SP-9.21 R-8.72 Q-8.55	$100	$17,200 $17,200	$9,292
100	70	24	B-11 C-11 P-11 SP-11 R-10 Q-11	$100	$13,100 $13,150	$2,050
100	98	39	B-10 C-9.7 P-9.7 SP-9.8 R-9.0 Q-8.7	$100	$ 5,550 $ 8,300	$6,869
100	na	na	Required—scores not available	$ 0	$ 5,550 $ 8,300	$8,000
100	95	29	B-10.9 C-11 P-11.4 SP-11 R-9.5 Q-9.5	$ 50	$ 5,500 $ 8,900	na
100	97	39	B-10.3 C-9.9 P-10.2 SP-9.9 R-9.1 Q-8.9	$100	$ 5,550 $ 8,850	$6,255
100	60	29	Not required	$ 0	$12,300 $12,300	$7,018
100	60	31	B-9.62 C-9.43 P-9.59 SP-9.41 R-9.31 Q-9.14	$100	$ 8,400 $ 8,400	$6,900

Table 6. Basic Data on the Medical Schools *continued*

School	Fee	Filing Dates Earliest	Filing Dates Latest	Number of Applicants	Men	Women	Out-of-State	Class Size	% with 4 years College
*Duke University School of Medicine	$45	6/1	11/1	3100	158	93	49	113	99
*East Carolina University School of Medicine	$15	6/15**	12/1	1022	na	na	na	68	100
*University of North Carolina School of Medicine	$25	6/15**	11/15	2344	na	na	na	160	100
NORTH DAKOTA									
University of North Dakota School of Medicine	$15	7/1	11/1	177	40#	15#	5	55	98
OHIO									
*Case Western Reserve University School of Medicine	$30	6/15**	11/15	5583	77#	61#	55	138	100
*Medical College of Ohio	$30	6/15**	11/1	1692	93#	57#	3	150	100
*Northeastern Ohio Universities College of Medicine	$20	6/15**	11/1	869	na	na	na	105	na
*Ohio State University School of Medicine	$10	6/15**	11/15	2082	154#	79#	10	233	97
*University of Cincinnati College of Medicine	$25	6/15**	11/15	4206	126#	66#	38	192	99
*Wright State University School of Medicine	$25	6/15**	11/15	1573	72#	28#	2	100	100
OKLAHOMA									
*Oral Roberts University School of Medicine	$30	6/15**	11/1	1217	na	na	na	48	100
*University of Oklahoma College of Medicine	$50	6/15	11/1	848	na	na	na	176	97
OREGON									
*Oregon Health Sciences University School of Medicine	$25	none	11/15	676	67#	23#	0	90	100

*   AMCAS school
** early decision available
na data not available
figures given are for men and women *enrolled*

Admission Statistics			Academic Statistics		Expenses		
Class Profile							
% Interviewed	% Residents	% Women	Mean MCAT	Deposit		Tuition Res/Nonres	Other
100	27	31	Required—scores not available	$ 50		$ 9,180 $ 9,180	$7,441
100	na	na	Required—scores not available	na		$ 1,070 $ 3,826	$5,996
100	na	na	Required—scores not available	$100		$ 1,070 $ 3,826	$4,917
100	91	25	B-9 C-8.14 P-8.54 SP-8.34 R-9.34 Q-8.5	$ 75		$ 2,600 $ 5,200	$7,500
100	60	44	Required—scores not available	$ 0		$11,350 $11,350	$8,730
100	97	37	B-9.1 C-9.0 P-8.9 SP-9.0 R-9.3 Q-9.2	na		$ 1,800 $ 2,450	$8,600
100	99	31	B-9.5 C-8.8 P-9.5 SP-9.4 R-9.0 Q-9.0	$ 0		$ 3,750 $ 7,500	na
100	95	33	B-9.8 C-9.8 P-9.8 SP-9.8 R-9.8 Q-9.8	$ 0		$ 4,284 $11,685	$5,187
100	80	33	B-10.2 C-9.8 P-10.3 SP-10 R-9.2 Q-9.3	$ 0		$ 5,529 $ 8,648	$4,995
100	98	28	B-9 C-8 P-8 SP-8 R-8 Q-8	$ 0		$ 5,400 $ 7,980	$7,135
100	8	25	Required—scores not available	$100		$ 8,500 $ 8,500	$7,150
100	na	na	Required—scores not available	$100		$ 2,296 $ 5,751	$5,000
100	100	26	B-11 C-10.9 P-11.3 SP-10.9 R-9.8 Q-10.3	$ 0		$ 4,565 $ 9,254	$6,117

Table 6. Basic Data on the Medical Schools *continued*

School	Fee	Filing Dates Earliest	Filing Dates Latest	Number of Applicants	Men	Women	Out-of-State	Class Size	% with 4 years College
PENNSYLVANIA									
*Hahnemann University School of Medicine	$50	6/15**	11/15	6017	na	na	na	170	98
*Jefferson Medical College, Thomas Jefferson University	$55	6/15**	11/15	223	164#	59#	97	223	99
*Medical College of Pennsylvania	$50	6/15**	12/1	4243	na	na	na	101	92
*Pennsylvania State University College of Medicine	$40	6/15	11/15	1441	165	89	36	95	98
*Temple University School of Medicine	$35	6/1**	12/1	4677	133#	44#	37	177	100
*University of Pennsylvania School of Medicine	$50	6/15	11/1	5809	na	na	na	155	100
*University of Pittsburgh School of Medicine	$40	6/15**	11/1	3062	88#	48#	44	136	100
RHODE ISLAND									
*Brown University Program in Medicine	$60	8/15**	11/1	1112	86	70	130	73	77
SOUTH CAROLINA									
*Medical University of South Carolina College of Medicine	$15	6/15**	12/1	1004	na	na	na	159	97
*University of South Carolina School of Medicine	$20	6/15**	12/1	657	44#	20#	9	64	95
SOUTH DAKOTA									
*University of South Dakota School of Medicine	$50	6/15	11/15	393	45	15	4	50	98
TENNESSEE									
*East Tennessee State University College of Medicine	$15	6/15**	12/1	1015	35#	21#	2	56	100
*Meharry Medical College School of Medicine	$25	6/15**	12/15	3542	na	na	na	80	99

*   AMCAS school
** early decision available
na data not available
\# figures given are for men and women *enrolled*

Admission Statistics			Academic Statistics	Expenses		
Class Profile						
% Interviewed	% Residents	% Women	Mean MCAT	Deposit	Tuition Res/Nonres	Other
100	55	30	B-10 C-10 P-10 SP-10 R-9 Q-10	$100	$14,600 $14,600	$7,310
na	56	26	B-10.6 C-10.4 P-10.5 SP-10.3 R-9.3 Q-9.6	$100	$13,175 $13,175	$7,638
100	74	60	B-9.4 C-9.0 P-9.0 SP-9.0 R-9.0 Q-8.5	$100	$12,425 $12,425	$1,580
100	87	34	B-10 C-10 P-10 SP-10 R-10 Q-10	$100	$ 8,084 $12,628	$8,790
100	21	25	B-10 C-10 P-10 SP-10 R-10 Q-10	$100	$ 9,888 $13,426	$7,600
100	na	na	Required—scores not available	$100	$12,535 $12,535	$8,215
100	68	35	B-9.8 C-10.1 P-10 SP-9.8 R-9.2 Q-9.5	$ 0	$12,100 $16,900	$10,720
na	26	51	B-10.04 C-9.7 P-9.64 SP-9.85 R-9.08 Q-8.59	$100	$13,330 $13,330	$6,504
100	na	na	Required—scores not available	$ 50	$ 3,300 $ 6,600	$7,660
100	86	31	Required—scores not available	$100	$ 3,000 $ 6,000	$8,400
100	94	26	B-9.02 C-8.5 P-8.72 SP-8.86 R-8.76 Q-8.48	$100	$ 5,200 $10,800	$2,770
100	97	38	B-8.9 C-8.2 P-8.2 SP-8.0 R-8.3 Q-7.5	$100	$ 4,266 $ 6,820	$5,335
100	14	35	B-7.8 C-7.5 P-7.9 SP-7.3 R-7.2 Q-6.5	$100	$ 9,500 $ 9,500	$8,299

Table 6. Basic Data on the Medical Schools continued

School	Fee	Filing Dates Earliest	Filing Dates Latest	Number of Applicants	Men	Women	Out-of-State	Class Size	% with 4 years College
University of Tennessee College of Medicine	$25	none	10/15	699	164	51	22	180	99
*Vanderbilt University School of Medicine	$25	6/15**	11/1	4661	74#	29#	83	103	100
TEXAS									
Baylor College of Medicine	$35	6/15**	11/15	3118	109#	59#	50	168	99
Texas A & M University College of Medicine	$35	6/1	11/1	1260	30#	19#	5	49	65
Texas Tech University School of Medicine	$30	4/15**	11/1	992	73#	27#	0	100	97
University of Texas Medical Branch at Galveston	$35	3/15	10/15	2342	147	54	na	203	99
University of Texas Medical School at Houston	$35	5/1	10/15	2700	127#	75#	18	202	95
University of Texas Medical School at San Antonio	$35	4/15	10/15	2574	142#	62#	18	204	97
University of Texas, Southwestern Medical School at Dallas	$70	4/15	10/15	2681	141	66	20	208	97
UTAH									
*University of Utah School of Medicine	$25	6/15**	10/15	569	75#	25#	23	100	100
VERMONT									
*University of Vermont College of Medicine	$25	6/15	11/1	2890	45#	48#	52#	93	99
VIRGINIA									
*Eastern Virginia Medical School	$50	6/15**	11/15	1317	128	81	31	96	100
*Medical College of Virginia, Virginia Commonwealth University	$25	6/15**	11/15	2554	76#	44#	12	120	99

* AMCAS school
** early decision available
na data not available
\# figures given are for men and women *enrolled*

Admission Statistics			Academic Statistics	Expenses		
Class Profile						
% Interviewed	% Residents	% Women	Mean MCAT	Deposit	Tuition Res/Nonres	Other
100	93	21	B-10 C-10 P-10 SP-10 R-9 Q-9	$100	$ 4,350 $ 6,903	$6,000
100	20	28	B-11 C-11 P-11 SP-11 R-10 Q-11	$ 50	$ 9,500 $ 9,500	$6,662
100	70	35	B-11 C-10.6 P-10.9 SP-10.8 R-9.6 Q-9.8	$100	$ 400 $ 8,400	$12,035
80	90	19	Required—combined score 54.89	$ 0	$ 300 $ 900	$6,550
100	100	27	B-9.23 C-8.86 P-8.69 SP-8.9 R-8.42 Q-8.31	$100	$ 300 $ 900	$8,579
100	90	25	B-10.2 C-9.4 P-9.7 SP-9.8 R-8.9 Q-8.7	na	$ 400 $ 1,200	$11,047
100	90	37	B-9.6 C-9.0 P-9.3 SP-9.1 R-8.7 Q-8.5	$ 0	$ 300 $ 900	$8,445
99	91	30	na	$ 0	$ 400 $ 1,200	$12,011
100	90	32	B-10.6 C-10.2 P-10.5 SP-10.5 R-9.6 Q-9.6	$ 0	$ 300 $ 900	na
100	77	25	B-11 C-11 P-11 SP-11 R-9 Q-10	$100	$ 3,111 $ 6,741	$3,724
100	44	52	B-9.86 C-9.53 P-9.37 SP-9.46 R-9.69 Q-9.51	$100	$ 6,540 $16,350	$7,135
100	84	32	B-9.7 C-9.1 P-9.0 SP-8.9 R-8.9 Q-8.4	$100	$10,000 $14,000	$6,735
100	100	37	B-10.5 C-9.8 P-10 SP-9.8 R-8.7 Q-8.7	$100	$12,540 $12,540	$5,025

Table 6. **Basic Data on the Medical Schools** *continued*

School	Fee	Application Data		Number of Applicants	Admission Statistics				
		Filing Dates			Applicants Accepted			Class Profile	
		Earliest	Latest		Men	Women	Out-of-State	Class Size	% with 4 years College
*University of Virginia School of Medicine	$40	8/1**	11/15	2952	106#	33#	32	139	100
WASHINGTON									
*University of Washington School of Medicine	$35	6/15	11/1	1763	111#	65#	9	176	100
WEST VIRGINIA									
*Marshall University School of Medicine	$10	6/15	11/15	584	29#	19#	3	48	94
West Virginia University School of Medicine	$30	6/1	11/30	386	60#	28#	6	88	98
WISCONSIN									
*Medical College of Wisconsin	$35	6/15**	12/1	3311	260	114	209	202	90
*University of Wisconsin Medical School	$20	6/15**	11/15	1328	na	na	na	155	94
CANADA									
Dalhousie University Faculty of Medicine	$15	10/1	12/15	457	na	na	na	96	90
Laval University Faculty of Medicine	$25	3/1**	3/1	1367	65	80	10	150	na
McGill University Faculty of Medicine	$15	8/1	12/1	1483	105	53	53	160	69
*McMaster University Faculty of Medicine	$13	8/1	11/15	2866	47#	53#	0	100	43
Memorial University Faculty of Medicine	$25	10/19	1/15	56	39#	17#	14	56	43
Queen's University Faculty of Medicine	$13	7/1	11/15	2407	46#	30#	9	76	na
Université de Sherbrooke Faculte de Medecine	$15	12/1**	3/1	1775	37	68	7	na	na
University of Alberta Faculty of Medicine	$50	7/1	12/1	819	80#	40#	0	120	28

* AMCAS school
** early decision available
na data not available
figures given are for men and women *enrolled*

| Admission Statistics | | | Academic Statistics | Expenses | | |
| Class Profile | | | | | | |
% Interviewed	% Residents	% Women	Mean MCAT	Deposit	Tuition Res/Nonres	Other
na	75	23	B-10.58 C-10.37 P-10.78 SP-10.6 R-9.46 Q-9.77	$100	$ 4,918 $ 9,738	$4,148
100	95	37	B-10.7 C-10.5 P-10.6 SP-10.6 R-9.7 Q-9.5	$ 50	$ 3,054 $ 7,734	$5,625
100	94	40	B-8.0 C-8.0 P-7.8 SP-7.9 R-8.8 Q-7.9	$ 0	$ 1,690 $ 4,300	$4,212
100	93	32	B-9.5 C-9.7 P-9.4 SP-9.5 R-9.3 Q-8.9	$ 50	$ 2,090 $ 4,790	$2,700
100	54	27	B-9.95 C-9.77 P-9.76 SP-9.64 R-8.89 Q-8.69	$100	$ 7,500 $13,000	$12,619
100	na	na	Required—scores not available	na	$ 6,014 $ 8,732	$4,180
100	94	na	Required—scores not available	$100	$ 1,733 $ 3,033	$7,093
na	na	53	Not required	$ 0	$ 278 $ 566	na
100	37	37	B-11.07 C-10.98 P-10.85 SP-11.01 R-9.5 Q-9.7	$ 0	$ 718 $ 5,800	$8,615
100	93	53	Not required	$ 0	$ 2,308 $ 9,802	$8,720
65	75	31	Required—scores not available	$100	$ 936 $ 936	$4,947
39	62	30	B-10.9 C-9.5 P-9.9 SP-9.9 R-9.7 Q-9.6	$ 0	$ 1,401 $ 6,160	$4,502
na	na	na	na	na	$ 1,000 $ 5,800	na
100	96	33	B-9.7 C-9.3 P-9.1 SP-9.4 R-8.9 Q-9.1	$ 50	$ 1,340 $ 1,961	$5,845

Table 6. **Basic Data on the Medical Schools** continued

| School | Fee | Filing Dates | | Number of Applicants | Applicants Accepted | | | Class Profile | |
		Earliest	Latest		Men	Women	Out-of-State	Class Size	% with 4 years College
University of British Columbia Faculty of Medicine	$25	8/15**	1/15	593	85#	45#	1	130	na
University of Calgary Faculty of Medicine	$20	7/1	11/30	982	40#	32#	22	72	92
University of Manitoba Faculty of Medicine	na	11/1	1/2	250	66#	29#	0	95	18
University of Montreal Faculty of Medicine	$15	12/1	3/1	1874	108	131	4	102	35
University of Ottawa Faculty of Medicine	$13	7/15	11/15	2178	45	36	8	84	25
University of Saskatchewan College of Medicine	$25	9/1	1/15	271	32#	28#	0	60	21
University of Toronto Faculty of Medicine	$13	7/1	11/15	2508	167#	85#	18	252	21
University of Western Ontario Faculty of Medicine	$13	7/1	11/15	2069	74#	31#	0	105	19

* AMCAS school
** early decision available
na data not available
\# figures given are for men and women *enrolled*

IN-DEPTH SCHOOL PROFILES

The medical school profiles consist of in-depth descriptions of the 123 fully accredited medical schools and the 16 Canadian medical schools.

The profiles cover admission procedures and require-ments, curricula, grading and promotion policies, facilities, and special features, as described below.

Admissions Though the minimum requirement for most schools is at least three years (90 credit hours) of undergraduate study at an accredited college, the percentage of those accepted with only this background is small. *The MCAT is required by almost all schools*, although in exceptional circumstances admission can be secured without having taken this exam, or it may be made contingent on securing satisfactory scores when taken at a later date. *Basic or minimum science courses* means one year of biology, inorganic chemistry, organic chemistry, and physics plus appropriate laboratory work. Some schools have additional requirements such

Admission Statistics			Academic Statistics		Expenses		
Class Profile							
% Interviewed	% Residents	% Women	Mean MCAT	Deposit		Tuition Res/Nonres	Other
100	99	35	B-10.32 C-10.65 P-10.08 SP-10.5 R-9.28 Q-9.36	$100		$ 2,000 $ 2,000	$4,922
100	69	44	B-10.07 C-8.92 P-8.96 SP-9.23 R-9.37 Q-8.95	$100		$ 1,642 $ 2,463	$7,320
100	100	30	B-10.03 C-10.12 P-9.78 SP-9.96 R-9.53 Q-9.48	$100		$ 1,600 $ 1,600	$7,100
100	98	44	Not required	na		$ 740 $ 4,350	$5,500
100	75	48	Required—scores not available	$100		$ 1,574 $ 6,878	$8,634
100	100	47	Not required	na		$ 1,462	$ 5,015
100	93	34	Required—scores not available	$ 0		$ 1,472 $ 7,114	$4,763
100	100	30	B-9.4 C-9.6 P-9.6 SP-9.4 R-8.9 Q-9.2	$ 0		$ 1,607 $ 6,598	$3,500

as English, mathematics, or certain advanced science courses. These are indicated along with any recommended courses. Since an interview is almost always by invitation, it is not indicated in each entry as a prerequisite for admission. *Transfer and advanced standing:* Transferring from one American medical school to another may present problems because of variations in curricula and length of programs. When these issues present no problem and space is available, transfer can be made at the end of the academic year. American citizens studying at foreign medical schools may be considered for admission to advanced standing, usually into the third-year class, at some schools. Generally, they must have completed their basic science courses and have taken the Medical Sciences Knowledge Profile examination.

Curriculum Each curriculum is indicated as to length and type. The classifications used (except where a school preferred not to be identified in this manner) are: *traditional* (basic sciences are taught during first two years using departmental or non-integrated format. Last two years consist of clerkships in major and minor clinical specialties with little or no time allotted for electives); *semi-traditional* (basic sciences are taught in traditional manner. Third year is devoted to clerkships in major specialties. Fourth year is mainly devoted to electives. Clinical correlation with basic sciences is usually provided); *semi-modern* (one of the two years devoted to basic sciences is presented using a core or organ systems approach. Third year is devoted to clerkships in major specialties and fourth year is mainly for electives. Clinical correlation with basic sciences is emphasized and student is introduced to patient early in preclinical program); *modern* (both basic science years are presented using core or organ systems approach. Third year is devoted to clerkships in major clinical specialties and fourth year consists mainly of electives. Clinical correlation with basic sciences is strongly emphasized and student is introduced to patient very early in preclinical program). The following terms will be useful in understanding the various school curricula:

introductory basic medical science courses Generally means anatomy, physiology, and biochemistry.

advanced basic medical science courses Generally means microbiology, pharmacology, and pathology.

clerkships Service on a hospital ward where medical student works under direct supervision of a physician and becomes directly involved in the care of patients.

major clinical specialties Usually medicine, surgery, pediatrics, obstetrics-gynecology, and psychiatry-neurology.

minor clinical specialties Generally anesthesiology, dermatology, otolaryngology, ophthalmology, radiology, and public health-preventive medicine.

subspecialty Specialized area of major specialty. For example, subspecialties of surgery are orthopedic surgery, neurosurgery, thoracic surgery, cardiac surgery, urology, etc.

preceptorship Service in a medical office or home situation where student works under supervision of family physician and becomes initiated into patient care in nonhospital format.

Grading and Promotion Policies The system used is not the same in all schools, so it is specifically identified for each school. Promotion usually is determined by a faculty committee and specific details concerning the policy of individual schools is outlined. Some schools require students to take only Parts I and II of the NMBE examinations. Others may require a passing total score for promotion to the third year and graduation.

Facilities *Teaching:* Facilities are of two kinds: those used for basic sciences and those used in clinical instruction. The former usually contain teaching and research laboratories, lecture rooms, and departmental and faculty offices. Clinical teaching occurs in hospitals with major facilities usually located on campus adjacent to basic science building. Other hospitals in city or area may be affiliated with school (for example, have a contractual arrangement whereby medical school faculty partly or completely staffs the hospital and uses its beds in teaching). Campus hospitals are frequently owned by the school and are then referred to as University Hospitals. Major teaching and affiliated hospitals are noted in the descriptions and the number of beds indicated. *Other:* Facilities concern the research and library facilities associated with the medical school. *Housing:* Facilities include information for single and married students. Off-campus accommodations are available near most schools and the Office of Student Affairs of the school may be able to assist students in securing such facilities. Details as to size, furnishings, and rental costs may be given in the school catalog.

Special Features This section deals with two topics, *minority admissions* and *other degree programs*. In the former, the extent of a school's recruiting efforts of underrepresented students is identified and special summer programs are noted. Under the latter heading, combined programs (especially MD-PhD programs) are identified, and any unique areas of graduate training that are not part of the traditional basic sciences are mentioned.

ALABAMA

> **University of Alabama**
> School of Medicine
> University Station
> Birmingham, Alabama 35294

Admissions (AMCAS) Additional courses beyond the basic science requirements are recommended in the behavioral sciences. Only nonresidents of superior ability are accepted. Upon admission students are assigned to the Birmingham, Tuscaloosa, or Huntsville campus for clinical experience. The basic sciences are completed at Birmingham by all students.

Curriculum 4-year semi-traditional. *First and second years:* Consist of education in the basic medical sciences as related to human biology and pathology. This is followed by an integrated study of organ system function and disorders. The humanities as related to medicine are also studied, and the skills necessary for physical diagnosis are developed. *Third and fourth years:* Consist of required rotations through clinical science disciplines, including participation in the cases of patients in both hospital and ambulatory settings (under faculty supervision). The clinical training curriculum requirements are similar at all three training centers.

Grading and Promotion Policies A letter system is used for required courses and Pass/Fail for electives. All grades of *D* and *F* require remedial work satisfactory to the faculty. Obtaining a total passing score on Parts I and II of the NBME exam is required for promotion to the third year and graduation after the fourth, respectively.

Facilities *Teaching:* The school is part of the University's Medical Center. The Basic Science Building contains teaching facilities and administrative and faculty offices. The major clinical teaching facility is the University Hospital (817 beds) in Birmingham. Other facilities utilized are the VA Hospital (479 beds), the Children's Hospital, the Cooper Green Hospital, the Eye Foundation Hospital, and various community hospitals. *Other:* The Lyons-Harrison Research Building, Tinsley Harrison Tower and basic science research and education buildings are the primary research facilities. Clinical facilities utilized in Tuscaloosa are the Druid City Hospital, the VA Medical Center and the Capstone Medical Center. The Huntsville Hospital and the Ambulatory Care Center in Huntsville are also used. *Library:* The Lister Hill Library of the Health Sciences is a 4-story structure that contains over 150,000 volumes. *Housing:* There are 178 modern apartment units in the Medical Center consisting of 28 efficiency, 84 one-bedroom, 62 two-bedroom and 4 three-bedroom apartments. Preference is given to married students but consideration is given to single students for occupancy of the smaller units.

Special Features *Fellowships:* Minority Student Program to discover and encourage study of medicine among minority group members. The program awards summer fellowships to premedical and medical students. *Other degree programs:* Dual MD-PhD program; continuing education program for graduates.

> **University of South Alabama**
> College of Medicine
> Mobile, Alabama 36688

Admissions (AMCAS) Required courses include the basic premedical sciences, English composition, one year of calculus (or one semester of calculus and one of statistics), and one year of humanities. Recommended courses include quantitative analysis, comparative vertebrate anatomy, and vertebrate embryology. Nonresidents should have higher MCAT and grade point averages in order to be accepted. *Transfer and advanced standing:* None.

Curriculum 4-year semi-traditional. *First year:* Devoted to the basic sciences; includes a course in basic cardiac life support. Emphasis is on interdisciplinary teaching, largely based on organ systems, with early and integrative clinical exposure. Courses entitled Medical Ethics, Health and Human Values, and Medical Practice and Society are also offered. *Second year:* Consists of advanced basic science courses and an opportunity for clinical exposure. Behavioral science, medical genetics, and public health and epidemiology are also covered. *Third year:* Consists of 52 weeks of required clerkships, including one in family practice. *Fourth year:* Composed of twelve 4-week rotations. One must be in neurosciences and one in the surgical subspecialties.

Grading and Promotion Policies A number system is used in the basic and required clinical sciences. A system of Honors/Pass/Fail is used for courses for which numerical evaluation is not possible and for all fourth year electives. Passing Parts I and II of the NBME exam is needed in order to graduate.

Facilities *Teaching:* The basic sciences are housed in the Medical Sciences Building on the 1200-acre university campus in the western section of Mobile. Clinical teaching is conducted at the 400-bed University Medical Center. *Other:* Other facilities include the Moorer Clinical Sciences Building, a newer Clinical Sciences Building, Primate Research Laboratory, Laboratory of Molecular Biology, Family Practice Center, Mastin Building, Pediatric Outpatient Clinic, and Psychiatric Building. *Library:* The Biomedical Library contains over 65,000 volumes and receives about 2500 periodicals. *Housing:* Furnished residence halls on campus are available for unmarried students. A university-owned subdivision immediately adjacent to campus offers housing for both married and single students.

Special Features *Minority admissions:* An active recruitment program is coordinated by the Office of Student Affairs. *Other degree programs:* Combined MD-PhD degree programs are offered in the basic medical sciences.

ARIZONA

University of Arizona
College of Medicine
Tucson, Arizona 85724

Admissions (AMCAS) Basic premedical science courses plus two semesters of English are required for admission. Applicants from states other than those in the WICHE program are not considered. *Transfer and advanced standing:* Students attending 2-year medical schools and foreign schools are considered. Those attending approved schools may apply after 2 years of study; those in nonapproved schools should apply after 2 years of study. Foreign transfers must take the MSKP exam.

Curriculum 4-year semi-traditional. *First-year:* A 40-week period when the basic sciences are presented. Patient contact is provided and the behavioral sciences are emphasized. *Second year:* A 36-week period consisting of advanced basic science courses and a continuation of the introduction to clinical sciences. *Third year:* A 48-week period when the clinical sciences are presented with at least 6 weeks of clerkships in each of the principal departments. *Fourth year:* A 33-week period for electives in the student's career path.

Grading and Promotion Policies An Honors/Pass/Fail system is in operation. A written evaluation which characterizes specific student performance is also recorded with the Office of Student Affairs. The major criterion for promotion is that the student passes all required courses in the curriculum during each academic year. The student may repeat a course only once. A score must be recorded for both Parts I and II of the NBME exam.

Facilities *Teaching:* The Arizona Medical Center is located adjacent to the University campus and consists of four interconnected buildings: Basic Science Building, Clinical Science Building, Outpatient Clinic, and University hospital (300 beds). *Other:* Additional facilities used are the Tucson Veterans Administration Hospital and other area hospitals. *Library:* The Health Sciences Center Library is part of the Medical Center and houses 120,000 volumes and 3000 medical journals. It is the only major biomedical library in the area. *Housing:* Some rooms are available for single students in the University residence halls and for married students at the University's Family Housing Project (a 420-unit building).

Special Features First and second years of instruction take place in a specially designed multidisciplinary laboratory; each student occupies an assigned study area for personal use at any time. Students work with faculty in caring for the health needs of the Tucson Model Cities area. The Division of Social Perspectives allows students to attend seminars on drug abuse, community health, law and medicine, abortion, death, and sexual adjustment. Continuing education is available to graduates.

ARKANSAS

University of Arkansas
College of Medicine
4301 West Markham Street
Little Rock, Arkansas 72205

Admissions (AMCAS) Recommended courses beyond the premedical science requirements include genetics or embryology, quantitative analysis, statistics or calculus, psychology, anthropology, world history, and literature. Nonresidents should have a GPA of over 3.5 and MCAT scores of 10 or more in each subtest. *Transfer and advanced standing:* College accepts transfer students from foreign and domestic medical schools. Foreign students must take the MSKP exam. Advanced standing is offered for transfer students, depending upon previous medical school credits.

Curriculum 4-year semi-traditional. *First year:* (36 weeks) Introductory basic sciences as well as opportunity for patient contact by means of courses entitled Introduction to the Patient and Radiographic Anatomy. *Second year:* (32 weeks) Consists of the advanced basic sciences and courses in genetics and physical diagnosis. *Third year:* (48 weeks) Consists of clerkship rotation through the major clinical specialties. *Fourth year:* (from 36 to 48 weeks) Open to more than 200 electives selected with advice of a faculty adviser. Research may be carried out as part of elective. Off-campus study locally or elsewhere in U.S. or abroad may be selected.

Grading and Promotion Policies A letter grading system is used in basic sciences and required clinical sciences; a Pass/Fail system is used in electives. Subjective assessments are used by a Promotions Committee in determining a student's eligibility for promotion. A passing grade must be recorded for each section of Part I of the NBME exam for promotion to the third year.

Facilities *Teaching:* Medical Center includes a 9-story Education Building which provides basic science facilities. University hospital (400 beds) is the principal site for clinical training. The School is affiliated with the Arkansas Children's Hospital and VA Hospitals in Little Rock and North Little Rock. It cooperates with other Little Rock hospitals in its training programs. *Other:* T.H. Barton Institute of Medical Research, Child Study Center (a part of the Greater Little Rock Comprehensive Mental Health Program), Arkansas State Hospital for Nervous Diseases. *Housing:* All single students are required to live at Medical Center in the residence hall unless special exemption is received. Approximately 90 one-bedroom furnished apartments are available for married students.

Special Features *Minority admissions:* The college's Office of Minority Student Affairs conducts programs designed to identify and assist prospective admission candidates among minority and disadvantaged students in the state. *Other degree* *programs:* Dual MS-MD program available, offered in conjunction with Graduate School of the University. Medical Student Research Program enables students to work in selected areas of research. Work done under this program may be applied toward MS degree.

CALIFORNIA

Loma Linda University
School of Medicine
Loma Linda, California 92350

Admissions (AMCAS) Required courses include minimum science courses plus English. The MCAT also is required. Preference is shown to members of the Seventh-Day Adventist Church, but it is a firm policy of the Admissions Committee to admit each year a number of nonchurch-related applicants who have demonstrated a strong commitment to Christian principles.

Curriculum 4-year traditional. The freshman year is devoted to the basic sciences as well as behavioral science, community medicine, and physical diagnosis. The sophomore year includes the standard advanced basic science courses as well as continued work in community medicine and physical diagnosis. The last two are clinical years with the didactic work integrated with ward and clinic assignments. Three months are set aside for an elective experience.

Grading and Promotion Policies Students are evaluated on a Pass/Fail basis. However, class ranks are determined on a scaled system. Passing Part I of National Boards is required for promotion to clinical clerkships. Obtaining a total passing score on Parts I and II of the NBME exam is required for promotion to the third year and graduation after the fourth, respectively.

Facilities *Teaching:* School is located on the University campus. Clinical teaching takes place at the University hospital (500 beds) and several affiliated hospitals. *Other:* A medium-scale, general-purpose computer facility serves the students and faculty of the University in instructional and research functions. *Library:* Medical and related fields make up more than half of the holdings of the Vernier Radcliff Memorial Library located on campus.

Special Features *Minority admissions:* The school sponsors a summer program for recruitment of disadvantaged under-graduate juniors and some accepted freshman class members. *Other degree programs:* MD-MS and MD-PhD programs are available.

Stanford University
School of Medicine
851 Welch Road
Palo Alto, California 94304

Admissions (AMCAS) The standard premedical courses are required. Recommended courses are calculus, biochemistry,

physical chemistry, and behavioral sciences. School does admit a few students after 3 years of college. No preference is shown to California residents. *Transfer and advanced standing:* Foreign applicants must have completed a minimum of one year of study in a U.S., Canadian, or United Kingdom accredited college or university. Particular consideration is given to applicants with disadvantaged backgrounds.

Curriculum Semi-modern. The curriculum aims to develop students' capacities for innovative leadership in clinical practice and to maximize their opportunities to prepare for careers in research and teaching in the various branches of clinical and social medicine and biomedical sciences. The curricular plan affords wide opportunities for academic, research and cultural activities in the medical school and university. Educational requirements include work in the basic sciences and clinical experiences in medicine, surgery, pediatrics, gynecology-obstetrics, and psychiatry. All MD candidates must satisfactorily complete at least 13 quarters of academic work. Students are encouraged to take an optional fifth year to pursue research or other interests. Thus the duration of the medical school program is flexible, ranging from 3 to 5 years.

Grading and Promotion Policies The grading system is Pass/Fail/Marginal Performance in the basic sciences and clinical clerkships. Narrative evaluations are also used in the clerkships. Part I of the NBME exam must be passed at a level set by the NBME, and each section of Part II must be passed in order to graduate.

Facilities *Teaching:* The School is part of the Stanford University Medical Center and consists of a complex of 8 units under one roof. The basic science departments are located mostly in the complex (with 3 departments being in nearby buildings on campus). The major clinical teaching facility is the University hospital (663 beds) that occupies 3 full units of the complex with an additional unit housing the University clinics. There are 3 other institutions which provide additional sites for teaching. The Children's Hospital (65 beds) specializes in acute and chronic care for children with major illnesses. The Santa Clara Valley Medical Center, located near the campus, has 672 beds, including 78 for tuberculosis and 180 for long-term care. *Other:* The Palo Alto Veterans Administration Hospital, about 4 miles from the Medical Center, has 1000 beds, including 469 beds for neurology and psychiatry. *Library:* The Lane Medical Library contains over 280,000 volumes and over 3000 periodicals. It has one of the largest collections of medical books in the West. One of its features is its extensive historical collection, including Arabic manuscripts, incunabula, Eastern medicine, and early printed Greek and Roman classics. *Housing:* Apartments are available for single men and women and married students.

Special Features *Minority Admissions:* A Minority Admissions Program is available for students from minority groups not strongly represented in the medical profession: blacks, Mexican-Americans, American Indians. The school has an active minority recruitment program. An early matriculation program, which includes preclinical course work and research opportunities, has been developed for disadvantaged students. *Other degree programs:* Combined MD-PhD programs are offered in most basic medical sciences as well as in cancer biology, cell biology, genetics, and medical information sciences.

Combined MD-MS and MD-PhD programs are offered in a wide variety of disciplines including biomedical engineering, biophysics, endocrinology, genetics, nutrition, and psychology.

University of California—Davis
School of Medicine
Davis, California 95616

Admissions (AMCAS) Requirements include the basic premedical science courses plus one year of English and mathematics that includes integral calculus. First preference goes to residents and next to WICHE applicants. *Transfer and advanced standing:* Transfer students are admitted to the third year only. Students wishing to transfer from foreign medical schools must submit the results of Part I of the NBME exam.

Curriculum 4-year semi-modern. The curriculum seeks to provide a balanced blend of basic and clinical sciences. *First year:* Consists of the introductory basic medical sciences, immunology, and general pathology. These are combined with social sciences, an introduction to the art of communicating with patients, and emergency medicine. *Second year:* Provides for a transition between basic and clinical sciences with the presentation of pathology, nutrition, pharmacology, microbiology, human sexuality, pathological basis of disease, physical diagnosis, as well as laboratory diagnostic techniques, and community health. *Third year:* Consists of clerkship rotations in the major specialties, maternal and child health, and psychiatry. *Fourth year:* Individualized training in one of three specialty tracts.

Grading and Promotion Policies Letter grades are given in required courses and letter grades or satisfactory/unsatisfactory in elective courses. At the end of each year, the medical school's Promotion Board evaluates each student's record. Students must record a passing total score on Part I of the NBME exam for promotion to the third year and record a score on Part II to graduate.

Facilities *Teaching:* The basic sciences are taught at the Medical Sciences I complex in Davis. Clinical facilities are provided by the University Medical Center (464 beds), which has over 100 specialty clinics. *Other:* Clinical instruction also takes place at the UCD Medical Center in Sacramento, VA Medical Center in Martinez, Kaiser Foundation Hospital in Sacramento, and other affiliated hospitals and family practice centers. *Library:* The Health Sciences Library is located adjacent to the School of Medicine and has more than 130,000 volumes and 3700 periodicals. The library has terminal access to MEDLINE, an on-line retrieval system for medical periodical information. A branch library is operated at the Sacramento Medical Center. *Housing:* Some on-campus housing is available at residence halls for unmarried students; a number of 1- and 2-bedroom units are available for married students.

Special Features *Minority admissions:* A very active recruitment program is coordinated by the Director of the Health Resources Development Program. A 6-week summer prematriculation program is offered. *Other degree programs:*

University of California—Irvine
California College of Medicine
Irvine, California 92717

Admissions (AMCAS) Preference is given to applicants with 4 years of undergraduate work. Nonresidents are accepted, but very few spaces are allocated for them. Minority students are invited to apply. Application fees may be waived and efforts are made to secure financial aid if accepted.

Curriculum 4-year modern. The educational program is made up of 18 quintiles divided into three educational periods. *First period:* Consists of 8 quintiles devoted to preclinical core courses and introductory clinical courses. It extends for 80 weeks. *Second period:* Consists of 7 required clinical clerkships covered during 5 quintiles that last for 52 weeks. *Third period:* Consists of 5 required clinical clerkships and 25 weeks of electives covered during 5 quintiles that last for 52 weeks. A 10-week vacation is included in this 52-week period.

Grading and Promotion Policies Grading is by letter in both required and elective courses. Students receiving lower than a passing grade will be required to repeat the course or to show proficiency in the material. Students are required to maintain an overall numerical rating to remain in good scholastic standing. Obtaining a total passing score on Parts I and II of the NBME is required for promotion to the third year and graduation after the fourth, respectively.

Facilities *Teaching:* The campus is 40 miles south of Los Angeles. Preclinical instructions are conducted in facilities on campus. Clinical teaching takes place at the University of California Irvine Medical Center, the Long Beach VA Hospital, Memorial Hospital of Long Beach, and Children's Hospital of Orange County. A University hospital was occupied in 1976. Laboratories are organized on a multidisciplinary basis. *Other:* Other facilities include electron microscope, analytical ultracentrifuge, amino acid analyzer, biometrics, medical illustration, medical vivarium, and research and development shop. *Library:* The Medical Sciences library is located in the medical sciences facilities on the University campus. *Housing:* A limited number of apartments are available for single and married students.

Special Features *Minority admissions:* Applications are encouraged from minority students and the school utilizes the Med-MAR list. A 6-week summer premedical program and a 7-week summer preentry program are offered for disadvantaged students to facilitate their admission and retention. *Other degree programs:* Interdisciplinary courses include those in community environmental medicine, mechanisms of disease, examination of patients, and a variety of elective courses. Students may take a leave of absence to pursue special research. A continuing education program is provided; a combined MD-PhD program is available in a wide variety of areas, including psychobiology and radiological sciences.

University of California—Los Angeles
School of Medicine
Los Angeles, California 90024

Admissions (AMCAS) Prerequisites for admission include the required premedical science courses plus quantitative analysis (as part of inorganic chemistry), one year of advanced biology (including molecular, cellular, developmental, and genetic biology), and one year of mathematics (including college algebra). Introductory calculus is recommended. *Transfer and advanced standing:* Those who have completed 2 years in an approved U.S. medical school will be considered for the third-year class only.

Curriculum 4-year semi-traditional. Stress is on the holistic approach in medicine. *First year:* Introductory basic sciences and patient contact and experience in history and physical examination as well as an elective program and a preceptorship program. *Second year:* Study of the process of disease through advanced basic science courses using an organ-system approach; diagnosis and treatment through courses in clinical surgery, clinical neurology, outpatient psychiatry, radiology, and obstetrics. *Third year:* Clerkships in clinical sciences and work in wards and outpatient clinics. *Fourth year:* Consists of electives—advanced elective clinical clerkships with primary patient responsibility, and in-depth elective courses which can be centered on major area of clinical interest or a combination of related or diverse disciplines.

Grading and Promotion Policies Letter grading in basic sciences, clinical sciences, and electives. Promotion is contingent upon satisfactory completion of required work each year. Completion of Parts I and II of NBME exam is required.

Facilities *Teaching:* Medical School is located in the Center for Health Sciences, which is the largest building in California. The University Hospital (517 beds) is the major clinical training center. Many other hospitals, including Harbor General (800 beds), are affiliated with the medical school. *Other:* The Brain Research Institute is a 10-story wing, connected to the Neuropsychiatric Institute and also houses the Los Angeles County Cardiovascular Research Laboratory. The Reed Neurological Research Center is an 8-story unit devoted to clinical research in neuromuscular disease. *Library:* The Biomedical Library is an 8-level facility in the northeast corner of the campus. *Housing:* Living accommodations are available in the University's residence halls or married students' housing.

Special Features *Minority admissions:* The school has an active recruitment program and offers a 4-week summer Prologue to Medicine program for accepted students. *Other degree programs:* Combined MD-PhD degree programs are offered in a variety of disciplines including medical physics, biomathematics, engineering, and experimental pathology. An MD-MPH program is also offered.

University of California—San Diego
School of Medicine
La Jolla, California 92093

Admissions (AMCAS) It is recommended that students enter medical school after four years of undergraduate study, the absolute minimum requirement is attendance for 3 academic years at an approved college of arts and sciences. Students who have attended a foreign school must have completed at least one year of study in a college in the United States prior to application. A solid understanding of the fundamental sciences is essential for the study of medical sciences, and applicants are required to have completed the minimum premedical science courses and one year of mathematics, which may include calculus, statistics, or computer science. The ability to express oneself clearly in both oral and written English is essential. A broad base of knowledge is advantageous in preparing for the many roles of a physician and may include courses in behavioral sciences, the biology of cells and development, genetics, biochemistry, English, social sciences, or conversational Spanish. *Transfer and advanced standing:* Transfer students from either foreign or domestic medical schools are not accepted.

Curriculum 4-year modern. Program places emphasis upon human disease with aim of expanding scientific knowledge and in the context of social applicability. The curriculum is divided into two major components: the core curriculum and the elective programs. Both are pursued concurrently, with the core predominating in the early years and the elective in the latter. Elective programs offer students a set of choices suited to their unique background, ability, and career objectives. *Preclinical phase:* The first year includes social and behavioral sciences, biostatistics, and an introduction to clinical medicine as well as some introductory and advanced basic science courses. The second year includes anatomy as well as advanced electives. *Clinical phase:* An extended continuum consisting of rotation through the major clinical specialties and electives (which take up about half of the total time of these 2 years).

Grading and Promotion Policies Grading is either Pass or Fail, and a narrative of each student's performance in his individual courses is prepared. These narratives are collated yearly, summarized, and a copy of the summary is made available to the student and his/her principal adviser.

Facilities *Teaching:* The school is located on the university campus in La Jolla. The primary teaching hospitals include the Veterans Administration Medical Center, UCSD Medical Center, and Balboa Naval Hospital. *Other:* Clinical teaching is also done at Mercy Hospital, Sharp Hospital, Children's Health Center, and the Kaiser Permanente Health Maintenance Organization as well as a wide spectrum of front-line, outpatient clinics, ranging from tiny Indian reservation facilities in North San Diego County, to the Clinica de Campesinos to the west, and the Northern California Rural Health Project some 500 miles to the north. *Library:* The Biomedical Library is located on the UCSD medical school campus and houses a large collection of books and journals. *Housing:* Limited on-campus housing is available.

Special Features *Minority admissions:* The school conducts an active recruitment program and offers a summer preparatory program for disadvantaged students who have been accepted. *Other degree programs:* Combined MD-PhD programs available in a variety of disciplines, including biology, bioengineering, and chemistry. Also available is a MD-MPH program in conjunction with San Diego State University.

University of California—San Francisco
School of Medicine
San Francisco, California 94143

Admissions (AMCAS) Minimum premedical science courses are required; biology should include vertebrate zoology. Mathematics, upper-division biological sciences, and humanities courses are recommended. *Transfer and advanced standing:* None are accepted at any level.

Curriculum 4-year program that allows flexibility in course sequence, in choice of major clinical pathways, and in increased elective time. *First year:* Devoted to anatomy (including clinical anatomy), biochemistry, histology, immunology, endocrinology, physiology, psychiatry, epidemiology, and introduction to clinical medicine. *Second year:* Devoted to pharmacology, parasitology, pathology, infectious diseases, psychiatry, and radiology. Other courses are genetics; human sexuality; and reproduction, growth and development. *Third year:* Devoted to completion of the 50 weeks of clinical clerkships in the major specialties. *Fourth year:* Spent in the major pathways and electives. The major pathway is selected by the students with the help of advisers according to personal goals. Pathways are divided into 7 categories: general, medical, surgical, behavioral, social and administrative, family medicine, and research.

Grading and Promotion Policies The grading system used is Pass/Not pass. The Committee on Student Promotions assesses the performance of all students at the end of each quarter and recommends one of the following: promotion to the next quarter; promotion to the next quarter, subject to certain conditions; formal repetition of one or more quarters of work; or consideration of dismissal from the school. A passing total score must be recorded in Part I of the NBME exam for promotion to the third year; Part II must be taken only to record a score.

Facilities *Teaching:* Preclinical courses are offered at the Medical Sciences Building and the Health Sciences Instruction and Research Building. Core clinical instruction utilizes the Herbert C. Moffitt/Joseph M. Long Hospitals (560 beds), San Francisco General Hospital (449 beds), Veterans Administration Medical Center (378 beds), and Langley Porter Psychiatric Institute (70 beds), as well as other area hospitals. *Other:* There are 8 research facilities affiliated with the school: the Cancer Research Institute, Cardiovascular Research Institute, George Williams Hooper Foundation, Hormone Research Laboratory, Institute for Health Policy Studies, Laboratory of Radiobiology and Environmental Health, Metabolic Unit, and Reproductive Endocrinology Center. *Library:* The major portions of the library are housed in the Medical Sciences Building; there are over 500,000 volumes and 8000 periodicals.

Housing: The university operates Millberry Residence Hall for single students and Aldea San Miguel for married students.

Special Features *Minority admissions:* With the exception of Howard and Meharry, this medical school has the highest minority enrollment of continental U.S. schools. Its multifaceted program seeks to identify, recruit, and prepare disadvantaged students for careers in the health sciences. Included in these efforts are academic support services and counseling opportunities. *Other degree programs:* Students are encouraged to engage in research and other scholarly activities. Dual-degree programs offering MS, MPH, and PhD degrees are offered for this purpose, along with many opportunities not linked to dual-degree programs. MD-PhD programs are offered in a variety of disciplines including bioengineering, endocrinology, genetics, and medical information science, and in the social science programs in medical anthropology and health psychology.

University of Southern California
School of Medicine
2025 Zonal Avenue
Los Angeles, California 90033

Admissions (AMCAS) Minimum premedical science courses are required. Developmental biology, cell physiology, genetics, calculus, and biochemistry are strongly recommended. The student body comes from all parts of the United States as well as from several foreign countries. *Transfer and advanced standing:* Domestic transfers are considered for the third year only. All students applying for transfer into the third year must complete Part I of the NBME exam. U.S. citizens transferring from foreign medical schools must take the MSKP exam.

Curriculum 4-year modern. *First year:* (36 weeks) Organ system review—normal (anatomy, biochemistry, and physiology) and behavioral sciences. Introduction to Clinical Medicine I, Family and Preventive Medicine, and Nutrition. *Second year:* (36 weeks) Organ system review—abnormal (microbiology, pharmacology, and pathology including psychopathology) and Introduction to Clinical Medicine II. *Junior/Senior years:* Required clerkships include two 6-week clerkships in medicine, 6-week clerkships in pediatrics, obstetrics/gynecology, general surgery, and psychiatry and two 3-week clerkships selected from surgical subspecialties. The balance of the scheduled time includes one 6-week basic science period, three 6-week clerkships in a selective program, and 18 weeks of free electives.

Grading and Promotion Policies Honors, Satisfactory, or Unsatisfactory grades are given on the basis of certifying examinations for the first and second years. Descriptive comments of the student's overall performance are submitted. For promotion to the third year, a passing total score must be recorded in Part I of the NBME exam; Part II must be taken only to record a score. In the third and fourth years, required clerkships are evaluated on an Honors/Satisfactory/Unsatisfactory basis. All other clerkships are evaluated on a Satisfactory/Unsatisfactory basis. Faculty are encouraged to submit written comments as well.

Facilities Instruction is conducted in the buildings on the medical campus, in the Medical Center, and in affiliated hospitals, community clinics, and institutions under the instruction of the medical faculty. Through the elective program instruction is conducted in medical schools and hospitals throughout the world. The Medical Center is a 2045-bed hospital which is the prime teaching facility of the school. There are 13 other hospitals affiliated with the school. McKibben Hall houses teaching laboratories and lecture rooms; the Bishop Building is also a teaching facility and is adjacent. *Other:* The Mudd Building houses research laboratories. The Hoffman Medical Research Center is used by a number of departments and includes a 154-seat auditorium for seminars and lectures. The Raulston Medical Research Building, the first unit of the School to be built, houses laboratories. The Estelle Doheny Eye Foundation has constructed a building for teaching and research and a 35-bed hospital devoted to care for problems of the eye. The Kenneth Norris Jr. Cancer Hospital and Research Institute is a 60-bed hospital that houses treatment and research facilities and is headquarters for the USC Cancer Center. *Library:* The Norris Medical Library is designed to house 200,000 volumes and seat 250 readers. *Housing:* A 4-story residence building provides accommodations for 95 students. Off-campus apartments are available for married students.

Special Features *Minority admissions:* A year-round Med-Cor program seeks to identify interested high school and college students. A Health Professions Preparation program is also offered that consists of an 8-week summer studies program and tutorial assistance extending over the entire year. A special 4-week program for incoming freshman minority students has been developed. *Other degree programs:* MD-PhD programs are offered in a variety of disciplines including biophysics and nutrition.

COLORADO

University of Colorado
School of Medicine
4200 East Ninth Avenue
Denver, Colorado 80262

Admissions (AMCAS) Required courses include the minimum premedical science courses plus 1 year of college level mathematics and English literature, and 1 semester of English composition. Almost all of the approximately 125 first-year openings are awarded to residents. Preference is then given to residents of Western states participating in WICHE. *Transfer and advanced standing:* Applicants from approved schools who have completed 1 year of study will be considered when openings occur in sophomore class; applicants from both foreign and domestic medical schools will be considered for the junior class after completing 2 years of study. Preference is given to students from 2-year medical schools.

Curriculum 4-year semi-modern. *First year:* Introductory basic sciences and courses in biophysics, genetics, and biometrics. Also given is a course introducing quantitative

methods used in medical research, the assessment of quantitative evidence, and the formulation of medically sound conclusions. *Second year:* Advanced basic sciences and courses in psychiatry, preventive medicine, and technical surgery (basic principles of surgery, anesthesia, hemostasis, and asepsis). *Third and fourth years:* Clerkship rotations through the major clinical specialties, electives, and free time. Seminars in minor clinical specialties are held throughout the school year. A large number of clinical and basic science opportunities are offered for the elective quarters. This allows students to major in certain specialties or subspecialties or to have experience in programs in community medicine, family medicine, or rural practice. It also provides for additional work in basic sciences or in laboratory research. An elective rural preceptorship is available, and participation in independent research during vacation is strongly encouraged.

Grading and Promotion Policies System used is Honors/Pass/Fail. The performance of each student is considered by Curriculum and Promotion committees. These determine when students have satisfactorily completed the first 2 and last 2 years of medical school.

Facilities *Teaching:* Basic sciences are taught in the School of Medicine Building, which also has space for faculty offices and research laboratories. Clinical teaching takes place at the University Hospital (386 beds), at Colorado General Hospital (450 beds), at the VA Hospital (500 beds), and at Denver General Hospital (340 beds). *Other:* The Sabin Building for Cellular Research; the Webb-Waring Institute for Medical Research; the Clinical Research Wing of the Colorado General Hospital. *Library:* Denison Memorial Library is located in a building bearing the same name. The collection includes more than 150,000 volumes, and 2,000 periodicals are received regularly. *Housing:* No residence halls available.

Special Features *Minority admissions:* A minority-group students program gives special consideration to the applicants, offers a flexible curriculum, provides advisory and tutoring services, and grants financial aid for eligible students. The school also offers an 8-week summer course, "Introduction to Medical Science," for matriculating minority students. *Other degree programs:* Combined MD-PhD programs are offered in the basic medical sciences as well as in biometrics, biophysics, and genetics. An MD-MS program is also offered.

CONNECTICUT

University of Connecticut
School of Medicine
Farmington Avenue
Farmington, Connecticut 06032

Admissions (AMCAS) Required courses include the basic premedical sciences. Applicants must demonstrate facility in quantitative and communicative skills. The faculty believes a broad liberal arts education provides the best preparation for those entering the medical profession. Strong preference is given to residents. *Transfer and advanced standing:* None.

Curriculum 4-year modern. *Basic sciences:* The student is exposed to the basic sciences through an integrated, inter-departmental curriculum. The program begins with the study of human biology, consisting of general aspects of cellular and molecular biology, tissue biology, anatomy, and pathology. Courses in social and behavioral sciences, biostatistics, and law and ethics run concurrently. The second year is fashioned around the study of each organ system. *Clinical sciences:* During the first two years, the student learns history-taking and physical diagnosis skills. In the third year, the student completes courses in medicine, surgery, obstetrics/gynecology, pediatrics, and psychiatry. During the fourth year, the student completes at least seven electives and a primary care clerkship. Students are encouraged to participate in research.

Grading and Promotions Policies   A Pass/Fail system is used. Students must take Parts I and II of the NBME exams and record a score.

Facilities   *Teaching:* Students obtain most of their clinical experience in hospitals in the greater Hartford area and at the John Dempsey Hospital at the Health Center. The Health Center is a member of a consortium of hospitals that seeks to strengthen health education programs and improve patient care. Ten health care institutions are affiliated, and 11 are allied with the Health Center. *Library:* Lyman Maynard Stowe Library is centrally located in the Health Sciences Center. *Housing:* Provision for both single and married student housing is coordinated by the Office of Student Affairs.

Special Features   *Minority admissions:* The school actively recruits disadvantaged applicants by visits to area institutions and participation in informational programs. Its Minority Scholars Institute sponsors an 8-week summer program which simulates the first year of basic medical sciences. *Other degree programs:* MD-PhD programs are offered in a variety of disciplines including molecular biology and immunology.

Yale University
School of Medicine
333 Cedar Street
New Haven, Connecticut 06510

Admissions   Courses in the basic premedical sciences are required and courses in mathematics (calculus and statistics) and physical chemistry are recommended. *Transfer and advanced standing:* Students studying at other medical schools, domestic or foreign, are not encouraged to apply. In a few cases, students are accepted into second or third year.

Curriculum   4-year semi-modern. Attempts to adhere as closely as possible to the graduate-type of presentation and to permit a large degree of freedom. *First year:* This year is divided into two semesters, each having two 8- or 9-week terms. Aside from the basic sciences courses, time is allotted for the study of genetics, biostatistics, immunobiology, behavioral science, human genetics, and medical history. Clinical correlations is offered during each term. *Second year:* Devoted to the advanced basic sciences as well as epidemiology, public health, clinical correlations, Introduction to Clinical

Medicine, and a reading period. *Third year:* This consists of a 12-week course in physical diagnosis, history-taking, laboratory medicine, and pathophysiology. *Fourth year:* A program of required and elective clerkships. Time must also be spent in the outpatient clinic. The school requires each student to prepare a dissertation based on original investigation either in the lab or in the clinic.

Grading and Promotion Policies   A Pass/Fail grading system is used. Students must record a passing score in each section of the NBME exam for promotion to the third year and a passing total score to graduate.

Facilities   *Teaching:* The school is part of the Yale-New Haven Medical Center and occupies several city blocks about one-half mile southwest of the University Center. Basic sciences are taught at Sterling Hall of Medicine, Lander Hall, and Brady Memorial Laboratory. Clinical instruction takes place primarily at Yale-New Haven Hospital (762 beds) and the VA Hospital (849 beds) in West Haven. *Other:* Research facilities are located in Sterling Hall and in Brady Memorial Laboratory. *Library:* Yale Medical Library is located in Sterling Hall and contains over 333,000 volumes, receives 2600 journals, and has over 62,000 other books of the last 2 centuries. The library is one of the country's largest medical libraries. *Housing:* Edward S. Harkness Memorial Hall provides living accommodations for single men and women and married students.

Special Features   *Minority admissions:* The school receives a substantial number of minority group applications even though it does not have a special recruitment program. *Other degree programs:* Combined degree programs are available for an MD-PhD in a variety of disciplines including anthropology, biology, chemistry, economics, engineering, genetics, biophysics, and psychology. MD-MS and MD-JD programs are also offered.

DISTRICT OF COLUMBIA

George Washington University
School of Medicine
2300 Eye Street, N.W.
Washington, D.C. 20037

Admissions (AMCAS)   Courses in English composition and literature are required in addition to the standard premedical science courses. School accepts many students from out of state. An early selection program for second-year Columbian (G.W.U.) College students is available. *Transfer and advanced standing:* Transfer students are ordinarily limited to third year. All transfer applicants must take Part I of the NBME exam.

Curriculum   4-year modern. *First year:* Introduction to normal human function including anatomy, biochemistry, physiology, neurobiology; microbiology; and psychiatry, emergency medicine, and epidemiology minicourses. Electives are offered. *Second year:* Pharmacology and pathology are taught initially in a core curriculum and then integrated in the major Introduction to Clinical Medicine course that runs throughout the second year. *Third year:* 8-week rotations through the 5 major clinical disciplines and a 6-week rotation in ambulatory (primary care) medicine. *Fourth year:* A highly flexible year in which students can prepare themselves for their postgraduate training. It includes 17 weeks of required courses and 20 weeks of elective choices. Students with exceptional interests and ability may spend some elective time at other institutions.

Grading and Promotion Policies   System used is Honors/Pass/Conditional/Fail. Part I of the NBME exam must be taken. Part II is optional.

Facilities   *Teaching:* Walter G. Ross Hall is the basic science building. Clinical instruction takes place at the 550-bed University Hospital, University clinic, as well as at numerous affiliated hospitals. *Other:* The Research Building houses special laboratories for graduate and staff research in the basic sciences. Warwick Memorial Building houses surgical primate and cancer research laboratories. *Library:* The Health Sciences Library is expanding, with a capacity for 80,000 volumes. *Housing:* Most students live off campus.

Special Features   *Minority admissions:* Admission Committee members visit selected schools to discuss the school's program with minority students. *Other degree programs:* Combined MD-PhD degree programs are offered in all the basic sciences.

Georgetown University
School of Medicine
3900 Reservoir Road, N.W.
Washington, D.C. 20007

Admissions (AMCAS)   Required courses include the basic premedical sciences as well as one year of English and mathematics. Courses considered useful preparation are computer science, cellular physiology, genetics, embryology, biostatistics, quantitative analysis, and physical chemistry. Some preference is given to District residents and Georgetown University undergraduates. *Transfer and advanced standing:* Students from foreign or domestic medical schools may apply to transfer to the second or third year. Transfers must take Part I of the NBME exam or the MSKP exam.

Curriculum   4-year semi-traditional. *First and second years:* The curriculum for the first 2 years has 3 major components: departmental courses emphasizing normal and altered human structure and function, an Introduction to Clinical Sciences course; and electives. *Third year:* Consists of 46 weeks of instructional time that is allotted to clerkships in the major clinical specialties. During this time, the student receives intensive instruction in the care of patients and is given progressively more responsibility as skill develops. *Fourth year:* Consists of 48 weeks of instruction and is divided into 6 clerkships and a 20-week elective program. Substantial freedom is given in choosing the service and the hospital where these blocks are carried out.

Grading and Promotion Policies   Grades are Honors, High Pass, Pass, and Fail. A student who receives an F in any course will be considered in a position of jeopardy, and his/her case will be referred to the Committee on Students for Review. A failure could lead to dismissal, repeating a year, or doing additional work in a specific course. Taking the NBME exam is optional.

Facilities   *Teaching:* Basic sciences are taught in the School of Medicine Building (535 beds), the Preclinical Science building, and the Basic Science Tower. Clinical teaching takes place at the University hospital, and a complex of affiliated institutions providing access to approximately 7000 beds. *Other:* The District location provides students with opportunities such as federal laboratories, libraries, and museums. The National Library of Medicine and the laboratories of the Department of Agriculture and Bureau of Standards are affiliated with the University. *Library:* Dahlgren Memorial Library houses about 160,000 volumes and subscribes to 1650 periodicals. Also available for students' use are the Library of Congress, the National Library of Medicine, the National Institutes of Health Library, Agriculture Department Library, and the Public Library of District of Columbia. *Housing:* Presently, there is no University housing available.

Special Features   *Minority admissions:* Special admissions programs for minority group students include a summer enrichment program and a special tutorial program. *Other degree programs:* Combined degree programs are available for the MD-PhD degrees in some of the basic medical sciences.

Howard University
College of Medicine
520 W Street, N.W.
Washington, D.C. 20059

Admissions (AMCAS)   Requirements include a minimum of 62 credits (2 years) of undergraduate work, plus minimum premedical science courses and one year of English. There are no residence restrictions; 85% of the students are black, 40% are women. Selection is based not only on academic achievement and personal qualities, but also on the likelihood of practice in communities or facilities needing physician services. *Transfer and advanced standing:* Placement is infrequent, and usually at the end of the second year. Foreign transfers are not accepted.

Curriculum   4-year modern. Program is flexible in order to produce the physician-scientist. *First year:* Core concept presentation of introductory basic sciences and interdisciplinary courses, plus optional electives. *Second year:* Continued core concept presentation of advanced basic sciences plus interdisciplinary courses in pathophysiology of organ systems, infectious diseases, and principles of practice of medicine. Elective courses are offered. *Third year:* A series of clerkships rotated through the major clinical specialties. Possibility for involvement in community health care is also provided. *Fourth year:* A 9-month program similar to junior year, except that periods of specialization are increased by allotment of 20 weeks of elective time (4 of which can be used for vacation).

Grading and Promotion Policies System used is the Honors/Satisfactory/Unsatisfactory. Students must take Part I of the NBME exam and obtain a passing total score for promotion to the third year. To graduate, students must record a passing total score on Part II.

Facilities *Teaching:* The college is part of Howard University Center for the Health Sciences. It is housed in a modern building and is the site for teaching basic medical sciences. Clinical teaching is at the 500-bed Howard University Hospital. Several other hospitals in the District area provide additional training facilities. *Other:* Research is carried out in several buildings, including a Cancer Center. *Library:* The Health Sciences Library contains over 170,000 volumes and periodicals. National Institutes of Health and National Library of Medicine are available to students. *Housing:* Professional students are not usually allocated accommodations on campus.

Special Features *Minority admissions:* The college is dedicated to training minority applicants and has a strong recruitment program which includes early admissions and academic reinforcement for admitted students. *Other degree programs:* A dual-degree program is available for the MD-PhD in Pharmacology; a BS-MD program is also offered and an MS in Public Health is available. Continuing education is available for graduates.

FLORIDA

University of Florida
College of Medicine
Gainesville, Florida 32610

Admissions (AMCAS) Only the minimum premedical science courses are required. The college gives strong preference to those who have completed the requirements for a bachelor's degree and who are state residents. Ten percent of the class are usually nonresidents; out-of-state applicants should have a 3.5 or better GPA. *Transfer and advanced standing:* Transfer students are rarely considered. The state's program in medical sciences provides for the easy transfer of students from Florida State University and Florida A & M only.

Curriculum 4-year semi-traditional. *First year:* In addition to the basic sciences, courses in medical ethics, human behavior, and molecular genetics are presented. *Second year:* Aside from the advanced basic sciences, courses in ophthalmology, radiology, and physical diagnosis are offered. *Third year:* Eight clinical clerkships extending over 52 weeks. *Fourth year:* Surgical and medical clerkships, course work, and electives, in selected categorical areas related to medicine within the medical school or at 2 nonuniversity settings.

Grading and Promotion Policies The system used is letter/number. At the end of each quarter the Committee on Academic Status reviews each student's performance on the basis of grades and comments by faculty and recommends suitable action to the dean. Students who receive Fs in 2 major

courses in one semester will be dropped automatically. In order to graduate, the student must record a passing total score on Parts I and II of the NBME exam.

Facilities *Teaching:* Basic sciences are taught in J. Hillis Miller Health Center which includes the Shands Teaching Hospital (405 beds). Clinical teaching also takes place at the nearby VA Hospital (450 beds). *Other:* Research facilities are present in Health Center, VA Hospital, and Animal Research farm. *Library:* The Health Center Library has a collection of over 193,000 books and periodicals. Computer-based retrieval services are available. *Housing:* Accommodations available for single students in Beaty Towers and Schucht Village and for married in Cory, University, Maguire, and Diamond Memorial Villages. The latter contain 1-, 2-, and some 3-bedroom apartments.

Special Features *Minority admissions:* The college encourages well-qualified students from minority groups and women students to apply. A summer workshop for new minority matriculants is sponsored annually. It is an orientation and academic preparation program. *Other degree programs:* The Medical Sciences Program allows students at Florida State University and Florida A & M to combine baccalaureate study with first year of medical study for combination degree. The college also offers a dual MD-PhD program for Medical Scientist Training Program. Continuing education is available for graduates.

University of Miami
School of Medicine
P.O. Box 016159
Miami, Florida 33101

Admissions Required courses include minimum premedical science courses plus biochemistry (or molecular biology) and mathematics (through calculus). School gives strong preference to residents. *Transfer and advanced standing:* Students are accepted into second- and third-year classes only; applicants must take the MSKP examination.

Curriculum 4-year modern. *First year:* Designed to provide the student with a background of normal structure function and behavior. Basic sciences are integrated into study of organ systems. These courses include gross anatomy, cell biophysics, neuroscience, biochemistry, and systemic physiology. The latter is an interdisciplinary course dealing with structure and function of organ systems. A course on health and human values teaches various phases of human development and behavior and provides for patient contact. *Second year:* Initial weeks are devoted to general concepts of advanced basic sciences. A major course in mechanisms of disease emphasizes the disease processes which affect various organ systems. The transition to third-year work is prepared for by physical diagnosis. *Third year:* Consists of clerkship rotations through the major clinical specialties. *Fourth year:* Consists entirely of electives. Students may select from a number of programs at the school and at other institutions, if approved. They may spend time in the community with a practicing physician, take a course in biomedical engineering, or follow up didactic courses in the basic sciences.

Grading and Promotion Policies A letter grading system is used for all courses in the first three years and Pass/Fail for the fourth-year electives. Promotion is dependent upon satisfactory completion of academic material for each year. The student must record scores on Parts I and II of the NBME exam.

Facilities *Teaching:* Basic sciences are taught in the Rosenstiel Medical Sciences Building. Clinical teaching takes place at the Jackson Memorial Hospital (1246 beds) and the VA hospital (1035 beds). *Other:* The Medical Research Building is connected with the Rosenstiel Building Medical Sciences Building on all 8 floors. *Library:* The Calder Memorial Library, which houses over 128,000 volumes and over 1700 periodicals, is located in the Rosenstiel Building. *Housing:* No student housing exists at present, but residence halls are available for married and single students on the main campus (about 10 miles from the medical school). The space is limited, however.

Special Features *Minority admissions:* The school actively seeks to recruit disadvantaged students studying on college campuses in the Southeast. A 7-week summer program for college students offers a mini-medical school experience. *Other degree programs:* In addition to a standard combined MD-PhD program, the school offers a special program for those with PhDs who would like to earn an MD degree. This 2-year program is only open to those with degrees in a biological, physical, or engineering science field.

University of South Florida
College of Medicine
12901 North 30th Street
Tampa, Florida 33612

Admissions Required courses include minimum premedical science courses plus genetics, statistics, and English (two semesters). Preference is given to state residents, but a very limited number of out-of-state applicants are accepted. Residents should have at least a 3.0 GPA and 8 on each MCAT subtest.

Curriculum 4-year semi-traditional. The initial academic instruction is in the basic medical sciences. This is followed by a clerkship program in the major clinical specialties and finally there is a period of multiple electives in clinical and basic medical sciences.

Grading and Promotion Policies Students are awarded grades of Superior (A), Excellent (B), Average (C), Below Average (D), or Failing (F). The student must record a score on Part I of the NBME exam, but taking Part II is optional. Each student's records are reviewed periodically by the Committee on Promotion.

Facilities The medical school is located on the campus of the University of South Florida. The facilities include student laboratories and classrooms, research laboratories, the medi-

cal library, and administrative and departmental offices. Clinical instruction is carried out at the Tampa General Hospital (600 beds), VA Hospital (700 beds), and All Children's Hospital (100 beds). *Library:* The Medical Center Library seats 350 people and is built to house over 100,000 volumes.

Special Features *Minority admissions:* Disadvantaged students are invited to visit the medical center for guided tours of the facilities and seminars on admissions policies and procedures. A special two-year non-degree program is administered by the Premedical Sciences Committee of the College of Natural Sciences of the University of South Florida for students who hold a baccalaureate degree and are seeking to improve their academic record prior to applying to medical school. *Other degree programs:* None.

GEORGIA

Emory University
School of Medicine
Atlanta, Georgia 30322

Admissions (AMCAS) Required courses, aside from the standard premedical sciences, only include one year of English. Biochemistry is highly recommended. Applications from well-qualified students are seriously considered regardless of geographic origin; however, 50 percent of the positions are given to state residents. *Transfer and advanced standing:* Properly qualified students from LCME-accredited schools will be considered for the second- or third-year classes.

Curriculum 4-year semi-traditional. *First year:* Interdepartmental course in cellular biology and biochemistry and in neurobiology; and interdisciplinary core curriculum course in behavioral sciences, introduction to health and medicine, and biostatistics. *Second year:* Advanced basic sciences and courses in behavioral science, nutrition, and clinical methods. *Third year:* 8-week clerkship rotations through the major clinical specialties. *Fourth year:* 4-week clerkships in medicine, neurology, and neurosurgery with brief rotations in dermatology, anesthesiology, and radiology and 20 weeks of elective work in any area.

Grading and Promotion Policies Grades of A through F are used in required courses and grades of satisfactory/unsatisfactory are used in electives. At the end of the year, the promotion committees for each class review the records of all students to determine whether they should be unconditionally promoted to the next year's program, whether they may be re-examined, whether they must repeat work deemed unsatisfactory, or whether they are to be asked to withdraw. For promotion to the third year, a passing total score must be recorded in Part I of the NBME exam; Part II must be taken only to record a score.

Facilities *Teaching:* Basic sciences are taught in the Woodruff Memorial Research Building, the Scott Anatomy Building, and the Fishburne Physiology Building. Clinical instruction takes place primarily at the University hospital (600 beds), Grady Memorial Hospital (1000 beds), the VA hospital (495 beds) and at several other institutions. *Other:* The Emory Eye Center is devoted to basic and clinical research and patient care. The Woodruff Health Sciences Center Administration Building and the Glenn Memorial Building contain administrative offices of the School of Medicine, classrooms, and some clinical research laboratories. *Library:* The Calhoun Medical Library is housed in the Woodruff Memorial Research Building and has over 140,000 volumes and 2500 periodicals. A basic collection, the Grady branch, is maintained in the Glenn Memorial Building. *Housing:* Campus housing for single students is extremely limited. There are approximately 200 furnished and unfurnished campus apartments for single and married students.

Special Features MD-PhD programs are offered in a variety of disciplines including bioengineering and biometry. An MD-MPH program is also available. There is a continuing education program for graduates.

> **Medical College of Georgia**
> 1120 15th Street
> Augusta, Georgia 30901

Admissions (AMCAS) The basic premedical science courses are required as well as courses in English sufficient to satisfy baccalaureate degree requirements. Very strong preference is given to state residents, as well as to candidates with 4 years of undergraduate work. *Transfer and advanced standing:* Applicants from 2- and 4-year medical schools are considered when space permits.

Curriculum 4-year modern. *Year 1:* A 36-week core with elective time available in the third quarter. The core period is concerned with molecular, cellular, and human biology. Structure and function of the healthy human body is approached by classical methods. The elective courses, which can be chosen from a wide variety of offerings, are aimed at strengthening skills and deepening knowledge. In addition, the student begins his/her first contact with patients in the course in Physical Diagnosis starting in mid-year. *Year 2:* A 35-week program coordinating the advanced basic sciences which are concerned with the study of the biology of diseases. Physical diagnosis is taught in relation to the study of pathophysiology. Additional contributions are made by various clinical departments. *Year 3:* A 48-week period of rotating clerkships in the major clinical specialties. Up to 8 weeks of electives can be taken. *Year 4:* 24 weeks of electives which can be advanced clinical clerkships, basic science electives, or research electives. The electives may be taken in other institutions and community hospitals. It is possible to graduate in 36 months.

Grading and Promotion Policies Letter grades are used. Parts I and II of the NBME exam must be passed in order to graduate. Obtaining a total passing score on Parts I and II of the NBME exam is required for promotion to the third year and graduation after the fourth, respectively.

Facilities *Teaching:* Basic sciences are taught primarily in the Research and Education Building that was opened in 1971. Clinical teaching takes place at the Eugene Talmadge Memorial Hospital (450 beds) and 4 affiliated hospitals. *Other:* A 10-floor Clinical Research Annex at the teaching hospital contains special laboratories for research. *Library:* The library houses over 100,000 volumes and 1500 periodicals. *Housing:* Accommodations are available in 3 residence halls for single students. One- and 2-bedroom apartments are available for married students.

Special Features *Minority admissions:* The college conducts an intensive recruitment program and is committed to increasing minority representation in the student body. The college also conducts an 8-week summer program for high school and college students to strengthen their academic backgrounds and introduce them to the practical aspects of the health careers. *Other degree programs:* MD-PhD programs are offered in a variety of disciplines including endocrinology.

> **Mercer University**
> School of Medicine
> Macon, Georgia 31207

Admissions (AMCAS) Only the basic premedical science courses are required. State residents receive a strong preference. *Transfer and advanced standing:* Information not available.

Curriculum 4-year modern. A 5-phase educational scheme is used to train primary care physicians for service in rural areas of Georgia. The first 3 phases make up the Biochemical Problem Solving Unit. *Phase 1:* This 6-week introductory segment is concerned with communication at various structural levels. *Phase 2:* A 12-week interval devoted to the human organism and its response to the environment. *Phase 3:* Consists of 54 weeks and emphasizes structure and function in health and disease, using a systemic pathophysiological approach. *Phase 4:* This 48 week period makes up the Clinical Skills Program and consists of rotations through the major clinical specialties. *Phase 5:* This segment makes up a large part of the Community Science Program in which a student completes 8 weeks with his/her sponsoring physician in a rural comprehensive care clerkship. Other activities during the last phase involve psychiatric and acute care clerkships and electives.

Grading and Promotion Policies A Pass/Fail system is used. Students must record passing total scores on Parts I and II of the NBME exam for promotion to the third year and graduation, respectively.

Facilities *Teaching:* The basic sciences are taught at the Education Building, and clinical training is offered at the Medical Center of Central Georgia. A 40-room ambulatory care unit is also utilized. *Library:* A comprehensive medical library is available for student and faculty use. *Housing:* Information not available.

Special Features *Minority admissions:* A program that involves strong recruiting efforts directed towards traditionally black colleges in Georgia. *Other degree programs:* Combined programs are not currently available.

Morehouse School of Medicine
720 Westview Drive, S.W.
Atlanta, Georgia, 30310

Admissions (AMCAS) The basic premedical science courses plus mathematics and English are required. Courses in biochemistry, embryology, and genetics are recommended. *Transfer and advanced standing:* Information not available.

Curriculum 4-year traditional. *First and second years:* Devoted to the basic medical sciences as well as courses in human behavior and psychopathology, nutrition, community medicine, and biostatistics as well as courses entitled Human Values in Medicine and Introduction to Clinical Medicine. *Third and fourth years:* These 2 years involve rotation through the clinical specialties plus 20 weeks of electives.

Grading and Promotion Policies Letter grades are used. Students must obtain passing total scores on Parts I and II of the NBME exam for promotion to the third year and graduation, respectively.

Facilities *Teaching:* The first two years are taught at the Basic Sciences Building. Clinical training is available at a number of affiliated hospitals in Atlanta and surrounding areas. *Library:* The medical library collection meets both student and faculty needs. *Housing:* Information not available.

Special Features *Minority admissions:* The school's Recruitment Officer is actively involved in identifying, informing, and encouraging potential applicants. *Other degree programs:* No combined degree programs are available at this time.

HAWAII

University of Hawaii
Burns School of Medicine
1960 East-West Road
Honolulu, Hawaii 96822

Admissions (AMCAS) In addition to the standard premedical science courses, it is desirable that students choose electives from the following: statistics, microbiology, embryology, genetics, biochemistry, and physical chemistry. Residents of Hawaii and the Pacific Islands are given preference. A minimum GPA of 3.2 is necessary. *Transfer and advanced standing:* Applicants from domestic medical schools must take Part I of the NBME exam.

Curriculum 4-year semi-modern. *First year:* Introductory basic sciences as well as courses in genetics, introduction to

human behavior, community health problems, and clinical correlation conferences. *Second year:* Advanced basic sciences as well as courses in laboratory diagnosis, clinical judgment, psychopathology, community medicine and clinical conferences. *Third year:* At least 44 weeks of clerkships. *Fourth year:* 36 weeks of electives.

Grading and Promotion Policies Grading system is Credit/No Credit. Failures may be made up if the course is passed upon repetition or by other qualifications. The student must obtain a passing total score on Part I of the NBME exam for promotion into the third year, and a passing total score on Part II for graduation.

Facilities *Teaching:* The basic science building contains most of the departments, with others located in 3 other buildings on campus. Clinical teaching takes place at the affiliated hospitals and clinics in the area. *Library:* University libraries include the Sinclair Library, Hamilton Library, and Walker Medical Library. Together they contain over 1 million volumes. The Reichert Medical History Collection emphasizes Pacific and Oriental medical history. *Housing:* Limited accommodations are available for 104 men and 104 women in double rooms in Gateway House on campus.

Special Features *Minority admissions:* A special program provides students from socioeconomically and academically underprivileged areas with the opportunity to study medicine. Intensive tutorial assistance is available. *Other degree programs:* Dual MD-MS and MD-PhD programs are offered in a variety of disciplines including reproductive biology and tropical medicine.

ILLINOIS

Chicago Medical School
University of Health Sciences
3333 Green Bay Road
Chicago, Illinois 60064

Admissions (AMCAS) Only minimum premedical science courses are required. Completion of a minimum of 90 semester hours is required and a baccalaureate degree is preferred. The school does not impose geographical restrictions. *Transfer and advanced standing:* None.

Curriculum 4-year semi-traditional. Students may be permitted to finish requirements in 5 years, if they choose. *Period 1:* 35 weeks of work in the basic sciences. Clinical experience begins in first quarter and increases progressively. Interdepartmental cooperation between clinical and basic science departments is emphasized. *Period 2:* 36 weeks devoted to the advanced basic sciences, including behavioral science and two clinical preparation courses as well as an elective. *Period 3:* 60 weeks devoted to clerkships in major specialties. Correlation of clinical instruction with basic sciences in conferences and seminars. *Period 4:* 28 weeks devoted to electives, 16 of these in affiliated hospitals.

Grading and Promotion Policies Letter grades are used in required courses and Pass/Fail in electives. There is a monthly review of performance by departments and a quarterly review by an evaluation committee. Students must record passing scores in each section of Part I of the NBME exam for promotion to the third year and similarly in Part II for graduation.

Facilities *Teaching:* The basic science instruction takes place in the classroom and administration building in North Chicago. Primary clinical teaching occurs in affiliated hospitals: Cook County Hospital, St. Mary's Hospital, North Chicago Veterans Medical Center, Great Lakes Naval Hospital and Jackson Park Hospital. *Library:* The library contains 75,000 volumes and subscribes to 1500 periodicals. *Housing:* None available on campus.

Special Features *Minority admissions:* The school is actively involved in the recruitment of disadvantaged students and participates in the Chicago Area Health Careers Opportunity Program. *Other degree programs:* MD-PhD programs are offered in a variety of disciplines including medical physics, pathology, and psychology.

Loyola University of Chicago
Stritch School of Medicine
2160 South First Avenue
Maywood, Illinois 60153

Admissions (AMCAS) This school requires satisfactory completion of the basic premedical science courses. Recommended courses are best selected in view of a given student's interests and talents. About half of the first-year openings are reserved for residents. A GPA of 3.2 and MCAT scores above 8 are necessary for consideration. *Transfer and advanced standing:* Transfers are accepted from domestic schools.

Curriculum 4-year semi-modern. *First and second years:* Introductory and advanced basic sciences are presented in a manner that prepares the student to learn and function in a clinical setting. *Third year:* Clerkship rotation through major clinical specialties. *Fourth year:* Electives are designed to help the student prepare for graduate education.

Grading and Promotion Policies The system used is Honors/ High Pass/Pass/Fail. Student performance is regularly reviewed by a Promotions Committee. Students must record a score on Parts I and II of the NBME exam.

Facilities *Teaching:* The school is part of the University Medical Center. Clinical teaching takes place at the University Hospital, the VA Hospital at Hines, the Madden Zone Mental Health Center; the school is also affiliated with 3 large public hospitals. *Other:* Research facilities are available at the Medical Center. *Library:* The Medical Center library has a 110,000-volume capacity. *Housing:* There are accommoda-

tions for only 61 female medical and dental students on campus.

Special Features *Minority admissions:* The school has joined others in the area to offer a Chicago Area Health Careers Opportunity Program. Applications from women and minority group members from Illinois are encouraged. *Other degree programs:* Dual MS-MD and MD-PhD degree programs are available. Among the latter is a program in biophysics.

Northwestern University
Medical School
Chicago, Illinois 60611

Admissions (AMCAS) One year of English is required in addition to the minimum premedical science courses. About 50 openings are available to out-of-state students. *Transfer and advanced standing:* Applications to the second and third years are considered.

Curriculum 4-year semi-traditional. *Basic sciences:* Work related to fundamental principles of molecular, cellular, tissue and gross architecture and function, followed by study of alteration in functions and structure by disease. Some degree of patient contact occurs throughout the first 2 years through courses such as Introduciton to Clinical Medicine and Physical Diagnoses. *Clinical sciences:* One year of clerkships in major clinical areas, ward rounds, teaching conferences, seminars, and increasing responsibility for patient care. Senior year is devoted exclusively to a program of electives. There is the option of spending one academic quarter at another school in the U.S. or abroad.

Grading and Promotion Policies The system used is Honors/- Pass/Fail. A Committee on Promotion reviews student records at the end of each year and determines those qualified for promotion. Taking Part I of the NBME exam and recording a score is required. Taking Part II is optional.

Facilities *Teaching:* Basic science teaching takes place in the Montgomery Ward and Searle Buildings. Clinical facilities are provided by 5 area hospitals that, together with the medical and dental schools, make up the Northwestern-McGraw Medical Center. *Other:* The Northwestern Health Sciences Building houses the NU Cancer Center and NU Memorial Hospital's acute care services. Morton Building contains research laboratories. *Library:* The Archibald Church Medical Library, located in the Searle Building, houses 228,000 volumes and over 2500 periodicals. In addition, other libraries of Northwestern University are open to the students. *Housing:* Rooms are available for single men and women in Abbott Hall and two high-rise residence halls located on campus. A limited number of apartments for married students without children is also available in the facility.

Special Features *Minority admissions:* Recruitment is conducted on the high school and college levels. The school participates in the summer program of the Chicago Area Health and Medical Careers Group. *Other degree programs:* A combined MD-PhD program is available for students interested in research in a variety of disciplines including molecular biology, tumor cell biology, and clinical psychology. MD-MS and MD-MPH combined programs are also offered.

Rush Medical College
600 S. Paulina
Chicago, Illinois 60612

Admissions (AMCAS) The standard premedical courses are required. Consideration is given primarily to state residents, although competitive out-of-state residents are encouraged to apply. Rush Medical College students come from a wide variety of educational and social backgrounds. The Committee on Admissions considers both the academic and nonacademic qualifications of applicants in making its decisions.

Curriculum 4-year semi-traditional. *First year:* Provides students with exposure to the vocabulary and fundamental concepts upon which the clinical sciences are based. The first year is made up of 3 quarters of basic science material organized by disciplines and emphasizing the structure, function, and behavior of the normal person. *Student year:* Students study the causes and effects of disease and therapeutics and initiate their work with patients in programs which emphasize interviewing, history-taking and the physical examination. *Third and fourth years:* Provide students with training in clinical skills, diagnosis, and patient management in a variety of patient care settings. The clinical curriculum includes required core clerkships in family practice, medicine, neurology, pediatrics, psychiatry, obstetrics/gynecology, and surgery for a total of 54 weeks. A total of 24 weeks of elective study in areas of special interest to each student is also required. *Alternative Curriculum:* Rush has established an innovative preclinical curriculum for 18 students in each entering class. The Alternative Curriculum strives to give beginning medical students more experience with clinical problems, emphasizes personal responsibility for learning, and fosters the development of interpersonal skills. The new program involves individual and group assignments and uses elements of new information processing and computer technology.

Grading and Promotion Policies The final evaluation in course work is recorded at Honors, Pass, or Fail. The Committee on Student Evaluation and Promotion receives evaluations of each clinical period and determines when students are eligible for promotion. A total passing score must be obtained on Part I of the NBME exam and a score recorded on Part II.

Facilities Rush Medical College is located on the campus of Rush University at Rush-Presbyterian-St. Luke's Medical Center on Chicago's near west side. The Academic Facility houses the physical facilities for classroom instruction, laboratory research and private study. Clinical teaching takes place at Rush-Presbyterian-St. Luke's Hospital (903 beds) and other affiliated institutions. *Library:* The Library of Rush University

is located in the Academic Facility, has over 93,000 volumes, and subscribes to over 2050 journals.

Special Features *Minority admissions:* The school participates in the Chicago Area Health and Medical Careers Program to provide enrichment experiences for disadvantaged students. *Other degree programs:* MD-PhD programs are offered in a variety of disciplines including immunology and psychology.

Southern Illinois University
School of Medicine
P.O. Box 3926
Springfield, Illinois 62708

Admissions (AMCAS) The minimum premedical science courses are required. Admission is restricted to legal residents of the state. *Transfer and advanced standing:* School will consider applications from students in good standing at other LCME-accredited medical colleges. For requirements for consideration for advanced standing, contact the Office of Student Affairs.

Curriculum 4-year modern. Academic year begins in August. *First year:* Designed to develop competence in several disciplines basic to medicine such as physiology, biochemistry, anatomy, and behavioral sciences, the curriculum is organized around organ systems rather than traditional disciplines, focuses on the normal organism, and is taught in Carbondale. *Second year:* Presented in Springfield, instruction is integrated and organized around organ systems, but the focus is on abnormalities associated with disease. The major academic disciplines include pathology, pharmacology, microbiology, immunology, radiology, and clinical medicine. *Third year:* Clinical clerkships are provided in the following major specialties: internal medicine, surgery, obstetrics/gynecology, pediatrics, family practice, psychiatry, and anesthesiology. *Fourth year:* There are 32 weeks of elective study which may include advanced clinical clerkships, basic science research, and medical application of ancillary disciplines.

Grading and Promotion Policies An Honors/Pass/Fail system is used. Taking the NBME exam is optional.

Facilities *Teaching:* The educational program is conducted at both the medical education facilities in Carbondale and the medical center in Springfield. The split campus allows the School of Medicine to maximize the existing resources of a major university and the long-established clinical facilities in Springfield—Memorial Medical Center and St. John's Hospital. *Libraries:* One library is located within Carbondale's Morris Library Science Division, consists of more than 100,000 bound volumes, and subscribes to 1000 periodicals. In Springfield, the library is located in the Medical Instruction Facility, contains 85,000 bound volumes and subscribes to 1900 periodicals. *Housing:* In Carbondale, university-owned apartments for married students are available.

Special Features *Minority admissions:* The school sponsors a non-degree-granting Medical-dental Education Preparatory Program (MED-PREP) for disadvantaged students who are underrepresented. *Other degree programs:* None.

University of Chicago
Pritzker School of Medicine
Chicago, Illinois 60637

Admissions (AMCAS) In addition to the minimum required premedical science courses, studies in the social sciences, humanities, English composition, and mathematics must be included in the college educational training. Geographic location is not a consideration in the admissions decision. *Transfer and advanced standing:* Students from 2-year U.S. medical schools, and occasionally from 4-year schools, may be considered for transfer into the third-year class. The school does not consider foreign transfers.

Curriculum 4-year semi-modern. *First year:* Consists of courses in anatomy, biochemistry, infection and immunity, psychiatry, and social medicine. A clinical orientation program introduces students to patients with diseases illustrating principles and subjects taught concurrently. *Second year:* Courses in pharmacology, clinical pathophysiology, ophthalmology, medical statistics, and physical diagnosis. Elective time available in both semesters of this year. *Third year:* Rotating clerkships through major clinical specialties and some subspecialties. Students attend departmental seminars and conferences. *Fourth year:* At least one-third must be clinical electives and the remainder can be fulfilled by formal course work, research, or additional clinical or medically related electives.

Grading and Promotion Policies Required courses are graded Pass or Fail. Continuance of students is subject to recommendations made by the Committee on Promotions and Degrees. Taking the NBME exam is optional.

Facilities *Teaching:* Basic sciences are taught in Hull Biological Laboratories, Abbott Memorial Hall, and other buildings in the medical area. Clinical teaching takes place exclusively at the University Hospitals and Clinics—10 interconnected units with a total bed capacity of 710. *Other:* Armour Clinical Research Building contains laboratories for the surgery, radiology, and ophthalmology departments. *Library:* The Bio-Medical Libraries house over 290,000 volumes and 1400 periodicals. *Housing:* There are 8 residence halls for graduate students, including medical students. There are 1100 apartments for married students, ranging from 1 to 3 rooms.

Special Features *Minority admissions:* While the school does not have a special recruitment program, it does participate in the Chicago Area Health and Medical Careers Program for college students. *Other degree programs:* A special Medical Scientist Training Program is also offered for a combined MD-PhD degree in a 6-year period. This program is limited to from 8 to 12 students yearly; all students receive an annual stipend. The program is offered in all the biological sciences as well as chemistry and physics. An MD-MS program is also available.

University of Illinois
College of Medicine
1735 West Polk Street
Chicago, Illinois 60612

Admissions (AMCAS) The minimum premedical science courses as well as mathematics and behavioral science are required. Preference is given to state residents. The college of medicine consists of 4 semi-autonomous units located in Chicago, Peoria, Rockford and Urbana-Champaign. Students enrolled at the college in Chicago must attend for the entire four years. Students attending the first year at Urbana-Champaign for basic science study will remain there or be assigned to Peoria or Rockford for the next three years. *Transfer and advanced standing:* A limited number of students who pass the school's qualifying exam may be admitted.

College of Medicine at Chicago This unit is located about two miles west of downtown Chicago. In addition to basic science facilities and a library, it encompasses nine teaching hospitals, among them the University of Illinois Hospital (500 beds), the West Side VA Hospital (538 beds), and Cook County Hospital (1300 beds). The school offers a 4-year semi-traditional curriculum. *First year:* This covers the introductory basic sciences. Over 30 clinical conferences are offered to reinforce basic science principles relevant to the practice of medicine. An introductory course in behavioral science is also offered. *Second year:* In addition to the advanced basic sciences, courses are offered in medical ethics and human sexuality as well as physical diagnosis and problem solving. *Third year:* Rotation through the 5 major clinical specialties. *Fourth year:* Involves rotations through 4 or more minor clinical specialties and 4 weeks in primary care. The balance of the time is devoted to electives.

College of Medicine at Peoria The college is located a few blocks west of downtown Peoria. The school encompasses basic science facilities and is affiliated with the Methodist Medical Center of Illinois and St. Francis Hospital-Medical Center, which allows access to 1300 beds. Only the upper 3 years are taught, using a modern curriculum. *Second year:* This serves as an introduction to clinical medicine using a systemic pathophysiological teaching approach. *Third year:* The basic clerkship rotations begin after a 3-week bridging segment. *Fourth year:* Consists of 36 weeks of electives.

College of Medicine at Rockford Located near the northeast side of the city, the college consists of a teaching center and three associated hospitals—Rockford Memorial, St. Anthony Hospital Medical Center, and Swedish-American Hospital. Only the upper 3 years are taught, using a semi-modern curriculum. *Second year:* This consists of anatomical pathology, pharmacology, public health and preventive medicine, and clinical medicine skills, as well as a systemic-oriented introduction to clinical medicine. *Third year:* This consists of clerkships in most of the major clinical specialties and in orthopedics/urology as well as 3 months of electives. *Fourth year:* This consists of general surgery, neurology, general medicine, medical electives, and other electives.

College of Medicine at Urbana-Champaign Located on the university campus, the college has, in addition to its basic science facilities, affiliations for clinical training with almost all the hospitals in the east-central region of Illinois. The college offers a 4-year modern curriculum. *First year:* All the basic sciences except pharmacology are covered, as well as medical genetics, behavioral science, medical statistics, and nutrition. *Second year:* Courses offered are pharmacology, pathology, epidemiology, sociomedical seminars, pathophysiology, and clinical tutorials. *Third and fourth years:* The core clinical clerkships, medical electives and in-depth individual study experiences make up the last 2 years.

Grading and Promotion Policies A pass/fail system is used. Students must record passing total grades on Part I of the NBME exam for promotion to the third year and on Part II for graduation.

Special Features *Minority admissions:* Recruitment is conducted through the Urban Health Program and a 6-week summer prematriculation program is offered for accepted students. *Other degree programs:* Combined MD-MS and MD-PhD programs are offered by the College of Medicine at Chicago and at Urbana-Champaign in the basic sciences.

INDIANA

> **Indiana University**
> School of Medicine
> 1100 West Michigan Street
> Indianapolis, Indiana 46223

Admissions (AMCAS) Only minimum premedical science courses are required. Preference is given to residents; a few out-of-state residents are accepted yearly. *Transfer and advanced standing:* Only transfers of Indiana residents from American or foreign medical schools are considered.

Curriculum 4-year semi-modern. The major objectives of the curriculum are: the concentration of core material in both preclinical and clinical years, early exposure to patients, and extensive elective time. The first year is devoted to core basic science courses, second year to core basic science courses and some patient contact through the Introduction to Medicine courses. Third year (12 months) is devoted to clinical experience in pediatrics, obstetrics, gynecology, psychiatry, medicine, and surgery. Fourth year (9 months) is reserved exclusively for electives.

Grading and Promotion Policies System used is High Honors/Honors/Pass/Fail. Students must pass Parts I and II of the NBME exam to graduate.

Facilities The Medical Center is located in Indianapolis; the School of Medicine has students on eight other campuses. *Teaching:* In Indianapolis, preclinical teaching takes place in the Medical Sciences Building. Clinical facilities are provided by the University Hospital, Robert W. Long Hospital, William H. Coleman Hospital for Women, and James Whitcomb Riley

Hospital for Children. *Other:* Emerson Hall accommodates clinical departments; Fesler Hall houses clinical laboratories and offices. Riley Hospital has connecting wings for pediatric and cancer research. A Psychiatric Research Unit is also located at the Center. Combined hospitals of the Medical Center contain 647 beds. Neighboring hospitals provide some additional experience. *Library:* The medical library and nursing library combined house over 125,000 volumes and subscribe to 2500 periodicals. *Housing:* Accommodations for singles are available in the single-student dormitory on campus; apartments, both furnished and unfurnished, are available for married students.

Special Features *Minority admissions:* The school has an active program to identify, advise, and recruit disadvantaged students. *Other degree programs:* Students interested in Medical Science can work to combine an MD degree with either an MS or PhD. Combined MD-PhD programs are offered in a variety of disciplines including biophysics, medical genetics, pathology, and toxicology.

IOWA

> **University of Iowa**
> College of Medicine
> Jessup Hall
> Iowa City, Iowa 52242

Admissions (AMCAS) College requires minimum premedical science courses plus one advanced biology course and college algebra and trigonometry. Iowa residents are given strong preference, but some nonresidents are admitted. *Transfer and advanced standing:* Applications from students at both domestic and foreign schools are considered for the appropriate classes.

Curriculum 4-year semi-traditional. *First and second years:* The 2-year introductory phase comprises the basic medical sciences as well as some electives in each year. One semester of the second year is devoted to an introduction to clinical medicine. *Third year:* Comprises summer session and 2 semesters of rotating clinical clerkships in major specialties, in which student participates in patient care. *Fourth year:* Devoted to 32–47 weeks of electives in which the student focuses on whatever facet of medical education best relates to his/her professional interests. Elective courses are offered in alcoholism, biomedical engineering, community medicine, drug abuse, emergency medicine, medical ethics, medical jurisprudence, and nutrition.

Grading and Promotion Policies System used is Honors/Pass/Fail in basic and clinical sciences and Pass/Fail in the electives. Promotions committees consisting of faculty members review the accomplishments of their students and determine their eligibility for advancement at the close of the academic year. Students must record a passing total score on Part I of the NBME exam and take Part II to graduate.

Facilities *Teaching:* Preclinical sciences are taught at the Medical Laboratories Building and the Basic Science Building. Clinical teaching takes place at the University Hospital (1100 beds), VA Hospital (440 beds), Children's Hospital (167 beds), and Psychopathic Hospital (85 beds). *Other:* The major research facility is the Medical Research Center. *Library:* The Health Sciences Library houses 111,000 volumes and more than 125,000 periodicals. *Housing:* There are single, double, and triple rooms for single students; married students may use the efficiency, 1-, and 2-bedroom units.

Special Features *Minority admissions:* Recruitment is coordinated by means of the college's Educational Opportunities Program, which sponsors a summer program for accepted students. *Other degree programs:* Combined MD-PhD programs are offered in a variety of disciplines including radiation biology and community medicine.

KANSAS

University of Kansas
School of Medicine
39th Street and Rainbow Boulevard
Kansas City, Kansas 66103

Admissions (AMCAS) The school requires a bachelor's degree, minimum premedical science courses including quantitative analysis, and a course that includes differential and integral calculus. Statistics is recommended. Preference is given to residents, but a few nonresidents are accepted. *Transfer and advanced standing:* If vacancies exist, candidates for the third-year class are considered.

Curriculum 4-year semi-traditional. *First and second years:* Basic medical sciences are taught in structured course format of traditional curriculum. Courses in medical jurisprudence and introductory clinical medicine are included in preclinical years. Clinical correlation of various aspects of basic sciences is emphasized. *Third year:* Clerkship rotations and a preceptorship extending over 56 weeks. *Fourth year:* Five 4-week electives.

Grading and Promotion Policies Grading is by letter. A passing total score is required on Part I of the NBME exam for promotion to the third year and on Part II for graduation.

Facilities *Teaching:* The school is part of the University's Medical Center. Orr-Major Hall provides classrooms and labs for teaching basic science courses as well as space for individual research and departmental offices. The University Hospital provides facilities used in clinical training. *Library:* Dykes Medical Library contains more than 110,000 volumes. *Housing:* Living quarters for women are available in the Women's Residence; there are places for men and women also in the dormitory of the student center.

Special Features Combined MD-PhD programs are offered in a variety of disciplines.

KENTUCKY

University of Kentucky
College of Medicine
900 Rose Street
Lexington, Kentucky 40536

Admissions (AMCAS) In addition to the basic premedical science courses, one year of English is required. Courses in mathematics and in the psychological and social sciences are recommended. Preference is given to residents, but a number of nonresidents who have a clear interest in pursuing their medical education in Kentucky are accepted each year.

Curriculum 4-year semi-traditional. *First and second years:* Each of 34 weeks of scheduled class work in the basic sciences. Each week has about 29 hours of scheduled activities and 6–7 hours of elective time. *Third year:* Clerkship rotations through the major clinical specialties as well as forensic medicine and therapeutics. *Fourth year:* Selection of specialty and electives. One rotation is required in a surgery specialty, one off-site, one outpatient clerkship, one in either psychiatry, anesthesiology, or ophthalmology, and one in medicine or pediatrics.

Grading and Promotion Policies Grades are A, B, C, U (Unsatisfactory) and I (Incomplete). A student who is doing unsatisfactorily in 2 or more classes in one academic year may be dropped. Each year a Student Evaluation and Academic Committee for each class reviews the record of each student and makes recommendations relative to promotion, adjustment of academic load, repetition, or dismissal. Students must record total passing scores on Part I of the NBME exam for promotion to the third year and on Part II for graduation.

Facilities *Teaching:* The college is part of the University's Medical Center. Basic sciences are taught at the Medical Science Building and the major clinical teaching site is the 486-bed University Hospital. *Other:* The Warren Wright University Medical Plaza offers comprehensive outpatient medical services. The Saunder-Brown Research Center on Aging is a national gerontology resource facility. The Lucille Parker Markey Cancer Center is in mid-construction. *Library:* The Medical Center Library houses over 160,000 volumes and 2000 periodicals.

Special Features *Minority admissions:* The school has an active recruitment program and offers a summer prematriculation program. *Other degree programs:* Combined MD-PhD degree programs are offered in the basic medical sciences. An MD-MS program is also available.

University of Louisville
School of Medicine
Health Sciences Center
Louisville, Kentucky 40292

Admissions (AMCAS) Requirements include minimum premedical science courses plus 1 semester of calculus (or 2 semesters of other college mathematics course) and 2 semesters of English. Preference is given to state residents; nonresidents should have a GPA of 3.6 or higher and above-average test scores. *Transfer and advanced standing:* Applicants from 2-year medical schools and those who have completed 2 years of work at other American medical schools are considered.

Curriculum 4-year semi-traditional. First 2 years consist of basic science courses, and 4 hours of elective time per semester is required. Third year is devoted to required clerkships. Fourth year has two required clerkships, an ACLS course, and 15 weeks of electives.

Grading and Promotion Policies A grade of Pass or Fail is submitted at the completion of each course. The Committee on Student Promotions approves the scholastic activities of the individual or may recommend one of several courses of action if work is unsatisfactory. A passing total score on Part I of the NBME exam is needed for promotion to the third year. Taking Part II is optional.

Facilities *Teaching:* Basic sciences are taught in the Instructional Building at the Health Science Center near downtown Louisville. Primary clinical facilities are: Humana Hospital University, Kosair-Children's Hospital, and Veterans Administration Medical Center. Other clinical affiliates are: The Bingham Child Guidance Clinic, Inc., Humana Hospital Audubon, Frazier Rehabilitation Center, Jewish Hospital, James Graham Brown Cancer Center, Norton Hospital, St. Anthony Hospital, and Trover Clinic (Madisonville). *Other:* The Research Building is devoted entirely to scientific investigation by all departments of the school. A commons building houses the Health Sciences library, auditorium, cafeteria and bookstore. *Library:* No information available. *Housing:* Medical-Dental dormitory located near the Health Sciences Center has dormitory accommodations for single men and apartment accommodations for single women and married couples.

Special Features *Minority admissions:* The Office of Professional and Graduate Minority Affairs aids in recruitment and retention of minorities. *Other degree programs:* A combined MD-PhD program is available in a variety of disciplines including biophysics, immunology, and toxicology.

LOUISIANA

Louisiana State University
School of Medicine in New Orleans
1542 Tulane Avenue
New Orleans, Louisiana 70112

Admissions (AMCAS) Required courses beyond the minimum premedical science requirements include 3 hours of advanced chemistry (quantitative analysis, biochemistry, or physical chemistry). Recommended courses include advanced mathematics, statistical methods, public speaking, economics, history, foreign languages, philosophy, psychology, and social studies. State residents are given priority and they generally compose all of the first-year class.

Curriculum 4-year semi-traditional. *First and second years:* Main concentration is on fundamental medical sciences and their relation to clinical medicine. Introduction to Clinical Medicine course is taught during both semesters of the second year. All phases of physical diagnosis as well as a survey of clinical medicine in an organ system and problem-oriented format are covered. *Third year:* After a presentation of 3 weeks of ophthalmology and radiology, the basic clinical clerkships are taken in four 12-week blocks, including: medicine-dermatology, obstetrics/gynecology-psychiatry, pediatrics-vacation/elective, and surgery-otorhinolaryngology-urology. *Fourth year:* Consists of nine 4-week blocks. It provides additional clerkship experience in medicine and surgery. Other required clerkships are neural sciences and ambulatory care. Special topics in geriatrics, nutrition, federal regulation in the delivery of health care, computers in medicine, and substance abuse are presented in a single block while the remainder of the year is elective.

Grading and Promotion Policies Grades are Honors, High Pass, Pass, Fail, Withdrew Passing, and Withdrew Failing. Periodic reviews are made of student performance by means of exams, staff reports, and other forms of appraisal. Eligibility for promotion rests on completion of all course work and requirements and approval by the Promotions Committee. A score must be recorded for Part I of the NBME exam. Taking Part II is optional.

Facilities *Teaching:* The Medical Education Building is the site for basic science instruction. The school is located near the center of the New Orleans business district adjacent to the 2200-bed Charity Hospital. Ten other hospitals are affiliated with LSU. An auditorium equipped with the most up-to-date audio-visual facilities provides space for medical meetings and faculty/student assemblies and lectures. *Other:* Recent expansion near the campus has provided more space for existing educational and research programs and the development of new programs. *Library:* Three major library holdings provide 6 professional schools of the LSU Medical Center with more than 150,000 volumes and current periodicals in excess of 1500 titles. *Housing:* University-controlled housing is provided for 300 married and single students. Located 3 blocks from the school, the residence hall provides 1-, 2-, or 3-bedroom apartments for married students and double rooms for single men and women. Recreational facilities are located on the first floor.

Special Features *Minority admissions:* The Office of Minority Affairs coordinates recruitment. The school offers a Minority Summer Prematriculation Program for accepted first-year students to facilitate adjustment to medical school. *Other degree programs:* Combined MD-PhD programs are offered in a variety of disciplines including pathology and tropical medicine.

Louisiana State University
School of Medicine in Shreveport
1501 Kings Highway
Shreveport, Louisiana 71130

Admissions (AMCAS) Required courses, in addition to the minimum premedical sciences, include English (9 semester hours) and a classical or modern foreign language (6 semester hours).

Curriculum 4-year semi-traditional. *First year:* Courses include introductory basic sciences plus introductory classes in comprehensive health care, human ecology, radiology, psychiatry, and biometry. A course entitled Man and Medicine is offered. *Second year:* Advanced basic sciences with a major course in clinical diagnosis to prepare students for clinical years. Courses in genetics, community medicine, and epidemiology are introduced. *Third and fourth years:* Emphasis on supervised experience in patient care, especially long-term care of ambulatory patients. One-third of fourth year is electives with opportunities for extramural and intramural work in family practice, other clinical specialties, basic sciences, and research.

Grading and Promotion Policies A letter system is used for course work and Pass/Fail for electives.

Facilities *Teaching:* Confederate Memorial Medical Center (1000 beds) is the principal clinical teaching facility. The school is presently constructing a basic and clinical science building and a comprehensive care teaching facility. *Other:* Shreveport VA Hospital (450 beds) is affiliated with the school and some instruction takes place there. *Library:* Three major library holdings provide 6 professional schools of the LSU Medical Center with more than 150,000 volumes and current periodicals in excess of 1500 titles. The school maintains property which houses an animal farm and laboratories on a site off campus. *Housing:* None.

Special Features *Minority admissions:* Recruitment of disadvantaged students is facilitated by visits to Louisiana colleges and communication with other educational institutions. *Other degree programs:* The school has instituted a BS-MD program in conjunction with Louisiana State University in Shreveport which will enable students to complete medical training within 6 years of high school graduation. Combined MD-PhD programs are offered in a variety of disciplines.

Tulane University
School of Medicine
1430 Tulane Avenue
New Orleans, Louisiana 70112

Admissions (AMCAS) Only the minimum premedical science courses are required. Suggested elective courses are physical chemistry, comparative anatomy, embryology, genetics, and mathematics. Large numbers of out-of-state students and a few 3-year students are accepted. Half the students will be drawn each year from the South. *Transfer and advanced standing:* A few students are accepted annually as transfers to second- and third-year classes. These students usually come from 2-year medical schools. Very few transfers are accepted from foreign medical schools.

Curriculum 4-year semi-modern. *First year:* Core courses in the introductory basic sciences as well as community medicine and clinical correlation. Three hours each week are available in the second semester for enrollment in elective courses. *Second year:* Consists of core courses in the advanced basic sciences as well as neuropsychiatry, cancer clinics, epidemiology, and biostatistics which serve as preparation for clinical studies such as physical diagnosis and introduction to clinical medicine. *Third year:* Consists of 48 weeks devoted to basic core clerkships in the major clinical areas. The clerkships provide the opportunity to participate in direct responsibility for diagnosis and management of clinical problems presented by patients in the hospital. *Fourth year:* Consists of two components: required clerkships and electives. The electives are available in all clinical departments and include medically related topics such as ethics, jurisprudence, engineering, community medicine, and health delivery systems.

Grading and Promotion Policies Grades are High Pass, Pass, Conditional, and Failure. Any course grade of less than Pass constitutes an academic deficiency which must be removed by remedial work and/or examination. Passing grades in all required courses of the year are necessary for advancement to the succeeding year. Taking Parts I and II of the NBME exam is optional.

Facilities *Teaching:* Located in downtown New Orleans, the school occupies a full city block and consists of 4 units: the Hutchinson Memorial Building, the Libby Memorial Building, the Burthe-Cottam Memorial Building, and the Environmental Medicine Building. Clinical teaching takes place at the Tulane Medical Center Hospital (300 beds) and Charity Hospital (1877 beds). Six other hospitals in New Orleans provide supplementary teaching facilities and others located elsewhere in the area are available. *Other:* The Leon M. Wolf Graphic Arts Laboratories houses facilities for medical photography and illustration. A television network is utilized for instructional purposes; Souchon Museum of Anatomy is an award-winning collection of over 400 specimens; the Computer Center provides services to the medical center; the Delta Regional Primate Research Center is involved in work in communicable diseases, genetics, developmental disorders, and other medical problems. *Library:* The Rudolph Matas library houses about 130,000 volumes, and 1200 periodicals are received. *Housing:* Accommodations for single and married students are available at the Charles Rosen House and Julian Hawthorne Hall.

Special Features *Minority admissions:* The school has an active recruitment program targeted at the southeastern and southwestern parts of the country. A Summer Reinforcement and Enrichment Program is available for minority undergraduate premedical students. *Other degree programs:* Combined MD-PhD programs are offered in a variety of disciplines including biostatistics and parasitology. MD-MS and MD-MPH programs are also available.

MARYLAND

Johns Hopkins University
School of Medicine
720 Rutland Avenue
Baltimore, Maryland 21205

Admissions Bachelor's degree or its equivalent required, minimum premedical science course requirements plus one semester of calculus and 24 semester hours of social and behavioral sciences and humanities. Courses in quantitative analysis, physical chemistry, and advanced biology courses recommended. There are no residence requirements and no preference shown in selection of applicants. Aside from the regular program, the school has a multiple option Flexible Medical Admissions Program (FlexMed) that permits accelerated or delayed matriculation. This permits students to pursue alternate educational pathways, work experiences, and humanitarian service in keeping with their interests and career goals. *Transfer and advanced standing:* Transfers are accepted for the second- or third-year class. Transfers are accepted only into the standard 4-year curriculum.

Curriculum 4-year semi-modern. Curriculum includes core, preclinical, and clinical courses. Patient-oriented experience in the first year increases in elective opportunities. *First year:* Introductory basic sciences as well as behavioral sciences, basic emergency medicine, and medical ethics. *Second year:* Three quarters devoted to advanced basic sciences, medical history, clinical epidemiology, physical and laboratory diagnosis, and the elements of clinical medicine. *Third and fourth years:* Required clerkships in major clinical areas and electives.

Grading and Promotion Policies Letter grades are used in required courses and clerkships and Honors/Pass/Fail are used for electives. Grades are based on the composite judgment of responsible instructors, and not solely upon results of examinations. At the end of each academic year, the Committee on Student Promotions decides what actions will be taken regarding student status. Taking the NBME exam is optional.

Facilities *Teaching:* Most of the preclinical departments are situated in the W. Barry Wood Basic Science Building. The Johns Hopkins Hospital (1100 beds) occupies 14 acres of land adjacent to buildings that house the preclinical departments. Separate buildings contain specialty clinics. The School is also affiliated wth Baltimore City Hospital (622 beds), Good Samaritan Hospital (253 beds), and Sinai Hospital of Baltimore (516 beds), and is associated with other institutions. *Other:* Research facilities for the preclinical sciences are located in the Basic Science Building, while the Traylor Research Building augments the research facilities of the clinical departments and houses the Division of Laboratory Animal Medicine. *Library:* The Welch Medical Library is located in a separate building adjacent to the other buildings of the School of Medicine and houses over 267,000 volumes and 2700 periodicals. *Housing:* A residence hall for single students

and a garden apartment complex for married students are available.

Special Features *Minority admissions:* The school has an active admissions program. *Other degree programs:* Combined MD-PhD programs are available in all the basic sciences as well as in biomedical engineering, biophysics, medical history, human genetics, and molecular biology. The school also offers combined MD-MPH and MD-DSc in Public Health programs.

Uniformed Services University
School of Medicine
4301 Jones Bridge Road
Bethesda, Maryland 20814

Admissions (AMCAS) The basic premedical science courses plus one year of mathematics and one of college English are required. *Transfer and advanced standing:* None.

Curriculum 4-year semi-traditional. *First year:* After a 4-week officer orientation program, the introductory basic sciences are taught. In addition, courses are offered in epidemiology and biometrics, Human Context in Health Care, Military Studies and Medical History, diagnostic parisitology and medical zoology, medical psychology, and Introduction to Clinical Medicine I. *Second year:* In addition to the advanced basic sciences, courses presented include clinical concepts, preventive medicine, radiographic interpretation, and Introduction to Clinical Medicine II. A 48-week period of rotations through the major clinical specialties including family practice. *Fourth year:* Consists of medical, surgical, and psychiatric selective blocks, neurology, military preventive medicine, contingency and emergency medicine, subinternships, and elective clerkships.

Grading and Promotion Policies Letter grades are used for courses and clerkships and Pass/Fail for electives. Both parts of the NBME exam must be taken.

Facilities *Teaching:* The school is located on the grounds of the Naval Hospital. Four buildings contain faculty offices, classrooms, student multidisciplinary and other laboratories and various support units. Ten affiliated hospitals provide clinical teaching facilities. *Library:* The Learning Resources Center possesses about 65,000 volumes and receives about 1500 medical periodicals. *Housing:* None available on campus.

Special Features *Minority admissions:* Recruitment is sponsored by a program entitled AQUA (Accession of Qualified Underrepresented Applicants). *Other degree programs:* None.

University of Maryland
School of Medicine
655 West Baltimore Street
Baltimore, Maryland 21201

Admissions (AMCAS) In addition to the minimum premedical science courses, requirements include one year of English.

Applicants must also have completed a minimum of 90 semester hours at an accredited college or university. Strong preference is given to residents.

Curriculum 4-year semi-modern. *First year:* Introductory basic science courses as well as genetics, human behavior, and biophysics. Introduction to Clinical Practices begins training in diagnostic procedures. The correlative medicine course introduces the students to patients with clinical problems related to basic sciences. Embryology is presented in conjunction with patients having congenital anomalies. *Second year:* Advanced basic sciences with instruction shifting to an organ system approach and interdisciplinary emphasis. Patient contact is maintained. *Third year:* Clerkships through major medical specialties. *Fourth year:* Devoted to ambulatory care, student internship, clerkships and electives.

Grading and Promotion Policies A letter grade system is used. Only Part I of the NBME exam is required, but promotion to the third year is not dependent on passing; Part II is optional.

Facilities *Teaching:* The school is located a short distance from the newly developed downtown Charles Center. University hospital and affiliated hospitals around Baltimore have more than 1400 beds for teaching purposes. *Other:* The school also is affiliated with the Shock Trauma Center, Cancer Center, Institute of Psychiatric and Human Behavior, and the Sudden Infant Death Syndrome Institute. *Library:* The Health Sciences Library houses more than 240,000 volumes and subscribes to 3100 periodicals. It also provides access to a wide range of data bases. *Housing:* Dormitory rooms are available in the Baltimore Student Union; apartments are available a short distance from campus.

Special Features *Minority admissions:* The school has an active recruitment program which involves visits to colleges; seminars; and workshops. A 10-week preprofessional summer program is sponsored for undergraduates interested in health science careers and a prematriculation summer program is available for those accepted into the first year. *Other degree programs:* Combined MD-PhD programs are available in all the basic sciences as well as in epidemiology, human genetics, and preventive medicine.

MASSACHUSETTS

Boston University
School of Medicine
80 East Concord Street
Boston, Massachusetts 02118

Admissions (AMCAS) The school is known for offering more pathways leading to the MD degree than any medical school in the country. Students are accepted after high school, after 2 years of college, in addition to being able to complete the first year of medical school over 2 academic years. For the traditional applicant who plans to enter after completing college, one year of English and humanities is required in addition to the minimum premedical science courses. It is recommended that biology and chemistry courses include laboratory exercises and that the student have a knowledge of calculus and of quantitation in chemistry. *Transfer and advanced standing:* Applicants considered for third-year class; students may bypass some basic courses. Transfer students must pass Part I of the NBME exam.

Curriculum 4-year semi-modern. The curriculum provides the opportunity to study medicine in a flexible environment that stimulates a spirit of critical inquiry and provides sound knowledge in the biological, social, and behavioral sciences in order to deal with human problems of health and disease. *First year:* The basic medical sciences are emphasized in both departmental and interdisciplinary courses. Human Development and Community Medicine are also presented. Correlations between basic scientific information and clinical disease are integrated in the regular course work. *Second year:* This period is a continuation of the basic science courses and the introduction of the clinical sciences and physical diagnosis which are presented in an integrated multidisciplinary format. During this time the student learns the basic techniques of clinical medicine, including history taking and physical examination. *Third year:* Represents the major clerkship year. In addition to the conventional clerkships in medicine, surgery, pediatrics, obstetrics, and psychiatry, a clerkship in ambulatory-community care is provided in which the student sees and manages health problems in the home under close supervision of a preceptor. *Fourth year:* Devoted to developing specific elective programs under the supervision of a faculty member who will serve the particular needs of the students.

Grading and Promotion Policies The student's record contains for each course the appropriate Honors/Pass/Fail designation and a detailed written narrative. If the student is unable to pass any given course, the Promotion Committee determines the action to be taken. Taking Parts I and II of the NBME examination is optional.

Facilities *Teaching:* The 14-story Instructional Building includes space for student activities, administrative offices, two 130-seat auditoriums, teaching laboratories, faculty offices, research laboratories, and a 3-floor library. The 10-story Research Building is adjacent. The principal teaching hospitals are Boston City Hospital, University Hospital, and the Veterans Administration Hospitals. *Other:* The school is affiliated with a network of at least 12 community hospitals, neighborhood health centers and other private practice settings, all of which provide clinical settings for third- and fourth-year students. *Library:* The Library contains more than 80,000 volumes and receives approximately 1500 periodicals.

Special Features *Minority admissions:* The school is committed to the recruitment, admission, and retention of disadvantaged students. It conducts a 6-week, summer enrichment Pre-entrance Program for accepted students. *Other degree programs:* Combined MD-PhD progams in all basic sciences are offered as is an MD-MPH program.

Harvard Medical School
25 Shattuck Street
Boston, Massachusetts 02115

Admissions Minimum science courses are required in addition to one year of calculus and one year of English. Recommended courses include introductory psychology, statistics, humanities, and social sciences. Selection is not based on residence. *Transfer and advanced standing:* Limited number of students are admitted to third-year class.

Curriculum 4-year modern. *First year:* First semester provides an introduction to scientific basis of medicine. Basic science subjects are presented in a core curriculum. There is abundant opportunity to expand on this material during subsequent required and elective time. Clinics are scheduled to illustrate the clinical relevance of the basic sciences. *Second year:* Study of the gastrointestinal, endocrine, respiratory, renal, cardiovascular, neurologic, and reproductive systems, as well as hematology and infection. Practical instruction in taking histories and giving examinations. *Third and fourth years:* Include clerkships in medicine, surgery, pediatrics, psychiatry, obstetrics-gynecology, neurology, radiology, dermatology, ophthalmology, otolaryngology, and orthopedics, as well as elective time. While a great deal of flexibility exists to establish personalized programs, they must be distributed according to the following requirements: basic sciences, 28 credits; pathophysiology, 20 credits; behavioral science, social medicine, and preventive medicine, 6 credits; clinical, 56 credits.

Grading and Promotion Policies System used is Honors/Pass/Fail. Promotion Boards for each of the first 3 years determine those qualified to be promoted. Students must record total passing scores on Parts I and II of the NBME exam for promotion and graduation, respectively.

Facilities *Teaching:* Preclinical courses are taught in the buildings that compose Longwood Avenue Quadrangle. Clinical instruction takes place in Beth Israel Hospital (368 beds), Brigham and Womens Hospital (650 beds), Massachusetts General Hospital (1060 beds) and others. *Other:* Research facilities available in most of the medical school buildings. *Library:* The Countway Library of Medicine is one of the largest in the country. *Housing:* Dormitory housing is available for men and women; apartments for married students are nearby.

Special Features *Minority admissions:* A full-time administrator coordinates the active minority recruitment program which is geared to enroll students having academic strength, community commitment, and leadership ability. An 8-week prematriculation summer program is offered for a limited number of disadvantaged students to enhance their academic preparation and provide exposure to research. *Other degree programs:* Cooperative programs with Massachusetts Institute of Technology allow science- and engineering-oriented students to begin medical study while completing requirements for undergraduate degree. School also offers combined MD-PhD degree programs in a wide variety of disciplines including biophysics, developmental biology, genetics, immunology, and molecular genetics.

Tufts University
School of Medicine
136 Harrison Avenue
Boston, Massachusetts 02111

Admissions (AMCAS) Minimum premedical science courses are required, as is proficiency in written and spoken English. Courses in calculus, statistics, and computers are desirable. There is no preference for state residents. Applicants under 28 are preferred. *Transfer and advanced standing:* Acceptance into the second or third year is possible as seats become available.

Curriculum 4-year modern. *First year:* Major themes during this year include fundamental principles applicable to the normal human, the biopsychosocial determinants of human behavior, the impact of health care systems and society on the individual patient and physician, an introduction to the doctor-patient relationship, and an introduction to human nutrition. *Second year:* This year involves a progressive introduction to human abnormal biology and therapeutics through a series of interdisciplinary courses organized by organ system. A course in psychopathology is also offered, as is one in physical diagnosis. *Third year:* Consists of rotations through the major clinical specialties and rotations in neurology, rehabilitative medicine, ophthalmology, otolaryngology, and therapeutic radiology. *Fourth year:* Involves eight 4-week rotations, two of which are ward service. The remainder of the time is free for electives.

Grading and Promotion Policies The system used is Honors/Pass/Fail. Students must record a passing total score on Part I of the NBME exam for promotion to the third year and on Part II for graduation.

Facilities *Teaching:* The major school structure is the Medical-Dental Building, which is made up of 4 adjoining 8-story buildings with a central entrance. Clinical teaching facilities are provided by the New England Center Hospital (452 beds) and off campus by St. Elizabeth's Hospital (385 beds), Bayside Medical Center (950 beds), VA Hospital (769 beds), Lemuel Shattick Hospital (250 beds), and others. *Other:* Clinical research is carried out in the Ziskind Research Building of New England Medical Center Hospital. *Library:* The Health Sciences Library houses 92,000 volumes and subscribes to 1400 periodicals. *Housing:* A residence hall for men and women is located one block from the main building.

Special Features *Minority admissions:* Recruitment of minority applicants is directed primarily to the Boston, New England, and New York areas. A preadmission summer program is offered for accepted applicants. *Other degree programs:* Combined MD-PhD programs are offered in a variety of disciplines including immunology and molecular biology.

University of Massachusetts
Medical School
55 Lake Avenue, North
Worcester, Massachusetts 01605

Admissions (AMCAS) The standard premedical science courses and one year of English are required. Courses in calculus, psychology, sociology, and statistics are recommended. *Transfer and advanced standing:* Applicants will be accepted, provided there are vacancies in the class.

Curriculum 4-year semi-traditional with innovative curriculum. *First year:* A large portion of this year is devoted to the study of normal structure and function of cells, tissues, and organs in courses of anatomy, biochemistry, genetics, and physiology. Clinical correlations illustrate and emphasize the fundamental scientific nature of clinical knowledge. Clinical experience begins in the first year in courses in emergency medicine, physical diagnosis, communication skills, and a 3-week family and community medicine clerkship. Special lectures and conferences are designed to integrate material in the longitudinal courses of geriatrics, medical humanities, nutrition, and oncology. *Second year:* Emphasis is placed on physical abnormalities, pathological processes, and the development of disease states taught within the context of pharmacology, microbiology, pathology, and an Introduction to Clinical Medicine. Significant time is allotted to psychopathology and physical diagnosis. Each student receives individual instruction and constructive feedback in interviewing and physical examination skills during the physical diagnosis course. Epidemiology and preventive medicine courses focus on issues of disease prevention. Once again, special lectures and conferences allow for the integration of the longitudinal courses. *Third and fourth years:* These are considered a continuum of study. The third year consists of 40 weeks of clinical rotations which allow the students to participate in the day to day care of hospitalized and ambulatory patients as part of a health care team which includes interns, residents, attending physicians, nurses, and other allied health professionals. The fourth year consists of 8 weeks of required rotations in medicine and neurology plus a minimum of an additional 16 weeks of electives. It is expected that students will select electives which provide an intensive study in a field that holds special interest for the individual.

Grading and Promotion Policies System used is Honors/Satisfactory/Marginal/Unsatisfactory/Incomplete. Students are not required to take the NBME exam, although it is anticipated that most will elect to do so for purposes of subsequent licensure. Promotion from one phase of the curriculum to the next will be determined by the Committee on Promotions, consisting of instructors from each department involved in the curriculum of a given period of study.

Facilities *Teaching:* The Medical School was developed on 126 acres of land on the eastern edge of Worcester. A 10-story Basic and Clinical Sciences Building was completed in 1973. A 400-bed teaching hospital that adjoins the Sciences Building opened in 1976. The Medical Center is the designated regional trauma center for Central Massachusetts as well as the base of

operation for New England Life Flight, the first hospital air ambulance in New England. *Other:* Among the affiliated hospitals for clinical teaching are the St. Vincent Hospital (600 beds), Worcester City Hospital (250 beds), Worcester Memorial Hospital (379 beds), and Berkshire Medical Center (365 beds). *Library:* The Medical School Library is housed in the Sciences Building and its facilities include the capacity for more than 100,000 volumes. *Housing:* The school has limited on-campus facilities for housing single students, which are reserved for first-year students. Most students find housing in the local community.

Special Features *Minority admissions:* Minority students who are legal residents of Massachusetts are invited to apply for admission. A 4-week Summer Enrichment Program (SEP) is available for sophomore and higher level college students. *Other degree programs:* Combined MD-PhD programs are offered in all the basic medical sciences as well as in immunology and molecular genetics.

MICHIGAN

Michigan State University
College of Human Medicine
East Lansing, Michigan 48824

Admissions (AMCAS) Requirements include the basic premedical science courses, one year English, and psychology and/or sociology. Preference is given to applicants from Michigan. *Transfer and advanced standing:* Applicants are considered when vacancies exist.

Curriculum The curriculum is divided into 3 phases integrating the basic biological and behavioral sciences with clinical training and problem-solving skills, and a phase in which the student concentrates primarily on clinical training. *Phase I:* A one-term experience in which the student becomes oriented to the medical process. The goal is to impart to students the notion of drawing upon a variety of disciplines essential to the solution of patient problems. Interviewing skills and work with live anatomical models are stressed in this phase along with an introductory course in cell biology. *Phase II:* Offered in 2 tracks to meet the needs of individuals with different learning styles. One track is primarily lecture and laboratory in basic science courses, and the other a small group, problem-solving track which continues the approach initiated in Phase I. *Phase III:* Can normally be completed within 6 or 7 terms and is spent in one of the community hospitals associated with the college. Students usually live in the community for the total period of clinical training. The community physicians work closely with community-based members of the college to provide a unique learning environment.

Grading and Promotion Policies All grading in the school is Honors/Pass/Fail. A total passing score on Parts I and II of the NBME exam is required for promotion to the third year and graduation, respectively.

Facilities *Teaching:* The primary facilities utilized in basic science instruction are: Life Sciences Building, Fee Hall, and Giltner Hall. The Clinical Center is an ambulatory care facility where students are trained in clinical sciences during the first 2 years of the curriculum. Students receive their formal clinical training during the last 2 years in community settings in 17 hospitals in 8 Michigan communities. *Library:* Information not available. *Housing:* On-campus dormitory rooms and apartments for both single and married students. There is also a large selection of off-campus housing.

Special Features *Minority admissions:* A major effort is made to include applicants from inadequately represented geographic, economic, and ethnic groups. *Other degree programs:* Combined MA-MD and MD-PhD programs available in basic and behavioral science departments by individual arrangement.

University of Michigan
Medical School
1301 Catherine Street
Ann Arbor, Michigan 48109-0010

Admissions (AMCAS) One year of English and 2 years of nonscience subjects are required. Advanced courses in biology and/or chemistry are recommended. Preference is given to residents, but a significant number of nonresidents are admitted. Forty-four highly qualified high school graduates who have been accepted by the University of Michigan College of Literature, Science and The Arts will be admitted to the 7-year Integrated Premedical-Medical Program. They earn their BA degree after the fourth year. *Transfer and advanced standing:* No transfer students are accepted. Beginning students may receive advanced placement through examination to bypass basic science courses.

Curriculum 4-year semi-traditional. *First year:* Introductory basic sciences as well as 2 interdisciplinary courses, Neural and Behavioral Sciences, and Introduction to Clinical Sciences. *Second year:* Advanced basic sciences and a continuation of the above mentioned interdisciplinary courses. Following completion of the second year, students spend one month involved in an interphase program especially designed to assist in the transition from the basic to the clinical sciences. *Third year:* Clerkship rotation through major clinical specialties and some subspecialties. *Fourth year:* This year consists of a basic clerkship (subinternship), structured electives, and 12–16 weeks of electives. Electives include interdisciplinary courses like Forensic Medicine and Medical Jurisprudence, History of Medicine, Infection and Immunity, Neural and Behavioral Science, Nutrition, and Respiratory Problems. Electives may also be taken at Michigan State and Wayne State Universities.

Grading and Promotion Policies A modified Pass/Fail system is used (Honors, High Pass, Pass, Marginal Fail, Fail). This is supplemented by narrative statement sent to the Dean's office. Students are required to demonstrate passing total scores on Parts I and II of the NBME exam for promotion and graduation, respectively. Advancements are made by the Basic Science and Clinical Academic Review Boards.

Facilities *Teaching:* Basic sciences are taught in Medical Sciences Buildings Unit I and II in the Medical Center. Clinical instruction takes place at the University Hospitals (931 beds) supplemented by use of St. Joseph Mercy Hospital (522 beds), the VA Hospital (486 beds), Westland Medical Center (474 beds), and the Henry Ford Hospital (1043 beds). A new University Hospital is scheduled to open in 1986. *Other:* Medical Center includes: Simpson Memorial Institute devoted to cancer research and diseases of the blood; 3 Kresge buildings for clinical research; and the Buhl Research Center for Human Genetics. A new Medical Sciences Research Building is scheduled to open in 1986. *Library:* The A. Alfred Taubman Medical Library was completed in 1980 and houses over 200,000 volumes and 3000 periodicals. *Housing:* Some facilities available.

Special Features *Minority admissions:* The school has an active minority-student recruitment program. Students with poorer academic backgrounds may choose to extend the period of medical study under the flexible curriculum program. *Other degree programs:* School offers combination MD-PhD programs in a variety of disciplines including human genetics.

Wayne State University
School of Medicine
540 East Canfield Avenue
Detroit, Michigan 48201

Admissions (AMCAS) Applicants should have taken the basic premedical science courses plus a course in genetics and one year of English. School does consider some nonresidents for admission. *Transfer and advanced standing:* Applicants from domestic medical and osteopathic schools will be considered for second- and third-year classes.

Curriculum 4-year modern. Curriculum consists of a core program, early correlation of clinical medicine, coordinated clinical experience, and expanded elective studies. *First year:* Consists of study of structure and function of the normal human by an integrated organ system approach. Social and behavioral sciences as related to community health problems are also considered. *Second year:* Consists of a study of abnormalities in structure and function. Behavior is also considered. Time is allotted for an intensive course in interviewing techniques, taking medical histories, and physical examination. *Third year:* Consists of rotating clerkships through major specialties and family medicine. *Fourth year:* A broad program of 32 weeks of structured electives. Time can be spent at another university.

Grading and Promotion Policies System used is Honors/Pass/Fail. In order to qualify for promotion to next class, a student must pass 2 comprehensive examinations. The NBME exam must be taken to record a score on both Parts I and II.

Facilities *Teaching:* The medical school is located in the heart of the 236-acre Detroit Medical Center. The Basic Science Building houses the school's 6 basic science departments, as well as administrative and service offices. Clinical teaching takes place at the Harper Hospital (557 beds), Children's

Hospital (320 beds), Grace Hospital (957 beds), Hutzel Hospital (360 beds). *Other:* Clinical teaching also takes place off campus at the Detroit General Hospital (700 beds) and VA Hospital (890 beds). *Library:* Shiffman Medical Library houses over 150,000 volumes. *Housing:* Available in the campus area.

Special Features   *Minority admissions:* The school's Office of Recruitment is actively engaged in furthering minority-student enrollment. Entering students can participate in a summer program designed to facilitate the transition to medical school. *Other degree programs:* Combined MD-PhD degree programs are offered in a variety of basic science disciplines.

MINNESOTA

Mayo Medical School
200 First Street, S.W.
Rochester, Minnesota 55901

Admissions (AMCAS)   Only the minimum premedical science courses are required. A course in cell biology is recommended. Forty students comprise each class; 20 are from the State of Minnesota and 20 are from other states.

Curriculum   4-year modern. *First year:* An 11-month period that provides the student with integrated study of the basic sciences by system. Study of an individual patient's illness will be introduced when such an approach affords opportunity to apply basic pathophysiologic concepts. A core curriculum is followed. *Second year:* Junior clerkship and pharmacology/therapeutics. *Third and fourth years:* A 2-year period designed to permit the student to develop an academic major in a clinical and/or scientific discipline. A combined program leading to the MD degree and PhD in Biomedical Science degree is available for up to 4 students each year. Senior clerkship assignments are included in this period.

Grading and Promotion Policies   An Honors/Pass/Fail system is used and a score must be recorded on Parts I and II of the NBME exam. Promotion will be based on evidence of behavior and maturation, consonant with the student's talents and defined professional goals.

Facilities   *Teaching:* Located in Rochester, the school makes use of 3 buildings in its preclinical program. The Guggenheim Building houses the facilities for education and research in most of the basic sciences, the Plummer Building houses the library and Biomedical Communications, and the Hilton Building houses clinical laboratories of the Department of Laboratory Medicine, Microbiology, and Endocrine Research. Clinical teaching takes place at 2 hospitals, Rochester Methodist Hospital and St. Mary's Hospital, which provide 2000 beds and several clinical research facilities. *Other:* Facilities for research are located in the Medical Sciences Building, Guggenheim Building, and Rochester Methodist and St. Mary's Hospitals. *Library:* Information not available. *Housing:* Students are responsible for finding their own housing in the area.

Special Features   *Minority admissions:* The school actively

seeks minority students and welcomes their application for admission. *Other degree programs:* Combined MD-PhD programs are offered in several disciplines including immunology and pathology.

University of Minnesota
Duluth School of Medicine
2400 Oakland Avenue
Duluth, Minnesota 55812

Admissions (AMCAS)   Requirements include the minimum premedical science courses and one year of English composition, mathematics through calculus, humanities, and behavioral science. Only residents of Minnesota and certain counties of northwest Wisconsin are considered. School offers a 2-year program that prepares students for transfer to a clinical program at a degree-granting institution. A mechanism has also been established for transfer to the University of Minnesota Medical School in Minneapolis on a non-competitive basis for completion of MD requirements. Minority group applicants are encouraged to apply, particularly native Americans.

Curriculum   2-year traditional. *First year:* The basic medical sciences are covered in a course-oriented curriculum. About 10 hours of a 40-hour week remain as unprogrammed time. A preceptorship, during which students spend periods each week with a physician engaged in family practice, will be initiated during the first year. *Second year:* The curriculum is course-oriented with a heavier emphasis on clinical science.

Grading and Promotion Policies   An Honors/Pass/Fail system is used, and Part I of the NBME exam must be taken and passed for promotion to the third year of the medical curriculum in Minneapolis.

Facilities   *Teaching:* A basic medical sciences building was constructed on the main Duluth Campus. Clinical teaching takes place at St. Mary's, St. Luke's, and Miller-Dwan Hospitals of Duluth. *Other:* The original facilities for research purposes. *Library:* The Health Science Library is part of the Duluth Campus library system and presently includes 60,000 volumes, and more than 500 periodicals are received regularly. *Housing:* Housing is available on the main Duluth Campus and in the surrounding community.

MISSISSIPPI

University of Mississippi
School of Medicine
2500 North State Street
Jackson, Mississippi 39216

Admissions (AMCAS)   In addition to the basic premedical sciences, required courses include one year of mathematics, one year of English, and one of advanced science. High priority is given to state residents between the ages of 20 and 25.

Transfer and advanced standing: Applications are considered from those who are in good standing at their previous school.

Curriculum 4-year traditional. *First year:* Introductory basic sciences plus psychiatry and cardiopulmonary resuscitation. *Second year:* Advanced basic sciences as well as courses in parasitology, genetics, psychiatry, epidemiology, and biostatistics, all of which are covered in the first 2 quarters. The third quarter is devoted to multidepartmental Introduction to Clinical Medicine which provides classroom instruction in history-taking and physical examination. This is supplemented by weekly tutorial sessions conducted by members of the faculty and is correlated with instruction in clinical laboratory diagnosis. *Third year:* Rotating clerkships in major clinical specialties as well as in family medicine and radiology. *Fourth year:* Consists of 8 required calendar-month blocks of clinical subjects. One block must come from 3 of the 4 major clinical specialties. Two courses must be taken in an ambulatory setting and one block in neuroscience is required.

Grading and Promotion Policies A numerical grading system is used. Students must achieve not less than 70 in each course and a weighted average of not less than 75 each year. Students must record scores in specific individual exams of Parts I and II of the NBME.

Facilities *Teaching:* The school is part of the University of Mississippi Medical Center located on the 155-acre campus in the heart of the city. It consists of an 8-story complex whose north wing is occupied by the medical school. The east-west and south wings house the University Hospital (545 beds) that serves as the principal clinical teaching facility. Three other hospitals in the Jackson area cooperate in the teaching program. *Other:* A research wing of the Medical Center was completed in 1963. *Library:* Rowland Medical Library houses more than 100,000 volumes and 2500 periodicals and is located on the second floor of the north wing. *Housing:* A dormitory for women students and efficiency, 2-, and 3-bedroom apartments are available.

Special Features *Minority admissions:* The school has a strong commitment to enrolling and retaining minority and/or disadvantaged students. Its efforts are coordinated by its Office of Minority Affairs. It offers a 9-week preparatory reinforcement and enrichment program and a pre-entry summer program for accepted minority students. *Other degree programs:* Combined MD-PhD programs are offered in the basic sciences and preventive medicine.

MISSOURI

St. Louis University
School of Medicine
1402 South Grand Boulevard
St. Louis, Missouri 63104

Admissions (AMCAS) In addition to the basic premedical science courses, requirements include one year of English and 12 credits of humanities and behavioral science courses.

Recommended courses include calculus, biochemistry, and physical chemistry. More than half of each class are nonresidents. *Transfer and advanced standing:* Applicants from accredited U.S. medical schools are considered for the third-year class.

Curriculum 4-year semi-traditional. *Basic sciences:* First 2 years include the introductory and advanced basic sciences. Elective time is available each year, as are correlative conferences. Courses are offered on human sexuality and death and dying. Multidisciplinary courses are offered for neural sciences and genetics and medical communication skills are taught. *Clinical sciences:* Third year consists of clerkships in major clinical areas. Senior year is divided into required programs in clinical neuroscience and clinical floor service and 24 weeks of electives.

Grading and Promotion Policies The system used is Honors/Pass/Fail. Overall achievement and promise of students is taken into consideration in deciding promotion. Students must record a passing total score on Part I of the NBME exam for promotion to the third year and on Part II for graduation.

Facilities *Teaching:* The school occupies a full block and consists of a medical sciences building (Schwitalla Hall) from which E-shaped wings project. Clinical facilities consist of 4 hospitals: Firmin Desloge Hospital (267 beds), Cardinal Glennon Memorial Hospital for Children (190 beds), Saint Mary's Health Center (568 beds), and the David P. Wohl Memorial Mental Health Institute (40 beds). Several other hospitals are affiliated with the school. *Other:* Laboratory facilities are available at the University Hospital and School of Medicine. *Library:* The Medical Center Library has a collection of 97,000 volumes and receives 1250 periodicals. *Housing:* Two medical fraternities offer housing; other housing is available at Lewis Hall, the university's graduate residence facility.

Special Features *Minority admissions:* The school does not have a special recruitment or summer program. *Other degree programs:* Combined MD-PhD programs are available in the basic medical sciences and in molecular virology.

University of Missouri—Columbia
School of Medicine
One Hospital Drive
Columbia, Missouri 65212

Admissions (AMCAS) In addition to the basic premedical science courses, 2 semesters of advanced biology, of mathematics, and of English composition are required. State residents are given very strong preference, especially those from small cities, towns, and rural areas. *Transfer and advanced standing:* Limited number admitted into either second or third year. Transfers are considered from 2- to 4-year medical or osteopathic schools; foreign transfers must take the MSKP exam.

Curriculum 4-year traditional. *First year:* Introductory basic sciences as well as 2 courses entitled Social and Behavioral Sciences and Perspectives in Medicine. A multi-year course, Introduction to Clinical Medicine, begins in second semester.

Second year: Courses in advanced basic sciences and radiology, a continuation of Social and Behavioral Sciences, and a course entitled Introduction to Clinical Medicine. The latter is an integrated, interdepartmental course that facilitates transition to clinical years and involves skills of interviewing, history-taking, and physical diagnosis. *Third and fourth years:* Period is divided into blocks during which the student rotates as clerk in various major clinical specialties. Blocks are also devoted to neurology and emergency medicine. As part of this time, student takes a 4-week preceptorship which provides the opportunity to share in the role of practicing physician, usually in a small community. A large block of time is available for electives that must be spent in educational pursuit.

Grading and Promotion Policies System used is Honors/Pass/Fail. A student-faculty Committee on Student Promotion and Advising is actively involved in reviewing those students who may have difficulty in their work. Students must record total passing scores on Parts I and II of the NBME exam for promotion and graduation, respectively.

Facilities *Teaching:* Medical school is located on the main, or Columbia, campus of the University and is part of the Medical Center. Basic sciences are taught in the Medical Sciences Building; among the additions to this building is a unit with classrooms and multidisciplinary laboratories. Clinical teaching takes place at the University Hospital (495 beds), Mid-Missouri Mental Health Center (87 beds), the VA hospital (480 beds), and other affiliated off-campus hospitals. *Other:* The Rusk Rehabilitation Center is part of the Health Sciences Center complex. *Library:* The Medical Library is located in the wing which joins the University Hospital with the Medical Sciences Building and has over 140,000 volumes. About 2000 periodicals are received regularly.

Special Features *Minority admissions:* The school has an active program and offers a special summer program for prematriculating students. *Other degree programs:* Combined MD-MA program as well as MD-PhD in the basic sciences are offered.

University of Missouri
Kansas City School of Medicine
5100 Rockhill Road
Kansas City, Missouri 64110

Admissions Major emphasis of school is the combined 6-year BA-MD program for graduating high school seniors. Only limited number of places will be open for students completing the usual premedical college program. *For year 1:* High school students should have strong science background and take other courses that will prepare them for a medical school education that is community oriented. *For year 3:* Minimum of 3 years of college, with the minimum premedical science courses. Courses such as calculus and statistics are recommended. *Transfer and advanced standing:* Not applicable.

Curriculum 6-year modern. Program operates on a 48-week year and has the objective of preparing physicians committed to comprehensive health care. *Preprofessional years:* These years comprise liberal arts and introductory medical courses. Emphasis is on team approach and courses integrate patient interviews and examinations with basic medical sciences, psychology, and sociology. *Professional years:* A clinical scholar is assigned for each small group of students and will act as their guide during the balance of study. Preclinical sciences are taught in the affiliate hospitals, with a problem-centered approach. Student attains a specific set of clinical competencies as a precondition to attaining degree.

Grading and Promotion Policies A Pass/Fail system is used, and obtaining a total passing score on Parts I and II of the NBME exam is required for promotion and graduation, respectively.

Facilities *Teaching:* A new medical school building has been completed. Clinical facilities include Children's Mercy Hospital, a major acute Psychiatric Center, and a Mental Retardation Center. *Other:* Several community hospitals are associated with the school and provide beds for teaching. *Library:* Information not available. *Housing:* Information not available.

Special Features *Minority admissions:* A Minority Recruitment Committee works to identify and recruit health science students early in their secondary schooling. *Other degree programs:* None.

Washington University
School of Medicine
660 South Euclid Avenue
Saint Louis, Missouri 63110

Admissions (AMCAS) Required courses include the basic premedical sciences and differential and integral calculus. Physical chemistry is recommended. *Transfer and advanced standing:* 10–20 third-year class positions available to well-qualified individuals enrolled in U.S. medical schools.

Curriculum 4-year modern. *First and second years:* (36 weeks each) Devoted to basic medical sciences with preparatory courses for the clinical sciences included. *Third year:* (48 weeks) Clinical clerkships. *Fourth year:* (48 weeks) Students must complete 36 weeks of clinical electives or research.

Grading and Promotion Policies A Pass/Fail grading system is used for the first trimester of the first year. Thereafter, the grades are Honors, High Pass, Pass, Deferred, Incomplete, and Fail. In the third and fourth years, grades are accompanied by comments characterizing each student's performance. Promotions are made by Committees on Academic Review and Promotions for the respective classes. Taking Parts I and II of the NBME exam is optional.

Facilities *Teaching:* The 9-story McDonnell Medical Sciences Building contains lecture halls, teaching laboratories, research laboratories, and animal quarters. Local affiliated teaching hospitals were incorporated in 1962 to form the Washington University Medical Center. The Center is now a federation of several institutions owned by the University and Barnes, Jewish, Children's, and Bernard Hospitals and the Central

Institute for the Deaf. The recently completed 10-story Clinical Sciences Research Building provides research facilities for seven clinical departments. *Other:* Six other hospitals are affiliated with the School of Medicine. The Cancer Research Building contains laboratories, the library, and some departmental facilities. The Institute for Biomedical Computing, consisting of the Biomedical Computer Laboratory and the Computer Systems Laboratory, are located in adjoining buildings. *Library:* The library contains more than 181,000 volumes and subscribes to more than 2300 journals. *Housing:* The Spencer T. Olin Residence Hall accommodates approximately 250 single men and women.

Special Features *Minority admissions:* Recruitment is facilitated by the school's Assistant Dean for Minority Student Affairs. *Other degree programs:* 5-year MA-MD program offering a year of research training, and 6-year combined MD-PhD program in various basic sciences including biology, biophysics, and genetics.

NEBRASKA

Creighton University
School of Medicine
2500 California Street
Omaha, Nebraska 68131

Admissions (AMCAS) The basic premedical science courses and one year of English are required. There are no restrictions placed on applicants because of residence, and about two-thirds are from out of state. *Transfer and advanced standing:* Possible to the second or third year when spaces are available. Both domestic and foreign applicants are considered. Applicants must take either Part I of the NBME exam or the MSKP.

Curriculum 4-year semi-traditional. *First year:* The basic sciences are offered as well as a humanities elective and courses in preventive medicine and behavioral sciences. *Second year:* Devoted to the advanced basic sciences. The course Introduction to Clinical Medicine considers disease on an organ-system basis and presents physical-diagnostic techniques. *Third year:* Consists of rotation through the major clinical specialties. *Fourth year:* Consists of electives. Four periods must be devoted to medicine and 2 periods to surgery. Four elective periods may be completed in extramural settings.

Grading and Promotion Policies Grading policy is from A to F, with quality point values based on 4. Advancement to second year occurs with passing of all required courses and maintaining a GPA of 1.8. Advancement to later years requires 2.0 GPA. Pass/Fail system is used in electives. Students must take Part I of the NBME exam and record a passing total score for promotion to the third year. Taking Part II is optional.

Facilities *Teaching:* Beginning courses are taken in the Basic Medical Science Building. The principal clinical facilities are Creighton Memorial St. Joseph Hospital (495 beds), Chil-

dren's Memorial Hospital (137 beds), Douglas County Hospital (500 beds), and the Omaha VA hospital (486 beds). *Other:* The Criss Medical Center includes a Medical Research Wing (Unit I), the Basic Medical Science Building (Unit II), and Unit III which provides additional space for the Basic Science Departments and houses the School of Pharmacy. *Library:* The library is part of the Creighton University Bio-information Center. Present library holding capacity is 90,000 volumes and it includes most necessary periodicals as well as reference books. *Housing:* Space is available in residence halls for single men and women, but not for married students.

Special Features *Minority admissions:* The Office of Minority Affairs coordinates an active recruitment program. The school also offers a Summer Enrichment Program to prepare accepted minority students for the rigors of medical school. *Other degree programs:* Combined MD-MS and MD-PhD programs are offered in several basic sciences.

University of Nebraska
College of Medicine
Omaha, Nebraska 68105

Admissions (AMCAS) The basic premedical science courses, introductory calculus or statistics, 4 courses in social sciences and humanities, and a course in writing are required. Few out-of-state residents are accepted. *Transfer and advanced standing:* Students may apply for admission to second- and third-year classes. Foreign transfers who are Nebraska residents must take the MSKP exam to be considered.

Curriculum 4-year semi-traditional. *First year:* Introductory basic sciences as well as genetics, psychiatry, medical jurisprudence, clinical medical humanities. *Second year:* Advanced basic sciences as well as Introduction to Clinical Medicine. *Third year:* Required clerkships in major areas and a 2-month community preceptorship. *Fourth year:* Nine 4-week blocks for elective courses which can be carried out in a variety of settings.

Grading and Promotion Policies System used is letter grades and narrative comments from clerkship directors. A student must attain a C average each year to advance. Students are limited to five years of enrollment to complete the medical curriculum. Taking Parts I and II of the NBME exam is optional.

Facilities *Teaching:* Basic sciences are taught in 2 buildings—Wittson Hall and Eppley Cancer Research Institute. Clinical teaching takes place at University Hospital (320 beds). Seven other affiliated hospitals provide access to over 1600 additional beds for teaching purposes. *Library:* The Library of Medicine is situated in Wittson Hall and houses over 160,000 volumes and 2800 periodicals. *Housing:* Information not available.

Special Features *Minority admissions:* The school has an active recruitment program for disadvantaged students. It also offers summer enrichment programs for college juniors and seniors, depending on availability of grant funds. *Other degree programs:* Combined MD-PhD programs available in all the basic sciences.

NEVADA

University of Nevada
School of Medicine
Reno, Nevada 89557

Admissions (AMCAS) In addition to the basic premedical science courses, one additional year of biology and English composition, and 3 behavioral science courses are required. There is no quota for out-of-state residents, but few are accepted. However, residents of WAMI states are also considered. *Transfer and advanced standing:* Possible from U.S. schools only.

Curriculum 4-year semi-modern. *First year:* The introductory basic sciences plus psychiatry, Introduction to Clinical Medicine, and microbiology. *Second year:* Organ system module, pharmacy, psychiatry, physical diagnosis, and a summer preceptorship. *Third year:* Rotation through major clerkships, including one in family medicine. *Fourth year:* Completely devoted to electives, including one in rural medicine.

Grading and Promotion Policies Letters and numbers are used in addition to a Pass/Fail system. Both parts of the NBME must be taken. A passing total score must be recorded on Part I for promotion to the third year and a score must be recorded on Part II for graduation.

Facilities *Teaching:* Four buildings at the north end of the Reno campus house classrooms, office space, the library, and research labs. Clinical facilities are the Veterans Administration Medical Center, St. Mary's Hospital, Washoe Medical Center, and the Southern Nevada Memorial Hospital, which provide some 2000 beds. *Library:* A Life and Health Sciences Library holds a significant number of books and subscribes to a wide variety of journals.

Special Features *Minority admissions:* Recruitment of minorities is coordinated by the Minority Student Affairs Office. *Other degree programs:* A combined MD-PhD program in biochemistry exists and can be arranged in other disciplines.

NEW HAMPSHIRE

Dartmouth
Medical School
Hanover, New Hampshire 03755

Admissions (AMCAS) The basic premedical science courses and a course in calculus are required. There are no residence restrictions, but special consideration is given to applicants from New Hampshire. In addition to the 69 students accepted each year for the 4-year Dartmouth MD track, 20 students are accepted for a joint program with Brown, in which the first 2 years are spent at DMS and the last 2 at Brown. For this program, the MD is awarded by Brown. *Transfer and advanced standing:* Transfers are considered only when places are available in a class. Preference is given to students from other U.S. schools with compelling needs to be in Hanover.

Curriculum 4-year. *First year:* The first year includes major courses in the basic sciences as well as a clinical symposium and courses in psychiatry, genetics, cell biology, and mechanisms of nerve, muscle, and synapse. *Second year:* The major course is an interdisciplinary pathophysiology program that integrates the basic sciences with the mechanisms of disease and the principles of clinical medicine. Also offered are psychiatry, pharmacology, epidemiology, systems of health care, and physical diagnosis. *Third year:* Rotation through the major clinical clerkships and 11 weeks of required electives. *Fourth year:* A 6-week primary care family medicine clerkship, 2 courses: Health, Society, and the Physician; and Therapeutics, and 25 weeks of electives.

Grading and Promotion Policies System used is Honors/Pass/Fail. Promotion is by vote of the faculty and no student will be promoted who has not passed all courses. Taking Parts I and II of the NBME exam is optional.

Facilities *Teaching:* The school is located on Dartmouth College campus. Two Medical Science Buildings house instructional and laboratory facilities and administrative offices. The Mary Hitchcock Memorial Hospital (450 beds), part of the Dartmouth Hitchcock Medical Center, is a major teaching hospital. Associated with the hospital are a mental health center, the Hitchcock Clinic, and The Norris Cotton Cancer Center. The White River Veterans Hospital is also part of the Medical Center and a major teaching hospital. *Other:* Kellogg Medical Auditorium is located midway between the Medical School and the Hitchcock Hospital. *Library:* Dana Biomedical Library contains over 125,000 volumes and 2300 periodicals. *Housing:* Strasenburg Hall and other college facilities provide living quarters for 72 students. Several apartments are available for married students here and at a college-owned development.

Special Features *Minority admissions:* The school actively encourages applications from qualified minority students. *Other degree programs:* Combined MD-PhD programs are offered in several disciplines.

NEW JERSEY

New Jersey Medical School
University of Medicine and Dentistry
100 Bergen Street
Newark, New Jersey 07103

Admissions (AMCAS) Minimum premedical science courses, an additional semester of advanced biology, and one year of English are required. A course in mathematics is recommended. *Transfer and advanced standing:* Applications to the third-year class from those in other medical schools will be considered. Applicants must take the Medical Science Knowledge Profile (MSKP) exam.

Curriculum 4-year semi-traditional. *First and second years:* Consists of integration and correlation of basic sciences. Part of the second year is devoted to an introduction to the clinical sciences, during which student receives instruction in history-taking and physical diagnosis. In addition, courses in preventive medicine and community health, psychiatry, and mental health are offered. *Third year:* Teaching is centered on permitting student to evaluate ill patients in the major specialties. Teaching is largely by individual reviewing of cases, small group discussions, and intimate supervision by personal tutor. *Fourth year:* Senior is an active member of a group of individuals responsible for study and care of patients. This method provides the advantages of the apprentice system in scientifically supervised atmosphere. Twenty weeks of electives are available.

Grading and Promotion Policies An Honors/High Pass/Pass/Fail system is used. Decisions on promotion are made by Executive Faculty on recommendation of a Promotions Committee. Decisions are based upon a comprehensive evaluation of accomplishments A score must be recorded on Parts I and II of the NBME exam

Facilities *Teaching:* A new campus was developed on a 58-acre site in Newark, where it is the hub of a major medical educational complex. It consists of the Biomedical Science Building, the University Hospital, and a library. Additional facilities are provided by the VA hospital in East Orange (875 beds). *Other:* Some hospitals in Newark, Jersey City, and Hackensack are affiliated with the school. *Library:* Library of Medicine houses 70,000 volumes and 2000 periodicals. *Housing:* No facilities available on campus, but there are many rooms or apartments in the local area.

Special Features *Minority admissions:* The school conducts an extensive recruitment program. Accepted minority students attend an 8-week summer, pre-enrollment enrichment program. *Other degree programs:* Combined MD-PhD programs are offered in all the basic sciences.

Rutgers Medical School
University of Medicine and Dentistry
P.O. Box 101
Piscataway, New Jersey 08854

Admissions (AMCAS) The basic premedical science courses as well as one semester of mathematics and one year of English are required. Some nonresidents are accepted. In addition to the campus in Piscataway, the school has a division in Camden. Separate applications are not required. Students who matriculate into this program receive their basic science education in Newark and their clinical education in Camden. *Transfer and advanced standing:* Applicants to the third-year class are considered.

Curriculum 4-year. *Basic sciences:* Most basic science instruction is carried out in multidisciplinary teaching laborato-

ries where a high degree of individualized attention is possible. Students are exposed to clinical problems from the outset and may take clinically-oriented elective courses in the first 2 years. *Clinical years:* The third year consists of rotation through the major specialties. The fourth year consists of 24 weeks of electives as well as a clerkship in neurology and one subinternship in medicine, surgery, pediatrics, or family medicine. At the Camden campus the third year consists of rotation through the major specialties and family medicine. The fourth year requires four 4-week electives, a choice of three 4-week electives in obstetrics/gynecology, pediatrics, psychiatry, medicine, or surgery, and a 4-week course in "Environmental Factors Influencing the Practice of Medicine."

Grading and Promotion Policies System used is Honors/Pass/Fail. A passing score on the NBME Part I exam is required for promotion into the third year, and passage of the NBME Part II is required for graduation.

Facilities *Teaching:* The Basic Science Building was completed in 1970. Clinical teaching takes place at Middlesex General-University Hospital and other affiliated hospitals in Central New Jersey. *Other:* Research facilities for the faculty are located in a wing of the Basic Science Building on the Piscataway campus and in the Medical Education Building adjacent to Middlesex General-University Hospital. The Institute of Mental Health Sciences is part of the Medical School building complex in Piscataway and accommodates the activities of the Department of Psychiatry. In Camden, clinical teaching takes place principally at the Cooper Hospital/University Medical Center. *Library:* The George F. Smith Library of Health Sciences adjoins The Medical Sciences Building in Newark, and clinical libraries are available in Camden. *Housing:* Students are assisted in finding nearby housing.

Special Features *Minority admissions:* The school has an active recruitment program and offers a 10-week summer enrichment program for incoming minority students. *Other degree programs:* Combined MD-PhD programs are offered in the basic medical sciences.

NEW MEXICO

University of New Mexico
School of Medicine
Albuquerque, New Mexico 87131

Admissions (AMCAS) In addition to the basic premedical science courses, one year of college mathematics is required. Recommended courses include calculus, biochemistry, physical chemistry, genetics, cell physiology, embryology and comparative anatomy. Residents of New Mexico are given primary consideration for admission. Secondary consideration is given to residents of Alaska, Montana, and Wyoming. WICHE applicants and residents of other states (including former New Mexico residents) must apply under the Early Decision Plan. *Transfer and advanced standing:* Transfer to the second year will be considered for New Mexico and WICHE residents attending approved foreign medical schools who have completed the equivalent of the first year of course work in a graduate or professional school. Transfer to the third year is considered for students in U.S. medical schools that require a number of their students to transfer at the end of the second year. Acceptance of such students is conditioned on their obtaining a passing score on Part I of the NBME exam.

Curriculum 4-year modern. The school offers students a choice between a conventional and a problem-based curriculum.

Conventional curriculum. *First year:* Principles of Medical Biology—Normal is taken during the first year. It offers an interdisciplinary study of biological principles. There is progression to successively higher levels of biological organization such as from molecular and cellular to organ. Normal structure and function of each organ system are studied in detail. At the same time, students take courses in behavioral medicine and emergency medicine. *Second year:* Consists of Principles of Medical Biology—Abnormal. At the same time, students gradually progress from learning communications skills to developing skill in taking histories, performing physical examinations, identifying the problems presented, and proposing analytical approaches to problems. Time is allotted to a study of the person as a whole, growing and changing mentally and functioning within the family and social environment. *Third year:* Clerkship rotation through the major clinical specialties. Students participate in the structure and activities of health delivery term, including rounds and conferences. *Fourth year:* Students complete a block in direct patient care and then a block in neurology or neurosurgery. Each student then pursues a curriculum developed individually to correspond with his/her interests. The student chooses between the areas of primary patient care and further and more intensive clinical experience. Opportunities exist for exploring clinical subspecialties and clinical support areas, returning to interest in medical biology, or undertaking a research project. Students spend one month with a practicing physician in New Mexico.

Problem-based curriculum. *Phase I:* A 12-month sequence divided into two parts. The first is Introductory Basic/Clinical Science and consists of problem-based learning of basic science in a small-group tutorial format, focus on common problems seen in New Mexico, weekly focus on clinical skills and community clinic experience, and preparation for community clerkship. The second part involves developing a working relationship with a primary care physician as a teacher/role model, independent study of basic and clinical sciences around community practice problems, visiting community sites, and participating in community health projects. *Phase II:* A 10-month interval during which learning of the basic sciences continues, focus is on more complex biomedical problems, and the student receives advanced clinical skills training and community clinic experience. *Phase III:* A 22-month interval during which the required conventional in-hospital clerkships

are completed as are a community subinternship and elective rotations.

Grading and Promotion Policies The school uses grades of Outstanding, Good, Satisfactory, Marginal, and Unsatisfactory. Part I of the NBME exam must be passed for promotion into the third year and Part II must be taken to record a score.

Facilities *Teaching:* The school is located on the campus of the University, on 600 acres near the center of Albuquerque. First- and second-year courses are taught in the Basic Medical Science Building. Clinical teaching takes place at University of New Mexico/Bernalillo County Medical Center (270 beds) located on campus and the VA hospital (413 beds) located very near the school. Six other hospitals are affiliated with the school. *Other:* Research facilities are located adjacent to the Basic Medical Science Building. The Cancer Research and Treatment Center, Bernalillo County Mental Health-Mental Retardation Center, New Mexico Children's Psychiatric Center, Family Practice Center, and a variety of other institutions are affiliated with the school. *Library:* Students have use of the Medical Center Library as well as University Library. *Housing:* None is available on campus for medical students.

Special Features *Minority admissions:* The school has an active minority admissions program that encourages applications from Chicano, Native American, and Black residents of New Mexico. The school offers a summer Basic Science Enrichment Program. *Other degree programs:* A combined MD-PhD program is available.

NEW YORK

> **Albany Medical College,**
> Union University
> Albany, New York 12208

Admissions Applicants must have completed a minimum of 3 years of college work in an accredited college, university, or scientific school. Required courses include one year of general biology or zoology, inorganic chemistry, organic chemistry, and general physics. Applicants for first-year admission are also required to take the Medical College Admission Test and submit official scores. *Advanced standing:* Opportunities may exist for advance standing admission to the second and third years. Preference generally is given to New York State residents attending foreign medical schools.

Curriculum 4-year. *First year:* Largely concerned with the preclinical or basic medical sciences where the major part of the time is spent in didactic sessions, conferences, and laboratories. Included in the freshman curriculum are courses in biochemistry, physiology, histology, epidemiology and biostatistics, neurosciences, gross anatomy, and general pathology. A course entitled Focal Problems in Medicine offers early exposure to patient care concerns. *Second year:* Increasing emphasis is placed on the preparation of the student for his/her entrance into the clinical curriculum. Required courses include Systems Pathology, Pharmacology, Microbiology and Infectious Disease, Neurosciences II, Human Reproduction and Genetics, Introduction to Medicine, Physical Diagnosis, and Human Behavior. *Third year:* Students are assigned to clerkships in the Albany Medical Center Hospital and affiliated hospitals. The clinical clerks are responsible for following the progress of the patients assigned to them and will assume increasing responsibilities as their abilities and knowledge increase. *Fourth year:* During the senior year the student may select from a variety of electives in addition to the required courses in medicine, surgery, neurology, and ambulatory/emergency medicine. Eligible students may elect to spend up to 4 months in other approved teaching institutions in this country or abroad. Practice preceptorships are available with practitioners in Albany or the surrounding communities for students who desire experience in the practice of medicine in an office setting.

Grading and Promotion Policies Students are graded on a modified Pass/Fail system. Grades assigned are Excellent, Good, Pass, and Unsatisfactory. Distinguished performance is recognized by the grade of Excellent with Honors. Academic performance is reviewed periodically by a promotions committee, and students with an accumulation of Pass or Unsatisfactory grades will be required to remediate their deficiencies before they are eligible for promotion. Students must take Parts I and II of the NBME exam as candidates and record scores.

Facilities *Teaching:* The Albany Medical College is located in the state's capital among private, federal, and state operated health care and research facilities. The school consists of a 7-floor Medical Education building and a 5-story Medical Research building which together provide for teaching facilities, research laboratories, faculty and administrative offices, clinic areas, a bookstore, student lounge, and library. The College and the closely associated Albany Medical Center Hospital, provide comprehensive diagnostic procedures and medical care for nearly 2,000,000 inhabitants of 20 counties of eastern New York and western New England. The 800-bed Albany Medical Center Hospital, the nearby 750-bed Veterans Administration Medical Center and other affiliated hospitals in the Capital District and surrounding area provide excellent facilities for clinical instruction. *Library:* The library possesses about 90,000 volumes, 1000 audiovisual programs and receives 1200 medical periodicals on a regular basis. *Housing:* A residence hall accommodating 196 single students is located within easy walking distance.

Special Features *Minority admissions:* The school conducts an active minority recruitment program. During the summer, accepted applicants can receive outlines of first-year courses, some source material and other assistance. *Other degree programs:* Joint programs with 2 undergraduate schools, Rensselaer Polytechnic Institute and Union College, enable qualified students to earn both BS and MD degrees in 6 calendar years. It is also possible for individuals desiring to be trained as Medical Scientists, making research and academic medicine a career, to develop individualized pro-

grams leading to both MD and PhD degrees. A program of this type usually takes 6 years to complete.

Albert Einstein College of Medicine
Yeshiva University
1300 Morris Park Avenue
Bronx, New York 10461

Admissions (AMCAS) Required courses include the basic premedical sciences and one year of mathematics and English. Recommended courses are quantitative analysis, calculus, genetics, physical chemistry, and biochemistry. *Transfer and advanced standing:* None.

Curriculum 4-year modified modern. *First year:* Initially the focus is on normal biological structure and levels of organization. Then it turns to the basic mechanisms of disease and the role of the immune system. Finally, attention is given to pathology and pathophysiology of the endocrine system. *Second year:* This year begins in March and deals with advanced basic sciences as well as courses in infectious diseases and physical diagnosis. *Third year:* Rotation through the major clerkships with 3 weeks allotted to subspecialties. *Fourth year:* Required clerkships include a 2-month subinternship in medicine, 2 months in ambulatory care, and 1 month in neurology. There are 6 months open for electives.

Grading and Promotion Policies Grades are Honors, Pass, Fail. Narrative evaluations do not appear on transcript but are part of the permanent record of the student and are used in preparation of school recommendations. In order that students be promoted to clerkships, they must have passed all courses in Preclinical Core Program. A student with failures in 2 or more courses cannot be promoted to clerkships. Taking Parts I and II of the NBME is optional.

Facilities *Teaching:* The school is located in the Westchester Heights section of the Bronx. Facilities for teaching are mostly in the Bassine Building and to a lesser extent in the Forchheimer Medical Sciences Building. Clinical facilities are in the Abraham Jacobi Hospital (808 beds), Van Etten Hospital (392 beds), Bronx-Lebanon Hospital (568 beds), Montefiore Hospital (778 beds), and the College hospital (375 beds). *Other:* Ullmann Research Center is a 12-story building that houses research in basic biological sciences. *Library:* Gottesman Library houses over 125,000 volumes and 2300 periodicals. *Housing:* The college operates 2 apartment complexes that provide apartments for single as well as married students.

Special Features *Minority admissions:* The college's Educational Programs Coordinator is in charge of minority student recruitment. Several basic science departments offer 2-week summer preparatory courses for disadvantaged students. *Other degree programs:* The Medical Scientist Training Program leads to combined MD-PhD degrees in 6 years in all the basic science disciplines.

Admissions Requirements include the basic premedical science courses and one year of English. The college welcomes applications from candidates in all geographical areas. *Transfer and advanced standing:* Transfer students from colleges in United States or Canada are considered. Relatively few candidates whose previous education was not obtained in this country or in Canada are admitted to an entering class or with advanced standing.

Curriculum 4-year semi-traditional. *First year:* Basic science courses with frequent correlation clinics through which basic science material may be related to medical problems. An Introduction to Medical Practice course is also offered. *Second course:* One semester of advanced basic science course with the addition of interdepartmental courses in abnormal human biology and an introduction to the evaluation of patients and their problems. *Third year:* Consists of a rotation in or clerkships in the clinical discipline. *Fourth year:* Clinical and basic science electives. An elective in medicine in the tropics is available to fourth-year students who serve for 3 months in hospitals in South America, Africa, or Asia. An elective in the ambulatory care area is required.

Grading and Promotion Policies The system used is Honors/Pass/Fail. Students may be advanced to the next academic year or be allowed to repeat a year only upon the recommendation of the faculty members under which they studied during the previous year.

Facilities *Teaching:* The College of Physicians and Surgeons is in a 17-story building, each floor of which connects with the wards and service of the Presbyterian Hospital. In addition to the Presbyterian Hospital, seven other hospitals are affiliated with the college. The William Black Medical Research Building is a 20-story building connected with the College Building. The Hammer Health Sciences Center contains multidisciplinary teaching laboratories, classrooms, and research laboratories. A new research building was recently completed for the Psychiatric Institute. Other facilities include a Clinical Cancer Center and a General Clinical Research Center. *Library:* The medical library occupies the first four floors of the Hammer Health Sciences Center. In addition to its large collection of books and periodicals, the library contains extensive and comfortable areas for study. *Housing:* Bard Hall is the residence for men and women, and there are a limited number of apartments for married students available at Bard Haven.

Special Features *Minority admissions:* The school has designated its Office of Special Projects to coordinate its minority recruitment program. This office offers a 6-week summer MCAT preparation course. *Other degree programs:* Hospital residencies for the training of specialists and continuing education courses offer medical training beyond the MD degree. Combined MD-PhD programs are available in a variety of disciplines including chemistry, epidemiology, human genetics and development, mathematical statistics, nutrition, and psychology. An MD-MPH program is also available.

Admissions (AMCAS) A solid background in science is important. Required courses include the basic premedical science courses and one year of English. Calculus is strongly recommended. *Transfer and advanced standing:* When vacancies occur, students are considered for admission to the second or third year. Candidates must furnish evidence of satisfactorily completed work and must present a certificate of honorable dismissal from their previous U.S. accredited school.

Curriculum 4-year. Instruction is conducted in small groups whenever possible, using seminars, clinical tutorials, and special projects; interdisciplinary teaching is emphasized. Electives begin in the first year. *First year:* Introductory basic sciences and introductory medicine, which includes basic elements of physical examination, interviewing technique, and sociological and emotional aspects of disease. Clinical conferences are presented to illustrate application of basic sciences to clinical medicine. *Second year:* Advanced basic sciences and physical diagnosis, psychiatry, pediatrics, obstetrics/gynecology, neurology, and public health. Attendance in a weekly clinico-pathologic conference is required for first- and second-year students. *Third year:* 48 weeks devoted to clerkship rotations through major clinical specialties as well as neurology and public health. *Fourth year:* 36 weeks devoted entirely to electives. The elective program for each individual is decided on in consultation with an advisor. However, it must include a required advanced clinical clerkship and ambulatory care experience. Three other short courses must be selected from a variety of offerings. Each student has a faculty advisor, who throughout the four years provides counseling and guidance.

Grading and Promotion Policies Performance is graded by an Honors/Pass/Fail system, supplemented by detailed faculty evaluations. Taking the NBME exam is optional.

Facilities *Teaching:* Basic sciences are taught in a series of joined buildings. Clinical instruction is carried on in New York Hospital, Memorial Sloan-Kettering Cancer Center; the Hospital for Special Surgery; North Shore University Hospital in Manhasset, New York; the Catholic Medical Center of Brooklyn and Queens; and the Burke Rehabilitation Center in White Plains, New York. *Library:* The Library for the College houses over 125,000 volumes and 1700 periodicals. *Housing:* Housing owned by Cornell is available for both single and married students in the immediate vicinity of the Medical Center.

Special Features *Minority admissions:* The college makes a nationwide effort to enroll qualified minority group students, especially black and Hispanic-American students. It conducts a research fellowship program for minority college premedical students who have completed their junior year. *Other degree programs:* The school offers three fully funded combined MD-PhD programs which are coordinated with Rockefeller University, Memorial-Sloan Kettering Cancer Center, and the Cornell University Graduate School of Medical Sciences.

Mount Sinai School of Medicine,
City University of New York
One Gustave L. Levy Place
New York, N.Y. 10029

Admissions Requirements include the basic premedical science courses and one year of English. Recommended courses are psychology, embryology, comparative anatomy and/or physical chemistry, and advanced organic chemistry. *Transfer and advanced standing:* Students from domestic and foreign schools are considered for second- and third-year classes when vacancies occur.

Curriculum 4-year semi-modern. *First year:* Basic sciences are scheduled in block times and take up first two-thirds of year. Remainder of time is devoted to integrated study of 2 organ systems—the neurosciences and the musculoskeletal. Some time is allotted to biostatistics; a total of 300 hours of elective and free time are included. *Second year:* Greater portion of year is devoted to continued integrated study of organ systems. Courses include human ecology, growth and development, and disease processes. In this period, 300 hours of elective and free time are provided for study at all institutions affiliated with school as well as off-campus study. Up to 200 hours are devoted to the interdepartmental course Introduction to Medicine which is begun in the first year and carries through the second year. *Third and fourth years:* Devoted primarily to rotation through series of required clerkships in clinical specialties. Student is given 23 weeks of elective time during which he/she may continue with additional clinical studies or engage in lab work.

Grading and Promotion Policies During the first 2 years, grades of Pass or Fail are given. In the clinical years, students receive Honors, Pass, or Fail grades. Students are evaluated for promotion by a promotions committee. Taking Parts I and II of the NBME exam is optional.

Facilities *Teaching:* School is part of Mount Sinai Medical Center in upper Manhattan. The basic science departments and nearly all clinical departments have teaching and office facilities in the 31-story Annenberg Building. Clinical teaching is done at Mount Sinai Hospital (1200 beds) and at 4 off-campus hospitals. *Other:* Nathan Cummings Science Building provides facilities for a variety of educational programs. *Library:* The Levy Library occupies one and a half floors of the Annenberg Building. *Housing:* A limited number of apartments in buildings owned by Medical Center are available for married students; single students are housed in a separate residence hall.

Special Features *Minority admissions:* The school has an active recruitment program and offers a 2-month summer enrichment program for accepted students with educational deficiencies. *Other degree programs:* School offers a 6-year Medical Scientist Training Program for combined MD-PhD degrees in a variety of disciplines including cellular and molecular pathology and human genetics.

New York Medical College
Valhalla, New York 10595

Admissions (AMCAS) Requirements include the basic premedical science courses and one year of English. Residence is not a factor in the admissions decision. *Transfer and advanced standing:* Transfer is possible in special instances from U.S. or Canadian schools to the second- or third-year class. Foreign transfers may apply to the third-year class.

Curriculum 4-year semi-traditional. Classes will be held for 9 months of the year, with the last 3 months allotted for vacation. *Preclinical:* Basic medical sciences for first 2 years. Subjects are presented by lectures and conferences supplemented by laboratory exercises and demonstrations. In addition, lectures in the areas of immunology, clinical genetics, and behavioral sciences are presented. The lab-centered programs move in a gradual transition toward patient-centered program of clinical science. *Clinical:* "Case method" of instruction is used. Students are rotated as clerks in major clinical specialties. They also gain experience in management of geriatric and chronic diseases. Elective clinical or laboratory courses give seniors opportunities for advanced instruction in subspecialties and other areas. Opportunities for research also exist.

Grading and Promotion Policies An Honors/Pass/Fail system is used. Students who pass all courses in a given year are recommended for promotion. Students who have failed 3 or more courses will have to withdraw. A student with one or 2 failures may have to do remedial work or repeat a year. Students must take both parts of the NBME exam and record scores.

Facilities *Teaching:* The preclinical program is taught in the Basic Sciences Building at Valhalla in Westchester County. The clinical program utilizes facilities of 35 hospitals in New York, in the counties of Westchester, Rockland and Ulster, and in Fairfield County in Connecticut. *Other:* The Mental Retardation Institute and the Institute of Environmental Sciences are affiliated. *Library:* The library occupies space in the Medical College Building at Westchester Medical Center and houses about 100,000 volumes and subscribes to 1500 periodicals. *Housing:* Arrangements for renting 1- and 2-bedroom garden apartments are possible for first-year students.

New York University
School of Medicine
550 First Avenue
New York, N.Y. 10016

Admissions Requirements include the minimum premedical science courses and one year of English. Recommended are genetics and embryology. *Transfer and advanced standing:* Transfers are accepted to the third-year class from accredited U.S. medical schools.

Curriculum 4-year traditional. Basic sciences are introduced with interdepartmental correlations. *First year:* Concerned with the normal pattern of cellular and organ dynamics. An introduction to the physiologic and pathologic basis of human disease is provided which sets the stage for principles of clinical science and psychiatry. *Second year:* Devoted to general and organ pathology and neurological sciences. Continuation of the introduction to clinical science is correlated closely with studies in special pathology. Advanced basic sciences and principles of physical diagnosis provide the basis for clinical clerkships. *Third year:* Clinical clerkships in the major areas of medicine. *Fourth year:* A subinternship in a clinical area of interest for 2 months. An elective program of approved research or clinical studies at the school, at another U.S. school, or at a school abroad makes up the balance of the year.

Grading and Promotion Policies A Pass/Fail system is used in the basic sciences and a letter or number in required clinical sciences. Advancement from one year to the next is made by a Faculty Committee which can approve advancement or require the student to repeat. Taking Parts I and II of the NBME exam is optional.

Facilities *Teaching:* The medical school is located adjacent to the East River, between 30th and 34th Streets in Manhattan. The preclinical program is carried out in the Medical Science Building. Clinical teaching facilities are provided by the University Hospital (622 beds), Bellevue Hospital (3000 beds), New York Veterans Hospital (1218 beds). *Other:* The off-campus Goldwater Memorial Hospital (1250 beds) is also affiliated. *Library:* The library houses over 100,000 volumes and 1600 periodicals. In addition, the Institute of Environmental Medicine at Sterling Forest offers another reference library. *Housing:* A residence hall on campus contains single and double rooms and a few 2-room suites.

Special Features *Minority admissions:* The school has an active recruitment program. *Other degree programs:* The school offers the Medical Scientist Training Program for an MD-PhD in all basic science disciplines.

during the first 2 years are intended to supplement and enrich basic information provided in required courses. *Second year:* Consists of the advanced basic sciences as well as courses in medical genetics, clinical biophysics, human sexuality, hematology, human behavior, social and preventive medicine, family practice, and introduction to clinical medicine. *Third year:* A year of clerkships in major clinical areas. Students observe and participate in care of patients with a wide variety of illnesses. *Fourth year:* This year is entirely electives. Each student designs his/her own course of study under the guidance of an advisor. Four weeks must be devoted to each of the following: direct patient care, ambulatory-primary care, and neurology.

Grading and Promotion Policies An Honors/Pass/Fail system is used. A Promotion Committee reviews the progress of students at the end of the year and is responsible for recommendations based on all aspects of the student's work and departmental appraisals. Taking the NBME exam is optional.

Facilities *Teaching:* Basic science departments are located in Farber, Cary, and Sherman Halls of the Main Street Campus within the 5 acres of the Health Sciences complex. Additional facilities are located at the Ridge Tea Campus a mile away. Clinical teaching takes place at the Buffalo General Hospital, Children's Hospital, Erie County Medical Center, Mercy Hospital, Sisters of Charity Hospital, Millard Fillmore Hospital, and the VA Hospital, which have a combined bed capacity of 4000. *Other:* Aside from research space located within the basic and clinical science departments, the Rosewell Park Memorial Institute is affiliated with the school. The Institute has extensive experimental and clinical facilities for research in cancer and allied conditions. *Library:* The Health Sciences Library in Stockton Kimball Tower houses over 210,000 volumes and subscribes to about 3200 periodicals. *Housing:* Housing is available in university-operated residence halls.

Special Features *Minority admissions:* The active recruitment program is directed at prospective applicants in the Northeast. An 8-week residential research program is available. *Other degree programs:* A combined degree program for MD-PhD and MD-MS is offered in all the basic sciences.

SUNY at Buffalo
School of Medicine
Farber Hall, Bailey Avenue
Buffalo, New York 14214

Admissions (AMCAS) Requirements include the basic premedical science courses and one year of English. Only one semester of organic chemistry is required, however, although one year is recommended. Mathematics through calculus and quantitative and physical chemistry are recommended. High priority is given to residents.

Curriculum 4-year semi-traditional. *First year:* Courses in the introductory basic sciences as well as human behavior and social and preventive medicine. Electives that are offered

---

SUNY at Stony Brook
School of Medicine
Stony Brook, New York 11794

Admissions The basic premedical science courses are required. Few out-of-state residents are accepted. *Transfer and advanced standing:* Transfers to the third-year class must complete the equivalent of a 2-year medical education in a domestic 2- or 4-year school.

Curriculum 4-year semi-modern. Preclinical disciplines are taught at the School of Basic Health Sciences, a separate division of the Health Sciences Center. *First year:* Includes courses in the basic sciences, genetics, and community medicine. Also included are 4 courses entitled Introduction to Clinical Medicine, Social Issues in Medicine, Introduction to

Community and Preventive Medicine, and Basic Life Support. *Second year:* Interdepartmental teaching of organ systems. Pathological physiology, the matrix of clinical science, is taught within the framework of coordinated teaching. Clinical encounters give special relevance to each organ system explored. *Third year:* Consists of major clinical clerkships, one of which is in primary care. *Fourth year:* Consists of four months of selectives and four and a half months of electives.

Grading and Promotion Policies   A Pass/Fail system is used. Both Parts I and II of NBME exam must be taken to record a score.

Facilities   *Teaching:* Clinical teaching takes place at the University Hospital (540 beds), the Nassau County Medical Center (800 beds), Long Island Jewish Medical Center (800 beds), Northport VA Hospital (480 beds), and other institutions. *Library:* The Health Science Library is located in the Health Science Center. Presently the collection totals about 100,000 volumes with a planned goal of 450,000; periodicals received number about 2400. *Housing:* Residence halls are arranged in quadrangles, each having single and double rooms and four- or six-person suites.

Special Features   *Minority admissions:* Recruitment visits are made to groups in the Long Island and New York City area. *Other degree programs:* Combined MD-PhD programs are offered in the basic medical sciences.

SUNY Downstate Medical Center
College of Medicine
450 Clarkson Avenue
Brooklyn, New York 11203

Admissions (AMCAS)   In addition to the basic premedical sciences, requirements include one year of English. One mathematics course and at least one advanced science course are recommended. Although the school is state-supported, enrollment is not exclusively limited to residents. *Transfer and advanced standing:* Students are considered for admission to the third-year class. Those wishing to transfer from domestic schools must take Part I of the NBME exam. Foreign transfers must take the MSKP exam.

Curriculum   4-year semi-traditional. *First and second years:* Cover the basic medical sciences and include free half-days throughout the first 2 years for electives, correlation clinics in the second year to show relationships of basic sciences to clinical work, and introduction to patients during second year. *Third year:* Clerkship rotation in the major clinical specialties. *Fourth year:* Individualized selective programs making available a variety of courses and clinical experiences.

Grading and Promotion Policies   An Honors/Pass/Fail system is used; the NBME exam is optional.

Facilities   *Teaching:* The subject matter of the first 2 years is taught in the Basic Sciences Building. This building also contains administrative offices, a student lounge, a computer center, and animal quarters. Clinical teaching takes place at the University hospital (350 beds), Kings County Hospital

(2500 beds), and several other major institutions. *Other:* Facilities for research are located in the Basic Sciences Building. *Library:* The Medical Research Library houses over 250,000 volumes making it one of the largest medical school libraries in the country. There are 1900 periodicals available to students as well. *Housing:* Two 11-story residence halls provide a limited amount of housing for both single and married students.

Special Features   *Minority admissions:* The school has an active recruitment program aimed at the Northeast. It offers a summer enrichment program for college sophomores and one for prematriculating students. *Other degree programs:* Combined MD-PhD programs are available in some of the basic sciences.

SUNY Upstate Medical Center
College of Medicine
155 Elizabeth Blackwell Street
Syracuse, New York 13210

Admissions (AMCAS)   Required courses include one semester of English. Preference will be given to New York State residents. Applications are accepted from U.S. citizens and from permanent residents who have completed at least 3 years of college study (90 semester hours) in the U.S. or Canada; applicants from foreign schools must complete at least one year of study at an accredited American or Canadian institution prior to application, and must demonstrate competency in English composition and expression. Preference also is given to applicants who have completed the required premedical science courses. Achieving excellence in the sciences is essential; however, academic work in the humanities and social sciences is equally important, as is experience in dealing with people.

Curriculum   4-year modern. The peculiarly human aspects of human biology are emphasized by encouraging students to think constructively about the comprehensive care of individuals and communities of people of all ages and socioeconomic backgrounds. *First year:* The first term is devoted to the study of gross anatomy, embryology, microscopic anatomy, and cell biology. The clinical applicability of anatomical information is demonstrated by presenting correlation conferences at regular intervals. Psychological effects of aging are studied at the cellular level. Neuroscience and biochemistry are presented in the second term. In the third term, students take nutrition, genetics, endocrinology, pathology, and physiology. *Second year:* Preventive medicine and behavioral sciences are offered concurrent with microbiology, pathology, and pharmacology. A large portion of the second year is devoted to an extended course in pathology, with which topics in microbiology and pharmacology are coordinated. Physical diagnosis or an introduction to clinical medicine is offered throughout the second year. This program is intended to prepare the student for clinical medicine and to integrate the basic sciences as they relate to problems in this area. *Third and fourth years:* The third and fourth years are considered a single unit. Every student is required to complete 50 weeks of clerkships and 26 weeks of electives. Forty-two weeks of required clerkship and 6 weeks of electives are included in the third year; 8 weeks of required time and 20 weeks of electives are included in the fourth year. Required courses are: medicine—12 weeks; general surgery—6 weeks; opthalmology, otorhinolaryngology, radiology, anesthesiology, and orthopedic surgery—6 weeks; psychiatry—6 weeks; obstetrics and gynecology—6 weeks; neuroscience—4 weeks; and preventive medicineurology—4 weeks.

Grading and Promotion Policies The grading system used is Honors/Pass/Fail. Taking Parts I and II of the NBME exam is optional.

Facilities *Teaching:* Facilities for instruction and research are in Weiskotten Hall, 766 Irving Avenue. Most of the Upstate Medical Center's hospital affiliates are adjacent to the basic science building at Weiskotten Hall. St. Joseph's Hospital Health Center, Community General, and Van Duyn Home and Hospital are in other parts of Syracuse. *Other:* Upstate Medical Center's affiliates are the State University Hospital (350 beds), U.S. Veteran's Administration Medical Center (379 beds), Crouse-Irving Memorial Hospital (490 beds), Community-General Hospital (350 beds), Richard H. Hutchings Psychiatric Center, and St. Joseph's Hospital and Health Center (472 beds). The Clinical Campus at Binghamton, a branch campus, offers clinical educational programs for the third and fourth years. Community health resources include the United Health Services, Our Lady of Lourdes Hospital, and the Robert Packer Hospitals. The Clinical Campus program is designed to provide a quality education for medical students in their clinical years by developing a curriculum that defines attitudes and skills essential to every medical student regardless of subsequent career choice. The community orientation of the program fosters close working relationships with practicing physicians and other community professionals. Through emphasis on the "patient caring" function, the curriculum provides experiences in primary care and the ambulatory setting. *Library:* The library's collection numbers over 130,000 volumes. About 2200 rare books, such as the library of the Geneva Medical College, early American medical imprints, and an archival collection containing numerous artifacts pertaining to the history of the Medical Center and of medicine in Syracuse are included. The library also has access to 2 large online bibliographic services—Bibliographic Retrieval Services, Inc. (BRS) and the Online Services of the National Library of Medicine (NLM). *Housing:* Two modern 10-story residence halls on campus provide dormitory rooms, studios, and one-bedroom apartments for single and married students.

Special Features *Minority admissions:* The college established the Upstate Minority Educational Development Program (U-MED) to increase opportunities for disadvantaged applicants. In addition, the college offers an 8-week summer program in gross anatomy for enrolled first-year students who receive advanced standing and an exemption in this course. *Other degree programs:* Research is an important aspect of medical education at SUNY Upstate Medical Center. Four common options are Academic Research Track, MD-PhD Program, Research Electives, and Summer Research.

University of Rochester
School of Medicine
601 Elmwood Avenue
Rochester, New York 14642

Admissions Required courses include the basic premedical sciences and one year of English and mathematics. The MCAT is not required, but if taken, the results should be submitted. *Transfer and advanced standing:* Vacancies in second- and third-year classes are limited; transfers from domestic and Canadian schools are considered.

Curriculum 4-year semi-traditional. *First year:* Introductory basic sciences including gross structure and function, interdepartmental cell structure and function (histology, biochemistry, and genetics), and adaptive and regulatory mechanisms (including physiology, neural sciences, and endocrinology). Also included is a year-long interdisciplinary psychosocial and community medicine course and a clinical case/problem-oriented series of exercises introducing students to concepts of human health and illness. *Second year:* Advanced basic sciences in a multidisciplinary program focusing on mechanisms of human disease. An introductory section is followed by a systems-oriented multidisciplinary section including biopsychosocial perspectives and a case/problem-oriented series of exercises in human health and illness. *Third year:* Begins with an 8-week General Clerkship followed by 5 clerkships rotating through the major clinical specialties. One half day per week will be devoted to small seminars on topics of special interest. One day per rotation will be dedicated to multidisciplinary conferences organized by clinical students and faculty. *Fourth year:* Required clerkships in emergency medicine, surgical subspecialties, and an externship. Selective clerkships in 2 of the following: musculoskeletal, neurology, and rehabilitation medicine. Ambulatory care experience required. Broad range of elective programs offered with 10 weeks of open elective time (at or away from the school) and 4 weeks of vacation.

Grading and Promotion Policies An Honors/Pass/Fail system is used and taking of the NBME exam is optional.

Facilities *Teaching:* School is part of University of Rochester Medical Center, situated on 60 acres adjacent to the main campus. Basic sciences are taught in Medical Education Wing that was completed in 1971. Clinical teaching takes place primarily at Strong Memorial Hospital (750 beds) and at 5 other affiliated hospitals. *Other:* Research laboratory space for basic science departments is in the Medical Education Wing. The Vivarium is a centralized facility in which research using laboratory animals occurs; the facility has a staff of over 25 and about 10,000 animals. *Library:* The Edward G. Miner Library houses over 190,000 volumes and subscribes to about 3000 periodicals. In addition, the historical collection contains about 10,000 rare books. *Housing:* Facilities are available near the Medical Center in the form of 1–2-bedroom apartments for single and married students.

Special Features *Minority admissions:* The Office of Minority Affairs coordinates an active recruitment program. This involves also a Summer Research Fellowship Program for upper-level college students. *Other degree programs:* Combined degree programs are available for MD-MS and MD-PhD; a Medical Scientist Training Program is being established. The Rochester Plan for BA-MD began in fall of 1976.

NORTH CAROLINA

> **Bowman Gray School of Medicine,**
> Wake Forest University
> Winston-Salem, North Carolina 27103

Admissions (AMCAS) The basic premedical courses are required. English and history are strongly recommended. Completion of 90 semester hours is necessary, but 120 are advised. A total of 108 students enter annually, with 65 coming from North Carolina. Admission is without regard to race, creed, sex, religion, age, physical handicap, marital status or national origin. *Transfer and advanced standing:* Transfer to the second- or third-year classes is dependent upon vacancies.

Curriculum 4-year. *First year:* Covers anatomy, biochemistry, behavioral sciences, microbiology, and physiology. *Second year:* Introduction to Medicine course incorporates physiology, pathology, pharmacology, and clinical topics. This is followed by Introduction to Clinical Clerkship and physical diagnosis. *Third year:* Consists of rotations through the major specialties, neurology and anesthesiology. *Fourth year:* Consists of eleven 4-week rotations: 2 in community medicine, 3 in basic medical fields, and the rest in electives.

Grading and Promotion Policies Grading is on a 0 to 4 scale. Students are provided with progress evaluations at the end of each course or rotation. The Promotion Committee meets regularly to evaluate student performance and make evaluations. Students must record total passing scores on Part I of the NBME exam for promotion and on Part II for graduation.

Facilities *Teaching:* Much of the basic science instruction takes place in the James A. Gray Building. The main teaching hospital is the North Carolina Baptist Hospital (703 beds). *Other:* Affiliated institutions include Forsyth Memorial Hospital (795 beds), the Kate Bitting Reynolds Health Center, and the Northwest Area Health Education Center. *Library:* The Coy C. Carpenter Library contains over 110,000 volumes including approximately 2000 medical and scientific journals. It has on-line access to various computerized bibliographic services. *Housing:* The school maintains no housing facilities, but apartments and rooms are available in the surrounding residential area.

Special Features *Minority admissions:* An active recruitment program is sponsored by the school through its Office of Minority Affairs. It provides a summer enrichment program for accepted students prior to matriculation. *Other degree programs:* None.

> **Duke University**
> School of Medicine
> Box 3710, Medical Center
> Durham, North Carolina 27710

Admissions (AMCAS) Required courses include the basic premedical science courses, one year of calculus, and one year of English (consisting primarily of expository English composition). Courses in embryology and physical chemistry are strongly recommended. An introductory course in biochemistry also would be helpful. Residence does not influence admissions decision. *Transfer and advanced standing:* Transfer to the third-year class will be considered. Foreign transfers will also be considered.

Curriculum 4-year modern. *First year:* Consists of 2 terms that are devoted to the introductory and advanced basic sciences and an introductory clinical medicine course. *Second year:* Provides exposure to clinical science disciplines by rotation through the major specialties. The year is divided into 5 blocks of 8 weeks each. *Third and fourth years:* Made up of electives selected by student. Time is divided equally between basic sciences in the third year and clinical sciences in the fourth.

Grading and Promotion Policies The Honors/Pass/Fail system is used. A special examination is taken annually by all students. The results of this exam, comprising two 3-hour papers, are included in the student's record. All students also take Part I of the NBME exam at the end of the second year. Records of students are reviewed periodically by promotion committees comprised of department heads.

Facilities *Teaching:* Preclinical teaching takes place in the Thomas D. Kinney Central Teaching Laboratory. Clinical instruction takes place at Duke Hospital (1008 beds), and at the Durham VA hospital (489 beds). *Library:* The Medical Center Library houses over 191,000 volumes and subscribes to 5000 periodicals. The Trent Collection includes books on the history of medicine, and is considered noteworthy for the Southeast. *Housing:* Single students are eligible to apply for rooms in Town House Apartments, modular homes, or Central Campus Apartments. Married students may secure efficiency, 1-, 2-, and 3-bedroom apartments at the Central Campus Apartments.

Special Features *Minority admissions:* The school has an active minority recruitment program. *Other degree programs:* Combined-degree programs include the Medical Scientist Training Program for the MD-PhD, the Medical Historian Training Program for the MD-PhD, the MD-JD program for a joint medical and legal degree, and the MD-MPH for a medical degree and a degree of Masters in Public Health.

> **East Carolina University**
> School of Medicine
> Greenville, North Carolina 27834

Admissions (AMCAS) Only the basic premedical science courses and English are required. First preference for admission is given to qualified residents of North Carolina. *Transfer and advanced standing:* Applications for advanced standing are considered only if vacant positions exist. Such openings are infrequent.

Curriculum 4-year semi-traditional. *First year:* In addition to the introductory basic sciences, courses in microbiology, genetics, psychosocial basis of medical practice, philosophy, and medicine, and a primary care preceptorship are offered. *Second year:* In additoin to the advanced basic sciences, courses are offered in nutrition, biostatistics, human sexuality, clinical pathophysiology, obstetrics/gynecology, and pediatrics. *Third year:* Consists of the major clinical rotations which extend over a 57-week period. *Fourth year:* Consists of 36 weeks of clinical and/or basic science selectives. Of these 2 months must be spent in primary care, one month each in a surgical selective, radiology, and clinical community medicine.

Grading and Promotion Policies Letter grades are used in evaluating students. Both parts of the NBME exam must be taken and scores recorded.

Facilities *Teaching:* The Brody Medical Science Building contains lecture hall, classrooms, conference rooms, and well equipped laboratories as well as an auditorium and library. The primary affiliated clinical teaching institution is the 556-bed Pitt County Memorial Hospital. *Other:* Radiation Therapy Center, an adjacent facility, Eastern Carolina Family Practice Center, and the Developmental Evaluation Clinic. *Library:* The Health Sciences Library has 127,000 volumes and receives more than 1800 periodicals. *Housing:* Housing is available for single students in dormitory rooms, and unfurnished apartments are available for married students.

Special Features *Minority admissions:* An active recruitment program is coordinated by the Center for Student Opportunities. *Other degree programs:* None.

University of North Carolina
School of Medicine
Chapel Hill, North Carolina 27514

Admissions (AMCAS) The basic premedical courses plus one year of English are required. Recommended are advanced courses in chemistry, biology, and mathematics. Each entering class has a maximum limit of 15% nonresidents. *Transfer and advanced standing:* A very limited number of places are available for transfer to the third year. Students in good standing at accredited U.S. medical schools are considered.

Curriculum 4-year modern. The goals of the curriculum are to build problem-solving and communicative skills and to develop habits of self-assessment and continual learning that will remain with the physician throughout his/her professional life. *First year:* Consists of the introductory basic sciences and microbiology-virology, immunology, neurobiology, Introduction to Medicine, and Social and Cultural Issues in Medical Practice as well as a selective seminars program. *Second year:* Consists of several major courses: mechanisms of disease (includes 11 organ systems courses), pathology, pharmacology, epidemiology, psychiatry, and physical diagnosis, as well

as selective seminars. *Third year:* Rotation through clerkship of major clinical specialties extending over 42-week period. *Fourth year:* A 4-week family preceptorship and a 4-week acting internship are 2 required selectives of the senior year. In addition, there are 28–32 weeks divided into 7–8 periods of electives. Opportunities for specialized clinical activities are offered as well as opportunities for in-depth study and investigation in special areas of interest to the student.

Grading and Promotion Policies The system used is Honors/Pass/Fail. The Student Promotions Committee recommends promotion or dismissal to the dean. Taking Part I of the NBME exam is optional, but a score must be recorded on Part II.

Facilities *Teaching:* The school is part of the medical center located on campus. Berryhill Basic Medical Sciences Building and preclinical Education Facilities Building provide facilities for the basic sciences. Clinical teaching takes place at the North Carolina Memorial Hospital (450 beds) which has a tower addition (with 206 beds). The most recent building is the 11-story Faculty Laboratory and Office Building. Affiliation for teaching purposes has been established with a number of community hospitals. *Other:* The Medical Sciences Research building provides facilities for research. *Library:* The Health Sciences Library houses over 202,000 volumes and 4000 periodicals. *Housing:* Residence halls are available on campus for single as well as some married students.

Special Features *Minority admissions:* The school has an active recruitment program and sponsors an 8-week Medical Education Development program for minority college students. *Other degree programs:* Combined MD-PhD programs are available in a variety of disciplines including biomedical engineering, genetics, mathematics, neurobiology, and toxicology. MD-MS, MD-MPH, and MD-JD programs are also offered.

NORTH DAKOTA

University of North Dakota
School of Medicine
501 Columbia Road
Grand Forks, North Dakota 58201

Admissions The equivalent of three academic years or a minimum of 90 semester hours from an approved college is required for admission. Preference is given to applicants who will have completed 4 years of college prior to enrollment. Required coursework includes the basic premedical science courses (including qualitative chemistry); courses in college algebra; psychology or sociology; and English composition and literature. It is highly recommended that students be computer-literate. North Dakota residents are given strong preference for admission. The only out-of-state students admitted in recent years are through the minority program, INMED (Indians-into-Medicine).

Curriculum 4-year. The University of North Dakota School of Medicine is a university-based, community-integrated medical education program. A 5-phase curriculum is utilized and includes 3 transitional phases. *Phase I:* Occurs in Grand Forks and is a 2-week transition period from undergraduate study to medical school. *Phase II:* Also occurs on the Grand Forks campus over the next 2 academic years and includes basic and behavioral science courses as well as introductory clinical science courses: biochemistry, histology and organology, gross anatomy, physiology, neuroscience, pathology, pharmacology, microbiology, immunology, epidemiology, human behavior, focal problems, physical diagnosis, and Introduction to Clinical Medicine. *Phase III:* A 3-week transition from the basic sciences to the clinical sciences. Occurs in rural communities throughout North Dakota. *Phase IV:* Encompasses the majority of the next 2 years and includes the third-year core clerkships of Medicine, Surgery, Pediatrics, Obstetrics and Gynecology, and Psychiatry and the fourth-year Family Medicine core clerkships, as well as 6 electives of 4 weeks' duration. *Phase V:* During this phase students return to their original Phase III site for a final 5-week transitional period geared to final preparation for beginning residency training.

Grading and Promotion Policies The curriculum is criterion-referenced and evaluations are based on stated learning objectives. The minimum pass level is established at 75%. The grading system used is Honors/Satisfactory/Unsatisfactory. Honors are limited to 20% or fewer of the students enrolled in any specific course. Promotion from phase to phase and within a particular phase (e.g., Phase II, Year 01 to Year 02) requires satisfactory completion of all courses, clerkships and/or phase objectives in the preceding curricular segment.

Facilities *Teaching:* The school is located on the 470-acre University of North Dakota campus and is part of the North Dakota Medical Center. Courses in the first 2 years are taught primarily in either the Medical Sciences South or the Medical Sciences North Buildings which contain classrooms, laboratories, administrative offices, and the library. Clinical teaching is coordinated through the four Area Health Education Centers located on campuses in Bismarck, Fargo, Grand Forks, and Minot. *Other:* Community hospitals throughout the state are affiliated with the school as well as the VA Hospital in Fargo, the USAF Hospitals in Grand Forks and Minot, and the PHS Hospitals and Clinics which are part of the Indian Health Service. The Medical Center Rehabilitation Hospital, an 88-bed facility, also is part of the Medical Center. *Library:* The Harley E. French Library houses over 50,000 volumes and about 1000 periodicals. Specialized biomedical research is conducted through the Ireland Research Laboratory and the USDA Human Nutrition Research Center. *Housing:* A variety of on-campus housing is available to both single and married students.

Special Features *Minority admissions:* The INMED (Indians-into-Medicine) program admits up to 5 fully qualified American Indian students to medical school each year. The Office of Rural Health (ORH) serves both the school and rural communities throughout the state. *Other degree programs:* A combined MD-PhD program is being developed. Cooperative programs with the University of Manitoba Faculty of Medicine are being put in place.

OHIO

Case Western Reserve University
School of Medicine
2119 Abington Road
Cleveland, Ohio 44106

Admissions (AMCAS) The basic premedical science courses and one year of English are required. Mathematics through calculus is recommended. More than half the places are filled by residents. Applicants from minority groups are encouraged. *Transfer and advanced standing:* Transfer students are not accepted routinely; each candidate is considered individually.

Curriculum 4-year modern. *First year:* Consists of instruction in subject areas of cell biology, differentiated cell, metabolism, biostatistics, cardiovascular-respiratory and renal systems, tissue injury, and mechanisms of infection. *Second year:* Consists of instruction in the organ systems as well as biometry and legal medicine. *Third year:* Consists of clerkship rotation through the major clinical specialties and ambulatory medicine. *Fourth year:* Consists of 8 months of electives selected by the student.

Grading and Promotion Policies Evaluation of a student is based on interim examinations, comprehensive examinations at the end of the year, and instructor's observations of performance in laboratory and clinical work. Grading is Pass/Fail in the basic sciences and Honors/Pass/Fail in the required clinical sciences. The Committee on Students determines whether or not it is desirable to refuse further registration to any student. Taking Part I of the NBME is optional but a passing total score must be obtained on Part II to graduate.

Facilities *Teaching:* The school is located on the university campus about 5 miles east of the center of Cleveland. The Health Science Center is the site of teaching of the basic sciences. Clinical teaching is done at University Hospitals of Cleveland, Cleveland Metropolitan General Hospital, the Cleveland Veterans Administration Hospital, St. Luke's Hospital, and Mt. Sinai Hospital. *Other:* The Mather Memorial Building, the East Wing and Sears Administration Tower provide space for research facilities. *Library:* The collections of the Schools of Medicine, Dentistry, and Nursing are located in the Health Center Library. The collection totals more than 150,000 volumes and 3000 periodicals. *Housing:* A graduate residence hall for single men and women is located within a 10-minute walk of the central campus. University House, a residence primarily for married students, offers sleeping rooms, efficiencies, and 1-bedroom apartments.

Special Features *Minority admissions:* The school's active recruitment program is conducted by its Office of Minority Student Affairs. A 6-week summer enrichment program is offered incoming students. Combined MD-PhD degree programs are offered in a variety of disciplines including biomedical engineering, developmental genetics and anatomy, molecular biology, and pathology.

Medical College of Ohio
C.S. No. 10008
Toledo, Ohio 43699

Admissions (AMCAS) The basic premedical science courses and one year of English are required and additional courses in biology are recommended. Nonresidents with a superior background are accepted. *Transfer and advanced standing:* None.

Curriculum 4-year semi-traditional. *First year:* In addition to the introductory basic sciences and behavioral sciences, 2 courses entitled an Introduction to Clinical Medicine and Clinical Correlations are presented. *Second year:* Advanced basic sciences and continuation of freshman introductory clinical courses. *Third year:* Major clinical clerkships as well as minor clerkships in family medicine and neurosciences or anesthesiology. *Fourth year:* Electives at university and non-university settings.

Grading and Promotion Policies The system used is Honors/Pass/Fail. Both Parts I and II of the NBME exam must be taken and a score recorded.

Facilities *Teaching:* The basic sciences are taught in the Health Sciences Teaching and Laboratory Building and the Health Education Building. The primary teaching hospital is the Medical College of Ohio Hospital. *Other:* Four other hospitals in the city of Toledo participate in the undergraduate and residency training programs. The Eleanor Dana Center for Continuing Medical Education and the Child and Adolescent Psychiatric Hospital provide additional training facilities. *Library:* The Mulford Library contains a large collection of bound books and journals. *Housing:* Information not available.

Special Features *Minority admissions:* The school has an active recruitment program directed by its Assistant Dean of Minority Affairs. A 5-week summer prematriculation program is offered. *Other degree programs:* Combined MD-PhD programs are being developed.

Northeastern Ohio Universities
College of Medicine
Kent, Ohio 44272

Admissions (AMCAS) A BS-MD program is available to students entering directly from high school. The MD program is available to students who already have a premedical background. For the MD program, the required courses are one year of organic chemistry and one year of physics at the college level. Recommended courses are biochemistry, calculus, embryology, physiology, microbiology, psychology, sociology, and statistics. Very strong preference is given to Ohio residents. *Transfer and advanced standing:* A small number of places are available for applicants entering the MD (4-year) portion of the program based on attrition from the BS-MD (6-year) program.

Curriculum The first year of the medical curriculum covers the basic medical sciences, the second year is devoted to clinical

correlation; the third year is the core clinical year; and the fourth year consists of electives.

Grading and Promotion Policies The system used is Honors/Satisfactory/Conditional-Unsatisfactory/Unsatisfactory. Parts I and II of the NBME exam must be taken and a total passing score recorded to be promoted into the clerkship years and to graduate.

Facilities *Teaching:* The academic base consists of the University of Akron, Kent State University, and Youngstown State University. The Basic Medical Sciences Campus is located in Rootstown. Clinical facilities are utilized at 17 associated community hospitals in Akron, Canton, and Youngstown. *Library:* Located at the Basic Medical Sciences Center. *Housing:* Information is not available.

Special Features *Minority admissions:* Qualified minority and disadvantaged rural students are encouraged to apply. *Other degree programs:* Combined MD-PhD programs are offered in the basic sciences and in bioengineering.

Ohio State University
College of Medicine
370 West Ninth Avenue
Columbus, Ohio 43210

Admissions (AMCAS) A baccalaureate degree is expected, but 3-year candidates are considered. Only the basic premedical science courses are required. Recommended courses include physical or analytical chemistry, cellular or molecular biology, genetics, comparative anatomy, and advanced mathematics. *Transfer and advanced standing:* Transfer applicants are considered.

Curriculum 4-year semi-modern. *First year:* Introduction to professional problems in service to the patient and community, along with the introductory basic sciences. *Second year:* Advanced basic sciences and patient-oriented interdisciplinary study of life processes by means of history taking, physical examinations, and diagnostic techniques, including a study of patients' diseases and treatment thereof. Disease mechanisms, correlation of abnormalities of structure and function with cardinal systems, and manifestations of disease. *Third and fourth years:* This segment begins with 5 required clerkships which includes 2-month clerkships in the major disciplines of medicine, surgery, pediatrics, psychiatry, and obstetrics-gynecology. This is followed by 9 months of electives and selectives allowing a total of 3 months' vacation during these final 22 months of medical school.

Grading and Promotion Policies The system used is Honors/Pass/Fail. All unsatisfactory marks must be removed from student's record. Oral examinations at the completion of each major subject; written examinations at end of the first and second years. Faculty Appraisal Committee recommends promotions. Students must take Part II of the NBME exam and record a passing total score to graduate.

Facilities *Teaching:* The Nisonger Center for Mental Retardation is in McCampbell Hall. The Medical Science Building houses the departments of anatomy, medical microbiology, pathology, pharmacology, physiological chemistry, and physiology. Starling Loving Hall houses the Department of Preventive Medicine as well as laboratories and the Center for Continuing Medical Education and Outpatient Clinics. Construction of the new Ambulatory Teaching Facility has been completed. University hospitals include Means Hall, Wiseman Hall, Upham Hall, Dodd Hall, and the University Hospital. *Other:* Nine hospitals in Columbus are affiliated for teaching, research, and patient care. A clinical Medical Sciences Educational Facility provides additional hospital support. Wiseman Hall provides laboratories for aerospace medicine and underwater medicine as well as facilities for animal research. *Library:* The Health Sciences Library contains over 100,000 books and bound journals and subscribes to over 2000 journals. *Housing:* No on-campus housing is available.

Special Features *Minority admissions:* The school conducts an active minority recruitment program. It also offers an 11-week, pre-entry summer enrichment program for accepted students. *Other degree programs:* Combined MD-MS and MD-PhD programs are offered.

University of Cincinnati
College of Medicine
231 Bethesda Avenue
Cincinnati, Ohio 45267

Admissions (AMCAS) A minimum of 3 years at an accredited college is required. Preferential consideration will be given to college seniors; however, each year a few students with exceptional records are admitted after 3 years. Candidates are discouraged who are in the process of completing more than one of the required courses at the time of application. About 20% of each class are non-Ohio residents. The admission prerequisites are the basic premedical science courses and English. Additional courses in biology and adequate preparation in mathematics are recommended. *Transfer and advanced standing:* Applicants are considered for the second- and third-year classes. Students at non-AAMC schools must take the MSKP exam to transfer to the second year or the MSKP and NBME Part I to transfer to the third year.

Curriculum 4-year. *First and second years:* Basic sciences, Introduction to Clinical Science I and II, and non-credit electives. *Third year:* Three-week clerkships (internal medicine, pediatrics, and surgery); two 6-week clerkships (obstetrics/gynecology, and psychiatry); 4 weeks of primary care; 2 weeks of radiology; and 6 weeks of clinical specialty clerkships selected from a limited menu. *Fourth year:* Junior Internship (8 weeks of either internal medicine or pediatrics) and 24 weeks of electives.

Grading and Promotion Policies Grades of Honors, Pass, or Fail for the first two years; and Honors, High Pass, Pass, or Fail for the third and fourth years. Students must pass NBME Part I before advancement to the fourth year. Students must record a score for NBME Part II.

Facilities *Teaching:* The College of Medicine, housed in the Medical Sciences Building, is located in the center of the University of Cincinnati Medical Center (UCMC). The

UCMC includes the Pharmacy and Nursing colleges, two research institutes, and a university hospital which provides over 766 beds. *Other:* In close proximity are 6 associated teaching hospitals with an additional 2900 beds. *Library:* The Health Sciences Library is in the Medical Sciences Building, where 3 floors contain over 125,000 volumes and 2800 current journals. *Housing:* A limited number of on-campus apartments are available for single and married students. A variety of off-campus housing is available.

Special Features *Minority admissions:* The school actively recruits minority applicants on a state and national level. A 6-week summer prematriculation program is available for accepted applicants who are educationally disadvantaged. *Other degree programs:* A combined MD-PhD program is available in conjunction with any of the basic science departments.

Wright State University
School of Medicine
P.O. Box 1751
Dayton, Ohio 45401

Admissions (AMCAS) Basic premedical science courses as well as mathematics and English are required. Ohio residents are given strong preference, but a few nonresidents are accepted. *Transfer and advanced standing:* Information not available.

Curriculum 4-year semi-modern. *First year:* In addition to the introductory basic sciences, courses are offered in behavioral science, Medicine and Society, and Introduction to Clinical Medicine. *Second year:* Consists of the advanced basic sciences plus biometrics, genetics, and a continuation of Introduction to Clinical Medicine. *Third year:* Involves rotation through the major clinical specialties including family practice and emergency care. *Fourth year:* Consists of a 1-month postclerkship conference program and 8 months of selectives.

Facilities Information not available.

Special Features *Minority admissions:* The school has an active recruitment program and offers an 8-week summer prematriculation enrichment program for accepted students. *Other degree programs:* No combined programs are available at this time.

OKLAHOMA

Oral Roberts University
School of Medicine
7777 South Lewis Avenue
Tulsa, Oklahoma 74171

Admissions (AMCAS) The basic premedical science courses as well as English, calculus, and general psychology are required. Recommended courses include genetics, statistics, comparative vertebrate anatomy, physical chemistry, and 2 advanced psychology courses.

Curriculum 4-year traditional. *First year:* In addition to the introductory basic sciences, courses in medical genetics, behavioral science, and epidemiology are offered. *Second year:* Consists of the advanced basic sciences, courses in nutrition, and an Introduction to Clinical Medicine. *Third year:* Clinical clerkships in the major specialties as well as anesthesiology make up this year. *Fourth year:* Provides for medicine and family medicine clerkships, a surgery subspecialty block, advanced cardiac life support, and 12 weeks of electives.

Grading and Promotion Policies Both percentage and number grades are utilized. Students must record scores on both parts of the NBME exam.

Facilities *Teaching:* The school is located on the university campus. The basic sciences are taught at the Learning Resources Center, while clinical training is received at the City of Faith Medical and Research Center, which is located adjacent to the university. *Library:* The Health Sciences Library contains a large collection of books and journals for student and faculty use. *Housing:* Students must reside in university apartments opposite the campus.

Special Features *Minority admissions:* The university facilitates recruitment of underrepresented students by encouraging ORU students to participate in the school's Provisional Medical Student Program. *Other degree programs:* No combined degree programs exist at this time.

University of Oklahoma
College of Medicine
Oklahoma City, Oklahoma 73190

Admissions (AMCAS) Requirements include 3 semesters of English; 1 semester of vertebrate zoology with lab; 1 semester (any one) of cell biology, histology, embryology, genetics, or comparative anatomy; 3 semesters (any combination) of anthropology, psychology, sociology, foreign language, humanities, history, philosophy or political science; 2 semesters of physics; 2 semesters of general chemistry; and 2 semesters of organic chemistry. Strong preference is given to residents. Nonresidents make up no more than about 5% of each class. *Transfer and advanced standing:* Applicants from other medical schools may be admitted with advanced standing. Priority is given to those completing studies at a 2-year medical college.

Curriculum 4-year. *First and second years:* Each of these years is 36 weeks. The program provides an integrated overview of the basic sciences and is accented by clinical correlation demonstrations. Patient contact begins in the first year in a wide variety of settings, including physicians' private offices. Interdepartmental courses in clinical medicine are offered. *Third and fourth years:* These make up a 90-week continuum which is subdivided into 3-week blocks. Sixty-five weeks are devoted to required clerkships in major clinical

specialties. Eighteen weeks must be utilized for elective coursework.

Grading and Promotion Policies The letter grading system is used. All courses must be completed with a grade of "C" or better ("D" or better in courses of less than 30 clock hours.) The Promotions Committee for each year is charged with the duty of determining whether the student receives an unsatisfactory grade, is promoted, or is put on probation. Part I of the NBME exam must be taken to record a score and Part II must be taken as a candidate and a passing total score received for graduation.

Facilities *Teaching:* The college is located on the university's Oklahoma City and Tulsa campuses. Basic sciences are taught in the Basic Science Education Building. Clinical teaching takes place at five hospitals and numerous clinics located on campus and at 14 affiliated hospitals. *Library:* The Health Sciences Center Library contains more than 156,000 books, journals, and audio visual material. *Housing:* There are no university-operated housing facilities on campus.

OREGON

Oregon Health Sciences University
School of Medicine
3181 S. W. Sam Jackson Park Road
Portland, Oregon 97201

Admissions (AMCAS) The basic premedical science courses, college mathematics (12 quarter hours including some calculus), and general psychology are required. Embryology, cellular physiology, analytical chemistry, instrumental analysis, and physical chemistry are recommended. Primary consideration is given to Oregon residents. Second preference priority is given to residents of states that do not have medical schools and which are members of WICHE. *Transfer and advanced standing:* Third-year transfer students in upper 50% of class are considered.

Curriculum 4-year semi-modern. *First year:* Introductory basic sciences and courses in medical genetics, immunology, nutrition, medical psychology, general pathology, and introduction to patient evaluation, and a course entitled The Human Context of Medical Practice. *Second year:* Advanced basic science courses, including Systems Pathophysiology, a multidisciplinary presentation designed to correlate basic science with disease processes and to introduce the student to clinical medicine. The material is presented in organ and system blocks; within each block a series of selected case presentations serves to introduce and to focus attention on specific disease entities. A course in patient evaluation is also included. *Third year:* Clinical clerkships in medicine, neurosciences, child health, radiographic diagnosis, and special programmed instruction. *Fourth year:* Clerkships in the other major clinical areas and special programmed instruction.

Grading and Promotion Policies Grades are Honors, Acceptable, Marginal, or Fail. The Preclinical and Clinical Promotion Boards consist of faculty members and determines promotion. Students must record a passing total score on Part I of the NBME exam for promotion and a passing score in each section of Part II to graduate.

Facilities *Teaching:* The Basic Science Classroom and Laboratory Building is a 7-story structure providing classrooms, laboratories, and quarters for the biochemistry, microbiology, and pathology departments. The Medical Research Laboratories Building is used for medical research. The Medical School Farm houses and breeds animals for teaching and investigative programs. The University of Oregon Medical School Hospital is a teaching and research hospital. The Medical School Hospital Addition provides surgical and expanded radiology (therapy) facilities. The VA Hospital serves as one of the teaching units. The Portland Center for Hearing and Speech is also located on the Medical School Campus. *Other:* Mackenzie Hall is made up of 3 medical science units including a 3-story laboratory wing. The Outpatient Clinic affords teaching facilities for the clinical branches. Multnomah Hospital provides a successful affiliation for teaching, research, and care of the sick. The University State Tuberculosis Hospital has medical and surgical facilities for teaching. The Laboratory and Administration Building houses basic science departments and administrative offices. The Child Development and Rehabilitation Center provides facilities for demonstrations and instruction. The Doernbecher Memorial Hospital for Children houses clinical laboratories, clinic facilities, and student teaching laboratories. The Crippled Children's Division Building has clinical facilities. *Library:* The Library and Auditorium afford facilities for lectures and scientific meetings. The Library contains about 150,000 volumes of books and periodicals and subscribes to 2500 current periodicals. *Housing:* The Women's Residence Hall houses 170 women students from the Medical, Nursing, and Dental Schools.

Special Features *Minority admissions:* Active recruitment of ethnic or educationally disadvantaged minorities is carried out through the Office of Minority Student Affairs. *Other degree programs:* Combined MD-PhD degree programs are offered in a variety of disciplines including medical genetics, medical psychology, and pathology. An MS-MD program is also available.

PENNSYLVANIA

Hahnemann University
School of Medicine
235 North 15th Street
Philadelphia, Pennsylvania 19102

Admissions (AMCAS) In addition to the basic premedical science courses, one year of English, social sciences, and humanities are required. Courses in embryology, quantitative analysis, physical chemistry, and comparative anatomy are recommended. A significant number of nonresidents are accepted. *Transfer and advanced standing:* Applications for advanced standing from students in academic or professional programs related to medicine will be considered.

Curriculum 4-year modern. *First year:* Core basic sciences and introduction to medical practice through a course entitled Clinical Science. *Second year:* Core clinical year. Elements of clinical medicine and intensive clinical clerkship training in each of the major divisions of medical practice—medicine, surgery, obstetrics and gynecology, pediatrics, and psychiatry. *Third year:* Clinical Basic Science Program and the start of the Multiple Track Program which continues through the fourth year. The Clinical Basic Science Program is a period of intensive correlative study of the application of the basic sciences to clinical medicine through office practice and electives. *Fourth year:* Multiple Track Programs, each of which includes 3 major elements: electives, required basic science courses, and required clinical clerkships.

Grading and Promotion Policies A Pass/Fail system is used. Student must record a passing total score on Part I and Part II of the NBME exam in order to be promoted to the third year and graduate, respectively.

Facilities *Teaching:* The Hahnemann Medical College and Hospital is one corporation. The Hospital has a modern 19-story addition and the college building is adjacent to it. *Other:* The Hahnemann Ambulatory Health Services Center Building houses all of the clinics associated with the Hospital. The Cardiovascular Research Institute Building is just north of the hospital. The college is affiliated with 6 other hospitals in Philadelphia, 4 in other areas of Pennsylvania, and 2 in New Jersey. *Library:* There are over 100,000 volumes of biomedical books and journals and over 1400 periodicals in the library. *Housing:* A building across from the college and one a few blocks away offer single and multiple accommodations.

Special Features *Minority admissions:* Recruitment is carried out by the Minority Admissions Coordinator. The college offers a pre-enrollment Summer Academic Enrichment Program. *Other degree programs:* Combined MD-PhD programs are offered in the basic sciences.

Jefferson Medical College
Thomas Jefferson University
1025 Walnut Street
Philadelphia, Pennsylvania 19107

Admissions (AMCAS) The basic premedical science courses are recommended. Preference is given to Pennsylvania residents, but a large number of out-of-state residents are accepted. *Transfer and advanced standing:* Transfer students are accepted.

Curriculum 4-year semi-modern. *First year:* Courses in anatomy, biochemistry, biostatistics, histology, neuroscience, Introduction to Clinical Medicine, and physiology. Also two courses entitled Medicine and Society, and Mechanisms of Disease. *Second year:* Medicine and Society, Introduction to Clinical Medicine, microbiology, pathology, and pharmacology. *Third and fourth years:* The clinical years are divided into

2 phases. Phase I consists of 6 weeks each of family medicine, general surgery, pediatrics, psychiatry and human behavior, and obstetrics/gynecology, and 12 weeks of internal medicine. Phase II consists of 6-week combination of anesthesiology, orthopedic surgery and urology; 6-week combination of neurology/neurosurgery, ophthalmology, and otolaryngology; 4-week combination of oncology/radiation and rehabilitation medicine; 4 weeks of advanced basic science; 4 weeks of inpatient subinternship in either internal medicine or general surgery; 6 weeks of an outpatient subinternship in either family medicine, internal medicine, pediatrics, or psychiatry and human behavior; and 12 weeks of electives.

Grading and Promotion Policies *First and second years:* Courses in the basic medical sciences are given numerical grades with the passing grade established at 70. Numerical grades are the only grades accepted for recording on the permanent academic record which includes both the grade and the standard error measurement (SEM) of that grade. *Third and fourth years:* Clinical courses for all Phase I and Phase II required courses and all electives will be recorded in the student's academic record with the following grades: High Honors—4, Above Expected Competence—3, Expected Competence—2, Marginal Competence—1, Incomplete—I, Failure—F. An examination grade will also be recorded for all required Phase I courses. This grade will be numerical with the minimum passing grade established at 70, including the standard error measurement (SEM). In addition to grades issued to each student for each course, a written evaluation report describing the quality of the student's individual performance on each course or clerkship is completed by the faculty and is made a part of a student's permanent academic record. Students must record passing total scores on Part I of the NBME exam for promotion to the third year and on Part II for graduation.

Facilities *Teaching:* In addition to administrative offices, the College Building houses the clinical departments, laboratories, and lecture rooms. The Curtis Building houses clinical faculty offices, research laboratories and classrooms. Contained in the 9-story New Hospital Building are four 100-bed mini-hospitals, each with its own diagnostic and therapeutic facilities, teaching rooms, and physicians' offices. Three other Jefferson Hospital structures, the Main Building, Thompson Building, and Foerderer Pavilion, contain patient rooms and special facilities such as the Kidney Unit, Cardiopulmonary Laboratory, Clinic Research Center, Intensive Care Unit, and Physical Medicine and Rehabilitation Center. *Other:* The college is affiliated with 17 additional hospitals in Philadelphia, other areas of Pennsylvania, New Jersey, and Delaware. The Jefferson Alumni Hall Building, opened in 1968, houses all basic science departments and recreational facilities. Stein Research Center is dedicated to specific activities in radiology, embryology, and cancer research. *Library:* The Scott Library Building contains 130,000 volumes and receives 1600 periodicals. *Housing:* Orlowitz Residence Hall and Barringer and Martin buildings provide reasonable apartment rentals.

Special Features *Minority admissions:* The college encourages applications from minority and other disadvantaged students. *Other degree programs:* Selected students can earn BS and MD degrees in 6 calendar years from Jefferson Medical

College in cooperation with The Pennsylvania State University. Students can participate in a combined MD-PhD program with the College of Graduate Studies, Thomas Jefferson University.

Medical College of Pennsylvania
3300 Henry Avenue
Philadelphia, Pennsylvania 19129

Admissions (AMCAS) In addition to the basic premedical science courses, one year of English is required. Residents are given preference over nonresidents. Although originally a college for women only, men and women are now given equal opportunity for admission. *Transfer and advanced standing:* Applicants are considered for the second and third years.

Curriculum 4-year modern. *First year:* Basic sciences as well as courses in nutrition, psychiatry, emergency medicine, bioethics, legal medicine, oncology, human sexuality, geriatrics and biostatistics, and electives. *Second year:* Basic sciences, Introduction to Clinical Medicine, advanced psychiatry, biology of aging, and electives. *Third year:* Five required clerkships. *Fourth year:* Required clerkships in primary care, subinternship in medicine, surgery and critical care, and 20 weeks of electives.

Grading and Promotion Policies The grading system used is Honors/Pass/Fail. Both Parts I and II of the NBME exam must be taken to record a score.

Facilities *Teaching:* The college consists of a number of interconnected buildings that provide teaching, research, and patient care facilities. They include the central building, Ann Preston Hall, the Martha Tracy Preventive Medicine Wing, the Kaiser Auditorium, and the Clementine and Duane L. Peterson Teaching Laboratory, a 9-story building devoted to patient care. The college has assumed the management of the Eastern Pennsylvania Psychiatric Institute (EPPI). Clinical teaching is carried out at the 412-bed Hospital of the Medical College of Pennsylvania/EPPI in East Falls. *Other:* The teaching program provides opportunities for additional clinical experience at many affiliated hospitals. *Library:* The Florence A. Moore Library of Medicine contains over 37,000 volumes, and more than 1050 serials are received regularly. These holdings are supplemented by the Mental Health and Neurosciences Library on the EPPI campus. *Housing:* Information not available.

Special Features *Minority admissions:* The school has an active recruitment program. *Other degree programs:* Combined MS-MD and MD-PhD programs are available and there is a continuing education program for graduates. There is a BA-MD program in conjunction with Lehigh University and an AB-MD program with Bryn Mawr College.

Pennsylvania State University
College of Medicine
Hershey, Pennsylvania 17033

Admissions (AMCAS) Three years of college and the basic premedical science courses are required. Recommended courses include mathematics (calculus), behavioral science, genetics, and physical chemistry. Courses in the humanities and social sciences are also encouraged. *Transfer and advanced standing:* Transfer students are considered.

Curriculum 4-year semi-modern. *First year:* An integrated approach to the teaching of organ systems and correlations between scientific principles and patient material. First-year courses include microscopic anatomy, embryology, biological chemistry, gross anatomy, family and community medicine, molecular and human genetics, physiology, neurobiology, physical diagnosis, behavioral science, and radiobiology. *Second year:* Interdisciplinary organ system approach to clinical science and pathology integrated with microbiology, pharmacology, and physical diagnosis. Longitudinal courses in behavioral science and psychiatry with particular emphasis on preventive medicine. An organized system of health care delivery is scheduled. *Third year:* Consists of required clinical clerkship experiences distributed between medicine, obstetrics and gynecology, surgery, pediatrics, psychiatry, and neurology. *Fourth year:* From 24 to 36 weeks devoted to selectives and elective periods.

Grading and Promotion Policies Examinations may be written, oral, or practical. Grades of Pass or Fail or, in exceptional cases, Honors, are determined by the faculty. The faculty is also responsible for recommendations for promotion and graduation. Students must take Parts I and II of the NBME exam as candidates and record scores to graduate.

Facilities *Teaching:* The principal structure is the 9-story Medical Sciences Building and Hospital which contains basic teaching facilities, clinical sciences facilities, the teaching hospital, and research laboratories. *Other:* The Animal Research Farm is used for both teaching and research. The Central Animal Quarters, located in the Medical Sciences Building, is designed for teaching and acute experimentation. *Library:* The Harrell Library is in the center of the Medical Sciences Building and teaching hospital. Holdings total over 100,000 volumes. This includes more than 3200 medical history, humanities, and rare books. About 2000 journal titles are currently received. *Housing:* There are 1-, 2-, and 3-bedroom apartments on campus.

Special Features *Minority admissions:* The school is strongly committed to and actively involved in the recruitment of minority applicants. *Other degree programs:* Combined MD-PhD programs are available in a number of disciplines. An overseas study program is available to selected students in their fourth year. Educational innovations include teaching by the Department of Humanities and the Department of Behavioral Science within the medical curriculum.

Temple University
School of Medicine
3400 North Broad Street
Philadelphia, Pennsylvania 19140

Admissions (AMCAS) Only the basic premedical courses are required. Preference is given to Pennsylvania residents, but about 25% of the class are nonresidents. Strong preference is

given also to students with 4 years of college. *Transfer and advanced standing:* Transfer students are accepted for the third year; foreign transfers are considered.

Curriculum 4-year semi-traditional. *First and second years:* Fundamentals of basic medical sciences. In addition, courses are offered in human genetics, behavioral science, molecular biology, endocrinology, and nutrition. Early patient contact is provided in courses such as Introduction to Primary Care and Clinical Problem-Solving. *Third year:* Rotation through clerkships in the major clinical specialties and several courses. *Fourth year:* Electives for 20 weeks in 3- and 6-week blocks in addition to required rotations in emergency medicine, neuroscience, a surgical specialty, and a subinternship.

Grading and Promotion Policies 2 types of grades are given: Honors/Pass/Fail and, where desirable, a numerical or letter grade. A written evaluation of each student is required for each clinical clerkship and is encouraged for each basic science course. Both Parts of the NBME exam must be taken.

Facilities *Teaching:* Medical school activities during the first 2 years are housed in the School of Medicine and Kresge Science Hall. The latter is a teaching structure with student laboratories, demonstration classrooms, and a library. Clinical teaching takes place at Temple University Hospital, Albert Einstein Medical Center, Germantown Hospital, and St. Christopher's Hospital for Children. *Other:* There are formal agreements of affiliation with other hospitals and the Fels Research Institute. In addition there are letters of agreement with a number of institutions in Philadelphia, other parts of Pennsylvania, and New Jersey. *Library:* A modern library is available to students and faculty. It houses a large number of books and periodicals. *Housing:* No University-related dormitories are available.

Special Features *Minority admissions:* The school has an active recruitment program and offers an 8-week summer enrichment program for incoming students. *Other degree programs:* Combined MD-PhD programs available in the basic sciences as is an MD-MS program.

University of Pennsylvania
School of Medicine
Philadelphia, Pennsylvania 19104

Admissions (AMCAS) Required courses are the basic premedical science courses. Recommended courses include mathematics (students should have a basic knowledge of logarithms, college-level algebra, analytical geometry, and differential calculus), and English (2 years of college-level work are suggested). Students are encouraged to prepare themselves broadly in the arts, the humanities, and in the social and behavioral sciences. Some preference is given to Pennsylvania students. *Transfer and advanced standing:* Information is not available.

Curriculum 4-year. *First year:* Consists of 40 weeks of basic sciences emphasizing normal form and function and an integrated clinical program. *Second year:* Begins with 6 months of coordinated teaching of pharmacology, pathophysiology, infectious disease, and continuation of the clinical program. This is followed by clinical clerkships. *Third and fourth year:*

Programs consist of a mixture of required and elective courses chosen from over 100 offered which cover all basic and clinical sciences. New programs using seminars and minicourses help the student learn psychosocial and behavioral aspects of medicine, reinforce the student's knowledge of basic science, and reinforce an attitude favorable to later continuing self-education.

Grading and Promotion Policies   Each department submits a grade of Honors, Pass, or Fail for a student along with a description of the student's characteristics. At the end of 3 academic years, the student's performance is evaluated and recommendations for postgraduate training are made. Students must obtain total passing scores on Parts I and II of the NBME exam in order to graduate.

Facilities   *Teaching:* Students receive clinical instruction and experience in the Hospitals of the University of Pennsylvania Medical Center as well as in other hospitals in Philadelphia and its vicinity. The chief source of clinical experience is the Hospital of the University of Pennsylvania. Besides teaching facilities, it houses research institutions and laboratories. Students serve clerkships and preceptorships at the Graduate Hospital of the University of Pennsylvania. A program for teaching and training has been established at Philadelphia General Hospital. Teaching privileges at Pennsylvania Hospital are reserved for clerkships in medicine, obstetrics, and surgery and for certain electives. Services at the Children's Hospital of Philadelphia are used for pediatric and surgical teaching. Students are assigned to the services of Medicine and Surgery at Presbyterian-University of Pennsylvania Medical Center. In addition, certain elective courses are offered there. *Other:* Courses, clerkships, and research facilities are offered at several other closely affiliated hospitals in the vicinity. The Alfred Newton Richards Medical Research Building was completed in 1961. *Library:* The library, which is housed in the Johnson Pavilion, contains more than 100,000 volumes and receives over 2000 periodicals and other publications. *Housing:* On campus, Graduate Towers and High Rise North offer apartments and suites on a 12-month basis.

Special Features   *Minority admissions:* The school has short- and long-term recruitment programs to recruit underrepresented minority groups which is directed by its Office of Minority Affairs. *Other degree programs:* Combined MD-PhD programs are available in the basic medical sciences; MD-JD and MD-MBA programs are also offered.

University of Pittsburgh
School of Medicine
Pittsburgh, Pennsylvania 15261

Admissions (AMCAS)   Applicants must have completed the basic premedical science courses, one year of calculus, English composition and literature, and courses in the behavioral sciences (anthropology, psychology, or sociology). Biochemistry, physiology, microbiology, genetics, and biostatistics are recommended. Preference is given to residents. *Transfer and advanced standing:* Transfer students are considered when vacancies occur.

Curriculum   *First year:* (37 weeks) Introductory basic science plus genetics. *Second year:* (37 weeks) Pathology, pharmacology, introduction to medicine, psychiatry and clinical skills including physical diagnosis. *Third year:* (48 weeks) Clinical clerkships in major clinical specialties. *Fourth year:* (36 weeks) divided into 4-week periods or multiples. Electives in basic disciplines or clinical areas with one 4-week acting internship required. Students may elect up to 3 months' study at other medical centers subject to faculty approval.

Grading and Promotion Policies   Students are graded on the basis of their practical work and oral and written examinations. The system used is Honors, Satisfactory, Unsatisfactory. Students must record total passing scores on Part I of the NBME exam for promotion to the third year and on Part II for graduation.

Facilities   *Teaching:* All of the teaching in the basic science areas is conducted in the 12-story Alan Magee Scaife Hall of the Health Professions. The office and research space of the basic science departments and some of the clinical departments are also located there. Clinical teaching is conducted in the Health Center Hospitals as well as in hospitals in other parts of the city. The Western Psychiatric Institute and Clinic is a part of the University. The University Health Center at Pittsburgh is composed of 5 hospitals and the University. *Other:* The Terrace Village Health Center is an extension of the University Health Center into the community. Five hospitals and the Tuberculosis League are affiliated. *Library:* The Maurice and Laura Falk Library of the Health Professions is the main library. It has approximately 175,000 volumes and receives more than 2000 periodicals; there are 8 other libraries in which students have full privileges. *Housing:* No on-campus housing is available.

Special Features   *Minority admissions:* The school has an active recruitment program and offers an 8-week Summer Research Program for undergraduate college minority students. *Other degree programs:* Students selected for academic promise will be admitted to joint MD-PhD study programs in a variety of disciplines including biomedical engineering, epidemiology, and pathology.

RHODE ISLAND

Brown University
Program in Medicine
Providence, Rhode Island 02912

Admissions   Students should apply directly after completion of high school. Approximately 25 students with bachelor's degrees are accepted each year into the third year, which is equivalent to the first year of medical school. At the conclusion of the sixth year of the program, students are eligible to obtain an MD degree. *Transfer and advanced standing:* Qualified college freshmen and sophomores are eligible to apply for transfer with advanced standing.

Curriculum 7–8-year modern. Those enrolled in the program are expected to earn the BA or BS in whatever major they elect, subject to requirements of a bachelor's degree. *First and second years:* Consist of a minimum of 24 semester courses that include inorganic and organic chemistry, physical chemistry, physics, mathematics (calculus and statistics), basic and advanced biology courses (molecular biology, cell physiology, and histology), psychology, sociology of medicine, and electives. *Third and fourth years:* Consist of basic science courses including physiology, pharmacology, microbiology, anatomy, pathology, neurosciences, integrated organ systems, clinical medicine, psychosocial development, and electives. Students are required to take Part I of the NBME exam at the end of the fourth year. *Fifth and sixth years:* Clinical training, and electives.

Grading and Promotion Policies A Pass/Fail system is used. Students must formally apply for admission to the second half of the program and must submit MCAT scores before the end of the third year. Both parts of the NBME exam must be passed in order to graduate.

Facilities *Teaching:* The campus is in a residential area overlooking the center of Providence. Undergraduate and graduate courses utilize the school's departmental facilities. Faculties of 8 neighboring hospitals assist in medical course teaching. *Other:* Medical Research Laboratory, a 4-story structure with facilities for research in areas of neural sciences. *Library:* Information not available. *Housing:* Residence halls for single students are available.

Special Features *Minority admissions:* Recruitment is coordinated by the Office of Minority Affairs. Three summer programs are offered: one for prematriculation high school students, one for sophomore college students, and a third for admitted students. *Other degree programs:* Combined MD-PhD programs are offered in a variety of disciplines including ecology, molecular biology, and evolutionary biology. Also offered are a combined MD-MPH and an MD-MS in medical science.

SOUTH CAROLINA

Medical University of South Carolina
College of Medicine
171 Ashley Avenue
Charleston, South Carolina 29423

Admissions (AMCAS) While there are no specific course requirements, adequate performance on the MCAT presupposes exposure to college-level basic premedical science courses. Students are advised to pursue any college studies that they find intellectually challenging and satisfying. *Transfer and advanced standing:* Students in good standing at other U.S. medical schools will be considered for transfer as space permits. Students enrolled in foreign medical schools must be South Carolina residents and must score in the top 10% of the MSKP to be considered for advanced standing.

Curriculum 4-year. *First and second years:* There are two areas of emphasis in the first two academic periods, the traditional basic medical sciences and an umbrella course for all preclinical courses, Introduction to Clinical Medicine (ICM) I–IV. This course includes ethics, human behavior, introduction to clinical reasoning, analytic and community medicine, laboratory medicine, and physical diagnosis. The use of small-group teaching is increasing. Emphasis is placed on clinical reasoning and issues of humanistic concern. *Third and fourth years:* The third academic period consists of rotating clerkships through the major clinical specialties. The fourth academic period consists of 36 weeks of selectives/electives.

Grading and Promotion Policies A quality point grading system is used. Passing Part I of the NBME exam is required for graduation.

Facilities *Teaching:* The college is in the center of a 45-acre medical complex. The Basic Science Building consists of a 7-story structure. Clinical teaching is at the Medical University hospital (510 beds), VA Hospital (431 beds), and City-Council Hospital (175 beds). *Library:* The Health Affairs Library is located in the Administration Building and contains 155,000 volumes and receives more than 2700 periodicals. *Housing:* Student housing is available for single students on campus.

Special Features *Minority admissions:* The college has an active recruitment program directed by its Office of Minority Affairs. It also conducts an 8-week Summer Health Careers Program for upper-level minority undergraduates matriculating in South Carolina colleges. *Other degree programs:* Combined MD-PhD programs are offered for highly qualified students in a variety of disciplines including biometry, immunology, and pathology.

University of South Carolina
School of Medicine
Columbia, South Carolina 29208

Admissions (AMCAS) The basic premedical science courses plus one year of English (composition and literature) and one year of mathematics is required. Courses in integral and differential calculus and advanced natural science courses are recommended. *Transfer and advanced standing:* Transfer from other accredited U.S. medical schools into the second or third year is possible if space is available.

Curriculum 4-year traditional. *First and second years:* These two years are devoted to the introductory and advanced basic sciences that are integrated with clinical correlations. Courses in Introduction to Clinical Medicine, behavioral science, family medicine, and preventive medicine are part of the program of studies. *Third year:* This consists of eight-week clerkships in the major clinical sciences. *Fourth year:* Consists of clerkships in medicine, surgery, and neurology with the remainder of the year devoted to a selective/elective program.

Grading and Promotion Policies A letter grading system is used. Students are required to pass Part I of the NBME exam before being promoted to the third year, and Part II before graduation.

Facilities *Teaching:* The courses during the first two years are taught in the Medical Sciences Building, which also houses various departmental offices. The Physical Science Center houses the Biochemistry Division. Clinical training takes place at the VA Medical Center, Richland Memorial Hospital, Hall Psychiatric Institute, and other affiliated hospitals. *Other:* Some research facilities are located in the Coker Biological Sciences Center. *Library:* The Medical School library is located on the grounds of the VA Center and has a collection of more than 50,000 volumes and subscribes to more than 1200 periodicals. *Housing:* The school offers on-campus housing to both single and married students.

Special Features *Minority admissions:* The school has an active minority recruitment program. *Other degree programs:* Combined MD-PhD programs are offered in the basic sciences.

SOUTH DAKOTA

University of South Dakota
School of Medicine
Vermillion, South Dakota 57069

Admissions The basic premedical science courses plus one year of mathematics (preferably analytical geometry and calculus), one year of behavioral science, and 2 years of English are required. Courses in genetics, developmental biology, and cell physiology are recommended. *Transfer and advanced standing:* Candidates for transfer are accepted only under exceptional circumstances.

Curriculum 4-year semi-traditional. The aim of this program is to provide a firm foundation in the basic medical sciences and to correlate these disciplines with clinical teaching and practical medical experience. *First year:* Introductory basic sciences as well as Introduction to Clinical Medicine. *Second year:* Advanced basic sciences as well as laboratory medicine and continuation of Introduction to Clinical Medicine. Following a clinical experience, each student is assigned to a practical preceptorship with a physician in private practice. *Third year:* 52 weeks of required clerkships. *Fourth year:* 44 weeks of Family Practice Clerkship. Also, emergency room training and electives for 24 weeks in blocks of 4, 8, or 12 weeks.

Grading and Promotion Policies The grading system of A to F is used. Promotion to the sophomore class is determined by the judgment of the faculty and not solely by the student's academic record. As a general rule, students with one grade of D or F will be considered scholastically deficient. Students must take both parts of the NBME exam as candidates and record passing total scores to graduate.

Facilities *Teaching:* Preclinical instruction takes place in the Lee Memorial Medical Sciences Building. Clinical teaching takes place at the Yankton State Hospital and 3 affiliated hospitals in Sioux Falls. The Medical Facilities Addition was opened in 1969 and provides additional research facilities. *Library:* The Christian P. Lommen Health Science Library

contains approximately 65,000 volumes and subscribes to about 1000 national and international medical and scientific periodicals. *Housing:* Both University residence halls and off-campus housing is available.

Special Features *Minority admissions:* The school has a program designed to identify and assist Native American Indians interested in medicine. *Other degree programs:* None.

TENNESSEE

East Tennessee State University
College of Medicine
P.O. Box 19,9000A
Johnson City, Tennessee 37614

Admissions (AMCAS) The basic premedical sciences plus 3 communications skills courses are required. Preference is given to residents of Tennessee. *Transfer and advanced standing:* Transfer to the second or third year is possible, but places are limited.

Curriculum 4-year semi-traditional. *First and second years:* Devoted to the study of introductory and advanced basic science courses. In addition courses are offered in legal medicine, biostatistics, personality development, medical genetics, psychopathology, and Introduction to Clinical Medicine. *Third year:* Provides for rotations through the major clinical specialties including family practice. *Fourth year:* Involves required clerkships in internal medicine and surgery and 24 weeks of electives.

Grading and Promotion Policies Letter grades are used for all work except for clinical electives when a Pass/Fail system is used. Students must record a score on both parts of the NBME exam.

Facilities *Teaching:* Teaching facilities are located adjacent to the Johnson City campus, on VA Medical Center grounds. Affiliation with the VA Medical Center, Johnson City Medical Center Hospital, and the Medical Center in Kingsport provides access to more than 1700 beds for clinical teaching. *Library:* The medical library has over 50,000 volumes in its collection. *Housing:* Information is not available.

Special Features *Minority admissions:* The Office of Student Affairs coordinates recruitment. The school participates in a summer Premedical Enrichment Program. *Other degree programs:* Combined MD-PhD and MD-MS programs are offered in the basic sciences.

Meharry Medical College
School of Medicine
1005 D. B. Todd Jr. Boulevard
Nashville, Tennessee 37208

Admissions Requirements include one year of English in addition to the basic premedical science courses. Preference given to those students who have more than 3 years of premedical training. *Transfer and advanced standing:* None.

Curriculum 4-year semi-traditional. *First year:* An introduction to cell biology is followed by a progression from the cell through organ systems in the teaching of biochemistry, anatomy, and physiology. *Second year:* Includes courses in family and community health, genetics, and physical diagnosis. *Third and fourth years:* The clinical clerkships, beginning in the junior year and extending into the senior year, consist of 3 months in each of the following: internal medicine, pediatrics, surgery, obstetrics-gynecology, community medicine and family health, and psychiatry. An 8-week elective program is part of the senior year.

Grading and Promotion Policies Grades of A, B, C, and F, and a summary of the student's work are issued. Receiving total passing scores on Parts I and II of the NBME exam is required for promotion to the third year and graduation, respectively.

Facilities *Teaching:* The School of Medicine is housed primarily in a building which contains basic science departments and teaching laboratories, a teaching hospital with clinical departments, and research facilities. Hubbard Hospital houses the basic and clinical sciences departments including laboratories, classrooms, an amphitheater, teaching laboratories, and other facilities. Riverside Hospital is affiliated. The Basic Medical Sciences Building was completed in 1976. *Library:* The Library contains more than 50,000 volumes and 1000 journal titles and is located in the Learning Resources Center. *Housing:* Alumni Hall provides rooms for 96 male students, Dorothy Brown Hall houses 70 female students, and the Student-Faculty Apartment Complex contains 1- and 2-bedroom apartments.

Special Features *Minority admissions:* The college, which over the years has turned out nearly half of the 7000 black physicians graduated from American medical schools, is offering through the Kresge Learning Resources Center, an opportunity for alumni and other physicians to continue their education. Several 8-week summer programs are available for undergraduates. *Other degree programs:* Combined MA-MD and MD-PhD programs in a variety of disciplines.

University of Tennessee
College of Medicine
800 Madison Avenue
Memphis, Tennessee 38163

Admissions The basic premedical science courses as well as courses in English composition and literature are required. Preference is given to state residents; very few nonresidents are accepted. *Transfer and advanced standing:* Students are accepted for transfer but must spend a minimum of 2 years at the school to graduate.

Curriculum 4-year semi-modern. *First and second periods:* First 3 terms are in the basic sciences. In addition, behavioral, social, developmental, and environmental influences on human health and disease are covered. The first period extends

for 10 months. Students are introduced to clinical syndromes in the third term which lasts 6 months; clinical manifestations are correlated with basic sciences, particularly organ pathology. Courses in physical diagnosis and lab medicine are also presented in third term. *Third period:* (12 months) Devoted to clinical clerkships. Student becomes part of a team responsible for patients. Learning is supplemented by lectures, conferences, and seminars. *Fourth period:* (8 months) Consists of clerkships in neurology and family medicine, a selective in patient management, and 5 months of electives.

Grading and Promotion Policies A to F grading policy used. Students must achieve 1.5 GPA for promotion to second term and a 2.0 GPA for promotion to succeeding terms. Students must record total passing scores on Part I of the NBME exam for promotion to the third year, and on Part II for graduation.

Facilities *Teaching:* The college is part of Memphis Medical Center. Students may elect to spend their last 2 terms at the Clinical Education Center in Knoxville. *Other:* Three new facilities added in the past decade have expanded research programs: Dobbs Medical Research Institute, Clinical Research Center, and Dental-Pharmacy Research Building. *Library:* Mooney Memorial Library houses a large collection. *Housing:* Information not available.

Special Features *Minority admissions:* The school maintains a long-term program for recruiting disadvantaged students. It also sponsors 3 summer enrichment programs for undergraduate college as well as high school students. *Other degree programs:* Combined MD-PhD and MD-MS programs are offered in the basic medical sciences.

Vanderbilt University
School of Medicine
21st Avenue South at Garland Avenue
Nashville, Tennessee 37232

Admissions (AMCAS) The basic premedical science courses and one year of English are required. A bachelor's degree is required or seniors will be granted the bachelor's degree after 1 year of work at the School of Medicine. The present student body comes from a wide variety of states. *Transfer and advanced standing:* None.

Curriculum 4-year semi-traditional. *First year:* Anatomy, biochemistry, physiology, biostatistics, personality development, and electives. *Second year:* Advanced basic sciences with additional courses in epidemiology and psychiatry. Exposure to patients takes place during an interdepartmental course, Introduction to Clinical Science, wherein history taking, physical examination, and laboratory study of patients are taught. One day is open for electives. *Third year:* Clerkships in the major clinical areas as well as neurology and orthopedics. One-half day per week is open for electives. *Fourth year:* Courses of clerkships in medicine, pediatrics, surgery, and emergency room experience plus electives.

Grading and Promotion Policies Both numerical and Honors/Pass/Fail grading systems are used. Promotion is considered by a committee composed of the faculty at the end of each academic year. Students must take Parts I and II of the NBME exam as candidates and record scores which are put on the transcript.

Facilities *Teaching:* The basic sciences are taught at the Medical Center, and clinical teaching takes place primarily at the 514-bed Vanderbilt University Hospital. Three other hospitals are affiliated. *Other:* The Northwest Court Building, the Werthan Building, the Bill Wilkerson Hearing and Speech Center, the A. B. Learned Laboratories, and the Clinical Research Center are affiliated. *Library:* The Medical Center Library contains over 133,000 volumes and receives 1400 periodicals and serial publications. *Housing:* Apartments are available for single and married students at the 11-story Lewis House, Oxford House, and Highland-Forde apartments.

Special Features *Minority admissions:* The school conducts an active recruitment program. *Other degree programs:* Combined MD-PhD degree programs are offered in the basic medical sciences and biomedical engineering.

TEXAS

Baylor College of Medicine
One Baylor Plaza
Houston, Texas 77030

Admissions Required courses, in addition to the basic premedical sciences, include one semester of advanced biology and one year of English. A course in behavioral sciences is strongly recommended. A medical and dental examination is required. *Transfer and advanced standing:* Transfer students are considered when vacancies occur.

Curriculum 4-year. *Preclinical period:* (66 weeks) Basic medical science courses plus psychiatry. *Clinical period:* (76 weeks) The student serves as a clinical clerk, spending a varied period of time in each of 17 areas. This includes the major and some minor specialties as well as primary care.

Grading and Promotion Policies The student's grades for the basic science courses, clinical clerkships, and overall work for the year are recorded as Honors, Pass, Marginal Pass, and Fail. Students may not begin clinical clerkships until they have completed all the basic science courses. Taking Parts I and II of the NBME exam is optional.

Facilities *Teaching:* The basic sciences are taught at the De Bakey Biomedical Research Building, which also contains auditoriums with a seating capacity of about 735. Four more buildings, the Jesse H. Jones Building for Clinical Research, the M. D. Anderson Basic Science and Research Building, the Jewish Institute for Medical Research, and the Roy and Lillie Cullen Building, provide additional space for the basic science departments. Clinical teaching and research take place in 8 general and specialized hospitals in the area. *Library:* The Jesse H. Jones Library includes an audiovisual resource center by means of which medical educational broadcasts are received. The library contains over 180,000 volumes and

receives a wide variety of periodicals. *Housing:* A student dormitory, belonging to the Texas Medical Center, offers accommodations for single and married students without children and is located across the street from the college. Women students can generally also find housing in the Nurses' Dormitory of Texas Women's University.

Special Features *Minority admissions:* The school has an active recruitment program for minority students. *Other degree programs:* Combined MD-PhD degree programs are offered in a variety of disciplines including audiology and speech pathology, experimental biology, immunology, and virology.

Texas A & M University
College of Medicine
College Station, Texas 77843

Admissions In addition to the basic premedical science courses, calculus, English, and one advanced biology course are required. Strong preference is given to Texas residents. A number of those accepted have only 3 years of college, but have outstanding academic records. *Transfer and advanced standing:* Information not available.

Curriculum 4-year semi-traditional. *First year:* Consists of the introductory basic sciences, medical humanities, epidemiology/biomeasurements, environmental medicine, and working with patients. *Second year:* Consists of the advanced basic sciences and an introduction to the clinical disciplines and clinical psychiatry as well as a preceptorship. *Third year:* Involves rotating clerkships through the major clinical specialties, radiology, and basic EKG and echocardiography. *Fourth year:* Made up of selective clerkships, a clerkship in family practice, medical jurisprudence, and electives.

Grading and Promotion Policies Letter grades are used for the first 3 years and Satisfactory/Unsatisfactory for the fourth. Taking the NBME exam is optional.

Facilities *Teaching:* The basic sciences are taught at the Basic Sciences Building, while clinical training is obtained at the Olin E. Teague Veterans Center (630 beds), Scott and White Memorial Hospital and Clinic (125 beds), and other affiliated institutions. *Library:* The Medical Library has 63,000 books and subscribes to 1900 journals. *Housing:* On-campus housing is limited. Some apartments are available at the Veterans Center for students completing the last 2 years.

Special Features *Minority admissions:* Recruitment is coordinated by the School Relations Office (Admissions), and a summer research program is offered for minority high school students. *Other degree programs:* No combined degree programs are available at this time.

Texas Tech University
School of Medicine
Lubbock, Texas 79430

Admissions (AMCAS) The basic premedical science courses and a course in calculus are recommended. Preference is given to western Texas residents; very few nonresidents are admitted. A working knowlege of conversational Spanish is desirable. *Transfer and advanced standing:* Applicants will be considered when vacancies occur. School offers possibilities for advanced standing.

Curriculum   4-year semi-traditional. *First year:* Made up of two 16-week terms. In addition to the basic science courses, courses in emergency medical care and electives are offered. *Second year:* This 34-week interval is divided up into 2 terms which cover the advanced basic sciences as well as several introductory clinical sciences (e.g., psychiatry, radiology, and dermatology). *Third and fourth years:* This 76-week interval consists of clerkships and electives. Three clerkships including Family Practice must be completed by the end of the first 48 weeks. A 4-week preceptorship in family practice is required, and 20 weeks are available for electives.

Grading and Promotion Policies   A grading system of Satisfactory/Unsatisfactory or number is used. Taking the NBME exam is optional.

Facilities   *Teaching:* Basic sciences are taught at the Health Sciences Center Building in Lubbock. A 308-bed hospital there combined with affiliate teaching hospitals in the area provide 1000 beds. *Other:* There are 4 regional academic health centers for clinical training: Lubbock, Amarillo, Odessa, and El Paso. *Library:* The Library of The Health Sciences contains more than 100,000 volumes and receives more than 1600 periodicals regularly. *Housing:* None available on campus.

Special Features   *Minority admissions:* The school has a recruitment program and offers a summer 2-week Pre-Entry Enrichment Program. *Other degree programs:* A combined MD-MA program is offered.

University of Texas
Medical Branch at Galveston
Galveston, Texas 77550

Admissions   Undergraduate degree waived only in exceptional cases. Besides the basic premedical science courses, an additional year of biological sciences and English, and one half-year of calculus are required. A very limited number of nonresidents accepted. *Transfer and advanced standing:* Transfer students accepted into third year.

Curriculum   4-year modern. *First academic period:* (32 weeks) Includes basic sciences plus medical ethics, cell biology, immunology, and 2 patient-related courses. *Second academic period:* (42 weeks) Includes the advanced basic sciences, endocrinology, preventive medicine and community health, Introduction to Clinical Medicine I and II, and a continuation of the 2 patient-related courses from the first year. *Third academic period:* (82 weeks) Covers internal medicine, surgery, obstetrics-gynecology, and clerkships in pediatrics, neurology, and psychiatry. Lectures and clinical exposure in anesthesiology, dermatology, medical jurisprudence, ophthalmology, and otolaryngology are given during the clerkships, and advanced CPR also is required. Especially qualified students who obtain an approved university internship or

residency may elect to graduate and enter postgraduate training. *Fourth year:* Students who do not graduate enter this 36-week elective period. A 7-week rotation in ambulatory care is required during the senior year.

Grading and Promotion Policies   Letter/number grades in required courses and pass/fail in electives. No student will be promoted until all work of a given grading sequence is completed and passed. Students must record passing total scores on Part I of the NBME exam for graduation and take Part II.

Facilities   *Teaching:* The basic sciences are taught at the Libby Moody Thompson Basic Sciences Building. John Sealy Hospital (the principal clinical service and teaching facility), 6 other hospitals, and 2 outpatient clinics make up the Medical Branch Hospitals Complex. Other separately owned and operated hospitals offer educational and research opportunities. *Other:* There is a School of Nursing, a School of Allied Health Sciences, and a Graduate School of Biomedical Sciences at Galveston. The Chronic Home Dialysis Center was established in 1968. The Marine Biomedical Institute offers opportunities for research in the physiological processes of humans as related to an underwater habitat. The Regional Poison Control Center has files containing information on over 10,000 commercial products. The Clinical Study Center is an independent 12-bed unit located in the John Sealy Hospital. The Shriners Burn Institute is located on the campus and staffed largely by faculty members. The Birth Defects Center is involved in research and provides programs to help afflicted children under 15. *Library:* The Moody Medical Library houses about 240,000 bound books and subscribes to about 3000 biomedical periodicals. *Housing:* Dormitory rooms are available on campus.

Special Features   *Minority admissions:* An active recruitment program is conducted by the school's Office of Special Programs. A 4-week Medical School Familiarization Program is available for upper-level college minority students. *Other degree programs:* Combined MD-PhD programs are available in the basic sciences.

University of Texas
Medical School at Houston
Houston, Texas 77225

Admissions   In addition to the basic premedical science courses, one year of advanced biology, one year of English, and one-half year of college calculus are required. *Transfer and advanced standing:* None.

Curriculum   4-year semi-traditional. *First year:* Basic sciences plus courses in genetics, immunology, reproductive biology, biostatistics, and behavioral science. *Second year:* Advanced basic sciences plus courses in behavioral science, medical jurisprudence, mechanisms of disease, interviewing techniques, and Introduction to Clinical Medicine. *Third year:* Required clerkships in the major specialties. *Fourth year:* Required clerkships in neurology and in family practice. Also, electives consisting of seven 4-week blocks.

Grading and Promotion Policies System used is Honors/Pass/Fail. Only Part I of the NBME exam must be taken and a passing total score recorded.

Facilities *Teaching:* The basic sciences are being taught in The Medical Science Building. In addition to the Hermann Hospital and M. D. Anderson Hospital and Tumor Institute, clinical teaching takes place in Shriner's Hospital, St. Joseph's Hospital, Southwest Memorial Hospital, and Brackenridge Hospital in Austin, Texas. *Library:* The Houston Academy of Medicine-Texas Medical Center Library has over 100,000 volumes; the 25,000-volume M. D. Anderson Hospital and Tumor Institute Library is another valuable asset. *Housing:* The UT student housing complex is located at Cambridge and El Paseo, approximately one mile from the Texas Medical Center. Two student resident halls are located within the medical center.

Special Features *Minority admissions:* An Associate Dean directs an active recruitment program. The school offers an 8-week Summer Enrichment Program for Minority Students. *Other degree programs:* Combined MD-PhD programs are available in a variety of disciplines including reproductive medicine and biology.

University of Texas
Medical School at San Antonio
7703 Floyd Curl Drive
San Antonio, Texas 78284

Admissions Aside from the basic premedical science courses, one additional year of biology, one year of English and one semester of calculus are required. A few nonresidents are admitted. *Transfer and advanced standing:* Not possible at the present time.

Curriculum 4-year semi-modern. *First year:* Spans the disciplines of cellular and molecular biology, anatomy, and systems physiology to human ecology and the rudiments of human and clinical relationships. *Second year:* Pathology and pharmacology are covered, and 5 introductory courses are given for the major clinical disciplines (medicine, surgery, obstetrics-gynecology, pediatrics, and psychiatry). *Third year:* Clerkship rotation through the major clinical specialties and surgical subspecialties. *Fourth year:* Consists of a 6-week clerkship in ambulatory primary care plus 1 month of didactic courses. Also 24 weeks are allotted for electives, 6 weeks for optional time, and 4 weeks for 5 required courses.

Grading and Promotion Policies All final grades are reported as letter grades. Any student encountering academic difficulty shall be provided an opportunity to make up deficiencies and improve performance. The student must take Part I of the NBME exam and a total score not lower than 2.1 below the national mean is required for promotion to the third year. On Part II, a passing total score is required for graduation.

Facilities The basic sciences are taught in the Medical School Building. Clinical teaching takes place at the Medical Center Hospital, the Robert B. Green Memorial Hospital, the VA Hospital, and 3 other affiliated institutions. Research labor-atories are located in the Medical School Building. *Library:* The library is also located in the Medical School Building. *Housing:* Information not available.

Special Features *Minority admissions:* The school's Office of Special Programs coordinates an active recruitment program for minority students. It also offers a two-part summer program for college upper-level students to improve aptitude test performance and reinforce motivation. *Other degree programs:* Combined MD-PhD programs in the basic medical sciences are offered.

University of Texas
Southwestern Medical School at Dallas
5323 Harry Hines Boulevard
Dallas, Texas 75235

Admissions In addition to the basic premedical science courses, an extra year of biology (or zoology), one semester of calculus, and one year of English are required. Maximum of 20 nonresident freshmen accepted. *Transfer and advanced standing:* Students may seek advanced standing only after obtaining admission as freshmen.

Curriculum 4-year semi-traditional. *First year:* Medical biochemistry. Biology of Cell and Tissues, medical genetics, human anatomy and embryology, psychiatry, medical physiology, neurobiology, endocrinology and human reproduction. *Second year:* Introduction to Clinical Medicine, immunology and medical microbiology, anatomic and clinical pathology, medical pharmacology, and psychiatry. *Third and fourth years:* Divided into blocks and allocated to the departments of medicine, surgery, obstetrics/gynecology, pediatrics, neurology, and psychiatry. All instruction pertaining to these departments is given within its own block of time, so that the student can devote time to each subject without interruption. About half of the fourth year is open to electives.

Grading and Promotion Policies Traditional letter grading system within which A, B, and C are passing grades. D and F are failing grades. Each student's performance is computed on the basis of a system of quantitative and qualitative weighting. A student incurring a failing grade may be asked by the Promotions Committee to withdraw from school, to repeat the year's work, or to remove the deficiency by some other means. The Promotions Committee is made up of representatives of each teaching department. Taking Parts I and II of the NBME exam is optional.

Facilities *Teaching:* The 60-acre campus serves as the focus of a large medical complex which includes Parkland Memorial Hospital, Children's Medical Center, St. Paul Hospital, The University of Texas at Dallas Callier Center for Communication Disorders, Texas Woman's University Institute of Health Science, The University of Texas Regional Computer Center in North Texas, City of Dallas Health Department and Southwestern Institute of Forensic Sciences. The health science center anticipates construction of a 159-bed university hospital by a non-profit corporation. A new Clinical Sciences Building is scheduled to connect the new hospital with Parkland Memorial Hospital. *Other:* James W. Aston

Ambulatory Care Center, Animal Resources Center, and Fred F. Florence Bioinformation Center. *Library:* The library currently has a collection of about 175,000 volumes and receives 2400 serials annually. *Housing:* No on-campus housing is available.

Special Features *Minority admissions:* The school has an active minority student recruitment program. *Other degree programs:* Combined MD-PhD programs are offered in a variety of disciplines including biophysics, cell biology, and immunology.

UTAH

> **University of Utah**
> School of Medicine
> 50 North Medical Drive
> Salt Lake City, Utah 84132

Admissions (AMCAS) Requirements include the basic premedical science courses and one year of English. Also inorganic chemistry should include work in qualitative and quantitative analysis. About 75% of entering students are Utah residents; approximately 50% of out-of-state students are from WICHE states.

Curriculum 4-year semi-traditional. *First year:* Major courses in anatomy, biochemistry, and physiology and their relationships to clinical application. *Second year:* Major courses include pharmacology, pathology, microbiology, nutrition, and introductory courses in physical diagnosis. Electives are available. *Third year:* Rotation in the major clinical specialties. Student is assigned patients for study and is responsible for the patient's history, physical examination, and the laboratory work necessary to make the diagnosis. *Fourth year:* Entirely composed of elective time during which independent programs are arranged for each student.

Grading and Promotion Policies An evaluation on a Pass/Fail basis and a description of student performance is submitted by the faculty. Students must take Parts I and II of the NBME exam and record scores.

Facilities *Teaching:* All preclinical instruction can be received within the Medical Center. Most of the clinical training is obtained in the University Hospital and the VA Hospital. *Other:* Five hospitals in Salt Lake City and 2 in Ogden are affiliated. *Library:* The Library contains over 100,000 volumes and 1750 current medical journal subscriptions. *Housing:* Board and room is available in residence halls for single students as well as apartments for married students.

Special Features *Minority admissions:* The school has an active recruitment program and is prepared to provide financial and academic support for Indian, Mexican-American, and black students who come from economically disadvantaged communities and who are likely to complete the medical curriculum successfully. *Other degree programs:* Combined

MD-PhD degree programs are offered in the basic medical sciences as well as biophysics.

VERMONT

> **University of Vermont**
> College of Medicine
> Burlington, Vermont 05405

Admissions (AMCAS) In addition to the required premedical science courses, applicants are urged to pursue a broad and balanced educational program during their undergraduate years. Priority for admission is given to residents of Vermont, Maine, and New York, but there are usually a moderate number of places available for applicants from other states. *Transfer and advanced standing:* Information not available.

Curriculum 4-year. *Basic Science Core:* (57 weeks) Both introductory and advanced basic sciences are covered during this year and one-half period. *Clinical Science Core:* (48 weeks) Instruction in clinical sciences and work within the hospitals and clinics. Instruction is based on the care of patients by means of clerkships in the major specialties. *Elective period:* (72 weeks) This final academic period is devoted to electives. These are individually designed experiences which fulfill chosen pathway requirements and student needs.

Grading and Promotion Policies System used is Honors/Pass/Fail. Taking Parts I and II of the NBME exam is optional.

Facilities *Teaching:* There is a 3-building medical college complex, a 450-bed teaching hospital, and the Medical Center Hospital. *Other:* Research facilities are located within the medical school complex and there are 2 affiliated teaching hospitals. *Library:* The medical library has a large number of bound volumes and receives numerous periodicals. *Housing:* Information not available.

Special Features *Minority admissions:* The school has developed a program to identify prospective medical students from among minority-group members. A 4-week pre-college enrichment program is offered for such students. *Other degree programs:* Combined MD-PhD and MS-MD programs offered in a variety of basic science disciplines.

VIRGINIA

> **Eastern Virginia Medical School**
> 700 Olney Road
> Norfolk, Virginia 23501

Admissions (AMCAS) Applicants must have a minimum of 100 semester hours from an accredited American or Canadian college or university which must include the basic premedical science courses. Applicants are expected to have grades of C or better in all required courses. Credits earned in advanced placement programs or CLEP are acceptable. No application will be considered complete without scores of the MCAT taken within 2 years prior to application. *Transfer and advanced standing:* No transfer students accepted.

Curriculum 4-year. During the first 2 years of the curriculum, the basic sciences are presented as a basis for the practice of medicine. The application of small-group, problem-based sessions with basic and clinical scientists as facilitators is utilized. Students receive introductory education in clinical and interpersonal skills and attend preceptorships with a physician in private practice. During the last 2 years of the curriculum, students rotate through clinical clerkships in family medicine, internal medicine, obstetrics and gynecology, pediatrics, psychiatry, surgery, and through selectives designed to meet the student's special interests and career goals.

Grading and Promotion Policies Students are promoted on the basis of their ability to complete required objectives satisfactorily, with achievement being designated as Honors, Pass, Fail, or Incomplete.

Facilities *Teaching:* The school's primary teaching and research facilities are housed in buildings that are part of the 33-acre Eastern Virginia Medical Center. Clinical experience is provided through affiliation with 29 medical health care facilities located within Hampton Roads. *Other:* Research facilities are located in the Medical Tower. *Library:* The library has a large collection of books and receives a wide range of serial periodicals. *Housing:* Information not available.

Medical College of Virginia,
Virginia Commonwealth University
MCV Box 565
Richmond, Virginia 23298

Admissions (AMCAS) Requirements include the basic premedical science courses, one year of mathematics, and one year of English. Preference is given to those with baccalaureate degrees; residents preferred. *Transfer and advanced standing:* Transfer students are considered when vacancies occur. Residents are given preference.

Curriculum 4-year semi-modern. *First and second years:* The basic sciences are covered in the first 2 years. The body is divided into organ systems to permit integration of the basic science disciplines with one another and with the clinical aspects. Behavioral science, preventive medicine, public health, pathogenesis, emergency care, and physical diagnosis are also taught during this interval. *Third year:* This year is devoted to rotation through the major clinical specialties. Also included are a course entitled Community Practice and a course in neuroscience. *Fourth year:* Consists of 2 weeks devoted to clinical rotations in cardiopulmonary medicine, ophthalmology, emergency room, and radiology, and 24 weeks (six 4-week blocks) of electives.

Grading and Promotion Policies Grades of Honors/Pass/Fail are determined by the faculty. Parts I and II of the NBME exam must be taken to record a score.

Facilities *Teaching:* Classrooms and laboratories for the basic medical sciences are in Sanger Hall, McGuire Hall Annex, and the Egyptian Building. Clinical teaching is done at the Medical Center, which consists of the West, South, East, and North Hospitals, the Clinical Center, and at the A. D. Williams Memorial Clinic. *Other:* Students in their third year spend a month in 1 of 5 community hospitals located in Richmond or in nearby cities or towns. The Dooley Building houses research laboratories, and the Lewis L. Strauss Surgical Research Laboratory accommodates many important research projects. *Library:* The comprehensive collections of the Tompkins-McCaw Library support study and research needs. *Housing:* Cabaniss Hall, a 432-bed dormitory and 4 residence halls provide for student housing needs.

Special Features *Minority admissions:* The Director of the school's Health Careers Opportunity Program (HCOP) is actively involved in recruitment of minority students. The school also offers a Pre-Admissions Study Skills Workshop and a Summer Institute. *Other degree programs:* Combined MD-PhD programs are available in a variety of disciplines including biometry, biophysics, and genetics.

University of Virginia
School of Medicine
Charlottesville, Virginia 22908

Admissions (AMCAS) The basic premedical science courses are required. Preference is given to residents. *Transfer and advanced standing:* Only state residents are considered for transfer into the third year.

Curriculum 4-year modern. The curriculum is divided into 4 major components. *Basic sciences:* (18 months) Provides a basic knowledge, both psychological and physical, of the structure of the normal and diseased human. *Clinical Clerkships:* (11 months) Provides a learning experience by direct contact with patients. *Electives:* (8 months) Offers clinical rotations, graduate courses, or research activities.

Grading and Promotion Policies A letter grading system is used except in the fourth year, where pass/fail is used in grading electives. Students who have satisfactorily completed all the work of the session are eligible for promotion. Those who have incurred deficiencies, which can be reasonably removed by the opening of the next session, may be provisionally promoted. Students with serious deficiencies may be required to repeat the session's work. Students who are not considered competent to continue training in medicine may be required to withdraw. Students must record a score only on Part I of the NBME exam, but must record a passing total score on Part II to graduate.

Facilities *Teaching:* Thomas Jefferson founded the University in 1819. Students join faculty members in conducting basic and clinical research to help solve some of the many medical questions puzzling scientists today. They are aided by special facilities, including the central electron microscope facility, lymphocyte culture center and protein and nucleic acid sequencing center. Many of these facilities are located in Harvey E. Jordan Hall, which also houses classrooms and laboratories for the 5 basic sciences. *Other:* Other facilities include several vivarium sites and research buildings in the Medical Center complex, adjacent to historic Central Grounds, and the University of Virginia Hospitals, licensed for 900 beds, including the main hospital, Blue Ridge Hospital, and Children's Rehabilitation Center. Underway is construction of a 410-bed replacement hospital and renovation of part of the existing main hospital. Students also receive clinical training at other hospitals in Virginia. *Library:* The Claude Moore Health Sciences Library contains 140,000 volumes and receives approximately 1800 publications. *Housing:* Dormitory rooms and suites are available for single students, and apartments are available for married students who may or may not have children.

Special Features *Minority admissions:* The school has an active recruitment program. It also offers a Summer Enrichment Program for senior college students and graduates and applicants who have been conditionally or unconditionally accepted for admission. *Other degree programs:* Combined MD-PhD degree programs are offered in the basic sciences and jointly with other departments of the Graduate School or School of Engineering.

WASHINGTON

University of Washington
School of Medicine
Seattle, Washington 98195

Admissions (AMCAS) The basic premedical science courses and proficiency in mathematics and English are required. Primary preference is given to residents of the states of Washington, Alaska, Montana, and Idaho (WAMI Program). *Transfer and advanced standing:* None.

Curriculum 4-year modern. *First year:* The introductory basic sciences are taught in relation to their clinical relevance. Courses in epidemiology, psychology, and molecular and cellular biology are offered as well as a course entitled Introduction to Clinical Medicine. *Second year:* The advanced basic sciences are taught within a systems context. In addition, courses are offered in genetics, hematology, and health care systems. *Third and fourth years:* Students select from a variety of elective clerkships after completing the prescribed clerkships.

Grading and Promotion Policies A system of Honors/Satisfactory/Not satisfactory is used. A passing total score must be recorded on Parts I and II of the NBME exam to graduate.

Facilities *Teaching:* Clinical teaching programs are conducted in the Health Sciences Building and in the University Hospital. *Other:* Other affiliated hospitals in the city and throughout the Pacific Northwest provide opportunities for clinical training. *Library:* A comprehensive medical library is available for students and staff. *Housing:* Information not available.

Special Features *Minority admissions:* No students are admitted to the medical school on a preferential basis, but the school is interested in considering as many qualified applicants as it can from minority groups regardless of residence. *Other degree programs:* Combined MD-PhD programs are available in the basic sciences.

WEST VIRGINIA

Marshall University
School of Medicine
1542 Spring Valley Drive
Huntington, West Virginia 25701

Admissions (AMCAS) The basic premedical science courses, English composition and rhetoric, and social or behavioral science are required. Preference is given to state residents, but the length of residence in and commitment to West Virginia may be considered. *Transfer and advanced standing:* Information not available.

Curriculum 4-year semi-traditional. *First year:* In addition to the basic medical sciences, courses are offered in community medicine, emergency medical training, human sexuality, and Introduction to Medicine. *Second year:* Consists of the advanced basic sciences plus psychiatry, genetics, epidemiology, biostatistics, physical diagnosis, community medicine, Introduction to Medicine, and electives. *Third year:* Rotation through the major clinical specialties including family practice. *Fourth year:* Consists of a block devoted to community medicine and one devoted to emergency medicine plus 26 weeks of electives, 8 of which must be spent in rural West Virginia and 8 in ambulatory experience.

Grading and Promotion Policies A letter grading system is used. The Academic Standards Committee administers promotions. Students must record passing total scores on Parts I and II of the NBME exam for promotion to the third year and graduation, respectively.

Facilities *Teaching:* The school is affiliated with the Cabell Huntington Hospital (363 beds), St. Mary's Hospital (440 beds) the VA Medical Center, and many community hospitals. *Library:* The medical library collection is available to students as well as faculty and is constantly expanding its holdings. *Housing:* Housing is available in the Twin Tower Dormitory for single students and in furnished family dwelling units for married students.

Special Features *Minority admissions:* No special recruitment program is available. *Other degree programs:* None currently exist.

West Virginia University
School of Medicine
Morgantown, West Virginia 26506

Admissions Requirements include the basic premedical science courses and one year each of English and of behavioral or social sciences. Minimum of 3 years of college work. A few places are available for well-qualified non-residents. *Transfer and advanced standing:* Transfers will be considered for admission to the third-year class.

Curriculum 4-year semi-traditional. *First and second years:* Introductory and advanced basic sciences. Student is introduced to community medicine and receives emergency medical training in the first term of the freshman year. Elective opportunities are offered in the basic science years, beginning with the second term of the freshman year. *Third year:* Clerkships. A foundation in history-taking, examination, patient relations, laboratory aids, diagnosis, treatment, and the use of medical literature. *Fourth year:* Clerkships in community and emergency medicine. Elective rotations at University Hospital and some approved rotations at other academic institutions.

Grading and Promotion Policies All courses are graded on a Satisfactory/Unsatisfactory grading system. These designations are accompanied by a narrative report of the student's progress. Taking Part I of the NBME exam is optional, but Part II must be taken and a score recorded.

Facilities *Teaching:* The Basic Sciences Building opened for instructional purposes in September, 1957. The University Hospital and its outpatient clinics opened in 1960. Specialist services at the Hospital are provided through the staff of the clinical departments of the school. *Library:* The Medical Center Library has approximately 100,000 bound volumes and receives more than 1500 domestic and foreign periodicals. The Medical Center Library and the University Library maintain an interlibrary loan service. *Housing:* The University maintains 7 residence halls, 2 for men and 5 for women, as well as efficiency and one-bedroom apartments.

Special Features *Minority admissions:* The school has a minority recruitment program and offers a one-month, summer enrichment program. *Other degree programs:* Combined MD-PhD programs are offered in the basic medical sciences.

WISCONSIN

Medical College of Wisconsin
8701 Watertown Plank Road
Milwaukee, Wisconsin 53226

Admissions (AMCAS) Required courses include minimum premedical science courses plus one year each of English, algebra, and analytical geometry (if not taken in high school). A significant number of nonresidents are accepted. *Transfer and advanced standing:* Data not available.

Curriculum 4-year semi-traditional. *First and second years:* Basic medical sciences in addition to genetics, biostatistics, medical ethics, psychology, physical diagnosis, community health, preventive medicine, and Introduction to Clinical Medicine. Second-year students are introduced to clinical experiences and have contact with patients during their work in psychology. Students are also introduced to the problems of community health during their work in preventive medicine. *Third and fourth years:* This time is devoted to rotating clerkships in major and some minor specialties. Two months of electives, including possibility of studying at another school, are offered during senior year.

Grading and Promotion Policies A Pass/Fail system is used. Students must take Part I of the NBME exam and record a passing total score for promotion to the third year. Part II must be taken and a score recorded.

Facilities *Teaching:* Clinical instruction takes place at 4 major hospitals: Milwaukee County General Hospital, VA Hospital, Milwaukee Children's Hospital, and Milwaukee Psychiatric Hospital. *Library:* A comprehensive medical library is available for student and staff use. *Housing:* Information not available.

Special Features *Minority admissions:* The school's Office of Minority Affairs conducts an active recruitment program. It also offers a 6-week Summer Bridging Program for admitted students. *Other degree programs:* The school has combined MD-PhD programs in a variety of disciplines including biophysics and pathology.

University of Wisconsin
Medical School
1300 University Avenue
Madison, Wisconsin 53706

Admissions (AMCAS) The basic premedical sciences are required as well as one year of mathematics. An advanced biology course and English, biochemistry, and calculus are recommended. Few nonresidents are accepted. *Transfer and advanced standing:* Very few transfers accepted into third-year class.

Curriculum 4-year semi-modern. *First year:* Courses in basic sciences. *Second year:* Course in pathophysiology of disease organized in blocks of time by organ systems. Concurrent with this are courses in hematology and immunology. *Third year:* Rotation through the major clinical clerkships. *Fourth year:* Five 8-week periods, one of which must be spent in an 8-week preceptorship. The remaining periods must be spent taking elective courses.

Grading and Promotion Policies Examinations are given at the end of each semester during the first and second years and at the end of the third and fourth years. Grades, recorded by letter or number, are given by a committee of faculty members. Students must record a passing total score on Part I of the NBME exam for promotion to the third year and on Part II for graduation.

Facilities *Teaching:* The school's major teaching facility is the University of Wisconsin Hospitals, consisting of 6 hospitals under one administration. There are also Bardeen Laboratories for teaching and research and the McArdle Laboratory for cancer research. *Other:* The Medical Science Building provides research laboratories, and the Service Memorial Institute houses research laboratories, teaching laboratories, and lecture rooms. The State Laboratory of Hygiene is concerned with the diagnosis, control, and eradication of communicable diseases, and the Genetics Building accommodates classrooms and laboratories. *Library:* The William S. Middleton Medical Library holds about 150,000 volumes and receives about 2000 serial publications. *Housing:* A few students live in college dormitories, but most live either in rooms or apartments with other students. Married students are eligible for housing in the University Eagle Heights Apartments.

Special Features *Minority admissions:* Recruitment is coordinated by the Office of Student Services. Accepted students can enter a summer program. *Other degree programs:* Combined MD-PhD and MD-MS degrees are offered in the basic sciences.

CANADA

> **Dalhousie University**
> Faculty of Medicine
> Halifax, Nova Scotia, Canada B3H 4M4

Admissions In addition to the basic premedical science courses, requirements include one year of English and taking the MCAT. Preference is given to residents of the maritime provinces of Nova Scotia, New Brunswick, and Prince Edward Island. *Transfer and advanced standing:* Transfer students are accepted only under special circumstances.

Curriculum 4-year semi-modern. *First year:* (37 weeks) Core courses in the introductory basic sciences, some advanced basic sciences, some clinical and system courses, and electives. *Second year:* (37 weeks) Several systems courses, psychiatry, preventive medicine, pharmacology, patient contact, and electives. *Third year:* Mostly systems courses with a pathophysiological perspective. Also courses in genetics, ophthalmology, otolaryngology, human sexuality, and electives. *Fourth year:* (52 weeks) 8-week clerkships in major specialties and 4-week clerkships in subspecialties. Also, a 4-week elective.

Grading and Promotion Policies A letter or number is given in basic and clinical sciences, but a Pass/Fail system is used for electives. Students are assessed each year on aptitude and fitness for the medical profession. In addition, all required exams must be passed in order that a student may progress from one year to the next. Taking Part I of the NBME exam is optional, but taking Part II is required.

Facilities *Teaching:* The Tupper Medical Building provides facilities for basic science instruction, while hospitals in the area (total of over 2500 beds) are used for clinical instruction. *Other:* The Tupper Medical Building also houses research facilities in basic and clinical sciences. *Library:* The Kellogg Health Sciences Library has a large volume of books and periodicals for student and faculty use. *Housing:* University housing is available for students.

Special Features There are no combined degree programs at this time.

> **Laval University**
> Faculty of Medicine
> Sainte-Foy, Quebec, Canada G1K 7P4

Admissions The basic premedical science courses plus mathematics through calculus are required. Applicants should have a good command of the French language as it is the language of instruction. Priority is given to residents of Quebec, but outstanding French-speaking students from other provinces are considered. *Transfer and advanced standing:* Applications for transfer are accepted only under exceptional circumstances.

Curriculum 4-year non-traditional. *First and second years:* One trimester of departmental courses in anatomy, biochemistry, physiology, pharmacology, pathology, and microbiology. Starting in the second trimester and for the next 5 trimesters, integrated courses in different systems including digestive, locomotor, and nervous. There are also courses in ethics, epidemiology, and the psychosocial aspects of medicine. Most teaching is done through small group discussion. *Third and fourth years:* Eleven weeks of primary clerkship followed by 18 months of clerkship rotation through the major clinical specialties including family medicine and social and preventive medicine. During this period, 5 months are devoted to electives.

Grading and Promotion Policies Letter grades in basic sciences, required clinical sciences, and electives. Taking the NBME exam is optional.

Facilities *Teaching:* Clinical instruction takes place at the 360-bed Centre Hospitalier de l'Université Laval and about 10 other affiliated hospitals. Research facilities in most fields are available. *Library:* A comprehensive medical library is at the disposal of students and faculty. *Housing:* Accommodations are available for many students.

Special Features After 3 years students receive a Bachelor of Health Sciences (Medicine) diploma and after 4 years, a Doctor of Medicine diploma.

> **McGill University**
> Faculty of Medicine
> 3655 Drummond Street
> Montreal, Quebec, Canada H3G 1Y6

Admissions The Faculty offers 4-year, 5-year and advanced standing programs of undergraduate medical education. Entrance to the 5-year program is restricted to Quebec residents enrolled in one of the Quebec Colleges of General and Professional Education. Entrance to the 4-year program is not restricted geographically; applicants must have received or be in the final year of study leading to a bachelor's degree and must take the MCAT. *Transfer and advanced standing:* A very few students are admitted to advanced standing at the beginning or in the middle of the second year. Equivalency examinations may be required in certain subjects.

Curriculum 4-year semi-traditional. The program emphasizes the coordination of course content in basic sciences and clinical work. An extensive elective program enables students to explore the aspects of medicine that most appeal to them and thus aids them in making wise career choices. *First year:* Provides an introduction to the basic medical sciences with integrated courses in behavioral science and epidemiology. *Second year:* Instruction in advanced basic sciences is offered. During the second half of the first term, emphasis is placed on an Introduction to Clinical Science. *Third year:* Consists of periods of from 2 to 10 weeks in medicine, surgery, obstetrics, neurology, anesthesia, radiology, and an elective block. There are also 208 hours of didactic teaching for the whole class. *Fourth year:* Devoted to clinical clerkships with increasing responsibility given to the student. There is a 12-week elective period. From this level, the student may progress directly to straight internship in his/her specialty field.

Grading and Promotion Policies Grading is on a Pass/Fail basis. A student is evaluated by each department and students with academic difficulties are reviewed by a Faculty Promotions Committee.

Facilities *Teaching:* There are 5 university teaching hospitals, 7 affiliated teaching hospitals, and 7 special research centers and units. Classroom instruction is carried out mainly in the McIntyre Medical Sciences Building. Research opportunities, available at the undergraduate as well as graduate level, are provided in all of the basic medical sciences and in many fields of clinical medicine. *Library:* The Medical Library, located in the McIntyre Medical Sciences Building, contains approximately 170,000 volumes and an excellent journal collection. The Osler Library, located in the same building, has a large collection in medical history and biography. *Housing:* Housing for approximately 1000 students is available in university residences.

Special Features No combined degrees are offered.

McMaster University
Faculty of Medicine
1200 Main Street West
Hamilton, Ontario, Canada L8N 3Z5

Admissions Completion of at least 3 years of college and a B average are required. Priority is given to Hamilton area residents and residents of northwestern Ontario, but there are some openings for out-of-province citizens. Applicants need not take the MCAT. Nonbiology majors are given the same consideration as students with a more scientific orientation but should have some background in biochemistry. *Transfer and advanced standing:* Transfer students may be accepted for advanced standing depending on an assessment of previous training.

Curriculum 3-year semi-modern. *Phase I:* (6 weeks) A course is offered in the summer to introduce the basic elements of the health care system and the important areas of human structure and function. Groups of 5 to 8 students work closely with a faculty tutor to study major medical problems, to learn interviewing and examination techniques, and to study growth and development of the normal individual. *Phase II:* (18 weeks) Concentrates on the basic concepts of cells, tissues, organs, and organisms, their responses to stimuli, and the inherent variations in their biological processes. *Phase III:* (40 weeks) Presents a study of organ systems and the relation of each system's anatomy and physiology to specialized functions and possible malfunctions. The student learns clinical techniques in preparation for Phase IV. *Phase IV:* (58 weeks) Close work with health teams in major clinical specialties. A program of electives designed to encourage in-depth study in portions of the medical program. This includes a Horizontal Program which involves specific learning situations and runs concurrently with the 3-year program. The entire program works on a full-year schedule with month breaks.

Grading and Promotion Policies A Pass/Fail system is used. Taking the NBME exam is optional.

Facilities *Teaching:* The Health Sciences Centre provides classroom area for basic sciences instruction and contains a 418-bed teaching hospital. The major hospitals in Hamilton also provide clinical teaching for the McMaster program. *Other:* The Health Sciences Centre also houses research facilities. *Library:* The Health Science Library provides a large number of periodicals, clinical science references, and audiovisual materials for student use. *Housing:* University housing exists for male students in the Faculty of Medicine.

Special Features No combined programs are currently available.

Memorial University
Faculty of Medicine
Prince Phillip Drive
St. John's, Newfoundland, Canada A1B 3V6

Admissions A minimum of 20 courses taken or accepted for credit at a recognized university or university college, is required for entry to Medical School. These courses must include 2 courses in English, 2 courses in mathematics, 2 courses in general chemistry and 2 courses in organic chemistry. Preference is given to residents of Newfoundland, Labrador, and the Maritime provinces, but nonresidents are admitted. Applicants must take the MCAT. Recommended courses include biology, physical chemistry, physics, and behavioral science. Admissions will normally be to the first year of medical studies. *Transfer and advanced standing:* In exceptional circumstances, admission with advanced standing may be offered. It is the policy of the university not to accept transfer students from other medical schools.

Curriculum 4-year. *First year:* Courses are offered in cell structure and function, behavioral science, and community medicine. Patient contact is established in work in varied medical settings in the community. *Second and third years:* Instruction is based on a systems approach with an integration of anatomy, physiology, pathology, and introductory clinical studies. *Fourth year:* Rotating clerkships through the major specialties. Electives make up a large part of the program throughout the four years and involve either research or in-depth study of a specific topic.

Grading and Promotion Policies A Pass/Fail system is used. Taking the NBME exam is optional.

Facilities *Teaching:* The medical school complex includes the Health Sciences Centre with its medical sciences teaching facilities and the University Hospital (320 beds). Affiliated hospitals in St. John's participate in the school's clinical teaching programs. *Library:* A biomedical library and research facilities are also part of the medical complex. *Housing:* Accommodations on campus are limited but off-campus housing is available.

Special Features Combined MD-PhD programs are available on request.

Queen's University
Faculty of Medicine
Kingston, Ontario, Canada K7L 3N6

Admissions Candidates must be Canadian citizens, Canadian landed immigrants prior to the closing date for receipt of applications, the children of Queen's University alumni who are resident outside Canada, or foreign students with appropriate sponsorship (e.g., Canadian International Development Agency).

Curriculum 4-year structured. The major emphasis is the education of students as thinkers and problem solvers, skilled in sensing, formulating, and managing common health problems. *First year:* Emphasizes normal structure and function with contributions from departments of anatomy, biochemistry, and physiology predominating, and an Introduction to Clinical Medicine through medical science rounds. *Second year:* Emphasis in the basic medical sciences shifts to the study of the abnormal with the introduction of microbiology, pathology, and pharmacology. The student is introduced to psychosocial concepts in the psychosocial aspects of medicine course. The knowledge and skills necessary in the practice of medicine are studied in depth in the clinical skills course. *Third year:* Clinical subjects are dealt with exclusively. *Fourth year:* Is comprised of a 48-week clinical clerkship which includes 5- or 10-week rotations and an 8-week elective period.

Grading and Promotion Policies An Honors/Pass/Fail system is used. Taking the NBME examination is optional.

Facilities *Teaching:* Botterell Hall is the major facility, housing the library, some student facilities, major classrooms, and the Departments of Biochemistry, Microbiology and Immunology, Pharmacology and Toxicology, Physiology, a National Cancer Institute Research Group of the Department of Pathology, and animal facilities. The Old Medical Building houses the Department of Anatomy. The Department of Pathology has its major facility in the Richardson Laboratory which is connected to the Kingston General Hospital. Etherington Hall, devoted to clinical teaching and research, is also connected to KGH and contains a major auditorium. *Other:* Other major facilities include Abramsky Hall, major research space in the Hotel Dieu Hospital, and in the LaSalle Building. *Library:* The Health Sciences Library contains about

80,000 volumes and over 1300 serials, and offers interlibrary loan service. *Housing:* Information not available.

Special Features The school offers a combined masters-MD program.

Université de Sherbrooke
Faculté de Medecine
Sherbrooke, Quebec, Canada J1H 5N4

Admissions Mathematics through calculus is required. Preference is given to residents of Quebec province, although a small number of nonresidents of Quebec can be accepted. Applicants should have a background in humanities and behavioral sciences as well as a knowledge of the basic sciences. Fluency in French is necessary. *Transfer and advanced standing:* Information is not available.

Curriculum 4-year semi-modern. The program aims to produce capable physicians adaptable to rapid social change. Problem solving approaches are stressed throughout. An elective program allows students to pursue special interests and explore capabilities. *First year:* Includes an introduction to basic medical sciences and clinical work with an orientation toward the psychosocial aspects of medicine. *Second year:* Integration of basic science and clinical disciplines using a systems approach. Courses in psychiatry, public health, and sexology are offered. An elective program is available. *Third year:* Clinical work in the morning and discussions in the afternoon, accompanied by elective time. *Fourth year:* A full year of clerkships ranging from 2–12 weeks plus 16 weeks of electives.

Grading and Promotion Policies Grading is on a 4-point basis, A=4. Evaluations are made by examination results and reports of professors on student progress. A grade of C, based on these exams and evaluation reports, must be obtained for promotion at fourth year's end. Taking the NBME exam is optional.

Facilities *Teaching:* A Health Sciences Center provides teaching facilities and houses the 395-bed teaching hospital, La Clinique Universitaire. *Other:* Three other hospitals are affiliated with the school. *Library:* A medical library containing more than 75,000 volumes offers extensive reference material. *Housing:* Information not available.

Special Features Combined degree programs are available at the MS-MD level.

University of Alberta
Faculty of Medicine
2J2.11 Walter MacKenzie Center
Edmonton, Alberta, Canada T6G 2R7

Admissions Requirements include the basic premedical science courses in calculus, statistics, microbiology, genetics, and vertebrate zoology as well as English. Preference is given to Alberta residents and nonresidents who have done their undergraduate work in Alberta. *Transfer and advanced standing:* School only accepts transfer students under exceptional circumstances.

Curriculum 4-year semi-modern. The first 2 years consist of instruction from September to May, while the last 2 years are a combined 86-week program with one 4-week vacation break. *Phase I:* One academic year of instruction covering most of the basic sciences and an introduction to clinical skills. *Phase II:* A one-year program of interdepartmental teaching in a clinical setting relating clinical and basic medical sciences to human diseases. *Phase III:* Consists of rotated clerkships in affiliated hospitals with 18 weeks devoted to electives in a wide range of fields. Students are encouraged to organize individual programs with career and special interests in mind.

Grading and Promotion Policies Evaluations of student work are made at the conclusion of each phase of the program on the basis of performance on final, course, and interdisciplinary examinations. A number grading system is used. Each student must attain a GPA of at least 5.0 to progress to the next level of study. Taking both parts of the NBME exam is optional.

Facilities *Teaching:* The Faculty of Medicine is located on the campus of the University of Alberta. The Basic Sciences Building houses facilities for the teaching of basic science and the 1200-bed University Hospital provides for most of the clinical instruction. There are also several other hospitals affiliated with the school. *Other:* Facilities for research in experimental medicine are available at the Surgical-Medical Research Institute. The Cancer Research Institute is housed at the McEachern Cancer Research Laboratory. *Library:* A comprehensive medical library contains a large number of bound volumes and periodicals. *Housing:* There are residence halls available for single students and a 299-unit apartment building for married students.

Special Features Combined MD-PhD programs are available in a variety of disciplines including immunology and pathology. An MD-MS program is also offered.

University of British Columbia
Faculty of Medicine
2194 Health Sciences Mall
Vancouver, British Columbia
Canada V6T 1Z6

Admissions Required courses include the basic premedical sciences, one year of mathematics (including calculus), one year of English, and one year of general biochemistry or cell biology. Residents of British Columbia are given priority. Applicants must have 3 years of college work and take the MCAT. A personal interview is advisable. Recommended courses include those in the humanities and behavioral sciences. *Transfer and advanced standing:* None.

Curriculum 4-year semi-traditional. *First and second years:* For the first 2 years the program concentrates on the basic medical sciences. Instruction is given mainly on the University campus with some hospital teaching taking place during the second year. *Third and fourth years:* Instruction shifts entirely to the hospitals. The third year provides the essentials of modern diagnosis and treatment which the student uses in his/her work with hospital patients. By the fourth year, the

student has received enough experience through clerkships in major clinical specialties to enable him/her to practice medicine under supervision with increasing responsibility for patient care. An 8-week elective program is offered.

Grading and Promotion Policies Grades are letter or number. Promotion is determined by the Faculty Committee at the end of each session. The committee also decides whether unsatisfactory work can be corrected by a special examination or by repeating the course, or if the failing student must withdraw from studies completely. Taking the NBME exam is optional.

Facilities *Teaching:* The Health Sciences Center on campus provides for teaching basic sciences. Included in the complex are research facilities, classrooms, and audio-visual equipment. Vancouver General Hospital offers its facilities for clinical teaching along with Shaughnessy and St. Paul's Hospitals on campus and several off-campus institutions. *Other:* The Basic Sciences Center houses the Strong Laboratory for Medical Research and the Kinsman Laboratory for Neurological Research, both of which provide facilities for special research. *Library:* On-campus library facilities exist at the Woodward Biomedical Library and a branch library is maintained at Vancouver General Hospital. *Housing:* Single student accommodations are available on a room or room-and-board basis. Married students can find a limited number of unfurnished suites.

Special Features No combined programs are offered.

University of Calgary
Faculty of Medicine
3330 Hospital Drive, N.W.
Calgary, Alberta, Canada T2N 4N1

Admissions Priority is given to residents of Alberta, and non-Canadian citizens are not encouraged to apply. Applicants need not have a strict premedical background if their academic record is superior. The basic premedical science courses and biochemistry, cell biology, and physiology are recommended. All applicants must take the MCAT and have a personal interview. *Transfer and advanced standing:* Applications are considered from students attending accredited medical schools, but only for the final or clerkship year.

Curriculum 3-year modern. After graduation the student usually takes 2 years of post-graduate work. The initial program provides a basic education, while the graduate work furnishes opportunity for specialization. The main emphasis is on problem solving, with patient contact and responsibility throughout the entire program. *First and second years:* A short orientation program is followed by an introductory course to prepare the student for the 9 body systems courses. A Continuity course, lasting for the 2 years demonstrates the relevance of social and physical environments to the individual student. An independent study program of 16 hours per week is time set aside secure from encroachment by scheduled curricular activities. Four hours a week are allotted for electives. *Third year:* Consists of clinical clerkships where the concepts taught in the first two years are applied. Elective programs are available.

Grading and Promotion Policies Evaluation is based largely on day to day performance, but also on the student's factual knowledge and ability to apply this knowledge toward solving problems. Grading is on a Pass/Fail basis. Taking the NBME exam is optional.

Facilities *Teaching:* The Calgary Health Sciences Centre which includes the University of Calgary Medical Clinic provides a model of health care services, teaching and research areas, an audio-visual center, and space for labs, lecture halls, and study areas. Clinical teaching takes place at Foothills Hospital, Calgary General Hospital, and Holy Cross Hospital. *Library:* The Health Sciences Library contains about 50,000 volumes and subscribes to about 2000 periodicals. An inter-library loan service also exists. *Housing:* Both single and married students can find some housing.

Special Features No combined programs are offered.

University of Manitoba
Faculty of Medicine
753 McDermot Avenue
Winnipeg, Manitoba, Canada R3E 0W3

Admissions Applicants must have completed 2 years of college. Course work should include the basic premedical sciences plus one year of biochemistry and English. Undergraduates and graduates of the universities in Manitoba (who are Canadian citizens) are given preference. The MCAT is required.

Curriculum 4-year semi-modern. *First year:* Devoted to a study of normal human biology, both by individual disciplines and in an integrated manner, and the general mechanisms of disease. *Second and third years:* During the second year and the first half of the third year, the clinical sciences are studied. The balance of the third year is an elective period. *Fourth year:* Consists of clinical clerkships in the major specialties.

Grading and Promotion Policies The Pass/Fail system is used. Taking the NBME exam is optional.

Facilities *Teaching:* The medical buildings are adjacent to the Health Sciences Center which contains 2 teaching hospitals: General Centre (750 beds) and Children's Centre (220 beds). Other hospitals are also utilized in the clinical training program. These include the Deer Lodge Veterans Hospital (500 beds) and St. Boniface General Hospital (634 beds). *Library:* A comprehensive medical library serves student and faculty needs. *Housing:* Information not available.

Special Features Combined MD-PhD programs are offered in immunology, pharmacology, and physiology.

University of Montreal
Faculty of Medicine
P.O. Box 6207, Station A
Montreal, Quebec, Canada H3C 3T7

Admissions A thorough knowledge of the French language is a prerequisite. All candidates accepted must be either Canadian citizens or landed immigrants. Admission of foreign students is limited to a few candidates who are from countries having no medical school and who are supported by the Canadian International Development Agency (CIDA). Under the present Quebec educational system, the minimum requirement is 2 years of college (Sciences Program). The college curriculum should provide a wide cultural background. Course work must include philosophy, behavioral and social sciences, French, English, mathematics (analytical geometry, calculus, college algebra, and trigonometry), and the basic premedical sciences courses.

Curriculum The curriculum is divided into 3 phases over a period of 5 years, Phase 1 (3 sessions or 1½ years) is devoted to essentials in basic sciences. During Phase 2 (same duration as Phase 1), morphology and function, both normal and abnormal, are presented in 13 integrated multidisciplinary courses. Phase 3 consists of a clerkship of 80 weeks.

Grading and Promotion Policies A number grades system is used in basic sciences; letter grades in clinical sciences; Pass/Fail in electives.

Facilities *Teaching:* Clinical instruction is carried out at 14 affiliated teaching hospitals and research centers.

Special Features Internship and residency training in the teaching hospitals is under the direction of the Faculty of Medicine. Various courses and symposia are organized by the continuing medical education division. Many programs of graduate studies leading to MSc and PhD degrees are also available.

University of Ottawa
Faculty of Medicine
275 Nicholas Street
Ottawa, Ontario, Canada K1H 8M5

Admissions Successful completion of the first 2 years of a BA or BSc program and of the basic premedical science courses is required. Only Canadian citizens or permanent residents are considered for admission except in the case of children of alumni. *Transfer and advanced standing:* Applications for transfer by Canadian citizens or permanent residents from other medical schools are considered under certain conditions. Acceptance for advanced standing is based on past academic achievement.

Curriculum 4-year traditional. The program is aimed at giving each student a background in all phases of medical knowledge. *First and second years:* Basic medical sciences conducted in seminars and small groups. *Third year:* A combination of rotating clerkships and instruction in pathophysiology. *Fourth year:* Clerkships lasting for 48 weeks which can be used as the equivalent of the rotating internship after graduation. Four weeks allotted for electives.

Grading and Promotion Policies The grading scale is A (80–100%), B (70–79%), C (60–69%), and F (below 60%). A grade of 60% in all subjects must be maintained for promotion to the next year of study. A Pass/Fail system is used in electives. Taking the NBME exam is optional.

Facilities *Teaching:* The University's Medical Building houses the facilities for basic science instruction. Clinical instruction takes place at Ottawa General Hospital (450 beds), Ottawa Civic Hospital (900 beds). *Other:* Other facilities include Children's Hospital of Eastern Ontario (300 beds), Royal Ottawa Hospital (150 beds), and several smaller institutions. *Library:* The Health Sciences Library has 32,000 volumes and subscribes to about 2000 journals. *Housing:* Information is not available.

Special Features   A combined BSc-MD program is available.

University of Saskatchewan
College of Medicine
Saskatoon, Saskatchewan
Canada S7N 0W0

Admissions   Requirements include the basic premedical science courses, a language, and an elective. Exclusive priority is given residents of Saskatchewan. Applicants are not required to take the MCAT. Students should have a minimum of one year of college. *Transfer and advanced standing:* Information not available.

Curriculum   5-year traditional. The curriculum is aimed at educating doctors for entrance into all phases of the medical profession. *First year:* Largely devoted to basic science courses but also includes courses in nutrition and a general introduction to medicine. *Second year:* Introductory and some advanced basic sciences as well as radiology, psychiatry, and electives. *Third year:* Advanced basic sciences, genetics, medicine or surgery, systems, and electives. *Fourth year:* Medicine or surgery, systems, community medicine clerkship, and 12 weeks for electives. *Fifth year:* Rotating clerkships through major clinical specialties. There are also clerkships in anesthesia, family medicine, and emergency medicine. Also included is a 4-week elective program.

Grading and Promotion Policies   A Pass/Fail system is used in electives and letters or numbers are used in basic sciences and required clinical sciences.

Facilities   *Teaching:* Basic sciences are taught in the Medical Building. Clinical instruction takes place at the University Hospital, connected with the Medical Building. *Other:* Other affiliated hospitals are St. Paul's, Saskatoon City Hospital, Regina General Hospital, and Plains Health Centre in Regina. *Library:* The Medical Building also houses the school library.

Special Features   A BSc(medicine)-MD combined program is available.

University of Toronto
Faculty of Medicine
Toronto, Ontario, Canada M5S 1A8

Admissions   Requirements include completion of Grade XIII plus 2 years at a Canadian college, or Grade XII plus 4 years at a non-Canadian college, as well as taking the basic premedical science courses. Preference is given to residents of Ontario. Applicants must take the MCAT and have a personal interview. No preference for admission is given to science majors. *Transfer and advanced standing:* Transfer students from other medical schools are not considered because of enrollment limitations.

Curriculum   4-year semi-modern. *First year:* Includes basic sciences, pharmacology, and statistics. *Second year:* Includes some advanced basic sciences, clinically oriented courses, and genetics. *Third year:* Provides integration of basic sciences and clinical problems using a systems approach. Courses in medical jurisprudence, psychiatry, and other clinical areas are introduced. *Fourth year:* Rotation through specialties for 2–8 weeks. Also, 8 weeks of electives and 4 weeks of selective experience must be taken.

Grading and Promotion Policies   Grades are given on a Pass/Fail/Honors basis, with in-course evaluations and examination scores being the principal means of determination. Each system and topic are graded. All evaluations must be passed for promotion to the next program of study. Final grade assessment is made by the Board of Examiners.

Facilities   *Teaching:* The basic courses for the first 2 years are given at the Medical Sciences Building. The University is associated with 11 hospitals, the largest being Toronto General Hospital with over 1100 beds. *Other:* Research facilities are housed in the Medical Sciences Building. *Library:* The medical library contains a large volume of books and subscribes to many periodicals. *Housing:* Some University housing is available. For students unable to find accommodations on campus, the school maintains a list of local housing.

Special Features   A combined MD-PhD program is offered by the Faculty of Medicine and the School of Graduate Studies.

University of Western Ontario
Faculty of Medicine
London, Ontario, Canada N6A 5C1

Admissions   Students of western Ontario are considered first. Foreign applications are not accepted. Requirements include MCAT scores and a knowledge of organic chemistry. A course in behavioral science is recommended. *Transfer and advanced standing:* Information not available.

Curriculum   4-year semi-traditional. *First year:* Work with patients begins early. Courses include the basic medical sciences and studies of the relationship between medicine and society. *Second year:* A continuation of basic science courses with a consideration of their connection with body systems. More attention is focused on clinical work with an introduction to clerkship. *Third year:* A full year of rotating clerkships. *Fourth year:* 12 weeks of elective courses in a special field of interest and 2 required clerkships.

Grading and Promotion Policies   Letters or numbers are used and taking the NBME exam is optional.

Facilities   *Teaching:* Clinical teaching facilities exist at Victoria Hospital, University Hospital, and several other affiliated institutions. *Library:* A comprehensive medical library is available for student and staff use. *Housing:* Information not available.

Special Features Combined MSc-MD and MD-PhD programs are available. The latter include programs in the basic medical sciences as well as in biophysics, epidemiology, and biostatistics.

MEDICAL SCHOOLS IN DEVELOPMENT

City University of New York
Sophie Davis School of Biomedical Education

This two-year school is expanding to a four-year program with the third and fourth years of clinical training at hospitals in Queens County, and the MD degree to be awarded by the University. The first class in the new program will be enrolled in September 1985.

Planning for a new medical school, **The Western University School of Medicine** in Phoenix, Arizona, is in progress. The new school would endeavor to train minority students to practice in underserved areas, including inner cities, rural areas, and Indian reservations. Graduates would be expected to perform social service duties for two years.

Discussion is also taking place on a possible new medical school at **Queens College** of the City University of New York. One of the goals of the new school would be to recruit and train black and Hispanic physicians.

9

FOREIGN MEDICAL STUDY

☐ Admission
☐ Transfer to U.S. schools
☐ Internship and residency
☐ Requirements for practice
☐ Fifth pathway schools
☐ Foreign medical schools

During the early decades of this century it was relatively common to find Americans going to Europe for postgraduate medical training. Since World War II, significant numbers of Americans have gone overseas for their undergraduate medical education. Currently it is roughly estimated that there may be as many as 10,000 enrolled in foreign medical schools. Approximately 500 new students are thought to matriculate each year, but this figure will probably decline.

The fact that a significant number of Americans are studying medicine abroad should not be taken to mean that if you fail to gain acceptance in the U.S., you should automatically seek admission to a foreign school. You should first determine if rejection by American schools means that you genuinely lack the ability to complete your medical studies. You should realize that *only* well-qualified and highly motivated students stand a good chance of overcoming the obstacles of studying medicine in a foreign language and then facing the difficulties of securing suitable postgraduate training and a license to practice in the U.S. The obstacles to be faced in overseas medical study are reflected by the findings of a study that indicates that of all the American students entering foreign medical schools, one-third will not continue after their first year of study; one-third will complete their studies after many years but cannot qualify to practice in the U.S.; and one-third will finish their studies within the standard period (5 to 8 years) and eventually enter the U.S. physician manpower pool (although they may not end up practicing in the state of their choice).

Current estimates are that about 200 foreign-trained American physicians become practitioners each year; that is, less than half of those who have gone overseas. As a general rule those graduating from Swiss, Belgian, or English schools have succeeded better than those enrolled in German, Italian, Spanish, and French schools. If you are contemplating overseas study you should ask yourself if you really want to become a physician so much as to be willing to do so by this long and very arduous means; if you have a chance of gaining acceptance to a U.S. school if you reapply; and if you could be happy in some health science career other than medicine.

ADMISSION

The process of securing admission to a foreign medical school is cumbersome because there are no standard application procedures or forms, no standard documents required for submission, and no central clearing service for foreign schools. In spite of these difficulties, it is still advisable to avoid private placement agencies that advertise that they can get you into a foreign school. They provide their services at a high fee and you can gain admission on your own if you are qualified. The following sources of information will be of help:

1. *Foreign embassies and consulates.* They usually have catalogs of the medical schools in their countries. They frequently have staff members who are familiar with the current admission policies and procedures and whose advice should be sought. This source may have applications and descriptive literature or may provide the name and address of admissions officers.

2. *Institute of International Education.* 809 United Nations Plaza, N.Y. 10017, maintains a library of foreign university catalogs.

3. *Barron's Guide to Foreign Medical Schools* (1979). Prepared by Carla Fine to help students decide whether or not to study medicine abroad, this guide provides valuable information and advice on who should go to a foreign medical school, selecting an appropriate foreign school, how to apply for admission, how to prepare for study abroad and how to succeed once there. It also provides advice on how to re-enter the U.S. medical system to practice after obtaining a degree in a foreign country. It includes detailed, up-to-date profiles on the schools. (Price is $7.95.)

4. *Guide to Foreign Medical Schools* (4th edition, 1975). Prepared by Prof. D. Marien (published by the Institute of International Education). Contains a lot of useful and relevant information for prospective applicants regarding the major foreign schools that Americans are attending.

5. *World Directory of Medical Schools* (5th edition, 1979) published by the World Health Organization, Geneva. It is available from The United Nations Bookshop, G. A. Room 32, New York, N.Y. 10017 or The Q Corporation, 49 Sheridan Avenue, Albany, N.Y. 11210. This publication, while providing some helpful data, is not written especially for the potential American applicant and thus lacks such useful information as how to initiate an application, who is responsible for admissions at a particular school, and how many Americans are enrolled at the school. Thus this volume is also probably not worth purchasing but should nevertheless be examined at some reference library.

Most German, Austrian, and Belgian schools have relatively high admission standards and strict scholastic requirements. As many as from 30 to 50 percent of the students fail the basic science examination which is taken prior to beginning clinical studies. However, graduates from schools in these three countries have some of the best records for passing the ECFMG examination. Italian, Mexican, and Spanish schools have relatively low admissions requirements. They accept and graduate relatively large numbers of students. Graduates from schools in these countries have had the most difficulty passing the ECFMG examination. (This possibly may be due to the poor quality of the students and not necessarily the standards of education at the schools.)

The course of studies in foreign medical schools varies from 4 to 6 years. At some schools, examinations are usually taken voluntarily at the end of one- or two-year periods and can be retaken a number of times. This system of academic freedom adds to the existing problem of studying medicine in a foreign language.

TRANSFER TO U.S. SCHOOLS

In 1970, the Coordinated Transfer Application System (COTRANS) was established on an experimental basis to facilitate the transfer of students studying abroad to U.S. medical schools. This system involved taking Part I of the National Board Examinations at a U.S. or foreign test center. This program was terminated in 1979. During the decade of COTRANS existence less than half of those who took Part I of the NBME exam passed and only about half of those who passed managed to transfer to U.S. medical schools. This points up the inherent difficulties associated with overseas medical study.

Starting in June 1980, a special examination was developed and administered by the NBME for U.S. citizens enrolled in foreign medical schools who wish to apply for transfer with advanced standing to a U.S. medical school. It is known as the Medical Sciences Knowledge Profile (MSKP). This two-day examination is designed to provide medical schools with a method of evaluating such an applicant's knowledge in the basic medical sciences and in introductory clinical diagnoses. Each part of the examination is graded on a nine point scale. No total score or pass or fail is reported. It is too early to determine the impact of this test, but the difficulty of transferring to a U.S. medical school is reflected in the fact that only 200 to 400 students have succeeded each year, over the past five years. Moreover, the numbers transferring have been declining consistently over these five years.

INTERNSHIP AND RESIDENCY

There are five pathways for foreign graduates to follow in securing AMA-approved internship and residency appointments: (1) transferring with advanced standing to a U.S. medical school and repeating one or more years. (The policies of U.S. medical schools regarding transfer and advanced standing is given in the profiles for the individual schools in Chapter 8); (2) certification by ECFMG on the basis of satisfying the ECFMG educational requirements, as well as passing the ECFMG examination; (3) obtaining a full and unrestricted license to practice medicine, issued by a state or other U.S. jurisdiction authorized to license physicians; (4) successfully passing the complete licensure examination in any state or licensing jurisdiction where a full and unrestricted license is issued upon satisfactory completion of internship or residency without further examination; and (5) an approach that is especially popular among one segment of foreign medical students, and is for obvious reasons known as the "Fifth Pathway," discussed below.

FIFTH PATHWAY SCHOOLS

Students who have completed all of the formal requirements of the foreign medical school except internship and/or social service may substitute a year of supervised clinical training for the required foreign internship (that is, clinical clerkship or junior internship) under the direction of an AMA-approved school. Upon successful completion, students may enter the first year of an approved residency program without having to complete the social service requirement of the foreign country. Before beginning the supervised clinical training, students must have their academic records reviewed and approved by the school supervising the clinical training and must pass a screening examination acceptable to the Council on Medical Education. The ECFMG examination and/or Part I of the NBME exam are used for this purpose.

Currently about twenty U.S. medical schools offer Fifth Pathway clerkships. This option applies primarily to students in Mexican medical schools and is open only to physicians who have completed their undergraduate premedical studies in an acceptable manner at an accredited American college or university. The Fifth Pathway program allows U.S. students who have completed the requirements for a medical degree in Mexico to be eligible for a continuous academic year of supervised clinical training under the direction of a medical school approved by the Liaison Committee on Medical Education. The students who complete this supervised clinical training are then able to enter an AMA-approved graduate training program without completing the Mexican required internship or social science obligation. This program allows graduates of Mexican medical schools to pass easily into graduate medical programs in this country. The following schools are associated with this Fifth Pathway program. An inquiry should be addressed to the director of these programs.

California:

University of California—Davis

University of California—Irvine

University of Southern California

Florida:

University of Florida

Indiana:

Indiana University

Maryland:

University of Maryland

Missouri:

St. Louis University

New Jersey:

Rutgers

New York:

Albert Einstein

Mt. Sinai

New York Medical College

New York University

SUNY at Buffalo

SUNY at Stony Brook

SUNY, Downstate Medical Center

Pennsylvania:

Hahnemann University

Canada:

Dalhousie University

Memorial University

University of Saskatchewan

REQUIREMENTS FOR PRACTICE

FLEX Examination: The Federation Licensing Examination (FLEX) is prepared by the Federation of State Medical Boards for administration by the state medical boards of examiners which participate in the program. Admission to the examination for medical graduates, including foreign medical graduates, will depend upon the statutory regulatory requirements of the individual states. All states and the District of Columbia participate in the FLEX program except for Florida and Texas. Requests for applications should be addressed to the specific state boards.

In recent years, the Federation of State Medical Boards has devised a new two-part licensing examination, known as FLEX I and FLEX II. Currently the recommendation is that FLEX I need not be passed before entering a residency. Also, FLEX II can be taken immediately after FLEX I. Ultimately, each examination or licensing authority decides examination requirements for licensure.

ECFMG Examination: Students from the U.S. who are graduates of foreign medical schools and wish to secure an internship or residency in or practice in the U.S. must pass an examination given by the Educational Council for Foreign Medical Graduates (3930 Chestnut St., Philadelphia, Pa. 19104). This examination, which is given twice a year in many centers throughout the world, consists of 360 multiple-choice questions selected from a

pool of questions previously used in Parts I and II of the NBME exams. To pass, a student must attain a score of 75.

State Board Requirements: While the AMA recognizes a graduate of any foreign medical school who has been certified by the ECFMG as eligible for internship and residency training, licensure to practice in the U.S. is under the jurisdiction of state governments, each of which establishes its own standards. Some states accept no foreign graduates while others accept graduates from certain foreign schools. Information on the requirements in each state can be secured from the secretary of each of the State Boards of Medical Examiners. (Graduates of Canadian medical schools are considered equivalent to U.S. graduates but must meet the requirements for citizenship and internship.)

FOREIGN MEDICAL SCHOOLS

As noted, the majority of Americans studying at overseas schools are located in four countries: Mexico, Italy, Belgium, and Spain.

Australia

It is extremely difficult for a U.S. student to be admitted to an Australian medical school. The general policy is to discourage foreign applicants.

Austria

It is not recommended that students attempt to apply to any Austrian medical schools. None of the schools are currently accepting foreign students. However, it is possible that this situation may change.

Belgium

Belgium is a country whose language is divided; thus, at the Universities of Ghent and Antwerp, course are given in Flemish, while at Brussels, Liège, and Louvain, French is the standard language. A Flemish section, however, is also presented at Brussels and Louvain. Students can join the section they prefer, and most Americans enroll in the French schools. Students must apply individually to each school, preferably in the spring. Usually, Americans have had to start from the beginning of the six-year didactic program (which includes the premedical courses) and must also serve a year of internship in order to receive the medical degree. There is an unofficial 5% quota for non-Belgium students.

University of Antwerp: This school previously only offered the first three years of the medical curriculum; i.e., the basic sciences. The fourth year is now available and is similar to a rotating internship. *Contact:* Faculteit der Geneeskunde, Rijksuniversitair Centrum Antwerpen, Goemaerelei, 52, 2000 Antwerpen, Belgium.

University of Brussels: A request for admission can be directed to either the French or Flemish sections or both. Proof of proficiency in either language will be required. Students spend approximately half their study time for the full four years in clinical areas. *Contact:* Faculté de Médecine, Université Libre de Bruxelles, Rectorat-Affaires Étudiantes, Avenue A. Buyl, 131, 1050 Bruxelles, Belgium.

University of Ghent: This school offers courses in Flemish for foreign students. It requires certified copies of diplomas and letters of recommendation in order to be considered. *Contact:* Faculteit der Geneeskunde, Rijksuniversiteit te Gent, Voldersstraat, 13, 9000 Gent, Belgium.

University of Liège: This school considers applicants who have their bachelor's for admission to the first and possibly also the second year. The work at this school is considered especially difficult because there is an oral final for the entire term's work. *Contact:* Faculté de Médecine, Université de Liège, Service des Étudiants, Place de XX Août, 4000 Liège, Belgium.

University of Louvain: The French section is now located at Brussels. A language proficiency examination is required in both sections. In the French section, examinations are given in each course. *Contact:* (French) Faculté de Médecine, Université Catholique de Louvain, Secrétariat des Étudiants Etrangers, Avenue E. Mounier, 1200 Bruxelles, Belgium. (Flemish) Faculteit der Geneeskunde, Universiteit Katholik te Leuven, Studentensecretariaat, Universiteithal, Naamsestraat, 22, 3000 Leuven, Belgium.

Admission Requirements: Bachelor's degree. The documents required include: letter of recommendation from the pre-medical committee (or individual letters where a committee does not exist), transcript covering all four years of college, a copy of the diploma from college.

Caribbean

In recent years several medical schools were established in the Caribbean with the aim of being profit making institutions. Since their goal is to enroll rejected American students, they teach in English and have high tuition and fees. The academic standards of some of these schools have had adverse criticism, and potential applicants are strongly urged to evaluate such schools thoroughly before committing themselves.

For additional information, *contact:* St. George's University, c/o Foreign Medical School Services Corporation, One East Main Street, Bay Shore, NY 11706;

Ross University School of Medicine, Empire State Building, 350 Fifth Avenue, New York, NY 10001; American University of the Caribbean, School of Medicine, 100 N.W. 37th Avenue, Miami, FL 33125.

Dominican Republic

For a while medical study by Americans in the Dominican Republic was fairly popular. The principal school accepting Americans was the Universidad Central del Este. The school accepted a large number of U.S. students and in particular a large number of Puerto Ricans. Unfortunately a major scandal involving granting of fraudulent degrees has resulted in the closing of one school and has created a cloud of suspicion over the others.

Universidad Central Del Este: The standard medical program of this school extends over 10 semesters. Each semester is 18 weeks long and this time is lengthened by holidays that occur within the semester. Students can be expected to complete their studies in four and one-quarter years. *Contact:* Admissions Office for Foreign Students, Universidad Central del Este, Tampico, Dominican Republic.

Admission Requirements: Bachelor's degree and minimum science courses plus two semesters each of English, philosophy, and one of sociology. School requires the following documents: official SAT and MCAT scores, high school and college transcripts, photocopy of birth certificate, certificate of good conduct from local police department.

Universidad Nacional Pedro Henriquez Urena: The course of study takes 9 semesters and each semester is 20 weeks long. The first 2 years deal with the basic sciences, and the last 2½ years are devoted to clinical work. *Contact:* Director, Escuela de Medicina, Universidad Nacional Pedro Henriquez Urena, Santo Domingo, Dominican Republic.

Admission Requirements: Bachelor's degree and premedical average above 2.8. School requires the following documents: official college transcript, premedical committee evaluation, three letters of recommendation, MCAT scores, and certificate of good conduct from local police department.

France

U.S. students may not encounter too much trouble in being admitted to the first year at a French medical school. At the end of the first year, however, all medical students in France take a qualifying test in order to obtain entry to the second year. Since there are many more first-year medical students than second-year places, the competition is very stiff and is unlikely that a U.S. student would fare well. For additional information, *contact:* Théraplix, Secrétariat du Guide Théraplix des Études Médicales, 46–52 rue Albert, 75640 Paris Cedex 13.

Germany

The probability of being accepted to a German medical school is very slight, owing to the limited number of places available to foreign students and to the great difficulty of the entrance examinations, which are language tests. For more information on German schools, *contact:* Cultural Division, Consulate General of the Federal Republic of Germany, 460 Park Avenue, New York, NY 10022.

Hungary

The medical school of the University of Pécs has recently introduced a six-year English language program. *Contact:* Hungarian Consulate, 8 East 75 Street, New York, NY 10021.

Ireland

Ireland has one private institution that accepts foreign applicants and this is the Royal College of Surgeons. There is an entrance examination; the school also requires MCAT scores, academic courses, and a letter of recommendation. *Contact:* Royal College of Surgeons, 123 St. Stephen's Green, Dublin 2, Ireland.

Israel

Students need not consider applying to an Israeli medical school because, although such applicants may be considered, few would be accepted. A special program primarily for New York State residents exists at the Sackler School of Medicine of the University of Tel Aviv Medical School and English is the language of instruction. *Contact:* Office of Admissions, Sackler School of Medicine, 17 East 62 Street, New York, NY 10021.

Italy

Previously, Italy had a fairly open admissions policy. Americans were screened at the Consulate office in New York and, if accepted, were allowed to attend any of the medical schools in the country. Recent meetings between the Italian medical schools and American counterparts have resulted in a new law which requires the assignment of foreign applicants to particular schools. Until this law, most American students went to the universities at Bologna, Rome, and Padua. Another law that was passed requires all students to have a B average and to speak Italian. These laws have markedly reduced the number of Americans in attendance at Italian medical schools.

Preclinical course work is characterized by overcrowded classrooms. After finishing their didactic course work, students must pass a series of final examinations before they receive the degree of doctor of medicine and surgery. They must then complete a one-year internship to be eligible for admission to the Italian State Examination. The ECFMG requires graduation from an Italian school, the ECFMG examination, and fulfillment of all requirements for admission to the Italian State Examination before a graduate is eligible for ECFMG certification. The year of internship can be fulfilled by a year of clinical clerkship at an undergraduate medical school approved by the AMA Liaison Committee on Medical Education.

University of Bologna: This school enrolls the largest group of Americans studying in Italy. Its appeal over other schools appears to be the lack of "obstacle" courses along the path to the degree. In addition, the American students have organized an association that seeks to assist the membership to adjust to their new environment. *Contact:* Università degli Studi, Bologna, Italy.

University of Padua: This school enrolls a small number of Americans. Anatomy is strongly emphasized in preclinical teaching. The school has a reputation for being very demanding and, as a result, a significant number of students transfer to Bologna after three years at Padua. *Contact:* Università degli Studi, Padua, Italy.

University of Rome: This school enrolls a small number of Americans. Most seem to have little academic difficulty until they reach the third and fourth year when the pharmacology and pathology courses are taken. The cost of living in Rome is relatively high. *Contact:* Università degli Studi, Rome.

University of Turin: *Contact:* Università degli Studi di Torino, Turin, Italy.

University of Pisa: *Contact:* Università degli Studi, Pisa, Italy.

University of Pavia: *Contact:* Università degli Studi, Pavia, Italy.

University of Palermo: *Contact:* Università degli Studi, Palermo, Italy.

University of Florence: *Contact:* Università degli Studi, Florence, Italy.

University of Genoa: *Contact:* Università degli Studi di Genova, Genoa, Italy.

University of Milan: *Contact:* Università degli Studi, Milan, Italy.

University of Naples: *Contact:* Università degli Studi, Naples, Italy.

Address for Information: Italian Consulate, 690 Park Avenue, New York, NY 10021 (or the nearest consulate).

Admission Requirements: Bachelor's degree, minimum science courses, and adequate knowledge of Italian. The following documents are required and should be sent to the Consulate between April 1 and September 15: official college transcript, letter of recommendation from the premedical committee or individual letters from the heads of science departments. If requirements are met, students will be asked to submit photographs (2, passport size), original high school diploma, and affidavit of support.

Mexico

All of the Mexican medical schools but one are state schools. They follow the six-year, European-style curriculum and the applicant must apply in person. The only nonstate school is the Universidad Autónoma de Guadalajara, a four-year school where a large number of American medical students are studying.

Autonomous University of Guadalajara: This school is located in Guadalajara, which is the second largest city in Mexico. The weather there is ideal almost year-round; though it does get hot in May and June, it generally cools off at night. All course work and conversation with instructors is in Spanish. Americans are required to take special language instruction and must pass a language examination at the end of the first year. Spanish translations of most of the well-known English textbooks are available. Classes at the medical school are scheduled through most of the day, except between the hours of one and four in the afternoon. Attendance is required in 80% of all classes in order to be eligible to take the final examinations. While the didactic work is currently four years, a year of internship and a year of social service in a rural community, presentation of a thesis, and a final examination are required before the student is awarded the *Titulo de Medico Cirujano* (the title of physician and surgeon). The *Titulo* is required by the ECFMG for certification of a candidate who has passed the ECFMG examination. The ECFMG Board of Trustees has approved the substitution of a year of clinical clerkship, under the sponsorship of an American medical school, for a year of internship that is a postgraduate requirement in certain foreign medical schools. The acceptability of an American clerkship in lieu of the internship by the Universidad Autónoma de Guadalajara is uncertain at this time. *Contact:* Oficina de Información a Extranjeros, Universidad Autónoma de Guadalajara, Apartado Postal 1–440, Guadalajara, Jalisco, Mexico.

Admission Requirements: Bachelor's degree and minimum science courses. School requires the following documents: birth certificate (3 copies), letters of recommendation (2), certificate of health, photographs, high school transcript and diploma, college diploma, letter of financial solvency, certificate of completion of premedical requirements, and MCAT scores. Of these, the following must be legalized by the

Mexican Consulate: transcripts, diplomas, birth certificate, letter of financial solvency, and certificate of premedical studies.

Three other schools in Mexico enroll Americans:

Autonomous University of Ciudad Juarez: *Contact:* Universidad Autonoma de Ciudad Juarez, Instituto de Ciencias Biomedicas, Apartado Postal 1574, Sucursal "D", Ciudad Juarez, Chihuahua, Mexico.

University of Monterrey: *Contact:* Direccion de Admisiones, Seccion de Extranjeros, Apartado Postal 4435, Sucursal "J" de Correos, Monterrey, Nuevo Leon, Mexico.

University Del Noreste (Tampico): *Contact:* Universidad del Noreste, Admissions Office, 120 East 41 Street, Suite 1000, New York, NY 10017.

Netherlands

The Netherlands no longer accepts American students.

Philippines

Some Americans are seeking admission to medical schools in the Philippines. This is probably owing to the increasing difficulty in securing admission to European schools and the fact that the teaching methods and procedures employed in the Philippines are similar to those used in the United States. The language of instruction is English. The course of study is four years and the academic year is divided into two semesters. The following are the names and addresses of the six medical schools in the Philippines. An * indicates those schools that accept from 10 to 25 Americans each year; the others accept fewer than 10.

University of the Philippines: College of Medicine and Surgery, 547 Herren Street, Manila, Philippines.

University of Santo Tomas: College of Medicine, España Street, Manila, Philippines.

***Manila Central University:** College of Medicine, Samson Road, Caloocan City, Philippines.

***University of the East:** Ramon Magsaysay Memorial Medical Center, College of Medicine, Aurora Boulevard, Quezon City, Philippines.

***Far Eastern University:** Institute of Medicine, Science Building, Nicanor Reyes Sr. Street, Manila, Philippines.

Southwestern University: College of Medicine and Surgery, Cebu City, Philippines.

Address for Information: Consulate General of the Philippines, 556 Fifth Avenue, New York, NY 10009.

Admission Requirements: Bachelor's degree with a premedical major or appropriate courses completed. Applications for admission can be secured from the individual universities and must be returned with a transcript and other required credentials. A student visa will be issued only after an official letter of acceptance is received.

Poland

Students in the United States with Polish ancestry will have the most success in being accepted to Polish medical schools. The schools are state-supported and therefore a very limited number of foreign applicants will be accepted. *Contact:* Embassy of the Polish People's Republic, 2640 16th N.W., Washington, DC 20009.

Spain

Medical schools in Spain appear to be receptive to Americans. The majority of those attending are at the University of Madrid. A reform plan has gone into effect which has resulted in a 75% attrition rate for first-year students, and, therefore, students may want to attend a different school (for example, at Bilbao or Barcelona). Acceptance confers eligibility to attend the school you select. Spanish schools require a two-year internship. Medical facilities are to be found at the following universities:

Barcelona	La Laguna
Barcelona	Malaga
(AUTONOMOUS)	Murcia
Bilboa	Navarra
Cordoba	Oviedo
Granada	Salamanca
Santander	Sevilla in Cadiz
Santiago de	Valencia
Compostela	Valladolid
Sevilla	Zaragoza

In addition, there are several Colegios Universitarios that offer the first year of medical study. Eventually these schools will offer a full program:

Burgos	Soria
Vitoria	Toledo

Address for Information: Cultural Relations Department, Spanish Embassy, Columbia Road N.W., Washington DC 20001.

Admission Requirements: Bachelor's degree. Documents required include: birth certificates with city or county seal (2), college transcript with school seal, copy of high school diploma, and a college catalog. An application for admission (obtainable from the Embassy or consulate) plus the required documents should be taken to the embassy or consulate for legalization and then submitted to the former for transfer to Madrid.

Expenses: The cost of living is higher in Madrid than in other Spanish cities. However the cost of living in general is lower in Spain than in other European countries. The overall costs of travel plus tuition and living expenses is significantly less than the mean cost in the United States.

Switzerland

Swiss schools are no longer accepting U.S. students.

United Kingdom

There are very few openings for U.S. students at British medical schools but some students are occasionally accepted. Contact: Universities Central Council on Admissions, P.O. Box 28, Cheltenham GL50 1HY, England.

10

OSTEOPATHY

☐ Basic philosophy
☐ Educational data
☐ Internship, residency, and practice
☐ Relationship between osteopathy and conventional medicine
☐ Financial assistance
☐ Basic data for osteopathic medical schools
☐ Descriptions of the osteopathic medical schools

Aside from the 124 standard, or allopathic, medical schools, there are 15 osteopathic schools in the U.S., which in a recent year had an enrollment of over 4000 students. There were more than 20,000 osteopathic physicians listed in the directory published by the American Osteopathic Association. Thus this branch of medicine contributes a significant number of professionals to the physicians pool, and information about it is relevant both to those specifically interested in osteopathic medicine and to students interested in allopathic medicine (especially those whose chances for admission to standard schools may be in doubt). For this reason the philosophy, educational data, and training program leading to the Doctor of Osteopathy, or DO degree, is outlined.

BASIC PHILOSOPHY

The osteopathic approach was developed by a physician, Dr. Andrew Taylor Sill, in 1874 and is based upon a holistic view of the function of the human body. Osteopathy is structured on the principles that the human body is an integrated organism and therefore abnormal function in one part of the body exerts unfavorable influences on other parts and thus on the body as a whole; a complex system exists in the body which tends to provide for self-regulation and self-healing in the face of stress; adequate function of all body organs and systems depends on the integrating forces of the nervous and circulatory system; the body's musculoskeletal system (i.e., its bones, joints, connective tissues, skeletal muscles, and tendons) plays an important role in the body's continuous effort to resist and overcome illness and disease. Based on these principles osteopathy postulates that any stress—physical, mechanical, or emotional—that causes muscles to become tense (referred pain) intensifies the constant stream of sensory nerve impulses being sent *to* the central nervous system (CNS) by receptors in the muscles and tendons. If this "neural barrage" is severe enough, it may "spill over" and initiate an excessive volley of autonomic nerve impulses that pass *away* from the CNS to segmentally related organs and tissues. As a result muscular responses to referred pain may trigger a neural feedback that can become a secondary source of irritation and pain. This in turn may induce responses by the internal organs that again are referred back to the musculoskeletal system. Thus a vicious cycle of sensory-motor nerve excitation can be created. Unless this cycle is interrupted, it may perpetuate itself until the somatic response to referred pain becomes more severe than the original visceral disease. The somatic response in effect becomes a secondary disease.

The musculoskeletal system is easily accessible and thus it is believed that the treatment of it may be beneficial in altering the disease process by interrupting the vicious cycle of neural exchange. In practice, osteopathy involves the application of manipulative procedures to help tense muscles, tendons, and connective tissues to relax. The increase in muscle-fiber length resulting from the relaxation eases the tension on the impulse receptors in the muscles and tendons thus reducing sensory bombardment to the spinal cord. This reduction may allow the entire body to return to more normal homeostatic levels and permit segmentally related visceral structures to repair themselves under more normal conditions. It is important to note that *the osteopathic system of diagnosis and therapy is used in conjunction with the standard medical procedures of drug and surgical therapy*. Thus as part of the educational program, osteopathic colleges train their students in the standard medical diagnostic and therapeutic methods as well as those associated with osteopathy. For additional information write the American Osteopathic Association, 212 East Ohio Street, Chicago, IL 60611.

EDUCATIONAL DATA

In the United States, there are presently 15 osteopathic colleges. The establishment of colleges of osteopathic medicine is being discussed in other areas of the country.

In a recent year, the present 15 colleges admitted about 1700 freshmen out of an applicant pool of about 4000. Students coming from six states—Pennsylvania, Michigan, Ohio, Missouri, Texas, and Iowa—made up the largest segment of the enrollment of the first-year classes. The grade point average of the class was about 3.2 (where 4.0 = A). This represents a significantly lower average than that for the entering class at conventional medical schools. Thus some borderline students who may have difficulty gaining acceptance at a standard medical school may more readily secure places in osteopathic medical schools.

Admissions committees are putting increased emphasis on grade point average, recommendations, and interviews, and less emphasis on test scores. The committees seek the same general characteristics in prospective students as conventional medical schools (e.g., dependability, maturity, integrity), but they also look for special interest in and motivation to study osteopathic medicine. Thus letters of recommendation for osteopathic physicians (and possibly even students) adequately acquainted with applicants can be helpful.

The number of women in a recent freshman class was more than 26% of the total enrollment. This is relatively similar to the proportion of women enrolled in standard medical school. The number of entering students having less than 4 years of undergraduate education was a small percentage of the total entering class. This clearly reflects the fact that both osteopathic and standard medical schools still feel that the fourth year in the undergraduate college is desirable.

The average age of entering osteopathic students has been 25 years (range: 20–42); this is higher than those accepted in standard medical schools. It may be because many matriculants were motivated into this field after exposure to related community service careers. Thus among the older freshmen, many have backgrounds in teaching, allied health fields, and research. Also a significant number are veterans and, as a result, are older than the typical college graduate. In any case, as with the standard schools, applicants over 28 can expect to have special difficulties in gaining admission. The basic science course requirements for admission to osteopathic schools are the same as that for standard schools. The majority of freshmen, as would be expected, were biology or chemistry majors and almost all of them took the MCAT test.

The curriculum at an osteopathic school is almost identical with that offered at the standard schools. Study is divided into basic science and clinical science training. There is a required course in the basic theory and practice of osteopathic medicine. The philosophy of osteopathy, with its emphases on total health care, is incorporated where appropriate into the standard courses. Curriculum revision in line with that taking place at standard schools is also occurring at osteopathic schools.

INTERNSHIP, RESIDENCY AND PRACTICE

After obtaining the DO degree, those planning to practice osteopathic medicine are expected to spend at least a year in internship training. There are about 150 osteopathic hospitals distributed in 25 states which have been accredited by the American Osteopathic Association and 75 of these have been approved for internship training. Some of these hospitals offer residency training in some medical specialty. Training for specialization can extend over a three- to five-year period in an osteopathic hospital having an approved program, or can be service as a trainee under a certified osteopathic specialist, or can be a combination of both types of training. After the completion of the formal training period, two years of specialized practice are required before the applicant is eligible to take the examination for certification in a specialty field.

It should be noted that the majority of osteopaths are general practitioners and only about 20 percent of all osteopaths are engaged in specialty training or practice (full- or part-time). Thus while many osteopaths practice in large cities, others are found in small communities where there is a special need for family physicians and general practitioners. The income for osteopathic physicians is roughly comparable to that of conventional doctors and depends on the location of the practice.

It should be noted that DOs are eligible for appointment and are serving as medical officers in the U.S. Public Health Service, Veterans Administration, and armed forces. They also serve as examiners or may prepare certificates of health examinations required by various federal agencies, as coroners, and as members of state, county, and city boards of health. They provide medical and surgical care for those insured under Blue Cross and Blue Shield as well as private health insurance plans. In other words, the same general opportunities are on the whole open to DOs as to MDs, within the confines of this not so widely established group of medical practitioners.

An osteopathic physician may obtain a license to practice in one of three ways:

1. Examination administered by the state board, which is usually the FLEX.

2. Acceptance of the certificate issued by the National Board of Examiners for Osteopathic Physicians and Surgeons which is issued after meeting their requirements.

3. Reciprocity of a license previously received from another state.

RELATIONSHIP BETWEEN OSTEOPATHY AND CONVENTIONAL MEDICINE

In June, 1967, at its annual convention the House of Delegates of the AMA authorized the Board of Trustees to begin negotiations toward conversion of osteopathic schools to conventional medical schools. Progress along these lines has been meager and the likelihood of a total changeover in the foreseeable future is remote. In the light of those circumstances the AMA suggested: that AMA-approved internship and residency programs be opened to qualified graduates of schools of osteopathy; that American Boards for medical specialties accept for examination for certification those osteopaths who have completed AMA-approved internships and residency programs and have met the other regular requirements applicable to all Board candidates; that accredited hospitals accept qualified osteopaths for appointment to the medical staffs of hospitals; and that determination of qualification be made at the level of the medical staff of a hospital, or the Review Committees and Boards having appropriate jurisdiction.

The aforementioned recommendations have thus potentially opened the way for wider acceptance of DOs into the mainstream of medical training and practice. Eleven specialty boards have agreed to examine for certification osteopathic graduates who have completed AMA-approved internships and residency programs. They are: the American Board of Pathology, Pediatrics, Physical Medicine and Rehabilitation, Preventive Medicine, Radiology, Anesthesiology, Dermatology, Internal Medicine, Obstetrics and Gynecology, Orthopedic Surgery, Psychiatry, and Neurology.

The application of the AMA proposals is indicated by the fact that in a recent year about 300 hospitals had appointed about 1000 osteopathic physicians to their attending staff as house officers. These appointments were spread over 25 states with the largest number being in Pennsylvania, New Jersey, California, Michigan and Washington. These figures will undoubtedly rise steadily during the next few years.

FINANCIAL ASSISTANCE

1. *National Osteopathic Scholarships.* Annually 25 scholarships of $1500 are awarded to entering osteopathic students. These will be applied to tuition at the rate of $750 per year for the first two years. (Information is obtainable from the Office of Education,

American Osteopathic Association, 212 East Ohio St., Chicago, IL 60611.)

2. *Health Professions Educational Assistance Scholarships.* Scholarships of up to $2000 for students from low-income families are available for 10% of the first-year classes. (Information is obtainable from the deans of colleges of osteopathic medicine.)

3. *Texas Osteopathic Association Scholarships.* Two $750 and $1000 scholarships available for Texas students entering osteopathic schools. (Information is obtainable from Mr. T. Roberts, 512 Bailey St., Ft. Worth, TX 76107.)

4. *Canadian Osteopathic Scholarships.* A $3000 scholarship is available to a first- or second-year Canadian student enrolled in an osteopathic school. (Information is obtainable from Canadian Osteopathic Education Trust Fund, Suite 126, 3545 Cote des Neiges Road, Montreal 25, Quebec.)

5. *Maine Osteopathic Association Scholarships.* A minimum of two $750 scholarships are awarded annually to students who have received their undergraduate education in Maine or who are Maine residents accepted for admission to an osteopathic school. (Information is obtainable from L. M. Newth, D.O., 491 Sevens Avenue, Portland, ME 04103.)

6. *New Jersey Association of Osteopathic Physicians and Surgeons Scholarships.* Three scholarships are awarded to cover full tuition for first-year students who are New Jersey residents. (Information is obtainable from the Executive Director, New Jersey Association of Osteopathic Physicians and Surgeons, 1212 Stuyvesant Ave., Trenton, NJ 08618.)

7. *New York State Scholarships.* These are awarded to New York students in amounts ranging from $350 to $1000 a year on the basis of an examination given in Albany in October of each year. (Information is obtainable from the Regents Examination and Scholarships Center, The University of the State of New York, State Education Department, Albany, NY 12201.)

8. *Florida Osteopathic Medical Association Scholarship.* A $1000 a year scholarship for a Florida resident entering osteopathy school. (Information is obtainable from the Secretary, Florida Osteopathic Medical Association, P.O. Box 896, Palmetto, FL 33561.)

9. *Kansas Osteopathic Foundation Scholarships.* Two scholarships are awarded to Kansas residents attending osteopathic schools. (Information is obtainable from the Executive Vice-President, Kansas Osteopathic Foundation, 835 Western, Topeka, KS 66606.)

10. *U.S. Air Force and Navy Scholarships.* These cover full tuition, books, and living expenses for applicants to medical and osteopathic schools for four-year period. (Information is obtainable from the Director, Washington Office, American Osteopathic Association, Cafritz Building Suite 1009, 1625 Eye Street, N.W., Washington, DC 20006.)

11. *Michigan Osteopathic College Foundation Scholarships.* These scholarships are restricted to students attending the College of Osteopathic Medicine, Michigan State University. (Information is obtainable from the Executive Director, Michigan Osteopathic College Foundation, 306 Penobscot Building, Detroit, MI 48226.)

12. *Minnesota State Osteopathic Association Scholarships.* Two $500 scholarships are awarded annually to Minnesota residents attending colleges of osteopathic medicine. Recipients must demonstrate a financial need and agree to practice in Minnesota for five years after completion of their training. (Information is obtainable from the Chairperson, Minnesota Osteopathic Scholarship Fund, 1595 Selby Avenue, St. Paul, MN 55104.)

13. *National Osteopathic Foundation Student Loan Fund.* An approved candidate may borrow a sum not exceeding $1000 annually. (Information is obtainable from the National Osteopathic Foundation Student Loan Fund Committee, 212 East Ohio Street, Chicago, IL 60611.)

BASIC DATA FOR OSTEOPATHIC MEDICAL SCHOOLS

Table 7 reflects the admissions picture at the osteopathic medical schools presently in operation.

Note: Applications for most osteopathy schools are processed by a centralized application service, the American Association of Colleges of Osteopathic Medicine Application Service (AACOMAS). In the Appendix to this guide you will find a sample AACOMAS form. To secure an application, write to AACOMAS, 6110 Executive Boulevard, Suite 405, Rockville, MD 20852.

DESCRIPTIONS OF THE OSTEOPATHIC MEDICAL SCHOOLS

In these school descriptions, the admissions requirement of the basic premedical science courses refers to one year each of inorganic and organic chemistry, biology, and physics, plus laboratory work.

Table 7. Basic Data for Osteopathic Schools

School	Total Number Applicants	Number 1st Year Accepted			Applications Deadline	Tuition**
		MEN	WOMEN	OUT-OF-STATE		
*College of Osteopathic Medicine of the Pacific	1100	74	26	na	12/1	12,500
*Southeastern College of Osteopathic Medicine	1200	82	21	na	1/1	11,500
*Chicago College of Osteopathic Medicine	2100	75	50	50	12/1	9,650 12,775
*University of Osteopathic Medicine and Health Sciences (Des Moines)	1800	122	61	129	3/15	9,775 12,775
*New England College of Osteopathic Medicine	1382	47	21	24	12/1	12,000
*Michigan State University College of Osteopathic Medicine	1122	80	45	18	11/1	5,133 10,416
*Kirksville College of Osteopathic Medicine	1621	102	30	104	12/1	14,000
University of Health Sciences College of Osteopathic Medicine	515	125	35	132	12/1	11,750
*New Jersey School of Osteopathic Medicine	924	32	24	5	12/1	7,175 8,965
*New York Institute of Technology College of Osteopathic Medicine	1306	86	48	5	12/1	12,500
*Ohio University College of Osteopathic Medicine	1160	71	29	17	12/1	4,605 6,546
*Oklahoma College of Osteopathic Medicine	1140	59	25	12	11/1	2,500 5,400
Philadelphia College of Osteopathic Medicine	1393	154	61	48	12/1	11,250 11,550
*Texas College of Osteopathic Medicine	1112	67	33	9	11/1	300 900
*West Virginia School of Osteopathic Medicine	1115	44	16	23	12/1	1,892 4,512

*AACOMAS school
**Where two amounts are given, the first is for residents. All tuition figures subject to change.
na Data not available

College of Osteopathic Medicine of the Pacific
College Plaza
Pomona, California 91766

Admissions (AACOMAS) Completion of a minimum of 3 years of college with a GPA of at least C+ (2.5) and the MCAT is necessary. The basic premedical science courses plus one year of English and behavioral science are required. Preference is given to residents of western states (including Alaska).

Affiliated Teaching Hospitals The school is affiliated with many hospitals, physicians' offices, and ambulatory health care centers throughout the western states and a few midwestern and eastern states.

Housing There is no on-campus housing. A housing referral system is available.

Southeastern College of Osteopathic Medicine
1750 N.E. 168 Street
North Miami, Florida 33162

Admissions (AACOMAS) A bachelor's degree is required, although exceptional students will be considered with only 3 years of college, MCAT.

Affiliated Teaching Hospitals Information not available.

Housing Information not available.

Chicago College of Osteopathic Medicine
5200 S. Ellis Avenue
Chicago, Illinois 60615

Admissions (AACOMAS) Completion of a minimum of 3 years of college (degree preferred), at least a high C+ average and MCAT are necessary. The basic premedical science courses are required. A total of 100 students are admitted each September. Approximately one half of the class comes from Illinois.

Affiliated Teaching Hospitals Chicago Osteopathic Hospital (300 beds); Olympia Fields Osteopathic Medical Center (225 beds).

Housing A 23-unit apartment building for married students and private residencies in vicinity of the college.

University of Osteopathic Medicine and Health Sciences—Des Moines
3200 Grand Avenue
Des Moines, Iowa 50312

Admissions (AACOMAS) Minimum 3 years of college, bachelor's degree preferred, at least a C+ average, MCAT. The basic premedical science courses plus one year of English composition and rhetoric are required. Recommended courses include biochemistry, genetics, comparative anatomy, and psychology.

Affiliated Teaching Hospitals The University operates 9 clinics and is affiliated with selected rural and urban clinics throughout Iowa. Among the 11 affiliated hospitals are Des Moines General Hospital (150 beds).

Housing The University maintains a minimal number of student housing units. However, students can obtain accommodations in private homes and nearby apartment complexes.

University of New England College of Osteopathic Medicine
11 Hills Beach Road
Biddeford, Maine 04005

Admissions (AACOMAS) Minimum of three years of college, at least 2.5 GPA, MCAT.

Affiliated Teaching Hospitals James A. Taylor Osteopathic Hospital, Osteopathic Hospital of Maine, Waterville Osteopathic Hospital, Huntington General Hospital, Cranston General Hospital.

Housing A limited number of housing units are available on campus.

Michigan State University College of Osteopathic Medicine
East Fee Hall, Michigan State University
Lansing, Michigan 48824-1316

Admissions (AACOMAS) Completion of the MCAT and a minimum of 3 years of college (but virtually all students have bachelor's degree by enrollment). The basic premedical science courses are required as well as 3 courses (9 credits) in English and in the behavioral sciences. Overall and science grade point average must be no less than C+ (2.5). Suggested electives include biochemistry, anatomy, physiology, and histology.

Affiliated Teaching Hospitals Several throughout the state, including many in the Detroit metropolitan area.

Housing Some housing available on campus and in the Lansing/East Lansing area.

Kirksville College of Osteopathic Medicine
Kirksville, Missouri 63501

Admissions (AACOMAS) Completion of a minimum of 90 semester hours, the MCAT, and a B average are necessary. The basic premedical science courses plus one year of English are required. Courses in biochemistry and comparative or human anatomy are recommended.

Affiliated Teaching Hospitals Kirksville Osteopathic Health Center (254 beds); Twin Pines Adult Care Center (186 beds); Doctors Hospital (605 beds); Normandy Osteopathic Hospitals (377 beds); Oklahoma Osteopathic Hospital (416 beds); South Bend Osteopathic Hospital (107 beds).

Housing 44 student apartments and private residences.

The University of Health Sciences College of Osteopathic Medicine
2105 Independence Boulevard
Kansas City, Missouri 64124

Admissions Completion of a baccalaureate degree with a GPA of at least 2.5 and the MCAT is necessary. The basic premedical science courses plus one year of English are required.

Affiliated Teaching Hospitals The college is affiliated with 9 hospitals providing access to over 2000 beds.

Housing Dormitory housing for first year, University-owned apartments for married and other students, private boarding houses near campus, low cost townhouse developments for qualified married students.

New Jersey School of Osteopathic Medicine
40 East Laurel Road
Stratford, New Jersey 08084

Admissions (AACOMAS) Completion of the MCAT and a baccalaureate degree is necessary. The basic premedical science courses are required as is one year of English, mathematics, and behavioral science.

Affiliated Teaching Hospitals Kennedy Memorial Hospitals-University Medical Center (627 beds).

Housing There are no housing facilities at the school. Most students obtain off-campus housing.

New York College of Osteopathic Medicine
Wheatley Road, Box 170
Old Westbury, New York 11568

Admissions (AACOMAS) Bachelor's degree, MCAT, and a GPA of 2.5.

Affiliated Teaching Hospitals Information not available.

Housing Information not available.

Ohio University College of Osteopathic Medicine
Grosvenor Hall
Athens, Ohio 45701

Admissions (AACOMAS) Completion of a baccalaureate degree with a minimum GPA of 2.5 and the MCAT is necessary. The basic premedical science courses plus one year of English and behavioral science is required. Ohio residents are given admissions priority.

Affiliated Teaching Hospitals The school provides clinical training at hospitals which form regional training centers in 5 different areas of Ohio.

Housing Student housing is available in residence halls, 2 married-student complexes, and off-campus apartments and houses.

Oklahoma College of Osteopathic Medicine and Surgery
Ninth Street and Cincinnati Avenue
Tulsa, Oklahoma 74119

Admissions (AACOMAS) Completion of 3 years of college, the MCAT, and at least a C+ average are necessary. The basic premedical science courses are required.

Affiliated Teaching Hospitals Oklahoma Osteopathic Hospi-

tal (534 beds), Hillcrest Osteopathic Hospital (148 beds), Enid Memorial Hospital (104 beds), and other hospitals in Missouri, Kansas, and Texas.

Housing Information not available.

Philadelphia College of Osteopathic Medicine
4150 City Avenue
Philadelphia, Pennsylvania 19131

Admissions (AACOMAS) A bachelor's degree, at least a C+ average, and completion of the MCAT are required, as are the basic premedical science courses.

Affiliated Teaching Hospitals College Hospital (66 beds); F. H. Barth Pavilion of the College Hospital (228 beds).

Housing Two fraternity houses accommodating 60 men, private rooming houses, and apartments available in the vicinity.

Texas College of Osteopathic Medicine
Camp Bowie at Montgomery
Fort Worth, Texas 76107

Admissions (AACOMAS) Completion of baccalaureate degree with at least a C+ (2.5) average and the MCAT is necessary. The basic premedical science courses plus one year of English and behavioral science are required.

Affiliated Teaching Hospitals Agreements were made with 9 hospitals to provide minimum of 2400 beds.

Housing Apartments or rooms in private homes.

West Virginia School of Osteopathic Medicine
400 North Lee Street
Lewisburg, West Virginia 24901

Admissions (AACOMAS) Completion of 3 years of college, and the MCAT, and at least a C+ average are necessary. The basic premedical science courses plus one year of English are required. Additional courses in molecular and organismic biology are also required.

Affiliated Teaching Hospitals The college has contractual arrangements with a large number of off-campus hospitals and clinics, which provide training in the clinical years.

Housing There is no on-campus housing, but ample rentals are available in the immediate vicinity.

Part 2
DENTISTRY

11

DENTISTRY AS A CAREER

☐ Why study dentistry?
☐ The need for dentists
☐ Today's trends in dentistry
☐ Dental specialization
☐ Is dentistry for you?
☐ Dentistry as an alternative to medicine

Dentistry is a profession dealing with the prevention, diagnosis, and treatment of oral diseases and disorders, with primary emphasis on the health of teeth. In a sense, dentistry is a medical subspecialty. Good oral health is critical to man's psychological and physical well being since the state of your teeth affects your speech and expression, and, also, systemic diseases frequently manifest themselves in the oral cavity.

There are more than 125,000 active dentists in the United States; most of them are in private practice with the remainder working as salaried professionals. Of those in private practice, 85% are general practitioners who are contributing to the improvement of their communities' health standards and are rewarded by having favorable working conditions and ample financial remuneration.

Many thousands of dentists hold positions as commissioned officers in the armed forces. Others are employed by the Veterans Administration and in public health dentistry at the state or local level. There are also several thousand full- or part-time teachers, administrators, and investigators in dental schools and in dental research laboratories.

WHY STUDY DENTISTRY?

Dentistry provides young men and women of talent and dedication with an opportunity for a lifetime of professional satisfaction. The following are some of the attractive attributes of the dental profession:

1. It provides a strong sense of inner satisfaction derived from the knowledge that one is contributing to the physical well being of one's patients.

2. It provides a personal feeling of achievement which comes from the successful application of one's judgmental and manual skills in resolving problems.

3. It provides an opportunity for group leadership as the head of a dental care team, making use of one's managerial and organizational skills.

4. It provides a basis for economic security and long-term financial stability.

5. It provides an opportunity to gain status in the community and thereby serve one's neighbors outside of one's professional capacity.

THE NEED FOR DENTISTS

The demands for dental care by the public have increased annually. The three factors responsible for this situation are greater affluence, better education, and increased population growth. (Nevertheless, only about 50% of the general population sees a dentist with any regularity.) The response to the demand for increased dental care has been an increase in the number of patients handled by dentists. Nevertheless, it should be realized that the demand for dental services tends to fluctuate with changes in economic conditions. In any case, the national need for dental care will not only be maintained, but probably will be increased, thus suggesting a bright future for most prospective members of the dental profession.

A note of caution is necessary, for in its most recent report on employment prospects for dentists, the U.S. Department of Labor has said, "employment prospects to grow about as fast as average. . . . Increasingly abundant supply of practitioners will make it more difficult to start a practice. Competition for patients is likely to be intense in some localities, which could adversely affect earnings."

TODAY'S TRENDS IN DENTISTRY

Over the past several decades a gradual reevaluation of both the philosophy and the practice of dentistry has taken place. Whereas around World War II it was estimated that half of all Americans over sixty-five had lost all their teeth, by the end of this century this figure for the same age group will have been reduced dramatically. The reason for this is that there has been a profound improvement in the oral health of recent generations of Americans caused by water fluoridation and the associated change in the role of dentistry, from one of treatment to one of prevention of tooth decay and gum diseases.

In terms of dental practice, an arsenal of new tools, techniques, drugs, and restorative materials has been developed over the past thirty years. These have dramatically expanded and improved the dentist's capacity for providing care in all areas. Among these developments are: (1) the high speed air drill which minimizes the pain, time, and noise associated with drilling; (2) a variety of materials, both metal and plastic, that crowns and bridges can now be made from; (3) plastic sealants which can be applied as a coating film over children's teeth to prevent decay-causing bacteria from attacking them for up to two years; (4) an alternative to bridges and dentures whereby one or more teeth can be set over metal implants inserted into the jaw bone; (5) a new technique called bonding in which a composite material that is undetectable can be glued on to the tooth, enabling chipped teeth to be repaired, spaces between teeth to be filled, and worn-down teeth to be restored, all with aesthetically appealing results.

Advances have also been made in diagnostic techniques, and research is continuing with the focus on preventive dentistry. The prospects for better oral health, therefore, are much higher, provided that increasing numbers of people practice good oral hygiene and avail themselves regularly of competent dental care.

Another major change that may be in the offing is the way dental services will be delivered. The traditional approach since the development of modern dentistry has been to have services provided by the individual practitioner. During the last decade groups of specialists in a particular specialty area have joined together to utilize a common facility on a rotation basis, thereby cutting down significantly on operating expenses. Thus group practices devoted exclusively to endodontics, for example, have developed.

Since about 1977, multipractitioner dental clinics, that is, clinics that offer primarily general but also specialty services, have sprung up in department stores and shopping centers. It is estimated that currently there are at least 300 such facilities in the United States. Their expansion from only a handful in 1978 has primarily been stimulated by legal decisions allowing dentists to advertise. Other contributing factors are the high cost of quality dental care at private offices and the unequal distribution of dentists in some areas.

In 1979, about 125 million Americans spent more than $13 billion for dental treatment, 90% of which was provided by individual practitioners. Some estimates predict that by the year 2000 only 10% of dental care will be provided by small-office dentists. While this may well be an exaggeration, it is certain that the trend is away from private care and toward multipractitioner clinics. This will have enormous implications both for patients and for dentists already in practice and those planning careers in dentistry. The new approach to dental care delivery holds the promise of offering less expensive and more convenient quality care. Whether it will do so in reality remains to be seen.

DENTAL SPECIALIZATION

With advances in a variety of dental techniques and with the current focus on preventive and restorative dentistry, the need for special expertise in the various branches of dentistry has significantly increased. While general practitioners have training in and frequently do work in specialty areas, there are currently about 16,500 dentists whose practice is limited exclusively to one specialty. These dentists have had from one to four years of additional training (depending on the specialty), during which time their diagnostic and operative skills were further developed to achieve a superior degree of competence.

The following eight areas of specialization are recognized by the American Dental Association. (They are listed in order of the number of practitioners in each specialty.)

Orthodontics. This specialty has about 6,500 practitioners. It is concerned with correcting irregular and abnormal dental development. Orthodontic procedures are applicable to patients in any age group, but treatment is more easily and effectively achieved on youngsters. The goal is not only to improve appearance, but to correct the functioning of the teeth by altering the bite. Correcting a bad bite, or malocclusion, will aid in eating and speaking, and will prevent eventual loosening or even loss of teeth, in addition to having a positive cosmetic effect. A bad bite is generally the result of an incorrect relationship that developed during childhood between jaw shape and teeth size. It may also result from habits such as thumb-sucking, nail-biting, or night grinding. Since teeth are moved to improper positions by forces that are out of balance in the mouth, they can be moved back by opposing forces. This is done by the use of various fixed orthodontic appliances such as metal braces or rubber bands, or plastic brackets. Removable appliances may also be used on occasion.

Oral Surgery. There are more than 3,600 practitioners in this specialty. They use surgical procedures to deal with defects and diseases of the entire maxillofacial region—the middle and lower face. Their work encompasses the jaws, cheekbones, and other skeletal elements and their surrounding structures. In addition, the oral surgeon diagnoses and treats injuries, deformities, and growths in and around the jaw. When a tooth (or teeth) must be extracted, the procedure is usually carried out in an oral surgeon's office. Another common surgical procedure is apicoectomy, or surgical removal of a tooth's root tip. Reemplanting teeth knocked out in an accident or treatment of simple or compound jaw fractures are types of traumatic injuries requiring an oral surgeon's skills.

Periodontics. This specialty has about 2,000 practitioners. It is concerned with the diagnosis and treatment of diseases affecting the periodontal tissues that support the teeth, namely the gum, periodontal membrane, and surrounding bone. These diseases are very insidious and become increasingly prevalent with age. The earlier treatment is instituted, the more likely it is that teeth loss can be prevented. Periodontal diseases are diagnosed by several procedures: probing the depth of the space around a tooth, comparing bone level as reflected in x-rays taken at two different dates, and examining for tooth mobility. Slight or somewhat moderate disease can be readily treated by scaling—the removal of plaque or tartar, or root planing—a fine smoothing of the surface of the root. More advanced cases require curettage—scraping of the tissues lining the infected tooth pocket. In severe cases, surgical intervention to expose teeth, or even bone grafting, may be necessary. Various splinting techniques that join loose teeth to firm ones are also utilized.

Pedodontics. This specialty also has about 2,000 practitioners. It is concerned with the treatment of children, adolescents, and young adults exclusively. Pedodontists are in a sense equivalent to pediatricians. In their special facilities and in the approach they use, they strive to establish in the child a positive attitude towards dentistry and a disposition to develop good oral hygiene habits. It is essential to maintain the health of the primary ("baby") teeth for, if decay sets in or premature loss occurs, the health and shape of the permanent teeth could be adversely affected. Also, the overall health of a child will be influenced by the condition of the primary teeth. Undetected decaying teeth can cause poor eating and chewing habits and thereby influence the overall state of a child's health.

Endodontics. There are about 1,000 specialists in this field. It deals with the diagnosis and treatment of diseases of the pulp (nerve) of the tooth. With the current emphasis on saving teeth and utilizing extraction only as a last resort, root canal therapy is a vitally important dental specialty. A tooth needs endodontic treatment if the nerve has been damaged by decay, infection, irritation, or trauma. In such cases, the endodontist cleans out the nerve canal(s), removing the degenerated pulp. When the tooth is asymptomatic and has stabilized, the canal(s) can be filled. The complexity of the treatment is determined by how many canals the tooth may have. Also, a live (vital) tooth is more readily treated than a dead (nonvital) tooth, especially if the latter has abscessed.

Prosthodontics. There are about 750 dentists in this field. Only several decades ago it was a common assumption that as one grew older teeth would have to be lost, and a partial or even full set of dentures was thought to be unavoidable. While the current philosophy is that with good oral hygiene and prompt and competent treatment extraction can be minimized, there are nevertheless patients who will lose teeth and require a replacement for them. Replacement of even a single (non-wisdom) tooth is desirable, since if it is not replaced the teeth on either side of the gap may move. To replace missing or extracted teeth, a fixed or removable bridge can be attached to one or both adjacent teeth, or, in some situations, removable partial or full dentures may be required.

Oral Pathology. There are currently about 100 specialists in oral pathology. They are concerned with diseases of the mouth, studying their causes, processes, and effects. Essentially a diagnostician, an oral pathologist usually serves as a consultant to other specialists as well as a teacher of dental students.

Dental Public Health. This field also has about 100 specialists. They are involved in promoting the oral health of communities by stimulating development of programs that aid in the prevention and control of dental diseases. Such specialists also gather and analyze data that is useful in determining the effectiveness of the oral health methods being used in a community.

IS DENTISTRY FOR YOU?

In evaluating whether dentistry is a suitable career for you, consider the following:

1. Do you possess the attributes that are prerequisites for dentistry?

2. Do you have adequate native manual dexterity?

3. Does your family support you in choosing dentistry as a career?

4. Do your teachers and faculty adviser feel that dentistry is a desirable career for you?

5. After speaking with and observing one or more dentists at work, do you find their profession attractive?

6. After visiting a dental school and/or clinic and speaking with administrators, faculty, and students, are you still strongly in favor of pursuing a dental career?

DENTISTRY AS AN ALTERNATIVE TO MEDICINE

Dentistry offers an attractive alternate career for *borderline* premedical and preosteopathic juniors. In such circumstances you should carefully evaluate whether dentistry is of sufficient interest to you as an alternate career. If this is the case, you should consider applying for admission to both medical and dental schools simultaneously at the end of your junior year in college (although obviously not to both types of schools at the same university). This can be done because admission requirements are almost identical and the medical and dental aptitude tests are very similar. Students who apply to medical and dental schools should inform their pre-professional advisory office of this fact so that appropriate evaluations can be prepared.

Trying to gain admission to dental school with the intent of using this as an avenue or lever to get into medical school, however, is self-defeating. Medical schools will not be favorably impressed by an applicant who is taking a valuable dental class place and is obviously using it primarily to aid his transfer from one professional school to another. Where such a student lacks a genuine interest in dentistry he may also end up wasting time and money in dental school.

If you fail to gain admission to medical school and did not apply to dental school in your junior year, you can consider doing so in the senior year or even later. Dental school admission committees are well aware that premedical or former premedical students will also apply for admission to dental school. While they naturally prefer "straight" predental majors, they know that many able and successful practicing dentists were former premedical students.

12

PREPARING FOR AND APPLYING TO DENTAL SCHOOL

☐ Educational preparation
☐ Application procedures
☐ Admissions criteria

EDUCATIONAL PREPARATION

The discussion in Chapter 2 concerning high school and college education is generally applicable to predental students and should be reviewed.

High School

While in high school, you should acquire a broad liberal arts education and at the same time demonstrate that you have a genuine interest and good ability in the sciences, especially biology. Taking an advanced course in biology (if available) and/or undertaking a special science project may be particularly useful. In addition, completing a course in art, sculpture, mechanical drawing, or machine shop work will help determine and improve your manual dexterity. Active participation in a variety of extracurricular activities, such as a dramatics society or sports team, will assist you in judging your interest in and ability to work with people.

Undergraduate Studies

The criteria for selecting a college noted on page 8 are fully applicable to predental students.

The overwhelming majority of students entering dental school have completed four years of college. Thus you should plan your program on this basis (unless you

223

have valid reasons for applying earlier). There is no specific required major for predental students, although most quite naturally select biology or chemistry. It is essential that your college studies:

1. include the minimum science course requirements, namely, inorganic chemistry—1 year; biology—1 year; physics—1 year, and organic chemistry—1 year.

2. demonstrate that you have solid abilities in the sciences by satisfactorily completing the aforementioned required courses and any science electives you take.

3. provide you with a well-rounded background in the social sciences and humanities by completing courses in English composition, history, and psychology.

4. reinforce your manual dexterity by taking courses that require use of your hands (e.g., art, sculpture, drafting). If this is not possible, then an extracurricular program involving such activities as model building, chalk carving, or playing a musical instrument can substitute for formal experience.

APPLICATION PROCEDURES

General Considerations

The initial step in the application process is to select the schools to which you will seek admission. The selection process should take into consideration the following:

1. *School requirements*. Dental schools have varying requirements for organic chemistry, elective science courses, and even some non-science courses. School catalogs should be consulted to insure that you will be able to meet all the requirements prior to enrolling.

2. *Financial status*. The cost of dental education is high. The best means of keeping costs down is to attend a state school in the state where you are a legal resident. Also, transportation costs will be less if you go to school as close to your permanent home as possible.

3. *School curriculum*. There are different perspectives in dental education as reflected in the various types of curricula currently in use. These are defined in Chapter 17, and the individual school curriculum is identified as part of the profiles given for each dental school in that chapter.

4. *Alumni admission ratio*. Admissions Committees give careful consideration to the undergraduate school the applicant attends, and this can influence the chance of acceptance. By applying to schools which have consistently accepted a significant number of students

from your college, you will automatically improve your chances.

5. *Admission criteria*. The four factors determining admission are academic performance (both overall and in science), recommendations, DAT scores, and interview performance. Schools place varying degrees of emphasis on these factors as shown in Tables 8 and 9. By applying to schools where your weaknesses may be less significant, you can possibly improve your chances for admission.

As to the total number of schools to which one should apply, this depends on your basic admission potential (academic average and DAT scores) and the amount of money you are prepared to spend as part of the admissions process. It should be realized that being called for out-of-town interviews can substantially increase the costs of applying. Generally, the number of applications can vary from 5 to 15 for A to C students, respectively.

How to Apply

There are two methods of applying: either directly to the school or through an application service. In the former case, the application must be secured from the dental school and the applicant will have to have all transcripts and recommendations sent to each dental school he is applying to. When applying to one of the 50 (out of 60) schools participating in the American Association of Dental Schools Application Service (AADSAS), their Application Booklet must be used (see Appendix A). These can be secured from your predental adviser or from AADSAS, P.O. Box 4000, Iowa City, IA 52240.

As part of the AADSAS application, an essay dealing with your career motivation is expected. A sample essay is reproduced on the following page, to give you an idea of what may be submitted.

In addition to the completed Application Booklet, AADSAS receives copies of all transcripts and the processing fee ($55.00 for the first school and $7.00 for each additional school). AADSAS processes the information provided, computes GPAs, and sends a screening copy to the applicant for approval or correction. AADSAS then sends each of the dental schools selected a copy of the approved screening copy and copies of transcripts. Also, the applicant is sent a confirmation copy. Thus only one set of transcripts is needed when applying through AADSAS, but letters of recommendation and photographs must be sent directly to each of the schools. The school usually will have its own application fee that may be required either at the time you apply through AADSAS or at a later date.

My interest in dentistry is the result of the inspiration of two people: my maternal grandfather, and my family dentist. My late grandfather lived in our home and thus was personally aware of my ability, as a child to assemble plastic model kits and, more generally, to fix things around the house. He graduated the New York School of Mechanical Dentistry in 1941, and understandably channeled my interest toward the dental profession.

When I entered college, I enrolled as a pre-dentistry major. Nevertheless, I wanted to be certain that dentistry was the profession to which I wanted to devote my life. My family dentist allowed me to watch him at work. He patiently explained to me the basic problem of each patient and how he went about treating it. Each patient required a different type of therapy and the variety of cases thoroughly fascinated me.

My reason for preferring dentistry above any other health profession are that the former allows more eye contact and friendliness between doctor and patient. A good dentist must be concerned with more than just the patient's oral health, he must consider the patient's physical appearance, comfort and ability to properly maneuver his teeth. The teenager's teeth must be straightened for esthetic reasons. The older patient must be fitted with dentures that will serve him well in both speech and mastication. And the young child whose permanent teeth are now appearing must be observed, to prevent the development of speech impediments, as a result of abnormal tooth growth.

The first year in college represented, for me, an induction period in my academic growth. Since I entered college on early admission at the age of 16, I have gotten progressively better adjusted to the work load. This change is reflected in my gradually improving index. The transition from only three years of high school (which I finished with a 94 average) to the more intense pressure and heavier workload, on the college level, explains my unimpressive performance in my freshman year. This is despite the fact that I was as conscientious then, as I am now and as I have always been.

Besides underestimating my scholastic potential, my college transcript cannot reflect my interest in a highly specialized area of chemistry. During the Spring Semester of 1976, I presented a seminar on catenanes and knots (i.e., cyclic molecules that are mechanically linked or interlocked) which have been shown to be the basis of certain viral infections and cancers. I am currently investigating the possible role of catenanes in oral pathology.

As a result of my consistent improving academic performance, I was named to the Dean's list with high honor at my college. In an effort to gain experience toward my intended profession, I worked at a local dental hospital in New York, during the 1984-85 Academic Year. The preceding year, I worked as a volunteer dental assistant at a dental clinic affiliated with a New York dental school. I am currently volunteering at another local dental clinic, while completing my undergraduate studies. My extensive dental exposure and academic work have provided me with both the motivation and background to successfully complete a program of dental studies and develop into a competent and empathic practitioner.

ADMISSIONS CRITERIA

Aside from the applicant's personal qualifications as reflected in the grade point average, DAT scores, recommendations, and interview rating, the most important factor in determining admission to dental school is the number of people making up the pool of applicants from which the entering class is selected. Therefore this consideration will be discussed first and then the personal attributes next.

Applicant Pool

In 1983 there were about 7100 applicants for admission to dental schools in the United States. Of these a little more than 5000 were admitted to the freshman class, giving about a 1.4/1 applicant/acceptance ratio. Each of the applicants filed an average of 6 applications to secure a place.

The number of dental school applicants has tended to follow a pattern of cycles. During the post-World War II period (1945–57) there was an abundance of applicants. From 1958 to 1963 there was a sharp decline. Subsequently, from 1964 to 1974 a steady increase in the applicant pool was recorded. Since 1974, there has been a dramatic decrease (about 50%) in the number of male applicants. This has been reflected in the change in the applicant/acceptance ratios from 3.0/1 to 1.4/1 over the past 5 years. It seems likely that at least for the immediate future the favorable acceptance ratio (from the applicant's point of view) will be maintained.

Grade Point Average (GPA)

The applicant's overall and science grade point averages (especially at a school where grade inflation is not a factor) along with the DAT scores (see below) will provide Admissions Committees with the screening factors necessary to determine if an interview should be granted. Obviously the college's reputation is an important consideration in assessing the credibility of the applicant's GPA.

The GPA distribution for 1983 applicants was about 10% with a 3.6 or better and 53% with a 3.1 or better. This can be compared with the 1980 cycle in which the corresponding figures were about 30% and about 75%, respectively. It appears that not only has the applicant pool declined over the past 10 years, but the decline was proportionately greater among those students with higher academic averages.

DAT Scores

As indicated in Table 8, most dental schools place considerable emphasis on the DAT scores. However, the importance of the individual subtest scores varies considerably, as shown in Table 9.

The DAT is designed to predict capabilities in two areas, academic and manual. Thus in addition to the nine subtest scores, average scores are reported in both of these categories. The academic average represents the average of all but the two perception ability test (PAT) scores, while the manual ability is summarized by the average of the 2- and 3-dimensional PAT scores. Table 8 suggests that more importance is given to the academic average than to the PAT average.

Recommendations

These are usually provided by a committee and/or the predental adviser. The recommendations may be submitted in the form of a letter incorporating faculty comments and/or an evaluation form. This material serves to provide a personalized evaluation that makes your transcript more meaningful. Recommendations can serve to enhance your chances for admission by bringing to the Admissions Committee's attention information about your personality, motivation, and innate abilities, as well as clarifying any uncertain aspects relative to your credentials.

Letters of recommendation from former employers (especially dentist, research laboratories, and/or dental clinics) can provide useful information to the Admissions Committee. However, personal recommendations from your family dentist or clergyman are not especially meaningful.

Interview

Most dental schools require a personal interview as part of the admission procedure. Being granted one implies that the school is seriously considering your application. The interview provides an opportunity for you to "sell yourself" as well as to explain any discrepancies or weaknesses, and to elaborate on your strengths. The discussion of "The Interview" in Chapter 3 is, for the most part, relevant to predental students as well and should be reviewed.

Table 8. The Importance Given to Various Sources of Information Concerning the Dental School Applicant[1]
(10 = most, 1 = least)

School	Science GPA	Non-Science GPA	General GPA	Interview	Recom-mendations[2]	Manual Dexterity Test
University of Alabama	10	1	9	7	6	
Loma Linda University	10	9	9	10	8	9
University of California—Los Angeles	10	5	8	1	2	
University of California—San Francisco	9	8	10	7	6	
University of Southern California	7	7	6	5	4	
University of the Pacific	9		7	4		
University of Colorado	2	2	2	3	7	
University of Connecticut	10	5	10	10	7	1
Georgetown University	8	5	5	9	5	8
Howard University	8	7	10		8	
University of Florida	8	7	10	10	7	
Medical College of Georgia						
Loyola University of Chicago	10	9	10	5	8	
Northwestern University	10	10	10	8	7	
Southern Illinois University						
University of Illinois	10	9	9		9	
Indiana University	10	8	9	10	9	
University of Iowa						
University of Kentucky	10	10	10			
University of Louisville	9		7	8	5	
Louisiana State University	8	7	7	6	5	
University of Maryland	10		10	10	10	
Boston University	10	10	10	10	9	
Harvard	9		8	8	7	
Tufts University	9	7	10	10	8	
University of Detroit	10	9	10	6	6	
University of Michigan	5		10	7	7	8
University of Minnesota						
University of Mississippi						
University of Missouri	10		10	8	8	
Washington University	10	8	9	9	6	
Creighton University	4		1		6	
University of Nebraska	10	8	10	10	3	
Fairleigh Dickinson University	5	3	3	10	10	
New Jersey Dental School	10	9	8	10		
Columbia University	9	7	9	9	9	8
New York University	8	7	8	8	7	
SUNY at Buffalo	9		10	6	5	
SUNY at Stony Brook	10	10	10	10	10	5
University of North Carolina	9	9	9	9	6	
Case Western Reserve	8	5	6	8	6	8
Ohio State University	10	5	9	10	7	
Oral Roberts University	10	10	10	10	10	
University of Oklahoma	10	8	10	9	8	
Oregon Health Science University	10	7	9	7	5	
Temple University	10	5	10		5	
University of Pennsylvania	10	5	8	10	10	
University of Pittsburgh	10	7	9	10	10	
Medical University of South Carolina	10		10	10	5	
Meharry Medical College	9	7	9	7	7	8
University of Tennessee	10	7	7	10	1	

[1] Information in Table 8 from Fall 1984 *Handbook for Predental Advisors*, copyright © by the American Dental Association, reprinted by permission.
[2] Recommendations include letters of recommendation in general.

Table 8. The Importance Given to Various Sources of Information Concerning the Dental School Applicant[1]—*Continued*

(10 = most, 1 = least)

School	Science GPA	Non-Science GPA	General GPA	Interview	Recommendations[2]	Manual Dexterity Test
Baylor	10		10			
University of Texas—Houston	10		10	10	2	
University of Texas—San Antonio	10		10	6	3	
Virginia Commonwealth University						
University of Washington	10			8	8	8
West Virginia University	10	9	10	10	8	
Marquette University	10	5	10	3	2	5

[1] Information in Table 8 from Fall 1984 *Handbook for Predental Advisors*
[2] Recommendations include letters of recommendation in general.

© Copyright by the American Dental Association. Reprinted by permission from *Handbook for Predental Advisors.*

Table 9. The Importance Given to Dental Admission Test Scores[1]
(10 = most, 1 = least)

School	Academic Average	PAT	Science	Quantitative Reasoning	Reading Comprehension	Biology	General Chemistry	Organic Chemistry
University of Alabama	8	5	4	2	3	1	1	1
Loma Linda University	10	10	10	9	8	10	10	10
University of California—Los Angeles	10	8	10	5	5	5	5	5
University of California—San Francisco	10	9	8	3	7	6	4	5
University of Southern California	8	8	9	5	2	5	5	5
University of the Pacific								
University of Colorado	5	4	5	5	5	5	6	6
University of Connecticut	10	1	10	10	10	10	10	10
Georgetown University	6	8	5	7	7	6	5	7
Howard University	10	9	8	7	9	6	6	6
University of Florida	9	10	4	3	7	6	6	6
Medical College of Georgia								
Loyola University of Chicago	10	9	8	5	5	9	9	9
Northwestern University	9	9	9	9	9	9	9	9
Southern Illinois University								
University of Illinois	10	9	10	10	10	10	10	10
Indiana University	10	9	8	4	6	7	7	7
University of Iowa								
University of Kentucky	6	6						
University of Louisville	6	4						
Louisiana State University	5	3	8	7	7	8	8	8
University of Maryland	10	10				5		5
Boston University	10	10	9	7	7	7	8	8
Harvard	7	6	7	6	6	7	7	7
Tufts University	10	8	10	6	6	6	6	6
University of Detroit	10	10	9	7	7	7	7	7
University of Michigan	9	8						
University of Minnesota								
University of Mississippi								
University of Missouri	9	9				8	8	8
Washington University	5	10	6	3	4	10	10	10
Creighton University	2	3	10		5	7	8	9
University of Nebraska	10	10	7	6	7	10	8	10
Fairleigh Dickinson University	10	10	5	3	5	5	5	5
New Jersey Dental School	8	8	8	8	8	8	8	8
Columbia University	9	7	7	5	8	7	7	7
New York University	5	7	6	4	8	6	5	0
SUNY at Buffalo	8	7	3	1	4	1	1	2
SUNY at Stony Brook	8	5	10	8	5	7	7	7
University of North Carolina	8	8	7	7	7	5	5	5
Case Western Reserve	7	8	8	5	5	8	8	8
Ohio State University	10	8	8	5	5	5	5	5
Oral Roberts University	10	10	8	8	8	8	8	8
University of Oklahoma	8	8	7	7	7	5	5	
Oregon Health Science University	5	3	6	5	5	5	5	5
Temple University	10	10	9	8	9	7	7	
University of Pennsylvania	10	7	10	5	10	5	5	7
University of Pittsburgh	10	8	10	4	2	6	6	6
Medical University of South Carolina	10	10						
Meharry Medical College	9	8	10	8	5	9	9	9

[1] Information in Table 8 from Fall 1984 *Handbook for Predental Advisors*, copyright © by the American Dental Association, reprinted by permission.

Table 9. The Importance Given to Dental Admission Test Scores[1]—Continued
(10 = most, 1 = least)

School	Academic Average	PAT	Science	Quantitative Reasoning	Reading Comprehension	Biology	General Chemistry	Organic Chemistry
University of Tennessee	10	10	10	7	10	10	10	10
Baylor	8	9	5	5	8	8	7	8
University of Texas—Houston	10	1	7	6	8	5	3	4
University of Texas—San Antonio	10	10						
Virginia Commonwealth University								
University of Washington	10	8						
West Virginia University	10	10	9	8	9	9	8	9
Marquette University	10	10	5	5	6	5	4	6

[1] Information in Table 9 from Fall 1984 *Handbook for Predental Advisors*, copyright © by the American Dental Association, reprinted by permission.

13

THE DENTAL ADMISSION TEST (DAT)

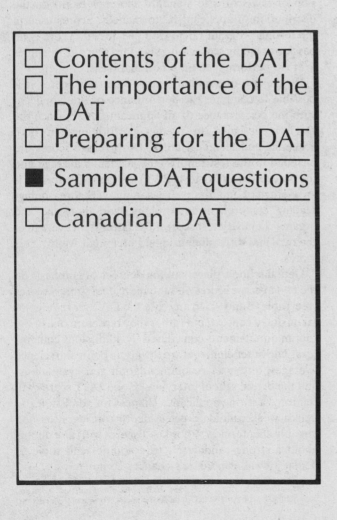

- ☐ Contents of the DAT
- ☐ The importance of the DAT
- ☐ Preparing for the DAT
- ■ Sample DAT questions
- ☐ Canadian DAT

This test is conducted two times a year (October and April) and is sponsored by the Division of Educational Measurements, American Dental Association, 211 East Chicago Avenue, Chicago, IL 60611. Students planning to enter in the fall of the following year should take the examination in the preceding April or October. The choice between these two dates is dependent on your state of preparedness (since admission announcements are not made before December 1). If you plan to use the summer to study, the DAT should be taken in October; otherwise, it should be taken earlier and gotten out of the way (as well as insure an opportunity to repeat it if necessary).

An application for the DAT can be obtained from the Division of Educational Measurements at the address above, or from the predental adviser. The application should include a recent photo and the $35 fee. This fee covers the cost of sending five official transcripts of scores to selected dental schools, as well as a copy for the applicant and the predental adviser, and DAT Preparation Materials. Additional official transcripts of scores can be sent if requested. The charge is $1 each if ordered at the time of applying and $2 each if requested later.

Testing centers for the Saturday administration are located in one or more cities in each state, as well as in the District of Columbia. Sunday (or Monday) administrations are provided in about 10 states and require a letter from a clergyman confirming the applicant's affiliation with a Sabbath observing religious group.

Foreign testing centers are set up as needed, but require special arrangements. The fee for a test administered in a foreign country is $25.

CONTENTS OF THE DAT

There are four examinations included in the Dental Admission Testing Program. The entire program requires one half for administration. The examinations included are:

1. Survey of Natural Sciences

BIOLOGY—Origin of Life. Cell Metabolism (including photosynthesis). Enzymology. Thermodynamics. Organelle Structure and Function. Biological organization and relationship of major taxa (e.g., Monera, angiosperms, arthropods, chordates, etc.) using the five-kingdom system. The structure and function of the following vertebrate systems: integumentary, skeletal, muscular, circulatory, immunological, digestive, respiratory, urinary, nervous, endocrine and reproductive. Fertilization, descriptive embryology and developmental mechanics. Mendelian inheritance, chromosomal genetics, meiosis, molecular and human genetics. Natural selection, population genetics, speciation, population and community ecology, animal behavior (including social behavior).

GENERAL CHEMISTRY—Stoichiometry (percent of composition, empirical formulas from percent of composition, balancing equations, weight/weight, weight/volume, density problems.) Gases (kinetic molecular theory of gases, Graham's, Dalton's, Boyle's, Charles' and ideal gas laws.) Liquids and Solids. Solutions (colligative properties, concentration calculations.) Acids and Bases. Chemical Equilibrium (molecular, acid/base, precipitation, equilibria calculations.) Thermodynamics and Thermochemistry (laws of thermodynamics, Hess's law, spontaneity prediction.) Chemical Kinetics (rate laws, activation energy, half life.) Oxidation—Reduction Reactions (balancing equations, determination of oxidation numbers, electro-chemical concepts and calculations.) Atomic and Molecular Structure (electron configuration, orbital types, Lewis-Dot diagrams, atomic theories, molecular geometry, bond types, quantum mechanics.) Periodic Properties (include categories of nonmetals, transition metals and non-transition metals.) Nuclear Reactions.

ORGANIC CHEMISTRY—Bonding (atomic orbitals, molecular orbitals, hybridization, Lewis structures, bond angles, bond lengths). Mechanisms (energetics, structure & stability of intermediates: S_N1, S_N2, elimination, addition, free radical and substitution mechanisms. Chemical & Physical Properties of Molecules (stability, solubility, polarity, inter- and intra-molecular forces: separation techniques). Organic Analysis (introductory infrared and ^1H NMR spectroscopy, simple chemical tests). Stereochemistry (conformational analysis, optical activity, chirality, chiral centers, places of symmetry, enantiomers, diastereomers, meso compounds). Nomenclature (IUPAC rules, identification of functional groups in molecules. Reaction of the Major Functional Groups (prediction of reaction products and important mechanistic generalities). Acid-Base Chemistry (resonance effects, inductive effects, prediction of products and equilibria). Aromatic (concept of aromaticity, electrophilic aromatic substitution). Synthesis (identification of the product of, or the reagents used in, a simple sequence of reactions).

2. Reading Comprehension (Dental and Basic Sciences)

3. Quantitative Ability (Math Problems)

4. Perceptual Ability (Two and three dimensional problem solving)[1]

THE IMPORTANCE OF THE DAT

About six weeks after taking the DAT, each applicant will receive a personal copy of the scores (with an explanation of them) at the permanent address listed on the original application form. DAT scores are based on the number of correct answers recorded. The scores are reported to the dental schools requested by the applicant as standard scores rather than raw scores. The conversion of raw scores to standard scores is based on the distribution of applicant performances. Scores used in the testing program range from −1 to +9. There is no passing or failing score, but a standard score of 4 signifies average performance on a national basis.

By the use of standard rather than raw scores it is possible to compare the performance of one applicant with the performance of all applicants. Also, since the DAT is designed to predict performance in both academic and technical areas, two average scores are included in the test report—the academic average and the perceptual ability test (PAT) average. The former is an average of quantitative reasoning, verbal reasoning, reading comprehension, biology, and inorganic and organic chemistry test scores; the latter is an average of the two- and three-dimensional Perceptual Ability Test scores.

Dental schools place varying degrees of emphasis on the two average scores and the individual subtest scores (see Tables 8 and 9). In any case the DAT scores are not taken out of context, but rather they represent one of the four major elements considered by admissions committees. The other elements are the grade point and science averages, letters of recommendation and evaluations, and the dental school interview. Good DAT scores will reinforce a strong applicant's chances for admission and help a weak candidate get in-depth consideration and possibly an interview. Poor DAT scores will raise doubts about a strong candidate's true abilities and serve to defeat a weak candidate's chances completely.

[1] This information from Fall 1984 *Handbook for Predental Advisors*, copyright © by the American Dental Association, reprinted by permission.

PREPARING FOR THE DAT

To do well on the DAT you should start preparing for the test two to three months prior to the test date. Preparation should be done on a regular basis, devoting a set number of hours each week exclusively to reviewing the necessary material. A study plan that takes into consideration your strong and weak areas of knowledge should be thoughtfully prepared prior to initiating your study program. Special emphasis should be placed on learning facts that are organized around principles and concepts, rather than on isolated details, since the former will be retained longer. Frequent review at regular intervals will be of special help in retaining details that are not of primary importance. Study and review sessions should be terminated as soon as signs of mental fatigue become evident.

Since the DAT is a multiple-choice test, some general considerations may prove helpful. Too much should not be read into a question; it is best to take the questions at face value. Avoid the impulse to change answers when some uncertainty develops. Look for the general principle involved in the question and try to recall specific details you have memorized.

When taking the DAT make certain that you:

1. have had a good night's sleep before the day of the exam. Also, try to relax between the various parts of the exam;

2. avoid taking medications that will inhibit your performance (e.g. antihistamines, tranquilizers);

3. use regular reading glasses rather than contact lenses;

4. Carefully read all directions before you start to answer the questions;

5. answer the questions in the exact manner and the exact place specified;

6. concentrate exclusively on the question under consideration;

7. determine how much time you have for each question (divide the number of questions in the subtest by the time allotted for that subtest);

8. respond first to all questions you are sure of the answers to;

9. next, answer those questions that require guessing (since the test score is based on the total number of questions answered correctly);

10. answer those questions that are time consuming last. (Coding these and "guessing" questions for identification at the outset may save time later.)

Sample DAT Questions

Following are typical questions likely to appear on the DAT.

Part 1 Science

Biology

1. Water absorption in the digestive system occurs principally in the: (A) duodenum (B) large intestine (C) islets of Langerhans (D) pancreas (E) greater omentum

2. The menstrual cycle of mammals is related in lower animals to (A) moulting period (B) mating season (C) metamorphosis (D) early spring (E) late fall

Organic Chemistry

3. Which would be easiest to chlorinate?

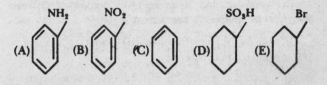

4. "Walden inversion" is found in (A) an Sn 7 reaction where optical activity is retained (B) an Sn 2 reaction where optical activity is retained (C) an Sn 7 reaction where optical activity is lost (D) an Sn 2 reaction where optical activity is lost (E) none of these.

General Chemistry

5. The reaction $NaOH + H_2SO_4 \rightarrow$ goes to completion because (A) it is a neutralization reaction (B) the laws of equilibrium are not valid here (C) H_2O is a strong electrolyte (D) sodium sulfate precipitates (E) a volatile product is formed

6. Aluminum is commercially produced by (A) Haber process (B) HC1 process (C) Bayer reaction (D) electrolysis (E) hydrolysis

Part 2 Reading Comprehension

During the fourth and fifth weeks of development of the human embryo a series of grooves, the pharyngeal pouches, appear along the lateral walls of the pharyngeal gut. At the same time, four ectodermal grooves appear on the surface of the embryo. The level of these grooves, known as the pharyngeal clefts, corresponds to that of the pharyngeal pouches, but although the clefts and pouches come in close contact, they rarely communicate with each other in the form of open gills. As a result of the formation of the deep clefts and pouches, the loose mesodermal tissue surrounding the pharyngeal gut is gradually pushed aside and a number of bars of dense mesodermal tissue, the branchial or pharyngeal arches, make their appearance.

7. From what germ layer are the pharyngeal pouches derived? (A) mesenchymal (B) ectodermal (C) cartilaginal (D) endodermal (E) mesodermal

8. Ectodermal grooves on the surface of the embryo are known as (A) pharyngeal pouches (B) pharyngeal gills (C) branchial arches (D) pharyngeal arches (E) pharyngeal clefts

Part 3 Verbal and Quantitative

Mathematics

9. If x is an integer, which of the following could *not* be even? (A) 3x (B) 2x (C) 3x−1 (D) 2x + 3 (E) 3x−2

10. $2/3 \sqrt{18} - \sqrt{9/2} + 2\sqrt{1/8}$ = ? (A) $\sqrt{2}$ (B) $2\sqrt{2}$ (C) $\sqrt{3}$ (D) $3\sqrt{3}$ (E) none of these

Verbal

11. capricious (A) spacious (B) loquacious (C) verbose (D) scrupulous (E) mercurial

12. tenacity (A) imperceptible (B) sobriety (C) casual (D) affluent (E) effrontery

Verbal Mathematics

13. The average height of each of six books is six inches. Two books are four inches each. If all the other books are all taller than 4 inches, and their heights are all integral, what is the tallest possible book? (A) four inches (B) seven inches (C) nine inches (D) eleven inches (E) thirteen inches

14. A right triangle has a hypotenuse of 15 inches and one of its acute angles has a tangent of .75. The area of the triangle is (in square inches): (A) 44 (B) 54 (C) 64 (D) 74 (E) 84

Analogies

15. Corruption is ____ in elected and appointed officials because of the ____ of the community in which these officials hold office. (A) engendered, integrity (B) prevalent, apathy (C) allowed, indifference (D) chastised, lassitude (E) encouraged, stupidity

16. The ____ for hoarding may be excessive precaution against possible future needs, or it may be the mere ____ gained from having possessions. (A) means, complacence (B) disdain, discontent (C) instinct, pleasure (D) expenditures, profit (E) motive, satisfaction

Part 4 Perceptual Motor Ability

17. Which of the following choices represents a constructed version of the model shown?

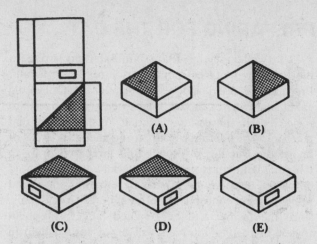

(A) (B)

(C) (D) (E)

18. Which of the following choices represents a constructed version of the model shown below?

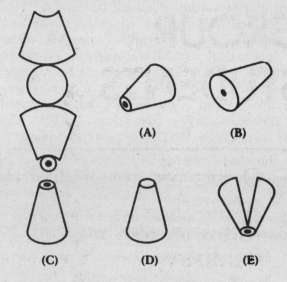

(A) (B)

(C) (D) (E)

Answers to Sample Questions

1. B	7. D	13. E
2. B	8. C	14. B
3. A	9. D	15. B
4. B	10. A	16. E
5. A	11. E	17. B,C
6. D	12. E	18. A,C

CANADIAN DAT

A Canadian Dental Aptitude Test has been developed by the Canadian Dental Association and the Association of Canadian Faculties. For information on this test contact the Canadian Dental Association (l'Association Dental Canadienne), 1815 Alta Vista Drive, Ottawa, Ontario K1G 3Y6.

14

OPPORTUNITIES FOR WOMEN AND MINORITY GROUP STUDENTS

☐ Doors are opening for women
☐ Minority students in dentistry

DOORS ARE OPENING FOR WOMEN

In many respects the United States is clearly a world leader in matters of progress. Yet the number of women in professional life in this country is disproportionate to the population as a whole. Less than 5% of the dentists here are women. This figure stands in marked contrast to that of Russia or Finland where about 80% of the dentists are women. It is also very different from some nations of the free world, such as Greece, France, Sweden, and Holland, where 25% to 50% of the dentists are women.

While the reasons for the sparsity of women dentists in this country are not positively known, one of the significant factors probably has been the belief that the profession is too physically demanding for women. While this widely held assumption is questionable to begin with, it has lost any possible validity in light of the drastic change in dentistry from a two-hand, stand-up profession to a four-hand, sit-down one.

Over the past decade, whatever barriers may have existed to prevent women from entering the field of dentistry have certainly fallen. This is evident from the dental school enrollment figures for women which show a 400% increase since 1972. Women have responded to favorable opportunities in dentistry. Thus, even though the pool of male applicants has been decreasing, the pool of female applicants has held constant or increased

235

somewhat over the past 5 years (see graph below). On the whole, from 1976 to 1983 the pool has increased from 10% to 30% of all applicants. Moreover the number of women accepted to the freshman 1983 class was about 1200, which represents about 25% of the class. The women were selected from a female applicant pool of about 1800. No evidence of sex bias is suggested from the application data of the past five years. Thus it is clear that motivated and qualified women can readily find a place in dental school. The profession is receptive to their admittance and it is likely that women will play a significant role in oral health care.

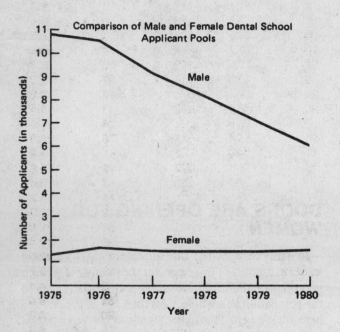

Comparison of Male and Female Dental School Applicant Pools

MINORITY STUDENTS IN DENTISTRY

Just as there has been a substantial decrease in the total applicant pool, to a comparable degree the minority applicant pool has decreased. Within this smaller pool of applicants the Hispanic segment has increased from 0.9% in 1975 to 8.0% in 1983. The number of blacks in the pool increased somewhat during this interval. In terms of minority enrollment as a whole for 1983, it stands at over 24% which represents a very significant increase during the past decade. The minority enrollment for freshmen in each of the dental schools is given in Table 10.

Minority Recruitment in Dental Schools

To help improve the proportion of minority students represented in the dental schools, special recruitment and retention efforts are employed by many schools. The following are some of the approaches used by dental schools to enhance recruitment and retention of minority and disadvantaged students.

1. Recruitment extends into high schools and community centers using seminars and workshops to inform prospective students of the opportunities that are available.

2. Contacts are developed and maintained with prospective applicants by means of college campus visits and communicating with predental advisors and other relevant faculty members.

3. In some cases application fees are waived.

4. Prematriculation orientation programs are frequently offered for from two to ten weeks during the summer. As part of such a program, learning skills, test taking methods and training to improve study habits and note taking abilities may be offered.

5. Prematriculation summer programs in dental anatomy, histology, or biochemistry are offered by some schools to lighten the freshman year load.

6. Students may be assigned special faculty and/or upper class student advisors. Personal professional counseling may also be offered.

7. Students may be provided with tutorial assistance when necessary.

8. Students may be permitted to extend their educational program to five instead of four years. Thus they can lighten their load each semester by one or two courses.

9. Individual teaching utilizing audiovisual learning modules may be offered.

10. Special scholarship and loan funds may be provided.

Table 10. 1983–84 Dental School Minority Enrollment[1]

Dental School	1st Year			1st through 4th Year		
	Total	Minority	Percent	Total	Minority	Percent
University of Alabama	55	6	10.9	217	24	11.1
Loma Linda University	86	22	25.6	355	75	21.1
University of California—Los Angeles	96	38	39.6	394	117	29.7
University of California—San Francisco	97	47	48.5	392	160	40.8
University of Southern California	130	50	38.5	530	190	35.8
University of the Pacific	142	47	33.1	402	115	28.6
University of Colorado	33	4	12.1	113	9	8.0
University of Connecticut	44	1	2.3	175	6	3.4
Georgetown University	157	25	15.9	621	53	8.5
Howard University	101	79	78.2	385	314	81.6
University of Florida	78	21	26.9	308	62	20.1
Medical College of Georgia	54	5	9.3	214	21	9.8
Loyola University of Chicago	149	20	13.4	575	47	8.2
Northwestern University	111	20	18.0	447	60	13.4
Southern Illinois University	50	5	10.0	201	24	11.9
University of Illinois	136	21	15.4	545	76	13.9
Indiana University	118	17	14.4	462	41	8.9
University of Iowa	73	3	4.1	325	19	5.8
University of Kentucky	47	0	0.0	193	7	3.6
University of Louisville	61	2	3.3	264	11	4.2
Louisiana State University	62	6	9.7	303	19	6.3
University of Maryland	112	27	24.1	463	88	19.0
Boston University	72	7	9.7	241	30	12.4
Harvard*	20	4	20.0	89	21	23.6
Tufts University	148	12	8.1	462	45	9.7
University of Detroit	69	3	4.3	298	13	4.4
University of Michigan	126	17	13.5	544	51	9.4
University of Minnesota	106	4	3.8	516	20	3.9
University of Mississippi	39	6	15.4	166	15	9.0
University of Missouri	120	18	15.0	551	52	9.4
Washington University	73	21	28.8	322	64	19.9
Creighton University	81	10	12.3	305	49	16.1
University of Nebraska	56	2	3.6	231	6	2.6
Fairleigh Dickinson University	85	25	29.4	321	65	20.2
New Jersey Dental School	89	9	10.1	337	68	20.2
Columbia University	62	7	11.3	231	22	9.5
New York University	144	17	11.8	633	54	8.5
SUNY at Buffalo	88	3	3.4	351	14	4.0
SUNY at Stony Brook	28	1	3.6	106	7	6.6
University of North Carolina	82	7	8.5	316	29	9.2
Case Western Reserve	102	12	11.8	410	26	6.3
Ohio State University	161	11	6.8	605	40	6.6
Oral Roberts University	20	1	5.0	89	11	12.4
University of Oklahoma	72	5	6.9	262	20	7.6
Oregon Health Science University	66	8	12.1	273	27	9.9
Temple University	140	7	5.0	544	22	4.0
University of Pennsylvania	109	12	11.0	555	46	8.3
University of Pittsburgh	99	3	3.0	423	22	5.2
Medical University of South Carolina	49	2	4.1	211	9	4.3
Meharry Medical College	53	44	83.0	203	168	82.8
University of Tennessee	90	4	4.4	410	24	5.9
Baylor	119	14	11.8	512	38	7.4

Table 10. **1983–84 Dental School Minority Enrollment**[1] *—Continued*

Dental School	1st Year			1st through 4th Year		
	Total	Minority	Per-cent	Total	Minority	Per-cent
University of Texas—Houston	108	22	20.4	466	100	21.5
University of Texas—San Antonio	123	22	17.9	514	95	18.5
Virginia Commonwealth University	94	19	20.2	405	58	14.3
University of Washington	52	12	23.1	272	51	18.8
West Virginia University	50	3	6.0	213	6	2.8
Marquette University	139	22	15.8	540	66	12.2

*Harvard University's figures under the headings of 1st through 4th include their 5th year.

[1] Information in Table 10 from Fall 1984 *Handbook for Predental Advisors*, copyright © by the American Dental Association, reprinted by permission.

15

FINANCING YOUR DENTAL EDUCATION

- ☐ The current financial aid crisis
- ☐ Scholarships and loans

The total cost of one's dental education depends on a number of factors, such as: (1) whether the dental school is a public or private institution, (2) whether or not you are a state resident, (3) whether you are single or married, (4) the location of the school, and (5) your life style. Obviously, there can be wide differences in total costs. For most students, selecting a school involves not only its reputation, location, and educational program, but first and foremost, its costs. A reliable estimate of costs for the freshman year can be readily ascertained by examining the last two columns of Table 14 and then multiplying by four to get the total costs for all four years.

THE CURRENT FINANCIAL AID CRISIS

Most students applying to dental school can expect to incur high educational costs. Moreover, with the inflation rate continuing to escalate unabated, these costs can expect to continue to rise. Unfortunately, while costs are rising dramatically, federal aid, which is the major source of scholarships and loans awarded to students in the health professions, is being cut back. This has had a strong negative impact on prospective applicants and their families and may be one of the most significant factors in the decline in the applicant pool.

SCHOLARSHIPS AND LOANS

The major portion of financial support that is made available to dental students is provided, either directly or indirectly, by the federal government. These funds are channeled through such programs as:

1. Scholarships for Health Professions Students of Exceptional Financial Need;

2. Armed Forces Health Professions Scholarship Programs;

3. National Health Corps Scholarship Program.

These three scholarship programs and loan programs are discussed in Chapter 6. Financial aid officers at the dental schools should be consulted regarding these and all other forms of support.

There are also regional groups that provide support for students living in certain states. These are:

Western Interstate Commission for Higher Education (WICHE). Students who are residents of western states that do not have dental schools (Alaska, Arizona, Idaho, Montana, Nevada, Utah, and Wyoming) may apply to the WICHE Student Exchange Programs. The home state contributes to the dental school to offset part of the educational costs of its resident. The student then has to pay only a relatively low resident's fee at a public school or no more than one third of the tuition at a private school. For more information contact: Director, Student Exchange Programs, Western Interstate Commission for Higher Education, P.O. Drawer P, Boulder, CD 80302.

Southern Regional Education Board (SREB). Students who are members of southern states, some of which do not have dental schools (Alabama, Arkansas, Florida, Louisiana, Maryland, Mississippi, North Carolina, Tennessee, and Virginia) may apply to SREB. Each home state contributes a fixed fee, while the student pays the resident's tuition at a public school and receives a $500 reduction in tuition at a private school. For more information contact: President, Southern Regional Education Board, 130 Sixth Street, N.W., Atlanta, GA 30313.

There are two services for loans that have no geographic prerequisites:

Robert Johnson Student Loan Guarantee Program. The aim of this program is to guarantee student loans made by lending institutions. To be eligible one has to be accepted or enrolled at a dental school and be recommended by the school for support. Loans of from $500 to $5,000 per year, up to a total of $17,500, can be secured, with repayment of the principal beginning three years after graduation. For information contact United Student Aid Fund at the address below, since they administer this program.

United Student Aid Funds. This fund endorses loans up to $5,000 per year for a total of $15,000 for all guaranteed loan programs. Repayment begins ten months after leaving school, with interest not exceeding 7%. For additional information contact: USA Funds Endorsement Center, 6610 North Shadeland Avenue, P.O. Box 50827, Indianapolis, IN 46250.

Two restricted sources of financial aid are:

American Fund for Dental Health Minority Scholarship Program. This program provides recipients with scholarships of up to $2,000 per year for the first two years of dental school. One must be accepted by a dental school and be a member of an under-represented minority (Black, American Indian, Mexican American, or Puerto Rican) to apply. For information contact: American Fund for Dental Health, 211 East Chicago Avenue, Suite 1630, Chicago, IL 60611.

Canadian Fund for Dental Education. This program provides information concerning scholarships and loans. For information contact: Canadian Fund for Dental Education, 1815 Alta Vista Drive, Ottawa, Ontario, K1G 3Y6.

Financial aid on a state level is also available for state residents. These sources are listed below by state.

Arizona
 Student Loan Fund
 Arizona State Dental Association
 3800 North Central Avenue
 Phoenix, AZ 85012

Florida
 Student Loan Fund
 Florida State Dental Society
 P.O. Box 18105
 Tampa, FL 33609

Indiana
 Student Loan Fund Program
 Indiana State Dental Association
 721 Hume Mansur Building
 Indianapolis, IN 46202

Kansas
 Loan Fund
 Kansas State Dental Auxiliary
 School of Dentistry
 University of Missouri at Kansas City
 Kansas City, MO 64108

Kentucky
Memorial Student Loan Fund
Kentucky Dental Association
1940 Bardstown Road
Louisville, KY 40205

Rural Scholarship
Kentucky State Board of Dental Examiners
2105 Bardstown Road
Louisville, KY 40205

Louisiana
Dental Student Loan Fund
Women's Auxiliary to the Louisiana Dental
Association
10 Stilt Street
New Orleans, LA 70124

Massachusetts
Dental Student Financial Aid Committee
Massachusetts Dental Society
The Prudential Tower Building
Boston, MA 02199

Minnesota
Student Loan Fund
Minnesota State Dental Association
2236 Marshall Avenue
St. Paul, MN 55104

Loan Funds
School of Dentistry
University of Minnesota
Washington Avenue and Union Street, S.E.
Minneapolis, MN 55455

New Hampshire
Memorial Scholarship Fund
New Hampshire Dental Society
19 Temple Court
Manchester, NH 03103

New Mexico
Student Loan Fund
New Mexico Dental Association
2917 Santa Cruz Avenue, S.E.
Albuquerque, NM 87106

Oklahoma
Oklahoma Dental Foundation for Research and
Education
222 Plaza Court Building
Oklahoma City, OK 73190

Virginia
Student Loan Fund
Virginia State Dental Association
Medical College of Virginia
School of Dentistry
521 North 11 Street
Richmond, VA 23219

Washington
Scholarship Fund
Women's Auxiliary
Washington State Dental Association
500 Wall Street
Seattle, WA 98121

West Virginia
Dental School Loan Fund
Auxiliary of the West Virginia State Dental
Society
School of Dentistry
West Virginia University
Morgantown, WV 26506

Wisconsin
Student Loan Fund Foundation
Wisconsin Dental Association
633 W. Wisconsin Avenue
Milwaukee, WI 53203

16

DENTAL EDUCATION

☐ Dental curriculum
☐ Other educational programs
☐ Postgraduate training

DENTAL CURRICULUM

Dental schools are located within or close to medical and hospital facilities. The traditional four-year program of studies corresponds to that of medicine and consists of two preclinical years of basic sciences and two years of clinical study. The basic sciences (anatomy, physiology, biochemistry, etc.) are taken by dental students in some schools together with medical students; in others, instruction is given exclusively in dental school. While most work consists of lecture and laboratory experiments, preclinical study also includes learning the basic techniques of dental restoration and treatment through practice on inanimate models.

The two clinical years are spent treating patients having a variety of oral diseases and disorders while working under the supervision of clinical instructors. A variety of clinical procedures and dental care for special patients (for example, the old and infirm) are mastered during this period. Making use of dental auxiliary personnel is outlined.

Beginning in the 1960s, the traditional curriculum in dentistry underwent change; the nature of this change was twofold. First there was a new approach that involved integration of the basic and clinical sciences with emphasis on relevance, and thus students were introduced to the patient earlier. Also, greater emphasis was placed on preventive dentistry, public health dentistry, practice management, and hospital dentistry.

The curricula of almost all dental schools have been updated to a greater or lesser extent along these lines.

A second major change that was attempted was the shortening of the curriculum to three years. This experiment, however, appears not to have been successful and, as of this time, all dental schools have a four year program leading to the D.D.S. or D.M.D. degree except the University of the Pacific, which has a three year program, and Harvard, which has a five year program.

To gain an insight into the various dental school courses and the approximate amount of time devoted to each, a summary is presented in Table 11.

Table 11. Dental School Courses and Hours Allotted

Basic Sciences

Course	Average number of hours
Anatomy (gross)	200
Anatomy (histology, general and oral)	135
Biochemistry	100
Microbiology	100
Pathology (general and oral)	185
Pharmacology	75
Physiology	100
subtotal	895

Clinical Sciences

Course	Hours
Anesthesiology	50
Auxiliary Utilization	140
Dental Materials	70
Diagnosis	120
Emergency Treatment	50
Endodontics	150
Hospital Dentistry	40
Nutrition	25
Occlusion	115
Operative Dentistry	475
Oral Surgery	140
Orthodontics	125
Pedodontics	150
Peridontics	220
Physical Evaluation	60
Prosthodontics (fixed and removable)	800
Special Care	70
Tooth Morphology	85
subtotal	2885
Total hours of training	3780

A sample breakdown of the major courses by year is shown in Table 12. Schools will allot varying amounts of time to the different courses and some courses may appear under different titles.

Table 12. Major Courses in the Dental Curriculum—By Year

First Year	Second Year	Third Year	Fourth Year
Biochemistry	Endodontics	Endodontics	Endodontics
Dental Anatomy	Complete Dentures	Crown and Bridge	Oral Surgery
Dental Materials	Removable Prosthodontics	Operative Dentistry	Operative Dentistry
Gross Anatomy	Pathology	Pharmacology	Periodontics
Histology	Partial Dentures	Oral Diagnosis	Partial Dentures
Physiology	Operative Dentistry	Periodontics	Pedodontics
Microbiology			

To appreciate the nature of the major courses taken in dental school, a brief description of their content follows. (Courses are listed alphabctically.)

Biochemistry. The course covers the biochemical proccsses that occur at the cellular and subcellular levels, and with tissue and organ metabolism and function. Emphasis is placed on the molecular basis of oral and other human disease.

Complete Dentures. Both the theoretical and practical aspects related to the construction of complete dentures are considered during this second year course. A complete denture is constructed for a mannequin.

Crown and Bridge (Fixed Prosthodontics). This course extends over the last three years. In the second year the student is introduced to the principles and basic techniques of fixed prosthodontics. Included are such topics as articulation, tooth preparation, impressions, working cast construction, waxing, casting, soldering, and finishing. The third year focuses on the research aspects, evaluating comparative studies of materials and techniques used in prosthodontics. The fourth year is devoted to seminars on current problems in the field and to clinical procedures for more complex problems.

Dental Anatomy. This freshman course deals with the anatomical structure, individual characteristics, and the functional arrangement of teeth and their development.

Dental Materials. This first year course serves to introduce the student to the basic principles and properties of materials used in dental treatment. Experience to gain and improve manipulative skills with selected materials is provided.

Endodontics. This subject is usually taught starting in the sophomore year. The differential diagnosis of dental pain is taught. Emphasis is placed on the technique used for preparing access cavities, preparing the root canal, obliterating the canal space, and utilizing endodontic instruments. The periodontal diseases and on the use of surgical techniques in their treatment. The fourth year emphasizes clinical work such as surgical treatment of pathological disorders of tissues and all phases of root canal therapy.

Gross Anatomy. The goal of this course is to familiarize the student with the anatomical basis for the study of the basic sciences and the clinical practice of dentistry. Emphasis is placed on the functional significance of various organ systems and regions by means of integrating the lectures and laboratory sessions. The latter uses predissected cadavers, skeletons, models, x-rays, and movies.

Histology. A study of the microscopic structure of tissues with special reference to the morphology of the oral cavity, particularly the teeth. Both light and electron microscopic levels of organization of tissues are analyzed.

Microbiology. The course introduces the student to bacteriology, virology, parasitology, immunology, and mycology as related to the oral cavity. The student learns the microbial diagnostic techniques and studies the bacteria of the nasopharynx and the processes of antibiotic resistance.

Operative Dentistry. In the second year, the basic concepts and procedures of tooth restoration are presented. Cavity preparation and restoration are taught in the laboratory. All types of cavities and the use of various restorative materials are covered. An anatomical mannequin is used to obtain experience. After a transition period from mannequin to patient, students are provided with an opportunity, over the last two years, to apply their theoretical knowledge in the clinic under supervision. Lectures, demonstrations, and seminars provide the opportunity to evaluate progress and receive individual guidance.

Oral Diagnosis. This course extends over the last two years. In the third year, students are taught how to take a history and carry out a clinical examination in light of the patient's complaint. The course serves to correlate the basic and clinical information by focusing on diseases and abnormalities of the oral cavity. Clinical work involving oral diagnosis is required. The fourth year consists of a seminar course devoted to diagnosis and treatment planning of specially selected cases.

Oral Surgery. Having had courses in anesthesiology, radiology, and exodontics in the first through third years, the student is prepared for this fourth year course in oral surgery. The course is devoted to the diagnosis and surgical treatment of diseases, injuries, and defects of the jaws and related structures.

Partial Dentures. The student is taught partial denture concepts and techniques. Technical experience is gained by fabricating dentures using a mannequin as a patient.

Pathology. Taught during the second and third years, this course stresses the recognition and treatment of oral diseases based on their clinical characeristics and an understanding of the disease process.

Pharmacology. Taught in the second or third year, this course aims to acquaint students with drugs currently in use, and to prepare them for the rational application of the drugs in dental practice.

Physiology. Taught in the first year, the course deals first with cell physiology and then with the function of the organ system. The physiological basis of dentistry and its application to clinical practice is emphasized.

Pedodontics. This subject is taught from the second to the fourth years. In the second year, the emphasis is on the procedures used with children of primary and mixed dentition ages, related to child management, oral pathology, preventive orthodontics, and operative techniques. The laboratory deals with restorative dentistry in the primary dentition. In the third year, the lectures deal with the procedures utilized, etiology, prognosis, and treatment of the dental problems of children. Supervised clinical experience is provided to learn the art of teaching dental hygiene to children and to develop the skills to diagnose and treat them. The fourth year is a continuation of the third year course.

Periodontics. This subject is usually taught during the last two years. The course includes a study of periodontal diseases, incorporating clinical and histopathological findings, etiological factors, and methods of prevention. The techniques of periodontal therapy are taught and clinical experience is provided.

OTHER EDUCATIONAL PROGRAMS

A small number of students enter dental school prior to completion of their undergraduate studies. In many such cases a bachelor's degree can be earned while completing the dental curriculum, but only if the college at which the individual did undergraduate work offers such a program and awards the degree independently.

Some schools provide the opportunity for selected students to earn their dental degree together with one of the following advanced degrees:

Master of Science (M.S.). This degree is usually offered in oral biology or a basic science. It usually requires about one additional year of study.

Masters in Public Health (M.P.H.). This is a program designed for those especially interested in dental public health. It requires from one summer to one year of additional study.

Doctor of Philosophy (Ph.D.). This degree is usually awarded for work completed in one of the basic sciences. It requires at least two additional years of study and is designed for those planning careers in academic dentistry.

Doctor of Science (D.Sc.). Boston University has a combined program leading to a D.M.D. and D.Sc. in nutritional sciences which requires two additional years of study.

Schools offering these advanced degrees are listed in Table 13.

Table 13. Dental Schools Providing Opportunities to Earn Other Degrees Concurrently

M.S.	M.P.H.	Ph.D.	D.Sc.
Alabama	Loma Linda	Alabama	Boston
California, Los Angeles	Illinois	Southern California	
California, San Francisco	Columbia	Connecticut	
		Iowa	
Medical College of Georgia		Illinois	
		North Carolina	
Illinois		Texas, San Antonio	
		Medical College of Virginia	
		West Virginia	

POSTGRADUATE TRAINING

There are eight dental specialties that are recognized by the American Dental Association. Becoming a specialist usually requires from one to four additional years of training beyond the dental degree and, in most instances, practical experience in the field.

Specialty training is offered at some dental schools and at many hospitals and medical centers. Further information on institutions offering postgraduate training can be secured from: The Commission on Dental Accreditation, American Dental Association, 211 East Chicago Avenue, Chicago, IL 60611.

17

DENTAL SCHOOLS

■ The dental scene in a
nutshell

■ In-depth school
profiles

This chapter consists of two components: tables and school profiles. The table in "The Dental Scene in a Nutshell" provides numerical data dealing with various items and serves as a quick source of information and a means for comparing elements of various schools. The "In-Depth School Profiles" offer detailed information that distinguishes the individual schools.

The Dental Scene in a Nutshell

Table 14, Basic Data on the Dental Schools, contains the kind of data that should be useful in helping you decide which schools to apply to. At a glance you can see and compare application data, admission statistics, academic statistics, and expenses.

Please note that while the information in this table is as up-to-date and accurate as possible, it is recommended that you check with the individual dental schools before applying.

How to Use This Table

The following list explains the column headings in Table 14.

Application Fee In many cases, this fee is required only at the time of final application. The preliminary application is usually the AADSAS application for which a fee is paid when submitting the form.

Earliest And Latest Filing Dates These are usually firm dates.

Number of Applicants This column gives an idea of how many applications were received for the 1984–85 class.

Entering Class The columns indicate the men, women, minority and out-of-state students who enrolled in the 1984–85 entering class. The ratio of the total number of men and women accepted to the total number of applicants gives an indication of the competitive nature of admissions at each school.

Two Years College This shows the relative chances of a second-year student gaining admission.

Three Years College This shows the relative chances of a third-year student gaining admission.

Mean Total GPA The mean grade point average. It is usually somewhat lower for residents.

Mean Science GPA The mean science grade point average.

DAT Academic Average The mean academic average test score for entering first-year students.

DAT PAT Average The mean perceptual ability test score for entering first-year students. This and the preceding score can serve as a guide for the standards and competitive nature of each school.

Tuition 1985–86 tuition costs (annual) for first-year students, unless otherwise indicated.

Other Expenses This estimate covers fees, books, instruments, and other supplies and materials for the first year.

Table 14. Basic Data on the Dental Schools

School	Fee	Application Data		Admission Statistics			
		Filing Dates		Number of Applicants	Entering Class		
		Earliest	Latest		Men	Women	Minority
ALABAMA							
*University of Alabama School of Dentistry	$25	6/1	1/31	314	41	15	2
CALIFORNIA							
*Loma Linda University School of Dentistry	$25	6/1	12/1	615	55	17	22
*University of California—Los Angeles, School of Dentistry	$35	4/1	10/1	658	80	20	6
*University of California—San Francisco, School of Dentistry	$35	6/1	11/1	500	64	32	20
*University of Southern California School of Dentistry	$35	5/1	2/1	1190	96	30	43
*University of the Pacific School of Dentistry	$35	7/1	12/15	860	109	28	52
COLORADO							
University of Colorado Medical Center, School of Dentistry	$20	6/1	2/1	321	16	11	na
CONNECTICUT							
*University of Connecticut School of Dental Medicine	$35	6/1	1/31	621	23	17	6
DISTRICT OF COLUMBIA							
*Georgetown University School of Dentistry	$35	8/1	2/28	1543	105	44	36
*Howard University College of Dentistry	$25	6/15	3/1	787	119	64	na
FLORIDA							
*University of Florida College of Dentistry	$15	5/1	10/15	481	54	22	21
GEORGIA							
Medical College of Georgia School of Dentistry	$10	7/1	12/1	125	38	13	5
ILLINOIS							
*Loyola University of Chicago School of Dentistry	$20	7/1	12/31	1227	89	33	na

* AADSAS school
na data not available

Admission Statistics			Academic Statistics				Expenses	
Entering Class			Accepted Out-of State Applicants		Entering Class			
Out-of-State	Percent with		Mean Total GPA	Mean Science GPA	DAT Academic Average	DAT PAT Average	Tuition Res/Nonres	Other
	Two Years College	Three Years College						
3	0	13	3.46	3.41	4.0	4.0	$ 1,800 $ 3,000	$ 9,400
20	1	16	3.09	2.97	4.38	5.69	$13,800 $13,800	$ 4,632
0	0	na			na	na	$ 0 $ 3,564	$ 5,441
5	0	3	3.5	3.5	3.3	6.0	$ 0 $ 2,100	$ 5,456
24	20	80	3.21	3.12	5.0	5.0	$14,706 $14,706	$ 2,000
20	0	13.1	2.91	2.77	4.5	5.7	$19,200 $19,200	$ 8,100
na	na	na	na	na	4.5	4.3	$ 4,770 $14,310	na
16	0	5	3.4	3.5	5.78	4.58	$ 5,555 $ 9,925	$ 9,000
na	na	na	3.04	2.88	4.69	4.90	$13,800 $13,800	$ 4,978
na	0	2.0	na	na	3.0	3.0	$ 3,700 $ 3,700	$ 5,055
4	0	na	na	na	5.2	4.9	$ 2,674 $ 6,081	$ 5,000
0	0	12			5.0	5.0	$ 2,886 $ 8,313	$ 5,109
36	0	11	2.89	2.72	4.0	4.25	$ 9,750 $ 9,750	$3,300

Table 14. **Basic Data on the Dental Schools** —Continued

| School | Fee | Filing Dates | | Number of Applicants | Entering Class | | |
		Earliest	Latest		Men	Women	Minority
*Northwestern University Dental School	$35	7/1	12/31	1373	75	34	
*Southern Illinois University School of Dental Medicine	$20	7/1	3/1	284	78	29	6
*University of Illinois at Chicago College of Dentistry	$20	7/1	12/31	548	99	34	18
INDIANA							
*Indiana University School of Dentistry	$20	6/1	12/1	488	80	37	19
IOWA							
*University of Iowa College of Dentistry	$10	6/1	2/1	451	53	19	6
KENTUCKY							
*University of Kentucky College of Dentistry	$10	5/1	3/1	498	30	15	5
University of Louisville School of Dentistry	$10	7/1	12/1	516	55	11	3
LOUISIANA							
Louisiana State University School of Dentistry	$20	7/15	1/15	142	50	10	6
MARYLAND							
*University of Maryland at Baltimore, College of Dental Surgery	$20	6/1	12/1	822	62	44	27
MASSACHUSETTS							
*Boston University—Goldman School of Graduate Dentistry	$35	7/1	1/1	914	na	na	na
*Harvard School of Dental Medicine	$50	7/1	12/1	242	18	6	8
*Tufts University School of Dental Medicine	$35	5/1	1/1	1243	86	44	13
MICHIGAN							
*University of Detroit School of Dentistry	$25	7/1	3/1	343	48	15	5
*University of Michigan School of Dentistry	$20	7/1	2/1	666	na	na	na

* AADSAS school
na data not available

Admission Statistics			Academic Statistics				Expenses	
Entering Class			Accepted Out-of State Applicants		Entering Class			
Out-of-State	Percent with		Mean Total GPA	Mean Science GPA	DAT Academic Average	DAT PAT Average	Tuition Res/Nonres	Other
	Two Years College	Three Years College						
69	na	na	na	na	4.64	4.58	$12,810 $12,810	$10,100
7	0	20	na	na	4.1	3.5	$ 1,848 $ 5,544	na
3	2.94	1.47	na	na	5.03	5.39	$ 2,706 $ 8,118	$ 4,709
14	0	5	3.13	3.02	4.49	4.26	$ 3,400 $ 7,200	$ 2,247
17	0	14	3.25	3.10	4.7	4.6	$ 2,820 $ 6,660	$ 3,160
3	1.8	4	3.14	na	3.39	3.22	$ 2,720 $ 6,005	na
8	2	25	3.27	3.04	3.51	3.10	$ 2,765 $ 6,006	na
11	0	15	2.86	2.67	4.3	3.13	$ 2,200 $ 5,250	$ 5,462
36	0	9	3.10	3.00	4.70	4.42	$ 4,254 $ 9,596	$ 3,074
na	na	na	na	na	4.1†	3.8†	$15,900 $15,900	$ 1,809
24	0	8.3	3.52	3.48	5.84	5.24	$13,100 $13,100	$ 1,905
68	0	4	3.0	3.0	4.4	4.3	$13,830 $13,830	$ 4,786
4	5	30	3.07	3.06	3.81	4.02	$ 9,600 $ 9,600	$ 4,184
na	na	na	na	na	5.42	5.45	$ 4,768 $ 9,064	$ 4,335

†figures are for 1983–84

Table 14. **Basic Data on the Dental Schools** —*Continued*

School	Application Data			Admission Statistics			
		Filing Dates				Entering Class	
	Fee	Earliest	Latest	Number of Applicants	Men	Women	Minority
MINNESOTA							
*University of Minnesota School of Dentistry	$20	7/1	2/1	567	na	na	na
MISSISSIPPI							
*University of Mississippi School of Dentistry	$10	7/1	3/15	183	29	6	4
MISSOURI							
*University of Missouri School of Dentistry	$ 0	6/1	3/1	549	89	30	18
*Washington University School of Dental Medicine	$35	7/1	1/1	977	47	17	11
NEBRASKA							
*Creighton University Boyne School of Dental Science	$25	6/1	3/1	915	73	9	1
*University of Nebraska Lincoln College of Dentistry	$ 0	5/1	12/1	389	45	11	4
NEW JERSEY							
*Fairleigh Dickinson University School of Dentistry	$25	7/1	na	798	71	26	12
*New Jersey Dental School, University of Medicine and Dentistry	na	na	na	na	na	na	na
NEW YORK							
*Columbia University School of Dental and Oral Surgery	$35	7/1	2/28	664	43	19	15
*New York University College of Dentistry	$35	5/1	2/1	1062	97	50	na
*SUNY at Buffalo School of Dentistry	$50	7/1	11/30	447	68	17	1
*SUNY at Stony Brook School of Dental Medicine	$50	na	na	409	11	16	0
NORTH CAROLINA							
*University of North Carolina School of Dentistry	$ 0	6/1	12/1	475	61	17	10

* AADSAS school
na data not available

Admission Statistics			Academic Statistics				Expenses	
Entering Class			Accepted Out-of State Applicants		Entering Class			
Out-of-State	Percent with		Mean Total GPA	Mean Science GPA	DAT Academic Average	DAT PAT Average	Tuition Res/Nonres	Other
	Two Years College	Three Years College						
na	na	na	na	na	4.94	4.97	$ 3,993 $ 7,986	$ 1,486
0	0	1			4.0	4.0	$ 4,000 $10,000	$ 2,000
12	3.4	19.2	2.92	2.62	3.97	4.37	$ 3,714 $ 5,856	$ 3,300
41	na	na	na	na	na	na	$12,720 $12,720	na
na	0	20	na	na	4.50	5.62	$ 8,876 $ 8,876	$ 1,950
16	0	30	3.40	3.29	4.54	5.20	$ 2,274 $ 5,008	$ 2,424
29	0	18	na	na	na	na	$13,052 $14,052	$ 3,100
na	na	na	na	na	4.56	5.69	$ 6,825 $ 8,530	$ 2,445
16	0	4.8	2.90	3.0	5.0	5.0	$12,416 $12,416	na
29	0	12	2.97	2.8	4.22	4.1	$14,936 $14,936	$11,540
4	0	4.7	2.97	2.99	5.31	5.19	$ 5,775 $ 8,775	$ 7,405
0	0	0	—	—	5.45	5.19	$ 5,550 $ 8,300	$ 8,153
24	0	6	3.1	2.9	4.6	4.4	$ 1,966 $ 5,372	$ 5,045

†figures are for 1983-84

Table 14. **Basic Data on the Dental Schools** —*Continued*

School	Fee	Filing Dates Earliest	Filing Dates Latest	Number of Applicants	Men	Women	Minority
OHIO							
*Case Western Reserve School of Dentistry	$35	8/1	3/1	918	64	22	10
*Ohio State University College of Dentistry	$10	7/1	12/15	995	122	29	11
OKLAHOMA							
*Oral Roberts University School of Dentistry	$30	6/1	2/1	296	17	3	1
*University of Oklahoma College of Dentistry	$15	7/1	1/1	382	47	10	9
OREGON							
Oregon Health Science University School of Dentistry	$25	7/1	10/1	107	50	15	1
PENNSYLVANIA							
*Temple University School of Dentistry	$30	7/1	3/1	1045	103	31	14
*University of Pennsylvania School of Dental Medicine	$35	6/1	1/1	1000	66	23	7
University of Pittsburgh School of Dental Medicine	$25	na	na	484	75	21	3
SOUTH CAROLINA							
Medical University of South Carolina, College of Dental Medicine	$20	7/15	2/15	120	38	10	3
TENNESSEE							
*Meharry Medical College School of Dentistry	$25	4/1	1/15	242	na	na	na
University of Tennessee College of Dentistry	$25	7/1	12/31	207	70	20	6
TEXAS							
Baylor College of Dentistry	$15	na	June	451	95	26	na
University of Texas—Houston Dental Branch	$35	4/15	10/15	410	74	36	40
University of Texas—San Antonio Dental School	$ 0	4/15	10/15	409	79	26	24

* AADSAS school
na data not available

Admission Statistics			Academic Statistics				Expenses	
Entering Class			Accepted Out-of State Applicants		Entering Class			
Out-of-State	Percent with		Mean Total GPA	Mean Science GPA	DAT Academic Average	DAT PAT Average	Tuition Res/Nonres	Other
	Two Years College	Three Years College						
45	5	10	2.8	2.71	4.0	4.0	$11,350 $11,350	$ 4,100
21	9	12	na	na	4.59	5.20	$ 3,024 $ 7,224	$ 3,376
18	5	5	2.9	2.7	3.95	4.2	$ 7,800 $ 7,800	$ 9,000
10	na	na	na	na	3.98	4.21	$ 2,296 $ 5,751	$ 4,674
13	0	na	3.3	na	4.0	5.0	$ 2,965 $ 7,035	na
41	0	27	na	na	2.87	4.0	$ 8,084 $12,992	$ 5,260
58	0	6	3.08	3.21	5.0	5.0	$15,540 $15,540	$10,050
7	0	15	3.12	2.97	4.64	4.47	$ 9,230 $13,870	$ 5,257
10	0	4	3.08	2.96	3.91	4.43	$ 2,688 $ 5,375	$ 2,450
na	na	na	na	na	2.57	2.96	$ 9,500 $ 9,500	$ 2,439
9	na	na	3.15	3.03	4.1	4.1	$ 2,850 $ 5,703	$ 3,449
20	0	1	na	na	4.64	4.59	$ 750 $ 3,600	$ 4,410
10	2	15	3.38	3.26	3.9	4.1	$ 400 $ 1,200	$ 3,767
10	2	10	3.33	3.25	4.4	4.7	$ 300 $ 900	$ 4,000

†figures are for 1983-84

Table 14. Basic Data on the Dental Schools —*Continued*

School	Fee	Filing Dates Earliest	Filing Dates Latest	Number of Applicants	Men	Women	Minority
VIRGINIA							
*Virginia Commonwealth University MCV—School of Dentistry	$35	6/1	12/15	580	64	29	11
WASHINGTON							
*University of Washington School of Dentistry	$50	6/1	11/1	405	39	17	14
WEST VIRGINIA							
*West Virginia University School of Dentistry	$30	6/1	11/1	462	27	13	3
WISCONSIN							
*Marquette University School of Dentistry	$20	7/1	3/1	1077	111	28	36
CANADA							
*Dalhousie University Faculty of Dentistry	$15	9/1	12/31	178	23	17	0
*McGill University Faculty of Dentistry	$15	9/1	3/1	385	30	10	0
Université de Montréal School of Dental Medicine	$ 0	1/1	3/1	532	48	37	na
Université Laval Ecole Médecine Dentaire	$15	na	3/1	421	28	10	na
University of Alberta Faculty of Dentistry	$24	9/1	2/1	301	44	6	na
University of British Columbia Faculty of Dentistry	$25	7/1	12/31	182	28	12	23
University of Manitoba Faculty of Dentistry	$ 0	9/1	1/1	30	22	8	8
*University of Saskatchewan College of Dentistry	$ 0	none	2/28	306	9	12	na
*University of Toronto Faculty of Dentistry	$20	9/1	12/1	774	78	26	na
University of Western Ontario Faculty of Dentistry	$ 0	9/1	12/1	464	29	11	na

* AADSAS school
na data not available

Admission Statistics			Academic Statistics				Expenses	
Entering Class			Accepted Out-of State Applicants		Entering Class			
Out-of-State	Percent with		Mean Total GPA	Mean Science GPA	DAT Academic Average	DAT PAT Average	Tuition Res/Nonres	Other
	Two Years College	Three Years College						
33	0	0	3.15	2.96	4.72	4.69	$ 4,582 $ 8,882	$ 2,949
9	0	20	na	3.49	5.67	5.33	$13,208 $33,488	$13,770
16	0	25	3.28	3.11	4.0	4.0	$ 2,620 $ 5,935	$ 7,222
69	0	39	na	na	3.78	4.3	$ 9,000 $14,500	$ 4,130
4	2.5	25	na	na	4.73	4.35	$ 1,988 $ 2,998	$ 2,576
4	33	66	na	na	4.0	4.0	$ 570 $ 4,350	$ 2,175
4	60	40	na	na	na	na	$ 640 $ 640	$ 3,300
1	60	25	na	na	4.0	5.0	$ 750 na	$ 3,000
5	34	66	na	na	na	na	$ 1,340 $ 1,340	$ 3,900
1	0	30	3.04	na	5.25	5.54	$ 2,000 $ 3,000	$ 1,725
2	63	13	3.51	3.44	4.8	5.13	$ 1,568 $ 3,452	$ 5,019
na	24	10	na	na	na	na	$ 1,400 $ 1,400	na
na	13	30	na	na	na	4.0	$ 1,472 $ 7,114	$ 2,538
0	100	40			na	5.6	$ 1,531 $ 1,531	$ 2,650

†figures are for 1983-84

In-Depth School Profiles

The dental school profiles consist of in-depth descriptions of the 60 accredited U.S. dental schools and the 10 Canadian dental schools. The profiles cover admission procedures and requirements, curriculum, grading and promotion policies, facilities, and special features as described below.

Admissions Although the minimum requirement for most U.S. schools is at least three years (90 semester hours) of undergraduate study at an accredited college or university, the percentage of those accepted with only this background is quite small. Most students hold a baccalaureate degree at the time they begin their dental school studies. (Some Canadian schools have a one- or two-year college prerequisite.) *The DAT is required for admission by essentially all U.S. schools* (but not by those in Canada). The basic or minimum predental science course requirements referred to in this section consists of one year each of biology, inorganic chemistry, organic chemistry and physics along with their appropriate laboratory work. Any additional required or recommended courses are indicated. Most other required courses include those covered by any regular general education program at an undergraduate college. An interview may or may not be required but it is given only at the invitation of the school. Since residence is in some cases a significant element in the admission process, the general policy is noted. (For a more definitive appreciation of this factor see Table 14, which lists the number of nonresidents accepted.)

Transfer and Advanced Standing The level to which transfer is possible varies from school to school. Foreign dental school graduates may be accepted at some undergraduate level at institutions that grant advanced standing (usually only the second year).

Curriculum The curriculum is described as to length and type. The classifications used are: *traditional* (basic science taught during the first two years, although some clinical exposure may be provided. Last two years consist of clerkships in major and minor clinical specialties with little or no time allotted for electives); *diagonal curriculum* (phases-in clinical experience to significant extent beginning in the first year, but the bulk of the clinics are still scheduled for the last two years); *flexible curriculum* (no rigid course curriculum and students complete the program in varying amounts of time).

Grading Policy Where known, the grading policy is described. These may be different in the basic and clinical sciences.

Facilities The facilities utilized in both the basic sciences and for clinical training are described.

Special Features Other degree programs or special programs for recruiting and retaining disadvantaged students are described in this section.

DENTAL SCHOOL PROFILES

ALABAMA

> **University of Alabama**
> School of Dentistry
> University Station
> Birmingham, Alabama 35294

Admissions (AADSAS) In addition to the basic predental science courses, one year of mathematics and English and one additional biology course are required. Recommended electives may be from biology (embryology, genetics, comparative anatomy, cell physiology), chemistry (quantitative analysis, physical chemistry), calculus, literature, foreign languages, business, art, and sculpting. Preference is given to residents of Alabama and neighboring states. *Transfer and advanced standing:* Occasionally a few students are admitted to advanced standing.

Curriculum 4-year traditional. The curriculum incorporates innovative interdisciplinary programs which emphasize the application of the basic sciences to various clinical problems. Initial clinical experience is provided during the latter part of the first year, at intervals during the second year, and intensively during the third and fourth years. Elective programs are offered to fourth-year students.

Facilities The School of Dentistry Building is located within the medical facilities campus in downtown Birmingham. A 5-story addition and renovation of this building were completed in 1975, providing increased space and modern equipment. Off-campus clinical experience is also provided at a hospital for the mentally ill.

Special Features A program exists that is designed to interest, recruit, and retain minority students and women. Programs leading to the MS, DMD or PhD in one of the basic sciences are available. The latter requires two to three years of additional study.

CALIFORNIA

> **Loma Linda University**
> School of Dentistry
> Loma Linda, California 92350

Admissions (AADSAS) In addition to the basic predental science courses one year of English and a business management course are required. A minimum GPA of 2.7 is required. Anyone scoring below a 5 on the PAT section of the DAT will be required to take a manual dexterity test.

Curriculum 4-year traditional. The courses in anatomy have clinical applications and the laboratories in physiology, bio-chemistry, and pharmacology are based on problem-oriented case presentations. Clinical experience begins with the second year. Thirteen electives are available during the senior year when more seminars are also offered.

Facilities The school is located on the university's campus in Loma Linda along with the university's other health profession training schools. The school operates three extramural programs. One is a 12-chair clinic in the Navajo Indian Reservation, another is a mobile unit, and the third is in a nearby hospital.

Special Features Remedial and tutorial programs are available for all students. Placement services for locating and evaluating practice opportunities are available at no cost to the student.

> **University of California—Los Angeles**
> School of Dentistry
> Center for Health Sciences
> Los Angeles, California 90024

Admissions (AADSAS) In addition to the minimum predental science courses, courses in English and introductory psychology are required. There are no residency restrictions. Minority and underprivileged students are encouraged to apply. *Transfer and advanced standing:* Students from other U.S., Canadian, or foreign dental schools may apply for advanced standing.

Curriculum 4-year flexible. In addition to the basic sciences, students are trained in the use of clinical preventive measures during the first year. They are also exposed to an integrated basic-clinical sciences program section on oral biology which begins in the first year and continues into the third. Clinical experience in comprehensive patient care begins in April of the second year. Numerous electives are available in the senior year.

Grading Policy The grading system used is a modification of the pass/not-pass rating system.

Facilities The Dental School building is located in the Center for Health Sciences on the UCLA campus. Off-campus clinical instruction is also provided.

Special Features A combined DDS/MS program exists which requires one additional year to complete.

> **University of California—San Francisco**
> School of Dentistry
> 1479 4th Avenue
> San Francisco, California 94143

Admissions (AADSAS) Two semesters of psychology are required. A minimum GPA of 2.00 for residents and 2.8 for nonresidents is required. Strong priority is given to California residents, but serious consideration will be given to a small number of outstanding non-California residents.

Curriculum As early as the first year the basic sciences are supplemented by orientation to clinical practice, participation in community clinical activities, and research projects. By the fourth year all didactic courses and 20–25% of clinical experience are elective.

Grading Policy Grades are reported as letter grades or as passed/not passed, depending on the wishes of the individual students.

Facilities The school is part of the health science campus. In addition to its own facilities, two community dental clinics, mobile clinics, and affiliated hospitals and schools contribute to providing additional opportunities for clinical experience.

Special Features A Health Sciences Special Services Program to assist socioeconomically disadvantaged applicants with the application and admission procedure is available. A Recruitment and Retention Program is also in existence.

University of Southern California
School of Dentistry
925 West 34th Street
Los Angeles, California 90007

Admissions (AADSAS) The school requires the basic predental science courses and one year of English composition, as well as one year of philosophy, history, or fine arts. Non-residents are evaluated and selected based on the same criteria as California residents. *Transfer and advanced standing:* Only transfers from American and Canadian schools are considered and these occur rarely.

Curriculum 3–4-year diagonal. Patient treatment is a dominant theme in the dental curriculum and begins during the first trimester. It increases until the fourth year when it occupies the student's total efforts. Honors and elective programs are also available, and research in the biomedical and dental sciences is encouraged.

Facilities The school is located on the USC campus and is housed in the Norris Dental Science Center. Other teaching resources include affiliated hospitals and a mobile clinic.

Special Features An Office of Minority Affairs coordinates all recruitment and retention programs.

University of the Pacific
School of Dentistry
2155 Webster Street
San Francisco, California 94115

Admissions (AADSAS) One year of English is required, plus the predental sciences courses. First consideration is given to applicants who have or will attain a baccalaureate degree prior to matriculation, have a GPA of 2.8 or above and DAT scores of 4 or better, and have financial resources adequate to meet the cost of dental education and living expenses. Established review procedures ensure applicants an equal opportunity to be considered for admission. The Admissions Committee has a firm policy of not discriminating against any applicant because of age, creed, handicap, national or ethnic origin, marital status, race, color or sex. *Transfer and advanced standing:* Not possible.

Curriculum Four academic/three calendar year (12 consecutive quarters), accelerated learning program. Biomedical sciences and preventive and community services instruction is presented throughout the curriculum. During the first year, students are introduced to comprehensive patient care and preclinical techniques. During the second year 18 hours per week are devoted to providing comprehensive dental care under the supervision of a multidisciplinary teaching faculty. In the final year, students spend 35 hours per week in a variety of school and community clinics. The Comprehensive Patient Care Program is based on the concept of private dental practice where the student assumed responsibility for assigned patients' treatment, consultation, and referral for specialty care. The Extramural Clinic Program serves critical Northern California urban and rural community needs where advanced students are provided with accelerated learning opportunities in the practice of dentistry.

Facilities The school is located on the university's San Francisco campus in the prestigious Pacific Heights neighborhood. It consists of a 9-story, modern, completely equipped building and a new, spacious housing facility within easy walking distance. The school has a major extended campus, the Union City Dental Clinic.

Special Features The school has an affirmative action program with regard to admission of qualified ethnic minorities, females, and members of underrepresented groups.

COLORADO

University of Colorado Medical Center
School of Dentistry
Denver, Colorado 80220

Admissions (AADSAS) The basic predental science courses, one year of mathematics and literature, and one semester of English composition are required. Preference is given to state residents and applicants from western states under the WICHE agreement. Non-residents are considered. *Transfer and advanced standing:* This is considered on an individual basis.

Curriculum 4-year traditional. Certain electives in the basic sciences are offered in the last two years. Clinical experience begins in the sophomore year and continues as increasing levels of competence are acquired. Dental ecology courses, including behavioral sciences, business administration, history, and ethics, are incorporated into the curriculum.

Facilities The school building was occupied in 1976 and contains the clinic, oral surgery suite, classrooms, laboratories, and offices. Certain facilities are available at the University of Colorado Medical Center.

CONNECTICUT

University of Connecticut
School of Dental Medicine
263 Farmington Avenue
Farmington, Connecticut 06032

Admissions (AADSAS) The basic predental courses are required. Students should have a strong facility in English and should be able to handle quantitative concepts. Credits in behavioral sciences and upper division biology courses are desirable. *Transfer and advanced standing:* Students from U.S., Canadian, and foreign dental schools may apply for advanced standing.

Curriculum 4-year diagonal. During the first two years students take an integrated course of study in the basic sciences which takes place in multidisciplinary laboratories. Simultaneously, students devote gradually increasing time to a 4-year program known as Correlated Dental Science, which serves as an introduction to clinical dentistry as well as a bridge between theoretical knowledge and its application to dental care. The clinical component begins in the third year and includes comprehensive patient care, self-paced clinics, and block rotations.

Facilities The school is part of the University of Connecticut Health Center. A satellite clinic is located in the Burgdorf Health Center in Hartford.

Special Features A combined DMD/PhD program is offered which takes about three years to complete.

DISTRICT OF COLUMBIA

Georgetown University
School of Dentistry
3900 Reservoir Road, N.W.
Washington, D.C. 20007

Admissions (AADSAS) Well-rounded predental applicants with courses in literature, arts, humanities, and social sciences are preferred. The requirements for admission are the predental courses and 6 semester hours in English (3 hours in English composition and 3 hours in public speaking). A minimum score of 4 is required on the DAT. There are no residence or other restrictions. *Transfer and advanced standing:* Students from other U.S. or Canadian dental schools may apply for advanced standing.

Curriculum 4-year traditional. Basic sciences are taught in the preclinical years; however, a certain amount of clinical experience is gained in community dentistry and periodontics. Electives are offered to a limited extent in the third and fourth years of the clinical experience.

Grading Policy A numerical grading system is used.

Facilities All instruction is conducted in the ultramodern facilities on the campus. Further training is available in various local hospitals.

Special Features Research opportunities are offered to all interested students in both science areas and clinical research problems. One research project is required of all candidates for the DDS degree.

Howard University
College of Dentistry
600 W Street, N.W.
Washington, D.C. 20059

Admissions (AADSAS) The basic predental courses and a year of English are required. Recommended electives are French or German, history, psychology, sociology, economics, humanities, behavioral sciences, and biostatistics. The GPA should be more than 2.0. Citizenship is not considered a requirement for admission, nor is residence within the District of Columbia. *Transfer and advanced standing:* Transfer from American schools is possible.

Curriculum 4-year traditional. Clinical experience begins in the second year. Basic and clinical sciences are integrated. Special features of the curriculum involve a program for the chronically ill and aged which takes dental care to the home- and institution-bound patient.

Facilities The college is housed in a 5-story complex with a 60-chair clinic located below-ground. Programs are also conducted at the university and other affiliated hospitals.

Special Features Many of the school's activities are devoted to the education of minorities, the educationally disadvantaged, and women. This involves a preentrance and academic reinforcement program.

FLORIDA

University of Florida
College of Dentistry
Gainesville, Florida 32610

Admissions (AADSAS) The basic predental courses are required and a course in biochemistry is recommended. Applicants with an overall B average as a minimum will receive strongest consideration for admission. A very limited number of nonresidents are admitted. *Transfer and advanced standing:* None admitted.

Curriculum 3–4-year self-paced. Consists of two components: (a) core-courses which are required of all, and (b) elective courses which are optional. The latter may include a research project. Basic sciences, correlated dental sciences, dental didactic activities, and dental clinical activities are presented in both the core and the electives.

Facilities The college is an integral part of the J. Hillis Miller Health Center located on the university campus. The 11-story dental clinical-science building was opened in August 1975.

GEORGIA

Medical College of Georgia
School of Dentistry
1120 Fifteenth Street
Augusta, Georgia 30912

Admissions The basic predental courses are required. A statistical screening which gives added weight to science grades and the academic scores of the DAT is used for preliminary selection. Occasionally a nonresident with demonstrated strong ties to the state is admitted. *Transfer and advanced standing:* A student with a PhD in one of the basic sciences may be admitted with advanced standing. Transfer is also possible from a compatible curriculum.

Curriculum 4-year flexible. Elementary clinical treatment of patients begins in the first year, including restorative dentistry in the third quarter. Conversely, some basic science courses are not completed until the senior year. Treatment of patients is carried out in a system of comprehensive care, rather than in block assignments, so as to simulate private practice of general dentistry.

Facilities The school is on the campus of Medical College of Georgia which is located on the fringe of the downtown area adjacent to a large complex of health-care facilities.

Special Features A combined DMD/PhD program is offered, requiring two additional years of study. Minority students who have been accepted but have recognizable deficiencies can attend a special presession. Students may be provided with tutors, special curricular loads, and self-paced learning packages, depending upon the severity of problems.

ILLINOIS

Loyola University of Chicago
School of Dentistry
2160 South First Avenue
Maywood, Illinois 60153

Admissions (AADSAS) In addition to the basic predental courses, two biology electives are required. A major in biology and, where possible, a minor in chemistry is recommended. Residents of Illinois, are given preferential consideration, but other out-of-state residents are invited to apply. *Transfer and advanced standing:* Not possible.

Curriculum 4-year traditional. Preclinical training and an introduction to patient care are included in the first two years of the curriculum. Specially designed "conjoint courses" integrate various basic and clinical sciences. An honors program is available for exceptional students.

Facilities The school is part of the university's Medical Center and is located about 10 miles west of metropolitan Chicago. The building rises 3 stories above a sub-ground level and contains classrooms, laboratories, clinics, and offices.

Northwestern University
Dental School
311 East Chicago Avenue
Chicago, Illinois 60611

Admissions (AADSAS) The basic predental science courses plus one year of English are required. Doing well in the required science courses, plus a selection of social science, language, speech and economics courses, is desirable. At least a B average is required. *Transfer and advanced standing:* Advanced standing may be granted under special circumstances.

Curriculum 3–4-year flexible. A special elective study-clinical program is available for junior and senior students. The multiphasic clinic provides the senior student with an opportunity to perform all types of clinical treatment using 16 different ultramodern dental office arrangements.

Facilities The school is located in the Ward Building on the shores of Lake Michigan, near downtown Chicago. A new clinical facility was completed in 1978. Cooperative arrangements are in effect with 4 hospitals and with satellite clinics.

Special Features An Early Selection Program in Dental Education (ESDDS) is available. It is designed for the newly matriculated college student who seeks a career in dentistry. It provides a plan whereby the student entering an undergraduate college or university cooperating with Northwestern University Dental School by formal agreement is admitted to that institution and during his/her first year of college may be admitted to Dental School.

Southern Illinois University
School of Dental Medicine
2800 College Avenue
Alton, Illinois 62002

Admissions (AADSAS) The basic predental school courses plus one year of English are required. Highest priority is given to state residents, with those having strongest credentials being invited for interviews. About three applicants are interviewed for each one accepted. *Transfer and advanced standing:* None admitted.

Curriculum 4-year. The first and second year of the curriculum present to the student biomedical information on the human organism and information necessary to recognize the disease states in man. In addition, these two years are preparation time for clinical dentistry. The students are first involved in direct patient treatment during the second semester of the second year. Year three consists of clinical sciences instruction, application-type courses in biomedical sciences, and increasing emphasis on patient care. The major portion of the fourth year is spent in comprehensive patient care; in addition, during this time, the student receives instruction in advanced clinical sciences and practice management.

Facilities The school is located within the metropolitan St. Louis area at a renovated facility in Alton, fifteen miles from the Edwardsville campus. Training is also available in hospital dental programs, private practices, and community health centers.

Special Features The school actively encourages applications from persons in those segments of society currently under-represented in the dental profession.

> **University of Illinois at Chicago**
> College of Dentistry
> 801 South Paulina Street
> Chicago, Illinois 60612

Admissions (AADSAS) The basic predental science courses plus one year of English are required. It is recommended that electives be chosen from the social sciences and humanities, and include at least one foreign language. Students interested in practicing in a rural community are encouraged to apply. A minimum GPA of 2.25 for residents and 3.5 for nonresidents is necessary. Very high priority is given to residents. *Transfer and advanced standing:* Students from other U.S. and Canadian dental schools are considered for advanced standing.

Curriculum 4-year traditional. Students are introduced to clinical experience in the winter quarter of the first year. From then on, clinical emphasis increases, the fourth year comprising clinical practice almost exclusively.

Facilities The college is located in the Health Sciences Center of the University of Illinois at Chicago.

Special Features Combined DDS/MS and DDS/MPH programs, which can usually be completed within the basic 4-year period, are offered. A DDS/PhD program is offered, but requires an additional 2 or 3 years.

INDIANA

> **Indiana University**
> School of Dentistry
> 1121 West Michigan Street
> Indianapolis, Indiana 46202

Admissions (AADSAS) The basic predental science courses as well as courses in English composition, interpersonal communications/speech, business, and psychology are required. Courses in genetics, solid art, medical terminology,

social sciences, humanities, and arts, as well as advanced biology electives (microbiology, endocrinology, biochemistry) are recommended. Minimum GPA for residents and nonresidents is 2.50. Indiana residents are given strong preference.

Curriculum 4-year traditional. Special clinical correlation lectures are scheduled to achieve an integration of basic and clinical sciences. Clinical experiences begin the first semester of the first year and gradually increase through the second semester of the third year. A multitrack curriculum allows the fourth-year student flexibility to develop a personalized program by electing both intramural and extramural courses of individual interest.

Facilities The school is an integral part of Indiana University's Medical Center. Dental clinics are maintained in Riley Hospital and the Rotary Building.

Special Features Following admission, an effort is made to assist any student needing financial, academic, or other types of counseling to ensure satisfactory progress toward graduation.

IOWA

> **University of Iowa**
> College of Dentistry
> Iowa City, Iowa 52242

Admissions (AADSAS) The applicant's background should include at least 3 years of college work incorporating the basic predental science courses and the English composition, rhetoric, and speech requirements for a bachelor's degree. *Transfer and advanced standing:* Only under exceptional circumstances on a space-available basis.

Curriculum 4-year. To achieve a close correlation of the basic sciences with clinical disciplines, students are introduced to clinical situations during the first year. The second-year program continues the basic sciences and technical courses, plus definitive clinical patient treatment. Third-year students rotate through a series of clinical clerkships in each of 8 clinical disciplines. Seniors are involved in the delivery of comprehensive dental care under conditions closely approximating those in private practice.

Facilities The Dental Science Building is part of the University's Health Sciences campus which includes the Colleges of Dentistry, Medicine, Nursing, and Pharmacy.

Special Features The Educational Opportunity Program is available to persons of all races and ethnic backgrounds. It provides both financial and academic assistance to a limited number of students who have experienced environmental, economic, or academic hardships which cause them to compete for admission at a disadvantage because their grade point average and DAT scores do not reflect true ability. Program eligibility must be formally requested by the applicant.

KENTUCKY

University of Kentucky
College of Dentistry
Lexington, Kentucky 40536

Admissions   The U.K. College of Dentistry seeks to enroll those students whose backgrounds, personalities and motivations indicate that they will make the best possible future dental practitioners. As a state-supported school, the college gives preference to those qualified applicants who are residents of Kentucky; however, a limited number of highly qualified out-of-state applicants are considered each year and such candidates are encouraged to apply. *Transfer and advanced standing:* Possible, but only on a space-available basis.

Curriculum   The curriculum is based on a diagonal plan. Basic science courses are taught along with clinical applications throughout the four-year program, with clinical work intensifying in the third and fourth years.

Grading Policy   The grading policy is based on three-tier rating of Honors, Pass and Unsatisfactory. This policy emphasizes learning and the development of professional competencies.

Facilities   The University of Kentucky College of Dentistry is an integral part of the University of Kentucky, The Commonwealth's flagship university. The 6-story dentistry building is linked to the University of Kentucky Albert B. Chandler Medical Center, which includes the five colleges—Dentistry, Medicine, Nursing, Pharmacy and Allied Health—and the university's teaching hospital. The main U.K. campus is across the street and downtown Lexington is a 10-minute bus ride away.

Special Features   Financial assistance is available, and the college has a full-time director of this program. Personal and career counseling are also an integral part of the curriculum. Entering students are assigned an advisor who works with them throughout their dental education. Tutorial support services are readily obtained for students needing assistance in developing study skills or mastering content/skill areas.

University of Louisville
School of Dentistry
Health Sciences Center
Louisville, Kentucky 40232

Admissions   Applicants are encouraged to have earned 90 semester hours, including 32 credits of science or health-related coursework. The basic predental science courses best meet this requirement. A very limited number of well-qualified, out-of-state residents are accepted. *Transfer and advanced standing:* Students from other U.S. dental schools may be considered for advanced standing.

Curriculum   4-year traditional. The basic and clinical sciences are integrated. Patient contact is initiated in the first year.

Electives may be taken from the first year on, including courses in the arts and sciences and those in the medical school. The majority of electives are usually taken in the fourth year. Self-instructional and self-pacing programs are available on a limited basis.

Grading Policy   Most grading is by letter grades, but several courses are offered, especially in the clinical program, on a pass/fail basis.

Facilities   The school occupies a new building in the Health Sciences Center located in downtown Louisville. The physical plant and all equipment are the most advanced available. Some off-campus programs are also available.

Special Features   An extensive support system of faculty advising, clinical monitoring, and student tutoring serves the needs of all dental students. Counseling services and assistance in developing study skills are also available.

LOUISIANA

Louisiana State University
School of Dentistry
1100 Florida Avenue
New Orleans, Louisiana 70119

Admissions   The basic predental science courses plus one year of English and one course in comparative anatomy or embryology are required. Additional courses in histology, genetics, and biochemistry are strongly recommended. High priority is given to state residents with a few out-of-state residents from Arkansas and Mississippi also being accepted. *Transfer and advanced standing:* Not available.

Curriculum   4-year diagonal. The basic, clinical, and social science courses are presented individually and then interrelated by the free use of correlation courses. As the emphasis on basic and preclinical sciences decreases from year 1 to year 4, the students' exposure to the clinical sciences increases.

Facilities   The school is an integral part of the LSU Medical Center. It is located in dental school buildings that were dedicated in 1972 and contain excellent preclinical and clinical facilities.

MARYLAND

University of Maryland at Baltimore
College of Dental Surgery
666 West Baltimore Street
Baltimore, Maryland 21201

Admissions (AADSAS)   The basic predental science courses plus one year of English are required and one additional year of advanced biology courses is strongly recommended. Nonresidents should have a minimum GPA of 3.3 and DAT of 5. *Transfer and advanced standing:* Students from other U.S. or Canadian schools may be admitted advanced standing.

Curriculum 4-year. Integration of biological and clinical sciences takes place by the use of the curriculum unit, "conjoint sciences." Elective basic science courses or clinical clerkship programs may be taken in the senior year. Students are required to complete a research project (essay or table clinic) to fulfill their requirements for graduation.

Facilities Each student has an individual space during preclinical laboratory instruction and an individual operatory in the clinical years. Training is also provided in affiliated hospitals.

Special Features An 8-week summer program is available for minority students admitted to the freshman class. Tutors and a special program are available for those in need of academic assistance while in attendance.

MASSACHUSETTS

Boston University
Goldman School of Graduate Dentistry
100 East Newton Street
Boston, Massachusetts 02118

Admissions (AADSAS) The basic predental sciences plus two years of English and one year of mathematics are required. Two courses in psychology, sociology or anthropology, and economics are strongly recommended. There are no geographical restrictions on attendance. *Transfer and advanced standing:* Students from other U.S., Canadian, and foreign dental schools are considered for advanced standing. This also applies to those holding a PhD in one of the basic sciences.

Curriculum 4-year traditional. The first-year teaching program is carried out together with the medical school. The subsequent three years are carried out at clinics and operating rooms at the dental school and its affiliated institutions including community-based clinics.

Grading Policy A letter grade system is used.

Facilities The school is a component of the BU Medical Center and its teaching and clinical facilities are located in Boston's South End. Facilities of affiliated institutions and community-based clinics are also utilized.

Special Features Combined programs leading to the DMD and an MSc and/or DSc in nutritional sciences are offered. These require one additional year of study for the former and two for the latter.

Harvard
School of Dental Medicine
188 Longwood Avenue
Boston, Massachusetts 02115

Admissions (AADSAS) The basic predental science courses plus a year's course in English and calculus are required. It is also recommended that two or three additional advanced science courses be taken such as physiology, genetics, and biochemistry. No residence restrictions exist. *Transfer and advanced standing:* Students from other U.S., Canadian, or foreign dental schools, as well as holders of a PhD in one of the basic sciences, are eligible to apply for advanced standing.

Curriculum 5-year traditional. All students are introduced to oral health during the Basic Science Core Courses in oral prevention, biostatistics and epidemiology, included in the first-year curriculum. The next year includes courses in oral biology, pathophysiology and introduction to clinical medicine. The major clinical period begins in the middle of the second year. The last semesters of the senior year and the fifth year are devoted to electives.

Grading Policy The Honors, Pass and Fail system is used.

Facilities Training is obtained at the dental school as well as at affiliated institutions such as Forsyth Dental Center, Massachusetts General Hospital, and VA Hospitals.

Special Features Tutorial assistance is available for all who need it. Significant numbers of women and minorities are accepted.

Tufts University
School of Dental Medicine
One Kneeland Street
Boston, Massachusetts 02111

Admissions (AADSAS) The basic predental science courses (but only one semester of organic chemistry) plus one year of English are required. Courses in histology, comparative anatomy, genetics, biochemistry, physiology, general psychology, mathematics, economics, statistics, and an anthropology course are recommended. A minimum GPA of 2.5 and DAT of 4 is required. *Transfer and advanced standing:* Students from other U.S. and foreign dental schools may be considered for advanced standing.

Curriculum 4-year. The curriculum of the School of Dental Medicine has been designed and modified over the years to reflect the changing needs of the dental profession. The school's primary goal is to develop dental practitioners who are able to utilize their knowledge of the basic principles of human biology and human behavior in conjunction with their technical skills in diagnosing, treating, and preventing oral disease. The DMD program, which extends over a 4-year period, consists of a series of didactic, laboratory, and clinical experiences, all of which are programmed to result in the logical development of concepts and skills.

Facilities The school is located in the Tufts Dental Health

Science Building, a 10-story structure located in midtown Boston in the Tufts-New England Medical Center.

Special Features The school encourages applications by women and minorities.

MICHIGAN

> **University of Detroit**
> School of Dentistry
> 2985 East Jefferson
> Detroit, Michigan 48207

Admissions (AADSAS) The basic predental science courses plus one year of English are required. Recommended courses include comparative anatomy, histology, and psychology. No priority is given to state residents. *Transfer and advanced standing:* Foreign dental graduates as well as those attending U.S. and Canadian schools are considered.

Curriculum 4-year traditional. Clinical experience begins on a limited basis during the first year and extends through the second year. Approximately one-half the time during the last 2 years is devoted to clinical dentistry, which is taught principally by the comprehensive patient-care method.

Facilities The school is located in downtown Detroit and contains well-equipped dental clinics and laboratories. Satellite clinical facilities are located nearby in a large medical center.

Special Features Women, veterans, and members of minority groups are encouraged to apply.

> **University of Michigan**
> School of Dentistry
> Ann Arbor, Michigan 48109

Admissions (AADSAS) The basic predental science courses plus a year of English composition are required. An introductory course in psychology is highly recommended, and an advanced course in psychology, sociology, or anthropology is also suggested. Preference is given to Michigan residents; the 10% nonresidents selected have excellent qualifications. *Transfer and advanced standing:* Not possible at this time.

Curriculum 4-year traditional. Clinical experience begins in the second semester of the freshman year. To integrate the curriculum, applied oral science courses are taught in conjunction with each basic science course. At least 5 credit hours of electives are required.

Facilities The school's modern quarters were designed to complement the changing concepts in dental education.

Special Features A Dental Research Institute is located in the dental school complex, women, veterans, and minority group members are encouraged to apply.

MINNESOTA

> **University of Minnesota**
> School of Dentistry
> 515 Delaware Street S.E.
> Minneapolis, Minnesota 55455

Admissions (AADSAS) The basic predental science courses and one semester of English, psychology, and mathematics (at least through college algebra) are required. Other recommended courses include speech, art (such as basic drawing and sculpturing), cell biology, genetics, and child and adolescent psychology. Strong preference is given to Minnesota residents, but residents from Montana, North and South Dakota, and Wisconsin also are given special consideration. *Transfer and advanced standing:* Opportunities are extremely limited.

Curriculum 3–4-year flexible. The basic sciences are taught throughout the first 3 years. Integration is accomplished by offering clinically oriented phases of the basic sciences. The students begin their clinical experience in oral radiology and occlusion during the first year in school. Some electives are offered during the second year, but most are taken during the last year.

Facilities The school is part of the university health center. Its facilities are located in an up-to-date health science building. Off-campus facilities of the Hennepin County Medical Center and VA Hospital are also utilized.

Special Features Academic counseling and tutorial assistance is available to students in need.

MISSISSIPPI

> **University of Mississippi**
> School of Dentistry
> 2500 North State Street
> Jackson, Mississippi 39216

Admissions (AADSAS) The basic predental science courses plus 2 years of English, one year each of mathematics, behavioral sciences, and communications, and one semester of advanced biology, chemistry, or comparative anatomy are required. Recommended courses include biochemistry, genetics, calculus, and a foreign language. Currently, only legal Mississippi residents are admitted. *Transfer and advanced standing:* Only a few students are admitted with advanced standing.

Curriculum 4-year traditional. A systems approach to a problem-oriented curriculum is used. Clinical experience begins in the first year and is designed to follow the team approach to patient care through all 4 years. Selective courses in the specialty areas of clinical dentistry are available in the last year.

Facilities The school is part of the UM Medical Center Clinics. Other facilities are located in the dental school building that was completed in 1977.

MISSOURI

> **University of Missouri**
> School of Dentistry
> 650 East 25 Street
> Kansas City, Missouri 64108

Admissions (AADSAS) A minimum of 2 years of predental education is required as well as attainment of other academic and nonacademic criteria. *Transfer and advanced standing:* students wishing to transfer are considered assuming availability of positions in the appropriate class.

Curriculum 4-year, 11 consecutive trimesters. Emphasis is on preventive and comprehensive dentistry. The student is introduced to clinical procedures during the first year and progresses to the comprehensive treatment of patients during the third and fourth years.

Facilities The school is located in midtown Kansas City. It maintains affiliations with 6 hospitals in the area. It has a complete computer system and a full-service library with an extensive instructional materials component.

Special Features Certain academic assistance, such as tutoring and counseling, is available as needed from the Study Skills Center.

> **Washington University**
> School of Dental Medicine
> 4559 Scott Avenue
> St. Louis, Missouri 63110

Admissions (AADSAS) The predental basic science courses and one year of English composition are required. Preference is given to students with a strong biological background. Residence restrictions are not imposed, but the school has enrollment support agreements with Arkansas and New Mexico. *Transfer and advanced standing:* Students from other U.S. and Canadian dental schools, as well as students with a PhD in one of the basic sciences, are considered for advanced standing on an individual basis.

Curriculum 4-year flexible. Clinical experience begins in the second half of the first year. Biological concepts and clinical practice are correlated within such courses as occlusion, growth and development, cariology, and physical evaluation. About 100 hours of elective course work or experience are required.

Facilities The school, which is associated with the medical school of the university, has extensive, modern preclinical and clinical facilities. A separate Learning Resources Center was established to accommodate study carrels, in which students participate in slide-tape and videotape programs.

Special Features Students with research interests are encouraged to participate in research to the extent possible.

NEBRASKA

> **Creighton University**
> Boyne School of Dental Science
> 2500 California Street
> Omaha, Nebraska 68178

Admissions (AADSAS) The basic predental science courses plus one year of English are required. Recommended courses include psychology, modern languages, history, speech, economics, and comparative anatomy. The school has admission agreements with Idaho, New Mexico, North Dakota, Utah, and Wyoming. *Transfer and advanced standing:* Students from other U.S. and Canadian dental schools are considered for advanced standing.

Curriculum 4-year traditional. Basic and clinical sciences are coordinated by the Department of Oral Biology. Clinical experience begins in the second year. A variety of electives are available in the fourth year. Off-campus clinical opportunities include private practice preceptorships and assignments to hospitals, schools, and clinics.

Facilities The dental facility is a modern, 3-level structure containing classrooms, teaching and research laboratories, television studios, and various clinics with over 175 patient treatment stations. The teaching hospital offers additional clinical facilities.

Special Features Financial assistance to minority, disadvantaged, and other traditionally underrepresented students in addition to that available to all students varies from year to year.

> **University of Nebraska**
> Lincoln College of Dentistry
> 40th and Holdrege Streets
> Lincoln, Nebraska 68503

Admissions (AADSAS) The basic predental science courses plus one year of English are required. The college has no specific requirements regarding the absolute minimal scholastic average or DAT scores. Priority is given to applicants from Nebraska, North Dakota, South Dakota and Wyoming. *Transfer and advanced standing:* Not possible.

Curriculum 4-year traditional. The basic sciences are taught by the team method. Students are introduced to clinical observation and personal participation during the first year. Patients are assigned and clinical activity is amplified in the sophomore year. Integration of the basic and clinical sciences is emphasized. Electives may be taken during the senior year. Off-campus clinical experience is possible.

Facilities Modern preclinical and clinical facilities exist in Lincoln. Hospital affiliations provide opportunities for additional clinical experience. A learning center is available in association with the school library.

Special Features Counseling is accessible to underrepresented minority applicants.

NEW JERSEY

Fairleigh Dickinson University
School of Dentistry
110 Fuller Place
Hackensack, New Jersey 07601

Admissions (AADSAS) The basic predental science courses plus one year of English are required. Most applicants have majors in one of the biological or physical sciences. More than half of the entering class are New Jersey residents. *Transfer and advanced standing:* Students from other U.S. dental schools are considered for advanced standing.

Curriculum 4-year. Clinical experience begins in the second half of the sophomore year. The clinic operates on a philosophy of total patient care rather than a block system. Elective courses are available in the second half of the senior year. Research work is encouraged.

Facilities The school is housed in a modern building on the Teaneck-Hackensack campus. Access to extramural community hospitals and clinics is provided.

Special Features A combined DMD/MS progam is available.

New Jersey Dental School
University of Medicine and Dentistry
100 Bergen Street
Newark, New Jersey 07103

Admissions (AADSAS) The basic predental science courses and one year of English are required. A strong background in the natural and biological sciences is necessary. Preference is given to state residents. *Transfer and advanced standing:* No students are admitted with advanced standing.

Curriculum 4-year flexible. Some basic science instruction continues beyond the second year. Clinical activity begins with an Introduction to Clinical Dentistry in the first year. In the next year students are rotated through clinical departments in a structured manner. During the last year a student may select a portion of his or her program from clinical courses or research.

Facilities The modern preclinical facilities and clinical facilities are located in Newark and are associated with the Newark campus of the University of Medicine and Dentistry of New Jersey.

Special Features A Students for Dentistry Program, consisting of 8 weeks of academic work, was established to aid in the recruitment and preparation of disadvantaged students for dental school.

NEW YORK

Columbia University
School of Dental and Oral Surgery
630 West 168 Street
New York, New York 10032

Admissions (AADSAS) The predental science courses plus one year of English composition and literature are required. Courses in chemistry, mathematics, foreign languages, sociology, history, and the fine industrial arts are recommended. A substantial number of out-of-state residents are admitted.

Curriculum 4-year traditional. Emphasis is placed on an understanding of broad biological principles integrated with clinical dentistry. Initially, students are exposed to the full spectrum of dental problems as observers; subsequently, they are introduced to surgical and manipulative procedures and to methods of diagnosis and prevention. Clinical training is broad in scope. All basic science courses are taken jointly with the medical students of the College of Physicians and Surgeons.

Facilities The school is an integral part of the Columbia Presbyterian Medical Center within which it occupies 3 floors. These house clinics, research facilities, faculty offices, and student facilities.

Special Features A combined DDS/MPH is available to selected students and requires an additional year of study.

New York University
College of Dentistry
421 First Avenue
New York, New York 10010

Admissions (AADSAS) The basic predental science courses and one year of English are required. Recommended courses include comparative anatomy, histology, embryology, genetics, physiology, sociology, psychology, and mathematics. Out-of-state residents are admitted. *Transfer and advanced standing:* Students who have completed graduate level courses in one of the basic sciences may be admitted with advanced standing.

Curriculum 4-year traditional. Emphasis is placed on preventive aspects of clinical practice. The curriculum is structured and integrated, but flexible. It introduces the student to clinical practice the first year. There is an innovative program for all seniors in Comprehensive Care and Applied Practice Administration.

Facilities The school is a component of the NYU Dental Center. A special building for the biomedical and clinical sciences (for the comprehensive care program) was dedicated in 1978. A close relationship exists with a number of affiliated hospitals. Dormitories are available.

Special Features Financial aid (loans and scholarships) is available for those who demonstrate need.

SUNY at Buffalo
School of Dentistry
196 Farber Hall
Buffalo, New York 14214

Admissions (AADSAS) The basic predental science courses are required. Recommended courses include biochemistry, embryology, calculus, quantitative chemistry, physical chemistry, genetics, advanced social sciences, and humanities. Strong preference is given to New York State residents. *Transfer and advanced standing:* Students from other U.S. and Canadian dental schools, graduates of foreign dental schools, and holders of a PhD in one of the basic sciences, may be admitted with advanced standing.

Curriculum 3–4-year flexible. Clinical training begins in the first semester with a course in preventive dentistry. Second year students have 150 clinic hours, while third and fourth year students spend 90 and 100% of their time in the clinic, respectively. Elective courses are available in the senior year, and off-campus experience is possible.

Grading Policy An A to F system is used.

Facilities The school is a component of the health sciences facility. It has 180 operatories within Farber Hall and is affiliated with 6 area hospitals and other satellite clinics.

Special Features A summer enrichment program for entering freshman is offered.

SUNY at Stony Brook
School of Dental Medicine
Stony Brook, New York 11794

Admissions (AADSAS) All applicants are required to complete the appropriate predental science courses prior to admission to the school. One year of mathematics (preferably calculus or statistics), and one year of social and behavioral sciences are also required. Strong preference is given to New York State residents. *Transfer and advanced standing:* Students from other U.S. and Canadian dental schools, as well as holders of a PhD in one of the basic sciences, are considered for advanced standing.

Curriculum 4-year. Clinical science begins in the first year. Emphasis is placed on the restorative dental areas by early introduction of students to patient care. Integration of basic and clinical sciences is emphasized and is especially evident in the courses in oral biology and oral pathology. Elective courses are available in the fourth year.

Facilities The school is one of 6 making up the Health Sciences Center. Clinical campus-affiliated hospitals are the Long Island Jewish-Hillside Medical Center and the Northport VA Hospital.

Special Features The school encourages applications from individuals from those groups which have been underrepresented in the dental profession in the past or which have been socioeconomically deprived.

NORTH CAROLINA

University of North Carolina
School of Dentistry
Chapel Hill, North Carolina 27514

Admissions (AADSAS) The basic predental science courses are required. A course in cell biology is recommended. About 85% of the students accepted are from North Carolina. *Transfer and advanced standing:* Students from other U.S. and Canadian schools and holders of a PhD in one of the basic sciences may be admitted with advanced standing.

Curriculum 3–4-year flexible. The curriculum is organized into 5 instructional tracts. Clinical experience is initiated in the first year, and integration of the first tract—the biological sciences—and the clinical sciences is emphasized. The second tract, oral medicine, contains the nonsurgical and nonrestorative aspects of clinical dentistry. The remaining tracts are surgery, restorative dentistry, and oral ecology. Ten credit hours of electives are required.

Grading Policy The traditional letter grading system is used, but some courses are Pass/Fail.

Facilities The school consists of the original dental building, and dental research center, and a 5-story addition. A basic science building and the Division of Health Science Library provide direct support to the programs. A Learning Resources Center is also available.

Special Features Both DDS/MPH and DDS/PhD are offered and require an additional 1 year and 2 years, respectively.

OHIO

Case Western Reserve
School of Dentistry
2123 Abington Road
Cleveland, Ohio 44106

Admissions (AADSAS) The basic predental science courses plus one year of English and mathematics are required. Recommended courses include comparative anatomy, developmental biology, genetics, cell biology, and/or biochemistry. A substantial number of out-of-state residents are admitted. *Transfer and advanced standing:* Students from other U.S. and Canadian schools may be admitted with advanced standing.

Curriculum 4-year traditional. Clinical experience is introduced early in the program. Recent curriculum innovations include an integrative experience in preclinical procedures basic to restorative dentistry, experience in the use of dental auxiliaries and in the comprehensive care concept. A number of multidisciplinary subjects are taught.

Facilities The school is located in the Health Sciences Center on the main campus. The dental facility consists of 2 underground and 4 above ground levels.

Special Features A preadmission academic reinforcement program is available for minority students.

Ohio State University
School of Dentistry
305 West 12th Avenue
Columbus, Ohio 43210

Admissions (AADSAS) The basic predental science courses and one year of English composition or literature are required. Advanced courses in biology are recommended. Very strong preference is given to Ohio residents. *Transfer and advanced standing:* Students from other U.S. schools may be admitted with advanced standing.

Curriculum 3-year traditional. Clinical experience begins after the first year-and-a-half. The basic and clinical sciences are integrated during both course work and practice sessions. Ten percent of the senior year must be devoted to electives. Off-campus clinical experience is available at hospitals and clinics.

Facilities The school is located on the main campus in a 4-story building. Dental clinics are also located in University and Children's Hospitals and in Nisonger Center. City Health Department clintcs, VA hospitals, and state institutions also offer facilities for student training.

Special Features Tutorial and financial assistance is available to qualified women, minorities, and disadvantaged students. A combined DDS/MS degree is offered, but requires additional time.

OKLAHOMA

Oral Roberts University
School of Dentistry
7777 South Lewis
Tulsa, Oklahoma 74171

Admissions (AADSAS) The basic predental science courses and one year of English composition or literature are required. A course in calculus and in statistics is recommended. *Transfer and advanced standing:* Applicants are considered on an individual basis.

Curriculum 4-year. The principal objective of the dental school curriculum is to prepare graduates to provide the best possible care for patients throughout the world in the general practice of dentistry and to be keenly aware of needs in areas of the world in which the graduates will work. The dental graduate will be concerned with spiritual and mental health, in addition to the prevention and treatment of diseases and their effects. The curriculum of study requires about 4,500 hours of actual assigned work. The curriculum is divided between didactic and clinical experience. Biomedical science courses are taught mainly during the first 2 years by 6 major departments: anatomy, biochemistry, microbiology, pathology, pharmacology, and physiology. The dental curriculum is taught by 3 major divisions: reconstructive dentistry, developmental dentistry, and diagnostic and therapeutic sciences.

Facilities The suburban ORU campus is noted for its ultramodern design and innovative, advanced educational technology; its physical fitness program with aerobic emphasis; its crosspollination perspective for graduate studies; and its Charismatic concern. Health professions educational programs are integrated with the City of Faith Medical and Research Center. The ORU Dental Center is located nearby in an office park complex.

Special Features Full-time students may not live off campus (except with their parents). ORU provides student apartments.

University of Oklahoma
College of Dentistry
P.O. Box 26901
Oklahoma City, Oklahoma 73190

Admissions (AADSAS) The basic predental science courses plus one year of English composition or literature are required. Preference is given to Oklahoma residents.

Curriculum 4-year traditional. Clinical experience in prevention, oral diagnosis, and simple treatment begins during the first year and increases thereafter. Basic sciences are taught by joint departments of the dental and medical schools. During the fourth year students may choose courses of special interest from a wide range of electives. Honors programs are available for outstanding proficiency.

Facilities A 5-floor school building was opened in May 1976. It houses 5 general practice clinics, 3 specialty clinics and 180 operatories, as well as the other standard dental school facilities.

Special Features A tuition fee waiver scholarship is available to all minority students qualifying academically and financially for the first academic year.

OREGON

Oregon Health Sciences University
School of Dentistry
611 S. W. Campus Drive
Portland, Oregon 97201

Admissions The basic predental science courses plus English are required. Applicants from Oregon, states certified under the WICHE program, and the remaining states and Canada are eligible for consideration in the priority order listed. *Transfer and advanced standing:* Not available.

Curriculum 4-year traditional. Students see their first patient during their freshman year in the preventive dentistry course. Some subjects are organized into conjoint courses, taught cooperatively by separate departments. Correlation and application of the biological and clinical sciences is emphasized.

Facilities The school is part of the Health Sciences Center.

Special Features A Disadvantaged Student Recruitment Program is in effect and a tutorial program is also available.

PENNSYLVANIA

> **Temple University**
> School of Dentistry
> 3223 North Broad Street
> Philadelphia, Pennsylvania 19140

Admissions (AADSAS) The basic predental science courses and one year of English are required. Where time permits, the following science courses are recommended: histology, biochemistry, mammalian anatomy, physiology, and microbiology. Strong preference is given to state residents; applicants with a college degree are also given preference. *Transfer and advanced standing:* Under exceptional circumstances, students from U.S. and Canadian schools are considered. Foreign dental graduates may be considered for admission at the first or second-year level.

Curriculum 3–4-year flexible. Some flexibility has been introduced into the curriculum, permitting students to progress at their own pace in certain courses and in clinical experience. It is also possible for students to gain additional experience in subjects in which they have special interest.

Facilities The school is situated in a densely populated section of Philadelphia. It has close affiliations with area hospitals and other teaching units of the Health Sciences Center.

Special Features Tutorial assistance and a Learning Team are available. Students may apply some of their predental course work credits towards either an MS or a PhD in physiology/biophysics.

> **University of Pennsylvania**
> School of Dental Medicine
> 4001 Spruce Street
> Philadelphia, Pennsylvania 19174

Admissions (AADSAS) The basic predental science courses plus one semester of mathematics (calculus preferred) and one year of English are required. A course in genetics is recommended. *Transfer and advanced standing:* Students from other U.S. dental schools may be admitted with advanced standing.

Curriculum 4-year flexible. Clinical experience begins with Preventive Dentistry Education in the first year and increases thereafter. Elective time is available in the third and fourth years. Fourth-year students spend six weeks gaining additional medical skills at selected hospitals.

Grading Policy The A,B,C,I evaluation system is used.

Facilities The school is located on the university campus. Use is made of closed circuit television with large screen monitors.

Special Features Qualified students are invited to participate in the ongoing programs of the Center for Oral Health Research. Interdisciplinary programs provide the opportunity to earn DMD/MBA or DMD/PhD degrees.

> **University of Pittsburgh**
> School of Dental Medicine
> 305 Salk Hall
> 3501 Terrance Street
> Pittsburgh, Pennsylvania 15261

Admissions The basic predental science courses plus one year of English are required. Recommended courses include mathematics, statistics, psychology, and sociology. *Transfer and advanced standing:* Not possible.

Curriculum 4-year. Interdisciplinary instruction in the natural sciences on a cell-to-systems basis. Major instructional areas of human biology, clinical biology and technology, methods of science, and social perspectives. Clinical experience begins in the first year. Elective program in third and fourth years provides in-depth study in area of student interest.

Facilities The school is located within the university health complex located in the city's Oakland district. Audiovisual instructional resources consist of 40 individual stations, areas for group study, and remote television transmission to laboratories.

Special Features The following combined degree programs, which take from 1 to 3 additional years, are offered: DMD/MS, DMD/MPH, DMD/MEd, DMD/MA, and DMD/PhD.

SOUTH CAROLINA

> **Medical University of South Carolina**
> College of Dental Medicine
> 171 Ashley Avenue
> Charleston, South Carolina 29403

Admissions (AADSAS) The predental science courses plus one year of English and mathematics are required. Recommended courses include comparative anatomy and microbiology. *Transfer and advanced standing:* Not possible.

Curriculum 4-year. Clinical experience in preventive dentistry is begun in the first year and increases each year. Students are required to complete a minimum of 3 credit hours of electives, usually in the senior year. Six weeks of extramural experience is required.

Facilities The school is located in the Basic Science–Dental Building of the Medical University complex. Use is also made of urban and rural clinics, comprehensive health care centers, and underserved communities.

TENNESSEE

Meharry Medical College
School of Dentistry
1005 18th Avenue North
Nashville, Tennessee 37208

Admissions (AADSAS) The basic predental science courses and one year of English composition are required. Recommended courses include those in engineering, design, human psychology, and sociology. State residents and students from states with which the school has admission agreements are given priority. *Transfer and advanced standing:* Students from other U.S. and Canadian dental schools can apply for advanced standing.

Curriculum 4-year flexible. The first year concentrates on the basic sciences. The middle years concentrate on a mixture of basic and clinical courses, and the last year largely on clinical courses. Integration of basic and clinical sciences is achieved by multidisciplinary councils and didactic/clinical hospital dentistry experiences. A system of audits, prescribed pacing, tailoring of schedules, and summer offerings allows broad self-pacing of required courses.

Facilities The school is located on the college campus. The basic science, learning resources, hospital, and modern dental facilities have been built or renovated since 1973. Audiovisual, computer assistance, and group and individual study rooms are available.

Special Features Research opportunities are available, as is counseling.

University of Tennessee
College of Dentistry
875 Union Ave.
Memphis, Tennessee 38163

Admissions The basic predental science courses plus one year of English composition are required. Additional course work in biology and chemistry is recommended. Qualified Tennesseans are given first priority, and a number of Arkansas students are also accepted under a formal agreement. A few additional out-of-state students may be accepted if they possess superior qualifications. *Transfer and advanced standing:* Not possible.

Curriculum 4-year traditional. Selected segments of the basic and clinical sciences are presented by an interdisciplinary,

team-teaching approach. Students are oriented to clinical activities in the first year. Delivery of patient care begins in the second year. During the senior year, 100 clock hours of selective courses from special clinical projects, lectures, and research projects are required.

Facilities The college is located on the Health Sciences Center campus and has a modern clinical facility that was occupied in 1977. Off-campus clinics are also used.

Special Features The school encourages applications from minority and disadvantaged students.

TEXAS

Baylor
College of Dentistry
3302 Gaston Avenue
Dallas, Texas 75246

Admissions The basic predental science courses and one year of English are required. Recommended courses include embryology, psychology, sociology, bookkeeping, speech, foreign languages, reading improvement, and mechanical drawing. Strong priority is given to state residents.

Curriculum 4-year traditional. First- and second-year students devote their time primarily to the basic biological and dental science courses. Starting with the second year, the various subdisciplines of dentistry are emphasized through clinical experiences and didactic instruction. Off-campus clinical experience is provided.

Facilities The facilities include a modern 7-story building plus a library, a seminar building, and a multilevel parking garage.

University of Texas—Houston
Dental Branch
Houston, Texas 77225

Admissions The basic predental science courses, one year of English, and one additional year of biology are required. High priority is given to state residents. *Transfer and advanced standing:* Students from other U.S., Canadian, and foreign dental schools may apply.

Curriculum 4-year flexible. This is a performance-based, self-directed program presented in a modular form. The subject matter is divided into 8 topics. Each topic is divided into modules and is presented in an integrated format. The modules are arranged sequentially so that they can be applied in the clinical training which begins in the first year.

Facilities The school is located in the Texas Medical Center and is housed in a self-contained, 6-floor building. Preclinical training is carried out in multidisciplinary laboratories provided with closed circuit television facilities. Clinical activities are performed in individualized clinical cubicles.

University of Texas—San Antonio
Dental School
7703 Floyd Curl Drive
San Antonio, Texas 78284

Admissions The basic predental science courses, one year of English, and one additional year of biology are required. Recommended courses include conversational Spanish and those that will assist in the development of manual skills (e.g., sculpturing, typing, etc.). Strong preference is given to legal residents of Texas. *Transfer and advanced standing:* Students from other U.S., Canadian, and foreign dental schools may apply for advanced standing.

Curriculum 4-year traditional. Some courses are offered in an integrated format. The basic sciences are offered throughout the 4 years. Clinical experience begins in the freshman year and increases thereafter. Juniors are taught the team approach. Seniors are provided with the opportunity to diagnose, plan treatment, and execute clinical procedures on patients. Two-and-a-half hours of selectives are required in the senior year.

Grading Policy A letter grade system is used.

Facilities The school building is designed to facilitate the educational process. It provides an individual cubicle for each lower-level student in multi-discipline laboratories and a fully-equipped, clinical cubicle for upper-level students. Off-campus facilities are also used.

Special Features Combined DDS/MS and DDS/PhD programs are offered. These require one to 3 additional years of study.

VIRGINIA

Virginia Commonwealth University
MCV—School of Dentistry
Richmond, Virginia 23298

Admissions (AADSAS) The basic predental science courses plus courses in English are required. Courses in general microbiology, biochemistry, and behavioral sciences as well as courses involving psychomotor skills are recommended. The school accepts both state residents and nonresidents. *Transfer and advanced standing:* Students from other U.S. dental schools may apply for advanced standing.

Curriculum 4-year. The subject matter of the curriculum is divided into the basic, clinical, and social sciences. The basic sciences, including preclinical didactic and laboratory preparation and comprehensive patient care, begin in the second year. The social sciences cover such topics as dental health needs, health care delivery systems, and practice management. Elective courses are offered in the senior year.

Facilities The facilities of the school are housed in 2 modern buildings, containing clinical facilities, classrooms/laborator-

ies, group and individual study areas, department offices, and a closed circuit color television studio. Dormitories, athletic facilities, and a student center are located on campus.

Special Features Combined DDS/MS and DDS/PhD programs are offered. They require additional time beyond the 4-year DDS program.

WASHINGTON

University of Washington
School of Dentistry
Seattle, Washington, 98195

Admissions (AADSAS) One year of introductory biology or zoology, one year of physics, and one semester/2 quarters each of inorganic and organic chemistry are required. Recommended courses are vertebrate zoology and embryology. Entering classes are 80% Washington state residents. *Transfer and advanced standing:* Advanced standing or transfer students may apply.

Curriculum 4-year. Strong emphasis is placed on integrating study in the basic sciences with study in clinical dental sciences. Seniors have the opportunity to participate in off-campus clinical experiences.

Facilities As an integral part of the Health Sciences Center, the school has a variety of facility resources available to students.

Special Features Students with special backgrounds can utilize the diverse resources of the Health Sciences Center to plan joint MS and/or PhD programs.

WEST VIRGINIA

West Virginia University
School of Dentistry
Morgantown, West Virginia 26506

Admissions (AADSAS) The basic predental science courses and one year of English composition and rhetoric are required. Preference is given to state residents. Nonresidents should have at least a GPA of 3.0 and DAT scores of 4–4. *Transfer and advanced standing:* Opportunities are extremely limited and open only to foreign dental graduates.

Curriculum 4-year flexible. Clinical experience begins during the second semester of the first year. The fourth year provides an option of 3 basic tracts: basic biological science, general practice, and a specific clinical tract. Students pursuing an approved tract must take at least 3 hours of electives each semester and must register for clinical courses. Off-campus clinical experience is available.

Facilities The school is part of the WVU Medical Center. It has modern, fully-equipped teaching and clinical facilities.

Special Features Combined DDS–MS and DDS–PhD programs are available on an individual basis. They require several additional years of study.

WISCONSIN

Marquette University
School of Dentistry
604 West 16th Street
Milwaukee, Wisconsin 53233

Admissions (AADSAS) The basic predental science courses and one year of English are required and additional courses in biology and chemistry are strongly recommended. *Transfer and advanced standing:* Students from other U.S., Canadian, and foreign dental school graduates can apply for advanced standing.

Curriculum 4-year traditional. A diagonal format allows the presentation of the basic science courses throughout the 4-year curriculum. Limited clinical experience commences early in the freshman year. Collaborative, interdepartmental coverage of selected topics has been used for the integration of relevant basic and clinical science topics. Elective courses are available in the senior year and off-campus experience is possible.

Facilities The school is located on the university campus. The dental building hås undergone extensive modernization over the past 10 years. An additional wing for basic science administrative offices and laboratories and for a self-instructional center was completed in 1976.

Special Features A combined DDS/BS program is available on an individual basis, and a combined DDS/MS program encompassing both dental and nondental fields is expected to be in place by the 1985–86 school year.

CANADA

Dalhousie University
Faculty of Dentistry
Halifax, N.S. B3H 3J5

Admissions The basic predental science courses plus one year of English and 5 electives (2 each from the humanities and social sciences) are required. Preference is given to students from the Atlantic Provinces of Canada. *Transfer and advanced standing:* Students from Canadian, U.S., and foreign dental schools may apply for advanced standing.

Curriculum Didactic teaching is emphasized during the first 2 years. The clinically oriented disciplines and total patient care

are emphasized during the third and fourth year, respectively. Selective study programs are required during the fourth year.

Facilities The basic science courses are presented by the Medical Faculty in their facilities. All other subjects are taught in the Dental Building which has ample and modern facilities. Three adjacent hospitals provide additional clinical facilities.

Special Features A limited number of student research fellowships are available on an irregular basis each summer.

McGill University
Faculty of Dentistry
3640 University St.
Montreal, Québec H3A 2B2

Admissions The basic predental science courses plus one year of mathematics are required. Very strong preference is given to provincial residents. *Transfer and advanced standing:* Students from other Canadian, U.S., and foreign dental schools may apply for advanced standing.

Curriculum Basic sciences are taught in the first 3 years of the program, the heavy component being in preclinical years. Introduction to clinical experience begins in the first year, and the integration of basic sciences into clinical dentistry in the second year.

Facilities The Faculty is located in downtown Montreal. The preclinical training is provided on the McGill campus and the clinical training takes place in the Dental Clinic of Montreal General Hospital and other teaching hospitals.

Université de Montreal
School of Dental Medicine
Montréal, Québec, H3C 3T9

Admissions The basic predental science courses plus 3 semesters of mathematics, physics, chemistry, and biology, as well as 4 semesters of philosophy and French, are required. All candidates must be Canadian citizens or landed immigrants. Strong preference is given to provincial residents. Instruction is given in the French language.

Curriculum Coverage of the basic sciences takes place during the first 2 years, and clinical training is secured during the last 2 years. Avenues are provided to permit continuous integration between the 2 segments. In addition to required course work, seniors must spend a full week in a hospital to become familiarized with dental surgery and another 2 weeks in pedodontics.

Facilities The Faculté is located in the main building of the university and occupies the street and second floor levels of the east end. Students have access to university audiovisual and computer facilities.

Université Laval
Ecole Médecine Dentaire
Sainte-Foy, Québec G1K 7P4

Admissions The basic predental science courses plus one semester of English, 4 semesters of French, and 3 semesters of mathematics are required. Only residents of Quebec are accepted. *Transfer and advanced standing:* Students from other Canadian dental schools can apply for advanced standing.

Curriculum 4-year nontraditional. The first 2 years are devoted to the basic and preclinical sciences. The last 2 years are devoted almost entirely to clinical work. In the senior year elective specialization is possible. Electives in hospital dentistry, public health, and basic research are available. Self-pacing is possible in a few courses.

Facilities The school is integrated into the university's health science complex. Its facilities have been expanded to accommodate doubled enrollment. A well-equipped learning resource center is available.

University of Alberta
Faculty of Dentistry
Edmonton, Alberta T6G 2N8

Admissions The basic predental science courses are required. Recommended electives include English, psychology, statistics, and genetics. High priority is given to provincial residents, but candidates from other provinces and other countries are admitted. Although it is not necessary to complete requirements for a degree prior to applying, it is to the student's advantage to register in a degree program for preprofessional study. *Transfer and advanced standing:* Foreign dental graduates may apply for advanced standing.

Curriculum The first 2 years of the program emphasize studies in the basic biological sciences with an introduction to the dental sciences. In the final 2 years, the emphasis shifts from classroom and laboratory learning to an application of knowledge and skills to clinical problems. Senior students are assigned to the Dental Department and the Department of Anaesthesia of the University Hospital as well as the Dental Utilization Clinic and a Mobile Clinic offering a community health service.

Facilities The school is located in the Dental-Pharmacy Center. The Dental Department of University Hospital is utilized by senior students. Also used is the Dental Utilization Clinic and a mobile clinic.

Special Features Limited research opportunities are available through employment as summer research assistants.

University of British Columbia
Faculty of Dentistry
2199 Westbrook Mall
Vancouver, B.C. V6T 1W5

Admissions The basic predental science courses plus one year of English, biochemistry, and mathematics are required, and electives in the social sciences and humanities are recommended. Preparatory study for entry must comprise at least 3 years at the college or university level. An overall GPA of 2.5 (65%) is also required. Very strong preference is given to provincial residents. *Transfer and advanced standing:* Students from other Canadian, U.S., and foreign dental schools may apply for advanced standing.

Curriculum Students are given clinic exposure early in their program and actual clinical instruction begins during the second half of the second year. Clinical experience is gained in a variety of environments both on and off campus.

Facilities The Faculty is located within the Health Sciences Center on the university campus. The facilities of community health clinics and other health care units are also utilized.

Special Features Establishing combined DMD/MSc and DMD/PhD programs is under consideration.

University of Manitoba
Faculty of Dentistry
Winnipeg, Manitoba R3T 2N2

Admissions The basic predental science courses and one year of mathematics and biochemistry plus 5 electives are required. Very high priority is given to provincial residents. *Transfer and advanced standing:* Students from other Canadian, U.S., and foreign dental schools may apply for advanced standing.

Curriculum The basic sciences are taught primarily in the first 2 years. Clinical experience begins in the second term of the second year. There are no electives; however, all senior students are required to spend 4 weeks in a rural community clinic and 4 weeks in a teaching hospital.

Grading Policy Letter grades are used in the didactic portion of the curriculum and Pass/Fail in the clinical segment.

Facilities The Faculty is located on the health science campus in downtown Winnipeg. Additional space is devoted to dental teaching and service in the Health Sciences Center, a consortium of 4 hospitals.

Special Features A limited number of undergraduate students are employed in research laboratories during the summer months.

University of Saskatchewan
College of Dentistry
Saskatoon, Saskatchewan S7N 0W0

Admissions A predental year of studies at the University of Saskatchewan, including the basic science courses is required. Also required is a course on psychology, sociology, philosophy, or anthropology. High priority is given to provincial residents. *Transfer and advanced standing:* Graduates of foreign dental schools may apply for advanced standing, and may be admitted if space is available.

Curriculum 5-year. The curriculum is diagonal. Clinical exposure begins in the first year with an introduction to clinical dentistry and restorative dentistry. Positive efforts are made at all levels to closely integrate the basic and dental sciences. Fifth-year students who have fulfilled the regular course requirements can select an option program.

Facilities The college is housed in the Health Sciences Building with clinical facilities in the adjoining Dental College Clinical Building. Hospital experience is acquired at the University Hospital Dental Department.

University of Toronto
Faculty of Dentistry
124 Edward St.
Toronto, Canada M5G 1G6

Admissions Students may apply for admission to the Faculty during the first year of a university program at a recognized university. The year must consist of five full courses (or equivalent), with acceptable courses in first year Biology, Chemistry and Physics (each to include a laboratory component). First priority is given to Canadian citizens who are provincial residents. A limited number of places will be available to all other Canadian citizens and permanent residents. Special consideration will be given to residents of the Yukon and the Northwest Territories. *Transfer and advanced standing:* Graduates of foreign dental schools will not be considered for admission with advanced standing. Only in very exceptional circumstances and space permitting will consideration be given to applicants enrolled in a Canadian Dental School, who wish to transfer to the Faculty of Dentistry at the University of Toronto.

Curriculum The dental program is designed to unify the fundamental sciences and dental studies, as it is believed that scientific and professional development cannot be sharply differentiated, but should proceed concurrently throughout the program. From first year, with an emphasis on sciences basic to dentistry, the instruction shifts gradually to a clinically-oriented program by fourth year.

Facilities The Faculty has been completely renovated and expanded making it the most modern facility in North America. New modern research laboratories, clinics, offices and ancillary services enable the Faculty to provide the best possible climate for teaching and research.

University of Western Ontario
Faculty of Dentistry
London, Ontario N6A 5C1

Admissions High priority is given to provincial residents. Requirements include successful completion of a second-year program at an Ontario university, or an equivalent second year at another university, provided that the program has included a minumum of 4 honors courses or equivalent within the first 10 courses completed. All applicants must have successfully completed the basic predental science courses. *Transfer and advanced standing:* Transfer is occasionally possible.

Curriculum 4-year traditional. The first 2 years provide exposure to the basic sciences. Clinical exposure is introduced to a limited extent during this period. During the last 2 years, major emphasis is placed on clinical studies.

Facilities Teaching takes place at the Dental Science Building.

APPENDIX A

MEDICAL AND DENTAL SCHOOL APPLICATION FORMS

For many students, a major obstacle to admission can be that of successfully completing the application forms. Many of the forms are lengthy and all should be completed when you are relaxed, not rushed. Read all instructions carefully and answer all questions completely. Don't jeopardize your chances for admission by submitting an incomplete application form. Type all your answers neatly and be sure to review your application before sending it off. If the appearance of your application is in question, obtain a new one and fill it out more carefully. For additional information on applications, read Chapter 3.

Note: You must obtain the current application forms from the schools directly or through one of the application services (AMCAS, AACOMAS, AADSAS). Do not use these sample forms as your final application. They will not be accepted by the schools.

This appendix contains several application forms. The first is a sample AMCAS application to which many but not all medical schools subscribe. An application like the one in this Appendix is completed and then sent to the service, which in turn will forward an evaluated copy to the medical schools you designate. Medical schools that do not subscribe to AMCAS have their own application form, and an example of that is the New York University form, which is shown next. All osteopathic medical schools belong to AACOMAS, which has its own standard application form. Most dental schools belong to AADSAS, and its application is presented last in this appendix. Nonsubscribing dental schools have their own application forms.

FOR PERSONAL COMMENTS & ADDITIONAL INFORMATION
SEE PAGE 2

1. SSN		AMCAS® APPLICATION FOR THE 1986–87 ENTERING CLASS		AMCAS USE ONLY

2A. LAST NAME	2B. FIRST NAME	2C. MIDDLE NAME	2D. SUFFIX

3A. PERMANENT ADDRESS — STREET		3B. CITY	3C. STATE	3D. ZIP

3E. COUNTY	4. TELEPHONE ( )

5. PARENTS OR GUARDIAN

NAME	LIVING? YES NO	OCCUPATION	LEGAL RESIDENCE	EDUCATION/COLLEGE (highest level)
FATHER				
MOTHER				
GUARDIAN				

6A. AGES OF YOUR BROTHERS	6B. AGES OF YOUR SISTERS	6C. AGES OF YOUR DEPENDENTS

7A. SECONDARY SCHOOL—NAME	7B. CITY, STATE	7C. YEAR GRAD.

8. ALL COLLEGES, GRADUATE AND PROFESSIONAL SCHOOLS ATTENDED:

INSTITUTION NAME	CAMPUS/CITY & STATE	DATES ATTENDED	CHECK IF SUMMER ONLY	CHECK IF JR/COMM COLLEGE	MAJOR	DEGREE GRANTED OR EXPECTED (with date)
A. UNDERGRADUATE (list in chronological order)						
		19 ___ to 19 ___				
		19 ___ to 19 ___				
		19 ___ to 19 ___				
		19 ___ to 19 ___				
		19 ___ to 19 ___				
B. GRADUATE/PROFESSIONAL (include previous medical school)						
		19 ___ to 19 ___				
		19 ___ to 19 ___				
		19 ___ to 19 ___				
		19 ___ to 19 ___				

9. HONORS RECEIVED WHILE IN COLLEGE (include honorary societies):

10. EXTRACURRICULAR, COMMUNITY AND/OR AVOCATIONAL ACTIVITIES WHILE IN COLLEGE OR AFTER:

11A. EMPLOYMENT DURING CURRENT SCHOOL YEAR (list type of work and approx. hours per week):

11B. EMPLOYMENT DURING PREVIOUS SCHOOL YEARS (list type of work and approx. hours per week):

12. HOW HAVE YOU SPENT YOUR SUMMERS DURING YOUR COLLEGE YEARS?

13. IF YOUR EDUCATION TO DATE HAS NOT BEEN CONTINUOUS OR HAS ALREADY BEEN COMPLETED, WHAT HAVE YOU DONE WHILE NOT IN SCHOOL?

14. WERE YOU EVER REQUIRED TO LEAVE ANY COLLEGE OR MEDICAL SCHOOL, OR DENIED READMISSION FOR ANY REASON?
IF "YES", EXPLAIN FULLY IN "PERSONAL COMMENTS" SECTION (PAGE 2). ☐ YES ☐ NO

15. MILITARY SERVICE (complete if applicable)	15A. BRANCH	15B. HIGHEST RANK	15C. ENTRY DATE	15D. DISCHARGE DATE

See AMCAS Instruction Booklet before completing this form. Type form using a dark ribbon only.
This form is most easily completed using a 10-character-per-inch (pica) typewriter.

[1]"Copyright 1985 Association of American Medical Colleges. Reprinted with permission
of the Association of American Medical Colleges."

SSN		ACADEMIC RECORD			AMCAS USE ONLY

LAST NAME		FIRST NAME		MIDDLE NAME		SUFFIX

COLLEGE	LOCATION	ACADEMIC STATUS	BCPM/A	ACADEMIC YEAR	TERM	COURSE NAME	NUMBER	TYPE	OFFICIAL TRANSCRIPT GRADE	SEMESTER HOURS ATTEMPTED	AMCAS GRADE	AMCAS USE

COLLEGE	LOCATION	ACADEMIC STATUS	BCPM/A	ACADEMIC YEAR	TERM	COURSE NAME	NUMBER	TYPE	OFFICIAL TRANSCRIPT GRADE	SEMESTER HOURS ATTEMPTED	AMCAS GRADE	AMCAS USE

MCAT TESTING STATUS

Number of MCATS taken ☐

Have you taken or do you plan to take the September 1985 MCAT? ☐ YES ☐ NO

ADVISOR RELEASE

Information regarding my application to medical school may be provided to the preprofessional advisory units at the college indicated as "Primary Undergraduate College" and "Other College 1" on the AMCAS Designation Form: ☐ YES ☐ NO

CERTIFICATION STATEMENT AND SIGNATURE

I have read and understand the instructions and other information in the AMCAS Instruction Booklet. I certify that the information submitted in this application and associated materials is complete and correct to the best of my knowledge.

_____
SIGNATURE (BLACK INK ONLY)

_____
DATE

No. E-6 Rev. 1/85   DCIC NO. 0547-85   COPYRIGHT 1985 ASSOCIATION OF AMERICAN MEDICAL COLLEGES

NEW YORK UNIVERSITY SCHOOL OF MEDICINE
A private university in the public service

APPLICATION FOR ADMISSION IN SEPTEMBER, 1986

> A 2"x2" passport-type photograph is required at the time of interview for purposes of identification and recall. You may enclose it with your application if you wish.

Name _____ Sex _____
       Last   First   Middle

Home Address _____

_____ Zip Code _____

Telephone (Please Include Area Code) _____

Mailing Address _____

_____ Zip Code _____

Telephone (Please Include Area Code) _____

Where should your mail be sent during the winter holidays? Give dates. _____

_____

Date of Birth _____ Place of Birth _____ Citizenship _____

Social Security No. _____

Have you applied previously to the NYU School of Medicine? _____ Year _____

Have you ever attended another medical school? _____ If so, when and where? _____

This application is for admission to the
☐ First Year
☐ Second Year
☐ Third Year

> The closing date for applications to the First Year Class is December 16, 1985. The closing date for transfer applications is May 1, 1986

Name of parents or nearest living relatives _____

Address _____

Parents' occupations _____ (If retired or deceased, former occupation)

How many brothers and sisters in your family? _____

Your high school _____ **City and State** _____ **Year of Graduation** _____

RECORD OF COLLEGES ATTENDED

Please include _all_ undergraduate and graduate level work, including summer school. Indicate any degree toward which you are now working, and date expected.

Name of College (and branch, if any)	Dates of Attendance	Field of Major Study	Degree	Mo/Yr

Has your education been continuous except for the standard vacations? _____

If not, or if not now in college, describe what you have done while out of school or since graduation. _____ _Please account, chronologically, for all periods of time._

_____

College academic honors _____

Extracurricular and summer activities, including employment _____

_____

_____

_____

_____

_____

_____

_____

APPLICANT'S SUMMARY OF COLLEGE COURSES

Please list *all* courses taken and grades received.
Please specify *all* advanced standing credits you received upon entering college.

Prerequisite Course Work	College	Course Title	Semester Hours†	Grade
English*				
Physics*				
Inorganic Chemistry*				
Organic Chemistry*				
General Biology or Zoology*				
Additional Sciences and Mathematics				
Humanities, Social Sciences and Foreign Languages				

(Use additional page if necessary.)

*Six semester hours minimum. If these course requirements have not yet been met, please indicate in the grade column when they will be completed (Mo/Yr).

†or equivalent (indicate unit used)

If there is any information you wish to bring to the attention of the Admissions Committee regarding a physical or emotional condition or a family problem which you feel may have affected your scholastic performance, please indicate below or on a separate sheet.

_____

_____

_____

_____

_____

The Medical College Admission Test is a requirement for admission. Please state, in the left column below, dates (Mo/Yr) when the test was or will be taken and/or repeated. You may enter your scaled scores if you know them.

Date	Biology	Chemistry	Physics	Problems	Reading	Quantitative

In the space below or on an accompanying sheet of paper please explain the key motivational factors in your decision to apply to medical school. Please feel free to supply any other information you would like to bring to the attention of the Committee on Admissions. Send completed application, completed statistical form, self-addressed acknowledgement card, $50 application fee and photograph (optional) to: *Committee on Admissions, New York University School of Medicine, P.O. Box 1924, New York, N.Y. 10016.*

Signature _____ Date _____

☐ If you have filed an application for the MD-PhD Program please check here.

NEW YORK UNIVERSITY

SCHOOL OF MEDICINE | **1986**

Instructions: Complete this Statistical Form and return with your application for admission. See reverse side.

SOCIAL SECURITY NUMBER

01
12

LAST NAME (FAMILY)
18

FIRST NAME
38

MIDDLE INITIAL
48

PERMANENT ADDRESS
49

02
12

CITY
12

STATE
27

ZIP CODE
29

NY COUNTY
34

COUNTRY (OTHER THAN IN U.S.)
36

MAILING ADDRESS
51

03
12

CITY
12

STATE
27

ZIP CODE
29

COUNTRY OF CITIZENSHIP IF OTHER THAN U.S.

CK. (GEOG. CODE)

▲ FOR OFFICE USE ONLY ▲

CITIZENSHIP

1	U. S. CITIZEN
2	U.S. PERMANENT RESIDENT VISA
3	STUDENT VISA
4	EXCHANGE VISITOR VISA
5	OTHER

36

SEX

M

F

34

PARENT'S FULL NAME IF ALUMNUS OF NYU SCHOOL OF MEDICINE
37

PARENT S YEAR OF GRAD.
67

FOR OFFICE USE ONLY:

USOE

| 1 |
| 2 |
| 3 |
| 4 |
| 5 |

69

APPLICATION NUMBER

12 (CARD 01)

USE ONLY THESE CODES FOR THE INFORMATION REQUESTED

STANDARD STATE ABBREVIATIONS	
AL Alabama	MT Montana
AK Alaska	NB Nebraska
AZ Arizona	NV Nevada
AR Arkansas	NH New Hampshire
CA California	NJ New Jersey
CO Colorado	NM New Mexico
CT Connecticut	NY New York
DE Delaware	NC North Carolina
DC District of Columbia	ND North Dakota
FL Florida	OH Ohio
GA Georgia	OK Oklahoma
GU Guam	OR Oregon
HI Hawaii	PA Pennsylvania
ID Idaho	PR Puerto Rico
IL Illinois	RI Rhode Island
IN Indiana	SC South Carolina
IA Iowa	SD South Dakota
KS Kansas	TN Tennessee
KY Kentucky	TX Texas
LA Louisiana	UT Utah
ME Maine	VT Vermont
MD Maryland	VA Virginia
MA Massachusetts	VI Virgin Islands
MI Michigan	WA Washington
MN Minnesota	WV West Virginia
MS Mississippi	WI Wisconsin
MO Missouri	WY Wyoming

NEW YORK STATE COUNTY CODES — Do not code if County is not known.

01	Albany	24	Kings	45	Saint Lawrence
02	Allegany	25	Lewis	46	Saratoga
03	Bronx	26	Livingston	47	Schenectady
04	Broome			48	Schoharie
		27	Madison	49	Schuyler
05	Cattaraugus	31	Manhattan	50	Seneca
06	Cayuga	28	Monroe	51	Steuben
07	Chautauqua	29	Montgomery		
08	Chemung			52	Suffolk
09	Chenango	30	Nassau	53	Sullivan
10	Clinton	31	New York	54	Tioga
11	Columbia	32	Niagara	55	Tompkins
12	Cortland	33	Oneida	56	Ulster
		34	Onondaga		
13	Delaware	35	Ontario	57	Warren
14	Dutchess	36	Orange	58	Washington
				59	Wayne
15	Erie	37	Orleans	60	Westchester
16	Essex	38	Oswego	61	Wyoming
17	Franklin	39	Otsego		
18	Fulton	40	Putnam		
19	Genesee			62	Yates
20	Greene	41	Queens		
21	Hamilton				
22	Herkimer	42	Rensselaer		
		43	Richmond		
23	Jefferson	44	Rockland		

AADSAS

APPLICATION FORM
1986
ENTERING CLASS

Please read instructions carefully before
attempting to complete the application.

YOU SHOULD RETAIN THESE INSTRUCTIONS AND A
PHOTOCOPY OF YOUR APPLICATION FORM UNTIL YOU
HAVE COMPLETED THE APPLICATION PROCESS. IT WILL
BE NECESSARY TO REFER TO THESE MATERIALS WHEN
YOU RECEIVE YOUR SCREENING COPY AND ACADEMIC
UPDATE FORM

INTRODUCTION

This AADSAS Application Form has been designed to assist you in providing detailed information to the dental schools that will receive your application materials. Because the transmission of accurate and complete data about your educational and personal history is so necessary if you are to be a successful applicant for admission to dental school, we strongly recommend that you familiarize yourself with the instructions before attempting to complete any part of the Application Form. Close attention to the specific instructions on the Application Form itself and in the Instruction Book will not only assist you in completing it more quickly, but will help insure that all information schools receive about you is timely and reliable.

Based upon the verification of an alleged irregularity (i.e., the misrepresentation of information) in an applicant's application materials, the American Association of Dental Schools reserves the right to notify member institutions of the irregularity.

Use a soft lead pencil to fill in the form beginning on the opposite page. If you make a mistake, erase it completely and enter the correct response as legibly as possible. Be sure to fill in the boxes in each item of the Form beginning with the first box on the left of the page. Enter only one character, including spaces, per box. For alphabetic data, leave remaining right hand boxes blank. For example, if your name were Jones, you would enter it in Item 1 like this:

| J | O | N | E | S | | | |

When you enter numerical data always use leading zeroes. For example, if your answer to Item 6 was $60.00 you would enter the figure like this:

$ | 0 | 6 | 0 | . | 0 | 0 |

If you should inadvertently damage your Application Form beyond use, notify AADSAS immediately and we will supply you with a replacement.

You should keep a copy of your completed application, with instructions, for future reference. Some information contained in the application booklet will be helpful in making corrections on your Screening Copy and in completing the Academic Update form at a later date.

FOR AADSAS USE ONLY
DO NOT WRITE HERE

AADSAS I.D.

DATE OF RECEIPT

$ | | | . | | | AMT. REC'D. | | | SCHOOLS

IDENTIFICATION

1 LAST NAME

2 FIRST NAME

3 MIDDLE INITIAL

4 [ ] [ ] – [ ] [ ] – [ ] [ ] [ ] [ ]   SOCIAL SECURITY NUMBER

INSTRUCTIONS

NAME
Enter your last name, first name, and middle initial.

SOCIAL SECURITY NUMBER
Enter your social security number. It will help insure identification of your application and all subsequent materials you provide either to AADSAS or dental schools. If you do not have a social security number, record 000-00-0000.

SELECTION OF DENTAL SCHOOLS
Place an X in the box next to each dental school to which you wish to apply. Mark the schools carefully. Once your application is submitted you may not change the schools you selected without incurring extra request fees. No new applications can be processed beyond March 1.

5

SCHOOLS	DEADLINE
01 California, U. of at Los Angeles	
02 Florida, U. of	10/15/85
03 Washington, U. of, at Seattle	
04 West Virginia University	11/1/85
05 SUNY at Buffalo	11/30/85
06 California, U. of, San Francisco	
07 Harvard University	
08 Indiana University	
09 Loma Linda University	
10 Louisville, U. of (03/01/86 — Kentucky residents)	12/1/85
11 Maryland, U. of	
12 Missouri, U. of, Kansas City	
13 Nebraska, U. of	
14 North Carolina, U. of	
15 Pittsburgh, U. of	
16 New Jersey Dental	
17 Pacific, U. of the	12/15/85
18 Puerto Rico, U. of	
19 Illinois, U. of	
20 Loyola University	12/31/85
21 Northwestern University	
22 Boston University	
23 Connecticut, U. of	1/1/86
24 Pennsylvania, U. of	

SCHOOLS	DEADLINE
25 Tufts University	1/1/86
26 Washington, U. of, St. Louis	
27 Alabama, U. of	1/31/86
28 SUNY at Stony Brook	
29 Columbia University	
30 Iowa, U. of	
31 Michigan, U. of	
32 Ohio State University	2/1/86
33 Oklahoma, U. of	
34 Southern California, U. of	
35 Virginia Commonwealth U.	
36 Case Western Reserve U.	
37 Colorado, U. of	
38 Creighton University	
39 Detroit, U. of	
40 Fairleigh Dickinson U.	
41 Georgetown University	
42 Howard University	3/1/86
43 Kentucky, U. of	
44 Marquette University	
45 Meharry Medical College	
46 Minnesota, U. of	
47 Mississippi, U. of	
48 New York University	

SCHOOLS	DEADLINE
49 Oral Roberts University	
50 Southern Illinois U.	
51 Temple University	3/1/86

HOW TO CALCULATE YOUR AADSAS PROCESSING FEE

The AADSAS Processing Fee is $60.00 for the first school and $7.50 for each additional school to which you apply at the time of your original application.

A. ☐ Enter the number of schools to which you are applying (the number of schools checked in Item 5).

B. ☐ Subtract 1 from the number entered in box A and enter the result in box B.

C. $ ☐ Multiply the number in box B by $7.50 and enter the total in box C.

D. $ ☐ Add $60.00 to the number in box C and enter the sum in box D.

E. Enter the amount in box D in Item number 6 to left of this page. This is your AADSAS Processing Fee. Please make your check or money order payable *in U.S. currency* to AADSAS (Do NOT send cash).

NOTE: If your check or money order is not sufficient to cover processing of your application to all the schools you selected in Item 5, your payment will be applied to schools in the order they are listed. Application materials will not be sent to any schools for which the entire processing fee has not been received. Any excess will be refunded to you.

6 $ ☐☐☐ . ☐☐ AMOUNT ENCLOSED

AADSAS POLICY FOR BAD CHECKS

A penalty of $10.00 will be assessed by AADSAS for processing fee checks that do not clear the bank after it has been deposited twice. Checks that are returned for "insufficient funds" will be deposited twice, and if returned a second time due to insufficient funds you will receive written notification from AADSAS advising you to pay the fee by Certified Check or Money order within a designated period of time. Checks returned for any reason must be paid within a designated period of time or your application will be held until payment is received. If the application has been transmitted to your schools, and you do not comply within the time designated, AADSAS will advise the schools of your default and you will not be considered as a candidate for admission during the cycle.

INSTRUCTIONS

CURRENT ADDRESS AND PHONE NUMBER
Enter your current mailing address. Since this is the address which AADSAS and dental schools will use to contact you, be certain it is correct. Abbreviate where necessary.

If your address is in the United States, use the State Codes listed in the Instructions. If your address is not in the United States, use the Non-U.S. codes listed in the Instructions, page 18.

Enter the Zip Code of your current address if you live in the U.S. If you have no Zip Code, enter 00000.

Enter the telephone number (including area code) where you can be reached now. If you do not have a telephone or have a phone number (including area code) of other than 10 digits, enter 000/000-0000.

PERMANENT ADDRESS AND PHONE NUMBER
Enter the street address and city of your permanent address. Dental schools will consider this as your legal residence.

Use the State Codes listed in the Instructions on page 18. If your address is not in the U.S., use the Non-U.S. Codes listed in the Instructions, page 18.

Enter the Zip Code of your permanent address. If your permanent address has no Zip Code, enter 00000.

CURRENT ADDRESS

7   STREET, LINE 1

8   STREET, LINE 2

9   CITY

10   STATE OR COUNTRY

11   ZIP CODE

12   / -   CURRENT TELEPHONE

PERMANENT ADDRESS

13   STREET, LINE 1

14   STREET, LINE 2

15   CITY

16   STATE OR COUNTRY

17   ZIP CODE

18 ☐☐☐☐☐☐☐☐☐☐ COUNTY

Enter the county (not country or city) of your legal residence. If you reside in a foreign country or area where the designation "county" is not used, enter "NOT APPLICABLE" for this item.

19 ☐☐☐/☐☐☐-☐☐☐☐ PERMANENT TELEPHONE

Enter your permanent telephone number, including the area code. If you do not have a permanent telephone or have a phone number (including area code) of other than 10 digits, enter 000/000-0000.

PARENTAL AND FAMILY INFORMATION

20 ☐☐☐☐☐☐☐☐☐☐ LAST NAME

21 ☐☐☐☐☐☐☐☐☐ FIRST NAME

PARENT'S NAME, ADDRESS AND PHONE NUMBER
Enter the full name of one of your parents (or legal guardian). If both parents are deceased and you have no legal guardian, enter "NONE" in Item 20 and leave Items 21-28 blank.

22 ☐ MIDDLE INITIAL

23 ☐☐☐☐☐☐☐☐☐☐ STREET, LINE 1

Enter your parent's address, using the appropriate State or Non-U. S. Codes. Page 18 of the Instruction Booklet.

24 ☐☐☐☐☐☐☐☐☐☐ STREET, LINE 2

25 ☐☐☐☐☐☐☐☐ CITY

26 ☐☐ STATE OR COUNTRY

27 ☐☐☐☐☐ ZIP CODE

Enter the Zip Code of your parent's address. If your parent's address has no Zip Code, enter 00000 in the Zip Code boxes.

28 ☐☐☐/☐☐☐-☐☐☐☐ TELEPHONE

Enter your parent's telephone number. If there is no telephone at the address you listed, or if the number (including area code) is other than 10 digits, enter 000/000-0000.

INSTRUCTIONS

PARENTS' STATUS
Indicate whether or not each of your parents is living by entering the appropriate number for Items 29 and 30.
1 Living
2 Deceased

PARENTS' EDUCATION
Indicate the highest level of education each of your parents attained by entering the appropriate number for each. These Items are to be completed even if your parents are deceased.

1 Graduate Degree
2 Some Graduate School
3 College Graduate
4 Some College
5 Business/Technical School
6 High School Graduate
7 Some High School
8 Elementary Education
9 Some Elementary
0 Unknown

PARENTS' OCCUPATION
Turn to the Occupation Codes, page 20 in the Instructions, and enter the appropriate Occupation Code for each parent. These items are to be completed even if your parents are deceased.

FAMILY SIZE
Indicate the number of brothers and sisters you have by entering the total. If you have more than 9 brothers and sisters, enter 9.

HIGH SCHOOL INFORMATION
Enter the name and city of the high school you last attended.

29 ☐ FATHER

30 ☐ MOTHER

31 ☐ FATHER

32 ☐ MOTHER

33 ☐ FATHER

34 ☐ MOTHER

35 ☐ FAMILY SIZE

EDUCATIONAL HISTORY

36 SCHOOL NAME

37 CITY

38 ☐☐ STATE OR COUNTRY

Enter the State Code. If your high school was not in the United States, enter the Non-U.S. Code, page 18 in the Instructions.

39 ☐☐ YEAR GRADUATED

Enter the last two digits of the year you completed high school.

40 ☐ RANK IN CLASS

Enter the appropriate number from the list below to indicate your percentile rank in your high school graduating class. (For example, if you were in the top 10% of your class, enter 1.)

1 90 and over	4 25-49
2 75-89	5 1-24
3 50-74	6 Not sure

41 ☐

UNDERGRADUATE (COLLEGE) INFORMATION
Enter the appropriate number from the list below to indicate your year in college as of Fall, 1985

1 Freshman
2 Sophomore
3 Junior
4 Senior
5 Graduate student (inc. professional school)
6 Other

42 ☐☐ UNDERGRADUATE MAJOR

Turn to the Major Fields of Study Codes in the Instructions. Enter the appropriate code for your undergraduate (college) major. Enter one code only, even if you had a second major.

43 ☐ UNDERGRADUATE DEGREE/CERTIFICATE EARNED

Enter the appropriate number or alphabet from the list below to indicate the highest undergraduate (college) degree/certificate which you have already earned. If you have not received a degree/certificate, enter D.

1 A.A.	A C.D.A
2 B.A.	B C.D.T.
3 B.S.	C Other
4 R.D.H.	D None
5 R.D.A.	

44 ☐☐ / ☐☐ DATE OF UNDERGRADUATE DEGREE/CERTIFICATE

Enter the month and year in which you received the undergraduate degree/certificate listed in Item 43. If you entered D for Item 43, enter 00/00 for this item.

45 ☐☐☐☐☐ SCHOOL CONFERRING UNDERGRADUATE DEGREE/CERTIFICATE

Turn to the College Codes in the Instructions, pages 27-54. Enter the appropriate code for the school which conferred the undergraduate degree/certificate reported in Item 43. If you entered D for Item 43, enter 000000 for this item.

46 ☐☐ GRADUATE MAJOR

GRADUATE SCHOOL INFORMATION
Turn to the Major Fields of Study Codes, page 21 in the Instructions. Enter the appropriate code for your graduate major. If you have not been or are not in a graduate program, enter 88 for "no major." If your major is not listed, enter 99 for "other."

47 ☐ GRADUATE DEGREE EARNED

Enter the appropriate number from the list below to indicate the highest graduate or professional degree you have earned. If you have earned no graduate or professional degrees, enter 8.

1 M.A.
2 M.S.
3 M.B.A.
4 Other Masters
5 Ph.D.
6 Other Doctorate
7 Other
8 None

48 ☐☐ / ☐☐ DATE OF GRADUATE DEGREE

Enter the month and year in which you received the degree in Item 47. If you entered 8 for Item 47, enter 00/00 for this Item.

49 ☐☐☐☐☐ SCHOOL CONFERRING GRADUATE DEGREE

Turn to the College Codes, pages 27-54 in the Instructions. Enter the code of the school which conferred your highest graduate or professional degree. If you entered 8 for Item 47, enter 000000 for this Item.

INSTRUCTIONS

ANTICIPATED DEGREE/CERTIFICATE

If you are currently in a degree or certification program, enter the appropriate number or alphabet from the list below to indicate the degree/certificate which you anticipate receiving. If you anticipate no degree or certificate enter D.

1 A.A.	4 M.A.	7 Ph.D.	A. C.D.A.
2 B.A.	5 M.S.	8 R.D.H.	B. C.D.T.
3 B.S.	6 M.B.A.	9 R.D.A.	C. Other
			D. None

If you anticipate a degree, enter your Major Field of Study Code. If you entered D in Item 50, enter 88 for this Item.

Enter the month and year you anticipate receiving the degree/certificate you reported in Item 50. If you entered D. for Item 50, enter 00/00 for this Item.

If you indicated an anticipated degree/certificate in Item 50, enter the College Code of the institution that will be conferring your degree/certificate. If you entered D for Item 50, enter 000000 for this Item.

DAT INFORMATION

Enter the month and year of the most recent time you took the Dental Admission Test (DAT). If you have not taken the DAT, enter 00/00. Enter scores below.

If your most recent DAT test was after April 1981, you will not have a 2-D and 3-D score to report. Leave these blocks BLANK. *DO NOT ENTER DASHES or ZEROS.*

If you plan to take DAT in the future, enter the number of the test date.
1   October, 1984
2   April, 1985

---

50 ☐ ANTICIPATED DEGREE/CERTIFICATE

51 ☐☐☐ ANTICIPATED MAJOR

52 ☐☐ / ☐☐ DATE OF ANTICIPATED DEGREE/CERTIFICATE

53 ☐☐☐☐☐☐ SCHOOL CONFERRING ANTICIPATED DEGREE/CERTIFICATE

DENTAL ADMISSION TEST

54 ☐☐ / ☐☐ MOST RECENT DAT

DAT SCORES

Most Recent									
Academic Avg.	PAT Avg.	Quant. Reas.	Verbal Reas.	Read. Comp.	Biology	Chem. Inorg.	Chem. Org.	Total Sci.	PAT 2-D	PAT 3-D

55 ☐ FUTURE DAT

EXTRACURRICULAR ACTIVITIES

56 ☐ MUSIC

57 ☐ ATHLETICS

58 ☐ DEBATE/WRITING

59 ☐ STUDENT GOVERNMENT

60 ☐ HEALTH SERVICES

61 ☐ ART/DRAMA

62 ☐ SORORITY/FRATERNITY

63 ☐ RELIGIOUS GROUP

64 ☐ COMMUNITY SERVICE

65 ☐ POLITICAL GROUP

66 ☐ OTHER ACTIVITY

PERSONAL DATA

67 ☐☐ / ☐☐ / ☐☐ DATE OF BIRTH

68 ☐☐☐☐☐☐☐☐☐☐☐☐☐☐☐☐☐☐ CITY OF BIRTH

69 ☐☐ STATE OR COUNTRY

70 ☐ CITIZENSHIP

71 ☐ SEX

INSTRUCTIONS

EXTRACURRICULAR ACTIVITIES
These items list various kinds of extracurricular activities you may have been involved in during your college or graduate school years. Enter one of the following numbers:

1. Participant
2. Participant and Leader
3. Not involved

BIRTH DATE AND PLACE
Enter the number of the month, day, and last two digits of the year you were born.

Enter the name of the city, and code of the state or country in which you were born.

CITIZENSHIP
If you are a citizen of the United States, enter 1. If not, enter 2.

SEX
Enter 1 Male
2 Female

ETHNIC IDENTIFICATION
Indicate your ethnic identification by entering the number of the appropriate category.

1 American Indian or Alaskan Native
2 Asian or Pacific Islander
3 Black or Negro (not of Hispanic Origin)
4 White or Caucasian (not of Hispanic Origin)
5 Hispanic
6 Do not wish to report ethnic data

FINANCIAL DATA
Do you consider yourself financially independent from your parents or guardian? Enter the appropriate number.
1 Yes   2 No

What percentage of your undergraduate expenses (including tuition, books, and living expenses) did you earn? Enter the estimated percentage. If you did not earn part of your undergraduate expenses, enter 000.

Enter the estimated amount (in U.S. dollars) you expect to receive annually from each of the sources listed to finance your dental education (including tuition, books, supplies, instruments and fees, but excluding living costs). Enter 0000 for sources from which you expect no funds; enter 9999 if the amount you expect to receive from any source exceeds $9,999 per year.

Enter the number of dependents you have (include yourself. If you have no other dependents than yourself, enter 1. If you have more than 9 dependents, enter 9.

SUPPLEMENTARY INFORMATION
These items should be answered by entering the appropriate response.
1 Yes   2 No

---

72 ☐ ETHNIC IDENTIFICATION

FINANCIAL DATA

73 ☐ FINANCIAL INDEPENDENCE

74 ☐☐☐ PERCENTAGE EXPENSES EARNED

75 $ ☐☐☐☐☐ .00 PARENTS/RELATIVES
76 $ ☐☐☐☐☐ .00 SAVINGS/PART-TIME WORK
77 $ ☐☐☐☐☐ .00 VETERAN'S BENEFITS
78 $ ☐☐☐☐☐ .00 OTHER

79 ☐ NUMBER OF DEPENDENTS

SUPPLEMENTARY INFORMATION

80 ☐ Have you previously attended a health professional school?

81 ☐ Have you previously applied to but not attended a health professional school?

INSTRUCTIONS

SUPPLEMENTARY INFORMATION (continued)
These items should be answered by entering the appropriate response.
1 Yes   2 No

82 ☐ Will you apply to a health professional school (other than dental) this year?

83 ☐ Has your education ever been interrupted or affected adversely because of deficiencies in conduct or scholarship?

84 ☐ Has your education ever been interrupted or affected adversely for reasons other than conduct or scholarship?

85 ☐ Were you employed while attending college?

86 ☐ Did you hold summer jobs during your college years?

87 ☐ Do you have relatives who are dentists or are in dental school?

88 ☐ Are you currently in school?

89 ☐ Did you receive any scholastic honors in college?

90 ☐ Have you had any previous military experience?

91 ☐ May AADSAS release the information on this form to your predental advisor?

Predental advisors use information reported by applicants to assist students who will apply to dental school in the future. To help both advisors and future applicants from your school, you should indicate whether the information you have reported may be released to the predental advisor at your undergraduate school by entering either:
1 Yes 2 No

92 ☐ Do you wish to participate in the AADSAS Application Clearinghouse?   1 Yes 2 No

The purpose is to provide an opportunity for AADSAS schools to consider applicants from a larger pool and assist applicants who have not been accepted to a dental school. On or about May 1, 1986 all applicants who have not received an acceptance to dental school and have answered yes to this question will have certain academic and demographic information extracted from their data file and entered on a roster with other applicants who qualify. This roster will be sent to all AADSAS schools requesting it. If the school is interested in you as an applicant, they will contact you.

INSTRUCTIONS

SAMPLE: Completed Coursework Entry

The information shown below (A) is a sample of coursework which might be found on a college transcript and (B) the way it should be entered using the codes provided in the Instruction Booklet.

A.

University of Alabama	2nd Semester	1/71-6/71
Course	Grade	Credit Hours
English	A	3
Biology	B+	4½
History	W	3
Physical Education	A	1
German	P	3

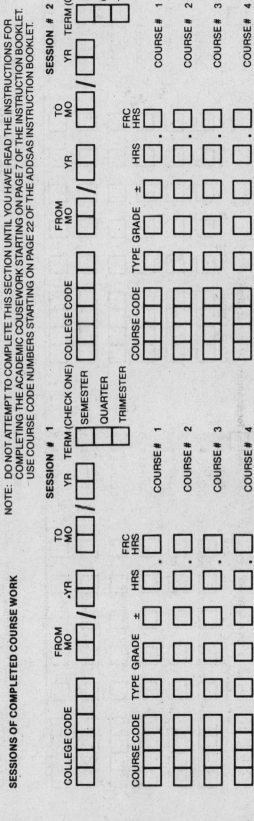

SESSIONS OF COMPLETED COURSE WORK

NOTE: DO NOT ATTEMPT TO COMPLETE THIS SECTION UNTIL YOU HAVE READ THE INSTRUCTIONS FOR COMPLETING THE ACADEMIC COUSEWORK STARTING ON PAGE 7 OF THE INSTRUCTION BOOKLET. USE COURSE CODE NUMBERS STARTING ON PAGE 22 OF THE ADDSAS INSTRUCTION BOOKLET.

SESSIONS OF COMPLETED COURSE WORK

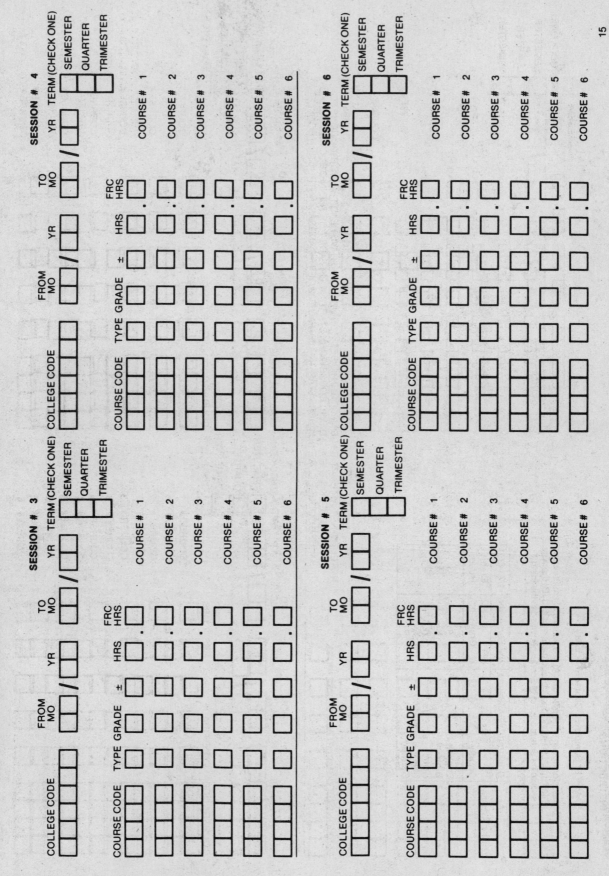

SESSIONS OF COMPLETED COURSE WORK

SESSION # 7

COLLEGE CODE

FROM MO / YR   TO MO / YR   TERM (CHECK ONE): SEMESTER / QUARTER / TRIMESTER

COURSE CODE   TYPE   GRADE ±   HRS   FRC HRS

COURSE # 1
COURSE # 2
COURSE # 3
COURSE # 4
COURSE # 5
COURSE # 6

SESSION # 8

COLLEGE CODE

FROM MO / YR   TO MO / YR   TERM (CHECK ONE): SEMESTER / QUARTER / TRIMESTER

COURSE CODE   TYPE   GRADE ±   HRS   FRC HRS

COURSE # 1
COURSE # 2
COURSE # 3
COURSE # 4
COURSE # 5
COURSE # 6

SESSION # 9

COLLEGE CODE

FROM MO / YR   TO MO / YR   TERM (CHECK ONE): SEMESTER / QUARTER / TRIMESTER

COURSE CODE   TYPE   GRADE ±   HRS   FRC HRS

COURSE # 1
COURSE # 2
COURSE # 3
COURSE # 4
COURSE # 5
COURSE # 6

SESSION # 10

COLLEGE CODE

FROM MO / YR   TO MO / YR   TERM (CHECK ONE): SEMESTER / QUARTER / TRIMESTER

COURSE CODE   TYPE   GRADE ±   HRS   FRC HRS

COURSE # 1
COURSE # 2
COURSE # 3
COURSE # 4
COURSE # 5
COURSE # 6

SESSIONS OF COMPLETED COURSE WORK

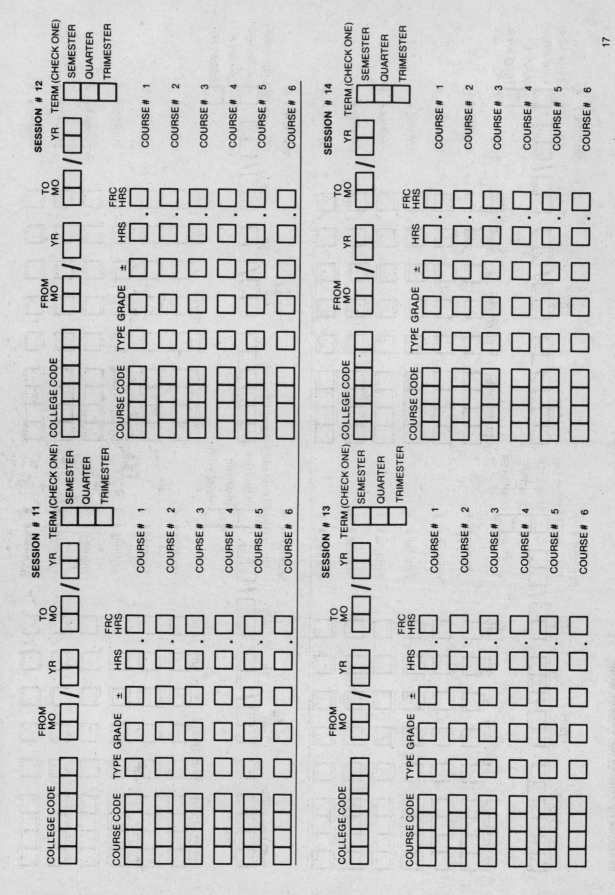

SESSIONS OF COMPLETED COURSE WORK

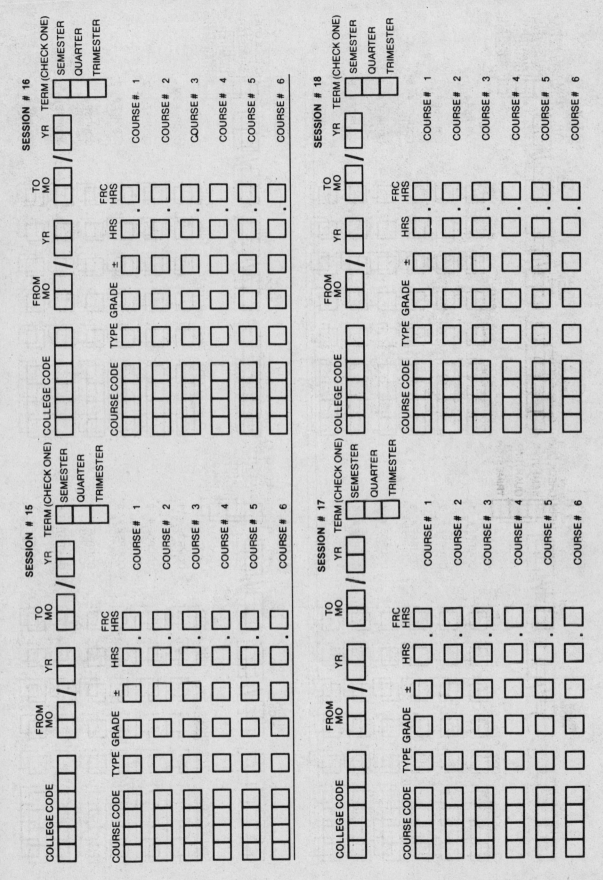

SESSIONS OF COMPLETED COURSE WORK

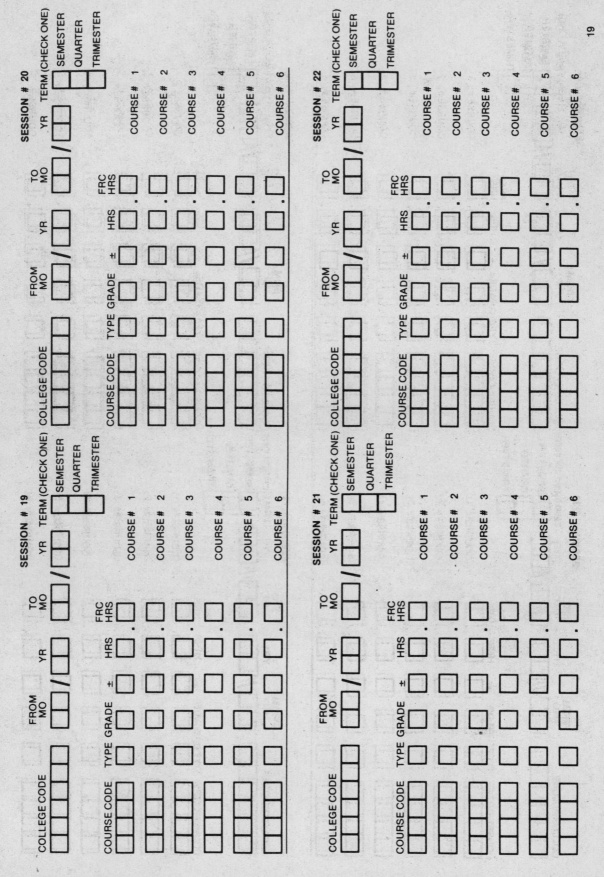

SESSIONS OF COMPLETED COURSE WORK

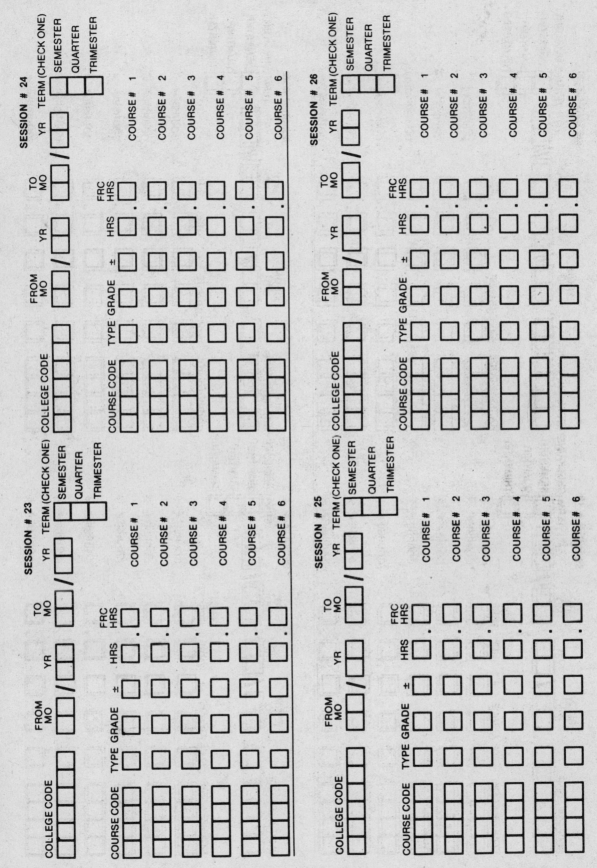

SESSIONS OF COMPLETED COURSE WORK

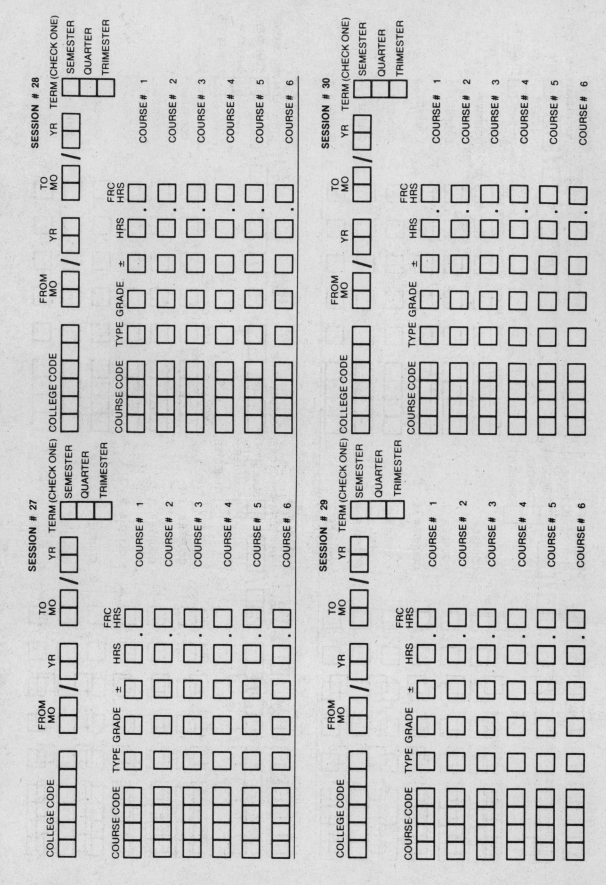

SESSIONS OF COURSES IN PROGRESS

INSTRUCTIONS

This page has been provided so that you may record coursework not currently completed but in which you are now enrolled.

COURSES IN PROGRESS
Record all coursework you are taking now. List the courses and hours as you registered for them. There will, of course, be no grades to report.

Refer to samples of coursework entries and other Instructions on page 14 of this Booklet.

SESSION IN PROGRESS # 1

FROM MO / YR   TO MO / YR   TERM (CHECK ONE)
SEMESTER
QUARTER
TRIMESTER

COLLEGE CODE

COURSE CODE   TYPE   HRS . FRC HRS

COURSE # 1
COURSE # 2
COURSE # 3
COURSE # 4
COURSE # 5
COURSE # 6

SESSION IN PROGRESS # 2

FROM MO / YR   TO MO / YR   TERM (CHECK ONE)
SEMESTER
QUARTER
TRIMESTER

COLLEGE CODE

COURSE CODE   TYPE   HRS . FRC HRS

COURSE # 1
COURSE # 2
COURSE # 3
COURSE # 4
COURSE # 5
COURSE # 6

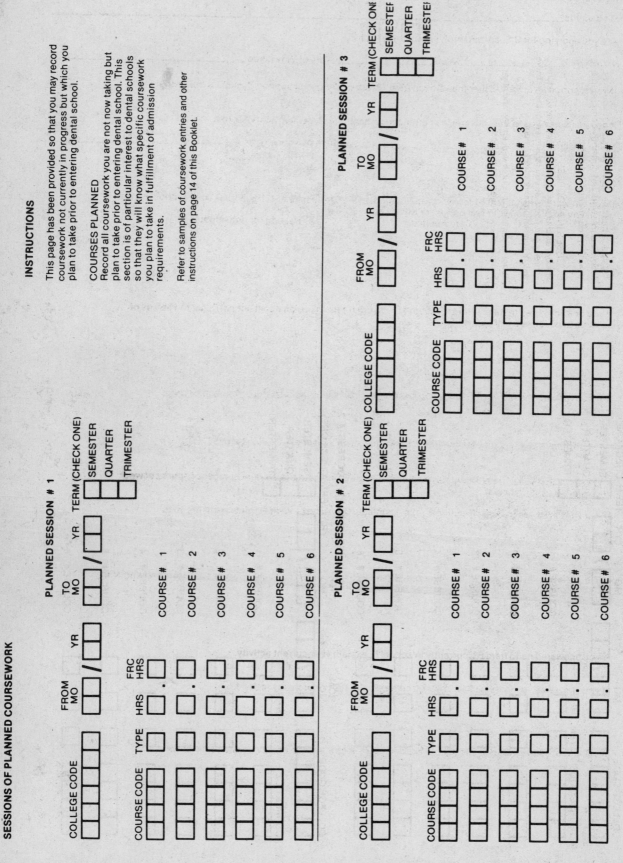

SESSIONS OF PLANNED COURSEWORK

INSTRUCTIONS

This page has been provided so that you may record coursework not currently in progress but which you plan to take prior to entering dental school.

COURSES PLANNED

Record all coursework you are not now taking but plan to take prior to entering dental school. This section is of particular interest to dental schools so that they will know what specific coursework you plan to take in fulfillment of admission requirements.

Refer to samples of coursework entries and other instructions on page 14 of this Booklet.

PLANNED SESSION # 1

COLLEGE CODE

FROM MO / YR. TO MO / YR. TERM (CHECK ONE) SEMESTER QUARTER TRIMESTER

COURSE CODE TYPE HRS FRC HRS
COURSE # 1
COURSE # 2
COURSE # 3
COURSE # 4
COURSE # 5
COURSE # 6

PLANNED SESSION # 2

COLLEGE CODE

FROM MO / YR TO MO / YR TERM (CHECK ONE) SEMESTER QUARTER TRIMESTER

COURSE CODE TYPE HRS FRC HRS
COURSE # 1
COURSE # 2
COURSE # 3
COURSE # 4
COURSE # 5
COURSE # 6

PLANNED SESSION # 3

COLLEGE CODE

FROM MO / YR TO MO / YR TERM (CHECK ONE) SEMESTER QUARTER TRIMESTER

COURSE CODE TYPE HRS FRC HRS
COURSE # 1
COURSE # 2
COURSE # 3
COURSE # 4
COURSE # 5
COURSE # 6

THE SPACE BELOW IS PROVIDED FOR EXPLANATION OF ITEMS 70, 78, AND 80-90.

70. If you answered no to Item 7 (U.S. Citizenship?), indicate:

Citizenship_____

Are you applying for U.S. citizenship? Yes ☐ No ☐

Visa Type _____ Visa# _____ City of Visa Issue _____

78. If you reported an amount other than zero in Item 78 (other sources of support?), explain the source.

80. If you answered yes to Item 80 (previous attendance, health professional school?), list:

Name of school_____ Dates of Attendance_____
Reasons for leaving

81. If you answered yes to Item 81 (previous application, health professional school?), list each school, the year which you applied and your reason for not attending.

School   Date Applied   Reason for not Attending

82. If you answered yes to Item 82 (current application, other health professional school?), list the names of schools to which you will apply.

83. If you answered yes to Item 83 (education interrupted, conduct or scholarship?), explain below.

84. If you answered yes to Item 84 (education interrupted, other reasons?), explain below.

85. If you answered yes to Item 85 (employed during college?), indicate the average number of hours per week you worked: _____ hours.

86. If you answered yes to Item 86 (summer jobs?), indicate the name of each employer and the year.

87. If you answered yes to Item 87 (relatives who are dentists?), indicate the name of each relative, his relationship to you, the school attended and the dates of attendance.

88. If you answered no to Item 88 (currently in school?), explain your current activity.

89. If you answered yes to Item 89 (scholastic honors?), list the honors you received.

90. If you answered yes to Item 90 (military experience?), list the branch of service and dates of service.

USE INK, BALLPOINT PEN OR SEPARATE THIS PAGE AND TYPE

In the space below, state concisely why you are interested in the dental profession. This space should also be used to provide any additional information of significance to your application, e.g., extracurricular activities, secondary majors or degrees, experience in a health care delivery setting, pertinent research, publications, etc. *You must limit your response to the space provided.*

I certify the information I have recorded to be complete and accurate to the best of my knowledge. I authorize AADSAS to release the information reported on this Application Form to the schools I designate, and to use this information for research purposes.

_____   _____   _____
NAME (printed)   SIGNATURE   DATE

APPENDIX B

MAJOR PROFESSIONAL ORGANIZATIONS

American Academy of Family Physicians
1740 West 92nd Street
Kansas City, Missouri 64114

American Academy of Ophthalmology and Otolaryngology
15 Second Street, S.W.
Rochester, Minnesota 55901

American Academy of Orthopaedic Surgeons
430 North Michigan Avenue
Chicago, Illinois 60611

American Academy of Pediatrics
1801 Hinman Avenue
Evanston, Illinois 60204

American Academy of Physical Medicine and Rehabilitation
30 North Michigan Avenue, Suite 922
Chicago, Illinois 60602

American Association of Colleges of Osteopathic Medicine
4720 Montgomery Lane
Bethesda, Maryland 20014

American Association of Dental Schools
1625 Massachusetts Avenue, N.W.
Washington, D.C. 20036

American Association of Neurological Surgeons
428 East Preston Street
Baltimore, Maryland 21202

American Association of Ophthalmology
1100 17th Street, N.W., Suite 304
Washington, D.C. 20036

American Association of Orthodontists
7477 Delmar Boulevard
St. Louis, Missouri 63130

American Association of Public Health Physicians
1703 Ridgemont
Austin, Texas 78723

American Board of Medical Specialties
1603 Orrington Avenue, Suite 1160
Evanston, Illinois 60201

American College of Cardiology
9650 Rockville Pike
Bethesda, Maryland 20014

American College of Chest Physicians
911 Busse Highway
Park Ridge, Illinois 60068

American College of Obstetricians and Gynecologists
One East Wacker Drive, Suite 2700
Chicago, Illinois 60601

American College of Physicians
4200 Pine Street
Philadelphia, Pennsylvania 19104

American College of Preventive Medicine
801 Old Lancaster Road
Bryn Mawr, Pennsylvania 19010

American College of Radiology
20 North Wacker Drive, Suite 2920
Chicago, Illinois 60606

American College of Surgeons
55 East Erie Street
Chicago, Illinois 60611

American Dental Association
211 East Chicago Avenue
Chicago, Illinois 60611

American Federation for Clinical Research
6900 Grove Road
Thorofare, New Jersey 08086

American Hospital Association
840 North Lake Shore Drive
Chicago, Illinois 60611

American Medical Association
535 North Dearborn Street
Chicago, Illinois 60610

American Ophthalmological Society
Mayo Clinic
200 First Street, S.W.
Rochester, Minnesota 55901

American Osteopathic Hospital Association
930 Busse Highway
Park Ridge, Illinois 60068

American Osteopathic Association
212 East Ohio Street
Chicago, Illinois 60611

American Psychiatric Association
1700 Eighteenth Street, N.W.
Washington, D.C. 20009

American Society of Anesthesiologists
515 Busse Highway
Park Ridge, Illinois 60068

American Society of Clinical Pathologists
2100 West Harrison Street
Chicago, Illinois 60612

Association of American Medical Colleges
One Dupont Circle, N.W.
Washington, D.C. 20036

College of American Pathologists
7400 Skokie Boulevard
Skokie, Illinois 60076

Educational Council for Foreign Medical Graduates
3624 Market Street
Philadelphia, Pennsylvania 19104

National Dental Association
735 Fifteenth Street, N.W.
Washington, D.C. 20005

National Medical Association
1720 Massachusetts Avenue, N.W.
Washington, D.C. 20036

Student American Medical Association
1400 Huks Road
Rolling Meadows, Illinois 60008

APPENDIX C

REGIONAL MAPS

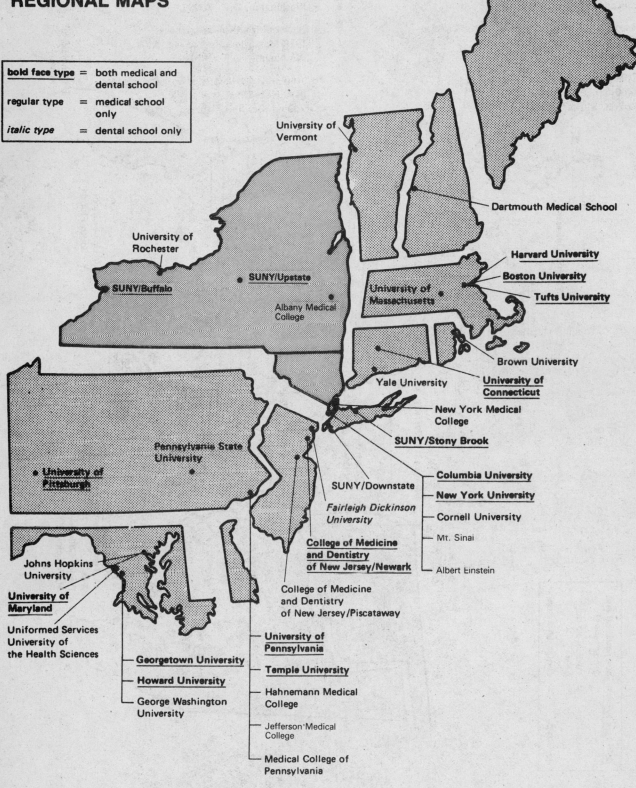

bold face type = both medical and dental school

regular type = medical school only

italic type = dental school only

University of Vermont

Dartmouth Medical School

University of Rochester

Harvard University

Boston University

Tufts University

SUNY/Upstate

University of Massachusetts

SUNY/Buffalo

Albany Medical College

Brown University

University of Connecticut

Yale University

New York Medical College

SUNY/Stony Brook

Pennsylvania State University

Columbia University

New York University

University of Pittsburgh

SUNY/Downstate

Cornell University

Fairleigh Dickinson University

Mt. Sinai

Albert Einstein

College of Medicine and Dentistry of New Jersey/Newark

Johns Hopkins University

College of Medicine and Dentistry of New Jersey/Piscataway

University of Maryland

Uniformed Services University of the Health Sciences

University of Pennsylvania

Georgetown University

Temple University

Howard University

Hahnemann Medical College

George Washington University

Jefferson Medical College

Medical College of Pennsylvania

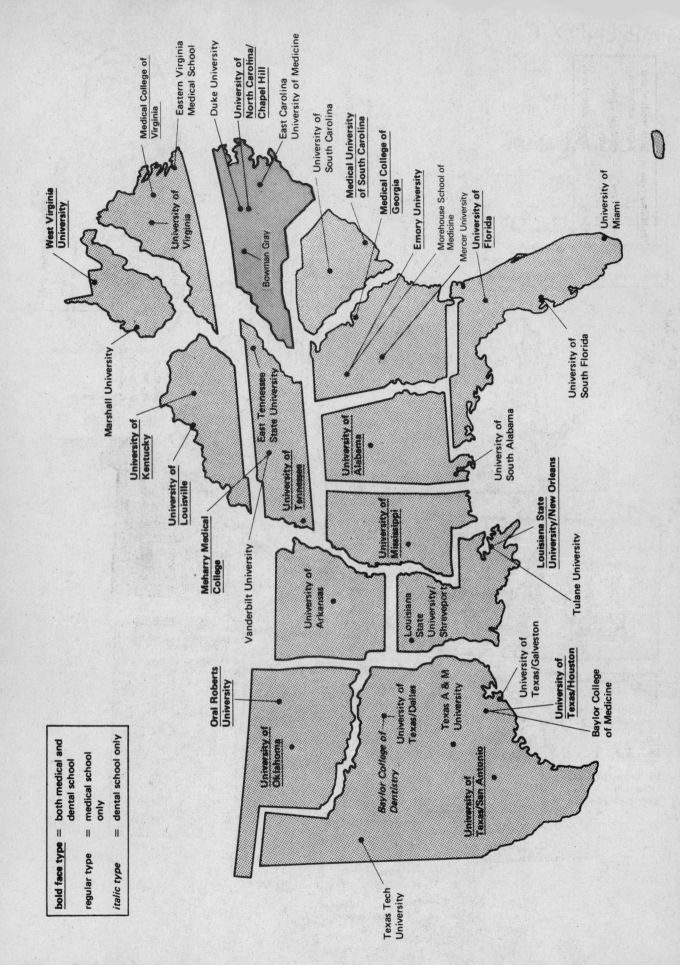

bold face type = both medical and dental school

regular type = medical school only

italic type = dental school only

West Virginia University

Medical College of Virginia

Eastern Virginia Medical School

Duke University

University of North Carolina/ Chapel Hill

East Carolina University of Medicine

University of South Carolina

Medical University of South Carolina

Medical College of Georgia

Morehouse School of Medicine

Emory University

Mercer University

University of Florida

University of Miami

University of Virginia

Marshall University

Bowman Gray

University of Kentucky

University of Louisville

East Tennessee State University

University of Tennessee

Meharry Medical College

Vanderbilt University

University of Alabama

University of South Alabama

University of South Florida

University of Mississippi

Louisiana State University/New Orleans

Tulane University

University of Arkansas

Louisiana State University/ Shreveport

Oral Roberts University

University of Oklahoma

Baylor College of Dentistry

University of Texas/Dallas

Texas A & M University

University of Texas/Galveston

University of Texas/Houston

Baylor College of Medicine

University of Texas/San Antonio

Texas Tech University

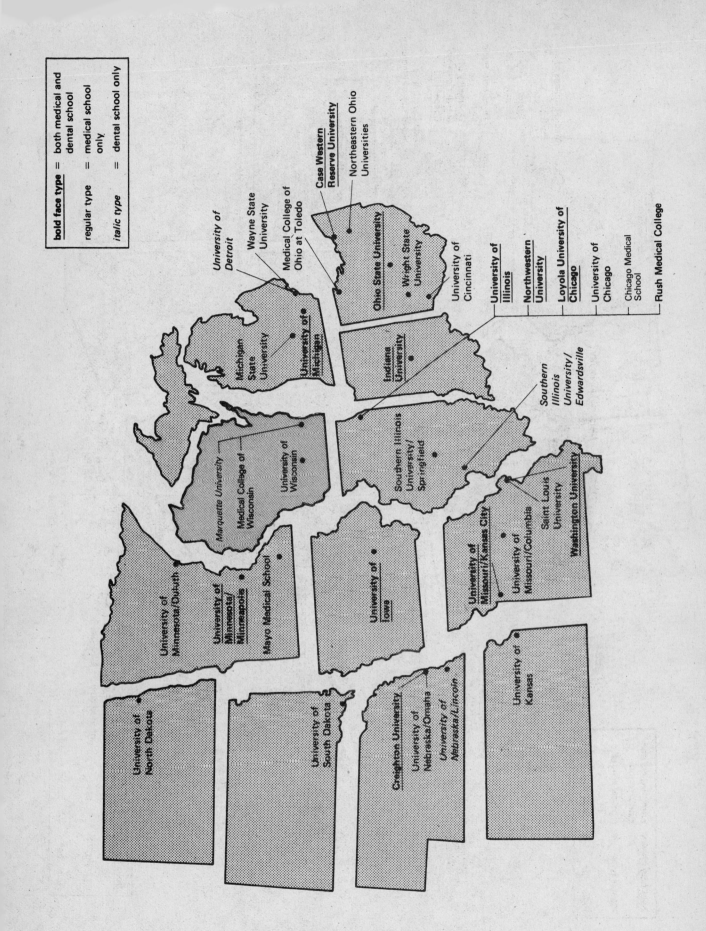

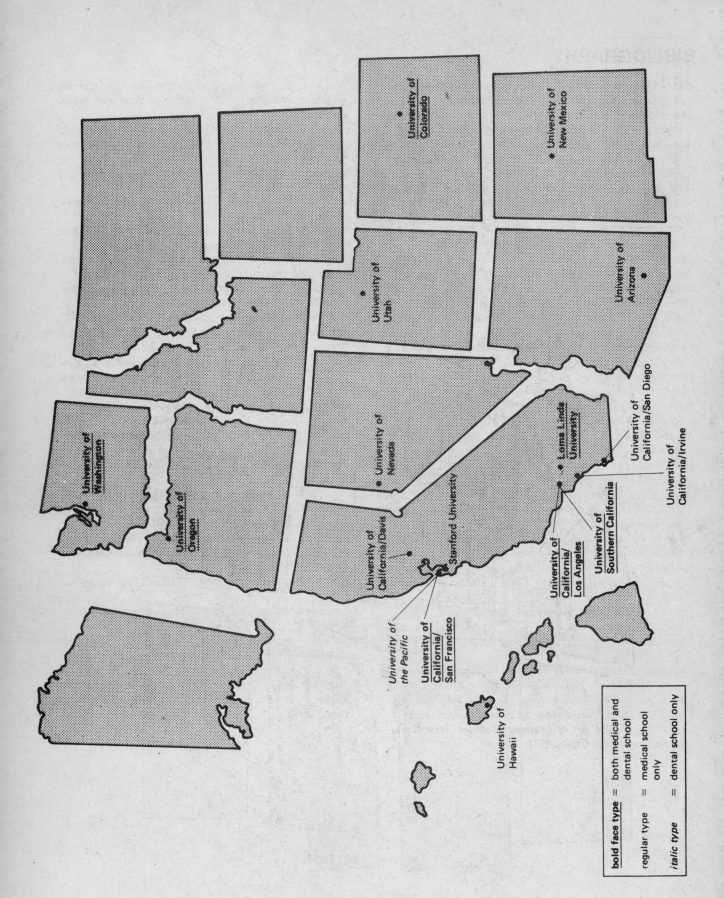

University of Colorado

University of New Mexico

University of Utah

University of Arizona

University of Washington

University of Nevada

University of Oregon

Loma Linda University

University of California/San Diego

University of California/Irvine

University of California/Davis

Stanford University

University of California/Los Angeles

University of Southern California

University of the Pacific

University of California/San Francisco

University of Hawaii

bold face type = both medical and dental school

regular type = medical school only

italic type = dental school only

BIBLIOGRAPHY

AAMC Curriculum Directory. Washington, D.C.: Association of American Medical Colleges, 13th ed., 1984.

Abernethy, V. *Frontiers in Medical Ethics: Applications in a Medical Setting*. Cambridge, Massachusetts: Ballinger, 1982.

Admission Requirements of U.S. and Canadian Dental Schools. Washington, D.C.: American Association of Dental Schools, 36th ed., 1985 (annual).

Bordley, J. and McGehee, H. *Two Centuries of American Medicine: 1776–1976*. Philadelphia: Saunders, 1976.

Brown, S. J., *Getting Into Medical School: The Complete Medical Student's Guidebook*. Woodbury, N.Y.: Barron's Educational Series, Inc., 6th ed., 1983.

Campbell, M. A., *"Why Would a Girl Go Into Medicine?"* Old Westbury, N.Y.: The Feminist Press, 1973.

Coombs, R. H. and St. John, J. *Making it in Medical School*. New York: SP Medical and Scientific Books, 1978.

Curtis, J. L. *Blacks, Medical Schools, and Society*. Ann Arbor: University of Michigan Press, 1971.

Duffy, J. *The Healers: The Rise of the Medical Establishment*. New York: McGraw-Hill, 1976.

Fine, C. *Barron's Guide to Foreign Medical Schools*. Woodbury, N.Y.: Barron's Educational Series, Inc., 1979.

Flexner, J. T. *Doctors on Horseback: Pioneers of American Medicine*. New York: Dover, 1979.

Hendin, D. *The Life Givers*. New York: William Morrow, 1976.

Howell, M. *On Becoming a Woman Doctor*. Boston: Harvard Medical School, 1975.

Hozed, J. L. *Pathways to a Career in Dentistry: A Source Book for Students Underrepresented in Dentistry*. Cambridge: Technical Education Research Center, 1976.

Jonas, S. *Medical Mystery: The Training of Doctors in the United States*. New York: Norton, 1978.

Kaufman, M. *American Medical Education: The Formative Years, 1765–1910*. Westport, Conn.: Greenwood Press, 1976.

Klein, K. *Getting Better: A Medical Student's Story*. Boston: Little, Brown, and Co., 1980.

Knight, J. A. *Medical Student: Doctor in the Making*. New York: Appleton-Century-Crofts, 1973.

Knowles, J. H., ed. *Hospitals, Doctors, and the Public Interest*. Cambridge, Mass.: Harvard University Press, 1965.

Lander, L. *Defective Medicine: Risk, Anger, and the Malpractice Crisis*. New York: Farrar, Straus and Giroux, 1978.

Lasser, M. H. *The Art of Learning Medicine*. New York: Appleton-Century-Crofts, 1974.

Lerner, M. R. *Medical School: The Interview and the Applicant*. Woodbury, N.Y.: Barron's Educational Series, Inc., 1981.

Lippard, V. W. *A Half Century of American Medical Education, 1920–1970*. New York: Independent Publishers Group, 1974.

Lygre, D. G. *Life Manipulation: From Test-Tube Babies to Aging*. New York: Walker, 1979.

Mamot, P. R. *Foreign Medical Graduates in America*. Springfield, Ill.: Thomas, 1974.

Mawardi, B. H. *Physicians and Their Careers*. Ann Arbor: University Microfilms International, 1979.

Medical School Admission Requirements. Washington, D.C.: Association of American Medical Colleges, 1981.

Mumford, E. *Interns: From Students to Physicians*. Boston: Harvard University Press, 1970.

Nolen, W. A. *A Surgeon's World*. New York: Fawcett, 1977.

Nolen, W. A. *The Making of a Surgeon*. New York: Pocket Books, 1976.

Parati, C. *Breakthroughs: Astonishing Advances in Your Lifetime in Medicine, Science, and Technology*. Boston: Houghton Mifflin, 1980.

Rabinowitz, P. M. *Talking Medicine: America's Doctors Tell Their Stories*. New York: Norton, 1981.

Rogers, D. E. *American Medicine Challenges for the 1980s*. Cambridge, Mass.: Ballinger, 1978.

Rubin, T. I. *Emergency Room Diary*. New York: Grosset & Dunlap, 1972.

Seibel, H. R. and Guyer, K. E. *Barron's How to Prepare for the New Medical College Admission Test*. Woodbury, N.Y.: Barron's Educational Series, Inc., 1980.

Shapiro, E. C. and Lowenstein, L. M., eds. *Becoming a Physician: Development of Values and Attitudes in Medicine*. Cambridge, Mass.: Ballinger, 1979.

Silverstein, A. *Conquest of Death*. New York: Macmillan, 1979.

Warner, H. R. *Computer-Assisted Medical Decision Making*. New York: Academic Press, 1979.

Wischnitzer, S. *Futures in Health: A Guide to Podiatry, Optometry, Pharmacy and 56 Other Professions*. Woodbury, N.Y.: Barron's Educational Series, Inc., 1985.

Zabarenko, R. *The Doctor Tree: Developmental Stages in the Growth of Physicians*. Pittsburgh: University of Pittsburgh Press, 1978.

Index of Medical School Profiles

Albany Medical College, Union University, NY   168

Albert Einstein College of Medicine, Yeshiva University, NY   169

Baylor College of Medicine, TX   188

Boston University, School of Medicine, MA   158

Bowman Gray School of Medicine, Wake Forest University, NC   175

Brown University, Program in Medicine, RI   184

Case Western Reserve University, School of Medicine, OH   177

Chicago Medical School, University of Health Sciences, IL   149

Columbia University, College of Physicians and Surgeons, NY   170

Cornell University, Medical School, NY   170

Creighton University, School of Medicine, NE   165

Dalhousie University, Faculty of Medicine, NS   195

Dartmouth, Medical School, NH   166

Duke University, School of Medicine, NC   175

East Carolina University, School of Medicine, NC   175

East Tennessee State University, College of Medicine, TN   186

Eastern Virginia, Medical School, VA   191

Emory University, School of Medicine, GA   147

George Washington University, School of Medicine, DC   144

Georgetown University, School of Medicine, DC   145

Hahnemann University, School of Medicine, PA   181

Harvard Medical School, MA   159

Howard University, College of Medicine, DC   145

Indiana University, School of Medicine, IN   153

Jefferson Medical College, Thomas Jefferson University, PA   181

Johns Hopkins University, School of Medicine, MD   157

Laval University, Faculty of Medicine, QB   195

Loma Linda University, School of Medicine, CA   139

Louisiana State University, School of Medicine in New Orleans, LA   155

Louisiana State University, School of Medicine in Shreveport, LA   156

Loyola University of Chicago, Stritch School of Medicine, IL   150

Marshall University, School of Medicine, WV   193

Mayo Medical School, MN   162

McGill University, Faculty of Medicine, QB   195

McMaster University, Faculty of Medicine, ON   196

Medical College of Ohio, OH   178

Medical College of Pennsylvania, PA   182

Medical College of Georgia, GA   148

Medical College of Virginia, Virginia Commonwealth University, VA   192

Medical College of Wisconsin, WI   194

Medical University of South Carolina, College of Medicine, SC   185

Meharry Medical College, School of Medicine, TN   186

Memorial University, Faculty of Medicine, NF   196

Mercer University, School of Medicine, GA   148

Michigan State University, College of Human Medicine, MI   160

Morehouse School of Medicine, GA   149

Mount Sinai School of Medicine, City University of New York, NY   171

New Jersey Medical School, University of Medicine and Dentistry, NJ   166

New York Medical College, NY   171

New York University, School of Medicine, NY   171

Northeastern Ohio Universities, College of Medicine, OH   178

Northwestern University, Medical School, IL   150

Ohio State University, School of Medicine, OH   178

Oral Roberts University, School of Medicine, OK   179

Oregon Health Sciences University, School of Medicine, OR   180

Pennsylvania State University, College of Medicine, PA   182

Queen's University, Faculty of Medicine, ON   197

Rush Medical College, IL   151

Rutgers Medical School, University of Medicine and Dentistry, NJ   167

Southern Illinois University, School of Medicine, IL   151

St. Louis University, School of Medicine, MO   163

Stanford University, School of Medicine, CA   139

SUNY at Buffalo, School of Medicine, NY   172

SUNY at Stony Brook, School of Medicine, NY   172

SUNY Downstate Medical Center, College of Medicine, NY   173

SUNY Upstate Medical Center, College of Medicine, NY   173

Temple University, School of Medicine, PA   183

Texas A & M University, College of Medicine, TX   188

Texas Tech University, School of Medicine, TX   188

Tufts University, School of Medicine, MA   159

Tulane University, School of Medicine, LA   156

Uniformed Services University, School of Medicine, MD   157

Universite de Sherbrooke, Faculte de Medecine, QB   197

University of Alabama, School of Medicine, AL   137

University of Alberta, Faculty of Medicine, AB   197

University of Arizona, College of Medicine, AZ   138

University of Arkansas, College of Medicine, AR   138

University of British Columbia, Faculty of Medicine, BC   198

University of Calgary, Faculty of Medicine, AB   198

University of California—Davis School of Medicine, CA   140

University of California—Irvine College of Medicine, CA   140

University of California—Los Angeles School of Medicine, CA   141

University of California—San Diego School of Medicine, CA   141

University of California—San Francisco School of Medicine, CA   142

University of Chicago, Pritzker School of Medicine, IL   152

University of Cincinnati, College of Medicine, OH   179

University of Colorado, School of Medicine, CO   143

University of Connecticut, School of Medicine, CT   143

University of Florida, College of Medicine, FL   146

University of Hawaii, Burns School of Medicine, HI   149

University of Illinois, College of Medicine, IL   152

University of Iowa, College of Medicine, IA   153

University of Kansas, School of Medicine, KS   154

University of Kentucky, College of Medicine, KY   154

University of Louisville, School of Medicine, KY   154

University of Manitoba, Faculty of Medicine, MB   199

University of Maryland, School of Medicine, MD   157

University of Massachusetts, Medical School, MA   160

University of Miami, School of Medicine, FL   146

University of Michigan, Medical School, MI   161

University of Minnesota—Duluth School of Medicine, MN   162

University of Minnesota, Medical School, Minneapolis, MN   162

University of Mississippi, School of Medicine, MS   162

University of Missouri, Columbia School of Medicine, MO   163

University of Missouri, Kansas City School of Medicine, MO   164

University of Montreal, Faculty of Medicine, QB   199

University of Nebraska, College of Medicine, NE   165

University of Nevada, School of Medicine, NV   166
University of New Mexico, School of Medicine, NM   167
University of North Carolina, School of Medicine, NC   176
University of North Dakota, School of Medicine, ND   176
University of Oklahoma, College of Medicine, OK   180
University of Ottawa, Faculty of Medicine, ON   199
University of Pennsylvania, School of Medicine, PA   183
University of Pittsburgh, School of Medicine, PA   184
University of Rochester, School of Medicine, NY   174
University of Saskatchewan, College of Medicine, SA   200
University of South Alabama, College of Medicine, AL   137
University of South Carolina, School of Medicine, SC   185
University of South Dakota, School of Medicine, SD   186
University of South Florida, College of Medicine, FL   147
University of Southern California, School of Medicine, CA   142
University of Tennessee, College of Medicine, TN   187
University of Texas, Medical Branch at Galveston, TX   189
University of Texas, Medical School at Houston, TX   189
University of Texas, Medical School at San Antonio, TX   190
University of Texas, Southwestern Medical School at Dallas, TX   190
University of Toronto, Faculty of Medicine, ON   200
University of Utah, School of Medicine, UT   191
University of Vermont, College of Medicine, VT   191
University of Virginia, School of Medicine, VA   192
University of Washington, School of Medicine, WA   193
University of Western Ontario, Faculty of Medicine, ON   200
University of Wisconsin, Medical School, WI   194
Vanderbilt University, School of Medicine, TN   187
Washington University, School of Medicine, MO   164
Wayne State University, School of Medicine, MI   161
West Virginia University, School of Medicine, WV   193
Wright State University, School of Medicine, OH   179
Yale University, School of Medicine, CT   144

Index of Osteopathic School Profiles

Chicago College of Osteopathic Medicine, IL   215
College of Osteopathic, Medicine of the Pacific, CA   214
Kirksville College of Osteopathic Medicine, MO   215
Michigan State University, College of Osteopathic Medicine, MI   215
New Jersey School of Osteopathic Medicine, NJ   216
New York College of Osteopathic Medicine, NY   216
Ohio University College of Osteopathic Medicine, OH   216
Oklahoma College of Osteopathic Medicine and Surgery, OK   216
Philadelphia College of Osteopathic Medicine, PA   216
Southeastern College of Osteopathic Medicine, FL   215
Texas College of Osteopathic Medicine, TX   216
University of New England, College of Osteopathic Medicine, ME   215
University of Health Sciences, College of Osteopathic Medicine—Kansas City, MO   215
University of Osteopathic Medicine and Health Sciences—Des Moines, IA   215
West Virginia School of Osteopathic Medicine, WV   216

Index of Dental School Profiles

Baylor College of Dentistry, TX   272
Boston University—Goldman School of Graduate Dentistry, MA   265
Case Western Reserve, School of Dentistry, OH   269
Columbia University, School of Dental and Oral Surgery, NY   268
Creighton University, Boyne School of Dental Science, NB   267
Dalhousie University, Faculty of Dentistry, NS   274
Fairleigh Dickinson University, School of Dentistry, NJ   268
Georgetown University, School of Dentistry, DC   261
Harvard School of Dental Medicine, MA   265
Howard University, College of Dentistry, DC   261
Indiana University, School of Dentistry, IN   263
Loma Linda University, School of Dentistry, CA   259
Louisiana State University, School of Dentistry, LA   264
Loyola University of Chicago, School of Dentistry, IL   262
Marquette University, School of Dentistry, WI   274
McGill University, Faculty of Dentistry, QB   274
Medical College of Georgia, School of Dentistry, GA   262
Medial University of South Carolina, College of Dental Medicine, SC   271
Meharry Medical College, School of Dentistry, TN   272
New Jersey Dental School, University of Medicine and Dentistry, NJ   268
New York University, College of Dentistry, NY   268
Northwestern University, Dental School, IL   262
Ohio State University, College of Dentistry, OH   270
Oral Roberts University, School of Dentistry, OK   270
Oregon Health Science University, School of Dentistry, OR   270
Southern Illinois University, School of Dental Medicine, IL   262
SUNY at Buffalo, School of Dentistry, NY   269
SUNY at Stony Brook, School of Dental Medicine, NY   269
Temple University, School of Dentistry, PA   271
Tufts University, School of Dental Medicine, MA   265
Universite de Montreal, School of Dental Medicine, QB   274
Universite Laval, Ecole Medecine Dentaire, QB   274
University of Alabama, School of Dentistry, AL   259
University of Alberta, Faculty of Dentistry, AB   275
University of British Columbia, Faculty of Dentistry, BC   275
University of California—Los Angeles, School of Dentistry, CA   259
University of California—San Francisco, School of Dentistry, CA   259
University of Colorado Medical Center, School of Dentistry, CO   260
University of Connecticut, School of Dental Medicine, CT   261
University of Detroit, School of Dentistry, MI   266
University of Florida, College of Dentistry, FL   261
University of Illinois at Chicago, College of Dentistry, IL   262
University of Iowa, College of Dentistry, IA   263
University of Kentucky, College of Dentistry, KY   264
University of Louisville, School of Dentistry, KY   264
University of Manitoba, Faculty of Dentistry, MN   275
University of Maryland at Baltimore, College of Dental Surgery MD   264
University of Michigan, School of Dentistry, MI   266
University of Minnesota, School of Dentistry, MN   266
University of Mississippi, School of Dentistry, MS   266
University of Missouri, School of Dentistry, MO   267
University of Nebraska, Lincoln College of Dentistry, NE   267
University of North Carolina, School of Dentistry, NC   269
University of Oklahoma, College of Dentistry, OK   270
University of Pennsylvania, School of Dental Medicine, PA   271
University of Pittsburgh, School of Dental Medicine, PA   271
University of Saskatchewan, College of Dentistry, SA   275
University of Southern California, School of Dentistry, CA   260
University of Tennessee, College of Dentistry, TN   272

University of Texas—Houston, Dental Branch, TX   272
University of Texas—San Antonio, Dental School, TX   273
University of the Pacific, School of Dentistry, CA   260
University of Toronto, Faculty of Dentistry, ON   276
University of Washington, School of Dentistry, WA   273
University of Western Ontario, Faculty of Dentistry, ON   276

Virginia Commonwealth University, MCV—School of
  Dentistry, VA   273
Washington University, School of Dental Medicine, MO
  267
West Virginia University, School of Dentistry, WV   273

Subject Index

Acceptance, 30
  dates, 113
  medical school, 30
Applying
  to dental school, 224
  to medical school, 15
  how, 20, 224
  when, 21
  where, 621
Attrition in medical school, 107
Basic data for schools
  dental, 246
  medical, 112
  osteopathic, 211
Canadian
  medical schools, 195
  dental schools, 274
College, 8
  premedical requirements, 9
  program of studies, 9
  selection of, 8
Combined programs, 106
Curriculum
  dental, 242
  medical in transition, 105
  traditional medical, 103
DAT, see Dental Admission Test
Dental
  curriculum, 242
  schools, 258
Dental Admission Test (DAT), 231
  sample questions, 233
Dentistry, 217
  as an alternative career, 222
  Is it for you? 222
Early admission, 16
Early decision plan, 21
Educational Council for Foreign Medical Graduates (ECFMG), 205
Family practice, 111
Federation Licensing Exam (FLEX), 205
Fifth pathway, 204
Financing
  current crisis, 99
  dental education, 239
  medical education, 98
  osteopathic education, 212
Foreign medical study, 202
  internship, 204
  residency after, 204
  transfer to U.S. schools, 203
High school
  preparation, 7
  program of studies, 7
Integrated programs, 106
Internship
  for foreign graduates, 204
  matching program, 109
  medical, 108
  osteopathic, 212
Interview, 25
  preparation for, 26
  questions asked at, 27
  significance of, 26
Matching program, 109
MCAT, see Medical College Aptitude Test

MS-MD And MD-PhD programs, 106
Medical College Admission Test (MCAT), 34
  contents of, 35
  preparation for, 36
  value of, 36
Medical Education, 102
  curriculum in transition, 105
  special programs, 106
  traditional programs, 103
Medical school
  acceptance, 30
  age limitation, 20
  applying to, 15
  basic data, 112
  early admissions, 16
  first-year applications, 16
  foreign, 205
  high school preparation for, 7
  how to apply to, 20
  osteopathic, 210
  preparation for, 7
  prospects for 1985-1990, 16
  race and, 20
  selection factors for, 16
  selection process, 29
  sex and, 20
  when to apply, 21
  where to apply, 21
Medicine
  as a career, 3
  attributes for a career, 5
  career placement, 111
  why study, 3
  women in, 91
Minority students, 96
  financial aid for, 96
  opportunities for, 96
National Board of Medical Examiners (NBME), 108
Osteopathy
  basic philosophy, 210
  educational data, 211
  financing education for, 212
  internship, 212
  medical schools, 212
  (and) medicine, 212
  practice, 212
  residency, 212
Physicians
  for the 21st century, 6
  major challenge to become, 5
  need for, 4
Premedical
  advisor, 12
  committee, 12
  requirements, 10
Preparation for
  dentistry, 223
  medicine, 7
Recommendations, 25
Residency
  matching program, 109
  medical, 204
  osteopathic, 212
Scholarships
  for medical schools, 99
  for osteopathic schools, 212

Selection factors for medical school, *16*
    college attended, *18*
    grade point average (GPA), *19*
    intellectual potential, *18*
    letters of recommendation, *19*
    MCAT scores, *18*

personal attributes, *19*
    science course grades, *18*
Summer activities, *11*
Women
    opportunities for, *91, 236*
    physician, *94*